# Companion Web site for ArcGIS data models

## http://support.esri.com/datamodels

A companion Web site provides a set of evolving sample geodatabases with both data and schemas that you can use to get started with your own design project.

ESRI recognizes that each design will have unique requirements and that no design is static. Your database schema will evolve over time just as many of the design examples included here will evolve. ESRI publishes and shares the most recent changes to each data model at http://support.esri.com/datamodels.

At this Web site, you can download posters, detailed white papers, and data model templates for use, extension, and adoption in your own systems. The Web page for each data model includes:

- A case study implementation for a selected user site, including a small sample database

- A geodatabase template that enables you to import each data model as a template on which to base your system

- A white paper explaining the design

- A data model poster

- Tips and Tricks documents on how to employ the data model from the case study in your work.

Some of the data models also have important community-based Web links so that you can collaborate with other users on the development of shared designs and concepts.

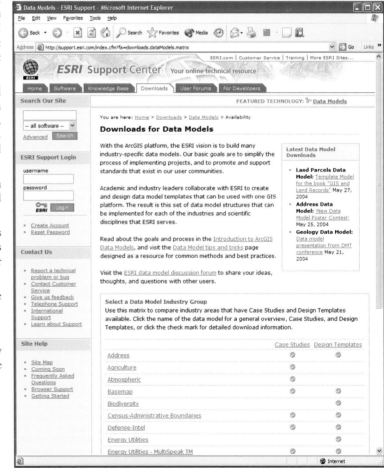

# How to use this book

This book was written with three goals in mind: (1) to teach you practical design concepts, (2) to present a series of commonly used design patterns for GIS databases, and (3) to get you started with geodatabase implementation for your projects.

Chapter 1, 'Geodatabase design', provides practical guidance on GIS database design principles and procedures. It provides ESRI's approach to document and graphically illustrate key parts of a GIS data model. These methods are applied throughout the book.

Chapters 2 through 8 are the heart of the book. Each chapter presents a real geodatabase design resulting from a case study for a specific GIS application domain, such as parcel management and tax assessment, address data management, and water resource applications.

Chapter 9, 'Building geodatabases', explains how to implement your geodatabase design using ArcGIS.

## Case study overviews

The data models presented in Chapters 2 through 8 are based on working implementations at a number of GIS sites. You can learn about practical designs implemented for each case study and gain insight into some common GIS design challenges in each chapter. Here is a brief overview of the specific design patterns you can learn about in each chapter.

| Case study overviews | Notes on design patterns and methods | |
| --- | --- | --- |
| 2<br><br>Streams and river networks | • How to extend surface water data models that support base mapping (blue lines and areas on maps) to add support for modeling network connectivity and flow and for hydraulic modeling and analysis of channel characteristics, volume and flow calculations, and flooding.<br><br>• Illustrates modeling of relationships between surface elevation (terrain) and water features. | • Illustrates 3D channel profiles and time series data model designs.<br><br>• Illustrates integration of external models, such as U.S. Army Corps of Engineers Hydrologic Engineering Center (HEC) models and DHI Water and Environment models. |
| 3<br><br>Census units and boundaries | • An example data model for applying and using U.S. census geography and how these features can be extended to access the rich sets of demographic attributes associated with census geographies.<br><br>• Design is based on an internal project performed by ESRI using published datasets from the U.S. Census Bureau.<br><br>• A strong example of how to use topology to model highly integrated feature geometry. The census topology illustrates behavior and integrity rules for more than 30 integrated feature classes derived from a single comprehensive set of line features (edges). | • This design addresses scalability and performance of complex topologies. It was tested at three implementation levels: local areas (200,000+ census features), large states (10+ million features), and the entire United States (50+ million features) with excellent performance results.<br><br>• This design case study primarily focuses upon the use of topology to enforce spatial relationships and behavior. It briefly illustrates how to work with census attribute tables. It does not address cartographic display of census boundaries for the U.S. Census Bureau's internal work flows, although it can be extended to support this. |

## Open GIS data models can be shared

ESRI ensures that the ArcGIS data models implement relevant standards as they evolve. For example, the land records and the Arc Hydro data models are based on strong standards development in these communities over the past decade. ESRI also monitors and participates in many standards-based efforts, such as ISO, ANSI, Open GIS Consortium, Inc. (OGC), the U.S. Federal Geographic Data Committee, and Geospatial One-Stop. ESRI will continue to incorporate appropriate standards into its data model work as these efforts evolve.

The ArcGIS data models presented here provide a starting point for each user-specific design project and incorporate industry-standard design techniques from information technology (IT), database management systems (DBMS), GIS, and various standards organizations.

The ArcGIS data model templates implement what users have found to be widely adopted best practices for building systems that really work. That will continue to be the main focus of these efforts.

Each ArcGIS data model includes commonly adopted spatial representations (for example, points, lines, and polygons), classifications, and map layer specifications that can be implemented in any GIS. Each also includes the commonly used integrity rules for key data layers and feature classes. These aspects of the ArcGIS data models can be widely adopted regardless of the user's system architecture.

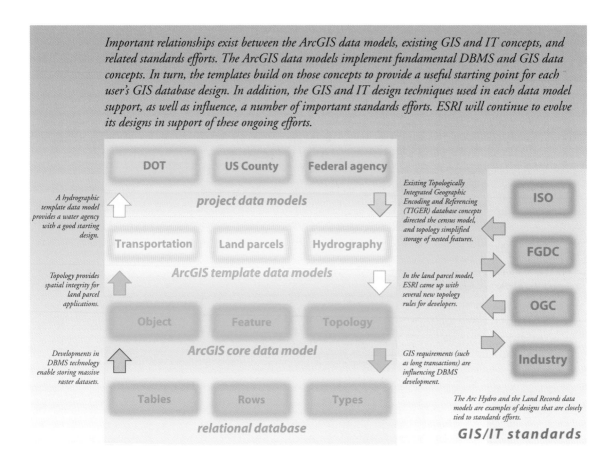

*Important relationships exist between the ArcGIS data models, existing GIS and IT concepts, and related standards efforts. The ArcGIS data models implement fundamental DBMS and GIS data concepts. In turn, the templates build on those concepts to provide a useful starting point for each user's GIS database design. In addition, the GIS and IT design techniques used in each data model support, as well as influence, a number of important standards efforts. ESRI will continue to evolve its designs in support of these ongoing efforts.*

DOT    US County    Federal agency

*project data models*

Transportation    Land parcels    Hydrography

*ArcGIS template data models*

Object    Feature    Topology

*ArcGIS core data model*

Tables    Rows    Types

*relational database*

*A hydrographic template data model provides a water agency with a good starting design.*

*Topology provides spatial integrity for land parcel applications.*

*Developments in DBMS technology enable storing massive raster datasets.*

*Existing Topologically Integrated Geographic Encoding and Referencing (TIGER) database concepts directed the census model, and topology simplified storage of nested features.*

*In the land parcel model, ESRI came up with several new topology rules for developers.*

*GIS requirements (such as long transactions) are influencing DBMS development.*

*The Arc Hydro and the Land Records data models are examples of designs that are closely tied to standards efforts.*

ISO

FGDC

OGC

Industry

**GIS/IT standards**

use–land cover classifications, could be documented and consistently applied across multiple databases. While not essential, adoption of common terms and classifications can simplify interoperability implementation. The goal is wider adoption of common data model terms, keywords, and attribute classifications.

- Integrity rules and spatial relationships—The primary set of integrity rules and spatial relationships should be specified to define the spatial behavior of features for each dataset. For example, road lines must connect at endpoints and not self-overlap (the same is true for hydrology and contour lines), connected contour lines must have consistent elevations, and county boundaries (and similar administrative units) cannot overlap one another and must nest within state boundaries.

For many users, understanding the integrity specifications of a dataset is critical in assessing its suitability for a particular application. Topology rules and networks are used to implement integrity rules and behavior. These are key GIS database design concepts that you'll see applied frequently throughout this guide.

- Map layout and map layer templates—Data models should include the definition of common map products and their associated map scales. A common cartographic standard for map sheets, symbols, and label specifications will be important for many application domains. Chapter 8, 'Cartography and the base map', presents advanced data models for a high-quality printed map series.

- Metadata templates—A common metadata description that adheres to appropriate Federal Geographic Data Committee (FGDC) or ISO standards for key layers of information. This is essential for the consistent discovery of information sets across hundreds of organizations. While every dataset covers its particular geography, common data layers should be consistently described among the participating organizations.

Each dataset's adherence to a specific data model guideline should also be noted (for example, hydrology data model) in the metadata. The data model can include a metadata template for each layer, with much of the general information already documented. The metadata templates can be copied and instance-specific information can be added. This practice helps ensure that much of the metadata content for each implementation will be consistent from site to site. This will result in adoption of common terms and keywords to improve the search and discovery process.

- Extraction guidelines and methods—All datasets are a sample of reality. Common data models require a set of rules for data capture and extraction. For example, is the collection of building footprints meant to capture all buildings or only prominent buildings? Will the stream representations be derived from a detailed digital elevation model to capture all drainage lines longer than 1,000 feet? What is the explicit methodology used to capture the features? What are the source materials and what is their vintage?

Understanding these properties for datasets is critical in determining appropriate uses of the data.

- Results of Case Study Implementation—Case studies illustrating how an organization solved particular data model requirements are useful in providing insight to other users. In this book, the results of actual case studies have been documented to illustrate many of the methods used to address specific design requirements. In each chapter, a lot of effort has been invested to graphically represent the key design elements of a GIS data model. You can read more about this presentation methodology in Chapter 1, 'Geodatabase design'.

# Preface

During the last several years, ESRI has worked with the geographic information system (GIS) user community to develop a set of "best practices" geodatabase designs for various application domains. These database designs are intended to help GIS users rapidly become productive with the geodatabase and to share "what really works" among users and developer communities.

The two primary goals of this book are to:

- Provide a series of domain data models that represent commonly used GIS datasets by applying best practices for GIS data modeling and collection. These data models are intended to provide a series of recipes or templates for implementing geodatabases for specific solutions.

- Communicate a practical GIS database design process.

As a GIS professional, you will need to learn and apply practical GIS database design methods. Gaining GIS design skills will be important to accomplish your job.

Many users learn from implementation examples. The data models presented here are based on working implementations at a number of GIS sites. The designs in this book are presented using a series of case studies that illustrate how to combine traditional relational database design techniques with GIS design methods. Each design includes a series of data modeling patterns that appear repeatedly in GIS. Understanding these design patterns will increase your ability to adopt many of these same methods for your own data modeling activities.

## ArcGIS data models build on traditional GIS database designs

In the data model case studies, ESRI found that, conceptually, there is nothing radically new in a geodatabase design. For example, parcels are represented as polygons. Lot lines are used for cartographically drawing parcels and will share geometry with parcels according to a well-defined set of rules. Parcels have a commonly used set of attributes and

relationships to tax rolls. Roads are still often represented as centerlines that connect at their endpoints, and so on.

GIS data design methods have been around for decades, are consistently applied, and have proven to be sound, especially when combined with best practices from relational database design. These are universal concepts that apply to all GIS usage. These best practices templates will be important for users as well as for the GIS community as a whole. All GIS users must collaborate and share datasets and data compilation responsibilities with users of many other GIS systems.

## Key elements in common data models

ESRI® ArcGIS® data models are built to be open for data sharing and use and for interchange of data between ArcGIS and other systems. In this book, you'll find a focus on some common elements in GIS database design. These include the following design elements:

- Series of thematic layers—Each application of GIS requires a minimum series of geographic layers of information. Specifying these layers is part of the conceptual design. These are referred to as thematic layers.

- Common spatial representations—Specify how each layer is to be represented as a collection of spatial datasets. For example, local roads at 1:25,000 scale will be represented as centerlines. Specific representations for each dataset will be defined as a collection of points, lines, polygons, map text (annotation), rasters, tabular attributes, and so on. These primarily consist of commonly agreed upon feature and image representations with a common set of names and terms.

- Minimum set of attributes—Attributes describe features and integrate related tabular information. Each data model includes a specification of the minimum set of attribution. Ideally, many of these common attributes would use similar terms and classifications. For example, agreed upon classifications, such as road class, soil types, and land

# contents

*chapter 1*

## geodatabase design  2

Spatial data modeling is an extension to conventional methodologies for conceptual, logical, and physical data modeling within a relational or object-oriented database. This chapter presents steps to design, a guide for reading data model illustrations, and recurring patterns used in geodatabase design.

*chapter 2*

## streams and river networks  36

Surface water flow is a fundamental part of many maps. It is also the subject of intense examination and research to understand and anticipate the effects of irrigation, storms, and flooding. This chapter summarizes the key points of Arc Hydro, a mature data model for hydrographic and hydrologic modeling applications.

*chapter 3*

## census units and boundaries  86

Census data comprises two main types of information: location and demographics. This data model focuses on the spatial hierarchy of physical features, census blocks, block groups, tracts, and higher-level administrative units. With these concepts, the rich demographic data can be easily joined to the spatial features for further analysis.

*chapter 4*

## addresses and locations  126

Streets can have multiple names and address ranges; buildings, parcels, and points of interest can have multiple addresses and subaddresses; and addresses can have many different styles and be used by multiple features. This case study from Calgary, Canada, shows how to support such complex relationships in a straightforward way.

ESRI Press, 380 New York Street, Redlands, California 92373-8100

Copyright © 2004 ESRI

All rights reserved. First edition 2004
10 09 08 07 06 05    2 3 4 5 6 7 8 9 10

Printed in the United States of America

Library of Congress Cataloging-in-Publication Data
Arctur, David, 1951–
    Designing geodatabases : case studies in GIS data modeling / David Arctur, Michael Zeiler.
      p.   cm.
    ISBN 1-58948-021-X (pbk. : alk. paper)
    1. Geographic information systems.  2. Information storage and retrieval systems—Geography.
  3. Database design.  4. Database management.  I. Zeiler, Michael.  II. Title.
  G70.2.A74 2004
  910'.285'573—dc22                       2004015047

Ask for ESRI Press titles at your local bookstore or order by calling 1-800-447-9778. You can also shop online at www.esri.com/esripress. Outside the United States, contact your local ESRI distributor.

ESRI Press titles are distributed to the trade by the following:

*In North America, South America, Asia, and Australia:*
Independent Publishers Group (IPG)
Telephone (United States): 1-800-888-4741
Telephone (international): 312-337-0747
E-mail: frontdesk@ipgbook.com

*In the United Kingdom, Europe, and the Middle East:*
Transatlantic Publishers Group Ltd.
Telephone: 44 20 8849 8013
Fax: 44 20 8849 5556
E-mail: transatlantic.publishers@regusnet.com

# Designing

# Geodatabases

## Case Studies in GIS Data Modeling

David Arctur • Michael Zeiler

*ESRI has been working with its user community over the last several years to develop a set of geodatabase designs reflecting best practices for various application domains. These database designs are intended to help ArcGIS users rapidly become productive with the geodatabase and to share what really works among users and developer communities.*

1

Geographic information systems (GIS) technology is founded upon the capability to organize information into a series of layers that can be integrated using geographic location. At a fundamental level, each GIS database is organized as a series of thematic layers to represent and answer questions about a particular problem set, such as hydrology, tax parcel management, transportation, or environment.

GIS database design is about identifying the thematic layers to be used and specifying the contents and representations of each thematic layer. This involves defining how the geographic features are to be represented (for example, as points, lines, polygons, rasters, or tabular attributes); how the data is organized into feature classes, attributes, and relationships; and the spatial and database integrity rules for implementing rich GIS behavior using topologies, networks, raster catalogs, and so forth. Ultimately, a design will be developed that can be implemented as a working geodatabase.

The process used to design a GIS database employs key GIS and database management system (DBMS) design methods. In this chapter, you'll read about fundamental GIS design principles, the design process, and some methods for graphically representing GIS designs.

The goal of this chapter is to provide you with a framework for understanding the designs that will be presented throughout the rest of this guide as well as the ability to interpret the data model diagrams you'll find in each case study.

# Geodatabase design

Evidence in the past two decades has shown that traditional GIS database design procedures are sound and need not change drastically with the migration of GIS data management toward object-based designs and DBMS applications. While object-oriented and DBMS design tools are useful when used appropriately, they are not enough for GIS database design. Fundamental GIS design principles and methods still apply. Here are some important GIS design concepts that you will use in your design work.

## Representation

A GIS database design is founded upon geographic representations. For example, individual geographic entities can be represented as features (such as points, lines, and polygons); continuous surfaces and imagery using rasters or triangulated irregular networks (TINs); and as map graphics, such as text labels and symbols.

## Thematic layers

Geographic representations are organized in series of thematic layers. A key concept in a GIS is one of map layers or themes. A thematic layer is a collection of common geographic elements, such as a road network, a collection of parcel boundaries, soil types, an elevation surface, satellite imagery for a certain date, or well locations.

The concept of a thematic layer was one of the early notions in GIS. Practitioners thought about how the geographic information in maps could be partitioned into logical information layers—as more than a random collection of objects. These early GIS users organized information in thematic layers that described the distribution of a phenomenon and how it should be portrayed across a geographic extent. These layers also provided a protocol for collecting the representations. For example, each and every area (polygon) in a specified extent could be assigned an explicit soil type, and the soil types could be described using properties or attributes of each polygon. A theme could be defined that delineated various areas representing the dominant soil type (that is, a layer collection of soil type polygons).

## GIS datasets are collections of representations

Many themes are represented by a single collection of homogeneous features, such as soil types and well locations, while other themes, such as a transportation framework, are represented by multiple datasets, such as streets, intersections, bridges, and highway ramps. Gridded datasets are used to represent continuous surfaces, such as elevation, georefer-

enced imagery, slope, and aspect. These data collections can be organized as feature classes and raster-based data layers in a GIS database.

| Some common GIS representations | |
|---|---|
| **Theme** | *Geographic representation* |
| Hydrography | Lines |
| Road centerlines | Lines |
| Vegetation | Polygons |
| Urban areas | Polygons |
| Administrative boundaries | Polygons |
| Elevation contours | Lines |
| Well locations | Points |
| Orthophotography | Raster |
| Satellite imagery | Raster |
| Land parcels | Polygons |
| Parcel tax records | Tables |

Both the intended use and existing data sources influence spatial representations in a GIS. When designing a GIS database, users have a set of applications in mind. They understand what questions will be asked of the GIS. Understanding these uses helps determine the content specification for each theme and how each is to be represented geographically. For example, there are numerous alternatives for representing surface elevation—as contour lines and spot height locations (hilltops, peaks, and so on), as a continuous terrain surface, or as shaded relief. The intended uses of the data will help determine its required representations.

Frequently, the geographic representations will be predetermined to some degree by the available data sources for the theme. If a preexisting data source was collected at a particular scale and representation, it will often be necessary to adapt your design to use it.

*In GIS, thematic layers are the organizing principle for GIS database design.*

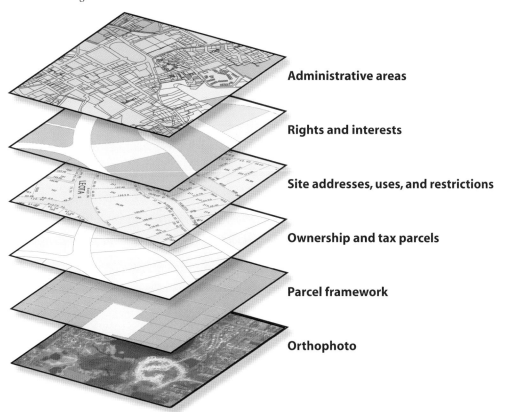

**Administrative areas**

**Rights and interests**

**Site addresses, uses, and restrictions**

**Ownership and tax parcels**

**Parcel framework**

**Orthophoto**

Each GIS will contain multiple themes for a common geographic area. The collection of themes acts as layers in a stack. Each theme can be managed as an information set independent of other themes. Each has its own representations (points, lines, polygons, surfaces, rasters, and so on). Because the various independent themes are spatially referenced, they overlay one another and can be combined in a common map display. GIS analysis operations, such as overlay, can fuse information between themes.

# INSIDE THE GEODATABASE

A geodatabase schema includes the definitions, integrity rules, and behavior for an integrated collection of datasets used to represent the collection of thematic layers in a GIS. Each design includes properties for feature classes, topologies, networks, raster catalogs, relationships, domains, and so forth. Understanding these geodatabase elements will be important for building a sound design.

Each geodatabase data model represents both the ordered collections of simple features and rasters, as well as the rules and schema properties that add rich GIS behavior. Here is a brief introduction to some of the more common geodatabase elements you will employ in your designs.

## Feature classes

A feature class is a collection of features representing the same geographic elements, such as wells, parcels, or soil types. All the features in a feature class have the same spatial representation (for example, point, line, or polygon) and share a common set of descriptive attributes. Individual features in a feature class can also share spatial relationships with other features. For example, adjacent polygons share boundaries according to well-defined integrity rules (such as that counties cannot overlap one another). Linear features often participate in an interconnected network for analytical use (for example, a street network).

Once you have identified a set of feature classes and how they will be represented, additional properties can be specified. These include how the features will be rendered and symbolized on maps, a specification of the attributes that will be used to describe each feature, and other rules that control feature representation and behavior. Additional geodatabase elements can be defined for representing spatial and attribute relationships and for maintaining data integrity.

## Feature datasets

Feature datasets are organized collections of related feature classes. Feature classes are organized in integrated feature datasets for many purposes—primarily to manage spatial relationships among related feature classes. In many, if not most GIS implementations, it is important to model both simple standalone features and higher level collections as a *system* of objects and relationships. Indeed, the ability to model and represent spatial relationships using topologies and networks is a key GIS capability.

## Topologies and networks

Topologies define how features share geometry and control their integrity through rules and editing behavior (for example, census blocks cannot overlap one another and share geometry with street centerlines). Networks are used to model connectivity and flow between features.

## Raster datasets and raster catalogs

Images and other raster datasets are an important GIS data resource that can be managed using relational databases. In recent years, DBMS and GIS have evolved to support massive image collections that can be simultaneously accessed by many users. Large multirow raster datasets can be used to manage national and global datasets that provide high performance levels and multiuser access in the GIS. A number of raster mechanisms are used to add behavior and to manage large multiuser raster collections.

A geodatabase is a store of geographic data implemented with the relational database of your choice. All geodatabase elements are managed in standard DBMS tables using standard SQL data types and adhere to the ISO/OGC Simple Features specifications. These are some of the structural elements of a geodatabase that you will use to develop your geographic data model.

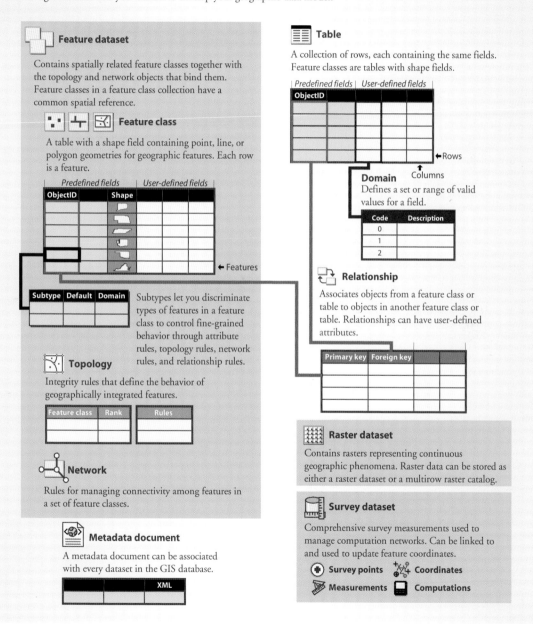

### Feature dataset

Contains spatially related feature classes together with the topology and network objects that bind them. Feature classes in a feature class collection have a common spatial reference.

### Feature class

A table with a shape field containing point, line, or polygon geometries for geographic features. Each row is a feature.

Subtypes let you discriminate types of features in a feature class to control fine-grained behavior through attribute rules, topology rules, network rules, and relationship rules.

### Topology

Integrity rules that define the behavior of geographically integrated features.

### Network

Rules for managing connectivity among features in a set of feature classes.

### Metadata document

A metadata document can be associated with every dataset in the GIS database.

### Table

A collection of rows, each containing the same fields. Feature classes are tables with shape fields.

### Domain

Defines a set or range of valid values for a field.

### Relationship

Associates objects from a feature class or table to objects in another feature class or table. Relationships can have user-defined attributes.

### Raster dataset

Contains rasters representing continuous geographic phenomena. Raster data can be stored as either a raster dataset or a multirow raster catalog.

### Survey dataset

Comprehensive survey measurements used to manage computation networks. Can be linked to and used to update feature coordinates.

- Survey points
- Coordinates
- Measurements
- Computations

A GIS design is built around the set of thematic layers of information that will address a particular set of requirements. A thematic layer is a collection of common features, such as a road network, a collection of parcel boundaries, soil types, an elevation surface, satellite imagery for a certain date, and well locations.

## Design starts with thematic layers

First, you define these thematic layers for your particular applications and information requirements. Then, you define each thematic layer in more detail. The characterization of each thematic layer will result in a specification of standard geodatabase data elements, such as feature classes, tables, relationships, raster datasets, subtypes, topologies, and domains.

The 10 steps presented on the following page outline a general GIS database design process. The initial conceptual design steps help you identify and characterize each thematic layer. In the logical design phase, you begin to develop representation specifications, relationships, and, ultimately, geodatabase elements and their properties. In the physical design stage, you will test and refine your design through a series of initial implementations. You will also document your design.

| Layer | Ownership parcels |
|---|---|
| Map use | Parcels define land ownership and are used for taxation. |
| Data source | Compiled from land ownership transactions at local government . |
| Representation | Polygons in survey-aware feature classes and related annotation. |
| Spatial relationships | Parcel polygons cannot overlap and are covered by boundary lines. |
| Map scale and accuracy | Typical map scales are 1:1,200 and 1:2,400. |
| Symbology and annotation | Parcels often drawn using boundary features and related annotation. |

When identifying thematic layers in your design, try to characterize each theme in terms of its visual representations, its expected usage in the GIS, its likely data sources, and its levels of resolution. These characteristics help describe the high-level contents expected from each theme.

Once you have identified the key thematic layers in a design, the next step is to develop specifications for representing the contents of each thematic layer in the physical database. These include how the geographic features are to be represented (for example, as points, lines, polygons, rasters, or tabular attributes); how the data is organized into feature classes, tables, and relationships; and how spatial and database integrity rules will be used to implement GIS behavior.

# Ten steps to designing geodatabases

*Identify the information products that will be produced with your GIS.*

Inventory map products, analytical models, database reports, Web access, data flows, and enterprise requirements.

*Identify the key thematic layers based on your information requirements.*

Specify the map use, data source, spatial representation, map scale and accuracy, and symbolology and annotation.

*Specify the scale ranges and spatial representations for each thematic layer.*

GIS data is compiled for specific scale use; feature representation often changes between points, lines, and polygons at larger scales. Rasters are sampled to include multiresolution pyramids.

*Group representations into datasets.*

Discrete features are modeled with feature datasets, feature classes, relationship classes, rules, and domains. Continuous data is modeled with raster datasets. Measurement data is modeled with survey datasets. Surface data is modeled with raster and feature datasets.

*Define the tabular database structure and behavior for descriptive attributes.*

Identify attribute fields, specify valid values and ranges, apply subtypes to control behavior, and model relationships.

*Define the spatial properties of your datasets.*

Use networks for connected systems of features and topologies to enforce spatial integrity and shared geometry. Set the spatial reference for the dataset.

*Propose a geodatabase design.*

Make informed decisions on applying structural elements of the geodatabase and prepare a design. Study existing designs for examples.

*Implement, prototype, review, and refine your design.*

From the initial design, build a geodatabase and load data. Test and refine your designs.

*Design work flows for building and maintaining each layer.*

Each layer has distinct data sources, accuracy, currency, metadata, and access. Define work flows to conform to your agency's business practices.

*Document your design using appropriate methods.*

Use drawings, layer diagrams, schema diagrams, and reports to communicate your data model.

conceptual design

logical design

physical design

As you build your design, documentation is important. Following is a series of diagrams that represent key design concepts and document the specifications of geodatabase elements, metadata, and map layers. This brief overview of how various geodatabase elements are presented in this book may be helpful to you as you read and as you document your own design.

In each of the data model case studies in later chapters, you'll find an initial discussion about key design concepts and requirements followed by a specification of the themes. Once the thematic layers are presented, you'll see a logical geodatabase schema representation for each layer and how each is implemented as a geodatabase element.

There are five key parts to schema representation.

- Datasets—These are specifications for a feature class, a raster catalog, or an attribute table and the set of columns in each table. For spatial representations, you'll see some geometric properties (such as point, line, and polygon). Often you'll see some specification for subtypes. These parts of the schema are always shown in blue.

- Domains—These represent the list or range of valid values for attribute columns. These rules control software behavior to maintain data integrity in certain attribute columns. Domains are shown in red.

- Relationships—Attribute relationships are widely used in GIS, just as they are in all relational database management system (RDBMS) applications. They define how rows in one table are associated with rows in another table. Relationships have a direction of cardinality and other properties (for example, is this a one-to-one, one-to-many, or many-to-many relationship?). Relationships and their properties are shown in green.

- Spatial rules—Spatial rules, such as topologies and their properties, are used to model how features share geometry with other features. This is a critical and widely used GIS mechanism to enforce certain spatial behavior and integrity in GIS databases. The geodatabase has an especially rich and powerful topological implementation to define complex spatial integrity rules. These and other rules, such as survey datasets and networks, are shown in orange.

- Map layers—GIS includes interactive maps and other views. A critical part of each dataset is the specification for how it is symbolized and rendered in maps. These are typically defined as layer properties, which specify how features are assigned map symbology (colors, fill patterns, line and point symbols) and labeling specifications. Layer specifications are shown in yellow.

*Map layers specify how datasets are drawn.*

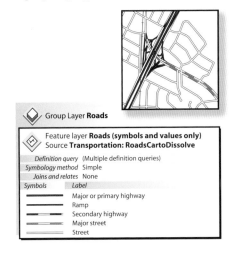

map layers

*Both spatial and nonspatial datasets are organized into DBMS tables with column definitions and optional subtypes. Feature classes (such as OwnerParcel shown here) will have geometric properties as well.*

*Domains provide a specification for valid values of a field. They can represent valid value ranges, lists of values, and standard classifications. Domains help enforce attribute value integrity.*

**1**

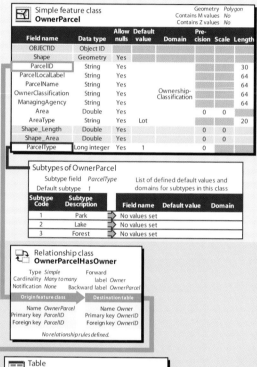

**Simple feature class**
**OwnerParcel**

Geometry *Polygon*
Contains M values *No*
Contains Z values *No*

| Field name | Data type | Allow nulls | Default value | Domain | Pre-cision | Scale | Length |
|---|---|---|---|---|---|---|---|
| OBJECTID | Object ID | | | | | | |
| Shape | Geometry | Yes | | | | | |
| ParcelID | String | Yes | | | | | 30 |
| ParcelLocalLabel | String | Yes | | | | | 64 |
| ParcelName | String | Yes | | | | | 64 |
| OwnerClassification | String | Yes | | Ownership-Classification | | | 64 |
| ManagingAgency | String | Yes | | | | | 64 |
| Area | Double | Yes | | | 0 | 0 | |
| AreaType | String | Yes | Lot | | | | 20 |
| Shape_Length | Double | Yes | | | 0 | 0 | |
| Shape_Area | Double | Yes | | | 0 | 0 | |
| ParcelType | Long integer | Yes | 1 | | 0 | | |

**Subtypes of OwnerParcel**

Subtype field *ParcelType*
Default subtype *1*

List of defined default values and domains for subtypes in this class

| Subtype Code | Subtype Description | Field name | Default value | Domain |
|---|---|---|---|---|
| 1 | Park | No values set | | |
| 2 | Lake | No values set | | |
| 3 | Forest | No values set | | |

**Relationship class**
**OwnerParcelHasOwner**

Type *Simple*
Cardinality *Many to many*
Notification *None*

Forward label *Owner*
Backward label *OwnerParcel*

| Origin feature class | Destination table |
|---|---|
| Name *OwnerParcel* | Name *Owner* |
| Primary key *ParcelID* | Primary key *OwnerID* |
| Foreign key *ParcelID* | Foreign key *OwnerID* |

*No relationship rules defined.*

**Table**
**Owner**

| Field name | Data type | Allow nulls | Prec-ision | Scale | Length |
|---|---|---|---|---|---|
| OBJECTID | Object ID | | | | |
| OwnerID | String | Yes | | | 60 |
| OwnerName | String | Yes | | | 60 |
| PercentOwned | Long integer | Yes | 0 | | |
| OwnershipRole | String | Yes | | | 30 |

*Relationships associate rows in one table to rows in another table. This is a common relational database modeling technique.*

**Coded value domain**
**OwnershipClassification**

Description
Field type *String*
Split policy *Default value*
Merge policy *Default value*

| Code | Description |
|---|---|
| CVT | City-Village-Town |
| County | County |
| Federal | Federal |
| Indian Tribe | Indian Tribe |
| International | International |
| Non-Profit | Nonprofit |
| Private | Private |
| State | State |
| Other | Other |
| PD | Public Domain |
| OC | Revested Oregon and California Railroad Lands |
| CB | Revested Coos Bay Wagon Road Lands |
| AQ | Land Acquired |
| LU | Land Utilization Projects |
| IND | Indian Trust and Fee Lands |
| HST | Historic State Lands |
| NF | Non-Federal |
| PE | Public Domain With Exception |
| AE | Acquired With Exception Right |

**Topology**
**ParcelFeatures_Topology**

Cluster tolerance *0.000247*

*Participating feature classes and ranks*

| Feature class | Rank |
|---|---|
| Boundary | 1 |
| Corner | 1 |
| SimultaneousConveyance | 2 |
| SurveyFirstDivision | 3 |
| SurveySecondDivision | 3 |
| Encumbrance | 4 |
| TaxParcel | 4 |
| SiteAddress | 5 |

*Topology rules*

| Origin feature class | Topology rule | Comparision feature class |
|---|---|---|
| Boundary | Must not have dangles | |
| Boundary | Endpoint must be covered by | Corner |
| Corner | Must be covered by endpoint of | Boundary |
| TaxParcel | Boundary must be covered by | Boundary |
| SimultaneousConveyance | Boundary must be covered by | Boundary |
| SurveyFirstDivision | Boundary must be covered by | Boundary |
| TaxParcel | Must not overlap | |
| SimultaneousConveyance | Must not overlap | |
| SurveyFirstDivision | Must be covered by | SimultaneousConveyance |
| SurveyFirstDivision | Must not overlap | |
| SurveySecondDivision | Must be covered by | SurveyFirstDivision |
| SurveySecondDivision | Must not overlap | |
| SiteAddress | Must be covered by | TaxParcel |
| TaxParcel | Contains | SiteAddress |

*Topologies and networks add advanced feature behavior and integrity rules. This topology specification defines integration rules for parcels, boundary lines, and control networks.*

Part of your task is to document GIS data models. Trial and error have taught what works for clear and effective communication of GIS data model designs. Toward this end, ESRI has developed tools for the semiautomated generation of geodatabase diagrams. You can make custom geodatabase diagrams with the same tool that created the schema illustrations for this book.

In developing this book and other documentation on ESRI's support Web site, a simple notation was developed that captures all the properties of a geodatabase at a glance. Furthermore, this notation illustrates the structure within a geodatabase—how feature classes are organized into feature datasets, how relationship classes can reach across the geodatabase, and how spatially related data can be organized into topologies and networks.

## The Geodatabase Diagrammer

The requirement to efficiently document many data models led to the development of a Visual Basic® project implemented as an ArcCatalog™ command to automate the generation of graphics. This ArcCatalog add-in command, Geodatabase Diagrammer, uses ArcObjects™ to query elements of the geodatabase for their properties, then creates a Microsoft® Visio® document containing the graphic elements that describe the geodatabase schema.

**Search ArcScripts**

Use the following options to customize your search:

All languages    All ESRI software

10    Results per page    ☐ Show script summaries

Search for geodatabase diagramm    Search    Tips

To get Geodatabase Diagrammer, go to arcscripts.esri.com and search for "geodatabase diagrammer". Download the zip file and follow the installation instructions in the readme.txt file.

After you run this command in ArcCatalog, you can open the new Visio file and easily cut and paste graphics from Visio into Microsoft

Word®, PowerPoint®, and any application that can insert Windows Metafile (WMF) files.

The data model diagrams, such as the land parcel data model shown on the next page at the bottom right, were finished in Adobe® Illustrator® with conceptual graphics and map graphics exported from ArcMap.

When you document your model, take time to make conceptual diagrams of its key aspects, such as how addresses, streets, and buildings are related. Augment these with instance diagrams showing sample table and record values and their relationships.

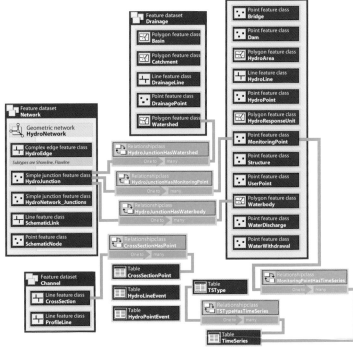

In ArcCatalog, select a geodatabase and start the Geodatabase Diagrammer command.

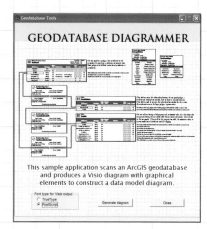

This sample application scans an ArcGIS geodatabase and produces a Visio diagram with graphical elements to construct a data model diagram.

Type a description of this feature class or table in this placeholder text.

Geodatabase Diagrammer launches Microsoft Visio and interrogates the structure of the geodatabase. Schema graphics are generated that you can insert in your own documentation.

You will derive great benefit from diagramming your data model—the active participation of stakeholders in examining your data model poster, the perspective you will gain on data model patterns, and the assurance that your schema is correct. The act of diagramming drives changes that will improve your data model.

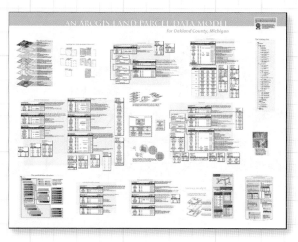

You'll discover a set of common data design patterns in any data modeling exercise. This set is far from complete but covers several important decision points. Like any design effort, geodatabase design involves a series of trade-offs. The right data model for you meets your organization's requirements by finding the right balance in the model for data integrity, cartographic production, and information access. Data model effectiveness is also often driven by budgetary constraints and the use of suitable, existing data.

These are decisions that commonly arise in developing data models.

## Feature datasets

Once you have a list of feature classes, relationship classes, and tables, you need to decide how to group them in feature datasets. Generally, if features have geometric relationships or thematic similarity, they will be organized in the same feature dataset.

## Subtypes

Subtypes of feature classes and tables are a powerful modeling technique to preserve a coarse-grained model, advantageous for display performance, geoprocessing, and data management, while allowing a rich set of behaviors for features and objects. Use subtypes when appropriate in your data model.

## Relationships

Once you've exhausted the spatial and topological capabilities of the GIS to form relationships, you have several ways to implement general associations for features and objects, depending on your display and query requirements.

## Topology

Topological integrity is enforced in ArcGIS by defining topology rules as part of the geodatabase schema and working with a set of topological editing tools that enforce these rules. There is a rich environment to discover and correct topological errors.

## Networks

For network connectivity, geometric networks offer a feature-based interface for performing high-speed traces on an underlying logical network model. You can model complex edge and junction features and set connectivity rules that specify what feature types can be connected to another and how many edge connections at a junction are valid.

## Survey data

Survey datasets allow you to integrate a computation network with features in a GIS. As the survey computation network is refined and new positions calculated, the linked features in survey-aware feature classes will have their geometry shifted to the more accurate location.

## Raster data

You can manage high-performance rasters of massive size as a catalog in a database management system. Two alternative types of models are available: many raster datasets or one big raster dataset that represents a mosaic of your area. Other data modeling choices will affect compression, band settings, and cell properties.

## Labeling and annotation

Placing descriptive text on a map involves a choice between automatic labeling, based on feature attribute values, and the use of annotation features, each edited and positioned manually.

## Classifications and domains

Simple classification systems can be implemented with coded value domains in ArcGIS. But some agencies define and manage complex classification hierarchies of objects. It's better to manage complex classification systems through related valid value tables (VVTs).

# Design patterns

*Some modeling issues recur across many data models. This set is a distillation of frequently encountered patterns, with some guidance on the considerations.*

## Feature datasets

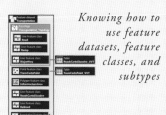

*Knowing how to use feature datasets, feature classes, and subtypes*

## Subtypes

*Using subtypes for fine control of feature behavior while keeping the model simple*

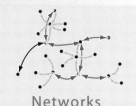

## Relationships

*Modeling how features and objects are related to each other*

## Topology

*Defining topologies to enforce valid connectivity between features*

## Networks

*Making geometric networks for tracing and network analysis*

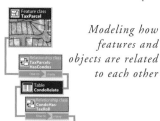

## Survey data

*Integrating survey projects with vertices and points in survey-aware feature classes*

*Using catalogs for time-related data and mosaics for base maps*

## Raster data

*Placing descriptive text efficiently on a map*

## Labeling and annotation

*Applying attribute domains for simple classifications and valid value tables for complex classifications*

## Classifications and domains

There are several reasons to group feature classes into feature datasets. First, you must group features that participate in topologies and networks into a common feature dataset. This is because when you are working with rules that specify how features touch, coincide, intersect, or contain one another, they must be in the same spatial reference. Second, when you are editing feature classes, all feature classes in a feature dataset are open for editing as well. Group only feature classes that you would naturally edit together. Finally, you can use feature datasets for grouping thematically similar feature classes.

Feature datasets are a way of organizing your feature classes, much as folders help you organize files in your computer's operating system.

Feature datasets are also the containers for spatially related sets of features. Each feature dataset has a defined spatial reference common to all its feature classes; that's how the geodatabase enforces the connectivity and topology of features that touch, coincide, overlap, cover, and intersect each other.

Here are three sample feature datasets from various data models. The Channel feature dataset contains a geometric network. The LandBase feature dataset contains thematically related feature classes. The ParcelFeatures feature dataset contains a topology.

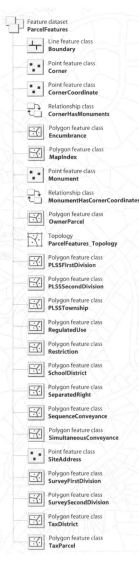

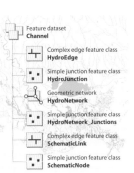

# Grouping feature classes into feature datasets

Feature dataset
**Administrative**

A — Annotation feature class
**AdminAnnotation**

Geodatabase topology
**Administrative_Topology**

Line feature class
**CountyBoundaries**

Polygon feature class
**LegalBoundaries**

Line feature class
**MilitaryResBoundaries**

Line feature class
**MunicipalBoundaries**

Polygon feature class
**MunicipalAreasCarto**

Line feature class
**ParkBoundaries**

*Use feature datasets to group feature classes for which you want to define topologies or networks or those you wish to edit simultaneously.*

A feature dataset is a container for feature classes that share the same spatial reference, along with relationship classes, geometric networks, and geodatabase topologies.

Feature datasets are necessary when you want to construct geodatabase topologies and geometric networks. Feature datasets should be used to group feature classes that are edited simultaneously and can be used to group feature classes thematically.

## Rules

Feature classes edited together in ArcMap can be grouped into feature datasets.

Feature classes not typically edited together should be segregated into separate feature datasets or geodatabases.

Feature classes that participate in a geometric network or topology must be grouped in the same feature dataset.

A feature class can participate in no more than one topology or network.

*The feature classes placed in a feature dataset and bound in a topology can be edited and validated against spatial constraints, such as overlap, containment, contiguity, and exclusion.*

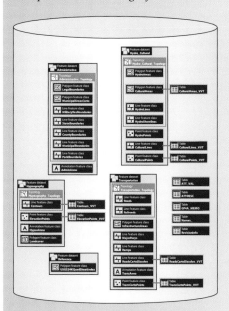

*Most often, the thematic layers in your logical data model design will correspond to feature datasets or other representations, such as rasters.*

*The number of feature datasets in a geodatabase, as well as the number of feature classes within a feature dataset, varies considerably. The census case study in this book has several dozen feature classes in one feature dataset, but most have several to a dozen feature classes per feature dataset.*

Well-designed data models contain a manageable set of feature classes along with the means to finely control feature behavior. Subtypes are one way to limit the number of feature classes required in your data model, while giving you a powerful set of rules to ensure attribute, relationship, network, and topological integrity. When choosing between defining a set of similar feature classes or one feature class with the same number of subtypes, you should choose subtypes unless the set of attributes or geometry type is different.

A table is a set of objects that all have the same set of attributes (and varying attribute values). A feature class is a table of features with the same set of attributes and a geometry column (for example, point, line, or polygon).

### Grouping by table

Tables are the cornerstone of relational databases, but an inevitable tension arises in data modeling—when is it better to split a set of features into distinct feature classes or lump them into one?

Part of the answer comes from looking at the sets of attributes of similar features. If two features share 15 out of 17 attributes, then it is reasonable to group them together in the same feature class; you can tolerate a few disused attributes for certain features.

An overriding factor, however, is the geometry type; for vector features, you will typically choose point, line, or polygon for each feature. This forces distinct feature classes, since you cannot group features with different geometry types in the same feature class.

But other than these two situations—more than a few disused attributes and distinct geometry types—you should generally seek ways to use subtypes before creating additional feature classes.

### Using subtypes

Subtypes provide a mechanism to add selected behavior to subsets of features in a feature class. An example would be subtypes such as highway, primary road, and secondary road for a street feature class.

When you design your logical data model, consider that there is merit in keeping the list of subtypes short. For example, in the Arc Hydro framework data model in Chapter 2, 'Streams and river networks', you will see that HydroEdge has two subtypes, Flowline and Shoreline. For hydrologic and hydrographic applications, these are the distinctions among edges of a stream network that really matter; hence the subtype definition. This feature class would be unwieldy if the subtypes represented the complete taxonomy of stream features, especially if its purpose is analysis and not classification.

## Roads with subtypes

| fid | geom | subtype | width | ln | name |
|-----|------|---------|-------|----|------|
| 102 | highway | 65 | 4 | US Highway 285 |
| 103 | highway | 75 | 4 | NM Highway 14 |
| 104 | highway | 75 | 4 | US Interstate 25 |
| 101 | primary | 45 | 2 | Cerrillos Road |
| 102 | primary | 35 | 2 | St Francis Blvd |
| 103 | primary | 40 | 2 | Paseo de Arjun |
| 104 | primary | 45 | 2 | Bishop's Lodge Rd |
| 101 | secondary | 25 | 2 | Korbinian Road |
| 102 | secondary | 15 | 1 | Camino Hasta Mañana |
| 103 | secondary | 20 | 1 | Petra Lane |
| 104 | secondary | 15 | 1 | Maximilian Road |

## Validation rules

| Default values | Attribute domains | Split/Merge policy | Connectivity rules | Relationship rules |
|---|---|---|---|---|
| A new highway is given a default value of four lanes. | Valid widths are 55, 65, and 75. Valid suffixes are "Highway" and "Interstate." | A split highway retains all highway designations. | A highway can connect to a primary road but not to a secondary road. | Two highway roadways can be associated with a highway route. |
| A new primary road is given a default width of 35 feet. | Valid widths are 30, 35, 40, and 45. Valid lane counts are 1, 2, and 4. | A merged primary road takes a default value for lanes. | A two-lane primary road can only connect to another two-lane road. | A primary road can be related with bridges or tunnel crosses. |
| A secondary road is given a default width of 15 feet. | Valid widths are 15, 20, and 25. Valid suffixes are "Road" and "Lane." | A split secondary road retains its width. | A secondary cannot directly connect to a freeway. | A secondary road cannot have more than four road segments at an intersection. |

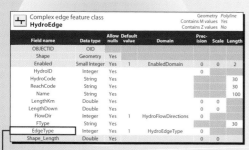

**Complex edge feature class**
**HydroEdge**

Geometry *Polyline*
Contains M values *Yes*
Contains Z values *No*

| Field name | Data type | Allow nulls | Default value | Domain | Precision | Scale | Length |
|---|---|---|---|---|---|---|---|
| OBJECTID | OID | | | | | | |
| Shape | Geometry | Yes | | | | | |
| Enabled | Small Integer | Yes | 1 | EnabledDomain | 0 | 0 | 2 |
| HydroID | Integer | Yes | | | 0 | | |
| HydroCode | String | Yes | | | | | 30 |
| ReachCode | String | Yes | | | | | 30 |
| Name | String | Yes | | | | | 100 |
| LengthKm | Double | Yes | | | 0 | 0 | |
| LengthDown | Double | Yes | | | 0 | 0 | |
| FlowDir | Integer | Yes | 1 | HydroFlowDirections | 0 | | |
| FType | String | Yes | | | | | 30 |
| EdgeType | Integer | Yes | 1 | HydroEdgeType | 0 | | |
| Shape_Length | Double | Yes | | | 0 | 0 | |

**Subtypes of HydroEdge**

Subtype field *EdgeType*
Default subtype *1*

List of defined default values and domains for subtypes in this class

| Subtype Code | Subtype Description | | Field name | Default value | Domain |
|---|---|---|---|---|---|
| 1 | Flowline | ⇨ | Enabled | 1 | EnabledDomain |
| | | | FlowDir | 1 | HydroFlowDirections |
| | | | EdgeType | 1 | HydroEdgeType |
| 2 | Shoreline | ⇨ | Enabled | 1 | EnabledDomain |
| | | | FlowDir | 1 | HydroFlowDirections |
| | | | EdgeType | 2 | HydroEdgeType |

*Subtypes let you apply a classification system within a feature class and apply behavior through rules. Subtypes are essential to good design because they help reduce the number of feature classes and improve performance.*

Subtypes are a powerful tool for data modeling because they let you control every configurable behavior in your geodatabase: attribute rules, relationship rules, network rules, and topology rules, without creating more tables. The result is a coarse-grained model, good for database performance, with finely discriminated object behavior.

| | Subtypes in a feature class* | Multiple feature classes |
|---|---|---|
| *Collections* | Subtypes define collections of features within a single feature class. | Feature classes store collections of features in the geodatabase. |
| *Behavior* | You can control behavior at the subtype level. | You can also control behavior by feature class. |
| *Benefit* | Subtypes reduce the number of feature classes. | Multiple feature classes give full modeling flexibility. |
| *Rules* | Subtypes define attribute domains, default attribute values, split–merge policies, connectivity rules, relationship rules, network rules, and topology rules. | Feature classes define attribute domains, default attribute values, split–merge policies, connectivity rules, relationship rules, network rules, and topology rules. |
| *Attributes* | Features in subtypes must have the same attributes. | Separate feature classes can have varied attributes. |
| *Geometry types* | Features in subtypes must share the geometry type (point, line, polygon). | Feature classes can have distinct geometry types. |
| *Pros* | Subtypes provide flexibility for applying rules to collections of features without requiring a separate feature class. Fewer classes result in fewer database queries for drawing and editing. | Multiple feature classes allow different attributes for collections of features. They also allow differing participation in topologies, networks, and relationship classes. |
| *Cons* | Subtypes cannot be used when there are distinct attributes, feature types, or topological rules among the collections of features. | Additional feature classes increase the number of queries required for operations such as drawing, editing, and topology validation. |
| *Recommendations* | Use subtypes liberally to reduce the number of feature classes in your data model. | Use multiple feature classes when you need more flexibility for defining attributes or geometry types. |

*\* This discussion applies to objects and tables as well.*

A geographic information system spatially integrates information. When you design relationships among features, use the GIS to discover spatial relationships, such as touch, overlap, intersect, and cover. For example, an electrical transformer that connects a secondary line with a pole could have that association defined exclusively by spatial proximity. When your design cannot use spatial relationships, ArcGIS supports many ways to implement associations, such as geometry snapping during editing, relationship classes, on-the-fly relationships, and joins.

There are many ways to associate features with each other in a geodatabase. Your job as a modeler is to find the method that represents the behavior associated with your data and the spatial integrative powers of the GIS.

## Modeling spatial relationships using topologies and networks

Your first choice for modeling relationships is to use the GIS to manage the spatial relationships inherent among features. Here are three examples.

- You can model the components of an electrical system on a geometric network, using complex edges for primary circuits with secondary taps and simple junctions for transformers, poles, and devices. To find an associated feature, do a trace on the network. A network is a set of relationships among edges and junctions.

- You can manage the nested geography in census mapping data with topology. Topology rules can be defined to enforce spatial relationships, such as how census blocks nest into block groups, and block groups nest into census tracts. Topology rules maintain the topological integrity of your data. Use the Identify tool to navigate nested geography.

- Some features can be associated by proximity, containment, or other relationship. You can use geospatial operators to aggregate features within other features and summarize feature values.

When you model spatial relationships, think first about how to use geodatabase topologies, geometric networks, shared-edge editing, and geospatial operators in your data model. That way, you'll gain efficiency in your data creation and maintenance costs.

## Modeling with general associations

There are also many associations that require attribute relationships to be defined. You can have an association between a geographic feature, such as a parcel of land, and a nongeographic entity, such as one or more parcel owners.

You may also need to capture relationships among features that may be close in proximity but, from the spatial context alone, for which there is ambiguity about the association. For example, a pad-mounted transformer may serve electrical power to several buildings, but unless you have the secondary lines mapped, you can't have a clean, unambiguous association between a transformer and the set of buildings it serves.

For these two general cases, you have three additional choices to make about representing that association. Relationship classes let you easily navigate related features and objects in ArcMap. On-the-fly relationships (relates) and joins are used to optimize editing and drawing performance.

# Using relationship classes, relates, and joins

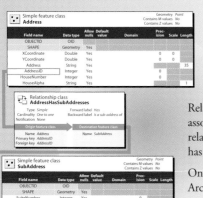

*Use relationship classes for referential integrity persisted in the geodatabase, on-the-fly relates for editing performance, and joins for labeling and symbology.*

Relationship classes provide a rich environment for ensuring consistent associations among features and objects. As part of the geodatabase data model, relationship classes participate in edit transactions as well as versioning. ArcMap has Identify and other tools to navigate through relationships between objects.

On-the-fly relationships, also called relates, are defined as a property of an ArcMap layer. They provide basic integrity with high performance.

Joins are defined through the relational database to make standard SQL queries cross the workspace as well as a variety of data sources.

|  | Relationship classes | On-the-fly relates | Joins |
|---|---|---|---|
| Scope | Geodatabase | Cross workspace or data source | Cross workspace or data source |
| Framework | Geodatabase data model | Defined in map layer | Relational database/SQL |
| Typical uses | Modeling compound objects | Editing with low overhead | Labeling, symbology |
| User interface for editing | ArcMap | VBA application in ArcMap | SQL queries |
| User interface for navigating | ArcMap | ArcMap | SQL queries |
| Composite objects | Yes | No | No |
| Referential integrity | Yes | No | No |
| Messaging | Yes, used for class extensions | No | No |
| Attributes | Yes | No | No |
| Relationship rules | Yes, by subtype | No | No |
| Cardinality | Up to many-to-many | One-to-one, one-to-many | One-to-one, one-to-many |
| Pros | Manages referential integrity and messaging behavior. Edited via ArcMap attributes inspector. | No editing overhead; can cross workspace and data source type. | No editing overhead; can cross workspace and data source type; can be used for SQL queries, labeling, and symbology. |
| Cons | Incurs editing overhead; must be defined only between tables in same geodatabase; still requires joins for SQL query, labeling, and symbology. | No referential integrity; no messaging; no support for many-to-many cardinality; still requires joins for SQL query, labeling, and symbology. | No referential integrity; no messaging; no support for many-to-many relationships. |

In earlier GIS systems, topology has been traditionally implemented as a data structure. The ArcInfo® coverage model is an example, storing right and left polygon values on arcs (line features). Advances in software development now permit a new and improved implementation of topology as a collection of feature classes with ranks and topology rules. Topology in ArcGIS is better than coverage topology because it offers a rich and configurable set of rules and allows any number of feature classes to share geometry and participate in a topology.

Topology in a GIS is used to ensure the integrity of spatial relationships among features that share geometry.

Here are some examples of topology rules in use:

- Voting districts must be covered by counties.
- States must not overlap.
- Census blocks tessellate block groups.

Topology can be considered a special type of relationship among features. Your data model will be more efficient if you can associate features by topology rather than with a relationship class.

There are two types of topologies in ArcGIS. Geodatabase topologies are stored in the geodatabase as a set of ranked feature classes and a defined set of topology rules. Map topologies are temporary, defined for the duration of an editing session, and allow quick shared-edge editing.

## Must be covered by

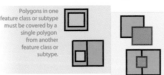

Polygons in one feature class or subtype must be covered by a single polygon from another feature class or subtype.

Polygon errors are created from polygons from the first feature class or subtype that are not covered by a single polygon from the second feature class or subtype.

*Use this rule when you want one set of polygons to be covered by some part of another single polygon in another feature class or subtype.*

Counties must be covered by states.

*The "must be covered by" rule is one of several dozen topology rules you can configure in a geodatabase topology.*

## Geodatabase topologies

A geodatabase topology is the grouping of feature classes along with a set of topology rules that define the behavior for feature geometry. When you edit a topology, a topological graph composed of edges, nodes, and vertices is used to control geometric editing and discover feature errors. The Topology Edit tool lets you select nodes and vertices and make simultaneous edits to all shared features.

## Map topologies

A map topology is a simple topology you can impose on simple features in a map during an edit session. A map topology allows you to simultaneously edit features that overlap or touch each other using the tools on the topology toolbar. These features can be in one or more feature classes and may have different geometry types. Line features and the outlines of polygon features become topological edges when you create a map topology. Point features, the endpoints of lines, and the places where edges intersect become nodes.

*Be sure to examine the geodatabase topology rules poster that comes in hardcopy and PDF form with your ArcGIS distribution.*

# Geodatabase topologies and map topologies

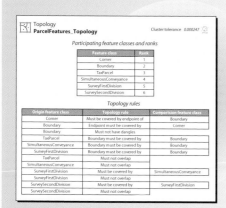

*You have two options for validating spatial relationships among features: geodatabase topologies, which give you a rich set of configurable topology rules, and map topologies, which make it easy to edit the shared edges of feature geometries.*

A geodatabase topology lets you accurately model geometric relationships between features. By selecting a set of feature classes with a ranking and a set of topology rules between those feature classes, you can enforce geometric relationships, such as making sure that land parcels don't overlap and census blocks aggregate into block groups.

A map topology performs efficient topological editing through shared-edge editing tools. It has the advantage of letting you edit feature classes across many feature datasets, as well as shapefiles.

| | **Geodatabase topology** | **Map topology** |
| --- | --- | --- |
| *Description* | A geodatabase topology manages a set of feature classes that share geometry; is used to integrate feature geometry, validate features, control editing, and define relationships between features. | A map topology manages a set of simple feature classes that share geometry; is used to integrate feature geometry and control editing tools. |
| *Scope* | Feature classes in a feature dataset. | Feature classes in multiple feature datasets or shapefiles in a folder. |
| *Definition* | Object in a feature dataset with topology rules. | Created for duration of ArcMap session. |
| *Rules* | User sets any of several dozen topology rules. | Rules such as coincidence, covering, crossing. |
| *Validation* | Rules evaluated when topology is validated. | Shared-edge validation applied during edits. |
| *Reporting errors* | Symbology for error shapes set in topology layer. | Errors cannot be created using Topology Edit tool. |
| *Correcting errors* | User interface for locating and correcting errors. | Errors cannot be created using Topology Edit tool. |
| *Pros* | Geodatabase topologies manage a set of rules and errors associated with the violations of those rules. They define valid spatial relationships between features. | Participant feature classes can be in different feature datasets. Map topologies can be used with shapefiles. They incur no editing overhead. |
| *Cons* | A geodatabase topology can incur editing overhead and work flow considerations. | Map topologies have no rules or errors. They are defined during an ArcMap session, not in the geodatabase data model. |
| *Recommendations* | Use geodatabase topologies when you want to apply a set of your organization's topology rules. | Use map topologies when you want to perform quick shared-edge editing. |

A network is a system of edges and junctions that convey objects and resources, such as cars, electricity, and water. Geometric networks are a mechanism to represent connectivity between edges (such as lines) and junctions where they connect. You can define connectivity rules on the network, which can constrain how many edges can be connected at a junction as well as valid network feature combinations.

The geodatabase has a dual representation of linear systems—the geometric network and the logical network. The geometric network is the set of features that participate in a linear system and is associated with a logical network, a pure network graph consisting of edges and junction elements. When you edit the geometric network, the logical network is concurrently updated. Simple network features are associated with one logical network element. Complex edge features can be associated with several logical network elements.

The main reason for creating geometric networks is to perform quick tracing tasks on large networks. Utility network tasks include establishing flow direction, tracing toward a source, locating isolated sections, and many other operations that benefit from having a connectivity graph.

## Connectivity rules

Network connectivity rules constrain the number and types of network features that can be connected. In most networks, not all edge types can connect to all junction types. For example, a hydrant lateral in a water network can connect to a hydrant but not a service lateral.

## Dynamic segmentation

Certain types of networks, such as transportation, employ a route measurement system. Dynamic segmentation is the process of computing the shape of route locations along calibrated linear features for which distance measures are available. A route is a calibrated line feature with m-values (measure values) and an identifier.

You can associate multiple attributes on routes with point events and line events. Examples of point events are road signs and accident locations. Examples of line events are pavement conditions and speed limits.

Dynamic segmentation works on linear networks independently of geometric networks. You can define a dynamic segmentation system for any line feature class in ArcGIS.

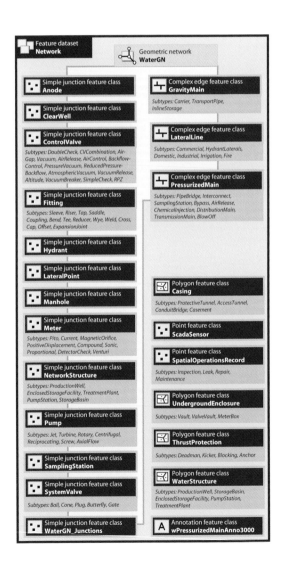

# Building geometric networks for tracing

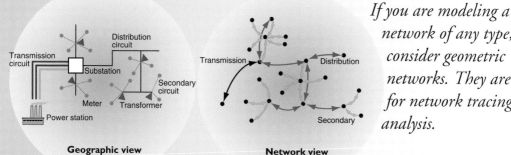

**Geographic view**

**Network view**

*If you are modeling a network of any type, consider geometric networks. They are used for network tracing and analysis.*

A geometric network is the representation of geographic features that comprise a network.

A logical network is a pure graph of junction elements and edge elements.

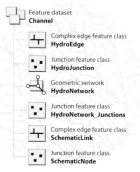

Feature dataset
**Channel**

Complex edge feature class
**HydroEdge**

Junction feature class
**HydroJunction**

Geometric network
**HydroNetwork**

Junction feature class
**HydroNetwork_Junctions**

Complex edge feature class
**SchematicLink**

Junction feature class
**SchematicNode**

## Two views of a network

You can view a network as a collection of geographic objects, such as rails, roads, and bridges, and also as a pure network of edges and junctions. The geometric network lets you interact with features and builds a logical network used for rapid tracing.

## Network features

Network features make up a geometric network. Use complex edge features for sections of line that might have secondary connections.

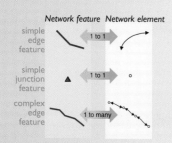

| | |
|---|---|
| *Description* | A geometric network is a set of network features that model systems, such as transportation, hydrography, and utilities. |
| *Scope* | A geometric network contains all the network feature classes in a feature dataset. |
| *Definition* | The set of all network features and integrity rules. |
| *Rules* | Users can constrain behavior with network rules. |
| *Validation* | Connectivity rules are enforced at edit time. |
| *Pros* | Geometric networks provide fast network tracing capabilities. They maintain connectivity during editing and updating. You can model junctions as well as simple and complex edge features. |
| *Cons* | The maintenance of the logical network adds overhead to editing and version management. |
| *Recommendations* | Use geometric networks when your data model and application require modeling network connectivity for the purposes of tracing. |

You can add survey datasets to a geodatabase to enhance the positional accuracy of GIS data. The survey dataset can accept raw survey data from data collectors or COGO measurements and calculate survey points, which can be linked to vertices of geographic features. The feature classes with linked vertices are called survey-aware feature classes. When new measurements are made, new survey points are computed with improved positions, which then update the feature geometry.

Survey datasets are part of the geodatabase and are managed by Survey Analyst, an ArcGIS extension. The key feature of Survey Analyst is the storage and management of survey data in a geodatabase tightly integrated with GIS data. You can visualize survey data, including error ellipses, as a survey layer in ArcMap.

### Integrating GIS and survey data

With Survey Analyst, you can manage data collected in the field using survey equipment as well as data entered by coordinate geometry from survey plans and field sketches.

Survey datasets contain survey projects. Typical survey projects are property, control network, and topographic surveys. Successive survey projects may revisit some survey points, such as common boundary points, and refine their spatial positions.

Survey datasets capture measurements, such as slope, distance, and horizontal angle observations, from a total station and perform and store computations, such as traverse adjustments, ray intersections, resections, and least-squares adjustments. Survey points, which are the best locations derived from multiple measurements and computations, can be associated with a vertex in a feature class.

A benefit of survey datasets is that you can trace the network of your computations. As a user, you interact with the computation network, and the measurement network is updated for you.

The illustration on the right shows an instance of two surveys and their data. You can see how the two survey projects have two shared survey points. Multiple survey projects in an area will successively improve the spatial accuracy of survey points.

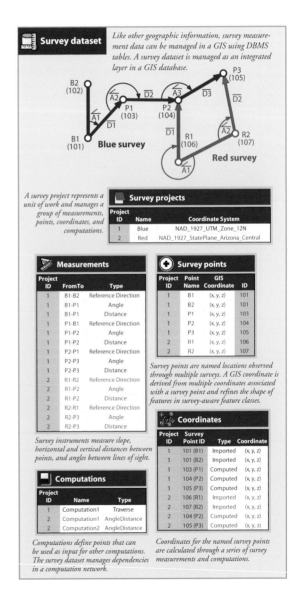

**Survey dataset** — *Like other geographic information, survey measurement data can be managed in a GIS using DBMS tables. A survey dataset is managed as an integrated layer in a GIS database.*

*A survey project represents a unit of work and manages a group of measurements, points, coordinates, and computations.*

**Survey projects**

| Project ID | Name | Coordinate System |
|---|---|---|
| 1 | Blue | NAD_1927_UTM_Zone_12N |
| 2 | Red | NAD_1927_StatePlane_Arizona_Central |

**Measurements**

| Project ID | FromTo | Type |
|---|---|---|
| 1 | B1-B2 | Reference Direction |
| 1 | B1-P1 | Angle |
| 1 | B1-P1 | Distance |
| 1 | P1-B1 | Reference Direction |
| 1 | P1-P2 | Angle |
| 1 | P1-P2 | Distance |
| 1 | P2-P1 | Reference Direction |
| 1 | P2-P3 | Angle |
| 1 | P2-P3 | Distance |
| 2 | R1-R2 | Reference Direction |
| 2 | R1-P2 | Angle |
| 2 | R1-P2 | Distance |
| 2 | R2-R1 | Reference Direction |
| 2 | R2-P3 | Angle |
| 2 | R2-P3 | Distance |

*Survey instruments measure slope, horizontal and vertical distances between points, and angles between lines of sight.*

**Survey points**

| Project ID | Point Name | GIS Coordinate | ID |
|---|---|---|---|
| 1 | B1 | (x, y, z) | 101 |
| 1 | B2 | (x, y, z) | 101 |
| 1 | P1 | (x, y, z) | 103 |
| 1 | P2 | (x, y, z) | 104 |
| 1 | P3 | (x, y, z) | 105 |
| 2 | R1 | (x, y, z) | 106 |
| 2 | R2 | (x, y, z) | 107 |

*Survey points are named locations observed through multiple surveys. A GIS coordinate is derived from multiple coordinates associated with a survey point and refines the shape of features in survey-aware feature classes.*

**Coordinates**

| Project ID | Survey Point ID | Type | Coordinate |
|---|---|---|---|
| 1 | 101 (B1) | Imported | (x, y, z) |
| 1 | 101 (B2) | Imported | (x, y, z) |
| 1 | 103 (P1) | Computed | (x, y, z) |
| 1 | 104 (P2) | Computed | (x, y, z) |
| 1 | 105 (P3) | Computed | (x, y, z) |
| 2 | 106 (R1) | Imported | (x, y, z) |
| 2 | 107 (R2) | Imported | (x, y, z) |
| 2 | 104 (P2) | Computed | (x, y, z) |
| 2 | 105 (P3) | Computed | (x, y, z) |

**Computations**

| Project ID | Name | Type |
|---|---|---|
| 1 | Computation1 | Traverse |
| 2 | Computation1 | AngleDistance |
| 2 | Computation2 | AngleDistance |

*Computations define points that can be used as input for other computations. The survey dataset manages dependencies in a computation network.*

*Coordinates for the named survey points are calculated through a series of survey measurements and computations.*

# Getting accurate with survey datasets

*Use survey datasets if you have survey control networks you want to integrate in your GIS. Using networks, you can incrementally enhance the positional accuracy of geographic features.*

Survey datasets store survey data as an integral part of the geodatabase. This is the marriage between the worlds of surveying and GIS.

**GIS geodatabase**

## feature

*Vertices in survey-aware feature classes can be linked and optionally adjusted when improved survey point locations are calculated.*

**measurement database**

## survey point

*Survey locations can be associated with feature geometry. When survey locations are adjusted, linked feature shapes are updated.*

## measurement

*A computation network stores dependencies among computations and refines positional accuracy with additional measurements.*

- Survey dataset
- Survey points
- Coordinates
- Measurements
- Computations

Polygon feature class
**PLSSFirstDivision**    Survey aware

*Subtypes are Sections, Sections R40, and Tracts cadastral.*

Feature classes anywhere in the geodatabase can contain vertices linked to survey points in survey datasets. These feature classes are said to be survey aware.

| | |
|---|---|
| *Description* | Survey datasets are managed by Survey Analyst, a comprehensive suite of surveying tools in ArcGIS. |
| *Scope* | A survey dataset contains survey projects, which manage measurements, computations, survey points, and coordinates. |
| *Definition* | Survey datasets manage measurement data from sources, such as survey equipment; store the measurements, survey points, and computations for later use; and associate these survey locations with vertices of geographic features. |
| *Pros* | Survey datasets are part of the geodatabase data model and incrementally improve the accuracy of GIS data as measurements are added. |
| *Cons* | Survey datasets incur overhead while editing and maintaining features. Survey datasets can only be edited in the default version, constraining some work flows. |
| *Recommendations* | Use survey datasets when you have survey data that you want to incorporate and use to manage the accuracy of your GIS features. |

Rasters are made of cells arrayed in a two-dimensional grid. From this simple data structure, you can model an incredible variety of phenomena: thematic data, such as vegetation type; continuous data, such as elevation surfaces and rainfall; rectified photomaps from planes or satellites; and pictures of features, such as buildings. The modeling decisions about rasters pertain to image compression, cataloging or mosaicking images, and cell size and properties.

Many raster datasets are used in GIS. Four classes in particular stand out—orthorectified imagery, raster elevation data, scanned maps, and raster time series.

### Orthorectified imagery

Orthorectified imagery is the base layer of many GIS data models. Topographic, hydrographic, and many other types of maps use imagery from aerial photogrammetry and satellite sensors. These are photographic maps with all distortions from camera aspect and projection removed.

Orthorectified images are, in essence, photographic maps. They may tolerate a lossy compression. These rasters can be organized either in a catalog or mosaic.

### Raster elevation data

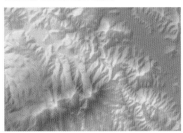

Medium- to small-scale elevation data may be available for your locale. Raster elevation data is kept as a single mosaic of elevation values at grid intersections. Since elevations are used in analysis, this data should use lossless compression.

### Scanned maps

Many government base maps have been scanned and are available as backgrounds to your feature layers. The U.S. Geological Survey (USGS) 7.5 minute topographic quadrangle map series is ubiquitous in the United States and familiar to the public.

### Raster time series

Certain resources or phenomena can be monitored over time, such as vegetative cover in this Landsat image, or the movement of a storm system using weather radar. These images are best captured in a raster catalog with lossless compression. While mostly used for visualization, these rasters are increasingly used for analysis.

# Mosaicking or cataloging rasters

*One important design decision is whether to merge all your rasters into one large continuous raster or to manage separate rasters as rows in a raster catalog.*

Raster datasets contain one single continuous raster, which is typically assembled as a mosaic of adjacent rasters.

Raster catalogs store a set of raster datasets, which can tile, overlap, or be of any irregular coverage.

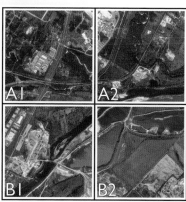

| | Raster dataset | Raster catalog |
|---|---|---|
| *Description* | A raster dataset stores a single raster. Many rasters may be combined, with more recent overlapping pixels replacing previous pixels, into a continuous raster, often called a mosaic. | A raster catalog is a container of raster datasets. It is organized as one table in the geodatabase. |
| *Scope* | Single row table in the geodatabase. | Multirow table in the geodatabase; each row is a raster. |
| *Uses* | When seamless coverages are needed, such as digital elevation models (DEMs), orthophoto base maps, or scanned map series. | For capturing massive raster datasets, aerial photography, data frequently or partially updated, or when historic conditions need to be archived. |
| *Pros* | Raster datasets with pyramids (downsampled rasters) provide good display performance. In maps, raster datasets are continuous coverages of an area of interest. | Raster catalogs can also have pyramids. They are good for capturing source data, such as aerial photogrammetry stereo pairs, and for preserving historic data about resources. Raster catalogs are easier to build and maintain. |
| *Cons* | Only one pixel per location is stored. The most recent pixel writes over the previous pixel. | In maps, it's sometimes difficult to work with multiple rasters because of overlaps, differing illumination, and slower display performance. |
| *Recommendations* | Use raster datasets when fast display performance is important. | Use raster catalogs for massive data collections, tiled rasters with irregular update cycles, and for raster time series. |

Maps convey information through map symbols and descriptive text. There are two basic choices for representing text: annotations, which are persistent instances of text that can be individually edited for high-quality cartographic display and positioning; and labels, which are driven by attribute values and positioning rules, placed on the map whenever it is redrawn. With annotation, you can choose simple or feature-linked annotation with the text strings derived from feature attributes, such as river names.

High-quality map labeling is complex—you need to define many rules to place descriptive text for several dozen map layers. Moreover, map data density varies considerably, so you need to handle text that won't fit in crowded areas. The main judgment you need to make as a data modeler about text is whether to use automatic labeling or more sophisticated annotation.

Your choices in handling descriptive text in your data model are influenced by the number of features, your agency's cartographic standards, and whether the text is static or dynamic.

### Dynamically displaying labels

The easiest way to draw descriptive text on a map is by labeling features based on their attribute values. You select an attribute to use for the label, properties such as font and size, and autolabeling properties, such as orientation and offset. This is done by setting labeling and display properties for a map layer in ArcMap.

### Map annotation and geodatabase annotation

When you require more precise control over label placement, you can work with annotation. One option is to convert dynamic text into annotation. When you do so, you can finely edit the placement of each character around the feature it's labeling.

You have the choice of storing annotation with the map in an annotation group or in the geodatabase in an annotation class. Store annotation in the map if you are producing a custom project map and the number of annotations is not great. Store annotation in the geodatabase if it is to be used in other maps or in substantial quantity.

### Simple and feature-linked annotation

You can have two types of annotation: simple or feature-linked. Simple annotation is for text fixed in location, static in text value, or describing indeterminate features such as general places. Feature-linked annotation lets you control

what happens to an annotation when its linked feature is deleted or moved. Feature-linked annotation can also be refreshed when an attribute value of the linked feature is updated.

### Descriptive text and map scale

A way of handling data density is to assign scale thresholds for labels or annotations. For example, one map layer could have labels for major cities for use at map scales ranging from 1:100,000 to 1:500,000, and another map layer could have all the cities, towns, and villages for map scales greater than 1:500,000. The two map layers could have two adjoining scale thresholds to prevent overcrowded text. At small scales (zoomed out), you would see just major cities; at large scales (zoomed in), you would see all populated places.

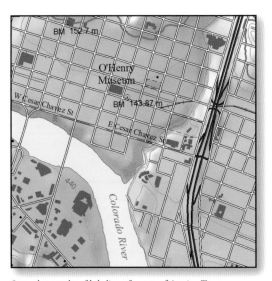

*Several examples of labeling of a map of Austin, Texas*

# Annotating and labeling features on a map

*Choosing whether to cartographically edit or automatically place text is an important design decision. The answer depends on the quality of source data, how much effort is to be expended, and the desired map quality.*

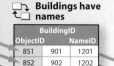

STOCKBRIDGE THEATRE

ALICE'S RESTAURANT

WHITEHALL APARTMENTS

There are two choices for representing descriptive text: as annotation objects in the geodatabase or as a set of labeling properties in an ArcMap layer. For simple map display, select labeling of attribute values for drawing descriptive text—you can label maps with little editing effort. When your map requires high-quality text placement, use annotation.

**Building feature class**

| ObjectID | Shape | Name | Square ft | Stories |
|---|---|---|---|---|
| 901 | | Stockbridge Theatre | 43600 | 1 |
| 902 | | Alice's Restaurant | 14100 | 2 |
| 903 | | Whitehall Apartments | 57500 | 7 |

**Buildings have names**

| BuildingID | | |
|---|---|---|
| ObjectID | | NameID |
| 851 | 901 | 1201 |
| 852 | 902 | 1202 |
| 853 | 903 | 1203 |

**A  BuildingName Annotation class**

| ObjectID | Shape | Element | FeatureID |
|---|---|---|---|
| 1201 | | STOCKBRIDGE THEATRE | 901 |
| 1202 | | ALICE'S RESTAURANT | 902 |
| 1203 | | WHITEHALL APARTMENTS | 903 |

| | Feature-linked annotation | Simple annotation | Labels |
|---|---|---|---|
| *Definition* | Annotation class joined in composite relationship with feature class. | Standalone annotation class. | Text properties, such as font and size, and a labeling field, defined in an ArcMap layer. |
| *Framework* | Geodatabase data model. | Geodatabase data model. | ArcMap document property. |
| *Typical uses* | Fine cartographic placement of annotation with attribute-based text. | Fine cartographic placement of annotation with fixed text. | When text values are attribute values that can be placed automatically on the map. |
| *Composite objects* | Yes | No | No |
| *Referential integrity* | Yes | No | No |
| *Pros* | The composite relationship lets you update, move, or delete annotation when features are edited. | Simple annotation lets you place fixed text with a high degree of control. | Labeling features is a quick and easy way to add descriptive text to your map. |
| *Cons* | Adds editing overhead; requires more work than labeling. | Requires more work than labeling; text values cannot be updated if attributes change. | While labels will not collide with each other, cartographic placement is rough. |
| *Recommendations* | Use feature-linked annotation for text, such as street names, building numbers, and gages. | Use simple annotation for static text or text describing large or indeterminate areas. | Use labeling for quickly placing descriptive text, such as addresses or measurements. |

# DESIGN PATTERNS—CLASSIFICATIONS AND DOMAINS

A major goal for many agencies is to capture detailed feature descriptions. Some systems implement a complex feature classification taxonomy using multiple feature attributes. When data integrity rules need to involve valid combinations of multiple attribute values, you should consider using valid value tables (VVTs). The modeling lesson is to not let a complex descriptive model become a complex data model. Instead, use VVTs to keep your model simple and clean yet capable of modeling any descriptive system.

National mapping agencies around the world use highly detailed feature classification systems for cartographic and analytical purposes. In some cases, the value of one feature attribute can determine which other feature attributes are to be part of the complete feature description.

When trying to implement this system in a GIS, some users went so far as to create a separate feature class for each distinct feature type, of which there could be several hundred. This is a burden on the DBMS for management and query. It also presents great difficulties for the user interface. Who would be willing to scroll through a list of hundreds of feature types, looking for one in particular?

The classification scheme need not drive the physical data model. A straightforward extension to the GIS has been developed that adds a small number of tables to implement the user's specific classification scheme. These tables, along with custom software, enable users to browse the geodatabase and access the full richness of their chosen classification system. They can create queries and assign symbology based on fields within the classification tables, performing queries such as "select all roads that are designated state highways with four lanes and concrete construction." Custom tools

are required to translate between the VVT identifier for each feature and the set of descriptive codes. This approach is described in more detail in Chapter 8, 'Cartography and the base map'.

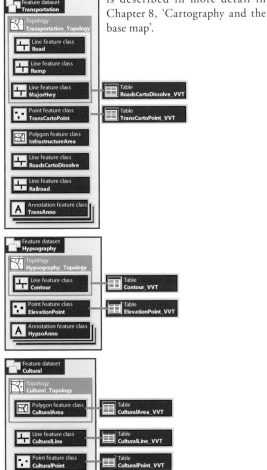

*These are some implementations of valid value tables from the topographic base map data model, documented in Chapter 8, 'Cartography and the base map'.*

*Most simple classification schemes rely on a small number of attributes to categorize each feature; these are well supported with coded-value attribute domains. When a classification needs to take into account combinations of multiple attribute values, consider the use of valid value tables for further data integrity and editing support.*

**Simple feature class — Contours**  
Geometry: Polyline  
Contains M values: No  
Contains Z values: No

| Field name | Data type | Allow nulls | Default value | Domain | Precision | Scale | Length |
|---|---|---|---|---|---|---|---|
| OBJECTID | Object ID | | | | | | |
| Shape | Geometry | Yes | | | | | |
| ELEVATION | Double | Yes | | | 0 | 0 | |
| SOURCE | Double | Yes | | | 0 | 0 | |
| UNITS | String | Yes | f | Units | | | 4 |
| SurfID | Long integer | Yes | | | 0 | | |
| LabelYN | Short integer | Yes | 0 | EnabledDomain | 0 | | |
| Index20 | Short integer | Yes | | | 0 | | |
| VVTID | Double | Yes | 0 | Contours | 0 | 0 | |
| Shape_Length | Double | Yes | | | 0 | 0 | |

**Table — Contours_VVT**

| Field name | Data type | Allow nulls | Precision | Scale | Length |
|---|---|---|---|---|---|
| OBJECTID | Object ID | | | | |
| VVTID | Double | Yes | 0 | | |
| FCODE | Long integer | Yes | 0 | | |
| ACODES | String | Yes | | | 254 |
| DESCRIPTIO | String | Yes | | | 254 |

| | Attribute domains | Complex coding systems |
|---|---|---|
| *Description* | Attribute domains control the allowable range or set of values for an attribute of a feature or object class and its subtypes. | Complex coding systems allow efficient storage and query of complex feature codes. |
| *Types* | Range and coded value sets. | Customizable types, especially multivalue sets. |
| *Definition* | A list of valid values in the geodatabase. | A set of validation tables you create with joins. |
| *Rules* | Attribute rules apply attribute domains to feature classes and subtypes. | You implement rules as a class extension in coordination with your validation tables. |
| *Pros* | Easily configurable; requires no custom coding. | Can handle complex domains and coding systems. |
| *Cons* | Can express simple attribute values only. | Requires customization and coding of ArcMap. |
| *Recommendations* | Use attribute domains to validate range and single-coded value sets for attributes. | Use a complex coding system if your feature coding system is complex and impacts your data models. Complex coding systems can reduce the number of feature classes to a manageable level. |

Geodatabase data models are designed to be used in practical application scenarios by a wide range of users. It is important to ensure that each design is easy to understand and implement. Each data model was built to support easy migration from existing data structures and designed to be flexible, extensible, and easily adapted by your organization. Here are a few final design tips to help you with your design implementations.

### Build on your existing GIS designs

Most existing database designs are suitable for moving forward. You can build on what has worked in the past and find new geodatabase capabilities that will improve over your past efforts.

### Use generic geodatabase types when feasible

It has been found that combining generic data structures with rich GIS tools provides the best solutions to scale and support multiple users and applications. Leverage the ArcGIS software logic as much as possible for your work. Only use customized GIS data structures as a last resort.

### Integrate spatially-related feature classes using topology

Legacy ArcInfo® users with coverages will find many opportunities to integrate feature classes using topologies in the geodatabase. Learn how to use geodatabase topology and its rules. This will create real savings in customization and user productivity. Even small cities will see 40 percent increases in efficiency for data maintenance.

### Combine GIS design concepts from this book with traditional relational database design methods

Both DBMS and GIS design methodologies are critical for good GIS design. One is not sufficient without the other. Learn to use and apply both techniques.

### Prototype and pilot your geodatabase design

Prototyping a design using personal geodatabases, ArcCatalog and ArcMap is easy, fun, and effective. You'll be surprised at how much insight you'll gain and how much more effective and efficient your design process will become.

During the final stage of design, you'll want to test scalability and work flows that represent the work that your organization will perform with your geodatabase. Use this to make final adjustments to your design. Be practical in your final test phase and adjust your design as necessary.

### for the Guadalupe River Basin, Texas

This diagram captures many of the elements that document the logical design. The presentation quality of the graphics is not paramount; what is essential is diagramming how key geographic features are modeled.

#### Network features

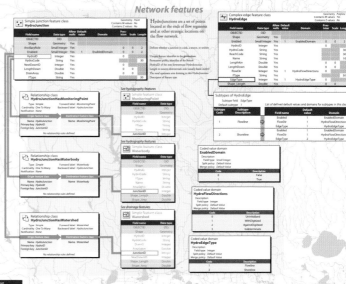

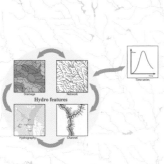

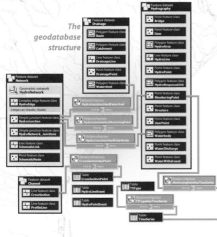

#### The geodatabase structure

#### Types of hydro edges

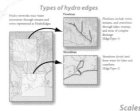

Hydro networks trace water movement through streams and rivers represented as HydroEdges.

Flowlines include rivers, streams, and centerlines through lakes, swamps, and areas of complex drainage (EdgeType=1)

Shorelines divide land from water for lakes and coastlines (EdgeType=2)

Flow direction is assigned going downstream on the hydro network.

#### Scales of representation of drainage systems

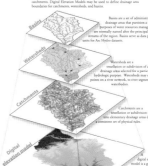

At the highest level are basins, which may be subdivided into watersheds or catchments. Digital Elevation Models may be used to define drainage area boundaries for catchments, watersheds, and basins.

#### HydroID to connect features

HydroID is a unique numerical integer identifier for all features within one Arc Hydro geodatabase.

#### Types of hydro junctions

HydroJunctions are generic locations where other hydro features are attached to the network.

HydroNetwork_Junctions are generic junctions created wherever two edges meet.

*Hydrography, hydrology, and hydraulics—these are all related fields in the study of water bodies and flow. From mapmaking to water quality analysis to flood prediction, there are many applications that can benefit from having a common data model for water features. This chapter explores a mature data model now in use in these related but diverse fields. Projects under way in the state of Texas and at the South Florida Water Management District illustrate the use of this model.*

2

**S**urface water location, depth, and flow data is collected and used for many purposes among local, regional, state, and national agencies, as well as in private industry. National agencies have traditionally compiled hydrographic data for base maps, such as the National Hydrography Dataset (NHD) created jointly by the U.S. Geological Survey and the U.S. Environmental Protection Agency (EPA). The NHD is also designed to represent the network connectivity of U.S. rivers and streams, enabling its use in hydrologic analysis.

Since 2001, the Center for Research in Water Resources (CRWR) at The University of Texas at Austin has coordinated the international GIS in Water Resources Consortium in the development of the Arc Hydro data model for surface water, which can be used to support hydrographic, hydrologic, and hydraulic applications. Some of the examples in this chapter are drawn from the use of Arc Hydro in modeling and managing water availability and quality in the state of Texas.

The South Florida Water Management District (SFWMD) is the largest of Florida's regional water management agencies and has several related projects that illustrate the need for a common data model across its organization. These projects include improving daily water monitoring and management efforts, restoration of key wetlands and river channels, and assisting with the generation of accurate Flood Insurance Rate Maps (FIRMs) for the Federal Emergency Management Agency (FEMA). The Arc Hydro data model appears well suited to supporting these projects, and plans are to extend it. In addition, since considerable talent and time goes into hydrologic and hydraulic mathematical modeling, SFWMD has learned that GIS can greatly improve the data management for such analysis. SFWMD anticipates implementing the Arc Hydro data model extensively throughout its organization.

Arc Hydro is more than a data model, however; it also includes a set of software, network analysis, and data management tools that complement ArcGIS.

# Streams and river networks

Ultimately, the content and structure of a GIS data model is based on application requirements and the set of information products you expect to generate with your GIS. Here are four projects that helped to define and shape the contents of the Arc Hydro data model.

## TEXAS

How much water do we have? How much are we using? How much do we need? These simple, reasonable questions, asked by then-Governor George W. Bush of Texas during a drought in 1996, had no ready answers. Accordingly, the Texas Legislature in 1997 launched an ambitious plan to overhaul water planning in the state and to construct detailed, statewide data layers of geospatial information on land surface terrain, soils, land use, and stream hydrography. Water availability in Texas is now managed using this digital geospatial infrastructure instead of stacks of paper maps. The Arc Hydro model described in this chapter is used to structure the geospatial information for Texas' water availability modeling.

The 1996 drought was hardly over when a severe storm in October 1998 caused a huge flood in south Texas. Flood flows in the lower Guadalupe River basin were more than twice as large as any recorded since stream-gaging stations were installed during the 1930s. The October 1998 flood killed more than 40 people and destroyed countless homes, resulting in $2.1 billion in damages.

The cleanup from this flood was still going on when Tropical Storm Allison hit Houston in June 2000. A total of 77,000 buildings were inundated in what became the most costly urban flood disaster in the history of the United States. The story continues. It is at times like these that understanding and managing water resources means so much more than understanding and managing information—it means life and death.

Accurate floodplain mapping is needed to be able to estimate flood risks precisely. One of the reactions to Tropical Storm Allison was a complete remapping of the floodplains of Houston using light detection and ranging (LIDAR), a remote sensing technique from aircraft that produces highly detailed and precise maps of land surface terrain.

In the United States, the Nexrad radar rainfall system provides maps of storm precipitation updated every few minutes. The South Florida Water Management District uses the Nexrad data, adjusted by actual rain gage measurements from across its jurisdiction, at 15-minute intervals (near real-time update). There would be a significant benefit for public safety if these radar rainfall maps could be quickly translated into anticipated flood inundation maps during storm events. Creating real-time flood inundation maps requires connecting map data on ground conditions with a time sequence of rainfall maps, and with flood simulation models, to produce a time sequence of flood maps on the ground.

*Flood control motivated the channelization of the Kissimmee River, Florida.*

## SOUTH FLORIDA

In South Florida, the network of canals through flat, swampy terrain resembles a transportation grid more than anything else. On this flat landscape, water can move in almost any direction with ease. Depending on the location of storms in its jurisdiction, the SFWMD will actually use pumps to change the direction of flow in these canals to draw water away from the storms, thereby reducing the potential for inundation. The daily monitoring and management of this system of canals and pumping stations requires sophisticated data management, modeling, and simulation. SFWMD is beginning to use the Arc Hydro data model to help them in this task.

## MANAGING WATER QUALITY AT EPA

Concern about water resources is not limited to the impacts of floods and droughts. Citizens want livable cities, where urban growth and development can coexist with a clean environment and healthy ecosystem. Water quality management in cities requires solutions that assess how regulation of land development will affect water quality and ecological resources. What combination of pollution prevention structures, education, and regulation best serves to enhance the quality of the urban water environment?

From a larger perspective, the goal of the 1972 Clean Water Act was to protect the environmental quality of the United States' waters. After 30 years of pollution prevention efforts, mostly aimed at controlling point sources of pollution, many of the nation's waters are still not fishable or swimmable because of nonpoint pollution sources, such as runoff from farmlands.

To rectify this problem, the U.S. Environmental Protection Agency has embarked on an ambitious program, called Total Maximum Daily Load, whose goals include setting regulatory standards on the quality of water within natural water bodies and regulating the outflows of wastewater discharge pipes. Trying to regulate water quality requires a much more comprehensive understanding of the impact of all types of pollution sources. The EPA has created a decision support system called Basins, built using ArcView®, to integrate water resources information and water quality models for improved water quality management. The Arc Hydro data model presented in this chapter can be used to support the Basins system.

## ENVIRONMENTAL RESTORATION

South Florida has further issues, brought about by the encroachment of human development. From 1962 to 1971, the Kissimmee River was channelized and its floodplain drained between Lake Kissimmee and Lake Okeechobee as part of the Central and South Florida Flood Control Project. Since this ambitious project was completed, many species of plants and animals have begun to disappear from the region. Efforts to restore the Kissimmee River began in 1992. From June 1999 to February 2001, 7.5 miles of canal were backfilled and converted to 15 miles of river.

This was the first step in returning a total of 43 miles of canals and floodplain back to their original state. To better understand and stimulate the return of plants and wildlife to this region, SFWMD is studying the inundated areas, to what depths, and for how long (this information is called the "hydro period"), and performing statistical interpolation to estimate values between monitoring points. The Arc Hydro data model is being used and extended to support this study.

This is the initial step for an even greater project, the Comprehensive Everglades Restoration Plan (CERP), which is intended to restore a significant portion of the Florida Everglades to its original state. Lessons learned from the Kissimmee restoration project should help in this effort.

*An aerial view of the Kissimmee River*

GIS applications for surface water systems are derived from surface elevation. Actual rivers, streams, and water bodies interact as a system of water features within this terrain. Drainage simulation—the expected behavior of raindrops hitting the ground—forms the primary concept of a GIS water resource data model.

The thematic layers presented here reflect the GIS datasets that are traditionally used for water resource applications.

## Surface terrain

Perhaps the most important source for defining a drainage network is the digital elevation model of surface terrain. Analytical methods have been developed to delineate stream networks and drainage basins from DEMs. Other elevation sources include LIDAR and digital surface models (DSM), such as those from the Shuttle Radar Topographic Mission (SRTM). LIDAR produces such highly detailed data that it is best used in focused areas. DSM data includes treetop surface, which is useful for some analyses but would need to be corrected for drainage network determination.

## Digital orthophotography

In flat terrain, traditional analytical methods are difficult to use to correctly delineate basins and stream networks from DEMs. Orthophotos and LIDAR can be used to fix errors in such DEMs. Orthophotos also provide useful backdrops in map displays.

## Hydrography

Topographic base maps typically include natural and man-made water features. The USGS has mapped the United States at 1:24,000 scale, and the National Hydrographic Dataset, compiled by the USGS and EPA, represents water networks at 1:100,000 and 1:24,000 map scales.

## Rainfall response areas

A complement to topographic maps and orthophotos is a layer illustrating broad patterns of land use, soils, and vegetation in terms of their contribution to rainfall runoff (response). This is useful for understanding and analyzing the environmental quality of streams and rivers.

## Drainage areas

Alternately called catchments, watersheds, and basins, drainage areas are of varying size, from the small catchment area that drains to a single creek or stream to multi-state regions that drain to a major river system. Watershed boundaries may be defined in purely technical terms from DEM source data or for various political purposes, such as to delineate water management jurisdictions.

## Streams

Cartographic data for mapping of streams and rivers can also be used for stream analysis, for example, flow analysis such as upstream or downstream tracing.

## Hydrographic points

Monitoring stations, dams, pumping stations, and other facilities are often located based on their river distance from the stream mouth or confluence. These provide important reference points for stream analysis.

## Channels

Detailed three-dimensional channel and cross section profile data is also required for hydraulic analysis, such as flood mapping.

# Thematic layers of the Arc Hydro data model

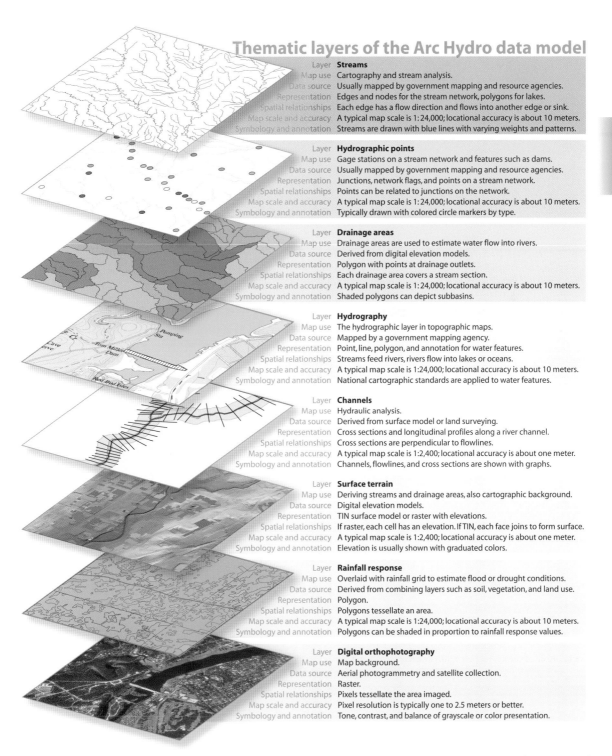

**Layer** **Streams**
**Map use** Cartography and stream analysis.
**Data source** Usually mapped by government mapping and resource agencies.
**Representation** Edges and nodes for the stream network, polygons for lakes.
**Spatial relationships** Each edge has a flow direction and flows into another edge or sink.
**Map scale and accuracy** A typical map scale is 1:24,000; locational accuracy is about 10 meters.
**Symbology and annotation** Streams are drawn with blue lines with varying weights and patterns.

**Layer** **Hydrographic points**
**Map use** Gage stations on a stream network and features such as dams.
**Data source** Usually mapped by government mapping and resource agencies.
**Representation** Junctions, network flags, and points on a stream network.
**Spatial relationships** Points can be related to junctions on the network.
**Map scale and accuracy** A typical map scale is 1:24,000; locational accuracy is about 10 meters.
**Symbology and annotation** Typically drawn with colored circle markers by type.

**Layer** **Drainage areas**
**Map use** Drainage areas are used to estimate water flow into rivers.
**Data source** Derived from digital elevation models.
**Representation** Polygon with points at drainage outlets.
**Spatial relationships** Each drainage area covers a stream section.
**Map scale and accuracy** A typical map scale is 1:24,000; locational accuracy is about 10 meters.
**Symbology and annotation** Shaded polygons can depict subbasins.

**Layer** **Hydrography**
**Map use** The hydrographic layer in topographic maps.
**Data source** Mapped by a government mapping agency.
**Representation** Point, line, polygon, and annotation for water features.
**Spatial relationships** Streams feed rivers, rivers flow into lakes or oceans.
**Map scale and accuracy** A typical map scale is 1:24,000; locational accuracy is about 10 meters.
**Symbology and annotation** National cartographic standards are applied to water features.

**Layer** **Channels**
**Map use** Hydraulic analysis.
**Data source** Derived from surface model or land surveying.
**Representation** Cross sections and longitudinal profiles along a river channel.
**Spatial relationships** Cross sections are perpendicular to flowlines.
**Map scale and accuracy** A typical map scale is 1:2,400; locational accuracy is about one meter.
**Symbology and annotation** Channels, flowlines, and cross sections are shown with graphs.

**Layer** **Surface terrain**
**Map use** Deriving streams and drainage areas, also cartographic background.
**Data source** Digital elevation models.
**Representation** TIN surface model or raster with elevations.
**Spatial relationships** If raster, each cell has an elevation. If TIN, each face joins to form surface.
**Map scale and accuracy** A typical map scale is 1:2,400; locational accuracy is about one meter.
**Symbology and annotation** Elevation is usually shown with graduated colors.

**Layer** **Rainfall response**
**Map use** Overlaid with rainfall grid to estimate flood or drought conditions.
**Data source** Derived from combining layers such as soil, vegetation, and land use.
**Representation** Polygon.
**Spatial relationships** Polygons tessellate an area.
**Map scale and accuracy** A typical map scale is 1:24,000; locational accuracy is about 10 meters.
**Symbology and annotation** Polygons can be shaded in proportion to rainfall response values.

**Layer** **Digital orthophotography**
**Map use** Map background.
**Data source** Aerial photogrammetry and satellite collection.
**Representation** Raster.
**Spatial relationships** Pixels tessellate the area imaged.
**Map scale and accuracy** Pixel resolution is typically one to 2.5 meters or better.
**Symbology and annotation** Tone, contrast, and balance of grayscale or color presentation.

2

To support these thematic layers, the GIS database is organized around five main categories of vector and tabular content: hydrographic features, drainage features, network elements, channel details, and time series. Features in one category may be created from features in another to suit specific analysis techniques. Users choose the features needed for a given project and may not require all those shown here. Users are also encouraged to expand on this schema.

Like some of the other data models presented in this book, the Arc Hydro data model is additive; the feature classes described here can be added to and, in some cases, derived from an existing base map data model.

The Arc Hydro data model is intended as a starting point for your specific applications; it is intentionally simplified to represent the core framework of the most common and generic components for hydrologic and hydraulic analysis. Early in the data model development, it was found to be impractical, and of benefit to very few users, to try to achieve a "superset" data model, from which users would just pick the components of interest to a given project and discard the rest. Instead, it was agreed by the GIS in Water Resources Consortium that the best balance between flexibility and interoperability of datasets was to standardize these core components.

## Drainage

Drainage features are derived from DEM or other surface topography. Drainage lines represent streams and rivers, and drainage points represent outlets from drainage areas. Catchments, watersheds, and basins represent different levels of drainage area delineations (this will be discussed in greater detail later in the chapter).

## Hydrography

Hydrography features are primarily base data from topographic maps and tabular data inventories.

## Network

These feature classes form connected sets of points and lines showing pathways of water flow. HydroEdges are network elements corresponding to DrainageLines or HydroLines (streams and rivers). HydroJunctions are user-defined nodes in the network, such as at confluences, and at the pour points of drainage areas. Notice the many relationships between HydroJunctions and other feature classes; these are important for connecting a project's alternate views of hydro data. HydroNetwork_Junctions are created by the GIS system wherever additional nodes are needed, beyond those defined by the user. SchematicLinks and SchematicNodes are an alternative "dual" representation of the network, in which drainage areas are represented by SchematicNodes, and the connections between drainage areas are represented by SchematicLinks.

Time series

Drainage

Network

Hydrography

Channel

## Channel

These feature classes are used to represent the three-dimensional model of stream channel bottoms, banks, and floodplains. This is done by capturing the stream bottom relief at specific cross section paths perpendicular to the stream direction. This level of detail is necessary to generate accurate maps of flood potential.

## Time Series

Time series are used for repeated periodic measurements at monitoring stations and other facilities. Each time series may be associated with one or more features, and each feature can have any number of time series. The TSType table provides a minimum set of metadata for each time series.

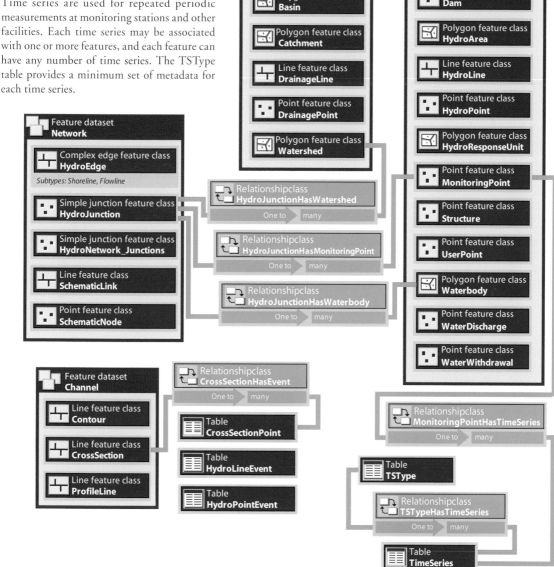

In an object-relational database, each object has a unique identifier maintained by the database management system. In this data model, it is useful for features to also have user-defined permanent identifiers independent of the DBMS. The Arc Hydro data model defines two public identifier fields, HydroCode and HydroID, for this purpose.

Throughout the United States, the USGS has installed gage stations to monitor stream stage (depth) and flow. Each gage is assigned a unique number that distinguishes it from all other gages in the United States. This identifier is a permanent, public key. In this data model, every feature class has a field called HydroCode that can be used as such an identifier. This is a text field, since public identifiers often have nonnumeric content.

## Identifying features with HydroID

However, not all hydro features have such a public identification system. Within the context of a GIS database, it is, therefore, useful to also define an identifier that is permanent and unique within, at least, the database. The DBMS-managed ObjectID field is not sufficient for this task because it can be reassigned by the system under various conditions, such as when copying features to another database. To better maintain the referential integrity of foreign keys with the many relationships in this data model, an integer field called

HydroID is defined in every feature class. The HydroID is the label that uniquely identifies features within Arc Hydro, while the HydroCode identifies features with labels used by other information systems external to Arc Hydro.

For example, many hydrology applications read stream flow time series data for USGS stream gages across the United States over the Internet from the National Water Information System (NWIS) Web site. One such application reads the stream flow data for a stream gage at the Guadalupe River at Victoria, Texas. Within the Arc Hydro geodatabase, this gage has a HydroID of 12000033; for the USGS, this gage has a site identifier of 08176500. The USGS site identifier is assigned to the HydroCode field, and knowing this, the application can programmatically extract the stream flow data for this gage from NWIS.

The HydroID is an important attribute within Arc Hydro. It is carefully managed in the Arc Hydro tools and must be carefully managed by users. The HydroID is defined using

### HydroID

HydroID is a unique numerical integer identifier for all features within one Arc Hydro geodatabase.

| LayerKeyTable | |
|---|---|
| LayerName | LayerKey |
| DrainageLine | Key A |
| Watershed | Key B |
| Catchment | Key B |
| HydroJunction | Key C |

| HydroIDTable | |
|---|---|
| LayerKey | HydroID |
| Key A | 100003 |
| Key B | 200007 |
| Key C | 300000 |
| Other | 1 |

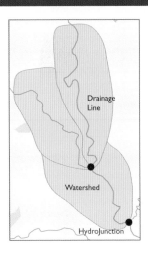

The HydroID for a new feature in a feature class is dispensed from a HydroID Table. A feature class points to its HydroID dispenser in the HydroID Table through its LayerKey defined in the LayerKeyTable.

Several feature classes can point to the same HydroID dispenser using the same LayerKey.

a pair of tables called the LayerKeyTable and the HydroID-Table. These tables are generated automatically (if not already present) by any of the Arc Hydro tools that need a HydroID. A default record in the HydroIDTable provides a starting value of 1 in case the user does not create layer keys for all (or any) feature classes. Each time a new ID is assigned to a feature in a particular class, the associated counter in the HydroIDTable is updated so that the same HydroID is never assigned again within the same geodatabase.

A number of alternative approaches for assigning HydroIDs could have been chosen, for instance, creating the identifier in terms of multiple subfields separated by a delimiter, similar to the format for domain names in Internet URLs. One subfield could identify the originating database, another subfield the feature class, and a third subfield the feature number, all separated by periods, vertical bars, or any other delimiter of your choice.

Such an approach would require additional programming within the Arc Hydro tools working with HydroID. However, this kind of ID-level processing can noticeably affect overall application performance and should be rigorously

minimized. After considering a number of alternatives, the hydrologists instrumental in developing the Arc Hydro tools sought the efficiency and speed of simple integers for this task.

Users should consider carefully when assigning HydroID ranges to layer keys to allow for potentially combining data from multiple separate databases. For example, it may make sense to compile the features of each major watershed in a separate database so multiple people can be working in parallel at remote locations, then merge the results into a single database. One approach for assigning HydroIDs in this situation is documented on the CD–ROM that comes with the definitive book on Arc Hydro (Maidment 2002). In this approach, you would assign different integer ranges to each feature class in each database so the HydroIDs in the combined datasets remain unique.

However you choose to define HydroID, the downloadable tools designed for the Arc Hydro data model will help populate and maintain the foreign key references for related feature classes.

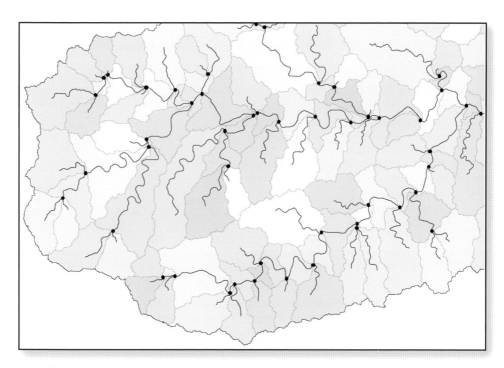

*Map of drainage lines, hydro junctions, and watershed—all related through the HydroID*

The hydro network is the backbone of Arc Hydro. The topological connection of HydroEdges and HydroJunctions in a network enables tracing of water movement upstream and downstream through streams, rivers, and other water bodies. Relationships built from the HydroJunctions connect drainage areas and point features, such as stream-gaging stations to the hydro network. Locations on the hydro network are defined by a river addressing scheme that allows measurement of distance along a flow path.

Networks of rivers and streams have always been fundamental to maps of a landscape. Traditionally, networks in GIS have been used to describe transportation systems of road networks. Such networks possess complications not typically seen in hydrology, such as flow moving in both directions along a road. Water flow in hydrology is normally driven by gravity and flows from higher to lower elevations. This rule simplifies the analytical tools needed in most cases.

## HydroEdge

A hydro network is a simplified representation of the blue lines on maps defining streams, rivers, and water bodies, in which centerlines can be drawn through all areal features to create a continuous, single-line network throughout the river system.

Fluid flow can be classified as one-dimensional, two-dimensional, or three-dimensional. A flowline traces the main direction of water movement in a one-dimensional flow. Flow properties, such as discharge, velocity, depth, and constituent concentrations, are allowed to vary only along the flowline, hence the term one-dimensional flow. A key virtue of the assumption of one-dimensional flow is that the flow equations are readily solved for a wide range of cases, from a small creek to a large river.

When water flows into a water body, such as a lake, its motion is no longer one-dimensional. However, many lakes can be approximated as one-dimensional flow systems, where the flow tends to follow the channels of

the inundated river. Hence, flowlines can be drawn through lakes from the point where a tributary inflow enters the lake to the point of discharge at the lake outlet. The process of drawing centerlines through water bodies can be automated, using raster processing of areal features, or the centerlines can be digitized in the GIS map editor.

## HydroEdge subtypes

Flowlines are used to trace water movement through streams, rivers, and water bodies, while shorelines form the interface between land and water for water bodies. Shorelines include those of lakes and reservoirs, coastlines to the sea

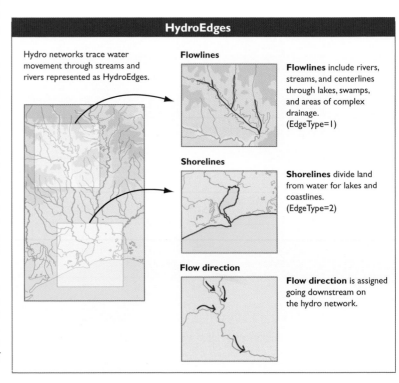

**HydroEdges**

Hydro networks trace water movement through streams and rivers represented as HydroEdges.

**Flowlines**

**Flowlines** include rivers, streams, and centerlines through lakes, swamps, and areas of complex drainage. (EdgeType=1)

**Shorelines**

**Shorelines** divide land from water for lakes and coastlines. (EdgeType=2)

**Flow direction**

**Flow direction** is assigned going downstream on the hydro network.

or ocean, and bank lines for wide streams or rivers that are considered areal or water body features. Users who wish to distinguish specific types of flowlines, such as natural channels, constructed channels, and pipelines (for example, for cartographic purposes), are encouraged to extend the set of subtypes of HydroEdge for this purpose.

### HydroEdge properties

HydroEdge is shown as a subclass of the ArcGIS complex edge feature class. This allows a single HydroEdge to have internal junctions, without having to split the HydroEdge feature.

Note the attribute of HydroEdge called ReachCode. A "reach" refers to a stream segment, typically a length of stream between two confluences. The USGS/EPA National Hydrographic Dataset (http://nhdgeo.usgs.gov) defines identifiers (reach codes) for stream segments throughout the United States at a scale of 1:100,000. In addition to stream reaches, the NHD defines reaches through water bodies, such as lakes and bays. Through collaborations with state governments, the NHD is being refined to a scale of 1:24,000.

The Enabled attribute is used by ArcGIS network tools. The default value of one (true) means that the HydroEdge feature participates in the connected network. A value of zero (false) means that the feature does not participate in the network and represents a break in the network connectivity.

The FlowDir attribute is used by some of the Arc Hydro tools. A value of 3 (indeterminate) means that flow can be in either direction, which allows some trace functions to still work. A value of zero will stop a network trace.

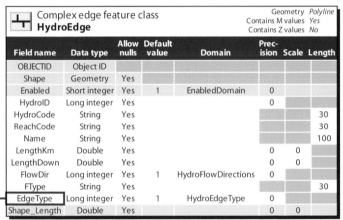

| Complex edge feature class **HydroEdge** | | | | | Geometry | *Polyline* | | |
| --- | --- | --- | --- | --- | --- | --- | --- | --- |
| | | | | | Contains M values | *Yes* | | |
| | | | | | Contains Z values | *No* | | |
| **Field name** | **Data type** | **Allow nulls** | **Default value** | **Domain** | **Prec-ision** | **Scale** | **Length** | |
| OBJECTID | Object ID | | | | | | | Unique feature identifier in the geodatabase |
| Shape | Geometry | Yes | | | | | | |
| Enabled | Short integer | Yes | 1 | EnabledDomain | 0 | | | |
| HydroID | Long integer | Yes | | | 0 | | | Permanent public identifier of feature |
| HydroCode | String | Yes | | | | | 30 | |
| ReachCode | String | Yes | | | | | 30 | An identifier for a river or stream segment |
| Name | String | Yes | | | | | 100 | Geographic name |
| LengthKm | Double | Yes | | | 0 | 0 | | Length of the edge in kilometers |
| LengthDown | Double | Yes | | | 0 | 0 | | Length to nearest downstream sink (usually the basin outlet) |
| FlowDir | Long integer | Yes | 1 | HydroFlowDirections | 0 | | | Defines the direction of flow on the edge |
| FType | String | Yes | | | | | 30 | Descriptor of feature type |
| EdgeType | Long integer | Yes | 1 | HydroEdgeType | 0 | | | Defines the edge as being either a flowline or a shoreline |
| Shape_Length | Double | Yes | | | 0 | 0 | | |

*Hydro edges are the network of lines describing map hydrography. There are two types: flowlines, which trace water movement, and shorelines, which form the interface between land and water.*

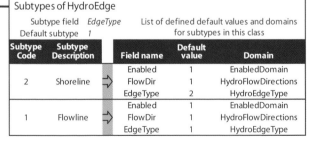

**Subtypes of HydroEdge**

Subtype field *EdgeType*
Default subtype *1*

List of defined default values and domains for subtypes in this class

| Subtype Code | Subtype Description | Field name | Default value | Domain |
| --- | --- | --- | --- | --- |
| 2 | Shoreline | Enabled | 1 | EnabledDomain |
| | | FlowDir | 1 | HydroFlowDirections |
| | | EdgeType | 2 | HydroEdgeType |
| 1 | Flowline | Enabled | 1 | EnabledDomain |
| | | FlowDir | 1 | HydroFlowDirections |
| | | EdgeType | 1 | HydroEdgeType |

**Coded value domain**
**HydroEdgeType**
Description
Field type *Long integer*
Split policy *Default value*
Merge policy *Default value*

| Code | Description |
| --- | --- |
| 1 | Flowline |
| 2 | Shoreline |

**Coded value domain**
**EnabledDomain**
Description
Field type *Short integer*
Split policy *Default value*
Merge policy *Default value*

| Code | Description |
| --- | --- |
| 0 | False |
| 1 | True |

**Coded value domain**
**HydroFlowDirections**
Description
Field type *Long integer*
Split policy *Default value*
Merge policy *Default value*

| Code | Description |
| --- | --- |
| 0 | Uninitialized |
| 1 | WithDigitized |
| 2 | AgainstDigitized |
| 3 | Indeterminate |

Network junctions bound network edge features, such as HydroEdges. In some cases, these junctions are important features in their own right, while others are only needed because the GIS network tools require at least a generic junction at every intersection of two edges.

Two kinds of network junction feature classes are used in this model: an application-specific feature class called HydroJunction and a generic class called HydroNetwork_Junction.

## HydroJunctions

HydroJunction features are used to represent significant point locations in the hydro network, such as the outlet of a watershed, the outlet of a lake or other water body, or the location of a monitoring station. In each of these cases, the HydroJunction is snapped to the hydro network at the appropriate location, and a relationship is then created between the HydroJunction and the desired feature, with the help of the Arc Hydro Tools. This serves one of the most important goals of the Arc Hydro data model, which is to enable connecting any hydrographic feature to the hydro network. This simple approach provides a unifying principle for navigating through the database among the various categories of water-related features.

Attributes on HydroJunctions include a link to the next downstream junction (NextDownID), length to the next downstream sink (basin outlet), and the total upstream area draining to the par-

ticular HydroJunction. These values are determined with the help of the Arc Hydro Tools.

## HydroNetwork_Junctions

In any GIS system that supports networks, a junction (or equivalent topological primitive) is required at the intersection of two edges. In ArcGIS, if there is not yet a user-defined junction at such an intersection, then the GIS network tools create a generic junction at this location. HydroNetwork_Junction class holds these generic junction features.

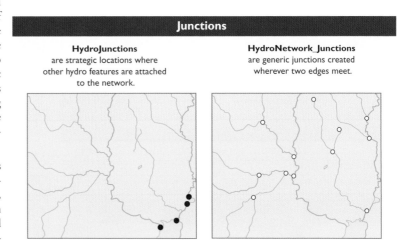

### Junctions

**HydroJunctions** are strategic locations where other hydro features are attached to the network.

**HydroNetwork_Junctions** are generic junctions created wherever two edges meet.

| Simple junction feature class **HydroNetwork_Junctions** | | | | Geometry *Point* Contains M values *No* Contains Z values *No* | | | |
|---|---|---|---|---|---|---|---|
| Field name | Data type | Allow nulls | Default value | Domain | Precision | Scale | Length |
| OBJECTID | Object ID | | | | | | |
| SHAPE | Geometry | Yes | | | | | |
| Enabled | Short integer | Yes | 1 | EnabledDomain | 0 | | |

*Generic junctions are created during the building of a geometric network at the ends of all the edges, except where a HydroJunction exists.*

## Simple junction feature class
### HydroJunction

| | |
|---|---|
| Geometry | Point |
| Contains M values | No |
| Contains Z values | No |

*HydroJunctions are points located at the ends of flow segments and at other strategic locations on the flow network*

| Field name | Data type | Allow nulls | Default value | Domain | Precision | Scale | Length | |
|---|---|---|---|---|---|---|---|---|
| OBJECTID | Object ID | | | | | | | |
| Shape | Geometry | Yes | | | | | | |
| AncillaryRole | Short integer | Yes | | | 0 | | | Defines whether a junction is a sink, source, or neither |
| Enabled | Short integer | Yes | 1 | EnabledDomain | 0 | | | |
| HydroID | Long integer | Yes | | | 0 | | | Unique feature identifier in the geodatabase |
| HydroCode | String | Yes | | | | | 30 | Permanent public identifier of feature |
| NextDownID | Long integer | Yes | | | 0 | | | HydroID of the next downstream HydroJunction |
| LengthDown | Double | Yes | | | 0 | 0 | | Length to nearest downstream sink (usually basin outlet) |
| DrainArea | Double | Yes | | | 0 | 0 | | The total upstream area draining to this HydroJunction |
| FType | String | Yes | | | | | 30 | Descriptor of feature type |

## Relationship class
### HydroJunctionHasMonitoringPoint

| | | | |
|---|---|---|---|
| Type | Simple | Forward label | MonitoringPoint |
| Cardinality | One to many | Backward label | HydroJunction |
| Notification | None | | |

| Origin feature class | Destination feature class |
|---|---|
| Name *HydroJunction* | Name *MonitoringPoint* |
| Primary key *HydroID* | |
| Foreign key *JunctionID* | |

## Simple feature class
### MonitoringPoint

| | |
|---|---|
| Geometry | Point |
| Contains M values | No |
| Contains Z values | No |

| Field name | Data type | Allow nulls | Precision | Scale | Length |
|---|---|---|---|---|---|
| OBJECTID | Object ID | | | | |
| Shape | Geometry | Yes | | | |
| HydroID | Long integer | Yes | 0 | | |
| HydroCode | String | Yes | | | 30 |
| FType | String | Yes | | | 30 |
| Name | String | Yes | | | 100 |
| JunctionID | Long integer | Yes | 0 | | |

## Relationship class
### HydroJunctionHasWaterbody

| | | | |
|---|---|---|---|
| Type | Simple | Forward label | Waterbody |
| Cardinality | One to many | Backward label | HydroJunction |
| Notification | None | | |

| Origin feature class | Destination feature class |
|---|---|
| Name *HydroJunction* | Name *Waterbody* |
| Primary key *HydroID* | |
| Foreign key *JunctionID* | |

## Simple feature class
### Waterbody

| | |
|---|---|
| Geometry | Polygon |
| Contains M values | No |
| Contains Z values | No |

| Field name | Data type | Allow nulls | Precision | Scale | Length |
|---|---|---|---|---|---|
| OBJECTID | Object ID | | | | |
| Shape | Geometry | Yes | | | |
| HydroID | Long integer | Yes | 0 | | |
| HydroCode | String | Yes | | | 30 |
| FType | String | Yes | | | 30 |
| Name | String | Yes | | | 100 |
| AreaSqKm | Double | Yes | 0 | 0 | |
| JunctionID | Long integer | Yes | 0 | | |
| Shape_Length | Double | Yes | 0 | 0 | |
| Shape_Area | Double | Yes | 0 | 0 | |

## Relationship class
### HydroJunctionHasWatershed

| | | | |
|---|---|---|---|
| Type | Simple | Forward label | Watershed |
| Cardinality | One to many | Backward label | HydroJunction |
| Notification | None | | |

| Origin feature class | Destination feature class |
|---|---|
| Name *HydroJunction* | Name *Watershed* |
| Primary key *HydroID* | |
| Foreign key *JunctionID* | |

## Simple feature class
### Watershed

| | |
|---|---|
| Geometry | Polygon |
| Contains M values | No |
| Contains Z values | No |

| Field name | Data type | Allow nulls | Precision | Scale | Length |
|---|---|---|---|---|---|
| OBJECTID | Object ID | | | | |
| Shape | Geometry | Yes | | | |
| HydroID | Long integer | Yes | 0 | | |
| HydroCode | String | Yes | | | 30 |
| DrainID | Long integer | Yes | 0 | | |
| AreaSqKm | Double | Yes | 0 | 0 | |
| JunctionID | Long integer | Yes | 0 | | |
| NextDownID | Long integer | Yes | 0 | | |
| Shape_Length | Double | Yes | 0 | 0 | |
| Shape_Area | Double | Yes | 0 | 0 | |

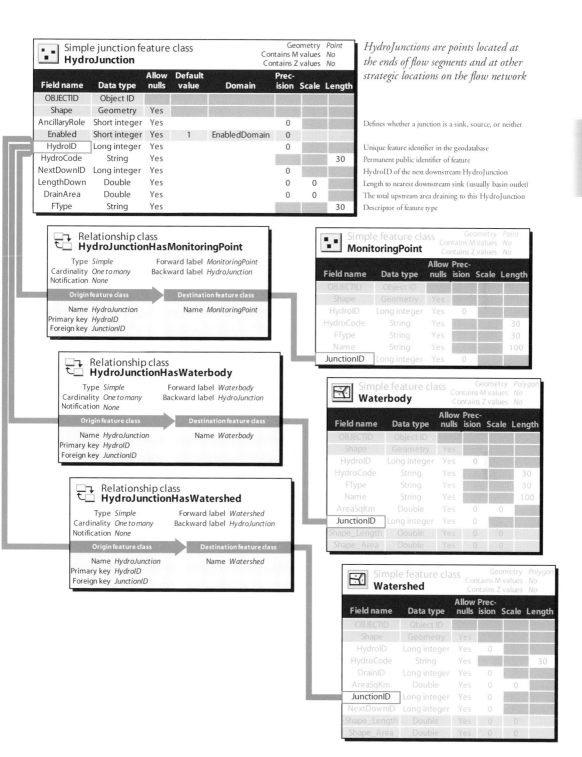

Event tables in ArcGIS are points or lines that are not explicitly defined with their own geographic coordinates but are, instead, referenced to a separate line feature class on which an addressing system has been defined. This is analogous to specifying that a house is located at 123 Oak Avenue, rather than giving its latitude and longitude.

Objects located by linear referencing on a hydro network are called hydro events. These may be HydroPointEvents (a point location on a HydroEdge) or HydroLineEvents (a line between two identified points on a HydroEdge).

## Hydro point and line events

Hydro events carry a ReachCode attribute to identify the HydroEdge or set of HydroEdges to which they are referenced.

In addition, HydroPointEvents have a Measure attribute to specify where along that reach the point is located. Similarly, HydroLineEvents contain FMeasure (from-measure) and TMeasure (to-measure) attributes to locate the endpoints of the linear event along a reach. Line events also carry the attribute Offset, which allows line events to be displaced to the left or right of the reference line, such as when information for the left bank of a river is defined separately from the right bank.

For example, some river-related features that are important for inventory purposes but not strictly part of the river network could be associated with the river network through the HydroPointEvent table. These may include reference locations where permits have been issued for water withdrawal or discharge.

Similarly, changes in various characteristics of a river channel, such as bed substrate type, could be referenced to the river network through the HydroLineEvent table.

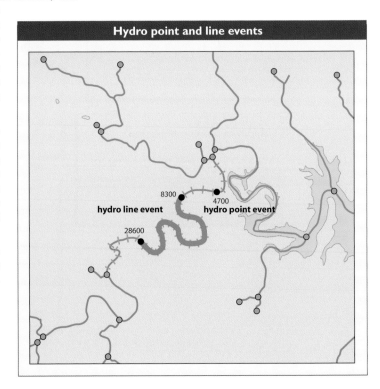

**Hydro point and line events**

8300

4700

hydro line event    hydro point event

28600

## Table
### HydroLineEvent

| Field name | Data type | Allow nulls | Prec- ision | Scale | Length |
|---|---|---|---|---|---|
| OBJECTID | Object ID | | | | |
| ReachCode | String | Yes | | | 30 |
| FMeasure | Double | Yes | 0 | 0 | |
| TMeasure | Double | Yes | 0 | 0 | |
| Offset | Double | Yes | 0 | 0 | |

*An attribute or set of attributes associated with a line segment through measure values*

An identifier for a river or stream segment
Measure value at the start of the line event
Measure value at the end of the line event
Distance from the center of the line to display event

## Table
### HydroPointEvent

| Field name | Data type | Allow nulls | Prec- ision | Scale | Length |
|---|---|---|---|---|---|
| OBJECTID | Object ID | | | | |
| ReachCode | String | Yes | | | 30 |
| Measure | Double | Yes | 0 | 0 | |

*An attribute or set of attributes associated with a location on a line segment through a measure value*

An identifier for a river or stream segment
Measure value for the point event

2

Drainage is the manner in which water flows on the landscape, into streams and rivers, and eventually to the sea. The shape of the landscape and related characteristics, such as soils and vegetation, control this flow. The Arc Hydro data model for drainage systems represents the landscape and drainage characteristics for specific areas. Drainages form a patchwork of basins used to model flow to river and stream networks.

Water and land interact with one another: The shape of the land surface directs the drainage of water through the landscape, while the erosive power of water slowly reshapes the land surface. Streams, rivers, and water bodies lie in the valleys and hollows of the land surface, and drainage from the ridges and higher land areas flows downhill into these water systems. Digital elevation models are used to analyze the drainage patterns of the land surface terrain, and drainage areas are delineated from outlets chosen either manually or automatically according to physical rules. Drainage areas can be traced upstream or downstream, either through their attachment to the hydro network or by using area-to-area navigation, thereby identifying the region of hydrologic influence upstream and downstream of a catchment or watershed.

Traditionally, drainage areas have been delineated from topographic maps, where drainage divides are located by analyzing contour lines. Arrows representing water flow direction can be drawn perpendicular to each contour, in the direction of the steepest descent. The location of a drainage divide is where flow directions diverge. The drainage area boundary is digitized by drawing a continuous line transverse to the contours, up from the outlet point to the ridge line, along the ridge line around the drainage area, then descending to the outlet point again.

Drainage areas can also be delineated automatically using DEMs of the land surface terrain. By determining how water flows from cell to cell in the DEM, the set of cells whose drainage flows through the cell at the outlet point location can be identified, and the drainage area determined.

The Arc Hydro toolset contains functions to accomplish automated drainage area and stream network delineation from DEMs, and there are many advantages to using them. Drainage patterns are complex, and automated processing removes the need for the hydrologist to spend endless hours trying to interpret these patterns from contour lines on maps. Nevertheless, DEMs are still an approximate representation of land surface terrain. Manual editing of drainage boundaries may be necessary, especially in regions with very flat terrain having many constructed, rather than natural, drainage channels (such as those that exist in southern Florida).

The Arc Hydro data model accepts drainage areas and connects them to the hydro network, whether the areas were automatically or manually delineated, and allows for the fact that the mapped stream hydrography may be drawn from data sources different from the land surface terrain used to determine drainage area or boundaries.

The Arc Hydro data model represents a system of behavior. In the most simplistic sense, the system follows the drainage of a raindrop from the time it hits the ground through streams and rivers to the point where it comes to its final destination, usually the sea. Working from DEMs, the path of a raindrop is straightforward to determine. However, working from vector maps is more difficult, since the only location that can be unambiguously identified is the drainage area outlet. In Arc Hydro, the connection "areas flow to lines at points" forms the basis of building the relationship between Watershed and HydroJunction features.

It is possible to associate drainage areas with streams more simply: Each stream segment has exactly one drainage area associated with it. In that case, following the path of a raindrop from anywhere on the land surface to the stream network consists of identifying the stream segment lying within the drainage area where the raindrop fell. This simpler "area to line" connectivity of the land surface to the stream network is used to determine catchments in Arc Hydro, subdividing the landscape into a large number of elementary drainage areas, each with its own DrainageLine and DrainagePoint at the outlet.

This data model distinguishes between three levels of drainage areas, which suit most studies. These are further described on the following pages.

# Scales of representation of drainage systems

At the highest level are Basins, which may be subdivided into Watersheds or Catchments. Digital Elevation Models may be used to define drainage area boundaries for Catchments, Watersheds, and Basins.

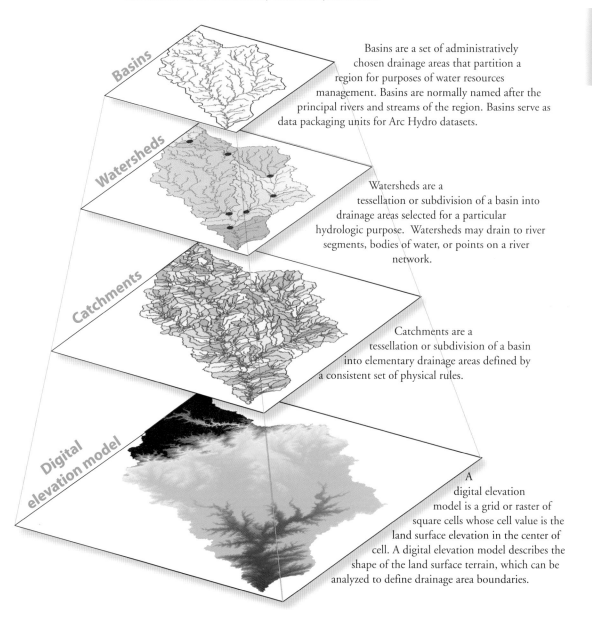

**Basins**

Basins are a set of administratively chosen drainage areas that partition a region for purposes of water resources management. Basins are normally named after the principal rivers and streams of the region. Basins serve as data packaging units for Arc Hydro datasets.

**Watersheds**

Watersheds are a tessellation or subdivision of a basin into drainage areas selected for a particular hydrologic purpose. Watersheds may drain to river segments, bodies of water, or points on a river network.

**Catchments**

Catchments are a tessellation or subdivision of a basin into elementary drainage areas defined by a consistent set of physical rules.

**Digital elevation model**

A digital elevation model is a grid or raster of square cells whose cell value is the land surface elevation in the center of cell. A digital elevation model describes the shape of the land surface terrain, which can be analyzed to define drainage area boundaries.

Three distinct levels of drainage areas are used, depending on the scope, purpose, and jurisdiction of a given project. Drainage area boundaries are used in water availability studies, water quality projects, flood forecasting programs, and many other engineering and public policy applications.

This data model uses three levels of drainage areas: basins, watersheds, and catchments. Each of these terms has a specific meaning in this data model, which may differ from the usage with which you are familiar. However, precision of concepts and terms is necessary for consistent and lossless data exchange. These terms were agreed on by consensus of the participants in the GIS Water Resources Consortium.

## Catchments

Catchments are elementary drainage areas delineated for each segment of a stream or river between confluences. These are defined by a consistent set of physical rules normally based on a DEM, so a catchment is defined by a line of raster cells, and its outlet is defined by a single cell. When converted from raster to vector features, these cells form the Arc Hydro feature classes Catchment, DrainageLine, and DrainagePoint, respectively. In the simplest approach for defining catchments, the DEM takes no account of water bodies, which appear as large flat areas. An alternative approach is to take a hydro network, with reach codes defined for all its segments, and use a DEM to delineate an elementary drainage area for

each reach. This approach involves more work but enables definitions of catchments for coastlines and water bodies, as well as stream segments.

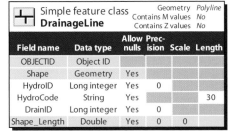

**Simple feature class — Catchment**

| | | Geometry | Polygon | | |
| | | Contains M values | No | | |
| | | Contains Z values | Yes | | |

| Field name | Data type | Allow nulls | Prec-ision | Scale | Length |
|---|---|---|---|---|---|
| OBJECTID | Object ID | | | | |
| Shape | Geometry | Yes | | | |
| HydroID | Long integer | Yes | 0 | | |
| HydroCode | String | Yes | | | 30 |
| DrainID | Long integer | Yes | 0 | | |
| AreaSqKm | Double | Yes | 0 | 0 | |
| JunctionID | Long integer | Yes | 0 | | |
| NextDownID | Long integer | Yes | 0 | | |
| Shape_Length | Double | Yes | 0 | 0 | |
| Shape_Area | Double | Yes | 0 | 0 | |

*Elementary drainage areas defined by subdividing the landscape according to a set of physical rules*

Unique feature identifier in the geodatabase
Permanent public identifier of the feature
HydroID of the reference drainage area feature
Area in square kilometers
HydroID of the HydroJunction at drainage outlet
HydroID of the next downstream catchment

**Simple feature class — DrainageLine**

| | | Geometry | Polyline | | |
| | | Contains M values | No | | |
| | | Contains Z values | No | | |

| Field name | Data type | Allow nulls | Prec-ision | Scale | Length |
|---|---|---|---|---|---|
| OBJECTID | Object ID | | | | |
| Shape | Geometry | Yes | | | |
| HydroID | Long integer | Yes | 0 | | |
| HydroCode | String | Yes | | | 30 |
| DrainID | Long integer | Yes | 0 | | |
| Shape_Length | Double | Yes | 0 | 0 | |

*A line drawn through the center of cells on a DEM-derived drainage path*

Unique feature identifier in the geodatabase
Permanent public identifier of the feature
HydroID of the reference drainage area feature

**Simple feature class — DrainagePoint**

| | | Geometry | Point | | |
| | | Contains M values | No | | |
| | | Contains Z values | No | | |

| Field name | Data type | Allow nulls | Prec-ision | Scale | Length |
|---|---|---|---|---|---|
| OBJECTID | Object ID | | | | |
| Shape | Geometry | Yes | | | |
| HydroID | Long integer | Yes | 0 | | |
| HydroCode | String | Yes | | | 30 |
| DrainID | Long integer | Yes | 0 | | |
| JunctionID | Long integer | Yes | 0 | | |

*A point at the center of a DEM cell that is the outlet of a DEM-derived drainage area*

Unique feature identifier in the geodatabase
Permanent public identifier of the feature
HydroID of the reference drainage area feature
HydroID of the HydroJunction at drainage outlet

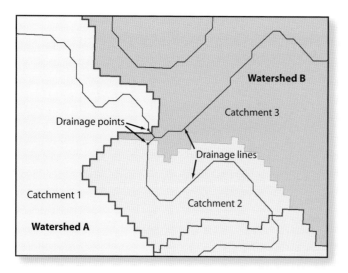

*DEM-based Watershed, Catchment, DrainageLine, and DrainagePoint features, seen at 1:5,000 scale*

## Basins

Although there is no unique way of defining a watershed layout, many agencies have a standardized set of watersheds that have been worked out over many years and that serve as reference units for water resources management. In Arc Hydro, these standardized watersheds are called Basins, and they serve as reference units for data management and data packaging. Regardless of the independence just mentioned between DEM-defined catchments and agency-defined watersheds, it is generally the case that catchments tessellate basins and watersheds tessellate basins. It is the interior watersheds of a basin whose boundaries may not coincide with catchments.

In the United States, a standard set of basins called hydrologic units has been developed by the U.S. Geological Survey and indexed by a Hydrologic Unit Code (HUC). These hydrologic units are arranged in a hierarchy. At the highest level, the United States is divided into 20 two-digit water resource regions.

## Watersheds

The subdivision of a given landscape into larger drainage units can vary greatly from one water resources agency to another and even within the same agency when different kinds of analysis are undertaken. In the United States, the National Weather Service (NWS) forecasts floods on all the major rivers and has divided the nation into one set of watersheds for this analysis. The Environmental Protection Agency manages water pollution using Total Maximum Daily Loads defined on watersheds draining to selected river segments or water bodies, a different watershed layout than that used by NWS. Regional agencies may have still other layouts for watersheds in their jurisdictions. There is no rule that Catchments must tessellate individual Watersheds.

**Simple feature class**
**Watershed**

Geometry: Polygon
Contains M values: No
Contains Z values: No

| Field name | Data type | Allow nulls | Precision | Scale | Length |
|---|---|---|---|---|---|
| OBJECTID | Object ID | | | | |
| Shape | Geometry | Yes | | | |
| HydroID | Long integer | Yes | 0 | | |
| HydroCode | String | Yes | | | 30 |
| DrainID | Long integer | Yes | 0 | | |
| AreaSqKm | Double | Yes | 0 | 0 | |
| JunctionID | Long integer | Yes | 0 | | |
| NextDownID | Long integer | Yes | 0 | | |
| Shape_Length | Double | Yes | 0 | 0 | |
| Shape_Area | Double | Yes | 0 | 0 | |

*Drainage areas defined by subdividing the landscape into units convenient for a particular analysis*

Unique feature identifier in the geodatabase
Permanent public identifier of the feature
HydroID of the reference drainage area feature
Area in square kilometers
HydroID of the HydroJunction at drainage outlet
HydroID of the next downstream watershed

**Simple feature class**
**Basin**

Geometry: Polygon
Contains M values: No
Contains Z values: No

| Field name | Data type | Allow nulls | Precision | Scale | Length |
|---|---|---|---|---|---|
| OBJECTID | Object ID | | | | |
| Shape | Geometry | Yes | | | |
| HydroID | Long integer | Yes | 0 | | |
| HydroCode | String | Yes | | | 30 |
| DrainID | Long integer | Yes | 0 | | |
| AreaSqKm | Double | Yes | 0 | 0 | |
| JunctionID | Long integer | Yes | 0 | | |
| NextDownID | Long integer | Yes | 0 | | |
| Shape_Length | Double | Yes | 0 | 0 | |
| Shape_Area | Double | Yes | 0 | 0 | |

*A set of administratively selected standard drainage areas, usually named after the principal streams and rivers of a region*

Unique feature identifier in the geodatabase
Permanent public identifier of the feature
HydroID of the reference drainage area feature
Area in square kilometers
HydroID of the HydroJunction at drainage outlet
HydroID of the next downstream basin

When defining drainage features, the user can apply topology rules in the GIS to enforce data integrity. The rules shown here are among those available in ArcGIS.

Due to the large number, size, and boundary complexity of catchments, watersheds, and basins, topology rules in the GIS can provide a useful tool for ensuring data integrity. Topology rules are not a required part of the Arc Hydro data model; the institutional heritage of watershed and basin boundaries within the United States has resulted in many quilts of arrangements in common use.

Regardless, in many studies covering an area small enough that consistent rules can be applied, they are expressed simply:

• Catchments tessellate basins.

• Watersheds tessellate basins.

• Drainage points must be coincident with a drainage line.

In ArcGIS, the tessellate rule is expressed as three separate rules so they can be applied independently:

• Features must not have gaps.

• Features must not overlap other features of the same class.

• Features must be covered by a single feature of the feature class it tessellates.

These are just suggested guidelines; you may choose to add or remove rules, depending on the nature of your project or data.

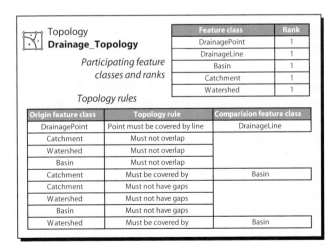

Topology
**Drainage_Topology**

*Participating feature classes and ranks*

| Feature class | Rank |
|---|---|
| DrainagePoint | 1 |
| DrainageLine | 1 |
| Basin | 1 |
| Catchment | 1 |
| Watershed | 1 |

*Topology rules*

| Origin feature class | Topology rule | Comparision feature class |
|---|---|---|
| DrainagePoint | Point must be covered by line | DrainageLine |
| Catchment | Must not overlap | |
| Watershed | Must not overlap | |
| Basin | Must not overlap | |
| Catchment | Must be covered by | Basin |
| Catchment | Must not have gaps | |
| Watershed | Must not have gaps | |
| Basin | Must not have gaps | |
| Watershed | Must be covered by | Basin |

# Topology rules in the Arc Hydro data model

**Catchment**

**must be covered by**

**Basin**

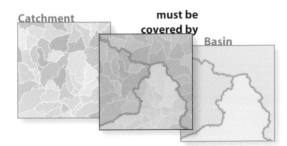

**Watershed**

**must be covered by**

**Basin**

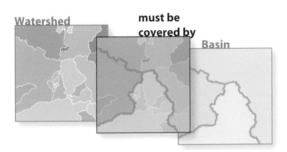

**DrainagePoint**

**point must be covered by line**

**DrainageLine**

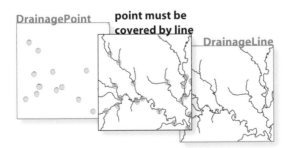

**Watershed**

**must not overlap**

*Also Catchment and Basin*

**Catchment**

**must not have gaps**

*Also Basin and Watershed*

2

Some hydrologic analysis techniques are designed to work with a simple connectivity model of watersheds or other water-related features. An example is to study downstream accumulation of contaminants for water quality analysis. One of the products created by Arc Hydro tools is a schematic network of nodes and links connecting watersheds. By associating programming scripts with such a schematic network, a certain amount of hydrologic analysis can be performed within the GIS.

Schematic networks provide a means of defining connectivity between features without the overhead of maintaining the complete geometry of such features. This can be useful in many analytical methods applied to a geographic dataset.

Analysis of drainage systems is facilitated by creating schematic networks from Watershed and HydroJunction feature classes. The connectivity is established by assigning the HydroID of a Watershed's outlet (a HydroJunction feature) to the JunctionID attribute for that Watershed. Similarly, the HydroID of the first downstream Hydro-Junction is assigned to the NextDownID attribute of a HydroJunction feature.

The schematic network consists of SchematicLink and SchematicNode features created from the connectivity information just described. SchematicNodes are located at the centroids and outlets of the Watershed polygon features, while Schematic Links are straight lines that connect SchematicNodes. The SchematicNodes contain a field called FeatureID, which stores the HydroID of the source feature that is represented by the schematic feature. SchematicLinks contain FromNodeID and ToNodeID, which identify the HydroID of the SchematicNodes connected to a given SchematicLink. FromNodeID identifies the starting (upstream) node, and ToNodeID identifies the target (downstream) node.

It is useful to further subdivide schematic network features into two types. Type 1 features are associated with a JunctionID–HydroID relationship from the source features, such as JunctionID on Watershed pointing to the HydroID of that Watershed's outlet HydroJunction (purple

nodes and links in the figure below). Type 2 features are associated with a NextDownID–HydroID relationship from the source features. These types could be specified by defining a SrcType attribute of SchematicNode and a LinkType attribute of SchematicLink.

Once the schematic network has been created, attributes from the source features may be joined to the schematic features using the FeatureID–HydroID association.

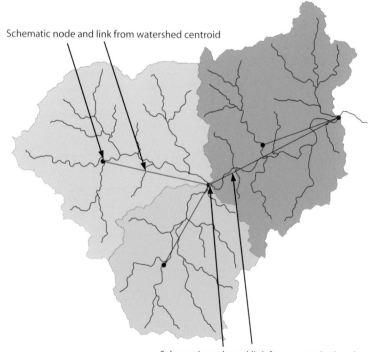

Schematic node and link from watershed centroid

Schematic node and link from watershed outlet

## SCHEMATIC VALUES

The schematic network structure just described was used to represent a system of behavior for simulating the movement of water (or contaminants in the water) across the landscape. This movement was managed by passing values down the schematic network. In this simulation, schematic network features incorporate four types of values: received, incremental, total, and passed values. These are held as additional attributes of the SchematicNode and SchematicLink features.

### Received values

Received values are values of a variable to be received by a schematic feature from adjacent upstream schematic features. The network was constrained such that a node could only receive values from adjacent upstream links, and a link could only receive a value from its adjacent upstream node, behavior representative of downhill gravity flow.

### Incremental values

An incremental value in this analysis is the value of a variable introduced into the schematic network at a given schematic feature's location. For example, a node might be located at a crop producing field, at which water may be withdrawn for irrigation. This use represents a drain from the schematic network and would be represented by a negative incremental value. An example of a positive incremental value would be the runoff produced at a watershed node from a given rainfall event.

### Total values

The total value for a schematic feature is the arithmetic sum of the received and incremental values.

### Passed values

A passed value is the value that a schematic feature passes to the next downstream feature in the network.

## SCHEMATIC BEHAVIORS

With the schematic values just defined, a system of behavior can be modeled for analysis, such as accumulated flow from a network of watersheds. Each schematic feature may have "receiving behavior" to control how it accepts values from upstream features, as well as "passing behavior" to control how it passes values to downstream features. Each behavior uses the schematic values described above, along with other attributes and algorithms as necessary, to determine the final value for a given attribute of that feature.

By linking programming scripts and dynamically linked library (DLL) modules implementing these behaviors, certain forms of hydrologic modeling can be performed within the GIS. At the University of Texas Center for Research in Water Resources, graduate students have written support tools in VisualBasic to work with ArcGIS ModelBuilder™ in linking a schematic network with hydrologic modeling modules for water quality analysis and floodplain mapping. The floodplain mapping example is presented later in this chapter.

2

| Simple feature class **SchematicLink** | | Geometry *Polyline* Contains M values *No* Contains Z values *No* | | | |
|---|---|---|---|---|---|
| **Field name** | **Data type** | **Allow nulls** | **Prec- ision** | **Scale** | **Length** |
| OBJECTID | Object ID | | | | |
| Shape | Geometry | Yes | | | |
| HydroID | Long integer | Yes | 0 | | |
| HydroCode | String | Yes | | | 30 |
| FromNodeID | Long integer | Yes | 0 | | |
| ToNodeID | Long integer | Yes | 0 | | |
| Shape_Length | Double | Yes | 0 | 0 | |

*A straight line connecting two schematic nodes in a schematic network*

Unique feature identifier in the geodatabase
Permanent public identifier of feature
HydroID of the schematic node at the from-end of the link
HydroID of the schematic node at the to-end of the link

| Simple feature class **SchematicNode** | | Geometry *Point* Contains M values *No* Contains Z values *No* | | | |
|---|---|---|---|---|---|
| **Field name** | **Data type** | **Allow nulls** | **Prec- ision** | **Scale** | **Length** |
| OBJECTID | Object ID | | | | |
| Shape | Geometry | Yes | | | |
| HydroID | Long integer | Yes | 0 | | |
| HydroCode | String | Yes | | | 30 |
| FeatureID | Long integer | Yes | 0 | | |

*A representative point for a hydro feature connected to a schematic network*

Unique feature identifier in the geodatabase
Permanent public identifier of feature
HydroID of the associated hydro feature

Water flows downhill—the river or stream channel is the conduit for carrying water along based on gravity. The data model includes elements to model these channels and their flow characteristics. Many water resource management issues are based on the three-dimensional properties of the channel at specified cross sections that transverse the direction of flow within a stream.

In recent years, GIS has become an excellent tool for spatial data storage, visualization, and analysis to support these studies. The Arc Hydro data model provides a framework for storing channel and cross section information in a systematic manner. In this data model, the river channel is considered a three-dimensional network of cross section lines, located transverse to the channel, and profile lines, drawn parallel to it.

## Channel cross sections

Cross sections are linear features that define the shape of the channel transverse to the stream flow. These are fundamental to all river studies. Elevations (depths) along the cross section line are measured or extracted from a digital terrain model (DTM), such as DEM grid or TIN, making the cross section a three-dimensional line where each vertex has x, y, and z coordinates.

## Channel profile lines

Profile lines identify the boundaries of a stream channel, typically including the left and right streamlines (looking downstream) of average water flow, the left and right banks, and the thalweg, which is the line of greatest depth along the streambed. It is important to note that the thalweg is not a "stream centerline," since the line of greatest depth is often close to one of the banks as the stream curves. A given stream valley may have one or multiple floodlines, depending on available data and analysis to determine the average flood stage (depth) at 10-year, 100-year, and other intervals.

Channel profile lines are typically created by one of two methods:

- Detailed cross section data can be entered into an analytical model developed by the U.S. Army Corps of Engineers Hydrologic Engineering Center (HEC) and called the River Analysis System (RAS), which determines the profile lines. These can then be imported as features back into the GIS.

- Alternatively, profile splines can be fit through bathymetric data (river bottom depth points), assuming sufficient data is available. An example of this approach is shown on the next page.

## Linear measure (m-coordinate)

In addition to the three standard coordinates, ArcGIS allows an m-coordinate, or linear measure, to be assigned at each vertex of a spatial feature (point, multipoint, polyline, or polygon). The purposes or uses of this m-coordinate is based on the application requirements. In the case of profile lines, the m-coordinate is often used to hold the distance (in either kilometers or as a percentage of the stream length) from the mouth of the stream. For cross sections, the measure could be used to define an absolute or relative distance from one bank to the other for purposes of defining cross section events.

*Three-dimensional view of a channel*

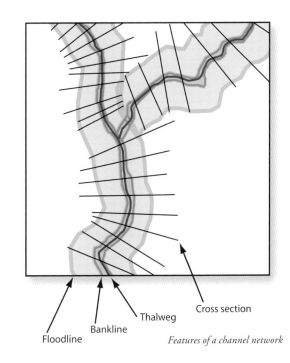

*Features of a channel network*

Floodline · Bankline · Thalweg · Cross section

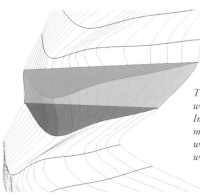

The blue longitudinal profile lines and red cross section lines were computed by spline fit through detailed bathymetric data. In this dataset, numerous profile lines were generated for more precise representation of the river bottom shape (most of these would be coded as streamlines). The shaded region depicts a volume of water between two cross sections.

*Longitudinal profile of a stream or river channel*

| | Simple feature class **ProfileLine** | Geometry | *Polyline* |
|---|---|---|---|
| | | Contains M values | *Yes* |
| | | Contains Z values | *Yes* |

| Field name | Data type | Allow nulls | Prec- ision | Scale | Length | |
|---|---|---|---|---|---|---|
| OBJECTID | Object ID | | | | | |
| Shape | Geometry | Yes | | | | |
| HydroID | Long integer | Yes | 0 | | | Unique identifier in the geodatabase |
| HydroCode | String | Yes | | | 30 | Permanent public identifier of the feature |
| ReachCode | String | Yes | | | 30 | An identifier for a river or stream segment |
| RiverCode | String | Yes | | | 30 | An identifier for a river |
| FType | String | Yes | | | 30 | A descriptor of feature type |
| ProfOrigin | String | Yes | | | 30 | A classifier for the method by which the ProfileLine was defined |
| Shape_Length | Double | Yes | 0 | 0 | | |

Coded value domain
**ProfileLineType**

Description
Field type *Long integer*
Split policy *Default value*
Merge policy *Default value*

| Code | Description |
|---|---|
| 1 | Thalweg |
| 2 | Bankline |
| 3 | Streamline |

Detailed attribution of stream cross sections is necessary for many forms of hydrologic analysis. Arc Hydro takes advantage of linear referencing in ArcGIS for this purpose. With linear referencing, cross section lines can have either or both linear or point events to describe arbitrary locations along the cross section.

## Cross section events

The geometry alone of a cross section is not sufficient for most water resources applications. For instance, a river model for hydraulic simulations requires roughness values along a cross section as well as the location of the left and right banks. Cross section properties—such as roughness values; land use and zone types; and the locations of the left and right banks, thalweg, and left and right floodplains—can be stored in a table corresponding to measure values along a cross section. These locations (points) and a part of the cross section (segments) can be displayed in the GIS as "point events" and "line events," respectively, using linear referencing utilities.

The CSPointEvent sample table on the next page identifies the location of thalweg, banklines, and streamlines in absolute measurement terms, typically specified as a distance from the left to the right across the stream as a viewer is looking downstream. The CSCode value identifies the cross section; Measure identifies the distance along the cross section line; and Type refers to the type of profile line (thalweg, bankline, or streamline) at that linear measure.

*DEM of river channel with cross sections shown in red*

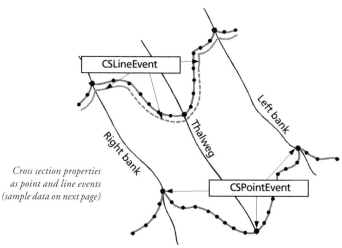

*Cross section properties as point and line events (sample data on next page)*

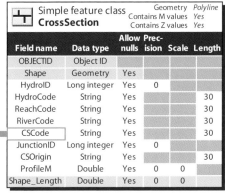

## Simple feature class
### CrossSection

| | | Geometry | Polyline |
| | | Contains M values | Yes |
| | | Contains Z values | Yes |

*The cross section of a channel, normally drawn transverse to the flow*

| Field name | Data type | Allow nulls | Prec- ision | Scale | Length | |
|---|---|---|---|---|---|---|
| OBJECTID | Object ID | | | | | |
| Shape | Geometry | Yes | | | | |
| HydroID | Long integer | Yes | 0 | | | Unique identifier in the geodatabase |
| HydroCode | String | Yes | | | 30 | Permanent public identifier of the feature |
| ReachCode | String | Yes | | | 30 | An identifier for a river or stream segment |
| RiverCode | String | Yes | | | 30 | An identifier for a river |
| CSCode | String | Yes | | | 30 | An identifier for a cross section |
| JunctionID | Long integer | Yes | 0 | | | HydroID of the related HydroJunction |
| CSOrigin | String | Yes | | | 30 | A classifier for the method by which the cross section was defined |
| ProfileM | Double | Yes | 0 | 0 | | The measure location of the cross section along the stream profile |
| Shape_Length | Double | Yes | 0 | 0 | | |

## Relationship class
### CrossSectionHasPoint

| | | | |
|---|---|---|---|
| Type | Simple | Forward label | CrossSection-Point |
| Cardinality | One to many | | |
| Notification | None | Backward label | CrossSection |

| Origin feature class | Destination table |
|---|---|
| Name *CrossSection* | Name *CrossSectionPoint* |
| Primary key *CSCode* | |
| Foreign key *CSCode* | |

## Table
### CrossSectionPoint

*A point of the cross section*

| Field name | Data type | Allow nulls | Prec- ision | Scale | Length | |
|---|---|---|---|---|---|---|
| OBJECTID | Object ID | | | | | |
| CSCode | String | Yes | | | 30 | An identifier for a cross section |
| CrossM | Double | Yes | 0 | 0 | | Measure location of point along cross section |
| Elevation | Double | Yes | 0 | 0 | | Elevation of the point above mean sea level |

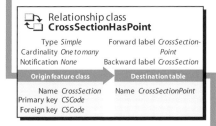

| OBJECTID* | CSCode | MEASURE | TYPE |
|---|---|---|---|
| 1 | 1 | 54.206 | 2 |
| 2 | 1 | 385.423 | 1 |
| 3 | 1 | 583.457 | 3 |
| 4 | 4 | 44.4 | 2 |
| 5 | 4 | 356.912 | 1 |
| 6 | 4 | 598.1 | 3 |
| 7 | 7 | 211.681 | 2 |
| 8 | 7 | 333.414 | 1 |

*CSPointEvent sample table*

These examples are representative of the kind of data that might be placed in cross section event tables. The Measure fields indicate where along the cross section a parameter value is located. The parameter value in the CSPointEvent table is TYPE, indicating whether the location is for a bankline, thalweg, or streamline. The CSLineEvent field CSPVALUE might be used to indicate channel properties, such as roughness.

| OBJECTID* | CSCode | FROMMEASURE | TOMEASURE | TYPE | CSPVALUE |
|---|---|---|---|---|---|
| 1 | 1 | 0 | 116.05 | 0 | 0.01 |
| 2 | 1 | 116.05 | 583.46 | 0 | 0.002 |
| 3 | 1 | 583.46 | 781.5 | 0 | 0.01 |
| 4 | 4 | 0 | 130.78 | 0 | 0.01 |
| 5 | 4 | 130.78 | 533.02 | 0 | 0.002 |
| 6 | 4 | 533.02 | 720.23 | 0 | 0.01 |
| 7 | 7 | 0 | 211.68 | 0 | 0.01 |

*CSLineEvent sample table*

Hydrography is the map representation of surface water features in the landscape. Hydrography data sources include point, line, and area data layers from map hydrography; point features derived from tabular data inventories; and hydro response units that account for vertical exchanges of water in the hydrologic cycle of a land surface. Arc Hydro was designed so that it can work with national and regional hydrography sets, including the National Hydrography Dataset.

Cartographic features can be classified in endless ways depending on each user's purpose of classification and other requirements, region of interest, available source data, and other factors. It is not the purpose of this data model to provide an exhaustive list of hydrographic features, but only to provide an essential set. Thus, the set of all hydrographic features is initially divided into categories of point, line, and area features. Point features are further categorized as shown in the diagrams below and on the next page. Line and area features are further described on the pages following point features.

## HydroPoint

HydroPoint is the root (generic) class of hydrographic point features. The most commonly used subcategories of HydroPoint are: Bridge, Dam, Structure, WaterDischarge, WaterWithdrawal, MonitoringPoint, and UserPoint. In this data model, these all have the same attributes but are represented by separate feature classes because of their distinctive purposes in hydrologic and hydraulic analysis. Any of these classes may be relationally connected to junction features for use in the hydro network for analysis, or they can simply represent cartographic point locations.

Various water resource data inventories can be used with Arc Hydro, such as the National Inventory of Dams, compiled by the U.S. Army Corps of Engineers, and the Permit Compliance System, developed by the EPA to monitor the status of wastewater discharge permits. Many tabular data inventories have now been associated with geospatial datasets that represent their locations, while others may contain latitude and longitude coordinate points that allow the data to be transformed to point features with attached attributes. The HydroPoint feature class is free of special attributes so attributes of the tabular inventory from which the points are developed can be used.

HydroPoints are used for many specific types of points in water resources analyses. However, they can also be used to store user-defined points for purely cartographic purposes. These are points that enrich the content of maps but are not used in analysis, such as locations of isolated (off-channel) ponds, rock outcrops, small islands, and small springs.

| Simple feature class **HydroPoint** | | Geometry | Point |
|---|---|---|---|
| | | Contains M values | No |
| | | Contains Z values | No |

*A point feature on a map, such as a gage, well, or spring*

| Field name | Data type | Allow nulls | Prec- ision | Scale | Length | |
|---|---|---|---|---|---|---|
| OBJECTID | Object ID | | | | | |
| Shape | Geometry | Yes | | | | |
| HydroID | Long integer | Yes | 0 | | | Unique feature identifier in the geodatabase |
| HydroCode | String | Yes | | | 30 | Permanent public identifier of feature |
| FType | String | Yes | | | 30 | Descriptor of feature type |
| Name | String | Yes | | | 100 | Geographic name |
| JunctionID | Long integer | Yes | 0 | | | HydroID of the related HydroJunction |

## Bridge

**Simple feature class — Bridge**  
Geometry: Point · Contains M values: No · Contains Z values: No

*A structure where a road or railroad crosses a river or stream*

| Field name | Data type | Allow nulls | Precision | Scale | Length | Description |
|---|---|---|---|---|---|---|
| OBJECTID | Object ID | | | | | |
| Shape | Geometry | Yes | | | | |
| HydroID | Long integer | Yes | 0 | | | Unique feature identifier in the geodatabase |
| HydroCode | String | Yes | | | 30 | Permanent public identifier of the feature |
| FType | String | Yes | | | 30 | Descriptor of feature type |
| Name | String | Yes | | | 100 | Geographic name |
| JunctionID | Long integer | Yes | 0 | | | HydroID of the related HydroJunction |

**Simple feature class — Dam**  
Geometry: Point · Contains M values: No · Contains Z values: No

*An embankment or structure that ponds water to create a reservoir*

| Field name | Data type | Allow nulls | Precision | Scale | Length | Description |
|---|---|---|---|---|---|---|
| OBJECTID | Object ID | | | | | |
| Shape | Geometry | Yes | | | | |
| HydroID | Long integer | Yes | 0 | | | Unique feature identifer in the geodatabase |
| HydroCode | String | Yes | | | 30 | Permanent public identifier of the feature |
| FType | String | Yes | | | 30 | Descriptor of feature type |
| Name | String | Yes | | | 100 | Geographic name |
| JunctionID | Long integer | Yes | 0 | | | HydroID of the related HydroJunction |

**Simple feature class — Structure**  
Geometry: Point · Contains M values: No · Contains Z values: No

*A water structure not represented as a bridge or dam, such as a weir or a waterfall*

| Field name | Data type | Allow nulls | Precision | Scale | Length | Description |
|---|---|---|---|---|---|---|
| OBJECTID | Object ID | | | | | |
| Shape | Geometry | Yes | | | | |
| HydroID | Long integer | Yes | 0 | | | Unique feature identifier in the geodatabase |
| HydroCode | String | Yes | | | 30 | Permanent public identifier of feature |
| FType | String | Yes | | | 30 | Descriptor of feature type |
| Name | String | Yes | | | 100 | Geographic name |
| JunctionID | Long integer | Yes | 0 | | | HydroID of the related HydroJunction |

## Bridge, Dam, and Structure

Bridge, Dam, and Structure points are intended to represent features, man-made or natural, that restrict or change the movement of water. The Structure class represents other hydraulic structures besides dams and bridges that change the hydraulic properties of the flow through the network. Typical examples of such structures include detention ponds on small streams, levees designed to hold back floodwaters, and weirs. Structures can also be natural features, such as waterfalls, if they have a significant effect on the hydraulic properties of the network. Typically, an irrigation turnout gate is not classified as a hydraulic structure, but as a WaterWithdrawal point (see next page). However, if the network or irrigation ditches are included in the network analysis, then the turnout structure would be a Structure point and would be modeled similarly to a valve on a pipe network. Any of these classes may be further extended, subtyped, or subclassed, depending on the kind of data they need to store.

Several other features are frequently used in cartography and hydrographic analysis. Point locations for monitoring stations, water discharge, and water withdrawal are the most widely used of these. For other applications, users may create additional feature classes or create subtypes of the UserPoint feature class.

## WaterWithdrawal and WaterDischarge

WaterWithdrawal and WaterDischarge represent points at which flow is removed or added to the stream network. Usually the corresponding flow data comes from agencies that give permits for water rights and withdrawal or from environmental agencies that permit discharges into the network. The points are significant to network analyses that deal with the mass balance of water and pollutants in the network and are used as flags (such as the beginning point for upstream or downstream tracing) in a network analysis.

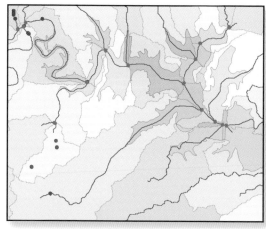

*Monitoring points, water discharge, and water withdrawals on a stream network*

| Simple feature class **WaterWithdrawal** | | Geometry | *Point* | | | |
| | | Contains M values | *No* | | | |
| | | Contains Z values | *No* | | | |

*A location where water is withdrawn from a river, stream, or water body*

| Field name | Data type | Allow nulls | Prec-ision | Scale | Length | |
|---|---|---|---|---|---|---|
| OBJECTID | Object ID | | | | | |
| Shape | Geometry | Yes | | | | |
| HydroID | Long integer | Yes | 0 | | | Unique feature identifier in the geodatabase |
| HydroCode | String | Yes | | | 30 | Permanent public identifier of feature |
| FType | String | Yes | | | 30 | Descriptor of feature type |
| Name | String | Yes | | | 100 | Geographic name |
| JunctionID | Long integer | Yes | 0 | | | HydroID of the related HydroJunction |

| Simple feature class **WaterDischarge** | | Geometry | *Point* | | | |
| | | Contains M values | *No* | | | |
| | | Contains Z values | *No* | | | |

*A location where water is discharged to a river, stream, or water body*

| Field name | Data type | Allow nulls | Prec-ision | Scale | Length | |
|---|---|---|---|---|---|---|
| OBJECTID | Object ID | | | | | |
| Shape | Geometry | Yes | | | | |
| HydroID | Long integer | Yes | 0 | | | Unique feature identifier in the geodatabase |
| HydroCode | String | Yes | | | 30 | Permanent public identifier of feature |
| FType | String | Yes | | | 30 | Descriptor of feature type |
| Name | String | Yes | | | 100 | Geographic name |
| JunctionID | Long integer | Yes | 0 | | | HydroID of the related HydroJunction |

## MonitoringPoint

MonitoringPoints store the locations of gages that measure water quantity or quality, including water quality monitoring stations, stream-gage stations, rain-gage stations, and any other type of fixed-location data collection point. These points can be tied to the time series data collected at their locations, as shown in the schema below. This allows the display of gage data in graphical format and comparison of gage readings at different locations. MonitoringPoints are well suited for subtyping, since most of them have similar attributes. Arc Hydro does not specify the attributes because of the wide variety of attribute data needed throughout the water resources community. For example, a stream gaging station is described differently from a water quality MonitoringPoint. More classes can be added to the model according to the user's needs.

## UserPoint

UserPoints are intended to store point data that does not fit into the model elsewhere. These points might include locations where a river crosses an aquifer or a political or administrative boundary. UserPoints are a good place to load data that can be organized and exported to other classes after the Arc Hydro schema is applied.

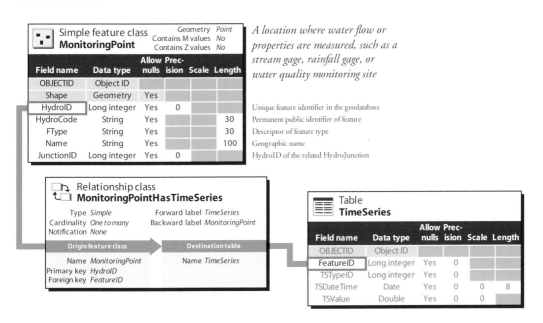

**Simple feature class — MonitoringPoint** · Geometry: Point · Contains M values: No · Contains Z values: No

*A location where water flow or properties are measured, such as a stream gage, rainfall gage, or water quality monitoring site*

| Field name | Data type | Allow nulls | Precision | Scale | Length | |
|---|---|---|---|---|---|---|
| OBJECTID | Object ID | | | | | |
| Shape | Geometry | Yes | | | | |
| HydroID | Long integer | Yes | 0 | | | Unique feature identifier in the geodatabase |
| HydroCode | String | Yes | | | 30 | Permanent public identifier of feature |
| FType | String | Yes | | | 30 | Descriptor of feature type |
| Name | String | Yes | | | 100 | Geographic name |
| JunctionID | Long integer | Yes | 0 | | | HydroID of the related HydroJunction |

**Relationship class — MonitoringPointHasTimeSeries**

Type: *Simple* · Forward label *TimeSeries*
Cardinality: *One to many* · Backward label *MonitoringPoint*
Notification: *None*

| Origin feature class | Destination table |
|---|---|
| Name *MonitoringPoint* | Name *TimeSeries* |
| Primary key *HydroID* | |
| Foreign key *FeatureID* | |

**Table — TimeSeries**

| Field name | Data type | Allow nulls | Precision | Scale | Length |
|---|---|---|---|---|---|
| OBJECTID | Object ID | | | | |
| FeatureID | Long integer | Yes | 0 | | |
| TSTypeID | Long integer | Yes | 0 | | |
| TSDateTime | Date | Yes | 0 | 0 | 8 |
| TSValue | Double | Yes | 0 | 0 | |

**Simple feature class — UserPoint** · Geometry: Point · Contains M values: No · Contains Z values: No

*A user-selected point location, such as where a river crosses an aquifer boundary*

| Field name | Data type | Allow nulls | Precision | Scale | Length | |
|---|---|---|---|---|---|---|
| OBJECTID | Object ID | | | | | |
| Shape | Geometry | Yes | | | | |
| HydroID | Long integer | Yes | 0 | | | Unique feature identifier in the geodatabase |
| HydroCode | String | Yes | | | 30 | Permanent public identifier of feature |
| FType | String | Yes | | | 30 | Descriptor of feature type |
| Name | String | Yes | | | 100 | Geographic name |
| JunctionID | Long integer | Yes | 0 | | | HydroID of the related HydroJunction |

Hydrographic features provide a visual, spatial reference on a map for viewers of the data and are necessary in this data model. Numerous detailed classifications of hydrographic features have been developed, especially by national agencies. It is not the purpose of Arc Hydro to replace any of these classification systems. These feature classes can be considered placeholders for users' own feature classes or subtypes.

## HydroLine

HydroLines are designed to contain line features important for the cartographic representation of a water study area. Some examples of hydrographic lines are:

- Natural streams and rivers

- Man-made canals and ditches

- Pipelines that carry water underground

- Connectors that are used when the original data had some obstruction covering the hydrologic feature, such as when a stream goes underground for a brief distance before appearing on the surface again

- Artificial paths that represent the centerlines of lakes and other water bodies

These features may also be represented in the hydro network. Of course, there are many other types of hydrographic lines, such as isolated ponds and lakes that are not part of the river network, shorelines, island boundaries, no-wake zones, swimming and recreation areas, roads, county and state boundary lines, jurisdictional boundaries for river authorities, and city limits. These are all marked off by lines important for cartography.

## HydroArea

Ordinary landmark areas are stored as HydroAreas. Examples of these include no-wake zones within water bodies, extents of counties or other jurisdictional areas, and inundation areas.

## Waterbody

The Waterbody feature class is a specialization of HydroArea used for lakes, large ponds, and wide rivers along a river channel included in the surface water network. These features are linked to the network through relationships with HydroJunction features so that properties of these areas can be attached to the hydro network for analysis.

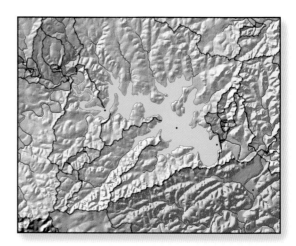

*Water body on a shaded relief map*

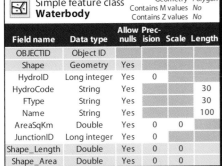

| Simple feature class **HydroLine** | | Geometry | Polyline | | |
|---|---|---|---|---|---|
| | | Contains M values | No | | |
| | | Contains Z values | No | | |

| Field name | Data type | Allow nulls | Precision | Scale | Length |
|---|---|---|---|---|---|
| OBJECTID | Object ID | | | | |
| Shape | Geometry | Yes | | | |
| HydroID | Long integer | Yes | 0 | | |
| HydroCode | String | Yes | | | 30 |
| FType | String | Yes | | | 30 |
| Name | String | Yes | | | 100 |
| Shape_Length | Double | Yes | 0 | 0 | |

*A line hydrography feature not represented by a HydroEdge, such as an administrative boundary*

Unique feature identifier in the geodatabase
Permanent public identifier of feature
Descriptor of feature type
Geographic name

| Simple feature class **HydroArea** | | Geometry | Polygon | | |
|---|---|---|---|---|---|
| | | Contains M values | No | | |
| | | Contains Z values | No | | |

| Field name | Data type | Allow nulls | Precision | Scale | Length |
|---|---|---|---|---|---|
| OBJECTID | Object ID | | | | |
| Shape | Geometry | Yes | | | |
| HydroID | Long integer | Yes | 0 | | |
| HydroCode | String | Yes | | | 30 |
| FType | String | Yes | | | 30 |
| Name | String | Yes | | | 100 |
| Shape_Length | Double | Yes | 0 | 0 | |
| Shape_Area | Double | Yes | 0 | 0 | |

*An areal hydrography feature not represented by a Waterbody, such as a swamp or inundation area*

Unique feature identifier in the geodatabase
Permanent public identifier of feature
Descriptor of feature type
Geographic name

| Simple feature class **Waterbody** | | Geometry | Polygon | | |
|---|---|---|---|---|---|
| | | Contains M values | No | | |
| | | Contains Z values | No | | |

| Field name | Data type | Allow nulls | Precision | Scale | Length |
|---|---|---|---|---|---|
| OBJECTID | Object ID | | | | |
| Shape | Geometry | Yes | | | |
| HydroID | Long integer | Yes | 0 | | |
| HydroCode | String | Yes | | | 30 |
| FType | String | Yes | | | 30 |
| Name | String | Yes | | | 100 |
| AreaSqKm | Double | Yes | 0 | 0 | |
| JunctionID | Long integer | Yes | 0 | | |
| Shape_Length | Double | Yes | 0 | 0 | |
| Shape_Area | Double | Yes | 0 | 0 | |

*Any significant pond, lake, or bay in the water system*

Unique feature identifier in the geodatabase
Permanent public identifier of feature
Descriptor of feature type
Geographic name
Area in square kilometers
HydroID of the related HydroJunction

A hydro response unit is an area of the land surface that has homogeneous precipitation, land surface characteristics, or both. Hydro response units account for the vertical exchange of water through the hydrologic cycle and are used in hydrologic modeling simulations to accurately describe and predict how water will move through the environment.

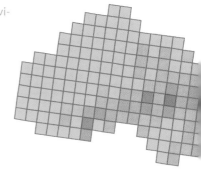

Hydro response units are polygon features, typically represented in a grid pattern as shown on the next page. Two general classes of hydro response units are defined in this data model: units linking atmospheric and surface processes and units linking surface processes and subsurface processes.

When defining hydro response units for linking atmospheric and surface processes that determine surface runoff from storm events, it is important to consider terrestrial characteristics, such as land use and soil type. A standard runoff prediction method, the Soil Conservation Service Curve Number method, considers both of these characteristics. In areas with high-porosity soils, infiltration is generally increased, which reduces the overall amount of surface runoff. Similarly, land use affects runoff by altering the permeability of the land surface. Urban areas with many buildings and much pavement have highly impervious surfaces and experience significant runoff. Agricultural areas, or areas of greater open space, tend to have less runoff for the same rainfall because the land surface is more receptive to infiltration. Even within a given "open space" away from urban land use, runoff can vary greatly as a function of the type of vegetation. Grasses enable much more rainwater to percolate into the ground than is possible under trees, such as ashe juniper, whose canopies prevent grass growth. Almost all the water falling on an ashe juniper forest (common in Texas) becomes runoff or evaporation directly from the trees, while most of the same amount of rain falling on grassy meadows stays in the soil.

Water is transferred between the atmosphere and the land surface through precipitation and evaporation. Each of these processes depends on the geographic location of the land area, and evaporation also depends on land use and season. Both processes are commonly recorded at specific points on the land surface, and methods have been determined to interpolate the respective values for the entire area based on only a few point measurements.

Another common method of representing precipitation on a land surface is through Nexrad cells. These cells describe atmospheric moisture using remote sensing technology. Data is available as rectangular polygons, commonly called a fishnet, as shown in the figure at right. The Nexrad data is intersected with a land surface grid to determine the quantity of precipitation that has fallen onto a land area. Ingesting Nexrad data into Arc Hydro is shown in a later section.

| Simple feature class **HydroResponseUnit** | | Geometry *Polygon* Contains M values *No* Contains Z values *No* | | | |
|---|---|---|---|---|---|
| Field name | Data type | Allow nulls | Prec- ision | Scale | Length |
| OBJECTID | Object ID | | | | |
| Shape | Geometry | Yes | | | |
| HydroID | Long integer | Yes | 0 | | |
| HydroCode | String | Yes | | | 30 |
| AreaSqKm | Double | Yes | 0 | 0 | |
| Shape_Length | Double | Yes | 0 | 0 | |
| Shape_Area | Double | Yes | 0 | 0 | |

*An area of the landscape possessing uniform properties for conversion of rainfall into runoff*

Unique feature identifier in the geodatabase
Permanent public identifier of feature
Area in square kilometers

*Fishnet map of rainfall values over Guadalupe River basin, Texas. Each cell is a HydroResponseUnit feature; the time series data is held in an Arc Hydro Time Series table. The color of each cell indicates the quantity of rainfall in a recent time period.*

The flow and quality of water are measured by numerous observations at gages and sampling stations. Some data is archived at regular intervals, such as daily mean discharge or daily rainfall, and other data is measured irregularly in time, such as water quality samples taken a few times a year at a particular location on a stream. The synthesis of spatial and time series data has been a challenge for GIS systems. The Arc Hydro data model incorporates a simple yet flexible approach to this issue.

Time series measurements of various aspects of the environment are an important data source for hydrologic and hydraulic modeling. As a storm moves across the landscape, rain collects from runoff in the streams and rivers, and increasing amounts of water swell the rivers downstream. In many regions of the world, it is a critical matter of safety and economic importance to predict the location, levels, and duration of flooding. Working with analytical models using current and historical data, hydrologists can often predict these effects.

Until recently, time series data has been difficult to integrate with GIS data. However, this was seen as a crucial part of the design of the Arc Hydro data model. The intention here was not only to build a complete hydrologic data model for use in a GIS environment but also to create a database that is accessible to many water resources models that operate independently of the GIS.

Time series data is often voluminous; a single time series file typically could hold 10 years of daily or hourly records made at irregular intervals. However, advances in RDBMS technology have brought direct support for various formats of time series in standard databases, such as Oracle®, IBM® DB2®, Informix®, and Sybase®. The purpose of the Arc Hydro data model for time series is to leverage the RDBMS technology and organize time series data for best use in hydrologic and hydraulic applications.

## Time series in Arc Hydro

A time series has three main aspects: location in space, location in time, and classification of the type of observation. The location in space is represented by the geographic feature associated with the time series, such as a river gage station located 10 miles from the mouth of a river. The location in time is given by a timestamp for each observation of the phenomenon being monitored. A given feature might be associated with any number of different types of observa-

tions, such as rainfall, runoff, stream stage (depth), stream flow rate, temperature, or pressure.

These basic concepts led to the initial design of the time series data model presented here. The TimeSeries table contains records of observations. Each observation is identified by its associated FeatureID; a timestamp value (TSDateTime); an observation value (TSValue); and a TSTypeID, which points to a descriptor for the time series.

TSTypes are records in a table that provide the core metadata needed to describe a particular type of observation. The figure on the next page describes each of the fields of this table. Notice the DataType field, which is shown as having a value domain called TSDataType. This domain distinguishes the most common types of time series, which users may extend as needed. Each type of time series has a specific role in hydrologic analysis:

1. Instantaneous data—A condition at a given instant in time

2. Cumulative data—The accumulated value since the beginning of the record

3. Incremental data—The difference in cumulative values at the beginning and end of a time interval

4. Average data—The average rate over a time interval, calculated as the incremental value divided by the duration of the data interval

5. Maximum data—The maximum value of a variable in a time interval

6. Minimum data—The minimum value of a variable in a given time interval

The Origin field of the TSType table is important metadata, as many time series are generated from postprocessing other time series. An example is the generation of daily average rainfall amounts from a source table of hourly data.

# Table
## TSType

| Field name | Data type | Allow nulls | Domain | Precision | Scale | Length |
|---|---|---|---|---|---|---|
| OBJECTID | Object ID | | | | | |
| TSTypeID | Long integer | Yes | | 0 | | |
| Variable | String | Yes | | | | 30 |
| Units | String | Yes | | | | 30 |
| IsRegular | Long integer | Yes | AHBoolean | 0 | | |
| TSInterval | Long integer | Yes | TSIntervalType | 0 | | |
| DataType | Long integer | Yes | TSDataType | 0 | | |
| Origin | Long integer | Yes | TSOrigins | 0 | | |

*Descriptive information for each type of time varying data stored in the TimeSeries table*

Identifier for the type of time series
The variable described by the time series, such as stream flow
Units of measurement
Whether data is regularly or irregularly measured by time
Time interval represented by each measurement
Type of time series data such as instantaneous, cumulative
Origin of the time series data

## Relationship class
### TSTypeHasTimeSeries

| | |
|---|---|
| Type *Simple* | Forward label *TimeSeries* |
| Cardinality *One to many* | Backward label *TSType* |
| Notification *None* | |

| Origin table | Destination table |
|---|---|
| Name *TSType* | Name *TimeSeries* |
| Primary key *TSTypeID* | |
| Foreign key *TSTypeID* | |

# Table
## TimeSeries

| Field name | Data type | Allow nulls | Precision | Scale | Length |
|---|---|---|---|---|---|
| OBJECTID | Object ID | | | | |
| FeatureID | Long integer | Yes | 0 | | |
| TSTypeID | Long integer | Yes | 0 | | |
| TSDateTime | Date | Yes | 0 | 0 | 8 |
| TSValue | Double | Yes | 0 | 0 | |

*A single large table storing all time varying values of feature attributes*

HydroID of feature described by time series
Identifier for the type of time series
Date and time of the time series table
Time series value

The timestamp held in the TSDateTime field of the Time-Series table is formatted as follows:

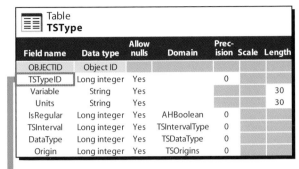

MM/DD/YYYY hh:mm:ss.sss

*year*
*day {01..31}*
*month {01..12}*
*fractions of second*
*second {01..59}*
*minute {01..59}*
*hour {01..24}*

Time series tables can have observations at regular intervals, such as hourly or daily, as well as observations at irregular intervals, such as whenever a storm event occurs. This information is held in the TSType table with two fields, IsRegular and TSInterval. If IsRegular is true (equals one), then TSInterval holds the value of the time between observations. If IsRegular is false (equals zero), then the value of TSInterval has no meaning and would not be used.

Coded value domain
**TSDataType**
Description
Field type *Long integer*
Split policy *Default value*
Merge policy *Default value*

| Code | Description |
|---|---|
| 1 | Instantaneous |
| 2 | Cumulative |
| 3 | Incremental |
| 4 | Average |
| 5 | Maximum |
| 6 | Minimum |

Coded value domain
**TSOrigins**
Description
Field type *Long integer*
Split policy *Default value*
Merge policy *Default value*

| Code | Description |
|---|---|
| 1 | Recorded |
| 2 | Generated |

Coded value domain
**AHBoolean**
Description
Field type *Long integer*
Split policy *Default value*
Merge policy *Default value*

| Code | Description |
|---|---|
| 1 | True |
| 0 | False |

Coded value domain
**TSIntervalType**
Description
Field type *Long integer*
Split policy *Default value*
Merge policy *Default value*

| Code | Description |
|---|---|
| 1 | 1Minute |
| 2 | 2Minute |
| 3 | 3Minute |
| 4 | 4Minute |
| 5 | 5Minute |
| 6 | 10Minute |
| 7 | 15Minute |
| 8 | 20Minute |
| 9 | 30Minute |
| 10 | 1Hour |
| 11 | 2Hour |
| 12 | 3Hour |
| 13 | 4Hour |
| 14 | 6Hour |
| 15 | 8Hour |
| 16 | 12Hour |
| 17 | 1Day |
| 18 | 1Week |
| 19 | 1Month |
| 20 | 1Year |
| 99 | Other |

2

Due to the large amounts and patterns of data in time series, specialized tools have evolved for working with them. These tools can be integrated with the GIS to provide the user with a seamless transition between the spatial and temporal domains. The tools shown here have evolved to display time variations in rainfall, stream characteristics, and water quality.

Several tools have evolved to help represent, display, and manage time series data. A widely used system familiar to the general public is Nexrad Doppler radar data, which is continually updated over the entire United States. An example display of Nexrad data for one cumulative 15-minute period is shown below. The South Florida Water Management District has further established an automatic system whereby actual rainfall data from its field monitoring stations is used to fine-tune the Nexrad data in near real-time, resulting in gage-adjusted rainfall grids to be posted within 15 minutes of receiving each delivery of the original Nexrad data.

## ArcGIS Tracking Analyst

The ArcGIS Tracking Analyst can be used to display animated maps of Nexrad data in ArcMap. It does this by associating the table of Nexrad time series in Arc Hydro format with the feature class containing the shapes of the Nexrad cells as a temporal layer in ArcMap.

ArcGIS Tracking Analyst is used in the upper figures on the next page. These figures show water quality in terms of bacteria levels at numerous monitoring stations in Galveston Bay, Texas. The time series contains bacteria levels sampled at irregular intervals from January 1995 to December 2001. The size of the orange dots represents a nominal range of bacteria level (the larger the dot, the higher the concentration). The user can animate this time series with Tracking Analyst, enabling visual identification of temporal–spatial patterns.

## DHI rainfall tools

DHI Water and Environment has developed a set of tools for time series analysis based on Arc Hydro. In the figure at the bottom of the next page, the BlueRiver geodatabase is being viewed by variable, where the variable refers to the type of observation having time series data. It is also possible to view the data by Data Type, Table Name, Origin, Group, Location, or Feature Class. In this case, the user has imported or otherwise generated eight rainfall time series, one evapora-

tion time series, and six discharge time series. The lower pane shows plots of user-selected time series values, in this case, rainfall in millimeters (plotted in blue) and runoff in cubic meters per second (plotted in black).

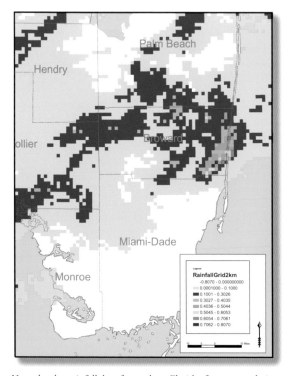

*Nexrad radar rainfall data for southern Florida, for one cumulative 15-minute period*

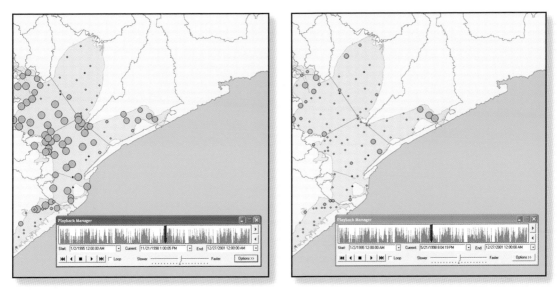

*Water quality levels for two months at monitoring stations in Galveston Bay using ArcGIS Tracking Analyst*

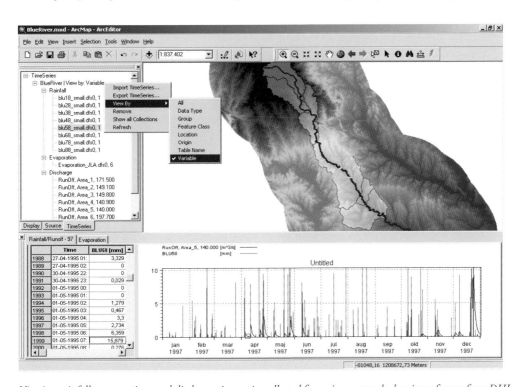

*Viewing rainfall, evaporation, and discharge time series collected for a given watershed, using software from DHI*

Since the initial development of the time series data model for Arc Hydro, numerous applications have been created. This has led to a deeper understanding of the use of time series in GIS and to the concept of temporal geoprocessing. This extends the capabilities of GIS and provides an important means of applying GIS data to analytical models from other scientific and engineering domains.

Lessons learned from numerous projects by Dr. Maidment's team at the University of Texas have led to the following distinctions among time series used in GIS. This is not just a set of different applications of time series, but the basis of a powerful framework for temporal–spatial analysis.

These are the types of temporal series:

- Time series—The most common type of time series is a sequence of records containing time and value attributes for a given type of observation, expressed in tabular form. A single time series may be related to one or more geographic features, as in the case of rainfall from one gage that applies to several catchments or watersheds in a hydrologic model.

- Attribute series—When a time series is associated with just one geographic feature, it could be considered an attribute of that feature. When all features of the same class have such time series for a given attribute, the series is said to be an attribute series, such as the bacterial data from the monitoring points on Galveston Bay. These are the same as static events in Tracking Analyst; that is, each feature shape and location remain fixed, but one or more properties of each feature may vary over time. This is the usual form for an Arc Hydro time series. A given feature may have several attribute series, one for each type of observation.

- Feature series—A feature series is a sequence of records in which the feature shape varies over time. This is the same as a dynamic event in Tracking Analyst and is appropriate for the case in which shapes are in motion or the geometry changes through time. The figure on the next page shows flood inundation polygons classified by depth. These polygons changes over time as the storm moves across the landscape.

- Raster series—A time series of raster data could be represented as a sequence of records containing raster and time attributes. Each raster represents a snapshot in time. The rasters could also be stored in external files, but a better approach is to store the rasters in records of an ArcGIS raster catalog, with additional DateTime and TSType fields to provide indices for timestamp and type of time series information in the raster.

## Temporal geoprocessing

The figure on the next page shows how all four of these types of temporal series can be utilized for geoprocessing, in this case, to study river depth and flooding. Incoming data from field measurement equipment may originate in a raw tabular form (time series), then be migrated (step 1 in the figure) to an attribute series of water surface elevations for different monitoring points.

This attribute series may then be processed into a raster series (step 2) using an approach such as inverse distance weighting (IDW) to create a water surface elevation raster, one such raster for each step in the time series. Water depth surface rasters can be computed from these, then reclassified and dissolved into polygons representing locations and shapes of various depth classes over time (step 3). A depth class refers to a range of depth, such as 6 to 8 inches. A set of depth class polygons over an area would be like contour lines that move across the landscape, depending on the amount of rainfall. The raster data also lends itself to zonal analysis for determining average, minimum, and maximum depths over an area. Polygons for watershed areas could now be assigned attribute series of this statistical information (step 4).

This methodology for temporal geoprocessing is validated by the ease with which non-GIS modeling and simulation software has been adapted to support hydrologic analysis with the GIS. Because many external simulation models structure temporal data in a similar way to that just described for time series and attribute series, it has taken little effort to integrate the GIS temporal data with these external tools—much less effort, in fact, than that normally required to integrate spatial data with external modeling tools.

# Temporal–Spatial analysis of inundation

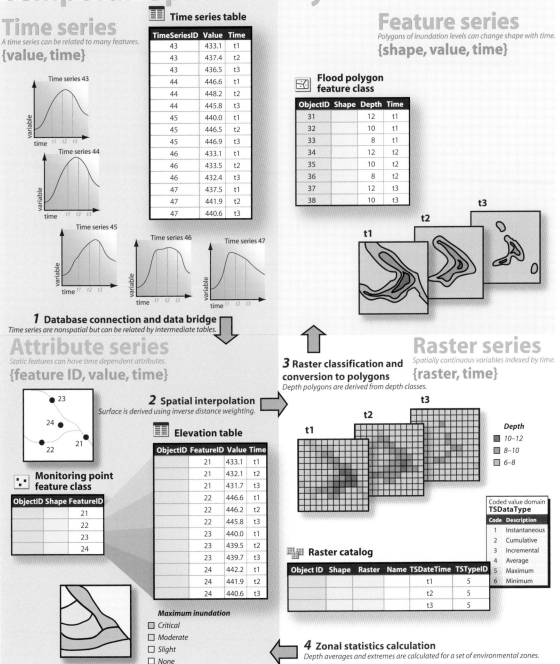

## Time series
*A time series can be related to many features.*
**{value, time}**

Time series 43
Time series 44
Time series 45
Time series 46
Time series 47

### Time series table

| TimeSeriesID | Value | Time |
|---|---|---|
| 43 | 433.1 | t1 |
| 43 | 437.4 | t2 |
| 43 | 436.5 | t3 |
| 44 | 446.6 | t1 |
| 44 | 448.2 | t2 |
| 44 | 445.8 | t3 |
| 45 | 440.0 | t1 |
| 45 | 446.5 | t2 |
| 45 | 446.9 | t3 |
| 46 | 433.1 | t1 |
| 46 | 433.5 | t2 |
| 46 | 432.4 | t3 |
| 47 | 437.5 | t1 |
| 47 | 441.9 | t2 |
| 47 | 440.6 | t3 |

## Feature series
*Polygons of inundation levels can change shape with time.*
**{shape, value, time}**

### Flood polygon feature class

| ObjectID | Shape | Depth | Time |
|---|---|---|---|
| 31 | | 12 | t1 |
| 32 | | 10 | t1 |
| 33 | | 8 | t1 |
| 34 | | 12 | t2 |
| 35 | | 10 | t2 |
| 36 | | 8 | t2 |
| 37 | | 12 | t3 |
| 38 | | 10 | t3 |

t1  t2  t3

**1 Database connection and data bridge**
*Time series are nonspatial but can be related by intermediate tables.*

## Attribute series
*Static features can have time dependent attributes.*
**{feature ID, value, time}**

23
24
22  21

### Monitoring point feature class

| ObjectID | Shape | FeatureID |
|---|---|---|
| | | 21 |
| | | 22 |
| | | 23 |
| | | 24 |

**2 Spatial interpolation**
*Surface is derived using inverse distance weighting.*

### Elevation table

| ObjectID | FeatureID | Value | Time |
|---|---|---|---|
| | 21 | 433.1 | t1 |
| | 21 | 432.1 | t2 |
| | 21 | 431.7 | t3 |
| | 22 | 446.6 | t1 |
| | 22 | 446.2 | t2 |
| | 22 | 445.8 | t3 |
| | 23 | 440.0 | t1 |
| | 23 | 439.5 | t2 |
| | 23 | 439.7 | t3 |
| | 24 | 442.2 | t1 |
| | 24 | 441.9 | t2 |
| | 24 | 440.6 | t3 |

**3 Raster classification and conversion to polygons**
*Depth polygons are derived from depth classes.*

## Raster series
*Spatially continuous variables indexed by time.*
**{raster, time}**

t1  t2  t3

**Depth**
- 10–12
- 8–10
- 6–8

### Raster catalog

| Object ID | Shape | Raster | Name | TSDateTime | TSTypeID |
|---|---|---|---|---|---|
| | | | | t1 | 5 |
| | | | | t2 | 5 |
| | | | | t3 | 5 |

Coded value domain
**TSDataType**

| Code | Description |
|---|---|
| 1 | Instantaneous |
| 2 | Cumulative |
| 3 | Incremental |
| 4 | Average |
| 5 | Maximum |
| 6 | Minimum |

**Maximum inundation**
- ☐ Critical
- ☐ Moderate
- ☐ Slight
- ☐ None

**4 Zonal statistics calculation**
*Depth averages and extremes are calculated for a set of environmental zones.*

A recent research project ties together many of the concepts discussed so far in this chapter. The project was funded by the San Antonio River Authority and carried out by the University of Texas Center for Research in Water Resources, with PBS&J as the consulting firm. The purpose of the project was to develop a floodplain map from Nexrad rainfall data.

Generating 100- and 500-year floodplain maps is a difficult process, requiring large amounts of data and geoprocessing. Until recently, floodplain maps corresponding to a given storm event could not be generated quickly enough to be of immediate use, for example, to anticipate downstream flooding and warn residents in time to evacuate. However, advances in GIS technology allow automation of hydrologic and hydraulic models, leading to near real-time mapping of floodplains.

A component of the San Antonio Regional Watershed Modeling Project uses GIS as an integration framework for floodplain modeling and mapping. In this approach, the GIS provides a spatial framework as the common ground for connectivity between existing, well-tested, and agency-approved hydrologic and hydraulic analytical models.

These analytical models are from the U.S. Army Corps of Engineers HEC Hydrologic Modeling System (HMS) for determining stream flow based on rainfall and runoff as well as the HEC–RAS for determining water surface elevation and extent as a function of this flow. The HEC Decision Support System (DSS) provides an underlying time series data storage system for both of these models. A crucial step in this framework is the transfer of time series data between linked model features at three levels: from the HEC–DSS to the geodatabase, within the geodatabase, and from the geodatabase to the HEC–DSS.

*Nexrad radar rainfall data is published in a series of text files containing hourly data for a storm event on July 1, 2002.*

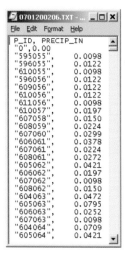

*Nexrad time series files are converted to geodatabase tables with Arc Hydro format (TimeSeries and TSType tables) as well as an HEC Time Series Type table to store the HEC–DSS descriptors of the data.*

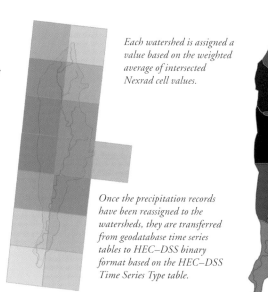

*Each watershed is assigned a value based on the weighted average of intersected Nexrad cell values.*

*Once the precipitation records have been reassigned to the watersheds, they are transferred from geodatabase time series tables to HEC–DSS binary format based on the HEC–DSS Time Series Type table.*

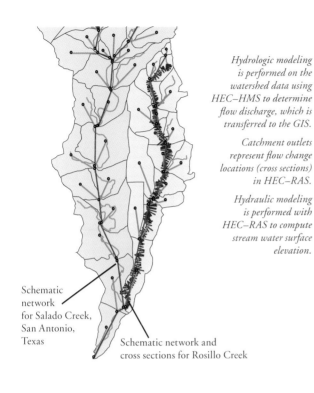

*Rosillo Creek channel profile*

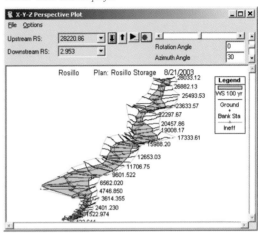

*Hydrologic modeling is performed on the watershed data using HEC–HMS to determine flow discharge, which is transferred to the GIS.*

*Catchment outlets represent flow change locations (cross sections) in HEC–RAS.*

*Hydraulic modeling is performed with HEC–RAS to compute stream water surface elevation.*

Schematic network for Salado Creek, San Antonio, Texas

Schematic network and cross sections for Rosillo Creek

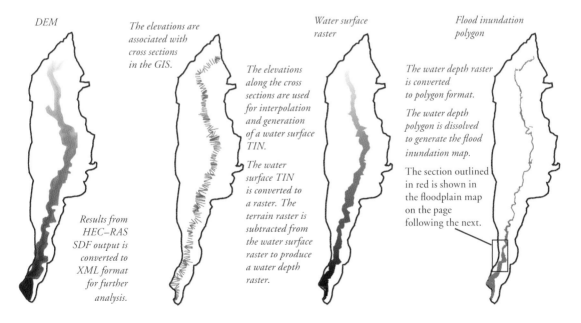

*DEM*

*Results from HEC–RAS SDF output is converted to XML format for further analysis.*

*The elevations are associated with cross sections in the GIS.*

*The elevations along the cross sections are used for interpolation and generation of a water surface TIN.*

*The water surface TIN is converted to a raster. The terrain raster is subtracted from the water surface raster to produce a water depth raster.*

*Water surface raster*

*Flood inundation polygon*

*The water depth raster is converted to polygon format.*

*The water depth polygon is dissolved to generate the flood inundation map.*

The section outlined in red is shown in the floodplain map on the page following the next.

This analytical model represents an integration between a GIS using the Arc Hydro data model, the HEC–HMS hydrologic modeling system, the HEC–RAS hydraulic modeling system, and the HEC–DSS time series and decision support system. The steps shown in this model diagram are not new; this kind of analysis has been performed for decades. What is new here is the degree of hydrologic model integration and work flow automation handled by the GIS.

The model shown here was implemented with ArcGIS ModelBuilder, allowing the user to change input sources and operational parameters and rerun the model without extensive data management overhead. It is important to note that the analytical models are industry standards; the only roles of the GIS are to prepare input data for the analytical models and automate the transfer of intermediate results between the different analytical models (Whiteaker 2004).

Now that the necessary input data has been assembled and structured, which required substantial initial effort, the model shown here executes in just a few minutes on a standard desktop computer for the stream network shown on the previous page. This means the flood map can be regenerated in sync with each 15-minute update of the Nexrad data.

The model shown computes the maximum flood inundation polygon for the highest water surface elevation at each point. This model can be extended to compute a feature series of flood inundation polygons as the flood passes along a river.

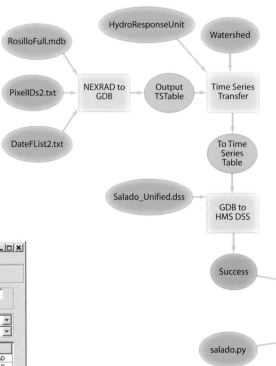

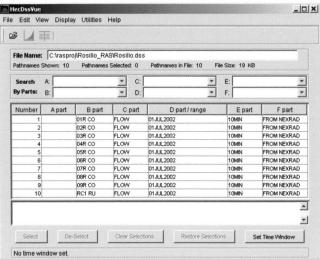

*The HEC–DSS software helps manage the time series data for rainfall used in this model.*

*In this project, the GIS time series data is converted for use in HEC–DSS and, later, the DSS data is converted back for use in the GIS. This procedure is used at several steps in the framework.*

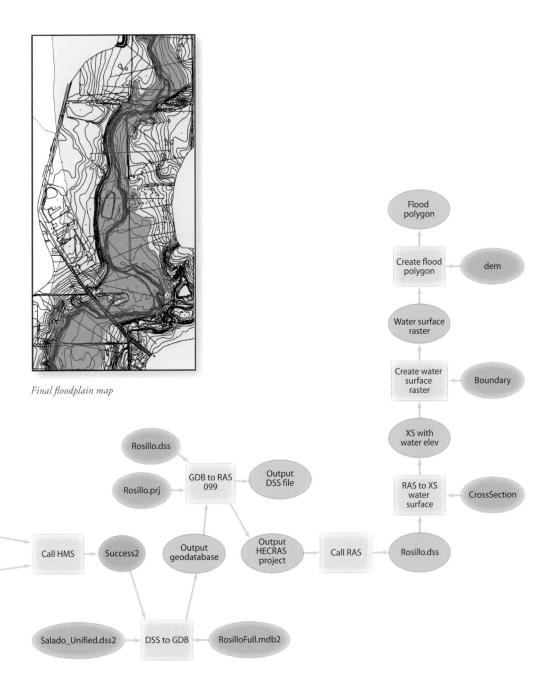

*Final floodplain map*

The water features in a vast area in southern Florida have undergone tremendous change from a natural system to an artificial state. This region is so flat that a canal system has evolved that looks more like a road network than streams.

The Arc Hydro data model and tools are based on assumptions of dendritic stream networks having gravity-based, unidirectional flow characteristics. This is a reasonable starting point for a hydrological data model that works in most traditional situations.

However, estuaries and river segments can have reversible direction of flow, generally due to tides, storm surges, pumps, or floodwaters from intersecting rivers. One striking exception to the general rule can be found in the region surrounding and to the south of Lake Okeechobee in southern Florida. The linear features on the map on the next page are not roads; they are canals. Canal levels are closely managed as storms pass over the landscape. To preclude or at least mitigate flooding, canals carry irrigation waters during dry periods and drainage waters during storms, often in opposite directions.

South Texas has a similar situation, with a complex network of irrigation canals over a large, relatively flat agricultural region. This canal grid with reversible flow has significant implications for many of the hydrologic analysis techniques mentioned in this chapter.

The Arc Hydro data model as it is documented in this chapter does not address these types of requirements. The ability to model two-directional flow based on time can be implemented as an extension to the model. Refer to http://support.esri.com/datamodels for the most recent information on these design extensions.

*Southern Florida has a grid of canals that resembles a road network.*
*Pumping stations move water in any direction, based on the location*
*of storms and projected flooding potential.*

## REFERENCES AND FURTHER READING

Gopalan, Hema; Tim Whiteaker, and David Maidment. Determining Watershed Parameters Using Arc Hydro. Paper presented at the GIS Hydro 2003 Conference, July 2003, San Diego, California.

Maidment, David, ed. Arc Hydro: GIS for Water Resources. Redlands, CA: ESRI Press, 2002.

Merwade, Venkatesh. Geospatial Representation of River Channels. Paper presented at the GIS Hydro 2003 Conference, July 2003, San Diego, California. URL: http://www.crwr.utexas.edu/gis/gishydro03/Channel/Channels.htm.

Strassberg, Gil, and Suzanne Pierce. Arc Hydro Groundwater Data Model. Paper presented at the GIS Hydro 2003 Conference, July 2003, San Diego, California. URL: http://www.crwr.utexas.edu/gis/gishydro03/Groundwater/Groundwater.html.

U.S. Army Corps of Engineers. Hydrologic Engineering Center. 2002. HEC-GeoRAS: An Extension for Support of HEC-RAS Using ArcView, Users Manual, CPD-76. Davis, California.

U.S. Environmental Protection Agency and U.S. Department of Interior. 2000. The National Hydrography Dataset: Concepts and Contents. URL: http://nhd.usgs.gov/techref.html.

U.S. Environmental Protection Agency and U.S. Department of Interior. 1999. Standards for National Hydrography Dataset, Draft Technical Instructions. URL: http://rmmcweb.cr.usgs.gov/public/nmpstds/nhdstds.html.

U.S. Environmental Protection Agency and U.S. Department of Interior. 1999. Standards for National Hydrography Dataset—High Resolution, Draft Technical Instructions. URL: http://rmmcweb.cr.usgs.gov/public/nmpstds/nhdstds.html.

U.S. Environmental Protection Agency and U.S. Department of Interior. 1996. Standards for 1:24,000-Scale Digital Line Graphs and Quadrangle Maps, Part 1: Template Development and Use, Technical Instructions. URL: http://rmmcweb.cr.usgs.gov/public/nmpstds/nhdstds.html.

Whiteaker, Tim. 2004. Geographically Integrated Hydrologic Modeling Systems. Ph.D. diss., University of Texas, Austin.

Whiteaker, Tim. 2003. Hydrologic Simulation With Arc Hydro, libHydro, and ModelBuilder. White paper, University of Texas Center for Research in Water Resources.

Whiteaker, Tim. 2003. Processing Schematic Networks With ArcToolbox. White paper, University of Texas Center for Research in Water Resources.

## ACKNOWLEDGMENTS

David Maidment and his team at the University of Texas Center for Research in Water Resources have been invaluable, in particular, Jon Goodall, Tim Whiteaker, and Oscar Robayo. The discussion of schematic networks in this chapter is based on a white paper by Tim Whiteaker.

We wish to thank the staff at South Florida Water Management District who contributed their time, photos, and maps: Jim Cameron, Michele Maierhofer, Chandra Pathak, Scott Huebner, Chris Carlson, Ken Stewart, Ken Konyha, and Clay Brown.

Michael Blongewicz at DHI Water and Environment, in Hørsholm, Denmark, was helpful with the time series discussion. The time series tool photo and explanation is courtesy of DHI Water and Environment.

Some of the illustrations, such as those for HydroID, hydro edges, hydro junctions, and cross section properties, were done by Savi Brant with ESRI Press for *Arc Hydro, GIS for Water Resources*, edited by David Maidment.

## FURTHER RESOURCES

View the data models at ESRI ArcOnline by clicking the Hydro link at http://support.esri.com/datamodels. In addition to sample database design templates and data, this site offers the free downloadable Arc Hydro Tools, mentioned throughout this chapter.

The GIS Water Resources Consortium Web site (http://www.crwr.utexas.edu/giswr) is maintained by the University of Texas Center for Research in Water Resources (http://www.crwr.utexas.edu). Both of these sites offer support for the Arc Hydro data model. A particularly useful link is the Arc Hydro Online Support System (http://www.crwr.utexas.edu/giswr/hydro/ArcHOSS/index.cfm).

The U.S. Army Corps of Engineers Hydrologic Engineering Center has developed several analytical modeling systems in widespread use, including the Hydrologic Modeling System (HEC–HMS and HEC–GeoHMS) and River Analysis System (HEC–RAS and HEC–GeoRAS). Visit http://www.hec.usace.army.mil/default.html for more information.

The USGS and EPA have collaborated to develop the National Hydrographic Dataset. One version of this has been developed as an ArcGIS geodatabase in Arc Hydro format, viewable at http://nhdgeo.usgs.gov.

2

*Many GIS users are faced with the task of modeling administrative boundaries. For the U.S. Census Bureau and corresponding census agencies in other nations, this is a critical GIS task. The data model presented here is designed for editing, data integrity, maintenance, and other direct census data use operations by various agencies. This model allows such users to share census and administrative boundary datasets and to collaborate on their update and maintenance.*

**3**

Government agencies in the United States and many other countries have the daunting task of generating hundreds of thousands of maps showing the boundaries of various districts for use in aggregating the extensive demographic data they collect. Over the last several decades, the U.S. Census Bureau has achieved a high degree of automation of this task and regularly publishes updates to the district boundaries and demographic tables describing population characteristics across the country. The TIGER database is downloaded and used by numerous agencies at the federal, state, and local levels, as well as at a wide variety of businesses that incorporate this wealth of information into their own databases for further analyses.

This case study focuses on administrative boundaries, which are related to linear features, such as rivers, roads, and railroads. Identifying address ranges for road segments is also important to this model. As a result, the data model incorporates several themes derived from a common series of linework.

Topology rules and enforcement play a large role in this census data model. Depending on your application requirements, you may choose to create a single topology for the entire database or, instead, leave some of the feature classes out of the topology.

# Census units
# and boundaries

Every 10 years, the U.S. Census Bureau performs the daunting task of counting all individuals who reside in the United States and accumulating a number of demographic statistics and characteristics of the population. These are summarized and published for many geographic units—blocks, block groups, and counties. These geographic boundaries of the census units also form the basis for school districts, voting precincts, federal election voting districts, and numerous other administrative activities. This forms the geographic framework that unifies the management of a vast range of government services.

Census data has two principal components: geographic mapping data of physical features and tabular population and demographic data at many levels of aggregation units. The map data is used to support census field staff in collecting the data and as a spatial reference for the published tabular data. The quantity of geographic data required to create maps for the entire United States is almost overwhelming. Managing, correcting, and updating this data is a major task, requiring considerable resources and coordination between local governments and the U.S. Census Bureau.

In the 1960s, before implementing topology in its census data, the Census Bureau had a computerized file that listed all street segments in the country with address ranges and left and right boundary information. Each of the millions of records required three 80-character punch cards. Data entry error was great and it was not feasible to systematically proof the database. In addition, an update to one record could require a number of changes to related records, which could not be checked automatically.

To better manage and enable automated validation of the mapping data, the Census Bureau developed the Geographic Base Files/Dual Independent Map Encoding (GBF/DIME) and later the TIGER® systems for tagging and relating geographic features in the census database. The GBF/DIME system implemented a topology to manage this vast geographic database as a hierarchy of features built on a common set of linework.

In the census data model, linear feature collections, such as street centerlines, railroads, streams, and administrative boundaries, were used to define a series of areal units—blocks collected into block groups that were further collected into tracts, and so on. Each boundary segment was defined as a series of topological elements and assigned its role or participation as a boundary in these nested area features. Traditionally, boundary lines had a from- and to-node, which specified the line's direction.

Each side of the line could be assigned an address range as well as many other unit values—the ID number of the block, block group, census tract, and so on.

The result of explicitly recording this topology as attributes within the GBF/DIME file (and maintaining it with the move to TIGER) was that a system administrator could then verify the geographic data. An algorithmic test could find and walk along the segments bounding atomic polygons to check, for example, that all of the left-side segments referenced a common block ID and subsequent hierarchy of geographies. Even though it could take three days to validate a single county, this provided an incredible improvement in the way the Census Bureau could manage its data and allowed a level of confidence in the topological integrity of the data not previously possible. However, rich feature coordinate representation was not addressed.

Since the 1980s, modern GIS software has included topology engines to automate geometric validation of such topologies. This has allowed the various user agencies at the local government, county, and state levels to enrich the geometric representation of census features and integrate census data with other GIS data layers.

The tasks and problems of collecting, updating, and validating census data continue to challenge local, state, and federal agencies. But today, U.S. census data is routinely available for live viewing or download via the Internet, for example, using the Geography Network℠ (http://www.geographynetwork.com). Businesses and government agencies at all levels use this data for numerous projects. Independent, value-added services also process and repackage census data for many different purposes.

Because of the extensive customer base and applications of this data across both public and private sectors, this census data model has been developed to enable users to rapidly put such data to use. The database structure and thematic layers presented in this chapter are designed to closely match the information content in U.S. Census TIGER/Line® files. By modeling and capturing this data within a GIS database, each user can better integrate the census data with other map layers and tabular data.

*These cartoons are from DIME Comix & Stories (Census, 1976).*

The key thematic layers shown here are based on two important design concepts incorporated across these layers: (1) the boundaries of all administrative areas are derived from the linework for several types of physical features, and (2) a contiguous set of administrative areas form a spatial hierarchy subject to topological integrity rules. Blocks are collected into block groups, block groups into census tracts, and so on. The boundaries of all area features are derived from a common set of linear features. Hence, the use of topology is critical.

There are five logical groups of features in this census data model. The first two are the foundation layers on which the administrative units are based.

## Census boundaries

Physical features, such as rivers, railroads, and even power lines, form the boundaries of census and other administrative units.

## Streets and addresses

Streets also form census boundaries but are placed in a separate layer because of their functional role in locating address ranges. Address ranges are a fundamental part of census data, both for field data collection efforts and for validation of street connectivity.

Road segments form both block and block group boundaries (pink).

Road and river segments form census block boundaries (yellow).

Not all road or river segments form block or block group boundaries.

*Other physical features, such as railroads, lakes, and power lines, can be used as census block and block group boundaries.*

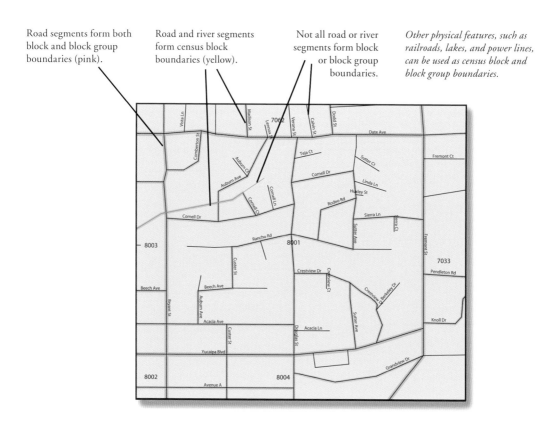

## Census administrative units

The primary administrative units for aggregating population and demographic data are the census block, block group, and census tract. These polygons are formed by connecting linear physical features, such as streets, railroads, and rivers.

## Other administrative units

There are many kinds of political and other administrative units, such as voting precincts, congressional districts, and so on. These are typically aggregations of census administrative units.

## Points of interest

Various landmark points and areas may be represented, such as parks or state and federal land.

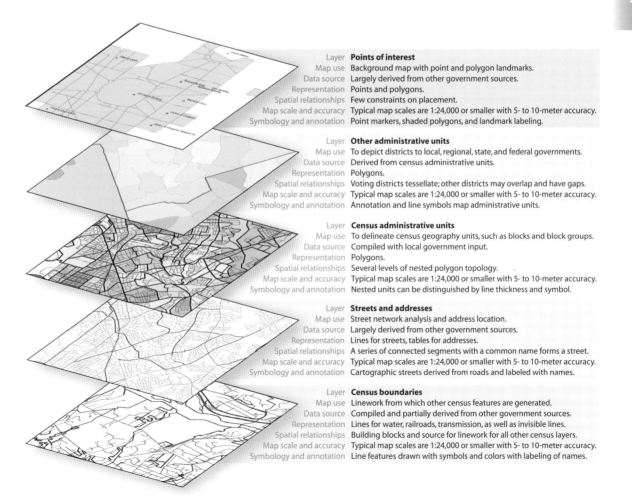

| | Layer | **Points of interest** |
| --- | --- | --- |
| | Map use | Background map with point and polygon landmarks. |
| | Data source | Largely derived from other government sources. |
| | Representation | Points and polygons. |
| | Spatial relationships | Few constraints on placement. |
| | Map scale and accuracy | Typical map scales are 1:24,000 or smaller with 5- to 10-meter accuracy. |
| | Symbology and annotation | Point markers, shaded polygons, and landmark labeling. |

| | Layer | **Other administrative units** |
| --- | --- | --- |
| | Map use | To depict districts to local, regional, state, and federal governments. |
| | Data source | Derived from census administrative units. |
| | Representation | Polygons. |
| | Spatial relationships | Voting districts tessellate; other districts may overlap and have gaps. |
| | Map scale and accuracy | Typical map scales are 1:24,000 or smaller with 5- to 10-meter accuracy. |
| | Symbology and annotation | Annotation and line symbols map administrative units. |

| | Layer | **Census administrative units** |
| --- | --- | --- |
| | Map use | To delineate census geography units, such as blocks and block groups. |
| | Data source | Compiled with local government input. |
| | Representation | Polygons. |
| | Spatial relationships | Several levels of nested polygon topology. |
| | Map scale and accuracy | Typical map scales are 1:24,000 or smaller with 5- to 10-meter accuracy. |
| | Symbology and annotation | Nested units can be distinguished by line thickness and symbol. |

| | Layer | **Streets and addresses** |
| --- | --- | --- |
| | Map use | Street network analysis and address location. |
| | Data source | Largely derived from other government sources. |
| | Representation | Lines for streets, tables for addresses. |
| | Spatial relationships | A series of connected segments with a common name forms a street. |
| | Map scale and accuracy | Typical map scales are 1:24,000 or smaller with 5- to 10-meter accuracy. |
| | Symbology and annotation | Cartographic streets derived from roads and labeled with names. |

| | Layer | **Census boundaries** |
| --- | --- | --- |
| | Map use | Linework from which other census features are generated. |
| | Data source | Compiled and partially derived from other government sources. |
| | Representation | Lines for water, railroads, transmission, as well as invisible lines. |
| | Spatial relationships | Building blocks and source for linework for all other census layers. |
| | Map scale and accuracy | Typical map scales are 1:24,000 or smaller with 5- to 10-meter accuracy. |
| | Symbology and annotation | Line features drawn with symbols and colors with labeling of names. |

The most striking aspect of the geodatabase structure for census data is that the topology includes most, if not all, of the feature classes. Topology integrity tools in the GIS help enforce coincidence of geometry between the administrative areas and the underlying physical features. There are many feature classes in this data model that are only used in certain portions of the United States; therefore, you should consider using only the feature classes relevant to your locale and expected uses.

## Features forming census boundaries

This group consists of mostly linear feature classes and a polygon class for water bodies. These physical features form the primitive boundary elements of census blocks.

## Census administrative units

Census administrative units are all polygon feature classes that represent census geographies (blocks, block groups, tracts, and so on). They form a containment hierarchy in which census blocks are aggregated into block groups. Block groups are further aggregated into census tracts, census tracts into counties, and counties into states. Native American Indian block groups and census tracts are used in specific local areas of the United States.

## Administrative boundaries: county, state, federal

Different types of districts are also assembled from census boundaries. These form various administrative units for local, county, state, and federal use.

## Points of interest

Points of interest are primarily landmarks, which could be point, line, or polygon features, and are not so much used in building administrative areas as in providing aids to navigation for field enumerator staff collecting census data.

## Topology

TIGER data provides an excellent example of topological integration of shared linework for numerous data layers. Units, such as blocks, block groups, and tracts, are assembled out of the underlying topological linework that represents features, such as roads, rails, and hydrography.

Topological rules can be defined to maintain the integrity and behavior of these layers. Examples of topological rules include:

- Census blocks cannot overlap and must nest within block groups.

- Block groups cannot overlap and must nest within census tracts.

- Traffic analysis zones must be covered by counties.

- The voting district layer must be covered by the county layer.

A more complete and detailed look at topological rules follows later in this chapter.

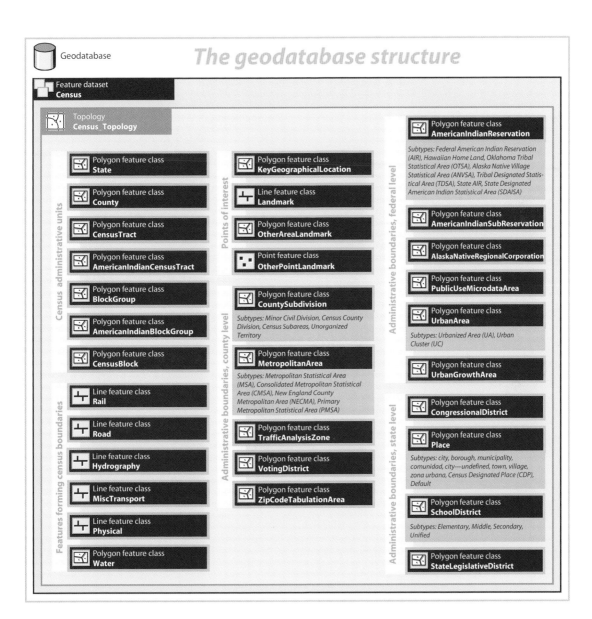

# The geodatabase structure

**Geodatabase**

**Feature dataset**
**Census**

**Topology**
**Census_Topology**

### Census administrative units

Polygon feature class
**State**

Polygon feature class
**County**

Polygon feature class
**CensusTract**

Polygon feature class
**AmericanIndianCensusTract**

Polygon feature class
**BlockGroup**

Polygon feature class
**AmericanIndianBlockGroup**

Polygon feature class
**CensusBlock**

### Features forming census boundaries

Line feature class
**Rail**

Line feature class
**Road**

Line feature class
**Hydrography**

Line feature class
**MiscTransport**

Line feature class
**Physical**

Polygon feature class
**Water**

### Points of interest

Polygon feature class
**KeyGeographicalLocation**

Line feature class
**Landmark**

Polygon feature class
**OtherAreaLandmark**

Point feature class
**OtherPointLandmark**

### Administrative boundaries, county level

Polygon feature class
**CountySubdivision**

*Subtypes: Minor Civil Division, Census County Division, Census Subareas, Unorganized Territory*

Polygon feature class
**MetropolitanArea**

*Subtypes: Metropolitan Statistical Area (MSA), Consolidated Metropolitan Statistical Area (CMSA), New England County Metropolitan Area (NECMA), Primary Metropolitan Statistical Area (PMSA)*

Polygon feature class
**TrafficAnalysisZone**

Polygon feature class
**VotingDistrict**

Polygon feature class
**ZipCodeTabulationArea**

### Administrative boundaries, federal level

Polygon feature class
**AmericanIndianReservation**

*Subtypes: Federal American Indian Reservation (AIR), Hawaiian Home Land, Oklahoma Tribal Statistical Area (OTSA), Alaska Native Village Statistical Area (ANVSA), Tribal Designated Statistical Area (TDSA), State AIR, State Designated American Indian Statistical Area (SDAISA)*

Polygon feature class
**AmericanIndianSubReservation**

Polygon feature class
**AlaskaNativeRegionalCorporation**

Polygon feature class
**PublicUseMicrodataArea**

Polygon feature class
**UrbanArea**

*Subtypes: Urbanized Area (UA), Urban Cluster (UC)*

Polygon feature class
**UrbanGrowthArea**

### Administrative boundaries, state level

Polygon feature class
**CongressionalDistrict**

Polygon feature class
**Place**

*Subtypes: city, borough, municipality, comunidad, city—undefined, town, village, zona urbana, Census Designated Place (CDP), Default*

Polygon feature class
**SchoolDistrict**

*Subtypes: Elementary, Middle, Secondary, Unified*

Polygon feature class
**StateLegislativeDistrict**

**3**

Geodatabases with national census data contain hundreds of millions of features. This data was constructed by the U.S. Census Bureau with a rich set of defined spatial relationships, such as tracts cannot overlap. On conversion, the TIGER data becomes multilevel nested polygon features in the geodatabase, modeling the stacked levels of census geography. With this simple data model and topology rules, you can edit census unit and boundary features and maintain spatial integrity.

Potentially all of the feature classes in this census data model may participate in a single topology, depending on your needs. The goal of a topology model for U.S. Census geography is to integrate numerous feature classes that share common boundaries and define a set of integrity rules for the shared boundaries. This section describes the types of topology rules commonly applied in this data model.

While there are a large number of topological relationships in the data model, there are only five types of rules used:

• Must not overlap
• Must not overlap with
• Must be covered by
• Must be covered by class of
• Must cover each other

## Must not overlap

The Must not overlap rule is a single-layer rule pertaining to the relationship between features in the same layer.

**County subdivisions** **must not overlap**

Features in the layer must not overlap with other features in the layer. The features can, however, share vertices and edges, such as two adjacent blocks that do not overlap, yet share a common boundary between them. This rule is used to model instances when each polygon in the layer must be spatially discreet. Examples include census blocks, ZIP Code tabulation areas (ZCTAs), voting districts, and counties.

## Must not overlap with

The Must not overlap with rule is similar to the Must not overlap rule except that the relationship is established between two layers that use mutually exclusive classifications.

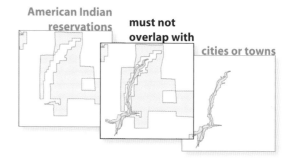

**American Indian reservations** **must not overlap with** **cities or towns**

Only two instances of this rule exist within the census data model: between the AmericanIndianReservation layer and the city and town subtype of the Place layer. Features from the AmericanIndianReservation layer cannot overlap features of type city or town from the Place layer. Having subtypes defined for the Place layer allows the rule to be defined for specific types of Place features.

## Must be covered by

The rule, Must be covered by, is a relationship between two layers in which each feature in one layer must be contained within or covered by a single feature from the second layer.

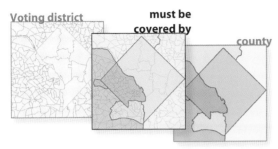

This rule is useful for relationships in which features of one layer are a subset of another layer. One example is the relationship between census blocks and block groups, where block groups are composed of census block features. Each feature in the census block layer must be covered by one and only one feature from the block group feature class.

This rule is critical to the census data model and is defined between all layers in the census boundaries group. The rule is also established between the layers in the other administrative units group and its respective subgroups, state and county.

## Must be covered by class of

The next rule, Must be covered by class of, is a relationship between two layers in which one layer must be entirely covered by any number of features from the second layer.

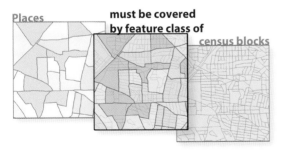

This rule differs from the previous rule in that a feature from the layer being covered need not fit exactly within the boundaries of individual features of the other layer.

The census blocks layer is the foundation of the data model. As such, there is a relationship between the census blocks layer and the layers in the other administrative units group: The census block layer must cover each of these layers. However, the other administrative units layers do not have to represent a continuous surface across the entire extent of the data model.

## Must cover each other

The relationship, Must cover each other, is between two layers in which both layers must share the same extent.

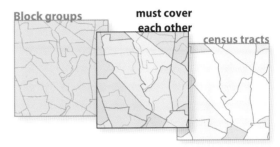

When two systems of classification are used for the same area, this rule can be used to ensure that any area covered by a feature from one layer must also be covered by a feature from the second layer. This relationship exists between layers in the census administrative units group, for example, between census blocks and block groups. Block groups are created from census blocks; any census block feature must contribute to the geometry of a block group feature. Conversely, any block group feature must be covered entirely by census block features.

This rule works in conjunction with another rule, Must be covered by, to maintain the topological relationship between the layers in the census administrative units group.

3

The previous section described the types of topology rules used in this data model. This section lists the complete set of topology rules that have been defined. It further illustrates how many of the administrative units are nested within others.

The diagram below illustrates the most fundamental feature classes in the spatial containment hierarchy for the administrative units of the U.S. census. This data model implements spatial units at the state level and below and topology rules for the county level and below.

The diagram on the next page provides the complete list of topology integrity rules used in this data model. However, it is likely that many users will choose not to enforce all the same rules for every application.

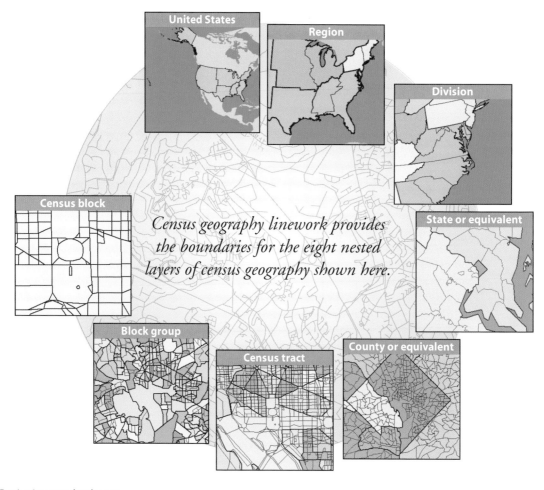

*Census geography linework provides the boundaries for the eight nested layers of census geography shown here.*

## Topology
## Administrative_Topology

*Participating feature classes and ranks*

| Feature class | Rank | Feature class | Rank | Feature class | Rank |
|---|---|---|---|---|---|
| OtherPointLandmarks | 2 | AmericanIndianSubReservation | 2 | PublicUseMicrodataArea | 2 |
| Hydrography | 1 | BlockGroup | 2 | SchoolDistrict | 2 |
| Landmarks | 1 | CensusBlock | 2 | StateLegislativeDistrict | 2 |
| MiscTransport | 1 | CensusTract | 2 | States | 2 |
| Physical | 1 | CongressionalDistrict | 2 | TrafficAnalysisZone | 2 |
| Rails | 1 | County | 2 | UrbanArea | 2 |
| Roads | 1 | CountySubdivision | 2 | UrbanGrowthArea | 2 |
| AlaskaNativeRegionalCorporation | 2 | KeyGeographicalLocation | 2 | VotingDistrict | 2 |
| AmericanIndianBlockGroup | 2 | MetropolitanArea | 2 | Water | 2 |
| AmericanIndianCensusTract | 2 | OtherAreaLandmarks | 2 | ZipCodeTabulationArea | 2 |
| AmericanIndianReservation | 2 | Place | 2 | | |

*Topology rules*

| Origin feature class | Topology rule | Comparison feature class |
|---|---|---|
| AmericanIndianReservation | Must not overlap with | Place : City |
| AmericanIndianReservation | Must not overlap with | Place : Town |
| TrafficAnalysisZone | Must be covered by | County |
| CountySubdivision | Must be covered by | County |
| VotingDistrict | Must be covered by | County |
| ZipCodeTabulationArea | Must be covered by | County |
| Place | Must be covered by | States |
| CongressionalDistrict | Must be covered by | States |
| StateLegislativeDistrict | Must be covered by | States |
| SchoolDistrict | Must be covered by | States |
| AlaskaNativeRegionalCorporation | Must be covered by | States |
| PublicUseMicrodataArea | Must be covered by | States |
| County | Must be covered by | States |
| CensusTract | Must be covered by | County |
| BlockGroup | Must be covered by | CensusTract |
| CensusBlock | Must be covered by | BlockGroup |
| AmericanIndianReservation:ANVSA | Must be covered by | AlaskaNativeRegionalCorporation |
| AmericanIndianBlockGroup | Must be covered by | AmericanIndianCensusTract |
| AmericanIndianCensusTract | Must be covered by | AmericanIndianReservation |
| AmericanIndianBlockGroup | Must cover each other | AmericanIndianCensusTract |
| AmericanIndianCensusTract | Must cover each other | AmericanIndianReservation |
| County | Must cover each other | States |
| CensusTract | Must cover each other | County |
| BlockGroup | Must cover each other | CensusTract |
| CensusBlock | Must cover each other | BlockGroup |
| AmericanIndianReservation | Must be covered by feature class of | CensusBlock |
| AlaskaNativeRegionalCorporation | Must be covered by feature class of | CensusBlock |
| AmericanIndianBlockGroup | Must be covered by feature class of | CensusBlock |
| CountySubdivision | Must be covered by feature class of | CensusBlock |
| Place | Must be covered by feature class of | CensusBlock |
| StateLegislativeDIstrict | Must be covered by feature class of | CensusBlock |
| TrafficAnalysisZone | Must be covered by feature class of | CensusBlock |
| UrbanGrowthArea | Must be covered by feature class of | CensusBlock |
| UrbanArea | Must be covered by feature class of | CensusBlock |
| VotingDistrict | Must be covered by feature class of | CensusBlock |
| ZipCodeTabulationArea | Must be covered by feature class of | CensusBlock |

| Origin feature class | Topology rule |
|---|---|
| AmericanIndianReservation | Must not overlap |
| AmericanIndianSubReservation | Must not overlap |
| AmericanIndianBlockGroup | Must not overlap |
| AmericanIndianCensusTract | Must not overlap |
| AlaskaNativeRegionalCorporation | Must not overlap |
| CountySubdivision | Must not overlap |
| TrafficAnalysisZone | Must not overlap |
| CongressionalDistrict | Must not overlap |
| Place | Must not overlap |
| States | Must not overlap |
| PublicUseMicrodataArea | Must not overlap |
| UrbanArea | Must not overlap |
| CensusBlock | Must not overlap |
| BlockGroup | Must not overlap |
| CensusTract | Must not overlap |
| County | Must not overlap |
| SchoolDistrict : Elementary | Must not overlap |
| SchoolDistrict : Middle | Must not overlap |
| SchoolDistrict : Secondary | Must not overlap |
| SchoolDistrict : Unified | Must not overlap |
| MetropolitanArea : PMSA | Must not overlap |

3

The extensive topological rules for census geography provide a natural and useful set of integrity constraints for editing spatial data. This section provides an example of applying these rules within a GIS.

One of the major purposes of using topology is to maintain data integrity and quality. During work flows for editing and updating the database, the special behaviors and rules defined for census features come to life in ArcGIS. The editing tools in ArcMap enforce the business rules that control the topological relationships among the GIS features.

The editing example below illustrates several operations on the database that take advantage of the ability to manage topology in a GIS. Suppose several road features need to be updated and corrected to match the latest data. This scenario outlines:

- Correcting an offset of road features

- Modifying a road feature

- Extending a road to intersect a perpendicular road feature

### Resolving an offset

In this first diagram, the two endpoints of Church Avenue are offset from each other. It's been determined that there should be no offset with Church Avenue and that the road should be continuous through Randall Avenue.

The editing steps that would be performed to achieve this using ArcMap follow.

- Set the snapping environment so that road vertices and topology nodes will snap to each other.

- Using the Topology Edit tool, select the upper end point of the southernmost Church Avenue feature to modify.

- Select the node feature and move it toward the end of Church Avenue.

- See that the Church Avenue and two Randall Avenue road features are also selected and are rubberbanding. The topological relationships between the features are maintained.

The node is snapped to the endpoint of Church Avenue, and the offset is removed. Church Avenue continues smoothly across Randall Avenue, as shown below.

## Extending a road feature across a gap

The next task is to modify Alru Street to remove a gap, identified by a blue circle in the figure below. The ArcMap editing steps follow.

- Select the Alru Street feature on the right of the gap, and set the target layer to Roads.

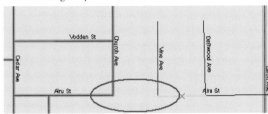

- Set the editing task to Modify Feature and click the Edit Sketch tool; a new segment sketch is added at the endpoint of Alru Street.

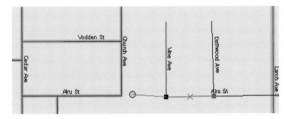

- Snap the new segment across the gap to the endpoint of the second Alru Street feature to finish the sketch. The Alru Street feature has been modified to span the gap.

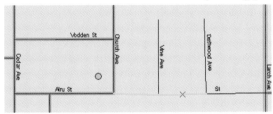

## Extending a road feature to intersect another feature

Finally, extend the end of Church Street to meet the just-modified Alru Street, filling the gap circled in blue.

- With Alru Street still selected, click the Extend tool on the Advanced Editing toolbar.

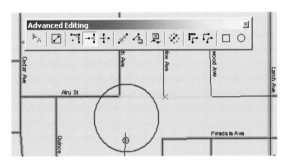

- Click the line to extend to Alru Street, in this example, Church Street.

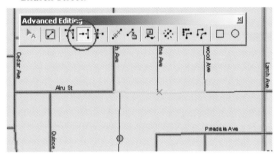

These examples show some of the ways topological rules and behavior can be used to support editing. A common editing task not shown here is to enforce coincidence of adjacent area feature boundaries, such as census blocks, block groups, or tracts.

## Summary statistics

The table below shows some of the statistics on recent projects built using ArcGIS to manage census geography datasets over study areas of different sizes. The database size is indicated by the number of features. The difference in the number of feature classes and topology rules between each study area is due to differing needs for special administrative area features. In all cases, the database and applications performed well for queries, edits, and updates.

| Case study area | Number of features | Feature classes | Topology rules |
|---|---|---|---|
| *Large metro area (Washington, D.C., plus five counties)* | *200,000* | *57* | *84* |
| *Large state (California)* | *3.4 million* | *32* | *57* |
| *Nation (USA)* | *53.5 million* | *57* | *84* |

Census boundaries are the most fundamental feature classes in the census data model. These linear features form the boundaries of each census block.

The census boundaries group includes the underlying linework of all other layers within the data model. Census block features are constructed from the underlying linework and from this, the other features in the data model are assembled topologically.

## Feature classes

This group includes:

- Road—Contains transportation features such as highways, major roads, and city streets. This information can be used to generate cartographic layers representing continuous road features.

- Rail—Contains features identified for rail transport.

- Hydrography—Contains hydrographic features, such as rivers, creeks, and ponds.

- Physical—Contains features such as canyons and firebreaks.

- Miscellaneous transport—Contains features such as power lines and pipelines.

## Principal attributes

For all of these feature classes, populated fields of interest include:

- FENAME—Contains the name of the physical feature. This can be used to group multiple features having a common name for cartographic purposes, such as to create long, continuous road or rail features.

- FEDIRP—The cardinal direction of the feature, such as N, SE, W, and so on.

- FETYPE—The type of road feature, such as street, avenue, or boulevard (not necessarily used for all boundary features).

- CFCC—Census Feature Class Code is the census classification code that can be used to symbolize the feature.

- SOURCE—Identifies the origin of the physical feature data (see the table at the bottom of the next page).

- TLID—The original TIGER/Line ID of the feature.

## Attributes for addressing

Addressing along roads and other physical features is an extension of the census boundaries group. Additional address information can be stored as attributes of features of the census boundaries group. GIS users have several key requirements for address data management. They must be able to:

- Associate multiple addresses per line feature.

- Associate a single address with multiple features.

- Associate multiple names (aliases) with features.

- Identify address locations for data collection efforts.

From these attributes, address matching analysis and the production of cartographic road features can be performed. Many other issues and details of a complete addressing data model are explored and discussed in Chapter 4, 'Addresses and locations'. Users can adapt various portions of the address data model to this census data model, according to their needs.

For the linear features on the next page, the relevant addressing fields include address range details following the DIME scheme (see Chapter 4 for a discussion of the DIME methodology). These include the following fields:

- FRADDL is the from address, left side.

- TOADDL is the to address, left side.

- FRADDR is the from address, right side.

- TOADDR is the to address, right side.

These fields provide bounds on the physical addresses found along each road segment or other physical feature. The left or right side orientation of a feature is based on traversing the feature from lower to higher address values.

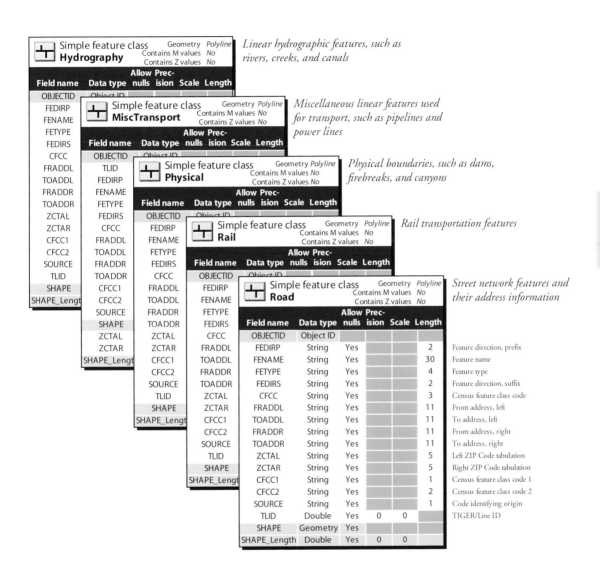

**Simple feature class — Hydrography**
Geometry: Polyline; Contains M values: No; Contains Z values: No
*Linear hydrographic features, such as rivers, creeks, and canals*

Fields: OBJECTID, FEDIRP, FENAME, FETYPE, FEDIRS, CFCC, FRADDL, TOADDL, FRADDR, TOADDR, ZCTAL, ZCTAR, CFCC1, CFCC2, SOURCE, TLID, SHAPE, SHAPE_Length

**Simple feature class — MiscTransport**
Geometry: Polyline; Contains M values: No; Contains Z values: No
*Miscellaneous linear features used for transport, such as pipelines and power lines*

Fields: OBJECTID, TLID, FEDIRP, FENAME, FETYPE, FEDIRS, CFCC, FRADDL, TOADDL, FRADDR, TOADDR, ZCTAL, ZCTAR, CFCC1, CFCC2, SOURCE, SHAPE, SHAPE_Length

**Simple feature class — Physical**
Geometry: Polyline; Contains M values: No; Contains Z values: No
*Physical boundaries, such as dams, firebreaks, and canyons*

Fields: OBJECTID, FEDIRP, FENAME, FETYPE, FEDIRS, CFCC, FRADDL, TOADDL, FRADDR, TOADDR, ZCTAL, ZCTAR, CFCC1, CFCC2, SOURCE, TLID, SHAPE, SHAPE_Length

**Simple feature class — Rail**
Geometry: Polyline; Contains M values: No; Contains Z values: No
*Rail transportation features*

Fields: OBJECTID, FEDIRP, FENAME, FETYPE, FEDIRS, CFCC, FRADDL, TOADDL, FRADDR, TOADDR, ZCTAL, ZCTAR, CFCC1, CFCC2, SOURCE, TLID, SHAPE, SHAPE_Length

**Simple feature class — Road**
Geometry: Polyline; Contains M values: No; Contains Z values: No
*Street network features and their address information*

| Field name | Data type | Allow nulls | Prec-ision | Scale | Length | |
| --- | --- | --- | --- | --- | --- | --- |
| OBJECTID | Object ID | | | | | |
| FEDIRP | String | Yes | | | 2 | Feature direction, prefix |
| FENAME | String | Yes | | | 30 | Feature name |
| FETYPE | String | Yes | | | 4 | Feature type |
| FEDIRS | String | Yes | | | 2 | Feature direction, suffix |
| CFCC | String | Yes | | | 3 | Census feature class code |
| FRADDL | String | Yes | | | 11 | From address, left |
| TOADDL | String | Yes | | | 11 | To address, left |
| FRADDR | String | Yes | | | 11 | From address, right |
| TOADDR | String | Yes | | | 11 | To address, right |
| ZCTAL | String | Yes | | | 5 | Left ZIP Code tabulation |
| ZCTAR | String | Yes | | | 5 | Right ZIP Code tabulation |
| CFCC1 | String | Yes | | | 1 | Census feature class code 1 |
| CFCC2 | String | Yes | | | 2 | Census feature class code 2 |
| SOURCE | String | Yes | | | 1 | Code identifying origin |
| TLID | Double | Yes | 0 | 0 | | TIGER/Line ID |
| SHAPE | Geometry | Yes | | | | |
| SHAPE_Length | Double | Yes | 0 | 0 | | |

*Codes for source information used in Census 2000*

| Value | Description |
| --- | --- |
| (Blank) | Not Documented Elsewhere |
| A | Updated 1980 GBF/DIME File |
| B | USGS 1:100,000-Scale DLG-3 File |
| C | Other USGS Map |
| J | Pre-1990 Census Updates |
| K | Post-1990 Census Updates (1990–1994) |
| L | Pre-Census 2000 Local Official Updates (1995–Census 2000) |
| M | Pre-Census 2000 Field Operations (1995–Census 2000) |
| N | Pre-Census 2000 Office Update Operations (1995–Census 2000) |
| O | Post-Census 2000 (2000–2002) |

The census administrative units group comprises the main census objects, such as census blocks, block groups, census tracts, American Indian block groups, and American Indian census tracts. These layers are produced from the line features in the census boundaries group and share a close topological relationship.

## Census blocks

Census blocks are represented with polygon features bounded on all sides by features from the census boundaries group. The size of census block features can vary from small, within urbanized areas, to relatively large features in sparsely populated areas. Census block features form a continuous fabric across the United States, covering all areas within the United States and its territories. Census blocks do not cross the boundaries of features from the other administrative units group, subgroups county and state.

Each census block feature has a unique identifier, a composite of the unique identifiers for the state, county, census tract, and block group in which the census block is contained. A breakdown of the census block unique identifier and its relation to other features follows.

*Parsing a Census ID*

The numeric content of this identifier is defined by the Federal Information Processing Standards (FIPS). This identifier serves as a foreign key to the extensive demographic tables published with each census. With this identifier, users can create relationships between the demographic tables and census block geographic features (as well as block groups, tracts, counties, and states). This is illustrated later in this chapter.

If a water body is wholly contained within a census block feature, there will be no corresponding census block feature identifying the water body. Instead, the water body will be covered by its containing census block. If the water body shares a boundary with two or more census block features, a feature corresponding to the water body feature will exist in the census block layer and have a unique identifying number. The numbers begin with the block group number and 999, with each additional water body feature being assigned a unique number in decreasing order, for example, 999, 998, 997, until all census block features corresponding to bodies of water have been assigned identifiers. There are instances when the number of census block features within a census tract is larger than 900. Because of this, census blocks with

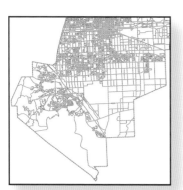

| Simple feature class **CensusBlock** | | Geometry | *Polygon* |
|---|---|---|---|
| | | Contains M values | *No* |
| | | Contains Z values | *No* |

| Field name | Data type | Allow nulls | Precision | Scale | Length | |
|---|---|---|---|---|---|---|
| OBJECTID | Object ID | | | | | |
| FIPSSTCO | String | Yes | | | 5 | FIPS state and county code |
| TRACT2000 | String | Yes | | | 6 | Census tract ID |
| BLOCK2000 | String | Yes | | | 4 | Census block ID |
| TABFLAG | String | Yes | | | 50 | |
| TAB9F | String | Yes | | | 50 | 2000 tabulation flag |
| UR | String | Yes | | | 50 | Tab90 block flag |
| ENTHSE | Long integer | Yes | 0 | | | Urban/Rural code |
| WORKING_POPULATION_COUNT | Long integer | Yes | 0 | | | Working housing count |
| SHAPE | Geometry | Yes | | | | Working population count |
| STFID | String | Yes | | | 15 | Unique census block ID |
| SHAPE_Length | Double | Yes | 0 | 0 | | |
| SHAPE_Area | Double | Yes | 0 | 0 | | |

*Areas bounded on all sides by linear features, such as roads and streams*

IDs in the 900 range are not guaranteed to correspond to water bodies. Census blocks that represent water bodies can be confirmed with the water layer.

Census blocks and block groups share a tessellate relationship. Tessellate is a composite relationship between two layers involving three topological integrity rules: (1) census block features cannot overlap each other, (2) the block groups layer must entirely cover the census blocks layer, and (3) each feature in the census blocks layer must be contained within a single block group feature.

## Block groups

A block group is a collection of census block features in a census tract that share the same first digit of the four-digit identifier that uniquely identifies the block group within the census tract. They generally contain a population of 800 to 3,000, with an ideal size of 1,500. Block groups may not cross the boundaries of features from the other administrative units group, census tracts, or features from the census boundaries group. Local participants in the Census Bureau's Participant Statistical Area Program identify the majority of block groups. Any areas for which block groups are not identified are done by the Census Bureau. Block groups are the lowest level of the data model hierarchy for which the U.S. Census Bureau tabulates and presents sample data.

Block groups and census tracts share a tessellate relationship. Block group features cannot overlap each other, the census tracts layer must entirely cover the block

groups layer, and each block group feature must be contained within one census tract feature.

## American Indian block groups

American Indian block groups are very similar to block groups; they are collections of census block features. They differ from block groups in that they are located within an American Indian reservation area and must have a minimum of 300 people, with an optimum size of 1,000. An American Indian block group may cross county and state lines as long as the American Indian reservation within which it is contained crosses the county or state line. American Indian block groups of this type are contained within American Indian census tracts with an identifier between 9400 and 9499.

American Indian block groups and American Indian census tracts share a tessellate relationship, as described above, for block groups and census tracts. In addition, the census blocks layer must cover the American Indian block groups layer.

| Simple feature class **BlockGroup** | | Geometry | *Polygon* | | | |
|---|---|---|---|---|---|---|
| | | Contains M values | *No* | | | |
| | | Contains Z values | *No* | | | |
| Field name | Data type | Allow nulls | Precision | Scale | Length | |
| OBJECTID | Object ID | | | | | |
| T0BLKBG | String | Yes | | | 50 | 2000 tabulation block group |
| FS | String | Yes | | | 50 | Functional status |
| ENTHSE | Long integer | Yes | 0 | | | Working housing count |
| WORKING_POPULATION_COUNT | Long integer | Yes | 0 | | | Working population count |
| LSAD | String | Yes | | | 2 | Legal/Statistical area description |
| NAME | String | Yes | | | 13 | |
| FIPSSTCO | String | Yes | | | 5 | FIPS state and county code |
| SHAPE | Geometry | Yes | | | | |
| TRACT | String | Yes | | | 6 | Census tract ID |
| BLOCKGROUP | String | Yes | | | 1 | Block group ID |
| STFID | String | Yes | | | 12 | Unique block group ID within the USA |
| SHAPE_Length | Double | Yes | 0 | 0 | | |
| SHAPE_Area | Double | Yes | 0 | 0 | | |

*Clusters of census blocks; smallest unit for which statistical information is presented*

| Simple feature class **AmericanIndianBlockGroup** | | Geometry | *Polygon* | | | |
|---|---|---|---|---|---|---|
| | | Contains M values | *No* | | | |
| | | Contains Z values | *No* | | | |
| Field name | Data type | Allow nulls | Precision | Scale | Length | |
| OBJECTID | Object ID | | | | | |
| IDCODE | String | Yes | | | 50 | Census AIR block ID code |
| FS | String | Yes | | | 50 | Functional status |
| SHAPE | Geometry | Yes | | | | |
| SHAPE_Length | Double | Yes | 0 | 0 | | |
| SHAPE_Area | Double | Yes | 0 | 0 | | |

*Block groups within the same tribal census block*

Census 2000 was the first decennial census for which the entire United States was covered by census tracts. For the 1990 census, some counties had census tracts, and others had block numbering areas (BNAs). For Census 2000, all BNAs were replaced by census tracts, which may or may not represent the same areas.

## Census tracts

Census tracts are collections of block groups identified by participants in the Census Bureau's Participant Statistical Area Program or by the Census Bureau where no participant exists. Census tracts are relatively permanent areas whose main purpose is to provide a consistent format for the presentation of decennial census information. Census tract numbers range from 1 to 9999 and are unique within the county or equivalent unit within which the tract is contained. Census tract numbers from 9400 to 9499 identify tracts in American Indian reservations and off reservation trust lands that exist in multiple states or counties (see 'American Indian census tracts' on the next page).

Census tracts and counties share a tessellate relationship. Census tract features cannot overlap each other, the county layer must entirely cover the census tract layer, and each feature in the census tract layer must be contained in a single county feature.

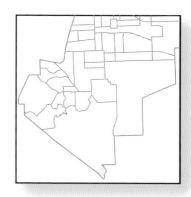

| Simple feature class **CensusTract** | Geometry | *Polygon* | | | |
|---|---|---|---|---|---|
| | Contains M values | *No* | | | |
| | Contains Z values | *No* | | | |

| Field name | Data type | Allow nulls | Precision | Scale | Length | |
|---|---|---|---|---|---|---|
| OBJECTID | Object ID | | | | | |
| TRT2000 | String | Yes | | | 6 | Census tract ID |
| TRACTID | String | Yes | | | 10 | Census tract ID |
| UR | String | Yes | | | 50 | Urban/Rural code |
| FS | String | Yes | | | 50 | Functional status |
| ENTHSE | Long integer | Yes | 0 | | | Working housing count |
| WORKING_POPULATION_COUNT | Long integer | Yes | 0 | | | Working population count |
| CBD | String | Yes | | | 50 | Central business district |
| LSAD | String | Yes | | | 2 | Legal/Statistical area description |
| NAME | String | Yes | | | 12 | |
| FIPSSTCO | String | Yes | | | 5 | FIPS state and county code |
| SHAPE | Geometry | Yes | | | | |
| STFID | String | Yes | | | 11 | Unique census tract ID within the nation |
| SHAPE_Length | Double | Yes | 0 | 0 | | |
| SHAPE_Area | Double | Yes | 0 | 0 | | |

*Small, relatively permanent subdivisions of counties*

## American Indian census tracts

American Indian census tracts are relatively permanent subdivisions of American Indian reservations composed of a collection of block group features with a minimum of 1,000 people and an optimum size of 2,500. American Indian census tracts may cross county and state lines if the American Indian reservation within which it is contained crosses the county or state line. American Indian census tracts of this type are identified with census tract numbers between 9400 and 9499.

American Indian census tracts and American Indian reservations share a tessellate relationship. American Indian census tract features cannot overlap each other, the American Indian reservations layer must entirely cover the American Indian census tracts layer, and each American Indian census tract feature must be contained within one American Indian reservation feature.

| Simple feature class **AmericanIndianCensusTract** | | Geometry | Polygon |
|---|---|---|---|
| | | Contains M values | No |
| | | Contains Z values | No |

| Field name | Data type | Allow nulls | Prec-ision | Scale | Length | |
|---|---|---|---|---|---|---|
| OBJECTID | Object ID | | | | | |
| CENSUSTRACTCODE | String | Yes | | | 50 | Census tract code |
| FS | String | Yes | | | 50 | Functional status |
| SHAPE | Geometry | Yes | | | | |
| SHAPE_Length | Double | Yes | 0 | 0 | | |
| SHAPE_Area | Double | Yes | 0 | 0 | | |

*Small, relatively permanent statistical areas within reservations*

**3**

*These census layers—blocks, block groups, and tracts—form the bottom three levels of the nested geography of census administrative units. Blocks are drawn with thin light gray lines, block groups with medium thick gray lines, and tracts with thick dark lines.*

Every census gathers various statistical data from each household, such as household size, ethnicity, gender, and age groups represented. This data is aggregated at the census block, block group, and higher levels of spatial hierarchy and used for the next several years as the basis for numerous governmental programs and funding allocations. Private individuals and companies also acquire this data, often for direct marketing campaigns. It is important to be able to link this data to the GIS.

The U.S. Census TIGER/Line files contain no demographic data, only geographic features. However, extensive demographic data is collected as part of the census and published in separate summary files, such as SF1, SF2, and PL94 (see references at the end of this chapter). These are published in aggregations at many levels in the spatial hierarchy, including the block, block group, tract, place, county, and state levels. A subset of the complete range of statistics in SF1 is shown in the figure on the next page, aggregated for one census tract.

These illustrations show how the demographic statistics can be easily linked to their associated spatial features using the unique census identifier introduced earlier in this chapter. For census blocks, block groups, and census tracts, this

identifier field is called STFID. The identifier field for place features is FIPS_ID_CODE, and for county features is FIPSSTCO.

The subset of SF1 statistics shown in the figure opposite is readily available for download from the Census Bureau via the Geography Network (www.geographynetwork.com).

*This figure shows the attributes of a census tract feature and identifies several other spatial units that overlap this census tract. The STFID field at the bottom right is a foreign key to the SF1 table containing demographic statistics for all census tracts in the state.*

## Table
### tgr06000sf1trt

This table lists a subset of the demographic content available in Summary File 1. These statistical values are used for census blocks, block groups, places, counties, and states.

| Field name | Data type | Allow nulls | Precision | Scale | Length | |
|---|---|---|---|---|---|---|
| OBJECTID | Object ID | | | | | |
| STATE | String | Yes | | | 2 | |
| COUNTY | String | Yes | | | 3 | |
| TRACT | String | Yes | | | 6 | |
| STFID | String | Yes | | | 11 | |
| POP2000 | Long integer | Yes | 0 | | | Population in year 2000 |
| WHITE | Long integer | Yes | 0 | | | White alone |
| BLACK | Long integer | Yes | 0 | | | African American alone |
| AMERI_ES | Long integer | Yes | 0 | | | American Indian or Alaskan native alone |
| ASIAN | Long integer | Yes | 0 | | | Asian alone |
| HAWN_PI | Long integer | Yes | 0 | | | Native Hawaiian or Pacific islander alone |
| OTHER | Long integer | Yes | 0 | | | Some other race alone |
| MULT_RACE | Long integer | Yes | 0 | | | Two or more races |
| HISPANIC | Long integer | Yes | 0 | | | Hispanic alone |
| MALES | Long integer | Yes | 0 | | | Males |
| FEMALES | Long integer | Yes | 0 | | | Females |
| AGE_UNDER5 | Long integer | Yes | 0 | | | Male and female under 5 years |
| AGE_5_17 | Long integer | Yes | 0 | | | Male and female 5 to 17 years |
| AGE_18_21 | Long integer | Yes | 0 | | | Male and female 18 to 21 years |
| AGE_22_29 | Long integer | Yes | 0 | | | Male and female 22 to 29 years |
| AGE_30_39 | Long integer | Yes | 0 | | | Male and female 30 to 39 years |
| AGE_40_49 | Long integer | Yes | 0 | | | Male and female 40 to 49 years |
| AGE_50_64 | Long integer | Yes | 0 | | | Male and female 50 to 64 years |
| AGE_65_UP | Long integer | Yes | 0 | | | Male and female 65 years and over |
| MED_AGE | Double | Yes | 0 | 0 | | Median age, both sexes |
| MED_AGE_M | Double | Yes | 0 | 0 | | Median age, males |
| MED_AGE_F | Double | Yes | 0 | 0 | | Median age, females |
| HOUSEHOLDS | Long integer | Yes | 0 | | | Number of households |
| AVE_HH_SZ | Double | Yes | 0 | 0 | | Average household size |
| HSEHLD_1_M | Long integer | Yes | 0 | | | One-person households, male |
| HSEHLD_1_F | Long integer | Yes | 0 | | | One-person households, female |
| MARHH_CHD | Long integer | Yes | 0 | | | Family households, 2 parents with children |
| MARHH_NO_C | Long integer | Yes | 0 | | | Family households, 2 parents, no children |
| MHH_CHILD | Long integer | Yes | 0 | | | Single-parent family, male with children |
| FHH_CHILD | Long integer | Yes | 0 | | | Single-parent family, female with children |
| FAMILIES | Long integer | Yes | 0 | | | Number of families |
| AVE_FAM_SZ | Double | Yes | 0 | 0 | | Average family size |
| HSE_UNITS | Long integer | Yes | 0 | | | Housing units |
| URBAN | Long integer | Yes | 0 | | | Housing units, urban |
| RURAL | Long integer | Yes | 0 | | | Housing units, rural |
| VACANT | Long integer | Yes | 0 | | | Housing units, vacant |
| OWNER_OCC | Long integer | Yes | 0 | | | Housing units, owner occupied |
| RENTER_OCC | Long integer | Yes | 0 | | | Housing units, renter occupied |

## Attributes

- CensusTract
  - 06071
    - SF1
      - 4608

| Property | Value |
|---|---|
| OBJECTID | 4608 |
| STATE | 06 |
| COUNTY | 071 |
| TRACT | 000112 |
| STFID | 06071000112 |
| POP2000 | 10872 |
| WHITE | 6290 |
| BLACK | 897 |
| AMERI_ES | 55 |
| ASIAN | 2008 |
| HAWN_PI | 8 |
| OTHER | 1065 |
| MULT_RACE | 549 |
| HISPANIC | 2746 |
| MALES | 5387 |
| FEMALES | 5485 |
| AGE_UNDER5 | 1158 |
| AGE_5_17 | 2529 |
| AGE_18_21 | 378 |
| AGE_22_29 | 1034 |
| AGE_30_39 | 2596 |
| AGE_40_49 | 1777 |
| AGE_50_64 | 1055 |
| AGE_65_UP | 345 |
| MED_AGE | 31.3 |
| MED_AGE_M | 31.1 |
| MED_AGE_F | 31.4 |
| HOUSEHOLDS | 3235 |
| AVE_HH_SZ | 3.36 |
| HSEHLD_1_M | 136 |
| HSEHLD_1_F | 124 |
| MARHH_CHD | 1667 |
| MARHH_NO_C | 826 |
| MHH_CHILD | 58 |
| FHH_CHILD | 136 |
| FAMILIES | 2850 |
| AVE_FAM_SZ | 3.56 |
| HSE_UNITS | 3302 |
| URBAN | 0 |
| RURAL | 0 |
| VACANT | 67 |
| OWNER_OCC | 3041 |
| RENTER_OCC | 194 |

1 features

3

A number of additional administrative units are based on the census boundary lines for managing a range of government activities, such as voting, federal funding, and statistical reporting. Twenty-five feature classes separate collections of administrative units and are divided into three subgroups: County, State, and Federal. Each of these subgroups contains two main types of layers: Legal and Statistical. The Census Bureau is the legal maintainer of city, county, and state boundaries for the country. Local government agencies are required to notify the Census Bureau of all boundary changes.

County-level boundaries include county, county subdivision, metropolitan area, traffic analysis zone, voting district, and ZIP Code tabulation area. These are described on the next four pages. Of these, the county and voting district are considered legal entities to the U.S. Census Bureau.

## County

The main subdivisions of states are counties or their equivalents, such as parishes in Louisiana or census areas, cities, and boroughs (as in Juneau City and Juneau Borough) in Alaska. In four states (Maryland, Missouri, Nevada, and Virginia), there are one or more incorporated areas that are independent of any county organization and thus constitute primary divisions of their states; these incorporated places are known as "independent cities" and are treated as counties for data presentation purposes. The District of Columbia has no primary division, and the entire area is considered equivalent to a county for data presentation purposes. In American Samoa, the primary divisions are districts and islands; in the Northern Mariana Islands, municipalities; in the Virgin Islands of the United States, the principal islands of St. Croix, St. John, and St. Thomas. Guam has no primary divisions, and the entire area is considered equivalent to a county for data presentation purposes. Each county or statistically equivalent entity is assigned a code that is unique within the state.

Counties and states share a tessellate relationship. County features cannot overlap each other, the state layer must entirely cover the county layer, and each

county feature must be contained within a single state feature.

## County subdivisions

County subdivisions are the major subdivisions of counties or their statistical equivalents. Types of subdivisions include minor civil divisions, census county divisions, census subareas, and unorganized territories. County subdivisions are assigned a unique five-digit FIPS code alphabetically, within the state. Since county subdivisions are the primary subdivi-

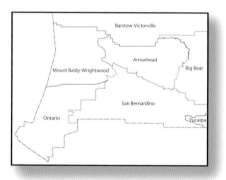

*Primary legal divisions of a state or their equivalent*

| Simple feature class **County** | | Geometry *Polygon* Contains M values *No* Contains Z values *No* | | | | |
|---|---|---|---|---|---|---|
| Field name | Data type | Allow nulls | Prec- ision | Scale | Length | |
| OBJECTID | Object ID | | | | | |
| STATE | String | Yes | | | 66 | State name |
| UR | String | Yes | | | 50 | Urban/Rural code |
| ENTHSE | Long integer | Yes | 0 | | | Working housing count |
| WORKING_POPULATION_COUNT | Long integer | Yes | 0 | | | Working population count |
| FS | String | Yes | | | 50 | Functional status |
| LSAD | String | Yes | | | 2 | Legal/Statistical area description |
| FIPS_ID_CODE | String | Yes | | | 5 | FIPS code |
| SHAPE | Geometry | Yes | | | | |
| COUNTY | String | Yes | | | 66 | County name |
| FIPSSTCO | String | Yes | | | 5 | FIPS state and county code |
| SHAPE_Length | Double | Yes | 0 | 0 | | |
| SHAPE_Area | Double | Yes | 0 | 0 | | |

sions of counties, they must be covered by a single county feature and cannot overlap each other. County subdivisions must not cross census block boundaries.

Minor Civil Division (MCD)—Represents the major subdivision of counties or their equivalent within many states. MCDs represent different legal entities with a wide range of uses and generally vary from state to state.

Census County Division (CCD)—Identified by the Census Bureau in concert with state and local governments in areas where MCDs are insufficient or nonexistent. CCDs are created to coincide with visible features, such as roads and hydrography, and generally correspond to census tracts.

Census Subareas—Identified through a combined effort between the state of Alaska and the Census Bureau. They are confined to the state of Alaska.

Unorganized Territory—Identified in areas where an MCD or incorporated place has not been identified.

## ZIP Code Tabulation Area

ZIP Code tabulation areas are identified by the Census Bureau for statistical purposes and are collections of census blocks that share the same predominant ZIP Code. ZCTAs do not accurately represent ZIP Code areas. ZCTAs must not cross the boundaries of census block features, must be covered by the census block layer, and each ZCTA must be contained within one county feature.

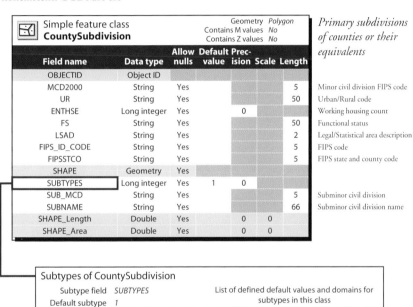

*Primary subdivisions of counties or their equivalents*

**Simple feature class**
**CountySubdivision**

Geometry *Polygon*
Contains M values *No*
Contains Z values *No*

| Field name | Data type | Allow nulls | Default value | Precision | Scale | Length | |
|---|---|---|---|---|---|---|---|
| OBJECTID | Object ID | | | | | | |
| MCD2000 | String | Yes | | | | 5 | Minor civil division FIPS code |
| UR | String | Yes | | | | 50 | Urban/Rural code |
| ENTHSE | Long integer | Yes | | 0 | | | Working housing count |
| FS | String | Yes | | | | 50 | Functional status |
| LSAD | String | Yes | | | | 2 | Legal/Statistical area description |
| FIPS_ID_CODE | String | Yes | | | | 5 | FIPS code |
| FIPSSTCO | String | Yes | | | | 5 | FIPS state and county code |
| SHAPE | Geometry | Yes | | | | | |
| SUBTYPES | Long integer | Yes | 1 | 0 | | | |
| SUB_MCD | String | Yes | | | | 5 | Subminor civil division |
| SUBNAME | String | Yes | | | | 66 | Subminor civil division name |
| SHAPE_Length | Double | Yes | | 0 | 0 | | |
| SHAPE_Area | Double | Yes | | 0 | 0 | | |

### Subtypes of CountySubdivision

Subtype field *SUBTYPES*
Default subtype *1*

List of defined default values and domains for subtypes in this class

| Subtype Code | Subtype Description | | Field name | Default value | Domain |
|---|---|---|---|---|---|
| 1 | Minor Civil Division | ➡ | No values set | | |
| 2 | Census County Division | ➡ | No values set | | |
| 3 | Census Subareas | ➡ | No values set | | |
| 4 | Unorganized Territory | ➡ | No values set | | |

**Simple feature class**
**ZipCodeTabulationArea**

Geometry *Polygon*
Contains M values *No*
Contains Z values *No*

*A statistical geographic entity that approximates ZIP Code areas*

| Field name | Data type | Allow nulls | Precision | Scale | Length | |
|---|---|---|---|---|---|---|
| OBJECTID | Object ID | | | | | |
| ZIPPREF | Long integer | Yes | 0 | | | ZIP Code prefix |
| ZIPSUFF | Long integer | Yes | 0 | | | ZIP Code suffix |
| LSAD | String | Yes | | | 2 | Legal/Statistical area description |
| FIPSSTCO | String | Yes | | | 5 | FIPS state and county code |
| SHAPE | Geometry | Yes | | | | |
| SHAPE_Length | Double | Yes | 0 | 0 | | |
| SHAPE_Area | Double | Yes | 0 | 0 | | |

3

Metropolitan area, traffic analysis zone, and voting district complete the description of county-level administrative units. Voting districts are legal entities to the U.S. Census Bureau. All of these units tend to change significantly from one decennial census to the next, as urban areas grow and change.

## Metropolitan areas

Metropolitan areas (MA) generally represent central areas of high population, along with surrounding areas that have a high degree of economic and social ties with the central area. MAs are identified by the federal Office of Management and Budget. The MA layer contains the following subtypes: metropolitan statistical area, consolidated metropolitan statistical area, primary metropolitan statistical area, and New England county metropolitan area.

**MSAs**—MAs that are not associated with any other MAs but are associated with surrounding counties that are not part of an MA.

**CMSAs and PMSAs**—If the population of an MA is at least 1 million, it can be subdivided into two or more PMSAs and become a CMSA. The same guidelines used to delineate MAs are used for PMSAs. MAs are converted to PMSAs and CMSAs at the discretion of the local government.

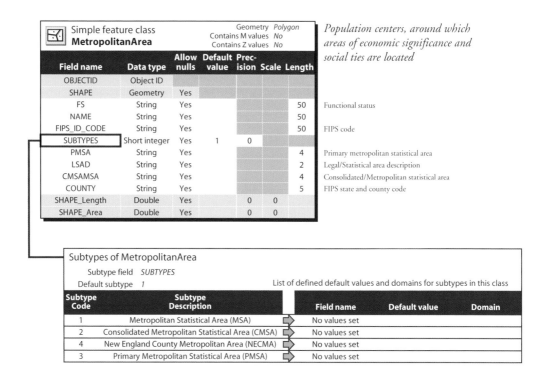

*Population centers, around which areas of economic significance and social ties are located*

Simple feature class **MetropolitanArea**
Geometry *Polygon*
Contains M values *No*
Contains Z values *No*

| Field name | Data type | Allow nulls | Default value | Precision | Scale | Length | |
|---|---|---|---|---|---|---|---|
| OBJECTID | Object ID | | | | | | |
| SHAPE | Geometry | Yes | | | | | |
| FS | String | Yes | | | | 50 | Functional status |
| NAME | String | Yes | | | | 50 | |
| FIPS_ID_CODE | String | Yes | | | | 50 | FIPS code |
| SUBTYPES | Short integer | Yes | 1 | 0 | | | |
| PMSA | String | Yes | | | | 4 | Primary metropolitan statistical area |
| LSAD | String | Yes | | | | 2 | Legal/Statistical area description |
| CMSAMSA | String | Yes | | | | 4 | Consolidated/Metropolitan statistical area |
| COUNTY | String | Yes | | | | 5 | FIPS state and county code |
| SHAPE_Length | Double | Yes | | 0 | 0 | | |
| SHAPE_Area | Double | Yes | | 0 | 0 | | |

**Subtypes of MetropolitanArea**

Subtype field  *SUBTYPES*
Default subtype  *1*

List of defined default values and domains for subtypes in this class

| Subtype Code | Subtype Description | | Field name | Default value | Domain |
|---|---|---|---|---|---|
| 1 | Metropolitan Statistical Area (MSA) | ⇨ | No values set | | |
| 2 | Consolidated Metropolitan Statistical Area (CMSA) | ⇨ | No values set | | |
| 4 | New England County Metropolitan Area (NECMA) | ⇨ | No values set | | |
| 3 | Primary Metropolitan Statistical Area (PMSA) | ⇨ | No values set | | |

**NECMA**—A county–county subdivision alternative to city- and town-based MSAs and CMSAs. NECMAs are defined as the county containing the first-named city in that MSA/CMSA title (this county may include the first-named cities of other MSAs or CMSAs as well). Each additional county must have at least one-half of its population in the MSAs/CMSAs whose first-named cities are in the previously identified county. NECMAs are not identified for individual primary metropolitan statistical areas. NECMAs are identified by a four-digit FIPS code.

| Simple feature class **TrafficAnalysisZone** | | Geometry *Polygon* Contains M values *No* Contains Z values *No* | | | |
|---|---|---|---|---|---|
| **Field name** | **Data type** | **Allow nulls** | **Prec- ision** | **Scale** | **Length** |
| OBJECTID | Object ID | | | | |
| TAZ | String | Yes | | | 6 |
| CTPP | String | Yes | | | 50 |
| ZTP | String | Yes | | | 50 |
| LSAD | String | Yes | | | 2 |
| FIPSSTCO | String | Yes | | | 5 |
| SHAPE | Geometry | Yes | | | |
| SHAPE_Length | Double | Yes | 0 | 0 | |
| SHAPE_Area | Double | Yes | 0 | 0 | |

*Statistical entity for delineating traffic-related census data*

Transportation analysis zone
Census transportation planning package
Traffic analysis code
Legal/Statistical area description
FIPS state and county code

## Traffic analysis zone

Traffic analysis zones (TAZs) are statistical bodies identified by state and local transportation officials mainly for the purpose of tabulating traffic-related data. A six-digit, alphanumeric code that is unique within counties identifies TAZ features. TAZs generally consist of a collection of census blocks, block groups, or census tracts. As such, a TAZ must not cross census block boundaries, and each TAZ feature must be covered by one county feature. TAZ features do not overlap.

## Voting district

The voting district (VTD) layer represents areas identified by state, local, and tribal governments for the purpose of conducting elections. State participation in providing VTD information is not mandatory and, as such, VTDs do not exist for all states. VTDs must not cross the boundaries of census block features, must be covered by the census block layer, and must be contained within a single county feature.

| Simple feature class **VotingDistrict** | | Geometry *Polygon* Contains M values *No* Contains Z values *No* | | | |
|---|---|---|---|---|---|
| **Field name** | **Data type** | **Allow nulls** | **Prec- ision** | **Scale** | **Length** |
| OBJECTID | Object ID | | | | |
| VOTE00 | String | Yes | | | 6 |
| NAME | String | Yes | | | 66 |
| VTDD | String | Yes | | | 50 |
| FS | String | Yes | | | 50 |
| LSAD | String | Yes | | | 2 |
| VTD | String | Yes | | | 6 |
| PDC | String | Yes | | | 1 |
| FIPSSTCO | String | Yes | | | 5 |
| SHAPE | Geometry | Yes | | | |
| SHAPE_Length | Double | Yes | 0 | 0 | |
| SHAPE_Area | Double | Yes | 0 | 0 | |

*Generic name for geographic entities used in elections*

Voting district code—2000

Voting district indicator
Functional status
Legal/Statistical area description
Voting district code
Place description code
FIPS state and county code

Government district layers at the state level include states; congressional, state legislative, and school districts; and places. These are all legal entities to the U.S. Census Bureau.

### State

States, or their equivalent entities, are the major subdivisions of the United States and the top level layer in the administrative boundaries data model. Equivalent entities include the District of Columbia, American Samoa, the Commonwealth of the Northern Mariana Islands, Guam, Puerto Rico, and the Virgin Islands of the United States. Each state is assigned a two-digit FIPS code in alphabetical order followed by the equivalent entities. States must not overlap each other. The states layer participates in several topological relationships with layers in the other administrative units group.

| Simple feature class **State** | | Geometry | Polygon | | | |
| | | Contains M values | No | | | |
| | | Contains Z values | No | | | |
| Field name | Data type | Allow nulls | Prec-ision | Scale | Length | |
| OBJECTID | Object ID | | | | | |
| NAME | String | Yes | | | 90 | |
| CENTRAL_STATUS_CODE | String | Yes | | | 50 | Census code |
| UR | String | Yes | | | 50 | Urban/Rural code |
| USPS_STATE_ABBR | String | Yes | | | 50 | Two-letter state abbreviation |
| ENTHSE | Long integer | Yes | 0 | | | Working housing count |
| WORKING_POPULATION_COUNT | Long integer | Yes | 0 | | | Working population count |
| FS | String | Yes | | | 50 | Functional status |
| LSAD | String | Yes | | | 2 | Legal/Statistical area description |
| FIPS_ID_CODE | String | Yes | | | 5 | FIPS code |
| SHAPE | Geometry | Yes | | | | |
| SHAPE_Length | Double | Yes | 0 | 0 | | |
| SHAPE_Area | Double | Yes | 0 | 0 | | |

*States and their equivalents—the major subdivisions of the United States*

### Congressional district

Congressional districts (CDs) are the 435 areas from which people are elected to the U.S. House of Representatives. Each state is responsible for delineating congressional districts within its boundaries based on census population counts. Congressional districts are assigned a two-digit FIPS code. Code 0 is used for states with a single representative; 98 for territories, such as American Samoa and Puerto Rico, which have nonvoting representatives; and 99 for the Northern Mariana Islands. Congressional districts must not overlap, and each feature in the CD layer must be covered by one state feature.

| Simple feature class **CongressionalDistrict** | | Geometry | Polygon | | | |
| | | Contains M values | No | | | |
| | | Contains Z values | No | | | |
| Field name | Data type | Allow nulls | Prec-ision | Scale | Length | |
| OBJECTID | Object ID | | | | | |
| CD | String | Yes | | | 20 | Congressional district code |
| INCUMBENT_NAME | String | Yes | | | 50 | Incumbent |
| INCUMBENT_CONTACT_INFO | String | Yes | | | 50 | Incumbent information |
| LSAD | String | Yes | | | 2 | Legal/Statistical area description |
| FS | String | Yes | | | 50 | Functional status |
| FIPS_CODE | String | Yes | | | 6 | FIPS code |
| FIPSSTCO | String | Yes | | | 5 | FIPS state and county code |
| SHAPE | Geometry | Yes | | | | |
| SHAPE_Length | Double | Yes | 0 | 0 | | |
| SHAPE_Area | Double | Yes | 0 | 0 | | |

*Area from which people are elected to the U.S. House of Representatives*

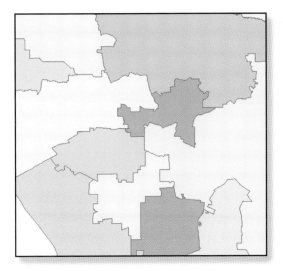

*Map showing legislative district boundaries*

## State legislative district

State legislative districts represent areas from which states elect members to both the upper and lower chambers of their respective legislature. Nebraska has a unicameral legislature, which is identified as an upper chamber. States identify legislative districts with a three-digit code, unique within the state. The state legislative districts layer must be covered by the census blocks layer, and each state legislative district feature must be covered by one state feature.

*Areas from which members are elected to state legislature*

| Simple feature class **StateLegislativeDistrict** | | Geometry *Polygon* Contains M values *No* Contains Z values *No* | | | |
|---|---|---|---|---|---|
| **Field name** | **Data type** | **Allow nulls** | **Precision** | **Scale** | **Length** |
| OBJECTID | Object ID | | | | |
| LSAD | String | Yes | | | 2 | Legal/Statistical area description
| FS | String | Yes | | | 50 | Functional status
| LEGISLATIVE_SESSION_DATE | Date | Yes | 0 | 0 | 8 | Legislative session date
| INCUMBENT_NAME | String | Yes | | | 50 | Incumbent
| INCUMBENT_INFO | String | Yes | | | 50 | Incumbent information
| SLDL | String | Yes | | | 6 | State Legislative District—Lower
| SDLU | String | Yes | | | 6 | State Legislative District—Upper
| NAME | String | Yes | | | 20 |
| FIPSSTCO | String | Yes | | | 5 | FIPS state and county code
| SHAPE | Geometry | Yes | | | |
| SHAPE_Length | Double | Yes | 0 | 0 | |
| SHAPE_Area | Double | Yes | 0 | 0 | |

3

School districts and places, such as cities, are state-level administrative units and are both legal entities to the U.S. Census Bureau. As seen by the many subtypes of place, this feature class encompasses a wide variety of urban communities.

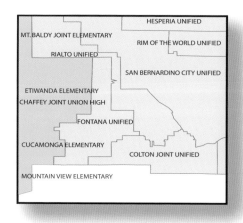

*Some of the school districts in San Bernardino County*

## School districts

School districts are geographic entities within which public educational services are provided. States supply the school districts. There are four types of school districts: elementary, middle, unified, and secondary. The Department of Education assigns each school district a code that is unique within the state. Each school district feature must be covered by one state feature, and school district features of the same type must not overlap.

*Areas within which education is offered*

### Simple feature class — SchoolDistrict

Geometry *Polygon*
Contains M values *No*
Contains Z values *No*

| Field name | Data type | Allow nulls | Default value | Precision | Scale | Length | |
|---|---|---|---|---|---|---|---|
| OBJECTID | Object ID | | | | | | |
| NAME | String | Yes | | | | 60 | |
| LSAD | String | Yes | | | | 2 | Legal/Statistical area description |
| ID_CODE | String | Yes | | | | 5 | Census school district ID code |
| FIPSSTCO | String | Yes | | | | 5 | FIPS state and county code |
| SHAPE | Geometry | Yes | | | | | |
| COUNTY | String | Yes | | | | 5 | |
| SUBTYPES | Long integer | Yes | 1 | 0 | | | |
| SHAPE_Length | Double | Yes | | 0 | 0 | | |
| SHAPE_Area | Double | Yes | | 0 | 0 | | |

### Subtypes of SchoolDistrict

Subtype field *SUBTYPES*
Default subtype *1*

List of defined default values and domains for subtypes in this class

| Subtype Code | Subtype Description | | Field name | Default value | Domain |
|---|---|---|---|---|---|
| 1 | Elementary | ⇨ | No values set | | |
| 2 | Middle | ⇨ | No values set | | |
| 3 | Secondary | ⇨ | No values set | | |
| 4 | Unified | ⇨ | No values set | | |

## Places

In the context of census data, the term "place" can refer to both legal and statistical entities. Legal places include consolidated cities and incorporated places, while statistical places include census designated places and consolidated city (Balance) portions.

Places are identified by a five-digit FIPS code, assigned alphabetically and unique within the state. Places with duplicate names in the same state but representing distinct areas are assigned a FIPS code alphabetically based on their respective counties. If the places are in the same county, they are assigned FIPS codes alphabetically based on their legal description, for example, "city" before "town".

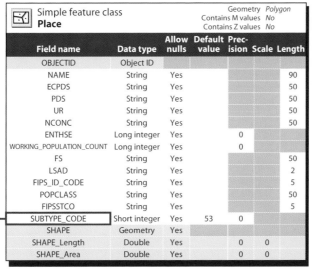

*Areas for reporting decennial census data*

Simple feature class
**Place**

Geometry *Polygon*
Contains M values *No*
Contains Z values *No*

| Field name | Data type | Allow nulls | Default value | Precision | Scale | Length | |
|---|---|---|---|---|---|---|---|
| OBJECTID | Object ID | | | | | | |
| NAME | String | Yes | | | | 90 | |
| ECPDS | String | Yes | | | | 50 | Economic census place description |
| PDS | String | Yes | | | | 50 | Place description |
| UR | String | Yes | | | | 50 | Urban/Rural code |
| NCONC | String | Yes | | | | 50 | Consolidated city 2000 code |
| ENTHSE | Long integer | Yes | | 0 | | | Working housing count |
| WORKING_POPULATION_COUNT | Long integer | Yes | | 0 | | | Working population count |
| FS | String | Yes | | | | 50 | Functional status |
| LSAD | String | Yes | | | | 2 | Legal/Statistical area description |
| FIPS_ID_CODE | String | Yes | | | | 5 | FIPS code |
| POPCLASS | String | Yes | | | | 50 | Population range |
| FIPSSTCO | String | Yes | | | | 5 | FIPS state and county code |
| SUBTYPE_CODE | Short integer | Yes | 53 | 0 | | | |
| SHAPE | Geometry | Yes | | | | | |
| SHAPE_Length | Double | Yes | | 0 | 0 | | |
| SHAPE_Area | Double | Yes | | 0 | 0 | | |

*Some places in Southern California*

### Subtypes of Place

Subtype field   *SUBTYPE_CODE*
Default subtype   *53*

List of defined default values and domains for subtypes in this class

| Subtype Code | Subtype Description | | Field name | Default value | Domain |
|---|---|---|---|---|---|
| 53 | city and borough | | No values set | | |
| 54 | municipality | | No values set | | |
| 55 | comunidad | | No values set | | |
| 56 | borough | | No values set | | |
| 58 | city | | No values set | | |
| 59 | city-undefined | | No values set | | |
| 60 | town | | No values set | | |
| 61 | village | | No values set | | |
| 62 | zona urbana | | No values set | | |
| 57 | CDP - Census Designated Place | | No values set | | |
| 0 | Default | | No values set | | |

Federal-level layers include American Indian reservations and subreservations, Alaska Native regional corporations, public use microdata areas, urban areas, and urban growth areas. While all these are included in the census data model, users need not keep feature classes that do not apply to their state or local area.

American Indian reservations are areas that have been set aside for government-recognized tribes. Features in the AIR layer do not generally conform to the standard relationship between layers in the census administrative units group. The AIR layer is subtyped based on its census code value. Each feature in the AIR is assigned a four-digit census code that falls within one of the categories shown in the table below.

*Census code ranges for American Indian reservations*

| Type | Census Code Range |
| --- | --- |
| Federal AIR | 0001 to 4999 |
| Hawaiian Home Land | 5000 to 5499 |
| OTSA | 5500 to 5999 |
| ANVSA | 6000 to 7999 |
| TDSA | 8000 to 8999 |
| State AIR | 9000 to 9499 |
| SDAISA | 9500 to 9999 |

## Federal American Indian reservations

Federal American Indian reservations are areas that have been set aside by the federal government of the United States for use by tribes. Each tribal government identifies the boundaries of its respective AIR. Federal AIRs may cross state, county, county subdivision, and place boundaries. Federal AIRs are identified with a unique four-digit census code ranging from 0001 to 4999 in alphabetical order nationwide. Federal AIRs are also assigned a FIPS code alphabetically within the state. For federal AIRs that cross state boundaries, different FIPS codes are assigned for each area of the federal AIR that is within each state.

## Hawaiian home lands

Hawaiian home lands are areas held in trust for native Hawaiians by the state of Hawaii. Each feature in the Hawaiian home lands layer is assigned a unique four-digit census code and a FIPS code that is unique within the state.

Both the census and FIPS codes are assigned in alphabetical order. The Hawaiian home lands subtype layer has the same topological relationships as its containing layer, AIR.

## Oklahoma tribal statistical areas

Oklahoma tribal statistical areas are identified by the U.S. Census Bureau in collaboration with federally recognized American Indian tribes. OTSAs represent areas previously designated as reservations within Oklahoma, except where grouped with neighboring tribes for presentation purposes. Each OTSA feature is assigned a unique census code alphabetically based on the name of the OTSA. OTSA features are also assigned a FIPS code unique within Oklahoma. The OTSA subtype layer has the same topological relationships as its containing layer, AIR.

## Alaska Native village statistical areas

Alaska Native village statistical areas identify densely populated native village areas within the state of Alaska. ANVSAs are delineated by officials from Alaska Native regional corporations (ANRCs). Each ANVSA feature is assigned a unique four-digit census code and a FIPS code that is unique within the state; both codes are assigned alphabetically based on the ANVSA name. The ANVSA subtype layer has the same topological relationships as its containing layer, AIR. In addition, ANVSA features must be covered by a feature from the ANRC layer.

## Tribal designated statistical areas

Tribal designated statistical areas are entities used for federally recognized tribes that do not have a corresponding federally recognized reservation (state recognized tribes are identified by the SDAISA layer). TDSAs are identified for the Census Bureau by federally recognized American Indian tribes. A TDSA generally encompasses a compact and contiguous area with a concentration of people who identify with a federally recognized American Indian tribe and in which there is structured or organized tribal activity. TDSAs may cross state boundaries but cannot overlap with any other type of AIR feature. Each TDSA feature is assigned a unique four-digit census code and a FIPS code that is unique within the state; both codes are assigned alphabetically based on the TDSA name.

## State American Indian reservation

State governments set state AIR areas for state-recognized tribes. A governor-appointed liaison provides the names and boundaries of state AIRs with each name suffixed with "State" in census data presentations. State AIRs may cross county, county subdivision, and place boundaries. State AIRs are identified with a unique four-digit census code ranging from 9000 to 9499 in alphabetical order within the state. State AIRs are also assigned a FIPS code alphabetically within the state.

## State-designated American Indian statistical area

State-designated American Indian statistical areas are used for state-recognized tribes that do not have a corresponding state-recognized reservation. SDAISAs are identified for the Census Bureau by the state. SDAISAs generally encompass a compact and contiguous area with a concentration of people who identify with a state-recognized American Indian tribe and in which there is structured or organized tribal activity. SDAISAs can only cross state boundaries if the tribe is recognized in both states. Each SDAISA feature is assigned a unique four-digit census code and a FIPS code that is unique within the state; both codes are assigned alphabetically based on the SDAISA name.

The Trust Land field in the AIR layer is associated with the Trust Land domain that designates areas for which the United States holds the land in trust for tribes (denoted by a T), individuals (I), residents of Hawaii (H), or if it is not applicable, zero (0).

**3**

*American Indian reservations*

| Field name | Data type | Allow nulls | Default value | Domain | Prec-ision | Scale | Length | |
|---|---|---|---|---|---|---|---|---|
| | | Geometry | *Polygon* | | | | | |
| | | Contains M values | *No* | | | | | |
| | | Contains Z values | *No* | | | | | |
| OBJECTID | Object ID | | | | | | | |
| AIANHHCE | String | Yes | | | | | 4 | American Indian/Alaska Native area/Hawaiian home land census code |
| TRUST | String | Yes | | Trust Land | | | 1 | Trust land indicator |
| NAME | String | Yes | | | | | 66 | |
| AIANA | String | Yes | | | | | 50 | American Indian/Alaska Native Area |
| FS | String | Yes | | | | | 50 | Functional status |
| LSAD | String | Yes | | | | | 2 | Legal/Statistical area description |
| FIPSCODE | String | Yes | | | | | 5 | FIPS code |
| ITP | String | Yes | | | | | 50 | American Indian/Alaska Native/Hawaiian Native entity type |
| FIPSSTCO | String | Yes | | | | | 5 | FIPS state and county code |
| SHAPE | Geometry | Yes | | | | | | |
| SUBTYPES | Long integer | Yes | 1 | | 0 | | | |
| SHAPE_Length | Double | Yes | | | 0 | 0 | | |
| SHAPE_Area | Double | Yes | | | 0 | 0 | | |

Simple feature class — **AmericanIndianReservation**

Subtypes of AmericanIndianReservation

Subtype field *SUBTYPES*
Default subtype *1*

List of defined default values and domains for subtypes in this class

| Subtype Code | Subtype Description | | Field name | Default value | Domain |
|---|---|---|---|---|---|
| 1 | Federal AIR | → | No values set | | |
| 2 | Hawaiian Home Land | → | No values set | | |
| 3 | OTSA - Oklahoma Tribal Statistical Area | → | No values set | | |
| 4 | ANVSA - Alaska Native Village Statistical Area | → | No values set | | |
| 5 | TDSA - Tribal Designated Statistical Area | → | No values set | | |
| 6 | State AIR | → | No values set | | |
| 7 | SDAISA - State Designated American Indian Statistical Area | → | No values set | | |

Two of the administrative units are for Native American entities, and the other is for general use by each state. The American Indian subreservations and public use micro-data areas are statistical in nature, while the Alaska Native regional corporations are legal entities.

## American Indian subreservations

American Indian subreservations are administrative subdivisions of American Indian reservations that serve social, economic, and cultural purposes. American Indian subreservations are supplied by their respective reservations. Each subreservation is assigned a census code identifier in alphabetical order that is unique within each reservation.

Each subdivision is also assigned a FIPS code alphabetically that is unique within the state. For subreservations that cross state boundaries, FIPS codes are assigned for each area of the subreservation that is within each state. American Indian subreservation features must not overlap each other.

*Administrative subdivisions of reservations*

| Simple feature class **AmericanIndianSubReservation** | | | | | | |
|---|---|---|---|---|---|---|
| Geometry | | | | *Polygon* | | |
| Contains M values | | | | *No* | | |
| Contains Z values | | | | *No* | | |

| Field name | Data type | Allow nulls | Precision | Scale | Length | |
|---|---|---|---|---|---|---|
| OBJECTID | Object ID | | | | | |
| AIANACE | String | Yes | | | 4 | American Indian/Alaska Native area census code |
| AIRSUBCE | String | Yes | | | 3 | American Indian subreservation census code |
| NAME | String | Yes | | | 90 | |
| FIPS_CODE | String | Yes | | | 50 | FIPS code |
| LSAD | String | Yes | | | 2 | Legal/Statistical area description |
| ISA | String | Yes | | | 3 | AI tribal subdivision code |
| FIPSSTCO | String | Yes | | | 5 | FIPS state and county code |
| SHAPE | Geometry | Yes | | | | |
| SHAPE_Length | Double | Yes | 0 | 0 | | |
| SHAPE_Area | Double | Yes | 0 | 0 | | |

## Alaska Native regional corporations

Alaska Native regional corporations are legally defined entities in the state of Alaska. Created pursuant to the Alaska Native Claims Settlement Act of 1972 (Public Law 92-203), the main purpose of ANRCs is to conduct the affairs of Alaska Natives. There are 12 ANRCs, each with a unique FIPS code assigned in alphabetical order by the ANRC name. ANRCs cover the state of Alaska except for the Annette Island Reserve American Indian reservation, which is not included in any ANRC. A thirteenth, nonspatial ANRC represents Alaska Natives who do not live in Alaska and do not identify with any of the 12 corporations. No data is supplied for this ANRC.

The topological relationships of the ANRC layer include: ANRC features must not overlap, each ANRC feature must be contained within a single state feature, and the ANRC layer must be covered by the census block layer.

| Simple feature class **AlaskaNativeRegionalCorporation** | | Geometry | Polygon | | |
|---|---|---|---|---|---|
| | | Contains M values | No | | |
| | | Contains Z values | No | | |
| **Field name** | **Data type** | **Allow nulls** | **Prec- ision** | **Scale** | **Length** |
| OBJECTID | Object ID | | | | |
| ANRC | String | Yes | | | 50 |
| LSAD | String | Yes | | | 2 |
| FIPS_ID_CODE | String | Yes | | | 5 |
| SHAPE | Geometry | Yes | | | |
| SHAPE_Length | Double | Yes | 0 | 0 | |
| SHAPE_Area | Double | Yes | 0 | 0 | |

*Areas within which Alaska Native affairs are managed*

Alaska Native regional corporation (FIPS code)
Legal/Statistical area description
FIPS code

## Public use microdata areas

Public use microdata areas (PUMA) are decennial areas for which the Census Bureau provides snapshots of raw data from long form census records. PUMAs are identified by states or their equivalent entities and can be of two types: 5 percent sampling of at least 100,000 people or 1 percent sampling of at least 400,000 people. The topological relationships of the PUMA layer require that PUMAs must not overlap, and that each PUMA feature must be contained within a single state feature.

| Simple feature class **PublicUseMicrodataArea** | | Geometry | Polygon | | |
|---|---|---|---|---|---|
| | | Contains M values | No | | |
| | | Contains Z values | No | | |
| **Field name** | **Data type** | **Allow nulls** | **Prec- ision** | **Scale** | **Length** |
| OBJECTID | Object ID | | | | |
| NAME | String | Yes | | | 50 |
| FS | String | Yes | | | 50 |
| LSAD | String | Yes | | | 2 |
| FIPSSTCO | String | Yes | | | 5 |
| SHAPE | Geometry | Yes | | | |
| SHAPE_Length | Double | Yes | 0 | 0 | |
| SHAPE_Area | Double | Yes | 0 | 0 | |

*Areas for which snapshots of raw data from long form census records are reported*

Functional status
Legal/Statistical area description
FIPS state and county code

Urban growth areas (UGAs) are only used in Oregon, while urban areas are used across the United States. These are used to help monitor the spread of urban areas over time, along with their associated demographics.

## Urban growth areas

An urban growth area is a legally defined feature within the state of Oregon. UGAs are defined around incorporated places and are used to regulate urban expansion and growth. UGAs are identified by a unique five-digit census code, generally the same as the FIPS code, assigned alphabetically within Oregon. The UGA layer must be covered by the census block layer.

| Simple feature class **UrbanGrowthArea** | | Geometry | Polygon | | |
|---|---|---|---|---|---|
| | | Contains M values | No | | |
| | | Contains Z values | No | | |
| **Field name** | **Data type** | **Allow nulls** | **Prec-ision** | **Scale** | **Length** |
| OBJECTID | Object ID | | | | |
| UGA | String | Yes | | | 50 |
| FS | String | Yes | | | 50 |
| NAME | String | Yes | | | 50 |
| LSAD | String | Yes | | | 2 |
| SHAPE | Geometry | Yes | | | |
| SHAPE_Length | Double | Yes | 0 | 0 | |
| SHAPE_Area | Double | Yes | 0 | 0 | |

*Areas defined around incorporated places in Oregon and used to regulate urban expansion and growth*

Urban growth area code

Functional status

Legal/Statistical area description

## Urban areas

Urban areas are densely settled areas containing a cluster of one or more block groups or census blocks, each of which has a population density of at least 1,000 people per square mile at the time; surrounding block groups and census blocks, each of which has a population density of at least 500 people per square mile at the time; and less densely settled blocks that form enclaves or indentations or are used to connect noncontiguous areas with qualifying densities. Urban areas are divided into two groups based on the legal–statistical attribute description code (LSADC) attribute, 76 for an urban cluster and 75 for an urbanized area.

Urban clusters must contain at least 2,500 people, with a maximum of 50,000. If fewer than 35,000 people live in an area that is not designated as a military installation, the UC may have more than 50,000 people. UCs are assigned a unique five-digit code in alphabetical order, which also includes urbanized areas.

Urbanized areas must contain a minimum of 50,000 people, of which at least 35,000 must not live on a military installation. UAs are assigned a unique, five-digit code in alphabetical order, which also includes urban clusters.

**3**

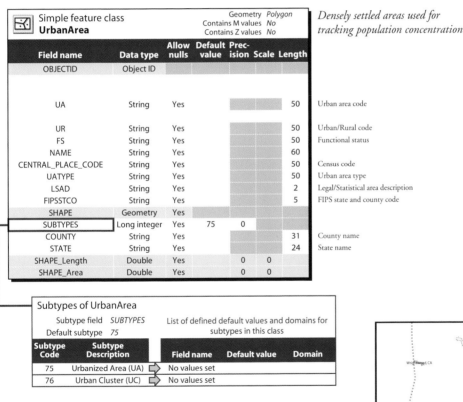

| Field name | Data type | Allow nulls | Default value | Prec-ision | Scale | Length | |
|---|---|---|---|---|---|---|---|
| OBJECTID | Object ID | | | | | | |
| UA | String | Yes | | | | 50 | Urban area code |
| UR | String | Yes | | | | 50 | Urban/Rural code |
| FS | String | Yes | | | | 50 | Functional status |
| NAME | String | Yes | | | | 60 | |
| CENTRAL_PLACE_CODE | String | Yes | | | | 50 | Census code |
| UATYPE | String | Yes | | | | 50 | Urban area type |
| LSAD | String | Yes | | | | 2 | Legal/Statistical area description |
| FIPSSTCO | String | Yes | | | | 5 | FIPS state and county code |
| SHAPE | Geometry | Yes | | | | | |
| SUBTYPES | Long integer | Yes | 75 | 0 | | | |
| COUNTY | String | Yes | | | | 31 | County name |
| STATE | String | Yes | | | | 24 | State name |
| SHAPE_Length | Double | Yes | | 0 | 0 | | |
| SHAPE_Area | Double | Yes | | 0 | 0 | | |

Simple feature class
**UrbanArea**

Geometry *Polygon*
Contains M values *No*
Contains Z values *No*

*Densely settled areas used for tracking population concentration*

### Subtypes of UrbanArea

Subtype field *SUBTYPES*
Default subtype *75*

List of defined default values and domains for subtypes in this class

| Subtype Code | Subtype Description | | Field name | Default value | Domain |
|---|---|---|---|---|---|
| 75 | Urbanized Area (UA) | ⇨ | No values set | | |
| 76 | Urban Cluster (UC) | ⇨ | No values set | | |

The points of interest group differs from the other groups in the data model in that layers are of different feature types (point, line, and polygon layers). These layers represent important geographic locations needed for typical administrative boundary datasets and maps. Layers include key geographical locations; buildings; and other point, line, and area landmarks, such as airports, airfields, and military bases.

## Key geographical location

Key geographical locations (KGL) are features such as post offices, libraries, and shopping centers. They are landmarks with special address information that facilitates location and address management. The CFCC field can be used to symbolize KGL features. Each KGL feature is identified by a five-digit POLYID code.

## Landmark

Landmarks are prominent features within an area, such as airports, libraries, or parks. Included in TIGER as an aid to enumerators, the landmarks list is not meant to be exhaustive. There are three landmark layers of shape type: point, line, and polygon. A landmark feature may be represented more than once in each layer.

The point landmark layer contains features such as schools, churches, and other civic points of interest. The point landmark features can be symbolized using the CFCC field.

The line landmark layer is composed of line features identifying airports, airstrips, and airfields. Landmark features rarely designate census boundaries. However, many of the fields are the same as for linear transportation features. Where data is available for street and addressing fields, these features can be treated as any other transportation feature. While there is no guarantee that the spelling of landmark names in the FENAME field will be consistent, the FENAME field can be used to group the features based on a unique name for cartographic purposes. Users may wish to edit the names of landmark features in their areas of interest to make them more consistent and useful for local analysis.

The area landmark layer contains features such as airports, military installations, national parks, and national monuments. Area landmark features can be symbolized using the CFCC field.

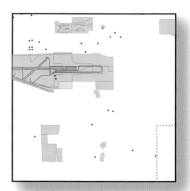

*Landmarks with special address information*

| Simple feature class **KeyGeographicalLocation** | | Geometry *Polygon* Contains M values *No* Contains Z values *No* | | | | |
|---|---|---|---|---|---|---|
| **Field name** | **Data type** | **Allow nulls** | **Prec- ision** | **Scale** | **Length** | |
| OBJECTID | Object ID | | | | | |
| SHAPE | Geometry | Yes | | | | |
| COUNTY | String | Yes | | | 5 | FIPS state and county code |
| CFCC | String | Yes | | | 3 | Census feature class code |
| KGLNAME | String | Yes | | | 30 | Name |
| ADDRESS | String | Yes | | | 50 | |
| USE | String | Yes | | | 50 | Usage flags |
| ZIP4L | Long integer | Yes | 0 | | | ZIP+4 add-on |
| PAZIP | Long integer | Yes | 0 | | | ZIP Code designator |
| DESFL | String | Yes | | | 50 | Description flags |
| WITYPE | String | Yes | | | 50 | Type of within-structure complex addressing |
| CIMPUT | Float | Yes | 0 | 0 | | Inputted coordinate |
| POLYID | Double | Yes | 0 | 0 | | Polygon identification code |
| SHAPE_Length | Double | Yes | 0 | 0 | | |
| SHAPE_Area | Double | Yes | 0 | 0 | | |

## Landmark

**Simple feature class — Landmark**

Geometry: Polyline
Contains M values: No
Contains Z values: No

*Prominent features within an area, such as airports*

| Field name | Data type | Allow nulls | Precision | Scale | Length | |
|---|---|---|---|---|---|---|
| OBJECTID | Object ID | | | | | |
| TLID | Double | Yes | 0 | 0 | | TIGER/Line ID |
| FEDIRP | String | Yes | | | 2 | Feature direction, prefix |
| FENAME | String | Yes | | | 30 | Feature name |
| FETYPE | String | Yes | | | 4 | Feature type |
| FEDIRS | String | Yes | | | 2 | Feature direction, suffix |
| CFCC | String | Yes | | | 3 | Census feature class code |
| FRADDL | String | Yes | | | 11 | From address, left |
| TOADDL | String | Yes | | | 11 | To address, left |
| FRADDR | String | Yes | | | 11 | From address, right |
| TOADDR | String | Yes | | | 11 | To address, right |
| CFCC1 | String | Yes | | | 1 | Census feature class code 1 |
| CFCC2 | String | Yes | | | 2 | Census feature class code 2 |
| SOURCE | String | Yes | | | 1 | Code identifying origin |
| SHAPE | Geometry | Yes | | | | |
| ZCTAL | String | Yes | | | 5 | Left ZIP Code tabulation |
| ZCTAR | String | Yes | | | 5 | Right ZIP Code tabulation |
| SHAPE_Length | Double | Yes | 0 | 0 | | |

## OtherPointLandmark

**Simple feature class — OtherPointLandmark**

Geometry: Point
Contains M values: No
Contains Z values: No

*Other point landmarks*

| Field name | Data type | Allow nulls | Precision | Scale | Length | |
|---|---|---|---|---|---|---|
| OBJECTID | Object ID | | | | | |
| SHAPE | Geometry | Yes | | | | |
| CFCC | String | Yes | | | 3 | Census feature class code |
| NAME | String | Yes | | | 30 | Landmark name |
| TYPE | String | Yes | | | 50 | Landmark type |
| FIPS_CODE | String | Yes | | | 50 | FIPS code |

## OtherAreaLandmark

**Simple feature class — OtherAreaLandmark**

Geometry: Polygon
Contains M values: No
Contains Z values: No

*Area landmarks, such as parks and military installations*

| Field name | Data type | Allow nulls | Precision | Scale | Length | |
|---|---|---|---|---|---|---|
| OBJECTID | Object ID | | | | | |
| SHAPE | Geometry | Yes | | | | |
| COUNTY | String | Yes | | | 5 | FIPS state and county code |
| CFCC | String | Yes | | | 3 | Census feature class code |
| LANDNAME | String | Yes | | | 30 | Landmark name |
| LANDPOLY | Double | Yes | 0 | 0 | | Landmark polygon identification |
| TYPE | String | Yes | | | 50 | Landmark type |
| FIPS_CODE | String | Yes | | | 50 | FIPS code |
| CENID | String | Yes | | | 50 | Census file identification code |
| POLYID | Double | Yes | 0 | 0 | | Polygon identification code |
| SHAPE_Length | Double | Yes | 0 | 0 | | |
| SHAPE_Area | Double | Yes | 0 | 0 | | |

## REFERENCES

Census 2000 Redistricting Data (Public Law 94-171) Summary File—Technical Documentation. 2002. Washington, D.C.: U.S. Census Bureau.

Census 2000 Summary File 1—United States. 2001. Washington, D.C.: U.S. Census Bureau.

Census 2000 Summary File 2—United States. 2001. Washington, D.C.: U.S. Census Bureau.

Census 2000 TIGER/Line Files (machine-readable data files). 2002. Washington, D.C.: U.S. Census Bureau.

Census 2000 Tiger/Line Files Technical Documentation. 2002. Washington, D.C.: U.S. Census Bureau. URL: http://www.census.gov/geo/www/tiger/ rd_2ktiger/ tgrrd2k.pdf.

Census TIGER Overview. 2003. Washington, D.C.: U.S. Census Bureau. URL: http://www.census.gov/geo/ www/tiger.

Census TIGER/Line Files Metadata. 2002. Washington, D.C.: U.S. Census Bureau. URL: http://www.census.gov/geo/www/tiger/rd_2ktiger/ tlrdmeta.txt.

DIME Comix & Stories: Using the Census Bureau's GBF/DIME System. 1976. Washington, D.C.: U.S. Census Bureau.

Redistricting Census 2000 TIGER/Line Files Technical Documentation. 2000. Washington, D.C.: U.S. Census Bureau.

TIGER Tales: A Presentation of the Automated Geographic Support System for the 1990 Census. 1985. Washington, D.C.: U.S. Census Bureau.

## FURTHER RESOURCES

For more information and a template for the administrative boundaries data model, visit ESRI ArcOnline and click the Census-Administrative Boundaries link at http://support.esri.com/datamodels.

## ACKNOWLEDGMENTS

Craig Gillgrass of ESRI provided data modeling and content for this chapter.

*This chapter presents a data model for representing address information for streets, buildings, parcels, and points of interest. This case study is based on the address management requirements of The City of Calgary in Alberta, Canada, and can be readily adapted in many countries and provinces by modeling the address styles that match the address practices of local culture and policies.*

4

Addresses describe the locations of places and events and provide directions for finding them. Addresses are broadly used in society for a host of purposes. This means that massive sets of information can be incorporated within the GIS by using addresses to find locations.

However, locating any address on a map is challenging. Address styles and assignment vary by locale and culture. This affects how addresses are expressed as a series of structured components and how addresses are used to assign locations. Special fuzzy logic is required to match an address against a master database of all addresses.

Knowing what kind of location you want to find is also important. This requires that you define a strategy for how you want address locations to be expressed. Should the address location be expressed as a point location for nonpoint features, such as a parcel or street segment? Or should the location be a building entrance or mail delivery location? For emergency response, accident locations may be reported by cross streets or city block. You may need to identify the street segment and its location. Even in organizations where the address location strategy is clear, maintaining the appropriate level of detail in the address information can be costly.

The potential payoff in information use and integration is tremendous and worth the effort required to support address management in a GIS despite the challenges. By associating addresses with geographic features, many types of information can be accurately geocoded and incorporated into the GIS. This information can be used to support such activities as emergency response, trouble call analysis in utilities, business planning, permitting, and routing. Therefore, many GIS users wish to build a comprehensive address database and integrate and manage it within their GIS.

The fundamental data model requirement is to associate robust, accurate, and complete address information with many types of geographic features: streets, land parcels, buildings, other landmarks, or even canals and rivers. Any one of these features could have multiple addresses, and one address could be used by multiple features.

# Addresses and
# locations

Geocoding is the process of finding the location of an address with a GIS. The location can be represented as a point location or as a feature (for example, a street segment, building, or mail delivery location). One of the main geocoding challenges is to provide good reference data. This includes the set of geographic features you need to match against as well as robust address characteristics that enable you to match address records to feature locations in the GIS.

Locating an address in a GIS is much like finding an address on a city map. Initially, you have to ensure that your city map contains enough detailed information so you can find the address location. Then, to match the address to a location, you break the address down into components (city, zone, street, and house number). Then you look up the zone on the map, search for the street name, and find the city block that contains the address. Often, the street map provides sufficient detail to find the side of the street and the house or building location of the address.

A similar process is used in a GIS. Assuming you have good reference data, special geocoding locators and logic will automate address lookup and location for you. Building a strong reference database of geographic features and associating address properties with those features is paramount.

A number of challenges to building good address reference data in a GIS are addressed in the design presented for The City of Calgary. In this chapter, you'll learn more about some of these key design challenges:

- Addresses can be associated with many types of feature classes in a reference database. You'll read how a common set of address elements can be associated with multiple feature classes.

- Addresses have multiple components that help you systematically express a location. You can organize the components of any address style as columns in tables. The complexities of the address relationships dictate that some address elements are organized in separate, related tables in the DBMS.

- Addresses and features in the GIS can share complex relationships. A feature can potentially have multiple addresses, and a single address can be associated with multiple features. Relational database design methods for managing many-to-many relationships can be applied to address these requirements.

- In some cases, a feature might have subaddresses. For example, ESRI has an address—380 New York Street, Redlands, California 92373. Yet individual buildings that comprise ESRI also have their own addresses. In addition, the company has multiple delivery locations for mail and other large shipments. Sections in this chapter describe a mechanism to model these types of scenarios in the geodatabase.

- The set of address components can vary by locale and culture. ArcGIS uses a series of formats, called address styles, to represent the set of address components for many local areas. Often users will define new address styles for their local needs. These are based on a specification of the elements in your addresses.

- Address locators must be built for geocoding addresses against your reference database (features that have addresses). An ArcGIS address locator references the address feature datasets, specifications of the address styles, and the geocoding rules that control the lookup process for matching addresses to feature locations in the GIS.

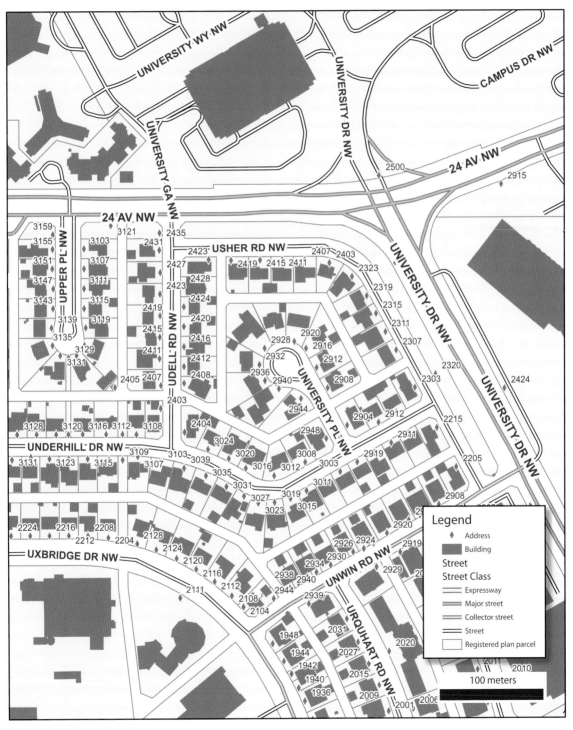

An address identifies and describes a specific geographic location and can be attached to many kinds of features, such as buildings, landmarks, and streets. Addresses have several elements, which can vary according to the purpose and locale of the address. The elements needed in any specific application often depend on the user's purpose for the addresses. Regardless how many types of features have addresses, all should point to a single, common set of address data.

Throughout the world, addresses are used to locate homes, offices, landmarks, and other places of interest along streets and rivers and within malls, buildings, and condominiums. Any piece of land or physical structure on the earth can be addressed in numerous ways, and many of these have more than one address. For example, many buildings have an address for the shipping and receiving dock that is different from that of the front entrance.

Addresses typically have several elements, such as:

• House or building number, or numeric range.

• Street name, such as "Main" in "Main Street".

• Street type, such as Street, Road, or Avenue.

• Directional component, usually N, NW, W, SW, S, SE, E, or NE. These may appear as a prefix, suffix, or both.

• Zones, such as city, state, or postal code.

Some regions and nations have additional components or different values for the components listed here. This addressing model can easily be adapted in such situations, even to the extent of storing more than one national style of address component values for each address. This is important in parts of Canada, for example, that use French and English together in many situations.

The example below shows the most common address style in the United States.

## 816 High Street, Redlands CA 92391

| House number | Street name | Street type | City | State | Postal code |

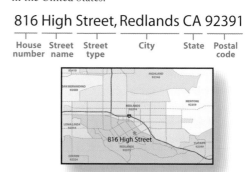

Often, the street name has a directional prefix and, just as often, the street type may have a separate directional suffix. Salt Lake City, Utah, typifies this throughout the city's addressing standard, as shown in the example below.

## 1052 N 300 W, Salt Lake City, UT 84119

House number | Prefix Direction | Street name | Suffix Direction | City | State | Postal code

In Salt Lake City, there are potentially four streets with the name "300". The particular street is indicated using the suffix direction, which specifies on which side of the temple the street is located.

## Addresses are locale based

In other countries, the same elements may be found as just described but in a different order. This is common in any country that uses Romance languages, such as Spanish, French, Italian, or Portuguese. The next example shows a typical address style used in Brazil.

# Rua Aurora 754, 01209001 São Paulo

| Street<br>type | Street<br>name | House<br>number | Postal<br>code | City |

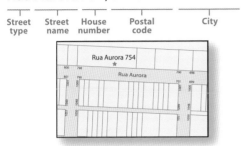

Still another style is found in countries that use a Germanic language, where the street name and street type are concatenated.

# Wendenstrasse 403, 20537 Hamburg

| Street name and<br>street type | House<br>number | Postal<br>code | City |

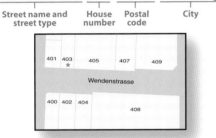

An address can also be used as a key that defines relationships between features of different types. This is an important concept elaborated on in several examples later in this chapter.

The conceptual model of addressing begins with an understanding of the relationship between geographic features and their names. This section shows how relational tables can be used to represent these associations specifically for street features. This approach for handling street names can then be applied to any other class of named features, such as buildings, landmarks, land parcels, rivers, and lakes.

In the real world, a feature, such as a street or landmark, can have multiple names. This is modeled with two tables, one for the street as a geographic feature class having a linear shape property and the other table for all the names used.

In the figure on the right, the shaded road feature in the upper right is associated with three names: West Main Street, Arlington Highway, and Highway 66.

**A street can have several names.**

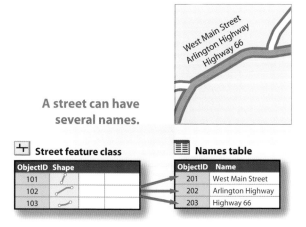

In addition, any one of these names could be used by multiple distinct features. This can be handled by a reverse relationship between the Street feature class and Names table.

In the figure on the left, the shaded road feature consists of three distinct segments, in this case, caused by intersections with other roads. The name Highway 66 is associated with all three of these street segments.

In relational database design, this is referred to as a many-to-many relationship.

**Many street segments can share a common street name.**

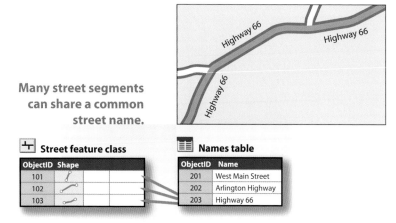

A common RDBMS practice is to use join tables to model many-to-many relationships. In the figure below, the first road segment (object ID 101) has two entries in the join table, one for each of two names, Highway 66 and West Main Street. This corresponds to the road segment in the lower left corner of the map inset.

**There is a many-to-many relationship between street features and names.**

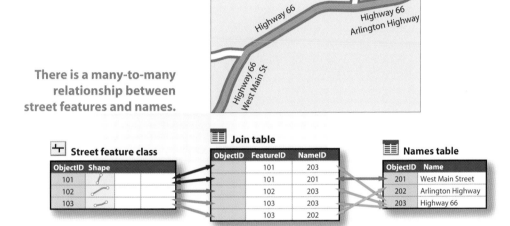

One of these names, Highway 66, is also associated with the two other road segments, object IDs 102 and 103.

This join table will become the basis for associating address ranges with streets, as seen in the next section.

The many-to-many relationships between streets and names can also apply to all address components, such as house numbers, street names, and zones. Both sides of each street can be associated with different house numbers. In the United States, a common convention is to assign even house addresses on one side of the street and odd numbers on the other side.

Streets have address ranges that can be modeled as additional attributes on the join table discussed in the previous section.

A street can have many address ranges, such as 100–198, 101–199, 200–248, and 201–249. The figure below shows a series of address ranges for each of three road features.

Furthermore, each address range can have multiple names, such as "100–198 Hwy 66" and "100–198 W. Main St." This can be seen by extending the role of the join table to include address ranges, as shown below.

Notice the Side column in the address ranges table below. This is used to indicate the side of the street to which a single address range applies, where Left and Right are indicated. Alternatives exist for encoding this level of detail in an actual database, as will be seen later.

Address range categories may be used to distinguish between multiple address ranges and names assigned to the same street. There can be many reasons for this:

- Address ranges might be used for different applications, such as actual versus theoretical address ranges.

- Addresses might be assigned differently by separate jurisdictions.

- Address ranges might be used for labeling or other user interface purposes.

To illustrate this example, one address range is considered the primary range, while a different address range is used for secondary purposes. In the Category column of the address ranges table below, the letter P indicates the primary range, and S indicates a secondary range. The choice of categories is based on user requirements.

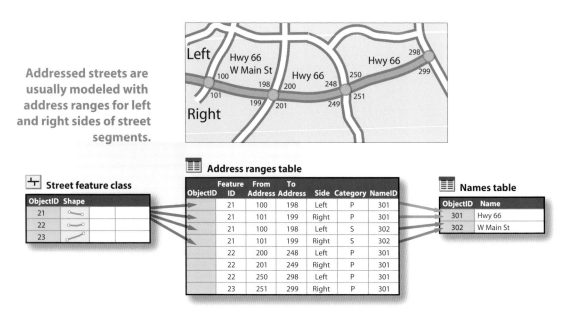

**Addressed streets are usually modeled with address ranges for left and right sides of street segments.**

### Street feature class

| ObjectID | Shape |
|---|---|
| 21 | |
| 22 | |
| 23 | |

### Address ranges table

| ObjectID | Feature ID | From Address | To Address | Side | Category | NameID |
|---|---|---|---|---|---|---|
| | 21 | 100 | 198 | Left | P | 301 |
| | 21 | 101 | 199 | Right | P | 301 |
| | 21 | 100 | 198 | Left | S | 302 |
| | 21 | 101 | 199 | Right | S | 302 |
| | 22 | 200 | 248 | Left | P | 301 |
| | 22 | 201 | 249 | Right | P | 301 |
| | 22 | 250 | 298 | Left | P | 301 |
| | 23 | 251 | 299 | Right | P | 301 |

### Names table

| ObjectID | Name |
|---|---|
| 301 | Hwy 66 |
| 302 | W Main St |

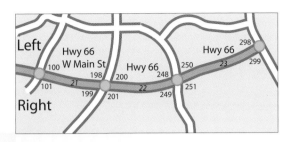

**By modeling many-to-many relationships among streets, address ranges, and names, you can represent every case.**

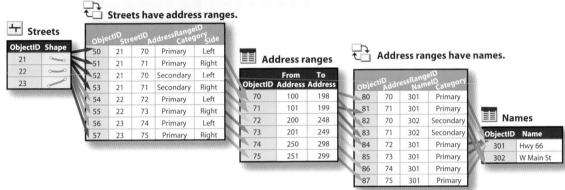

**Streets have address ranges.**

**Streets**

| ObjectID | Shape |
|----------|-------|
| 21 | |
| 22 | |
| 23 | |

| ObjectID | StreetID | AddressRangeID | Category | Side |
|----------|----------|----------------|----------|------|
| 50 | 21 | 70 | Primary | Left |
| 51 | 21 | 71 | Primary | Right |
| 52 | 21 | 70 | Secondary | Left |
| 53 | 21 | 71 | Secondary | Right |
| 54 | 22 | 72 | Primary | Left |
| 55 | 22 | 73 | Primary | Right |
| 56 | 23 | 74 | Primary | Left |
| 57 | 23 | 75 | Primary | Right |

**Address ranges**

| ObjectID | From Address | To Address |
|----------|--------------|------------|
| 70 | 100 | 198 |
| 71 | 101 | 199 |
| 72 | 200 | 248 |
| 73 | 201 | 249 |
| 74 | 250 | 298 |
| 75 | 251 | 299 |

**Address ranges have names.**

| ObjectID | AddressRangeID | NameID | Category |
|----------|----------------|--------|----------|
| 80 | 70 | 301 | Primary |
| 81 | 71 | 301 | Primary |
| 82 | 70 | 302 | Secondary |
| 83 | 71 | 302 | Secondary |
| 84 | 72 | 301 | Primary |
| 85 | 73 | 301 | Primary |
| 86 | 74 | 301 | Primary |
| 87 | 75 | 301 | Primary |

**Names**

| ObjectID | Name |
|----------|---------|
| 301 | Hwy 66 |
| 302 | W Main St |

**4**

### Normalizing range–name relationships

In an organization responsible for managing shared address data, this model can be made still more flexible by normalizing the address range information across multiple tables. The figure above shows how each address range can be stored once, avoiding duplication of data (and potential errors) for address ranges appearing more than once. This normalized data model allows:

- Multiple names for the same street or other feature
- Multiple address ranges for the same feature
- Multiple zone combinations for the same feature (to be explored more fully in a later section)

Furthermore, the use of multiple feature classes participating in an integrated data model allows more thorough cross validation of address information.

This enables development and management of a centralized repository of address ranges and names tables that can be used across an organization or group of related organizations.

### DIME versus nickel address range models

The DIME model was originated by Don Cooke and Marvin White for use by the U.S. Census Bureau in the 1970s. In the DIME model, each street segment has attributes such as LeftFromAddress, LeftToAddress, RightFromAddress, and RightToAddress. This model continues to be widely used today because it enables fast address lookup and cartographic display from a single flat file.

An alternative model for storing address ranges is also widely used. In this model, each street segment is associated with two separate range records, one for each side of the street. This is the model shown in the above figure. Because each range has half as many columns as in the DIME model (just a single FromAddress and ToAddress), this came to be called the nickel model in the United States.

The nickel model facilitates storing different names and address ranges for different sides of the street and enables easier validation of cases where there is no address range for one side of the street, such as along a coastal beach road. It also better supports cases where streets have multiple address ranges and names.

Buildings, points of interest, parcels, and many other kinds of features also have addresses that can be modeled using the same design as streets, extended for subaddresses. However, the conceptual model for building and parcel addresses requires an extended structure and set of relationships for managing subaddresses.

## BUILDINGS, PARCELS, AND SUBADDRESSES

Buildings, points of interest, and parcels can have both addresses and subaddresses. For example, a land parcel with multiple lots may have a separate subaddress for each of its lots. A building or parcel with multiple points of entry might have subaddresses for each point of entry, such as for a main entrance, shipping/receiving entrance, or rear parking entrance. Each unit of a multiunit office building, apartment building, or condominium can have subaddresses.

A subaddress can be represented as a feature with spatial location (as in the data model presented on the next page), or it can be a record in a table. The design alternative you use depends on the available data and your intended purpose. Each subaddress is always associated with its "parent" building, parcel, or other feature.

## ADDRESSES AND SUBADDRESSES

Addresses themselves may have subaddresses. A subaddress is a subdivision of an address, such as units of an apartment building, office building, or condominium. An address can have many subaddresses, and each subaddress is always associated with one address (its parent address).

A parcel can have many addresses and subaddresses.

*To simplify this illustration, only Building features are shown with subaddresses. However, the model allows for parcels and points of interest to also have subaddresses through the use of appropriate relationships, such as Parcels-have-subaddresses, or Points-of-Interest-have-subaddresses.*

**Parcels have addresses.**

**Parcel feature class**

| ObjectID | Shape | | |
|----------|-------|---|---|
| 701 | | | |

| ObjectID | BuildingID | AddressID |
|----------|------------|-----------|
| 301 | 701 | 1101 |
| 302 | 701 | 1102 |
| 303 | 701 | 1103 |
| 304 | 701 | 1104 |
| 305 | 701 | 1105 |
| 306 | 701 | 1106 |
| 307 | 701 | 1107 |
| 308 | 701 | 1108 |
| 309 | 701 | 1109 |
| 310 | 701 | 1110 |
| 311 | 701 | 1111 |
| 312 | 701 | 1112 |
| 313 | 701 | 1113 |

**Address table**

| ObjectID | Address |
|----------|---------|
| 1101 | 1919 University Dr NW |
| 1102 | 1919 A University Dr NW |
| 1103 | 1919 B University Dr NW |
| 1104 | 1919 C University Dr NW |
| 1105 | 1919 D University Dr NW |
| 1106 | 1919 E University Dr NW |
| 1107 | 1919 F University Dr NW |
| 1108 | 1919 G University Dr NW |
| 1109 | 1919 H University Dr NW |
| 1110 | 1919 J University Dr NW |
| 1111 | 1919 K University Dr NW |
| 1112 | 1919 L University Dr NW |
| 1113 | 1919 M University Dr NW |
| 1114 | 2108 Uxbridge Drive NW |
| 1115 | 2919 Unwin Rd NW |
| 1116 | 2029 Unwin Rd NW |

4

A point of interest can have many addresses and subaddresses.

**Point of interest feature class**

| ObjectID | Shape | | |
|----------|-------|---|---|
| 801 | | | |

**Points of interest have addresses.**

| ObjectID | PointOfInterestID | AddressID |
|----------|-------------------|-----------|
| 450 | 801 | 1114 |

Buildings can share an address; a building can have subaddresses.

2919 Unwin Rd NW
*subaddresses 1,2,3,4,5*

2919 Unwin Rd NW
*subaddresses 6,7*

2029 Unwin Rd NW

**Buildings have addresses.**

| ObjectID | BuildingID | AddressID |
|----------|------------|-----------|
| 550 | 901 | 1115 |
| 551 | 902 | 1115 |
| 552 | 903 | 1116 |

*Parcels and points of interest can also have subaddresses, but that is not shown in this instance diagram.*

**Buildings have subaddresses.**

| ObjectID | BuildingID | AddressID |
|----------|------------|-----------|
| 851 | 901 | 1201 |
| 852 | 901 | 1202 |
| 853 | 901 | 1203 |
| 854 | 901 | 1204 |
| 855 | 901 | 1205 |
| 856 | 902 | 1206 |
| 857 | 902 | 1207 |

**Building feature class**

| ObjectID | Shape | | |
|----------|-------|---|---|
| 901 | | | |
| 902 | | | |
| 903 | | | |

**Subaddress table**

| ObjectID | Subaddress |
|----------|------------|
| 1201 | 1 2919 Unwin Rd NW |
| 1202 | 2 2919 Unwin Rd NW |
| 1203 | 3 2919 Unwin Rd NW |
| 1204 | 4 2919 Unwin Rd NW |
| 1205 | 5 2919 Unwin Rd NW |
| 1206 | 6 2919 Unwin Rd NW |
| 1207 | 7 2919 Unwin Rd NW |

Zones are important for locating groups of addresses and address ranges. The most common examples of zones are postal code areas, cities, counties, provinces, and states. There are two sets of zones in this data model: "zones," such as city, province, and postal codes for individual addresses; and "range zones," such as city, province, and forward sortation area (FSA) for address ranges.

Why have zones and range zones? Zones are used to

- Rapidly narrow a search for an address.

- Index addresses by general location.

- Provide contextual information about the location of an address.

- Distinguish between identical addresses in different locations.

Zones typically form a hierarchy, with the state or province at the highest level containing cities and towns, each of which, in turn, contains one or more postal codes.

In Canada, postal codes have two main parts: the first three characters represent the forward sortation area, and the last three characters represent the local delivery unit (LDU). The FSA is analogous to the five-digit ZIP Code used in the United States, and the LDU is analogous to the last four digits of a complete nine-digit ZIP Code (also called ZIP+4).

Canadian postal codes can be assigned to buildings, companies with a single mail stop, block faces, rural routes, general deliveries, mobile routes, post office boxes, and suburban services (community mailboxes).

The figure at the upper right is an outline of Calgary's boundary with FSA locations shown. A closer look at the sortation area T2P's district is shown at the lower right.

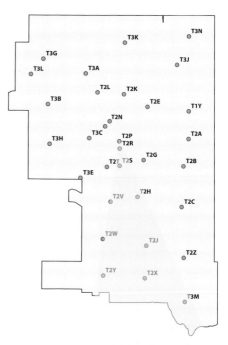

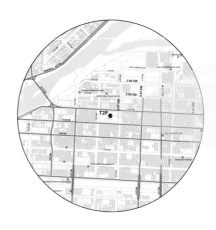

The figure below shows four addresses, each with its complete postal code assignment. This is a fictitious set of addresses, for illustration purposes only.

The address of one building is 199 Kent Street. It is an apartment building, so it has its own postal code (T2P 2K8), just as an apartment building in the United States might have its own ZIP+4 code.

Other street fronts on this block have their own addresses and have a different postal code (T2P 2M4). These are the only addresses with this postal code.

Notice that addresses located on this block face have different postal codes, but all of these postal codes have the same FSA. Therefore, the FSA is assigned to the block face (address range).

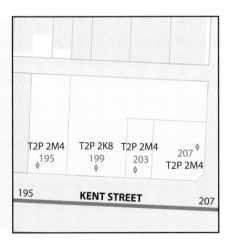

These pages show how features and addresses are organized as map layers and tables in the GIS. Addresses can be integrated with existing GIS databases as a set of shared tables for access across many applications. The thematic layers shown here represent the core information content in The City of Calgary's address database.

For viewing and editing purposes, addresses can be separated into four main types of data: addressable features, address numbers and ranges, names (as in street names or building names), and address zones. Each of these is briefly described below.

## FEATURES WITH ADDRESSES

Many types of features can be considered addressable, including buildings, points of interest, parcels, and streets.

### Buildings

Buildings could be polygon features, point features, or both, depending on the scale and intended use. At more detailed resolutions, building footprint polygons are used. Buildings may have a single address or multiple discrete addresses, such as for an office building or condominium. Not all buildings have names, and some buildings may have multiple names.

### Points of interest

Points of interest include (but are not limited to) monuments; museums; schools; houses of worship; community facilities; and offices for local, state, and federal government. While some of these might appear as building footprints at a large scale, they may be stored as point features at a smaller scale. Points of interest may have more than one address.

### Parcels

Land parcels delineate ownership and are used for taxation and ownership management. Parcels may be annotated with their street address and, possibly, with their parcel identification number for cross referencing.

### Streets

This layer consists of street centerline data in which street features meet at intersections or terminate at cul-de-sacs.

## ADDRESS FEATURES AND TABLES

There are three main entities in this data model for holding address information: Addresses, Names, and Zones. The large downward-pointing arrows along the right side of the diagram indicate that each of the feature layers has a relationship with Address features, and that the main Address features have relationships with Names and Zones tables.

### Addresses

The Addresses layer includes Address and SubAddress features as well as the AddressRange table. The SubAddress is for subdivisions of an Address, such as units of an apartment building, office building, or condominium. Both Address and SubAddress features provide label fields for annotation. The AddressRange table uniquely identifies each distinct address range used.

### Names

The GeoName table holds all the components of a name, whether used for a street, building, or parcel. Additional tables support abbreviations and other values used for directional octants (such as N, S, SW), street types (such as AV, ST, CT), and base names.

### Zones

There are four kinds of Zone tables in this model for specific addresses in Calgary: Province, CityLimit, PostalCode, and ForwardSortationArea. A ForwardSortationArea defines a major geographical area for primary mail sortation, similar to a five-digit U.S. ZIP Code. In addition to these, a RangeZone table contains a valid combination of City, Province, and ForwardSortationArea that can be assigned to address ranges.

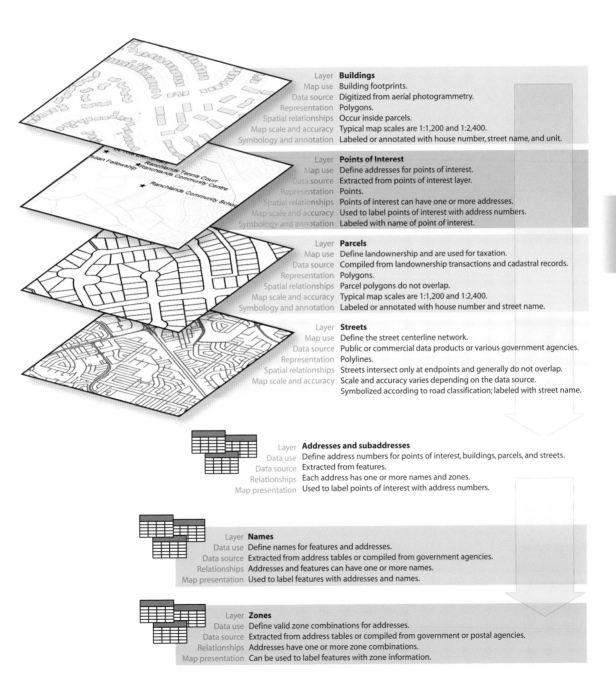

| Layer | **Buildings** |
|---|---|
| Map use | Building footprints. |
| Data source | Digitized from aerial photogrammetry. |
| Representation | Polygons. |
| Spatial relationships | Occur inside parcels. |
| Map scale and accuracy | Typical map scales are 1:1,200 and 1:2,400. |
| Symbology and annotation | Labeled or annotated with house number, street name, and unit. |

| Layer | **Points of Interest** |
|---|---|
| Map use | Define addresses for points of interest. |
| Data source | Extracted from points of interest layer. |
| Representation | Points. |
| Spatial relationships | Points of interest can have one or more addresses. |
| Map scale and accuracy | Used to label points of interest with address numbers. |
| Symbology and annotation | Labeled with name of point of interest. |

| Layer | **Parcels** |
|---|---|
| Map use | Define landownership and are used for taxation. |
| Data source | Compiled from landownership transactions and cadastral records. |
| Representation | Polygons. |
| Spatial relationships | Parcel polygons do not overlap. |
| Map scale and accuracy | Typical map scales are 1:1,200 and 1:2,400. |
| Symbology and annotation | Labeled or annotated with house number and street name. |

| Layer | **Streets** |
|---|---|
| Map use | Define the street centerline network. |
| Data source | Public or commercial data products or various government agencies. |
| Representation | Polylines. |
| Spatial relationships | Streets intersect only at endpoints and generally do not overlap. |
| Map scale and accuracy | Scale and accuracy varies depending on the data source. |
| | Symbolized according to road classification; labeled with street name. |

| Layer | **Addresses and subaddresses** |
|---|---|
| Data use | Define address numbers for points of interest, buildings, parcels, and streets. |
| Data source | Extracted from features. |
| Relationships | Each address has one or more names and zones. |
| Map presentation | Used to label points of interest with address numbers. |

| Layer | **Names** |
|---|---|
| Data use | Define names for features and addresses. |
| Data source | Extracted from address tables or compiled from government agencies. |
| Relationships | Addresses and features can have one or more names. |
| Map presentation | Used to label features with addresses and names. |

| Layer | **Zones** |
|---|---|
| Data use | Define valid zone combinations for addresses. |
| Data source | Extracted from address tables or compiled from government or postal agencies. |
| Relationships | Addresses have one or more zone combinations. |
| Map presentation | Can be used to label features with zone information. |

The diagram below provides an overview of the feature classes, tables, and relationships that implement the layers shown on the previous page. These implement the address data model for The City of Calgary. The relationship classes play an important role in the data model.

The entities in this data model are divided into four main groups: features with addresses, addresses, names, and zones. These may be all in the same feature dataset or in separate datasets, as long as the relationships can be established. The feature classes and tables are largely described on the preceding pages, but the properties of the relationships between them have not yet been discussed.

You may note that Address and SubAddress are shown here as point feature classes, while they are shown as tables in the previous diagram. These can be modeled either way; The City of Calgary chose to create these as feature classes for easier validation (for example, using the GIS to identify spatial relationships) and data availability reasons (they already maintain this feature data for subaddresses).

## OVERVIEW OF RELATIONSHIPS

Notice that Building, OwnershipParcel, and PointOfInterest feature classes all have relationships to both Address and SubAddress tables. This does not imply that all features of these classes participate in both relationships, just that a subset of these features do.

As mentioned in the conceptual model discussion earlier, Street has a relationship with Names and Zones through the AddressRange table. Addresses are related to Zones, and AddressRanges have associations with Zones through valid combinations of Province, CityLimit, and ForwardSortationArea identified in the RangeZones table.

All these features, tables, and relationships are discussed in more detail throughout the rest of this chapter.

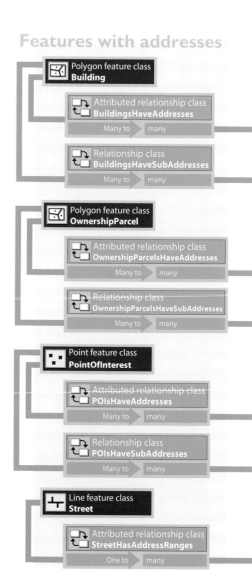

**Features with addresses**

Polygon feature class
**Building**

Attributed relationship class
**BuildingsHaveAddresses**
Many to many

Relationship class
**BuildingsHaveSubAddresses**
Many to many

Polygon feature class
**OwnershipParcel**

Attributed relationship class
**OwnershipParcelsHaveAddresses**
Many to many

Relationship class
**OwnershipParcelsHaveSubAddresses**
Many to many

Point feature class
**PointOfInterest**

Attributed relationship class
**POIsHaveAddresses**
Many to many

Relationship class
**POIsHaveSubAddresses**
Many to many

Line feature class
**Street**

Attributed relationship class
**StreetHasAddressRanges**
One to many

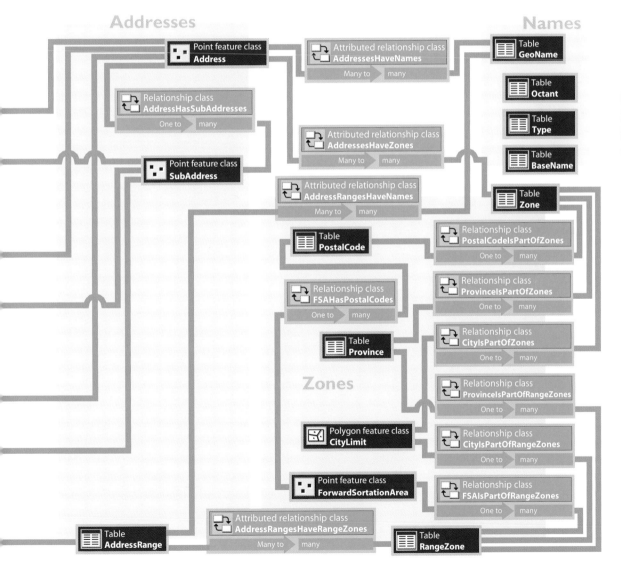

The physical data model and a working example of a street with multiple address ranges are shown here. Address ranges also are stored on the street features so that the address ranges can be labeled on a map.

The Street feature class contains records for street center-lines in Calgary. These records have polyline geometry. In this data model, a number of address elements are stored redundantly to support mapping. The LabelName attribute contains a name associated with the street in text form for labeling. The LeftFrom, LeftTo, RightFrom, and RightTo attributes contain the addresses found on each side and end of the street and, again, are used for labeling. The StreetID attribute is a unique identifier for records in the Street class. Other attributes are maintained by The City of Calgary but are not used in the context of the address model.

In the map inset on the right, one street feature is selected (highlighted in the data content window). This is part of Unwin Rd NW (see LabelName field). The term "Collector" refers to one type of street feature; other types are listed in the domain table for Class Codes shown opposite.

| Simple feature class **Street** | | | | | Geometry | *Polyline* | | |
|---|---|---|---|---|---|---|---|---|
| | | | | | Contains M values | *No* | | |
| | | | | | Contains Z values | *No* | | |
| Field name | Data type | Allow nulls | Default value | Domain | Prec-ision | Scale | Length | |
| OBJECTID | OID | | | | | | | |
| SHAPE | Geometry | Yes | | | | | | |
| StreetID | Double | Yes | | | 0 | 0 | | |
| LeftFrom | Integer | Yes | | | 0 | | | |
| LeftTo | Integer | Yes | | | 0 | | | |
| RightFrom | Integer | Yes | | | 0 | | | |
| RightTo | Integer | Yes | | | 0 | | | |
| ClassCode | String | Yes | | ClassCodes | | | 3 | |
| BuiltCode | String | Yes | | BuildCodes | | | 3 | |
| RegistrationCode | String | Yes | | RegistrationCodes | | | 2 | |
| BarrierCode | Small Integer | Yes | | BarrierCodes | 0 | 0 | 2 | |
| ClosureCode | String | Yes | | ClosureCodes | | | 1 | |
| PrivateCode | String | Yes | | PrivateCodes | | | 3 | |
| DirectionCode | String | Yes | | DirectionCodes | | | 3 | |
| BridgeCode | Small Integer | Yes | | BridgeCodes | 0 | 0 | 2 | |
| BridgeName | String | Yes | | | | | 50 | |
| SHAPE_Length | Double | Yes | | | 0 | 0 | | |
| LabelName | String | Yes | | | | | 26 | |

*A street represents a street centerline, usually segmented at intersections.*

The unique identifier of the street
The first address found at the from node on the left side of the street
The last address found at the to node on the left side of the street
The first address found at the from node on the right side of the street
The last address found at the to node on the right side of the street
A code indicating the road class of the street
A code indicating the built status of the street
A code indicating the registration status of the street
A code indicating the navigability of the street
A code indicating the closure status of the street
A code indicating if the street is private
A code indicating the directionality of the street
A code indicating if the street passes over a bridge
The name of the bridge over which the street passes

The name of the street used for labeling

Note that the Unwin Rd NW street feature shows fields for address ranges on both sides of the street (left from, left to, right from, right to). This is to support labeling the address ranges on the map.

By navigating from the Street feature to its associated AddressRange records, the FromAddress and ToAddress for each side of the road are seen.

The relationship depicted below is the link between streets and address ranges. The Side field is for values of L (left) or R (right) corresponding to the side of the street with which an address range is associated. The Side field might have had a domain defined, but in this case does not.

The AddressRange class contains the unique set of address ranges that can be assigned to Street features. An AddressRange record represents the set of addresses that can be found along one side of a Street segment. The FromAddress and ToAddress attributes indicate the first and last addresses, respectively, that can be found along the Street feature as the feature is traversed from its start node to its end node. The Parity attribute describes the parity of address numbers found in the address range; its values are taken from the ParityCodes domain.

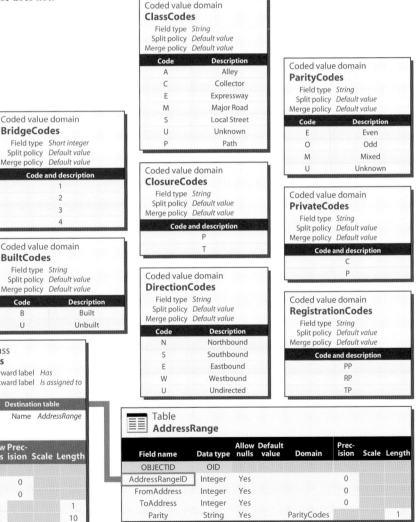

**Coded value domain**
**ClassCodes**
Field type — String
Split policy — Default value
Merge policy — Default value

| Code | Description |
|---|---|
| A | Alley |
| C | Collector |
| E | Expressway |
| M | Major Road |
| S | Local Street |
| U | Unknown |
| P | Path |

**Coded value domain**
**ParityCodes**
Field type — String
Split policy — Default value
Merge policy — Default value

| Code | Description |
|---|---|
| E | Even |
| O | Odd |
| M | Mixed |
| U | Unknown |

**Coded value domain**
**BridgeCodes**
Field type — Short integer
Split policy — Default value
Merge policy — Default value

| Code and description |
|---|
| 1 |
| 2 |
| 3 |
| 4 |

**Coded value domain**
**BarrierCodes**
Description — Barrier codes for streets
Field type — Short integer
Split policy — Default value
Merge policy — Default value

| Code and description |
|---|
| 1 |
| 2 |
| 3 |
| 4 |
| 5 |
| 6 |
| 7 |
| 8 |
| 9 |
| 10 |

**Coded value domain**
**ClosureCodes**
Field type — String
Split policy — Default value
Merge policy — Default value

| Code and description |
|---|
| P |
| T |

**Coded value domain**
**PrivateCodes**
Field type — String
Split policy — Default value
Merge policy — Default value

| Code and description |
|---|
| C |
| P |

**Coded value domain**
**BuiltCodes**
Field type — String
Split policy — Default value
Merge policy — Default value

| Code | Description |
|---|---|
| B | Built |
| U | Unbuilt |

**Coded value domain**
**DirectionCodes**
Field type — String
Split policy — Default value
Merge policy — Default value

| Code | Description |
|---|---|
| N | Northbound |
| S | Southbound |
| E | Eastbound |
| W | Westbound |
| U | Undirected |

**Coded value domain**
**RegistrationCodes**
Field type — String
Split policy — Default value
Merge policy — Default value

| Code and description |
|---|
| PP |
| RP |
| TP |

**Attributed relationship class**
**StreetHasAddressRanges**
Type — Simple
Cardinality — One to many
Notification — None
Forward label — Has
Backward label — Is assigned to

| Origin feature class | | Destination table | |
|---|---|---|---|
| Name — Street | | Name — AddressRange | |
| Primary key — StreetID | | | |
| Foreign key — StreetID | | | |

| Field name | Data type | Allow nulls | Precision | Scale | Length |
|---|---|---|---|---|---|
| OBJECTID | Object ID | | | | |
| StreetID | Long integer | Yes | 0 | | |
| AddressRangeID | Long integer | Yes | 0 | | |
| Side | String | Yes | | | 1 |
| Category | String | Yes | | | 10 |

**Table**
**AddressRange**

| Field name | Data type | Allow nulls | Default value | Domain | Precision | Scale | Length |
|---|---|---|---|---|---|---|---|
| OBJECTID | OID | | | | | | |
| AddressRangeID | Integer | Yes | | | 0 | | |
| FromAddress | Integer | Yes | | | 0 | | |
| ToAddress | Integer | Yes | | | 0 | | |
| Parity | String | Yes | | ParityCodes | | | 1 |

The physical data model and a working example of a building with an address and multiple subaddresses are shown here. This example demonstrates two buildings having the same address, as well as having separate subaddresses.

The Building class contains building roof lines in Calgary. These roof lines were digitized from aerial photography and have polygon geometry representations. The AddressLabel attribute contains an address associated with the building in text form for labeling. The BuildingID attribute is a unique identifier for records in the Building class. Other attributes in this class are maintained by The City of Calgary but are not significant in the context of the address data model.

Because records in the Building class are digitized from aerial photography, each record in this class does not necessarily represent an individual building. Records in this class may represent several buildings that share a roof line. This sometimes makes it impossible to associate addresses with records in this class. In cases where it is possible, such as in single-family residential areas of the city, Building records can be related to Address records and SubAddress records. Each Building can have several Addresses and several SubAddresses, and each Address and SubAddress can be associated with multiple Building records.

For example, a record for an apartment building might be associated with one Address record that represents the building entrance and several SubAddresses that represent the addresses of apartments within the building. Each of these relationships has a Category attribute, which identifies the type of relationship between the Building record and a particular Address or SubAddress record.

The map inset and object inspector at right provide an example of the table structures and relationships just discussed. The BuildingID, AddressID, and SubAddressID fields link the three tables, enabling navigation from the building to its associated records in the Address and SubAddress tables.

These relationships are bidirectional; that is, one can also navigate from an Address or SubAddress record to its Building feature.

In this map inset, two apartment buildings are shown that have a common street address, 2919 Unwin Rd NW. The larger building has apartment units 1–5, while the smaller building has units 6 and 7.

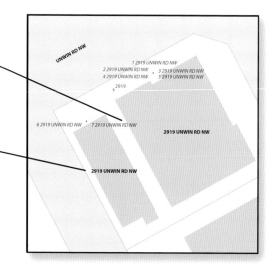

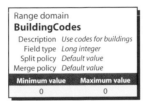

## Simple feature class
## Building

| | Geometry | Polygon |
|---|---|---|
| | Contains M values | No |
| | Contains Z values | No |

| Field name | Data type | Allow nulls | Default value | Domain | Precision | Scale | Length |
|---|---|---|---|---|---|---|---|
| OBJECTID | OID | | | | | | |
| SHAPE | Geometry | Yes | | | | | |
| BuildingCode | Integer | Yes | | BuildingCodes | 0 | | |
| XCoordinate | Double | Yes | | | 0 | 0 | |
| YCoordinate | Double | Yes | | | 0 | 0 | |
| BuildingID | Integer | Yes | | | 0 | | |
| SHAPE_Length | Double | Yes | | | 0 | 0 | |
| SHAPE_Area | Double | Yes | | | 0 | 0 | |
| AddressLabel | String | Yes | | | | | 50 |

*A Building is a polygon that represents the roof outline of a structure, as digitized from aerial photography.*

An integer code that represents the type of building
The x coordinate of the building centroid
The y coordinate of the building centroid
The unique identifier for the building

The address of the building used for labeling

## Range domain
## BuildingCodes

| Description | Use codes for buildings |
|---|---|
| Field type | Long integer |
| Split policy | Default value |
| Merge policy | Default value |

| Minimum value | Maximum value |
|---|---|
| 0 | 0 |

4

## Attributed relationship class
## BuildingsHaveAddresses

| Type | Simple | Forward label | Has |
|---|---|---|---|
| Cardinality | Many to many | Backward label | Is assigned to |
| Notification | None | | |

| Origin feature class | | Destination feature class | |
|---|---|---|---|
| Name | Building | Name | Address |
| Primary key | BuildingID | Primary key | AddressID |
| Foreign key | BuildingID | Foreign key | AddressID |

| Field name | Data type | Allow nulls | Precision | Scale | Length |
|---|---|---|---|---|---|
| Category | String | Yes | | | 10 |
| RID | Object ID | | | | |
| BuildingID | Long integer | Yes | 0 | | |
| AddressID | Long integer | Yes | 0 | | |

## Simple feature class
## Address

| | Geometry | Point |
|---|---|---|
| | Contains M values | No |
| | Contains Z values | No |

| Field name | Data type | Allow nulls | Default value | Domain | Precision | Scale | Length |
|---|---|---|---|---|---|---|---|
| OBJECTID | OID | | | | | | |
| SHAPE | Geometry | Yes | | | | | |
| XCoordinate | Double | Yes | | | 0 | 0 | |
| YCoordinate | Double | Yes | | | 0 | 0 | |
| Address | String | Yes | | | | | 35 |
| AddressID | Integer | Yes | | | 0 | | |
| HouseNumber | Integer | Yes | | | 0 | | |
| HouseAlpha | String | Yes | | | | | 1 |

## Attributed relationship class
## BuildingsHaveSubAddresses

| Type | Simple | Forward label | Has |
|---|---|---|---|
| Cardinality | Many to many | Backward label | Is assigned to |
| Notification | None | | |

| Origin feature class | | Destination feature class | |
|---|---|---|---|
| Name | Building | Name | SubAddress |
| Primary key | BuildingID | Primary key | SubAddressID |
| Foreign key | BuildingID | Foreign key | SubAddressID |

| Field name | Data type | Allow nulls | Precision | Scale | Length |
|---|---|---|---|---|---|
| Category | String | Yes | | | 10 |
| RID | Object ID | | | | |
| BuildingID | Long integer | Yes | 0 | | |
| SubAddressID | Long integer | Yes | 0 | | |

## Simple feature class
## SubAddress

| | Geometry | Point |
|---|---|---|
| | Contains M values | No |
| | Contains Z values | No |

| Field name | Data type | Allow nulls | Default value | Domain | Precision | Scale | Length |
|---|---|---|---|---|---|---|---|
| OBJECTID | OID | | | | | | |
| SHAPE | Geometry | Yes | | | | | |
| SuiteNumber | Integer | Yes | | | 0 | | |
| SuiteAlpha | String | Yes | | | | | 1 |
| AddressID | Integer | Yes | | | 0 | | |
| SubAddressID | Integer | Yes | | | 0 | | |
| UnitDesignator | String | Yes | | UnitDesignators | | | 10 |
| AddressLabel | String | Yes | | | | | 50 |

The physical data model and a working example of a parcel with an address and multiple subaddresses are shown here. As with buildings, parcels can have multiple addresses and subaddresses, and each address or subaddress can be associated with several parcels.

The OwnershipParcel class contains landownership parcels within Calgary. These records are constructed from the land survey framework and have polygon geometry representations. The AddressLabel attribute contains an address associated with the parcel in text form for labeling. The Calgary Parcel ID (CPID) attribute is a unique identifier for records in the OwnershipParcel class and is the main identifier by which The City of Calgary identifies ownership parcels. Other attributes in this class are maintained by The City of Calgary but are not significant in the context of the Address data model.

Parcels can have one or more Addresses and SubAddresses, and each Address or SubAddress can be associated with several OwnershipParcel records. The multibuilding parcel outlined below has a principal address of 1919 University Dr NW but also has a distinct address for each building.

Another common pattern of multiple addresses for a single parcel is illustrated in this example, as well. Notice that this large parcel has entrances on Ulster Rd NW and Uxbridge Dr NW in addition to University Dr NW. In many cases, separate parcel addresses might be assigned for each road entrance, perhaps to identify the entrances for shipping or receiving, emergency response, snow removal routing, or some other internal reference.

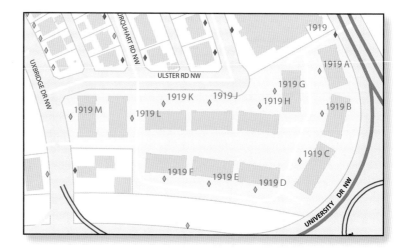

## Simple feature class
### OwnershipParcel

| | Geometry | Polygon |
|---|---|---|
| | Contains M values | No |
| | Contains Z values | No |

*An ownership parcel is a unit of landownership.*

| Field name | Data type | Allow nulls | Default value | Domain | Precision | Scale | Length | |
|---|---|---|---|---|---|---|---|---|
| OBJECTID | Object ID | | | | | | | |
| SHAPE | Geometry | Yes | | | | | | |
| XCoordinate | Double | Yes | | | 0 | 0 | | The x coordinate of the parcel centroid |
| YCoordinate | Double | Yes | | | 0 | 0 | | The y coordinate of the building centroid |
| SectionNumber | String | Yes | | | | | 6 | The section number in which the parcel is located |
| CPIDChar | String | Yes | | | | | 10 | |
| AddressLabel | String | Yes | | | | | 50 | The address of the ownership parcel used for labeling |
| CPID | Long integer | Yes | | | 0 | | | The unique identifier for the ownership parcel |
| SHAPE_Length | Double | Yes | | | 0 | 0 | | |
| SHAPE_Area | Double | Yes | | | 0 | 0 | | |

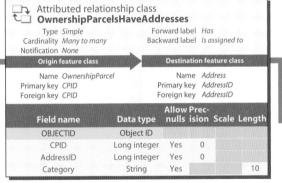

## Attributed relationship class
### OwnershipParcelsHaveAddresses

| Type | Simple | Forward label | Has |
|---|---|---|---|
| Cardinality | Many to many | Backward label | Is assigned to |
| Notification | None | | |

| Origin feature class | | Destination feature class | |
|---|---|---|---|
| Name | OwnershipParcel | Name | Address |
| Primary key | CPID | Primary key | AddressID |
| Foreign key | CPID | Foreign key | AddressID |

| Field name | Data type | Allow nulls | Precision | Scale | Length |
|---|---|---|---|---|---|
| OBJECTID | Object ID | | | | |
| CPID | Long integer | Yes | 0 | | |
| AddressID | Long integer | Yes | 0 | | |
| Category | String | Yes | | | 10 |

## Simple feature class
### Address

| | Geometry | Point |
|---|---|---|
| | Contains M values | No |
| | Contains Z values | No |

| Field name | Data type | Allow nulls | Default value | Domain | Precision | Scale | Length |
|---|---|---|---|---|---|---|---|
| OBJECTID | OID | | | | | | |
| SHAPE | Geometry | Yes | | | | | |
| XCoordinate | Double | Yes | | | 0 | 0 | |
| YCoordinate | Double | Yes | | | 0 | 0 | |
| Address | String | Yes | | | | | 35 |
| AddressID | Integer | Yes | | | 0 | | |
| HouseNumber | Integer | Yes | | | 0 | | |
| HouseAlpha | String | Yes | | | | | 1 |

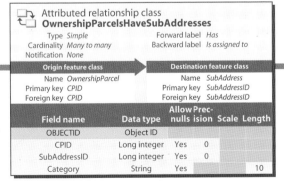

## Attributed relationship class
### OwnershipParcelsHaveSubAddresses

| Type | Simple | Forward label | Has |
|---|---|---|---|
| Cardinality | Many to many | Backward label | Is assigned to |
| Notification | None | | |

| Origin feature class | | Destination feature class | |
|---|---|---|---|
| Name | OwnershipParcel | Name | SubAddress |
| Primary key | CPID | Primary key | SubAddressID |
| Foreign key | CPID | Foreign key | SubAddressID |

| Field name | Data type | Allow nulls | Precision | Scale | Length |
|---|---|---|---|---|---|
| OBJECTID | Object ID | | | | |
| CPID | Long integer | Yes | 0 | | |
| SubAddressID | Long integer | Yes | 0 | | |
| Category | String | Yes | | | 10 |

## Simple feature class
### SubAddress

| | Geometry | Point |
|---|---|---|
| | Contains M values | No |
| | Contains Z values | No |

| Field name | Data type | Allow nulls | Default value | Domain | Precision | Scale | Length |
|---|---|---|---|---|---|---|---|
| OBJECTID | OID | | | | | | |
| SHAPE | Geometry | Yes | | | | | |
| SuiteNumber | Integer | Yes | | | 0 | | |
| SuiteAlpha | String | Yes | | | | | 1 |
| AddressID | Integer | Yes | | | 0 | | |
| SubAddressID | Integer | Yes | | | 0 | | |
| UnitDesignator | String | Yes | | UnitDesignators | | | 10 |
| AddressLabel | String | Yes | | | | | 50 |

4

The physical data model and a working example of points of interest are shown here. Points of interest may be associated with a building and parcel through a common Address record.

The PointOfInterest class contains point feature locations for community facilities, such as museums, sports arenas, religious centers, police and fire stations, and day care centers in Calgary. The AddressLabel attribute contains an address associated with the facility in text form for labeling. The POIID attribute is a unique identifier for records in the PointOfInterest class. Other attributes in this class are maintained by The City of Calgary but are not used in the context of the address data model. Note that these fields illustrate the additive nature of the address data model, which is used to extend other models to integrate address data management. These other attributes are important in the context of other applications.

Like Building and OwnershipParcel records, each record in the PointOfInterest class can have several Addresses and SubAddresses, and each Address or SubAddress can be associated with several PointOfInterest records. Each relationship has a Category attribute for distinguishing among multiple relationships between PointOfInterest and Address or SubAddress records.

In this example, a day care center at 2108 Uxbridge Dr NW is shown, along with its associated building and parcel. Note that they all share a common address.

```
☐ Point of Interest
   ☐ Dominican Sisters Day Care Centre
      ☐ has addresses
         ⊞ 2108 UXBRIDGE DR NW
         has sub-addresses
☐ Building
   ⊞ 2108 UXBRIDGE DR NW
☐ Ownership Parcel
   ⊞ 2108 UXBRIDGE DR NW
```

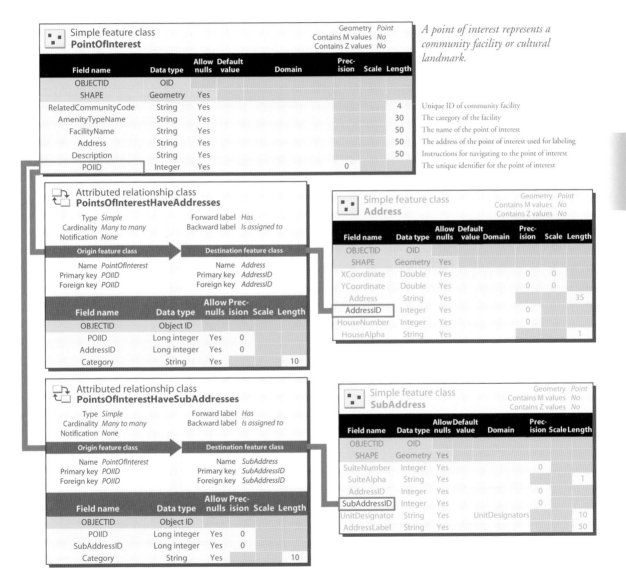

**Simple feature class**
**PointOfInterest**

Geometry *Point*
Contains M values *No*
Contains Z values *No*

| Field name | Data type | Allow nulls | Default value | Domain | Precision | Scale | Length |
|---|---|---|---|---|---|---|---|
| OBJECTID | OID | | | | | | |
| SHAPE | Geometry | Yes | | | | | |
| RelatedCommunityCode | String | Yes | | | | | 4 |
| AmenityTypeName | String | Yes | | | | | 30 |
| FacilityName | String | Yes | | | | | 50 |
| Address | String | Yes | | | | | 50 |
| Description | String | Yes | | | | | 50 |
| POIID | Integer | Yes | | | 0 | | |

*A point of interest represents a community facility or cultural landmark.*

Unique ID of community facility
The category of the facility
The name of the point of interest
The address of the point of interest used for labeling
Instructions for navigating to the point of interest
The unique identifier for the point of interest

**4**

**Attributed relationship class**
**PointsOfInterestHaveAddresses**

Type *Simple*
Cardinality *Many to many*
Notification *None*

Forward label *Has*
Backward label *Is assigned to*

| Origin feature class | | Destination feature class | |
|---|---|---|---|
| Name *PointOfInterest* | | Name *Address* | |
| Primary key *POIID* | | Primary key *AddressID* | |
| Foreign key *POIID* | | Foreign key *AddressID* | |

| Field name | Data type | Allow nulls | Precision | Scale | Length |
|---|---|---|---|---|---|
| OBJECTID | Object ID | | | | |
| POIID | Long integer | Yes | 0 | | |
| AddressID | Long integer | Yes | 0 | | |
| Category | String | Yes | | | 10 |

**Simple feature class**
**Address**

Geometry *Point*
Contains M values *No*
Contains Z values *No*

| Field name | Data type | Allow nulls | Default value | Domain | Precision | Scale | Length |
|---|---|---|---|---|---|---|---|
| OBJECTID | OID | | | | | | |
| SHAPE | Geometry | Yes | | | | | |
| XCoordinate | Double | Yes | | | 0 | 0 | |
| YCoordinate | Double | Yes | | | 0 | 0 | |
| Address | String | Yes | | | | | 35 |
| AddressID | Integer | Yes | | | 0 | | |
| HouseNumber | Integer | Yes | | | 0 | | |
| HouseAlpha | String | Yes | | | | | 1 |

**Attributed relationship class**
**PointsOfInterestHaveSubAddresses**

Type *Simple*
Cardinality *Many to many*
Notification *None*

Forward label *Has*
Backward label *Is assigned to*

| Origin feature class | | Destination feature class | |
|---|---|---|---|
| Name *PointOfInterest* | | Name *SubAddress* | |
| Primary key *POIID* | | Primary key *SubAddressID* | |
| Foreign key *POIID* | | Foreign key *SubAddressID* | |

| Field name | Data type | Allow nulls | Precision | Scale | Length |
|---|---|---|---|---|---|
| OBJECTID | Object ID | | | | |
| POIID | Long integer | Yes | 0 | | |
| SubAddressID | Long integer | Yes | 0 | | |
| Category | String | Yes | | | 10 |

**Simple feature class**
**SubAddress**

Geometry *Point*
Contains M values *No*
Contains Z values *No*

| Field name | Data type | Allow nulls | Default value | Domain | Precision | Scale | Length |
|---|---|---|---|---|---|---|---|
| OBJECTID | OID | | | | | | |
| SHAPE | Geometry | Yes | | | | | |
| SuiteNumber | Integer | Yes | | | 0 | | |
| SuiteAlpha | String | Yes | | | | | 1 |
| AddressID | Integer | Yes | | | 0 | | |
| SubAddressID | Integer | Yes | | | 0 | | |
| UnitDesignator | String | Yes | | UnitDesignators | | | 10 |
| AddressLabel | String | Yes | | | | | 50 |

Just as buildings, parcels, and points of interest can have subaddresses, address features themselves can have subaddresses. This is for use in validation tasks. Subaddresses are always related to one "parent" address.

The Address class contains the unique set of addresses that can be assigned to addressable objects within Calgary. The Address attribute contains the full address in text form for labeling. The HouseNumber attribute contains the numeric part of the street address, while the HouseAlpha attribute contains the alphabetic part of the street address. Note that storing geometric representations for addresses is not a general requirement for the Address data model; however, since The City of Calgary already maintains geometry for each address, it was included in this case study. The AddressID is a unique identifier for records in the Address class.

In this figure, the larger Building feature has SubAddresses for units 1–5 while the smaller Building feature has SubAddresses for units 6 and 7. This figure shows that the Address feature for 2919 Unwin Rd NW has SubAddresses for all the units from both Buildings.

This design, in which SubAddresses can be held by both Address and Building features (or any other addressable features), provides a relationship path between Addresses and Buildings.

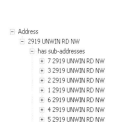

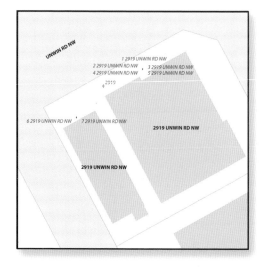

Unit Designators is an attribute value domain included in the model to provide a convenient place for holding standard abbreviations and descriptions of units such as building, suite, and apartment. It is empty in this case study because The City of Calgary does not use it.

In addition to SubAddresses, note all the other relationships in which Address features participate. This shows all the forward (has) and backward (is assigned to) relationship paths for the day care center used in the previous PointOfInterest feature example. These are all examples of standard relational database concepts.

```
Address
  2108 UXBRIDGE DR NW
    has sub-addresses
    has zones
    has names
    is assigned to ownership parcels
      2108 UXBRIDGE DR NW
    is assigned to buildings
      2108 UXBRIDGE DR NW
    is assigned to point of interest
      Dominican Sisters Day Care Centre
```

*An Address feature can participate in many relationships.*

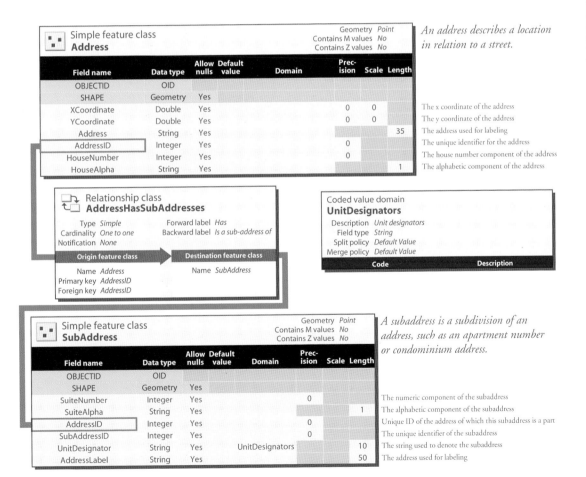

**4**

**Simple feature class**
**Address**

Geometry *Point*
Contains M values *No*
Contains Z values *No*

*An address describes a location in relation to a street.*

| Field name | Data type | Allow nulls | Default value | Domain | Precision | Scale | Length | |
|---|---|---|---|---|---|---|---|---|
| OBJECTID | OID | | | | | | | |
| SHAPE | Geometry | Yes | | | | | | |
| XCoordinate | Double | Yes | | | 0 | 0 | | The x coordinate of the address |
| YCoordinate | Double | Yes | | | 0 | 0 | | The y coordinate of the address |
| Address | String | Yes | | | | | 35 | The address used for labeling |
| AddressID | Integer | Yes | | | 0 | | | The unique identifier for the address |
| HouseNumber | Integer | Yes | | | 0 | | | The house number component of the address |
| HouseAlpha | String | Yes | | | | | 1 | The alphabetic component of the address |

**Relationship class**
**AddressHasSubAddresses**

Type *Simple*      Forward label *Has*
Cardinality *One to one*   Backward label *Is a sub-address of*
Notification *None*

| Origin feature class | Destination feature class |
|---|---|
| Name *Address* | Name *SubAddress* |
| Primary key *AddressID* | |
| Foreign key *AddressID* | |

**Coded value domain**
**UnitDesignators**

Description *Unit designators*
Field type *String*
Split policy *Default Value*
Merge policy *Default Value*

| Code | Description |
|---|---|
| | |

**Simple feature class**
**SubAddress**

Geometry *Point*
Contains M values *No*
Contains Z values *No*

*A subaddress is a subdivision of an address, such as an apartment number or condominium address.*

| Field name | Data type | Allow nulls | Default value | Domain | Precision | Scale | Length | |
|---|---|---|---|---|---|---|---|---|
| OBJECTID | OID | | | | | | | |
| SHAPE | Geometry | Yes | | | | | | |
| SuiteNumber | Integer | Yes | | | 0 | | | The numeric component of the subaddress |
| SuiteAlpha | String | Yes | | | | | 1 | The alphabetic component of the subaddress |
| AddressID | Integer | Yes | | | 0 | | | Unique ID of the address of which this subaddress is a part |
| SubAddressID | Integer | Yes | | | 0 | | | The unique identifier of the subaddress |
| UnitDesignator | String | Yes | | UnitDesignators | | | 10 | The string used to denote the subaddress |
| AddressLabel | String | Yes | | | | | 50 | The address used for labeling |

This section presents the table structures for representing names. Names can have several elements and styles, which vary by region and nation according to user needs.

Address names typically have many elements, such as:

- Prefix direction (N, NW, W, SW, S, SE, E, NE)
- Prefix type (when the street type occurs as a prefix, as in Avenue B, or Rue Madeleine)
- Street name
- Street type (St, Rd, Ave, Ct, Cir, and so on)
- Suffix direction (same content as prefix direction)

Name styles are a convenient means of identifying what components will be used in the name's construction and how the components are assembled to form the name. For example, the following are three specific name styles:

- U.S. streets (E State St.)
- Canadian English streets (MacLeod Trail SW)
- Canadian French streets (Rue Ste.-Catherine)

Some additional style examples were introduced at the beginning of this chapter.

The choice of name style indicates how to translate between the full name and its elements. Note that a name style defines not just the elements to be included in an address, but the order of those elements as well. This is important for building an address locator (also called a geocoding service), which is discussed later in this chapter. In this case, the name style "Canadian English street name" implies that the street name (Ulster) comes before the street type (Rd) and that the directional component is always a suffix, not a prefix.

The address data model described here simplifies the list of address name components to those used in Calgary: Base Name, Type, and Octant (direction suffix), as illustrated in the object inspector below. The Name field represents the fully assembled street name and is used to improve readability for users exploring and editing the data. Having the name elements as separate fields may seem redundant, but this enables easier validation and geocoding.

Address
- 2010 ULSTER RD NW
  - has sub-addresses
  - has zones
  - has names
    - 5374
  - is assigned to ownership parcels
  - is assigned to buildings
  - is assigned to point of interest

Location: [-8877.615808 5659365.281565]

| Field | Value |
| --- | --- |
| OBJECTID | 5374 |
| NameStyle | Canadian English street name |
| NamingAuthorityID | 1 |
| NameID | 5374 |
| BaseName | ULSTER |
| Type | RD |
| Octant | NW |
| Name | ULSTER RD NW |

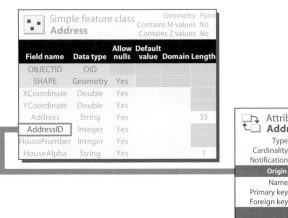

**Simple feature class**
**Address**

| | | Geometry | Point |
|---|---|---|---|
| | | Contains M values | No |
| | | Contains Z values | No |

| Field name | Data type | Allow nulls | Default value | Domain | Length |
|---|---|---|---|---|---|
| OBJECTID | OID | | | | |
| SHAPE | Geometry | Yes | | | |
| XCoordinate | Double | Yes | | | |
| YCoordinate | Double | Yes | | | |
| Address | String | Yes | | | 35 |
| AddressID | Integer | Yes | | | |
| HouseNumber | Integer | Yes | | | |
| HouseAlpha | String | Yes | | | 1 |

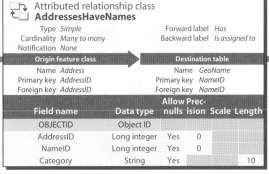

**Attributed relationship class**
**AddressesHaveNames**

| | | | |
|---|---|---|---|
| Type | Simple | Forward label | Has |
| Cardinality | Many to many | Backward label | Is assigned to |
| Notification | None | | |

| Origin feature class | | Destination table | |
|---|---|---|---|
| Name | Address | Name | GeoName |
| Primary key | AddressID | Primary key | NameID |
| Foreign key | AddressID | Foreign key | NameID |

| Field name | Data type | Allow nulls | Precision | Scale | Length |
|---|---|---|---|---|---|
| OBJECTID | Object ID | | | | |
| AddressID | Long integer | Yes | 0 | | |
| NameID | Long integer | Yes | 0 | | |
| Category | String | Yes | | | 10 |

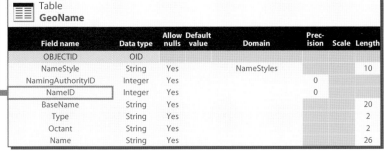

**Table**
**GeoName**

*Geographic names can be associated with geographic features.*

| Field name | Data type | Allow nulls | Default value | Domain | Precision | Scale | Length | |
|---|---|---|---|---|---|---|---|---|
| OBJECTID | OID | | | | | | | |
| NameStyle | String | Yes | | NameStyles | | | 10 | The style of the name |
| NamingAuthorityID | Integer | Yes | | | 0 | | | ID of the authority responsible for assigning the name |
| NameID | Integer | Yes | | | 0 | | | The unique identifier of the name |
| BaseName | String | Yes | | | | | 20 | The base component of the name |
| Type | String | Yes | | | | | 2 | The type component of the name |
| Octant | String | Yes | | | | | 2 | The directional (octant) component of the name |
| Name | String | Yes | | | | | 26 | The full geographic name |

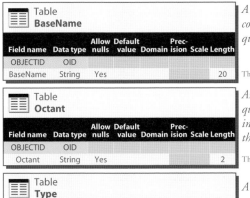

**Table**
**BaseName**

*A base name is a base component on which a fully qualified name is constructed.*

| Field name | Data type | Allow nulls | Default value | Domain | Precision | Scale | Length | |
|---|---|---|---|---|---|---|---|---|
| OBJECTID | OID | | | | | | | |
| BaseName | String | Yes | | | | | 20 | The base component of a name |

**Table**
**Octant**

*An octant is a directional qualifier for a name that indicates in which quadrant of the city the feature is located.*

| Field name | Data type | Allow nulls | Default value | Domain | Precision | Scale | Length | |
|---|---|---|---|---|---|---|---|---|
| OBJECTID | OID | | | | | | | |
| Octant | String | Yes | | | | | 2 | The quadrant component of a name |

**Table**
**Type**

*A type is a qualifier for a name.*

| Field name | Data type | Allow nulls | Default value | Domain | Precision | Scale | Length | |
|---|---|---|---|---|---|---|---|---|
| OBJECTID | OID | | | | | | | |
| Type | String | Yes | | | | | 2 | The type qualifier for a name |

**Coded value domain**
**NameStyles**

| | |
|---|---|
| Description | Geographic name styles |
| Field type | String |
| Split policy | Default value |
| Merge policy | Default value |

| Code | Description |
|---|---|
| CANENSTR | Canadian English street name |

For query and validation purposes, it is useful to identify and relate the various kinds of zones in which an address may occur. This diagram illustrates the structure and relationships between address records and the zones of most interest to The City of Calgary.

As in many nations, Canada's postal delivery system assigns postal codes for every address location in the country. These codes assist in mail sorting and delivery. Canada's postal codes contain two main parts: the FSA, which identifies primary centers from which mail is delivered, such as a post office; and the LDU, which is a subdivision of an FSA. The FSA serves the same role as the five-digit ZIP Code in the United States, and the LDU serves the same role as the last four digits of the nine-digit U.S. ZIP Code (also called ZIP+4).

In addition to the postal zones, the province and city are important, again, for query and validation of an address. Together, the valid combinations of province, city, and postal codes form what could be called the zone domains

of an address database. These are the lists of valid value combinations for zones. Different regions or nations might have alternative components for their zone domains.

The example object inspector on the next page shows sample postal code data for the address of 2010 Ulster Rd NW. In this case, the FSA is T2N, and the LDU is 4C2. The complete postal code would be labeled "T2N 4C2."

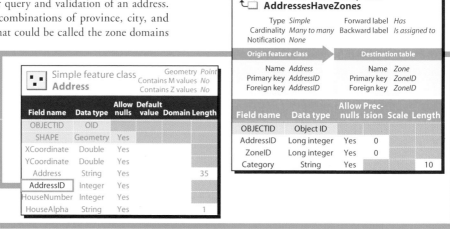

**Attributed relationship class**
**AddressesHaveZones**

| | | | |
|---|---|---|---|
| Type | *Simple* | Forward label | *Has* |
| Cardinality | *Many to many* | Backward label | *Is assigned to* |
| Notification | *None* | | |

**Origin feature class → Destination table**

| | | | |
|---|---|---|---|
| Name | *Address* | Name | *Zone* |
| Primary key | *AddressID* | Primary key | *ZoneID* |
| Foreign key | *AddressID* | Foreign key | *ZoneID* |

**Simple feature class**
**Address**

Geometry *Point*
Contains M values *No*
Contains Z values *No*

| Field name | Data type | Allow nulls | Default value | Domain | Length |
|---|---|---|---|---|---|
| OBJECTID | OID | | | | |
| SHAPE | Geometry | Yes | | | |
| XCoordinate | Double | Yes | | | |
| YCoordinate | Double | Yes | | | |
| Address | String | Yes | | | 35 |
| AddressID | Integer | Yes | | | |
| HouseNumber | Integer | Yes | | | |
| HouseAlpha | String | Yes | | | 1 |

| Field name | Data type | Allow nulls | Precision | Scale | Length |
|---|---|---|---|---|---|
| OBJECTID | Object ID | | | | |
| AddressID | Long integer | Yes | 0 | | |
| ZoneID | Long integer | Yes | 0 | | |
| Category | String | Yes | | | 10 |

**Table**
**Zone**

| Field name | Data type | Allow nulls | Default value | Domain | Precision | Scale | Length |
|---|---|---|---|---|---|---|---|
| OBJECTID | OID | | | | | | |
| ZoneID | Integer | Yes | | | 0 | | |
| PostalCode | String | Yes | | | | | 6 |
| ProvinceID | Integer | Yes | | | 0 | | |
| CityID | Integer | Yes | | | 0 | | |

*A valid combination of city, province, and postal code that can be assigned to addresses*

The unique identifier of the zone
The six-character postal code
The unique identifier of the province
The unique identifier of the city

Notice that CityLimit is a polygon feature class, in contrast to the other zones, which are table records. Postal codes could also have been implemented as geographic features, but the most correct type of feature would be a multipoint, since each postal code is actually defined by the address points it serves and not by a fixed polygon shape. However, maintaining the geometries of postal codes is not a primary business function of The City of Calgary.

FSAs may also be modeled as polygons approximating the spatial extent of a multipoint, but these are not always completely accurate. If spatial representation is not needed, FSAs may be modeled as nonspatial objects.

However, there is a significant benefit to modeling zones as polygons; this allows users to take advantage of GIS spatial relationships to help validate addresses. For example, to validate relationships between addresses and zones, the database contains two relationships: the explicit relationship defined in the address data model and the spatial relationship that can be discovered using GIS tools.

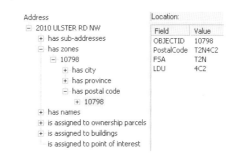

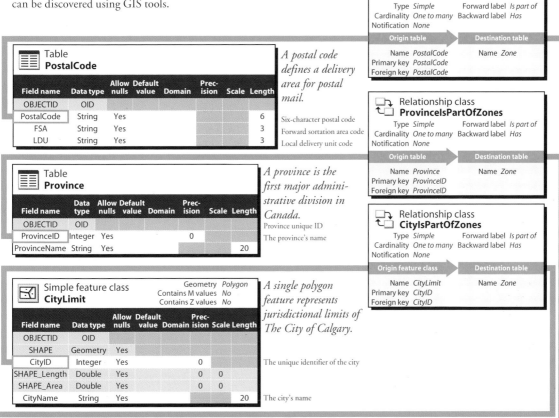

**4**

### Relationship class
**PostalCodeIsPartOfZones**

| | | | |
|---|---|---|---|
| Type | *Simple* | Forward label | *Is part of* |
| Cardinality | *One to many* | Backward label | *Has* |
| Notification | *None* | | |

| Origin table | Destination table |
|---|---|
| Name *PostalCode* | Name *Zone* |
| Primary key *PostalCode* | |
| Foreign key *PostalCode* | |

### Relationship class
**ProvinceIsPartOfZones**

| | | | |
|---|---|---|---|
| Type | *Simple* | Forward label | *Is part of* |
| Cardinality | *One to many* | Backward label | *Has* |
| Notification | *None* | | |

| Origin table | Destination table |
|---|---|
| Name *Province* | Name *Zone* |
| Primary key *ProvinceID* | |
| Foreign key *ProvinceID* | |

### Relationship class
**CityIsPartOfZones**

| | | | |
|---|---|---|---|
| Type | *Simple* | Forward label | *Is part of* |
| Cardinality | *One to many* | Backward label | *Has* |
| Notification | *None* | | |

| Origin feature class | Destination table |
|---|---|
| Name *CityLimit* | Name *Zone* |
| Primary key *CityID* | |
| Foreign key *CityID* | |

### Table
**PostalCode**

| Field name | Data type | Allow nulls | Default value | Domain | Prec-ision | Scale | Length |
|---|---|---|---|---|---|---|---|
| OBJECTID | OID | | | | | | |
| PostalCode | String | Yes | | | | | 6 |
| FSA | String | Yes | | | | | 3 |
| LDU | String | Yes | | | | | 3 |

*A postal code defines a delivery area for postal mail.*

Six-character postal code
Forward sortation area code
Local delivery unit code

### Table
**Province**

| Field name | Data type | Allow nulls | Default value | Domain | Prec-ision | Scale | Length |
|---|---|---|---|---|---|---|---|
| OBJECTID | OID | | | | | | |
| ProvinceID | Integer | Yes | | | 0 | | |
| ProvinceName | String | Yes | | | | | 20 |

*A province is the first major administrative division in Canada.*

Province unique ID
The province's name

### Simple feature class
**CityLimit**

Geometry *Polygon*
Contains M values *No*
Contains Z values *No*

| Field name | Data type | Allow nulls | Default value | Domain | Prec-ision | Scale | Length |
|---|---|---|---|---|---|---|---|
| OBJECTID | OID | | | | | | |
| SHAPE | Geometry | Yes | | | | | |
| CityID | Integer | Yes | | | 0 | | |
| SHAPE_Length | Double | Yes | | | 0 | 0 | |
| SHAPE_Area | Double | Yes | | | 0 | 0 | |
| CityName | String | Yes | | | | | 20 |

*A single polygon feature represents jurisdictional limits of The City of Calgary.*

The unique identifier of the city

The city's name

Range zones aid in the validation of address ranges by defining valid combinations of province, city, and FSA. While this design is tailored to Canada's postal delivery system, it is a useful approach that can be adapted to many local address databases.

While the zones just described provide important location and validation information, it is possible for users to create combinations of city, province, and postal code that are incorrect, even though the values for each zone, taken individually, might be correct. To prevent such errors, the RangeZone table is used to store all the valid combinations of the key zones. This type of table, containing valid combinations of multiple fields, is often called a valid value table and is used in many other application domains mentioned in this book.

The diagram below illustrates a relationship between the RangeZone table and three other tables, Province, City-Limit, and ForwardSortationArea, used in Canada's postal delivery system.

In the example to the right, a street's AddressRange has been opened, revealing associations with RangeZones and Names records. The associated RangeZone record shows the address range to be in the T2B forward sortation area. (In Canada, full postal codes are assigned to specific addresses, not to address ranges.) The CityID and ProvinceID refer to Calgary and Alberta, respectively.

Different sets of zones may be used for different features, depending on business requirements. For example, address ranges might have additional zones for emergency response (E-911), school districts, or voting districts.

| Table **RangeZone** | | | | | | | | |
|---|---|---|---|---|---|---|---|
| Field name | Data type | Allow nulls | Default value | Domain | Prec-ision | Scale | Length |
| OBJECTID | OID | | | | | | |
| ZoneID | Integer | Yes | | | 0 | | |
| FSA | String | Yes | | | | | 3 |
| CityID | Integer | Yes | | | 0 | | |
| ProvinceID | Integer | Yes | | | 0 | | |

*A range zone is a valid combination of city, province, and forward sortation area.*

The unique identifier of the zone
The forward sortation area code
The unique identifier of the city
The unique identifier of the province

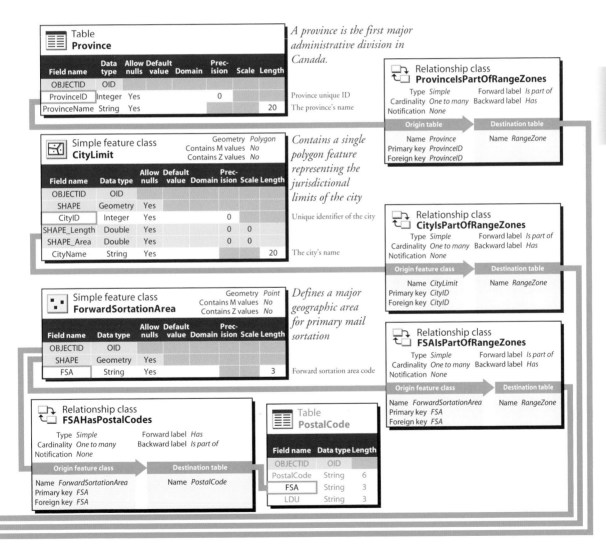

### Table
### Province

| Field name | Data type | Allow nulls | Default value | Domain | Precision | Scale | Length |
|---|---|---|---|---|---|---|---|
| OBJECTID | OID | | | | | | |
| ProvinceID | Integer | Yes | | | 0 | | |
| ProvinceName | String | Yes | | | | | 20 |

*A province is the first major administrative division in Canada.*

Province unique ID

The province's name

### Simple feature class
### CityLimit

Geometry *Polygon*
Contains M values *No*
Contains Z values *No*

| Field name | Data type | Allow nulls | Default value | Domain | Precision | Scale | Length |
|---|---|---|---|---|---|---|---|
| OBJECTID | OID | | | | | | |
| SHAPE | Geometry | Yes | | | | | |
| CityID | Integer | Yes | | | 0 | | |
| SHAPE_Length | Double | Yes | | | 0 | 0 | |
| SHAPE_Area | Double | Yes | | | 0 | 0 | |
| CityName | String | Yes | | | | | 20 |

*Contains a single polygon feature representing the jurisdictional limits of the city*

Unique identifier of the city

The city's name

### Simple feature class
### ForwardSortationArea

Geometry *Point*
Contains M values *No*
Contains Z values *No*

| Field name | Data type | Allow nulls | Default value | Domain | Precision | Scale | Length |
|---|---|---|---|---|---|---|---|
| OBJECTID | OID | | | | | | |
| SHAPE | Geometry | Yes | | | | | |
| FSA | String | Yes | | | | | 3 |

*Defines a major geographic area for primary mail sortation*

Forward sortation area code

### Relationship class
### ProvinceIsPartOfRangeZones

| | | |
|---|---|---|
| Type *Simple* | Forward label *Is part of* |
| Cardinality *One to many* | Backward label *Has* |
| Notification *None* | |

| Origin table | Destination table |
|---|---|
| Name *Province* | Name *RangeZone* |
| Primary key *ProvinceID* | |
| Foreign key *ProvinceID* | |

### Relationship class
### CityIsPartOfRangeZones

| | | |
|---|---|---|
| Type *Simple* | Forward label *Is part of* |
| Cardinality *One to many* | Backward label *Has* |
| Notification *None* | |

| Origin feature class | Destination table |
|---|---|
| Name *CityLimit* | Name *RangeZone* |
| Primary key *CityID* | |
| Foreign key *CityID* | |

### Relationship class
### FSAIsPartOfRangeZones

| | | |
|---|---|---|
| Type *Simple* | Forward label *Is part of* |
| Cardinality *One to many* | Backward label *Has* |
| Notification *None* | |

| Origin feature class | Destination table |
|---|---|
| Name *ForwardSortationArea* | Name *RangeZone* |
| Primary key *FSA* | |
| Foreign key *FSA* | |

### Relationship class
### FSAHasPostalCodes

| | | |
|---|---|---|
| Type *Simple* | Forward label *Has* |
| Cardinality *One to many* | Backward label *Is part of* |
| Notification *None* | |

| Origin feature class | Destination table |
|---|---|
| Name *ForwardSortationArea* | Name *PostalCode* |
| Primary key *FSA* | |
| Foreign key *FSA* | |

### Table
### PostalCode

| Field name | Data type | Length |
|---|---|---|
| OBJECTID | OID | |
| PostalCode | String | 6 |
| FSA | String | 3 |
| LDU | String | 3 |

4

Now that the relevant components have all been introduced, this diagram illustrates the structure and relationships between AddressRanges, Zones, and Names. These classes are joined through attributed relationship classes.

As previously discussed, a separate record in the Address-Range table is used for each side of the street. This approach enables a street to be associated with multiple address ranges, each with potentially different conditions on opposite sides of the street. There are many reasons why this may be useful:

- Different address sequencing or no addressing at all, such as along a beach front

- Different schemes assigned by different jurisdictions

- Different schemes for different applications

The Parity field value for an AddressRange record specifies whether the address range is even or odd, mixed, or unknown.

In addition, each side of a street can belong to a different postal delivery zone. The association between address ranges and range zones is illustrated below; an example is shown on the next page (see object inspector diagram).

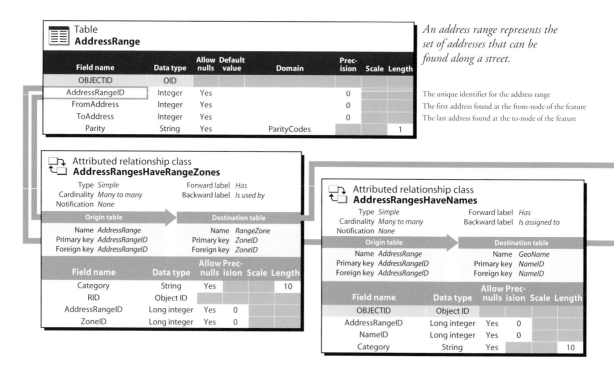

*An address range represents the set of addresses that can be found along a street.*

Table
**AddressRange**

| Field name | Data type | Allow nulls | Default value | Domain | Precision | Scale | Length |
|---|---|---|---|---|---|---|---|
| OBJECTID | OID | | | | | | |
| AddressRangeID | Integer | Yes | | | 0 | | |
| FromAddress | Integer | Yes | | | 0 | | |
| ToAddress | Integer | Yes | | | 0 | | |
| Parity | String | Yes | | ParityCodes | | | 1 |

The unique identifier for the address range
The first address found at the from-node of the feature
The last address found at the to-node of the feature

Attributed relationship class
**AddressRangesHaveRangeZones**

Type *Simple*          Forward label *Has*
Cardinality *Many to many*   Backward label *Is used by*
Notification *None*

| Origin table | | Destination table | |
|---|---|---|---|
| Name *AddressRange* | | Name *RangeZone* | |
| Primary key *AddressRangeID* | | Primary key *ZoneID* | |
| Foreign key *AddressRangeID* | | Foreign key *ZoneID* | |

| Field name | Data type | Allow nulls | Precision | Scale | Length |
|---|---|---|---|---|---|
| Category | String | Yes | | | 10 |
| RID | Object ID | | | | |
| AddressRangeID | Long integer | Yes | 0 | | |
| ZoneID | Long integer | Yes | 0 | | |

Attributed relationship class
**AddressRangesHaveNames**

Type *Simple*          Forward label *Has*
Cardinality *Many to many*   Backward label *Is assigned to*
Notification *None*

| Origin table | | Destination table | |
|---|---|---|---|
| Name *AddressRange* | | Name *GeoName* | |
| Primary key *AddressRangeID* | | Primary key *NameID* | |
| Foreign key *AddressRangeID* | | Foreign key *NameID* | |

| Field name | Data type | Allow nulls | Precision | Scale | Length |
|---|---|---|---|---|---|
| OBJECTID | Object ID | | | | |
| AddressRangeID | Long integer | Yes | 0 | | |
| NameID | Long integer | Yes | 0 | | |
| Category | String | Yes | | | 10 |

Local Street
⊟ ULSTER RD NW
   ⊟ has address ranges
      ⊟ 14055
         ⊞ has range zones
         ⊟ has names
            ⊞ 5374
      ⊟ 61207
         ⊞ has range zones
         ⊞ has names

Location: (-8886.743319 5659350.449359)

| Field | Value |
|---|---|
| OBJECTID | 5374 |
| NameStyle | Canadian English street name |
| NamingAuthorityID | 1 |
| NameID | 5374 |
| BaseName | ULSTER |
| Type | RD |
| Octant | NW |
| Name | ULSTER RD NW |

*In this data model, names are associated with streets through a specific address range. This allows a street to have different names, such as for different zones in which it might participate.*

**4**

Coded value domain
**ParityCodes**
Description *Address range parity*
Field type *String*
Split policy *Default value*
Merge policy *Default value*

| Code | Description |
|---|---|
| E | Even |
| O | Odd |
| M | Mixed |
| U | Unknown |

Table
**RangeZone**

| Field name | Data type | Allow nulls | Default value | Domain | Precision | Scale | Length | |
|---|---|---|---|---|---|---|---|---|
| OBJECTID | OID | | | | | | | |
| ZoneID | Integer | Yes | | | 0 | | | The unique identifier of the zone |
| FSA | String | Yes | | | | | 3 | The forward sortation area code |
| CityID | Integer | Yes | | | 0 | | | The unique identifier of the city |
| ProvinceID | Integer | Yes | | | 0 | | | The unique identifier of the province |

*A range zone is a valid combination of city, province, and forward sortation area.*

Table
**GeoName**

| Field name | Data type | Allow nulls | Default value | Domain | Precision | Scale | Length | |
|---|---|---|---|---|---|---|---|---|
| OBJECTID | OID | | | | | | | |
| NameStyle | String | Yes | | NameStyles | | | 10 | The style of the name |
| NamingAuthorityID | Integer | Yes | | | 0 | | | ID of the authority responsible for assigning the name |
| NameID | Integer | Yes | | | 0 | | | The unique identifier of the name |
| BaseName | String | Yes | | | | | 20 | The base component of the name |
| Type | String | Yes | | | | | 2 | The type component of the name |
| Octant | String | Yes | | | | | 2 | The directional (octant) component of the name |
| Name | String | Yes | | | | | 26 | The full geographic name |

*A geographic name is a name that can be associated with geographic features.*

Address lookup, also called geocoding, is a common use of an address database. The data model presented so far is designed to support address data editing and validation, with less attention to geocoding. This section discusses that distinction and explains how to adapt an address database for use in geocoding.

The most common use of address data in a GIS is for geocoding. This is the process of matching an address (called an input address) to reference geographic data features, then providing a location, such as a point (an x,y coordinate). This section discusses the geocoding process using a simple example, then presents a number of approaches for using composite locators.

## UNDERSTANDING AN ADDRESS LOCATOR

The figure on the right shows the main steps that a geocoding engine would perform in processing a map lookup request for the address 123 W. Burmingham Dr., with the postal code 92373. First the address is parsed, abbreviations standardized, and pertinent elements indexed.

To complete the spatial lookup, however, there must first be a reference geographic dataset with a spatial extent that completely encloses any potential address that might need to be geocoded. The reference dataset must also contain complete and current address data with the same style of address elements as the input addresses to be matched. This data model is about designing and building that reference geographic dataset.

The geocoding engine searches for matches between the input address and the reference dataset and may find a number of possible matches, some better than others. The geocoding engine allows the user to control the precision of matches; under different circumstances, users may wish more or less fuzziness in the matching process. User-defined filtering options result in matches presented to the user, such as the two candidate records in the example shown. The user would pick one of these, and the map view would highlight the location of the selected address.

In the reference dataset, each element of an address (house number, prefix direction, street name, street type, suffix direction, and so on) would be in a separate field and indexed for address geocoding performance, as illustrated in the previous pages. The key to achieving maximum performance is

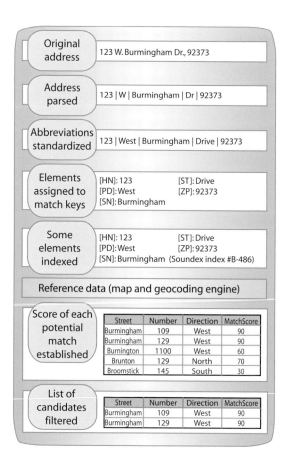

to keep all the address attributes within the same table as the addressable features, such as streets and buildings. In contrast to this, the data model described so far in this chapter divides the address elements among several tables that must be joined to construct a complete address. This eliminates considerable duplication of data and leads to a more maintainable address database. But this approach adversely affects the performance of geocoding. For high-speed geocoding, a flattened, denormalized data model is best, but this would not be the most appropriate model for editing. Therefore, a high-speed geocoding model is normally constructed from this normalized editing database and used for building an address locator in ArcGIS.

## COMPOSITE LOCATORS

Composite locators are built to work with multiple sources of address reference data to perform geocoding. This generally means working with more than one feature class having address data.

### Fallback locator

Different feature classes often have different levels of precision in their address information. For example, the address information in an AddressPoint feature would be much more precise than the address information in a forward sortation area. This difference in precision can be used to advantage in building what is called a fallback composite locator. You may have already encountered such a locator using one of the common Web-based address locator services, which may fall back from the precise address to just the street feature as a whole when the address number cannot be located on that street or in that postal code area.

However, a composite locator can be created that uses more feature classes for fallback, such as (in order of decreasing precision) AddressPoint, Parcel, Street, and FSA. In this example, if the user enters an address for lookup that is not contained in the reference set of AddressPoints, then the locator would fall back to the next level of precision, in this case Parcel feature class, and attempt to match the nearest parcels to the requested address. If this step fails, then the locator would fall back to the Street feature class and attempt to find the street indicated in the address. If this succeeds, the user is presented with the matched streets and taken to a point on the map interpolated on the selected street. If the street lookup fails, then the locator would attempt to find the closest FSA and position the user at an arbitrary location, such as the FSA mail distribution facility.

Besides serving as a means to assign at least general location information for an address that is not in the reference dataset, a fallback locator can serve well in other situations. For example, a police or emergency response operator might want to see in what zone (FSA, police or fire district, or other zone) the address falls to alert the correct response team. A property appraiser might want to know which parcel corresponds to an address point.

Fallback locators tend to be designed and programmed for specific applications. Such a locator must be designed to work with the fields and address styles of the feature classes included.

### Country-based locator

Another form of composite locator has been designed for use with ArcGIS StreetMap™. This locator actually consists of several country-specific locators. In the initial address lookup dialog box, the user may enter address information, such as street, city, postal code, and country. The country code is required, and through this selection, the initial dialog box knows which country-specific locator to invoke for the lookup. Each country locator is designed for a single address style and is thus able to carry out the lookup without troubling the user with the differences in format from one country to the next.

A higher level of sophistication for this approach could be achieved by incorporating a fallback locator for each country.

### Cross vendor locator

Street maps for address lookup and routing have become very competitive in North America, with vendors and datasets, such as Census TIGER/Line, GDT, Navtech, Tele Atlas, and StreetMap covering most or all of Canada, the United States, and Mexico. These sources vary in their content and accuracy, so it may be useful to try accessing them all in a particular address search. A composite locator can be built that searches through all of them from a single address lookup request. Such a locator would have to recognize the specific format and address style of each vendor's dataset and apply the lookup criteria accordingly.

As with the country-based composite locator, vendor- and country-specific fallback locators could be combined with each vendor-based address locator for further flexibility.

## FURTHER STUDY

If your address database will be used for geocoding, it is recommended that you read *Geocoding in ArcGIS* (ESRI 2003), which details the various aspects of creating, modifying, and maintaining address locators.

This case study for The City of Calgary's addressing database distills a considerable amount of design evolution that took place over the course of one year. With appropriate GIS tools, the resulting data model is well suited to the task of address management within the local government.

## SUMMARY

This chapter has presented several aspects and issues of address structure and composition. The main aspects affecting this data model design included:

### Some feature classes can have addresses

Streets, buildings, points of interest, and parcels were chosen as addressable feature classes by The City of Calgary. A single feature can have one or more addresses, and an address can be used by more than one feature. Other feature classes that could potentially require addresses might include rivers, canals, and lakes. For The City of Calgary, this choice was driven primarily by municipal functions, such as taxation, permitting, voter registration, and emergency services. Other communities may have alternative purposes and criteria for determining addressability.

### Some feature classes can have subaddresses

Buildings, points of interest, and parcels could have relationships to subaddresses, as well as to their main address. This is a simple and effective way of representing apartment, office, and condominium units, as well as other subdivisions of the primary feature. In addition, the address records themselves could have a relationship to relevant subaddress records. This provides an alternative means of navigating between features and their addresses.

### Streets can have address ranges

Numeric address ranges can be created and applied to street features. A different range can be defined for each side of a street, and additional ranges associated with alternative street names can be defined. A single street (made up of distinct street segments between intersections) can have multiple address ranges, and a particular address range can be used by multiple streets.

### Addresses have multipart names

A complete street address can have many parts, including but not limited to:

- Numeric address value or range
- Base name, such as "Main" in Main Street
- Street type, such as Street, Road, and Avenue
- Directional prefix and suffix

The address model used by The City of Calgary does not require a directional prefix, but it frequently uses a directional suffix. Other national and regional conventions may call for additional components. Numerous address styles can be managed.

To support efficient labeling and human readability, the fully assembled name may also be stored as a field of each addressable feature class.

### Addresses can have many zones

For editing and address validation purposes, it is useful to define various zones corresponding to states or provinces, city limits, and postal codes. Canada Post defines forward sortation areas as postal delivery districts, some form of which is used in many other nations as well (these correspond to U.S. postal ZIP Codes). Each address or address range then has a set of relationships with the relevant zones.

### The data model design is adaptive

This data model can be readily adapted to other national or regional conventions by changing or adding address elements, field names, and lookup tables of valid values (such as street names, street types, and direction codes).

### Centralized address databases are useful

In local governments and other large organizations, many different departments or agencies typically have responsibility for address maintenance at some level. To the extent that these agencies can work with a shared resource with a focus on completeness and correctness, considerable duplication of data (and potential errors) can be avoided. The data model design presented here lends itself to use in such an enterprise environment.

## REFERENCES AND FURTHER READING

Address Reference Guide (draft). 2002. The City of Calgary, Alberta, Canada.

Federal Geographic Data Committee. 2003. Address Data Content Standard, Public Review Draft, Version 2. Washington, D.C. URL: http://www.fgdc.gov/standards/status/sub2_4.html.

*Geocoding in ArcGIS*. 2003. Redlands, California: ESRI Press.

T575003 Version 2, The Canadian Addressing Standard Handbook. 2003. Canada Post Corporation. URL: http://www.canadapost.ca/personal/tools/pg/.

USPS Publication 28. 2000. Postal Addressing Standards. Washington, D.C. URL: http://www.usps.gov/publications.

## ACKNOWLEDGMENTS

Thanks to Glenn McKean and Gord Rasmussen of The City of Calgary and Dippan Shukle of Intera Solutions, Inc., for sharing data, time, and experience working with the addressing data model. Jonathan Bailey of ESRI provided data modeling and content for this chapter.

## CREDITS

Many of the graphics, photographs, and map data were provided by The City of Calgary.

The postal codes were extracted from The City of Calgary's address data, but the geometries for the FSAs are from the 2002 ESRI *Data & Maps* CD–ROM.

## FURTHER RESOURCES

Find more data models at ESRI ArcOnline. Follow the Addressing link from http://support.esri.com/datamodels.

*4*

*This chapter presents a working parcel data model case study that builds on contemporary GIS methods and practices. While this parcel data model case study is largely based on the needs of U.S. counties, many of the key concepts are of practical use worldwide. To reach the broad parcel user community, the thought processes and design decisions for this data model are documented in this chapter.*

5

**W**alk into any local government building and you will find a multitude of maps draped on the walls—maps of jurisdictional boundaries, maps showing land use and zoning, maps used to delineate electoral districts, maps for managing environmental areas, and maps of municipal utility service.

You will also see public sector staff using interactive map displays to assist property owners. Citizens can access public information through map-based interfaces on the Internet as well.

Parcel maps are the cornerstone of local government information management. Nearly all the information that flows through local governments contains a reference to a place: an address, a location, an area of land. The parcel is the basic unit of geography for local governments.

This parcel data model gives GIS professionals at local governments and other organizations a powerful start on the intelligent creation, mapping, maintenance, and analysis of parcel data. In this chapter, you will learn about cartographic practices for parcel maps, distinctions and issues for modeling different kinds of parcels, and the GIS database schema for parcels.

This chapter documents a GIS data model for land parcels developed by a consortium of interested agencies and individuals led by Nancy Von Meyer of Fairview Industries. This parcel data model was developed in conjunction with, and is an implementation that supports, the Federal Geographic Data Committee (FGDC) Cadastral Data Content Standard (FGDC, 1999). This chapter discusses both the general land parcel data model as well as the adoption and customization of this schema by Oakland County in Michigan. A link to the most recent version of the Oakland County parcel data model is provided in the Further Resources section at the end of this chapter.

# Parcels and
# the cadastre

Parcel maps are essential to government services and economic activity. Shown here are several tasks involved in creating new land parcels at a county government in the United States, from the time a subdivision of land is created to the sale of lots. Note that the department and agency names and tasks performed can vary among organizations. The departments and work flows described here are a generalization of a common process used in the United States for land division approval, recording, and maintenance.

## LAND DIVISION APPROVAL

Many departments at the local government level play a role in accepting, process-ing, evaluating, and approving a new subdivision. These can be planning agencies, highway or transportation departments, zoning departments, regional authorities, and even state agencies. These agencies work with developers, property owners, the public, and elected officials to formulate a subdivision document that can be submitted for approval.

## LAND DIVISION RECORDING

The Register of Deeds or County Recorder reviews the subdivision docu-ment for format and completeness. The subdivision docu-ment is recorded at a date and time, and an index describing the document is prepared. The index com-monly contains the grantor, which is the current owner; the grantee, which is the purchaser; the name of the subdivision; and a general indication of the location of the subdivision. The subdivision location is often kept in a tract index, which facilitates searching for and finding recorded documents based on general location.

Business process: **Establish new parcels**

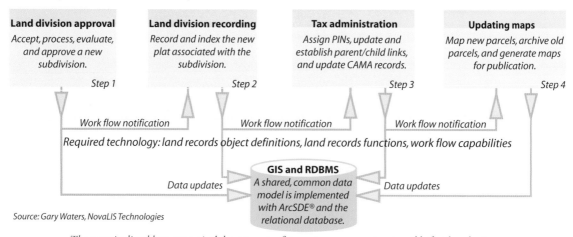

Source: Gary Waters, NovaLIS Technologies

*The agencies listed here are typical departments of a county government responsible for these business steps; however, considerable variation exists in the organization of county governments.*

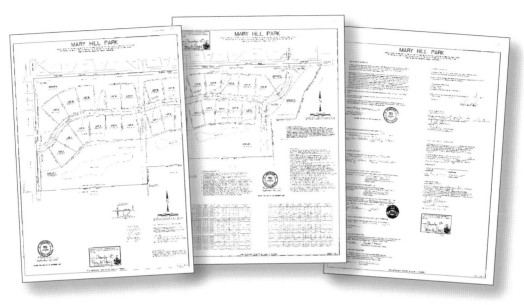

*Subdivision plats are courtesy of Waukesha County, Wisconsin.*

## TAX ADMINISTRATION

The assessment agency, also called the real property, property tax, or tax lister department, generates and maintains the value and tax information about newly created parcels.

This department assigns a parcel or tax identification number, called the parcel identification number (PIN) or tax map sheet number (TMS). The parcel number associates a parcel's appraised value, tax value information, ownership, site addresses, and mailing addresses for taxation and mapping. In some jurisdictions, the assessed and taxable values are managed in a computer-assisted mass appraisal (CAMA) system. In terms of work flow, the final appraised and taxable values may be assigned on an annual or semiannual basis rather than on a per-transaction basis. Another important function of the parcel number and the parcel mapping is to manage the historical lineage of the parcel. This historical lineage is important for tracking real property taxes and land division status over time.

## UPDATING MAPS

The mapping department is a generic title for a local government department or office that produces parcel maps. This mapping function may occur before the assessment process and involves mapping all land parcels onto the county or township maps. The specifics of how the maps are organized into map sheets or files vary widely from place to place. The general process is to determine the location of the new subdivision, archive the existing parcels, and replace them with the new parcels created by the subdivision. In some jurisdictions, a graphical lineage of the parcel ownership is maintained with the mapping so a graphical

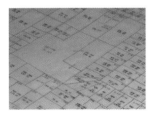

chain of title can be easily derived. The mapping department typically provides maps to other departments and to post on the agency's Web site or generates hardcopies and associated reports for the public and other users.

Parcel maps can be used to define and work with various segments of government information management, including rights and interests, land use zoning, public access areas, building permits, and public works projects. Understanding how parcel maps will be used in your own jurisdiction will help focus the database and system designs to better meet your needs. This section discusses a few common applications.

## RESEARCHING TITLES

Once a parcel is recorded, entered into the assessment system, and mapped, it becomes available for use by other agencies and the public. One common use, as a complement to working with a grantor–grantee index, is to properly research a title. This is a process of working through the chain of title from the current owner to each previous owner until all the owners for a piece of land have been documented. The resulting document is sometimes called an abstract or an abstract of title. In some states, these title searches go back 30 years in what is sometimes called a 30-year marketable title. In other states, the full title is researched.

Title research is a common task, and a GIS can be helpful in providing graphical support to the chain of title.

## HISTORICAL PARCEL MAPS

While historical parcel maps can support developing a chain of title, they are also important for establishing prior and historical land use, determining historical patterns of ownership, and supporting the initial automation of the parcel maps. In some areas, these historical hardcopy

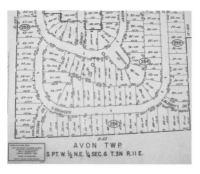

maps are scanned so the original image of the map can be referenced digitally. Many local governments also store historical aerial photography, which is useful for environmental analysis and other research.

## LOCATING CUSTOMER INFORMATION

The ultimate use of the parcel map is to serve the government and its citizens. In any jurisdiction it is important to find, retrieve, and present parcel information to a citizen, taxpayer, elected official, developer, department, state agency, or anyone requesting information. How customer information is located depends on how it is indexed. By linking information to the maps in a GIS, the tasks involved in determining the location of data and responding to requests becomes easier and faster.

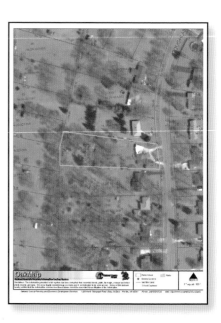

In Oakland County, Michigan, local governments provide citizen kiosks with simple, flexible tools to get answers to the most common queries as well as hardcopy maps for a nominal fee.

## EMERGENCY OPERATIONS

Parcel maps can be used to support emergency, fire, and police operations as well as other critical government functions. For emergency operations, the parcel maps and their related data can identify the current owner; determine whether there is a structure on the property and, if so, what type it is; and provide access to additional landownership information.

For example, police and fire officials may need to contact a commercial building owner if there is a fire at night or in the aftermath of a storm. The parcel maps, with their related information, can be useful for determining damage assessments, conducting followup checks of neighborhoods, and notifying landowners of remediation activities. The parcel information provides an important access point during emergencies for linking data from many sources. This is an increasingly urgent requirement, as the demands of responding to emergency situations are calling for greater integration and collaboration among all government GIS data holdings and services.

## Public sector uses for GIS

- Land use and urban growth planning and permit tracking
- Economic development planning
- Infrastructure and transportation planning and management
- Needs assessments and epidemiological analyses
- Legislative redistricting
- Crime tracking and law enforcement planning
- School districting and school bus routing
- Educational planning across secondary, university, and technical school levels
- Comparison of program effectiveness across jurisdictions
- Taxation analysis and record keeping
- Benchmarking in human services
- Public health risk analysis
- Site selection for service facilities, housing, and so on
- Site selection for locally unwanted land uses, such as landfills and prisons
- Emergency management
- Environmental monitoring and wildlife and greenway corridor siting
- Public housing and housing weatherization and rehabilitation planning
- Public information systems

Source: John O'Looney, *Beyond Maps: GIS and Decision Making in Local Government*, ESRI Press, 2000

5

This section covers some of the ways that data sources are transformed into parcel maps. These methods can be combined—Oakland County uses coordinate geometry supplemented with digital orthophotography. Data sources can vary greatly in accuracy and in automation cost. Methods that may be least expensive for initial compilation, such as scanning parcel maps and heads-up digitizing, can be the most expensive options for long-term maintenance due to lower accuracy and the resulting potential need for extra work to resolve property description conflicts that arise in the normal flow of updating parcel maps.

There are several options for counties to convert their hardcopy parcel maps to a GIS. To get the initial database constructed within a reasonable time and cost, users can digitize scanned maps or perform heads-up digitizing from orthophotos. However, for ongoing maintenance of the parcel information, they may choose to improve the accuracy of the GIS data with coordinate geometry (COGO) descriptions, derived from surveys or legal descriptions, or with actual survey measurement data in the database.

Each method varies considerably in terms of accuracy and cost. The potential error in digitized maps comes from many factors—accuracy of the original field measurements, scale of the source map, stretching of the map, original drafting accuracy, digitizing accuracy, and other factors. In contrast, the accuracy of primary sources depends predominantly on the survey measurements. The more accurate the data, the better suited it is to integration with other feature classes and map layers (vertical integration).

The use of COGO, or other survey-based approaches, implies different data models, such as COGO attributes on features, or survey datasets in the database. This level of sophistication is becoming increasingly important as communities and agencies seek to build "multipurpose cadastral systems where information about natural resources, planning, land use, land value, and land titles, including Western and indigenous interests, can be integrated for a range of business purposes" (Williamson and Ting, 1999).

*Historic tax maps are courtesy of Cook County, Illinois.*

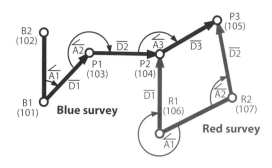

## COORDINATE GEOMETRY DESCRIPTIONS

COGO is a computational method and, in modern times, a widely used software tool for parcel mapping. COGO transforms field survey measurements into accurate geographical positions. Legal property descriptions from deeds and title reports may be used as COGO input as well.

In the parcel data model, the Boundary feature class (discussed later) has been made COGO-ready by including certain attributes to hold traverse data: Direction, Distance, Radius, Delta, Tangent, Arclength, and Side. These are used by COGO editing tools during parcel creation and updating.

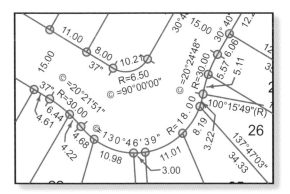

Topology rules for use with COGO editing are straightforward; any feature classes that define the parcels and their boundaries participate in the same topology. The COGO feature classes have a higher accuracy rank than other feature classes. This is discussed in more detail later in this chapter.

## MEASUREMENT-BASED CADASTRAL SYSTEM

Integrating direct land survey data with a GIS provides a way to achieve highly accurate tax maps. These could be computer assisted drafting (CAD) data converted to a GIS and georeferenced to the Public Land Survey System (PLSS) or other control network. For greatest accuracy, this approach would employ cadastral adjustment to reconcile differences between multiple surveys of the same points and lines. This is a mathematical process requiring actual survey field data. To take advantage of this approach, survey information in the form of survey points, measurements, computations, and coordinates would be linked to appropriate feature classes in the GIS. When an update to a survey occurs, these linked or survey-aware GIS features are also updated accordingly. Note that the ability to integrate survey data and define survey-aware feature classes depends on the GIS used. Survey-aware feature classes would typically include TaxParcel, SimultaneousConveyance, Corner, Boundary, and possibly others, as discussed later in this chapter.

The use of survey-aware feature classes influences how topology rules are defined. The geometry of survey-aware features can be adjusted as survey points are updated. The feature classes that share geometry with the survey-aware features must also be adjusted. Thus, the survey-aware feature classes should all participate in the same topology. Furthermore, all feature classes that share geometry in a topology with a survey-aware feature class must also be made survey-aware.

**5**

*Costs and benefits of methods for parcel map automation*

| | Vectorized maps | Digitized orthophotos | Coordinate geometry | Measurement-based cadastre |
|---|---|---|---|---|
| **Accuracy** | Lowest * | Better | Good | Highest |
| **Compilation cost** | Lowest | Moderately higher | Much higher | Higher |
| **Maintenance cost** | Highest | Moderately lower | Lower | Lowest |
| **Vertical integration** | Poor * | Slightly higher | Good | Best |
| **Benefits** | Fast way to get started | Fast way to get started | Detects conflicts | Integrates GIS and legal descriptions |

*\* Improves with quality of ground control network*

The collection of thematic layers in this section represents the key components of the conceptual design for the land parcel data model. Users often choose subsets of these layers to support their available data and institutional practices. All these layers need not be within the user's authority to control but could be drawn from other departments, agencies, or elsewhere on the Internet.

Data collection and maintenance policies can vary widely. This model can be adapted to suit a wide range of institutional settings and still support a set of common concepts that promote data sharing.

The parcel is the heart of the FGDC Cadastral Data Content Standard (FGDC, 1999). This geodatabase model has been developed to be consistent with the FGDC standard.

## PARCEL THEMATIC LAYERS

The parcel model has eight key thematic layers as shown on the next page. The foundation layers for cadastral information are parcel frameworks and corners and boundaries. Next, ownership parcels and tax parcels are the fundamental parcel information required by most jurisdictions. The top two themes, parcel-related uses and the administrative areas, are derived layers for using parcel data with local government.

Digital orthophotography represents the base spatial reference theme and is often used for heads-up digitizing of parcels.

A continuously maintained survey is often used to manage precise locations for corners and boundaries. Surveys are managed in a comprehensive survey dataset.

Corner and boundary information is used to construct parcels. In some jurisdictions, corners and boundaries may precede the parcel framework, but the thematic content is the same—points and lines build parcel polygons.

The parcel framework provides the supporting outline for parcel-related features. These are typically based on the boundaries of major subdivisions as defined by surveys. In the case of Oakland County, Michigan, and for a large portion of the United States, this is the PLSS.

Parcel and parcel framework boundaries can also include road and river networks. Transportation and hydrography are subjects of separate and extensive data modeling efforts

and are described in other chapters of this book. In practice, parcel mapping often includes separate layers for these features.

The ownership and tax parcel themes may have related tables that contain essential information for local government operations, such as tax rolls, condominium records, and grantor–grantee indices.

Rights and interests in land can be separated and limited in certain ways. For example, subsurface mineral rights can be separated from surface landownership. Encumbrances are limitations on the use of land, such as rights-of-way and utility easements.

Parcel-related uses include managing land use, such as zoning or master plans; regulations on land, such as limits on building sizes; and parcel site addresses, which are important for emergency management and public notification.

Administrative areas are the management and jurisdiction districts important to parcel management. Some examples are school districts, taxing authorities, sanitary districts, and parcels included in lake management associations.

Together, these themes form the basis of parcel management systems that support ongoing activities in governmental bodies and decision making in all sectors.

Layer **Administrative areas**
Map use Tax administration and map production.
Data source Derived using dissolve operation or by known relationship to parcels.
Representation Polygons.
Spatial relationships Districts of the same type do not overlap.
Map scale and accuracy Scale is typically 1:1,200 to 1:4,800, but accuracy varies.
Symbology and annotation District name and type by annotation.

Layer **Site addresses, regulated uses, and restrictions**
Map use Identify address locations, extent of regulated uses, and restrictions.
Data source Derived from tax parcels and other sources.
Representation Points and polygons.
Spatial relationships Polygons may overlap; points are contained within polygons.
Map scale and accuracy Scale is typically 1:1,200 to 1:4,800, but accuracy varies.
Symbology and annotation Regulated use by color, address annotation; restrictions by type.

Layer **Separated rights and encumbrances**
Map use Identify rights, interests, and limitations on landownership.
Data source Derived from legal descriptions.
Representation Polygons.
Spatial relationships Separated rights, encumbrances are overlapping and noncontinuous.
Map scale and accuracy Scale is typically 1:1,200 to 1:4,800, but accuracy varies.
Symbology and annotation Fills with transparencies can reveal polygon overlay patterns.

Layer **Ownership and tax parcels**
Map use Identify extent of parcels for assessment and land management.
Data source Plats, condominiums, and surveys.
Representation Polygon.
Spatial relationships Tax parcels do not overlap.
Map scale and accuracy Scale is typically 1:1,200 to 1:4,800, but accuracy varies.
Symbology and annotation Property identification numbers annotated.

Layer **Parcel framework**
Map use Boundary control and framework.
Data source Surveys, parcel control points.
Representation Points, lines, polygons, and survey dataset.
Spatial relationships Corners define PLSS shapes. Feature classes are all survey-aware.
Map scale and accuracy Submeter to millimeter.
Symbology and annotation Corner type, accuracy, and method of collection annotated.

Layer **Corners and boundaries**
Map use Identify extent of land divisions.
Data source Plats, condominiums, and surveys.
Representation Lines and points, optionally stored in a survey dataset.
Spatial relationships Primary parcel features for an area.
Map scale and accuracy Scale is typically 1:1,200 to 1:4,800, but accuracy varies.
Symbology and annotation Record dimensions, line types, and subdivision corners.

Layer **Survey network**
Map use Foundation for a map's positional accuracy.
Data source Survey measurements and computations.
Representation Survey dataset.
Spatial relationships Controls locations of points in survey-aware feature classes.
Map scale and accuracy Exceedingly high accuracy.
Symbology and annotation Survey-aware point features shown with error ellipses.

Layer **Digital orthophotography and hydrography**
Map use Map background and reference.
Data source Aerial photogrammetry and satellite collection.
Representation Raster and vector for hydrography.
Spatial relationships Pixels tesselate the area imaged; hydrography forms a boundary.
Map scale and accuracy Pixel resolution is typically 15 to 50 centimeters.
Symbology and annotation Tone, contrast, and balance of grayscale or color presentation.

The thematic layers are mapped to the geodatabase structure. In some instances, several thematic layers combine to form a set of feature classes in a feature dataset, with integrity constraints in the form of topologies and geometric networks. In other instances, a thematic layer is represented by a survey dataset, a raster dataset, or another georeferenced data source. Relationships bind features and objects, enable validation, and link behavior.

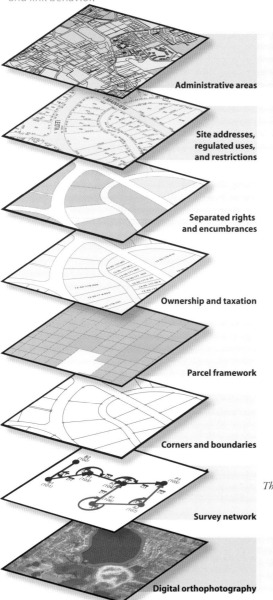

**Administrative areas**

*These thematic layers capture various ways of organizing parcels, as well as other important information used in different maps. This data is derived from other features for use by planners and others.*

**Site addresses, regulated uses, and restrictions**

**Separated rights and encumbrances**

*The parcel features dataset provides a linkage between parcels and tax rolls. It also provides a connection between parcel boundaries and actual survey data. For spatial integrity, the features in this dataset are topologically integrated.*

**Ownership and taxation**

*Feature classes for locating land parcels based on surveys and the PLSS represent the cadastral framework theme.*

**Parcel framework**

**Corners and boundaries**

*The survey dataset contains the survey points, measurements, computations, and coordinates that form the survey network and are obtained from field surveys.*

**Survey network**

*Raster data can be stored as a mosaic in a single raster dataset or as a series of rows in a raster catalog (one record per image).*

**Digital orthophotography**

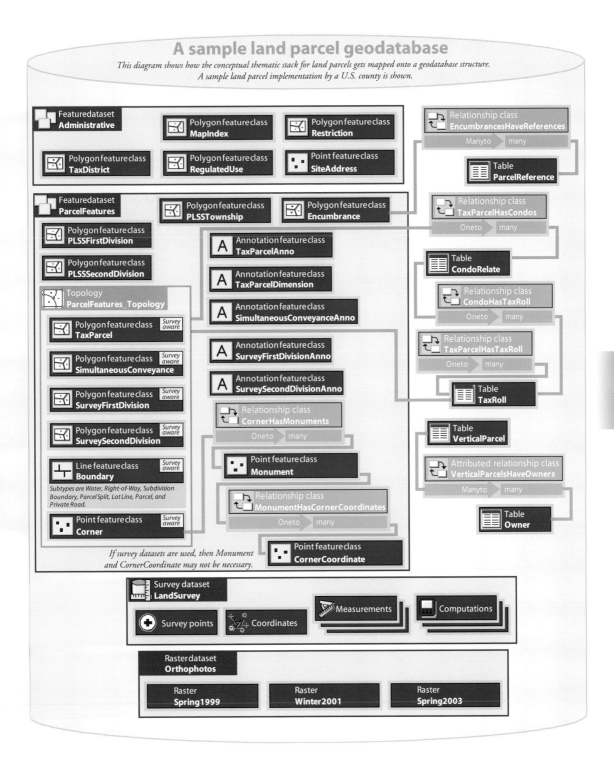

# A sample land parcel geodatabase

*This diagram shows how the conceptual thematic stack for land parcels gets mapped onto a geodatabase structure. A sample land parcel implementation by a U.S. county is shown.*

Feature dataset **Administrative**

Polygon feature class **MapIndex**

Polygon feature class **Restriction**

Polygon feature class **TaxDistrict**

Polygon feature class **RegulatedUse**

Point feature class **SiteAddress**

Relationship class **EncumbrancesHaveReferences**
Many to many

Table **ParcelReference**

Feature dataset **ParcelFeatures**

Polygon feature class **PLSSTownship**

Polygon feature class **Encumbrance**

Relationship class **TaxParcelHasCondos**
One to many

Polygon feature class **PLSSFirstDivision**

Annotation feature class **TaxParcelAnno**

Polygon feature class **PLSSSecondDivision**

Annotation feature class **TaxParcelDimension**

Table **CondoRelate**

Topology **ParcelFeatures_Topology**

Annotation feature class **SimultaneousConveyanceAnno**

Relationship class **CondoHasTaxRoll**
One to many

Polygon feature class **TaxParcel** — Survey aware

Annotation feature class **SurveyFirstDivisionAnno**

Relationship class **TaxParcelHasTaxRoll**
One to many

Polygon feature class **SimultaneousConveyance** — Survey aware

Annotation feature class **SurveySecondDivisionAnno**

Polygon feature class **SurveyFirstDivision** — Survey aware

Table **TaxRoll**

Relationship class **CornerHasMonuments**
One to many

Polygon feature class **SurveySecondDivision** — Survey aware

Table **VerticalParcel**

Line feature class **Boundary** — Survey aware

Point feature class **Monument**

Attributed relationship class **VerticalParcelsHaveOwners**
Many to many

*Subtypes are Water, Right-of-Way, Subdivision Boundary, Parcel Split, Lot Line, Parcel, and Private Road.*

Relationship class **MonumentHasCornerCoordinates**
One to many

Table **Owner**

Point feature class **Corner** — Survey aware

*If survey datasets are used, then Monument and CornerCoordinate may not be necessary.*

Point feature class **CornerCoordinate**

Survey dataset **LandSurvey**

Survey points

Coordinates

Measurements

Computations

Raster dataset **Orthophotos**

Raster **Spring1999**

Raster **Winter2001**

Raster **Spring2003**

5

In many jurisdictions, parcel maps begin with the definition of survey corners, followed by coordinate geometry or survey descriptions of the boundaries between them. Corners and boundaries also provide reference locations for the parcel framework. A local government may create a grid of surveyed monuments and other points throughout its jurisdiction to serve as a required reference grid for all property surveys. As in Oakland County, these reference corners can be colocated with the PLSS corners.

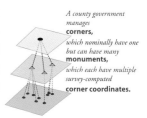

*A county government manages* **corners,** *which nominally have one but can have many* **monuments,** *which each have multiple survey-computed* **corner coordinates.**

Corners is a point feature class in this model, based on the FGDC Cadastral Data Content Standard (FGDC, 1999). In this standard, the parcel is defined by legal descriptions. Parcels are the spatial extents formed by record boundaries and corners. The attributes for the corners and record boundaries, as described in the standard, are information from public records.

There are 20 types of corner features in the data model, although not all will be used in every situation. These include Township Corner, Closing Township Corner, Section Corner, Closing Section Corner, Center of Section, Quarter Corner, Closing Quarter Corner, Aliquot Part, Closing Aliquot Part, Crossing Closing Corner, Intersection Point, Location Point, Location Monument, Meander Corner, Special Meander Corner, Mile Post/Mile Corner, Point on Line, Witness Point, Other, and Unknown. Of these, the corners related to Township, Section, and Quarter are especially for PLSS. Aliquots are further divisions of PLSS quarter sections.

Corners are best managed through survey information. The construction methods used to establish coordinates on corners determine the parcel boundaries. These methods are cartographic construction, computations, and adjustments. The methods used to determine coordinates are important because they help assure coordinate accuracy when survey datasets are employed.

This parcel model accommodates multiple monuments for corners and multiple coordinates for each monument. That is, a corner may be marked by more than one monument, and a monument may have more than one coordinate value. The CornerCoordinate feature class is not needed when the Corners are integrated with a survey dataset; this information is maintained in the survey data.

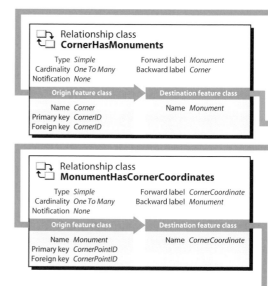

To make informed decisions about which coordinate to use in a GIS to represent a corner, it may be important to know the source and quality information of all coordinates and monuments. The FGDC Cadastral Data Content Standard (FGDC, 1999) addresses this issue. The attributes for corners, monuments, and coordinates in this parcel model are taken from the standard. The concept is to have GIS features that represent the physical realities of parcel corners and to capture sufficient information for complete parcel mapping. For example, notice the possible values for corner types listed above. The possible corner types support both simultaneous conveyances and the PLSS, to be discussed later in this chapter.

Note that the use of the Monument and CornerCoordinate feature classes is optional. If you choose to use survey projects to manage your surveyed points, then these two feature classes and related relationship classes are unnecessary because they are redundant with tables managed by ArcGIS Survey Analyst.

**Simple feature class**
**Corner**

Geometry *Point*
Contains M values *No*
Contains Z values *No*

| Field name | Data type | Allow nulls | Default value | Domain | Precision | Scale | Length |
|---|---|---|---|---|---|---|---|
| OBJECTID | OID | | | | | | |
| Shape | Geometry | Yes | | | | | |
| CornerID | String | Yes | | | | | 30 |
| CornerType | String | Yes | Other | Corner-Classification | | | 30 |
| CornerLabel | String | Yes | | | | | 100 |
| CornerLocalLabel | String | Yes | | | | | 60 |

*A corner is a legal location. It may mark the extremity of a parcel or a parcel framework polygon. A corner may have multiple monuments that serve as physical markers for the legal location of the corner.*

Primary key for the feature class polygon.
A named corner classification.
A name describing the legal location. For PLSS, names for corners on base land net.
Any number of alternative names or aliases for the corner.

**Simple feature class**
**Monument**

Geometry *Point*
Contains M values *No*
Contains Z values *No*

| Field name | Data type | Allow nulls | Precision | Scale | Length |
|---|---|---|---|---|---|
| OBJECTID | OID | | | | |
| Shape | Geometry | Yes | | | |
| CornerPointID | String | Yes | | | 30 |
| CornerID | String | Yes | | | 30 |
| MonumentType | String | Yes | | | 30 |
| MonumentDateSet | Date | Yes | 0 | 0 | 8 |
| CPSourceAgent | String | Yes | | | 100 |
| CPSourceIndex | String | Yes | | | 100 |
| CPSourceType | String | Yes | | | 100 |
| CPSourceDate | Date | Yes | 0 | 0 | 8 |
| CornerPointStatus | String | Yes | | | 100 |

*A monument is a point feature that marks the ends of record boundaries or the extremities of a parcel or a parcel framework polygon. A corner may or may not be monumented, and it is possible that there is only one monument per corner. The relationship allows multiple monuments for corners.*

A primary key for the point feature
Pointer to the corner point feature to identify the corner to which the monument is attached

The type of source for the monument information

**Simple feature class**
**CornerCoordinate**

Geometry *Point*
Contains M values *No*
Contains Z values *No*

| Field name | Data type | Allow nulls | Default value | Domain | Precision | Scale | Length |
|---|---|---|---|---|---|---|---|
| OBJECTID | OID | | | | | | |
| Shape | Geometry | Yes | | | | | |
| CornerCoordinateID | String | Yes | | | | | 30 |
| CornerPointID | String | Yes | | | | | 30 |
| XCoordinate | Double | Yes | | | 0 | 0 | |
| YCoordinate | Double | Yes | | | 0 | 0 | |
| ZCoordinate | Double | Yes | | | 0 | 0 | |
| CoordinateValue | String | Yes | | | | | 30 |
| CoordinateStatus | String | Yes | Active | CoordinateStatus | | | 30 |
| CSourceAgent | String | Yes | | | | | 100 |
| CSourceIndex | String | Yes | | | | | 100 |
| CSourceType | String | Yes | | | | | 100 |
| CSourceDate | Date | Yes | | | 0 | 0 | 8 |
| CSourceComments | String | Yes | | | | | 100 |
| XAccuracy | Double | Yes | | | 0 | 0 | |
| YAccuracy | Double | Yes | | | 0 | 0 | |
| ZAccuracy | Double | Yes | | | 0 | 0 | |
| Reliability | String | Yes | | | | | 30 |
| AccuracyComments | String | Yes | | | | | 30 |
| HorizontalDatum | String | Yes | NAD83 | HorizontalDatum | | | 30 |
| CoordinateSystem | String | Yes | | | | | 30 |
| VerticalDatum | String | Yes | North American Vertical Datum of 1988 | ElevationDatum | | | 60 |
| CoordinateMethod | String | Yes | Total Station | CoordinateMethod | | | 30 |
| CoordinateProcedure | String | Yes | Other | CoordinateProcedure | | | 30 |
| VerticalUnits | String | Yes | International Feet | ElevationUnits | | | 30 |

Primary key for the feature
Points to the monument represented by the coordinate

*The corner point measured coordinate is a x,y; x,y,z; or z-value for a monument. Note that being measured does not imply being surveyed. Digitizing from a map is a type of measurement.*

*Corner and boundary map data is courtesy of Oakland County, Michigan.*

5

Boundaries are the exterior lines that form the parcel or parcel framework. In many jurisdictions, coordinate geometry and least squares adjustments are used to compute the shape and extent of parcels. The information for the coordinate geometry and adjustments is usually extracted from public records, such as plats, condos, or surveys.

Each parcel polygon and parcel framework polygon is built from a set of distinct boundary line features. Boundary features have several attributes, as shown in the figure on the next page. A jurisdiction can collect some or all of these attributes, depending on the construction method and what information is available and required. For example, some attributes apply only to curved line segments (Radius, Delta, Tangent, ArcLength, and Side) and are used for COGO data. RecordDirection and RecordDistance are used for straight-line segments between two points, which may also be part of a COGO description. Any of the attributes can be used for boundary annotation.

Note the Boundary subtypes. In ArcGIS, subtypes are useful for assigning symbology; default attribute values; and relationship, connectivity, and topology rules. In the case of the Boundary feature class, the subtypes include Right-of-Way (ROW), Subdivision Boundary, Parcel, Lot Line, Parcel Split, Private Road, and Water. Parcel split and lot line might at first seem redundant, but these are created under different conditions. Lot lines are generally defined at the time a simultaneous conveyance is created and approved. However, over time, the original lot lines may not work as well for the owners as the original developer had intended.

For example, notice in the figure on the left how the lot lines (gray dashed lines) fall between the parcel split lines (heavier dash-dot lines). The original platted lots have been combined and recombined over time, so the actual parcel splits now appear at a wider spacing than the lot lines.

All Boundary features have an attribute called RecordBoundaryStatus that may hold values of ambulatory,

tidal, disputed, adjudicated, connecting line, computed, constructed, duplicate, archived, or unknown. Ambulatory boundaries are boundaries that can possibly shift. Rivers and other riparian features define the most common ambulatory boundaries. Natural features can be linked to boundaries to define an ambulatory boundary and are shown in the boundary feature. Users can also modify or extend this list of RecordBoundaryStatus values according to their jurisdiction's practice and needs.

In some situations, boundary features are used solely for cartographic purposes to symbolize and label boundary lines on parcel maps.

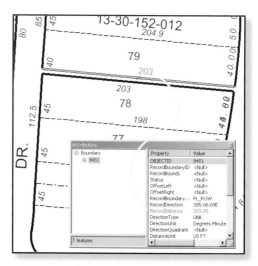

*Annotation, such as distance along a property line, can be linked to an attribute of a feature, such as Boundary.*

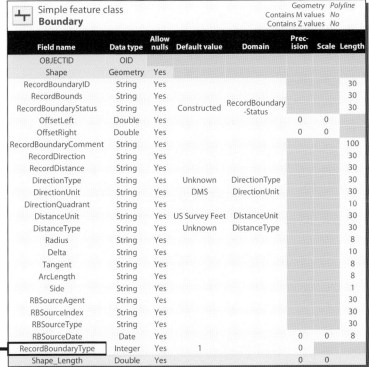

## Simple feature class
## Boundary

| | | | | | Geometry | Polyline |
|---|---|---|---|---|---|---|
| | | | | | Contains M values | No |
| | | | | | Contains Z values | No |

| Field name | Data type | Allow nulls | Default value | Domain | Precision | Scale | Length | |
|---|---|---|---|---|---|---|---|---|
| OBJECTID | OID | | | | | | | The primary key for the line entity. |
| Shape | Geometry | Yes | | | | | | |
| RecordBoundaryID | String | Yes | | | | | 30 | Boundary location by call, related document, or known location. |
| RecordBounds | String | Yes | | | | | 30 | Identifies the record boundary's status from a legal perspective. |
| RecordBoundaryStatus | String | Yes | Constructed | RecordBoundary-Status | | | 30 | Distance left of and perpendicular to a defined boundary line. |
| OffsetLeft | Double | Yes | | | 0 | 0 | | Distance right of and perpendicular to a defined boundary line. |
| OffsetRight | Double | Yes | | | 0 | 0 | | Information about record boundary in the public record. |
| RecordBoundaryComment | String | Yes | | | | | 100 | Direction is angle between a line and an arbitrary reference line. |
| RecordDirection | String | Yes | | | | | 30 | The quantity for the linear measure distance of a boundary. |
| RecordDistance | String | Yes | | | | | 30 | The basis of bearing or basis of azimuth for the direction. |
| DirectionType | String | Yes | Unknown | DirectionType | | | 30 | Indicates the units for a direction. |
| DirectionUnit | String | Yes | DMS | DirectionUnit | | | 30 | Directions can be measured as either bearings or azimuth. |
| DirectionQuadrant | String | Yes | | | | | 10 | Defines the units of measure and the distance reference plane. |
| DistanceUnit | String | Yes | US Survey Feet | DistanceUnit | | | 30 | Describes the reference surface for the distance. |
| DistanceType | String | Yes | Unknown | DistanceType | | | 30 | Distance from the center of a curve to any point on it. |
| Radius | String | Yes | | | | | 8 | The central angle of a circular curve. |
| Delta | String | Yes | | | | | 10 | Distance between the points of tangency and intersection. |
| Tangent | String | Yes | | | | | 8 | The arc length is the long chord length. |
| ArcLength | String | Yes | | | | | 8 | Side where radius point is located with respect to circular curve. |
| Side | String | Yes | | | | | 1 | Individual or organization determining record boundary values. |
| RBSourceAgent | String | Yes | | | | | 30 | Value assigned to record boundary document to identify source. |
| RBSourceIndex | String | Yes | | | | | 30 | Describes a family of documents, files, images, or other formats. |
| RBSourceType | String | Yes | | | | | 30 | The date of the record boundary document or other record. |
| RBSourceDate | Date | Yes | | | 0 | 0 | 8 | Classification of boundary line to support definition of subtypes. |
| RecordBoundaryType | Integer | Yes | 1 | | 0 | | | |
| Shape_Length | Double | Yes | | | 0 | 0 | | |

*A record boundary is the linear feature that represents the edge of a polygon feature, which may be a parcel or a parcel framework.*

**5**

## Subtypes of Boundary

Subtype field *RecordBoundaryType*
Default subtype *1*   List of defined default values and domains for subtypes in this class

| Subtype Code | Subtype Description | | Field name | Default value | Domain |
|---|---|---|---|---|---|
| 1 | Right of Way | ⇨ | | | |
| 2 | Subdivision Boundary | ⇨ | RecordBoundaryStatus | Constructed | RecordBoundaryStatus |
| 3 | Parcel | ⇨ | DirectionType | Assumed | DirectionType |
| 4 | Lot Line | ⇨ | DirectionUnit | Unknown | DirectionUnit |
| 5 | Parcel Split | ⇨ | DistanceUnit | US Survey Feet | DistanceUnit |
| 6 | Private Road | ⇨ | DistanceType | Ground | DistanceType |
| 7 | Water | ⇨ | | | |

These subtypes all share the same default values and domains.

Intersection point
Tangent distance
Side = Left
Point of tangency
Radius point

## Coded value domain
### DirectionUnit
Field type *String*
Split policy *Default Value*
Merge policy *Default Value*

| Description |
|---|
| Decimal Degrees |
| Degrees Minutes Seconds |
| Radians |
| Gradians |
| Gons |
| Other |
| Unknown |

## Coded value domain
### DirectionType
Field type *String*
Split policy *Default Value*
Merge policy *Default Value*

| Description |
|---|
| Assumed |
| Astronomical North |
| Astronomical South |
| Geodetic North |
| Geodetic South |
| Magnetic North |
| Magnetic South |
| Unknown |

## Coded value domain
### DistanceType
Field type *String*
Split policy *Default Value*
Merge policy *Default Value*

| Description |
|---|
| Ground |
| Sea Level |
| Grid |
| Unknown |

## Coded value domain
### DistanceUnit
Field type *String*
Split policy *Default Value*
Merge policy *Default Value*

| Description |
|---|
| Chains |
| US Survey Feet |
| International Feet |
| Meters |
| Pole |
| Arpent |
| Perch |
| Rod |
| Stick |
| Vara |
| Vara - California |
| Vara - Texas |
| Unknown |

## Coded value domain
### RecordBoundaryStatus
Field type *String*
Split policy *Default Value*
Merge policy *Default Value*

| Description |
|---|
| Ambulatory |
| Tidal |
| Disputed |
| Adjudicated |
| Connecting Line |
| Computed |
| Constructed |
| Duplicate |
| Archived |
| Unknown |

Parcels may be tied to a system of known reference points for the greatest benefit within a GIS. Parcel frameworks provide a reference structure for locating parcels in space. A parcel framework is a set of polygon features in a nested hierarchy that encloses land parcels. For example, a simultaneous conveyance exterior boundary defines and contains the individual blocks and lots within the subdivision; a block further defines and contains a set of lots. This system of subdivisions, blocks, and lots constitutes a type of parcel framework.

Corners form the reference points on which boundaries and parcel frameworks are based. Parcel frameworks, in turn, provide the structural units that contain collections of individual parcels.

## PROPERTIES OF PARCEL FRAMEWORKS

There are many types of parcel systems that form hierarchical frameworks for describing landownership. The most widely used frameworks in the United States are simultaneous conveyances and the PLSS. Other parcel frameworks include offshore parcel frameworks, original government grants of land, ranchos, French claims, and Georgia military districts.

Parcel frameworks have the following characteristics:

• They are measured, often by survey. Parcel frameworks can be described and expressed in a GIS. They are tied to the measurements and placement of corners and boundaries.

• They form a hierarchical framework. This means that the parcel frameworks provide a structure that often includes the definition of senior boundaries, and these polygons provide a basis for describing land or ownership.

• They form closed polygons. This means that the exterior boundaries of this framework are intended to close.

The Oakland County data model includes two parcel frameworks: simultaneous conveyances and the PLSS. These may differ somewhat from the parcel framework in your jurisdiction, but they serve to illustrate what is needed in any parcel framework. Consider what is presented here as suggestive, not prescriptive, and adapt these parcel frameworks to your own policies and requirements.

## SIMULTANEOUS CONVEYANCES

Simultaneous conveyances occur when several parcels are created at the same moment, such as lots in a subdivision, units in a condominium, or plots in a cemetery.

> A simultaneously created boundary results when several parcels of land are created in the same legal instant by the same person, persons, or agency, and by the same instrument. All parcels have equal standing, and no such portion can be said to have prior rights or seniority over any other portion (Brown, 1995).

Some texts describe PLSS townships as simultaneous conveyances, but they are modeled separately in the parcel data model because the PLSS hierarchical structure has special rules, as discussed below.

While state and local laws control the rules and definitions for simultaneous conveyances, there are some common features. For example, many simultaneous conveyances have a hierarchical structure in which the exterior boundary is senior to interior lines. A typical pattern is that lots are nested within blocks, and blocks are nested within a simultaneous conveyance. However, the simultaneous conveyance may contain only lots and not blocks.

For the purposes of this parcel data model, the SimultaneousConveyance feature class is a polygon feature class for the external boundary of the conveyance, such as the subdivision exterior. The same feature class is also used to represent roads, blocks, or other polygon features that form subdivision interior boundaries to the actual property parcels. The ConveyanceType field is used to specify which of several types of simultaneous conveyance applies to each feature.

One purpose of the SimultaneousConveyance feature class is to improve polygon rendering—for example, the external boundaries of plats may be shown with a heavier weight line or may be annotated differently.

Another purpose of the SimultaneousConveyance feature class is to provide a structure for parcel descriptions in subsequent feature classes. This feature class allows the parcel map to be related to underlying lots from which a parcel description is derived. Topology rules play an important role in parcel frameworks and will vary depending on your specific needs.

Conceptually, simultaneous conveyances would be nonoverlapping; that is, at any point in time, any piece of land in a simultaneous conveyance should be controlled or described by only one simultaneous conveyance. However, they may, in fact, overlap for several reasons. The two most common reasons are ambiguous legal descriptions and descriptions that are stacked over time. Therefore, the simultaneous conveyance features are potentially overlapping polygons that are noncontinuous; that is, simultaneous conveyances may not cover the entire jurisdiction, and they may overlap.

In this map, the Happy Acres Subdivision plat shows five lots. Later, a condominium plat was developed that included lots 3 and 4 of the subdivision and other lands outside the subdivision. In this case, the High-Rise Condominium overlaps the Happy Acres Subdivision. Many states would require that the

portion of the subdivision included in the condominium be vacated, but other states allow this overlap. Technically, the land that was in lots 3 and 4 would now be described as being in the condominium, even though the legal description of the condominium itself includes a portion of the plat.

See Chapter 6, 'Surveying federal lands', for more examples of simultaneous conveyances.

High-Rise Condominium
Lot 1 | Lot 3
Lot 4
Lot 2 | Lot 5
Happy Acres Subdivision

**5**

Coded value domain
**SimultaneousConveyanceType**

| Field type | String |
| Split policy | Default Value |
| Merge policy | Default Value |

| Code |
| --- |
| Assessor Plat |
| Cemetery |
| Condominium |
| Farm Lot |
| French Long Lot |
| Indian Allotment |
| Plat of Survey |
| Protraction Block |
| Small Holding Claim |
| Small Tracts Act |
| Subdivision |
| Survey |
| Townsite |
| United States Survey |
| Other |

Simple feature class
**SimultaneousConveyance**

Geometry *Polygon*
Contains M values *No*
Contains Z values *No*

| Field name | Data type | Allow nulls | Default value | Domain | Precision | Scale | Length |
| --- | --- | --- | --- | --- | --- | --- | --- |
| OBJECTID | OID | | | | | | |
| Shape | Geometry | Yes | | | | | |
| ConveyanceID | String | Yes | | | | | 64 |
| ConveyanceDesignator | String | Yes | | | | | 64 |
| ConveyanceType | String | Yes | Subdivision | Simultaneous-ConveyanceType | | | 30 |
| Shape_Length | Double | Yes | | | 0 | 0 | |
| Shape_Area | Double | Yes | | | 0 | 0 | |

*A named or numbered area of land that can be identified by a type and a designator. These types of survey systems are created at one time in one document and all of the interior lines will have equal standing with one another.*

Primary key for the polygon feature
Name for the conveyance, often a numeric value
The type of conveyance

The first division is the primary division of the survey system. Examples are blocks and lots. These are nested within the simultaneous conveyance and do not cross its boundaries. First divisions may or may not tessellate or uniquely divide the entire simultaneous conveyance. The second survey division is the subdivision of the first division. These are nested within the first division and do not cross its boundaries. The second division may not necessarily tessellate or uniquely divide the entire first division.

The SurveyFirstDivision and SurveySecondDivision feature classes support an internal hierarchy within a simultaneous conveyance. The use of these classes depends on the nature of the simultaneous conveyance. For example, in the case where a simultaneous conveyance represents a subdivision of multiple blocks, the survey first division might be used to describe each block, and the survey second division individual lots. On the other hand, where a conveyance represents just a single block, the survey first division might represent the individual lots. Another way to look at this is that lots can be in blocks, subdivisions, or simultaneous conveyances (for example, government lots). Notice that both of these survey division feature classes have the ConveyanceType attribute, so it will be easy to tell each survey division feature's exact use.

This map shows a subdivision in which the red line on the image is the external boundary. The first divisions are the blocks within the plat. The second divisions are the lots within the blocks. The first division polygons are not continuous because, as shown in this map, a road right-of-way separates the blocks. The second division polygons are the individual lots within the blocks. They are contained entirely within the block boundaries and are nonoverlapping and noncontinuous.

There is an important difference in the way some organizations manage conveyances from this example. It is often the intent of subdivision platting statutes to provide a legal description of all lands contained within the subdivision. If this applies, then the more strict "must not have gaps" polygon rule can be applied to the first and second divisions.

It is also important to note that in some cases, there are no blocks; that is, all the lots are numbered within the subdivisions. In this case, the first division is the lot.

| Coded value domain | |
|---|---|
| **FirstDivisionType** | |
| Field type | String |
| Split policy | Default Value |
| Merge policy | Default Value |

| Code | Description |
|---|---|
| Block | Block |
| Lot | Lot |
| Tract | Tract |
| Right of Way | Right of Way |
| Unit | Unit |
| Fractional Part | Fractional Part |
| Claim | Claim |
| Parcel | Parcel |
| Plot | Plot |
| Survey | Survey |
| Other | Other |

| Simple feature class **SurveyFirstDivision** | | | | | Geometry | Polygon | | |
|---|---|---|---|---|---|---|---|---|
| | | | | | Contains M values | No | | |
| | | | | | Contains Z values | No | | |

| Field name | Data type | Allow nulls | Default value | Domain | Prec-ision | Scale | Length |
|---|---|---|---|---|---|---|---|
| OBJECTID | OID | | | | | | |
| Shape | Geometry | Yes | | | | | |
| ConveyanceID | String | Yes | | | | | 64 |
| ConveyanceDesignator | String | Yes | | | | | 64 |
| ConveyanceType | String | Yes | Subdivision | Simultaneous-ConveyanceType | | | 30 |
| FirstDivisionID | String | Yes | | | | | 100 |
| FirstDivisionDesignator | String | Yes | | | | | 100 |
| FirstDivisionType | String | Yes | Block | FirstDivisionType | | | 30 |
| Shape_Length | Double | Yes | | | 0 | 0 | |
| Shape_Area | Double | Yes | | | 0 | 0 | |

*The primary division of the survey system, such as blocks and lots. These are nested within the simultaneous conveyance and do not cross its boundaries.*

See SimultaneousConveyance.

Primary key for the polygon feature.
An alphanumeric designator used to identify the first division.
The classification of the first survey system division.

When creating SurveyFirstDivision features representing right-of-way, it may be tempting to create a single feature to represent the boundary of an entire road network. However, it is generally considered good practice to break up such large polygon features at subdivision boundaries and other convenient breakpoints. Instead of managing all road casings as a single polygon, you can split them to simplify maintenance and improve performance.

*Second survey division polygons are shaded by type against an orthophoto background. This diagram shows blocks and lots within simultaneous conveyances.*

**Coded value domain**
**SecondDivisonType**
Field type *String*
Split policy *Default Value*
Merge policy *Default Value*

| Code | Description |
|---|---|
| Fractional Part | Fractional Part |
| Outlot | Outlot |
| Lot | Lot |
| Tract | Tract |
| Parcel | Parcel |
| Other | Other |

**Simple feature class**
**SurveySecondDivision**

Geometry *Polygon*
Contains M values *No*
Contains Z values *No*

| Field name | Data type | Allow nulls | Default value | Domain | Prec-ision | Scale | Length |
|---|---|---|---|---|---|---|---|
| OBJECTID | OID | | | | | | |
| Shape | Geometry | Yes | | | | | |
| ConveyanceID | String | Yes | | | | | 64 |
| ConveyanceDesignator | String | Yes | | | | | 64 |
| ConveyanceType | String | Yes | Subdivision | Simultaneous-ConveyanceType | | | 30 |
| FirstDivisionID | String | Yes | | | | | 100 |
| FirstDivisionDesignator | String | Yes | | | | | 100 |
| FirstDivisionType | String | Yes | Block | FirstDivisionType | | | 30 |
| SecondDivisionID | String | Yes | | | | | 100 |
| SecondDivisionDesignator | String | Yes | | | | | 100 |
| SecondDivisionType | String | Yes | Lot | SecondDivisonType | | | 30 |
| Shape_Length | Double | Yes | | | 0 | 0 | |
| Shape_Area | Double | Yes | | | 0 | 0 | |

*The second survey division is the subdivision of the first division. These are nested within the first division and do not cross the first division boundaries.*

*See SimultaneousConveyance.*

*See SurveyFirstDivision.*

The primary key for the polygon feature.
Alphanumeric designator used to identify the first survey division.
Describes the classification of the first survey system division.

**Annotation feature class**
**SurveyFirstDivisionAnno**

Geometry
Contains M values *No*
Contains Z values *No*

| Field name | Data type | Allow nulls | Default value | Domain | Prec-ision | Scale | Length |
|---|---|---|---|---|---|---|---|
| OBJECTID | Object ID | | | | | | |
| SHAPE | Geometry | Yes | | | | | |
| FeatureID | Long integer | Yes | | | 0 | | |
| ZOrder | Long integer | Yes | | | 0 | | |
| AnnotationClassID | Long integer | Yes | | | 0 | | |
| Element | Blob | Yes | | | 0 | 0 | 0 |
| SHAPE_Length | Double | Yes | | | 0 | 0 | |
| SHAPE_Area | Double | Yes | | | 0 | 0 | |

5

A set of baselines and principal meridians that define relatively equal divisions of land, the PLSS originated in the 1780s as a system for inventorying and selling federal land in the public domain to raise money for the new nation. Because it is the prevalent legal description framework in 32 of the United States, a set of PLSS feature classes is included in the parcel data model. The PLSS is implemented here as a hierarchical group of feature classes that define land descriptions. A more extensive PLSS data model is presented in Chapter 6, 'Surveying Federal Lands'.

## THE PUBLIC LAND SURVEY SYSTEM

In its idealized form, rectangular divisions begin with six-mile by six-mile townships numbered north and south of baselines and east and west from principal meridians. To account for the convergence of meridians, east–west correction lines are established at regular intervals.

The huge task of surveying such a large area quickly enough to accommodate the westward migration of population in the early 1800s resulted in less-than-perfect township and section boundaries in many places. However, corrections were made in the size of sections and townships so that, on the whole, the system forms a consistent fabric.

Townships are nominally divided into 36 sections, each being nominally one mile by one mile. The townships can be divided into sections, tracts, lots, and other types of divisions. If sections are the first division, these can be further divided into aliquot parts by quartering and lotting the sections. The PLSS nested feature classes are the polygon manifestations of the PLSS descriptions.

*Townships as defined in the United States Public Land Survey System*

| | | Allow | Default | | Prec- | | |
|---|---|---|---|---|---|---|---|
| **Field name** | **Data type** | **nulls** | **value** | **Domain** | **ision** | **Scale** | **Length** |
| OBJECTID | OID | | | | | | |
| Shape | Geometry | Yes | | | | | |
| PLSSID | String | Yes | | | | | 64 |
| PrincipalMeridian | String | Yes | NA | PrincipalMeridian | | | 64 |
| TownshipDesignator | String | Yes | | | | | 30 |
| TownshipDirection | String | Yes | | TownshipTown-Direction | | | 2 |
| TownshipFraction | Integer | Yes | | | 0 | | |
| RangeDesignator | String | Yes | | | | | 30 |
| RangeDirection | String | Yes | | TownshipRange-Direction | | | 1 |
| RangeFraction | Integer | Yes | | | 0 | | |
| TownshipType | String | Yes | PLSS | Township Type | | | 60 |
| StateCode | Integer | Yes | | | 0 | | |
| Shape_Length | Double | Yes | | | 0 | 0 | |
| Shape_Area | Double | Yes | | | 0 | 0 | |

Simple feature class
**PLSSTownship**

Geometry *Polygon*
Contains M values *No*
Contains Z values *No*

Primary key for the polygon feature.
Reference for numbering of townships and ranges within a public land survey area
The number of rows of townships north or south from a PLSS origin.
Direction of a row of townships from a PLSS origin.
Township fractions are created at gaps between surveyed township boundaries.
Indicates the number of columns of townships east or west from a PLSS origin.
Direction of a column of townships from a PLSS origin.
Range fractions are created at gaps between surveyed township boundaries.
Indicates whether the township is surveyed, protracted, or unsurveyed.
Indicates the state in which the PLSS township is located.

## SECTIONS IN A TOWNSHIP

This map illustrates the normal township section divisions with the sections numbered. However, there may be exceptions to this rule all across the public domain states. The township in this map is rectangular, but this is a generalization.

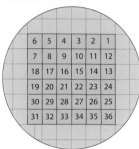

The nested components of the PLSS are described in the Cadastral Data Content Standard (FGDC, 1999).

The PLSS township is the first or top level of polygon in the public land survey system. The principal meridian or baseline identifies PLSS townships. If the first division is not a PLSS township, then there is a survey name and potentially a secondary survey name. The survey name and secondary survey name generally occur in Ohio, the original testing ground of the public land survey.

The first division of the PLSS township, as defined in the Cadastral Data Content Standard, is the division of the nominal six-mile by six-mile township areas. Townships are most commonly divided into sections but can also be divided into tracts, protraction blocks, and other divisions.

The first divisions of the townships are nonoverlapping, and more than one type of first division can exist in a PLSS township.

The second division of the PLSS township, as defined in the Cadastral Data Content Standard, is a division of the first division. The most common second division divides a section into aliquot parts, which are formed by halving and quartering. However, second divisions can include government lots and tracts.

## SUBDIVISIONS OF A SECTION

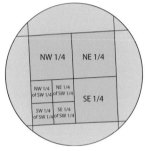

This map shows a section (640 acres) divided into quarter sections (160 acres) and one quarter section divided into sixteenth sections (40 acres).

The reason the quarter and sixteenth parts are included in the second division is that these are commonly occurring, nonoverlapping divisions. Typically, all divisions of the section are defined once the center of a section is established, even if they are not staked or described.

| Field name | Data type | Allow nulls | Default value | Domain | Prec-ision | Scale | Length |
|---|---|---|---|---|---|---|---|
| OBJECTID | OID | | | | | | |
| Shape | Geometry | Yes | | | | | |
| PLSSID | String | Yes | | | | | 64 |
| PrincipalMeridian | String | Yes | | | | | 64 |
| TownshipDesignator | String | Yes | | | | | 30 |
| TownshipDirection | String | Yes | | TownshipTownDirection | | | 2 |
| TownshipFraction | Integer | Yes | | | 0 | | |
| RangeDesignator | String | Yes | | FirstDivisionSectionRange | | | 30 |
| RangeDirection | String | Yes | | TownshipRangeDirection | | | 1 |
| RangeFraction | Integer | Yes | | | 0 | | |
| TownshipType | String | Yes | PLSS | Township Type | | | 60 |
| StateCode | Integer | Yes | | | 0 | | |
| FirstDivisionID | String | Yes | | | | | 30 |
| FirstDivisionDesignator | String | Yes | | | | | 10 |
| FirstDivisionSuffix | String | Yes | | | | | 10 |
| FirstDivisionType | String | Yes | Section | First Division Type | | | 30 |
| Shape_Length | Double | Yes | | | 0 | 0 | |
| Shape_Area | Double | Yes | | | 0 | 0 | |

Simple feature class
**PLSSFirstDivision**

Geometry: Polygon
Contains M values: No
Contains Z values: No

*Public Land Survey System township first divisions are normally tracts or sections. This entity is for the primary or first subdivisions of a township.*

*See PLSSTownship.*

The numeric identifier of the first division.

The primary or first subdivision category; in most cases, a section.

The tax parcel is a polygon feature designed to support a real estate tax system. Tax parcel management varies by jurisdiction. Regardless of how tax parcels are defined, the parcel data model links tax parcel features with their associated tax roll records, which are often maintained in a separate database. The parcel model also makes special provisions for handling condominiums as tax parcels.

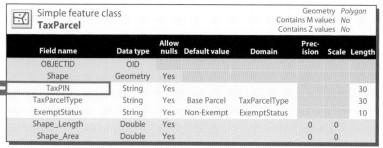

| Simple feature class **TaxParcel** | | | | | | | | Geometry *Polygon* Contains M values *No* Contains Z values *No* |
|---|---|---|---|---|---|---|---|---|

| Field name | Data type | Allow nulls | Default value | Domain | Precision | Scale | Length |
|---|---|---|---|---|---|---|---|
| OBJECTID | OID | | | | | | |
| Shape | Geometry | Yes | | | | | |
| TaxPIN | String | Yes | | | | | 30 |
| TaxParcelType | String | Yes | Base Parcel | TaxParcelType | | | 30 |
| ExemptStatus | String | Yes | Non-Exempt | ExemptStatus | | | 10 |
| Shape_Length | Double | Yes | | | 0 | 0 | |
| Shape_Area | Double | Yes | | | 0 | 0 | |

*The tax parcel is a polygon defined for the purposes of supporting a real estate tax system. How these polygons are defined varies by jurisdiction.*

Links to the tax roll, tax record, or assessment record
An attribute for the tax parcel use classification
Whether the tax parcel is subject to real property tax

At the heart of a tax parcel record is the parcel identification number assigned by the taxing authority. Several other tables refer to this number, which is called TaxPIN in this model.

In many cases, a TaxParcel feature—sometimes called a base parcel—includes a number of condominium units. These might be part of a single building, as in the case of office space, or they may be separate buildings, as in the case of a planned community. The tax parcel may have a single address or multiple addresses. The base parcel and each condominium will have its own assessment and tax bill.

For tax roll analysis purposes, it may be important to find the base parcel associated with a given condominium parcel, and vice versa. For this reason, a TaxParcelHasCondos relationship class was created to associate each base parcel feature with its condominiums by TaxPIN. A separate CondoRelate table contains the TaxPINs of all condominiums, along with the associated base parcel's TaxPIN (held in the PrimaryTaxPIN field). Editing and inspection tools in ArcMap allow the user to directly browse this relationship for a given base parcel or condominium.

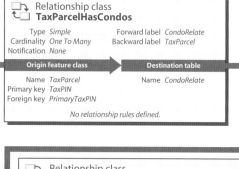

| Relationship class **TaxParcelHasCondos** | | |
|---|---|---|
| Type *Simple* | Forward label *CondoRelate* | |
| Cardinality *One To Many* | Backward label *TaxParcel* | |
| Notification *None* | | |

| Origin feature class | | Destination table |
|---|---|---|
| Name *TaxParcel* | | Name *CondoRelate* |
| Primary key *TaxPIN* | | |
| Foreign key *PrimaryTaxPIN* | | |

*No relationship rules defined.*

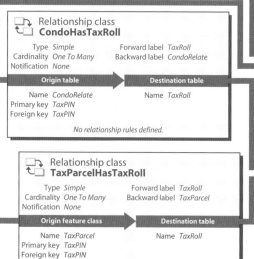

| Relationship class **CondoHasTaxRoll** | | |
|---|---|---|
| Type *Simple* | Forward label *TaxRoll* | |
| Cardinality *One To Many* | Backward label *CondoRelate* | |
| Notification *None* | | |

| Origin table | | Destination table |
|---|---|---|
| Name *CondoRelate* | | Name *TaxRoll* |
| Primary key *TaxPIN* | | |
| Foreign key *TaxPIN* | | |

*No relationship rules defined.*

| Relationship class **TaxParcelHasTaxRoll** | | |
|---|---|---|
| Type *Simple* | Forward label *TaxRoll* | |
| Cardinality *One To Many* | Backward label *TaxParcel* | |
| Notification *None* | | |

| Origin feature class | | Destination table |
|---|---|---|
| Name *TaxParcel* | | Name *TaxRoll* |
| Primary key *TaxPIN* | | |
| Foreign key *TaxPIN* | | |

*No relationship rules defined.*

Note that there is both a TaxParcel class and a TaxRoll class. TaxParcel is a feature (geometric) class, while TaxRoll is non-spatial. The TaxRoll class contains the detailed assessment and parcel owner contact information, while the TaxParcel class defines the location and geometry of the parcel, as well as its type. Tax parcel types include Base Parcel, Condominium, Right-of-Way Overlap, Unknown, and Other.

Tax parcels may also have some exemption from taxes. The exemption status codes indicate the reason for the tax exemption.

Any given parcel feature may appear in multiple tax rolls, that is, for multiple tax years. To link parcel features with their corresponding tax roll records, a simple one-to-many relationship class called TaxParcelHasTaxRoll has been created.

**Coded value domain**
**ExemptStatus**

Field type *String*
Split policy *Default Value*
Merge policy *Default Value*

| Code | Description |
|---|---|
| Bankrupt | Bankrupt |
| Exempt | Exempt - General |
| Local | Exempt - Local Govt |
| County | Exempt - County Govt |
| State | Exempt - State Govt |
| Federal | Exempt - Federal Govt |
| Tribal | Exempt - Tribal |
| Non-Exempt | Non-Exempt |
| Non-Profit | Non-Profit |
| For Profit | For Profit |
| Regulated | Regulated |
| Other | Other |

**Coded value domain**
**TaxParcelType**

Field type *String*
Split policy *Default Value*
Merge policy *Default Value*

| Code | Description |
|---|---|
| Base Parcel | Base Parcel |
| Condominium | Condominium |
| ROW Overlap | ROW Overlap |
| Unknown | Unknown Ownership |
| Other | Other |

5

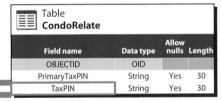

**Table**
**CondoRelate**

| Field name | Data type | Allow nulls | Length |
|---|---|---|---|
| OBJECTID | OID | | |
| PrimaryTaxPIN | String | Yes | 30 |
| TaxPIN | String | Yes | 30 |

*This table contains the relationships between the tax parcel polygons and multiple tax records, such as those in a condominium.*
*This table is used to connect the individual tax records for the units in the condominium to the larger polygon representation.*

The linkage to the larger polygon, such as a building polygon within which the multiple records are related
The tax key number that links to information contained in the tax roll, the tax record, or the assessment record

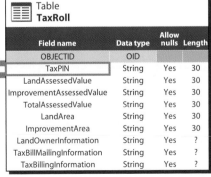

**Table**
**TaxRoll**

| Field name | Data type | Allow nulls | Length |
|---|---|---|---|
| OBJECTID | OID | | |
| TaxPIN | String | Yes | 30 |
| LandAssessedValue | String | Yes | 30 |
| ImprovementAssessedValue | String | Yes | 30 |
| TotalAssessedValue | String | Yes | 30 |
| LandArea | String | Yes | 30 |
| ImprovementArea | String | Yes | 30 |
| LandOwnerInformation | String | Yes | ? |
| TaxBillMailingInformation | String | Yes | ? |
| TaxBillingInformation | String | Yes | ? |

*The tax roll is a listing of all property and its assessed value, but this object class is a generic listing for any related table that contains information is linked to the tax parcels. This could include the property tax table, the assessment data, or a customized list of attributes used for mapping.*

Tax key number that links to information contained in the tax roll, the tax record, or the assessment record
Assessed value of the land
Assessed value of any improvements
Property value determined by the assessment authority and used to calculate a tax amount
Land area for assessment purposes
This is the size, in acres or square feet, to which the assessment is applied
Name of the owner or taxpayer, included to support queries, information displays, and feature-based annotation
Mailing address information, to be expanded for project needs
This could include tax amounts, tax years, lottery credits, or payment information

Most jurisdictions have condominiums or other structures that can form common interest areas and three-dimensional surfaces with different owners on different levels of the structures. Such a structure may have multiple addresses, one for each tenant's unit. Jurisdictions differ in the amount of information they require for tax purposes, such as whether to capture every unit's geographic footprint in the tax parcel database. This section describes the three most widely practiced approaches for modeling condominiums.

It is useful to review a formal definition of condominiums to clarify the issues this parcel data model must address.

A condominium is a separate system of ownership of individual units in a multiple unit building; a single real property parcel with all the unit owners having a right in common to use the common elements with separate ownership confined to the individual units, which are serially designated. The condominium concept was not rooted in English common law, and most condominiums in the United States are formed in accordance with specific state enabling statutes. A condominium is an estate in real property consisting of an undivided interest in common in a portion of the parcel of real property together with separate interest in a space in a residential, industrial, or commercial building on such real property, such as an apartment, office, or store (Black, 1991).

In some jurisdictions, condominiums may look like a subdivision plat with the units laid out as if they were lots and the common elements looking like rights-of-way, as shown in the left side of the image below. Other condominiums are stacked (sometimes called vertical) parcels that come into play when the condominium is a single large building, as shown on the lower right.

There are two special cases with condominiums: common elements and unit ownership.

## COMMON ELEMENTS

In many jurisdictions, values and assessments of the common elements are prorated across the individual ownership parcels in the condominium, but common elements may also be mapped, assessed, and managed separately. Common elements may be assigned to the condominium owners as a group, the condominium association, or the developer. The assessment on common elements may be assigned to the individual units, or the common elements may be exempt from assessment and taxes.

The decision of whether to create a separate ownership polygon for the common elements or manage the condominium as a single polygon depends on the assessment system and the level of detail and parcel maintenance the jurisdiction wants to employ.

## UNIT OWNERSHIP

The units or buildings in the condominium are part of the ownership parcels with a vertical aspect and are called vertical parcels in the parcel data model.

This illustration shows a vertical parcel that is a condominium building with condominium unit F on three separate floors. Unit F is connected by common elements, such as stairways and elevators.

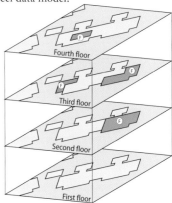

The common elements, which appear as holes or gaps through the elements of parcel F, provide access to parcels in the vertical condominium similar to how a right-of-way provides access to more traditional flat parcels.

In the parcel data model, there are several ways to model or represent vertical parcels:

- A single base polygon pointing to multiple parcel records

- A single base polygon pointing to another series of polygons that represent the levels or floor

- A single base polygon that points to a three-dimensional model of the building

A single base polygon pointing to a series of parcel records has one graphic of the condominium. In this approach, the information about multiple owners is stored in attribute tables, but there is not an accompanying graphic that outlines the footprints or polygons of the separate owners in the condominium.

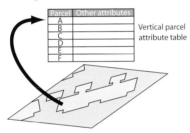

An image of the condominium plat could also be attached to the base polygon.

The second approach is to have the base polygon as part of the ownership object that points to or is related to another series of polygon objects. Each related polygon represents a layer or floor of the condominium with the individual owners and common elements indicated.

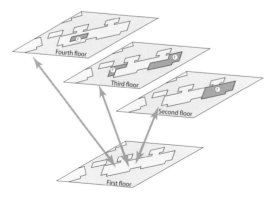

There are three polygons related to the base polygon; each of these is a level or floor. The area owned by owner F is indicated in each level polygon. An accompanying table could summarize all of the holdings of owner F. Conversely, a table could be associated with each level that describes the owner or owners on that floor.

The third approach is to have a three-dimensional model of the building. This is a more complex approach. However, like the first two approaches, the three-dimensional model would be related to the parcels through the condominium outline polygon. In the parcel polygons, the exterior of the condominium is shown on the parcel map with a polygon type indicating that it is a vertical parcel.

5

A land parcel has many meanings across different organizations, disciplines, and situations that go beyond its use for property tax administration. In a GIS, parcels are simply represented as polygons. Their data models become more complex to tie parcels to cadastral frameworks; manage ownership rights, interests, and restrictions; and for taxation. Various international conventions further complicate the picture, depending on the nationality of interest.

From a parcel mapping perspective, local governments in the United States frequently use property tax parcels as the basis for parcel management. Other organizations begin parcel mapping with an ownership parcel defined by the official Register of Deeds records. Still others use zoning, land use, mineral rights, or farmland conservation as the basis for parcel mapping.

The simplest and broadest definition used in the United States for a parcel is "a unit of real property with rights and interests" (Moyer and Fisher, 1973).

The FGDC expanded this definition slightly: "A parcel is a single cadastral unit, which is the spatial extent of the past, present, and future rights and interests in real property" (FGDC, 1999).

Both of these definitions portray the parcel as a set of rights and interests. This is because landownership parcels are not as simple as they may appear at first glance.

Although we speak of "owning" land, land, in fact, cannot be owned. It is the rights to use the land that are owned or held. Over time, rights and interests in land have passed from groups, or society, to individuals. These rights are conceptualized as a "bundle of sticks" (Danielsen, 1993).

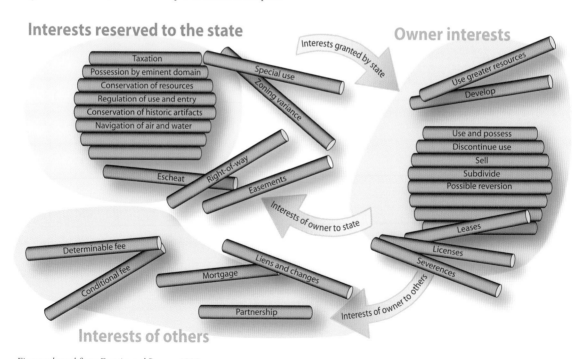

Figure adapted from Epstein and Brown, 1990

The sets of rights and interests individuals, organizations, or agencies hold define the uses that owners can enjoy.

> The collection of rights pertaining to any one land parcel may be likened to a bundle of sticks. From time to time the sticks may vary in number (representing the number of rights), in thickness (representing the size or "quantum" of each right), and in length (representing the duration of each right). Sometimes the whole bundle may be held by one person, or it may be held by a group of persons, such as a company or family or clan or tribe, but very often, separate sticks are held by different persons. Sticks out of the bundle can be acquired in different ways and held for different periods, but the ownership of the land is not itself one of the sticks; it must be regarded as a vessel or container for the bundle, the owner being the person (individual or corporate) who has the right to give out the sticks (Simpson, 1976).

This view of landownership in the United States is the result of centuries of evolving practices. According to Williamson and Ting (1999), countries influenced by Roman law or the Napoleonic Code generally view land as a commodity that can be owned in whole, while countries influenced by the British common law regard land as something to which one can have rights, that is, potentially, multiple independent owners. Most land tenure systems in Asia have been strongly influenced by the concepts of the British common law. All countries, regardless of their tenure system, have restrictions on land use in the interests of society.

In feudal times in Europe, cadastres were mainly used to publicly record ownership and support fiscal accounting. They have grown to support land transfer and land markets in the Industrial Age, and urban and regional planning in the post-World War II era. Since the 1980s:

> The focus has turned to wider issues of environmental degradation and sustainable development, as well as social equity. All of these issues will likely temper short-term economic imperatives. Planning issues have widened to include more community interests and deepened to address more detailed issues of land use. This has created a growing need for more complex information about land and land use, and the desire for multipurpose cadastres (Ting and Williamson, 1999).

It is not practical in this chapter to show examples of the parcel data model that would completely illustrate its use in every county and country. The examples in this chapter are largely drawn from Oakland County, Michigan, which does not map ownership parcels, but does reference ownership information via the Register of Deeds office. However, the essential data model showing all the feature classes developed through data model consortium activities is presented here, including ownership feature classes for completeness.

The ownership parcels in the parcel data model represent the surface ownership parcels. The specific set of rights and interests held in the surface are described in feature attributes and related objects. The mineral estate or subsurface ownership and overhead air rights are described in the separated rights. Easements across the land are represented in encumbrances. These are all described and illustrated in the sections that follow.

Most local governments in the United States do not manage both tax and ownership parcels. Ownership parcels are used where the Register of Deeds is tightly integrated with the parcel mapping function. In the United States, ownership parcels are normally of more interest in the context of federal lands management, such as to control mineral rights or grazing rights. However, there are a few local governments that manage ownership parcels instead of tax parcels, and even some that manage both.

Ownership parcels provide a geographic representation of deeds and surveys. If ownership parcels are included in your data model, they can be used to define the ownership characteristics of all land parcels and their chain of title.

Three polygon feature classes define ownership parcels in this parcel data model: OwnerParcel, SeparatedRights, and Encumbrance. These are basic parcel building blocks and can be used to support the many varied definitions of land parcels. The ownership parcels in the parcel data model represent *surface* ownership parcels. The specific set of rights and interests held in the surface are described in feature attributes and related objects. The mineral estate or subsurface ownership and overhead air rights are described in the separated rights. Easements across the land are represented in encumbrances.

OwnerParcel features are characterized as:

- Continuous—All land has ownership. The exact name of the owner may not be known. The exact spatial extent of ownership may not be known, but all land area has continuous ownership. There may be conflicts in ownership, but this does not negate that the ownership is intended to be continuous.

- Nonoverlapping—All land has a single set of current owners. If the surface ownership appears to be in conflict, this may be due to an error in a legal description or to some other ownership conflict or uncertainty.

According to Brown (1969), "Conflicts in ownership result where (a) two parties are given title to the same land, or (b) one party has title and another has possession, or (c) descriptions are ambiguous."

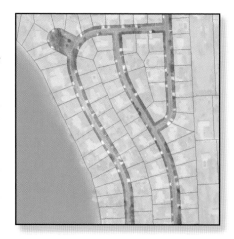

Notice the subtypes of OwnerParcel shown in the table on the next page. These are chosen to support many common queries, as well as for proper symbolization. No additional attributes are shown for OwnerParcel, since they would depend on each jurisdiction's policies and practices.

Each OwnerParcel is linked to its owner record through the parcel ID. This choice of key field, rather than owner ID, is preferred because parcel IDs are easier to control and maintain. The OwnerParcel also has an attribute for OwnerClassification (for example, local, state, or federal government or private sector) to support common queries and reporting requirements.

The VerticalParcel table shown is slightly different from the VerticalParcel table shown previously to illustrate the kind of adaptation users might make. Vertical ownership parcels are similar to the CondoRelate illustration given for tax parcels. This example uses BuildingID and UnitID attributes to identify an ownership parcel. The best choice of vertical parcel attributes depends on the purpose for the data and the level of detail available in the source data.

In the class descriptions shown so far, there are no implied relationships between owner parcels and tax parcels. However, in a jurisdiction that maintains both, these feature classes could be in the same topology, with rules such as "TaxParcel must be covered by OwnerParcel".

See Chapter 6, 'Surveying federal lands', for more examples and discussion of ownership parcels.

## Simple feature class
## OwnerParcel

| | Geometry | Polygon |
|---|---|---|
| | Contains M values | No |
| | Contains Z values | No |

*Represents a unit of real property on the surface with rights and interests*

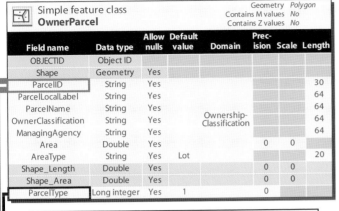

| Field name | Data type | Allow nulls | Default value | Domain | Precision | Scale | Length | |
|---|---|---|---|---|---|---|---|---|
| OBJECTID | Object ID | | | | | | | |
| Shape | Geometry | Yes | | | | | | |
| ParcelID | String | Yes | | | | | 30 | The primary key |
| ParcelLocalLabel | String | Yes | | | | | 64 | A cartographic name for the parcel |
| ParcelName | String | Yes | | | | | 64 | The common name for the parcel |
| OwnerClassification | String | Yes | | Ownership-Classification | | | 64 | Categories of public, private, and trust |
| ManagingAgency | String | Yes | | | | | 64 | Government agency managing this parcel if owner is public or trust |
| Area | Double | Yes | | | 0 | 0 | | The legal area of the parcel |
| AreaType | String | Yes | Lot | | | | 20 | Units used for the legal area |
| Shape_Length | Double | Yes | | | 0 | 0 | | |
| Shape_Area | Double | Yes | | | 0 | 0 | | |
| ParcelType | Long integer | Yes | 1 | | 0 | | | The cartographic classification of parcels |

## Subtypes of OwnerParcel

Subtype field *ParcelType*
Default subtype *1*

List of defined default values and domains for subtypes in this class

| Subtype Code | Subtype Description | Field name | Default value | Domain |
|---|---|---|---|---|
| 1 | Park | | No values set | |
| 2 | Lake | | No values set | |
| 3 | Forest | | No values set | |
| 7 | Other | | No values set | |
| 4 | Other water | | No values set | |
| 5 | Recreation area | | No values set | |
| 6 | Recreation trail | | No values set | |
| 8 | Private lands | | No values set | |
| 9 | Right-of-way | | No values set | |

## Relationship class
## OwnerParcelHasOwner

Type *Simple*  Forward label *Owner*
Cardinality *Many to many*
Notification *None*  Backward label *OwnerParcel*

| Origin feature class | Destination table |
|---|---|
| Name *OwnerParcel* | Name *Owner* |
| Primary key *ParcelID* | Primary key *OwnerID* |
| Foreign key *ParcelID* | Foreign key *OwnerID* |

*No relationship rules defined.*

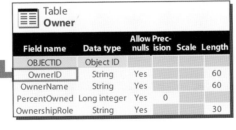

## Table
## Owner

*Represents the owner and interests*

| Field name | Data type | Allow nulls | Precision | Scale | Length | |
|---|---|---|---|---|---|---|
| OBJECTID | Object ID | | | | | |
| OwnerID | String | Yes | | | 60 | The primary key |
| OwnerName | String | Yes | | | 60 | Person or corporation with interest |
| PercentOwned | Long integer | Yes | 0 | | | The fraction of ownership |
| OwnershipRole | String | Yes | | | 30 | Type of interest the owner has in the parcel |

## Relationship class
## OwnerParcelHasVerticalParcel

Type *Simple*  Forward label *VerticalParcel*
Cardinality *One to many*
Notification *None*  Backward label *OwnerParcel*

| Origin feature class | Destination table |
|---|---|
| Name *OwnerParcel* | Name *VerticalParcel* |
| Primary key *ParcelID* | |
| Foreign key *PrimaryParcelID* | |

*No relationship rules defined.*

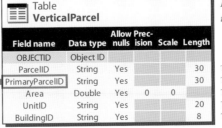

## Table
## VerticalParcel

*Represents buildings or units in a condominium*

| Field name | Data type | Allow nulls | Precision | Scale | Length | |
|---|---|---|---|---|---|---|
| OBJECTID | Object ID | | | | | |
| ParcelID | String | Yes | | | 30 | The primary key |
| PrimaryParcelID | String | Yes | | | 30 | The foreign key to OwnerParcel |
| Area | Double | Yes | 0 | 0 | | The legal area of the parcel |
| UnitID | String | Yes | | | 20 | The unit designation |
| BuildingID | String | Yes | | | 8 | The building identifier |

Separated rights are rights and interests in landownership that have been disconnected from the primary or fee simple surface ownership. For example, mineral and oil
rights are often separated from the surface ownership. Aboveground air rights may be
separated as well. Some countries do not recognize this notion, having the custom of
recognizing ownership of land "to the center of the earth." For those countries in which
certain rights can be separated, these rights are represented in the parcel data model
as polygon features.

## SEPARATED RIGHTS

Separated rights are represented as overlapping noncontinuous polygons. The separated rights are modeled similarly
to encumbrances (see below). Some of the idiosyncrasies of
separated rights are:

- There are often future estates and leases associated with
  minerals. In these cases, the mineral rights may be separated from the surface for a limited period of time.

- The mineral rights can be divided according to the mineral. For example, fossil fuels, oil and gas, sulfite minerals,
  and surface quarry rock are often considered as distinct
  separated rights.

- The apex rule for minerals that are found as defined
  veins and are claimed under the 1872 mining claims act
  provides for extralateral rights. This means that whoever
  claims the surface expression of a veined mineral deposit
  has the rights to the mineral deposit even though it may
  pass under the land of adjoiners. This is shown below.

There are also aboveground separated rights, such as solar
easements and transferable development rights (TDRs).
These, too, are potentially overlapping and noncontinuous
polygons. Overhead or aboveground separated rights tend
to be three-dimensional envelopes, although they can be
expressed with a flat or two-dimensional expression.

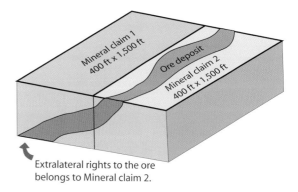

Extralateral rights to the ore
belongs to Mineral claim 2.

Separated rights are modeled as polygon features. There
could be any number of overlapping polygons based on the
type of mineral. Two examples of mineral claim types are
lode, a mineral that is in place and generally in a vein, and
placer, all forms of mineral deposits that aren't in place—
generally minerals in a loose state. The model includes a
ParcelReference table for storing additional details about
specific separated rights.

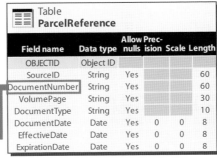

## Simple feature class
### SeparatedRight

| | | Geometry | Polygon | | |
|---|---|---|---|---|---|
| | | Contains M values | No | | |
| | | Contains Z values | No | | |

| Field name | Data type | Allow nulls | Precision | Scale | Length |
|---|---|---|---|---|---|
| OBJECTID | Object ID | | | | |
| Shape | Geometry | Yes | | | |
| SeparatedRightID | String | Yes | | | 30 |
| RightOwner | String | Yes | | | 30 |
| RightType | String | Yes | | | 30 |
| RightMineral1 | String | Yes | | | 30 |
| Area | Double | Yes | 0 | 0 | |
| AreaType | String | Yes | | | 30 |
| Shape_Length | Double | Yes | 0 | 0 | |
| Shape_Area | Double | Yes | 0 | 0 | |

*A separated right represents rights and interests in landownership that can be disconnected from the primary surface ownership.*

The primary key
Owner of the right
Type of right

The legal area of the separated right
Unit used for the legal area

## Table
### ParcelReference

| Field name | Data type | Allow nulls | Precision | Scale | Length |
|---|---|---|---|---|---|
| OBJECTID | Object ID | | | | |
| SourceID | String | Yes | | | 60 |
| DocumentNumber | String | Yes | | | 60 |
| VolumePage | String | Yes | | | 30 |
| DocumentType | String | Yes | | | 10 |
| DocumentDate | Date | Yes | 0 | 0 | 8 |
| EffectiveDate | Date | Yes | 0 | 0 | 8 |
| ExpirationDate | Date | Yes | 0 | 0 | 8 |

*A parcel reference contains additional information about the parcel.*

The primary key
Common reference for document
Page number in the volume
Which ownership rights are held
Date of the document
Date of approval or recording
Date the document expires

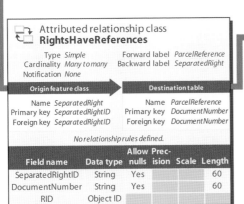

## Attributed relationship class
### RightsHaveReferences

| Type | Simple | Forward label | ParcelReference |
|---|---|---|---|
| Cardinality | Many to many | Backward label | SeparatedRight |
| Notification | None | | |

| Origin feature class | Destination table |
|---|---|
| Name *SeparatedRight* | Name *ParcelReference* |
| Primary key *SeparatedRightID* | Primary key *DocumentNumber* |
| Foreign key *SeparatedRightID* | Foreign key *DocumentNumber* |

*No relationship rules defined.*

| Field name | Data type | Allow nulls | Precision | Scale | Length |
|---|---|---|---|---|---|
| SeparatedRightID | String | Yes | | | 60 |
| DocumentNumber | String | Yes | | | 60 |
| RID | Object ID | | | | |

**5**

Encumbrances are limitations on the use of land. Rights-of-way and utility easements are two common types of encumbrances, but there are many others, such as the U.S. Army Corps of Engineers' right to flood an area when creating a lake. Encumbrances are polygon features that may cover part or all of a parcel or group of parcels and may have an associated legal description. Mortgages and liens are types of encumbrances that can be described using the ParcelReference table. Still more elaborate systems can be developed based on your specific needs.

## ENCUMBRANCES

Black defined encumbrances in 1991 as:

> Any right to, or interest in, land which may subsist the fee [ownership] by another to the diminution of its value, but consistent with the passing of the fee [ownership] by conveyance. A claim, lien, charge, or liability attached to and binding real property; examples are a mortgage, judgment lien, mechanic's lien, lease, security interest, easement, or right-of-way. If the liability relates to a particular asset, the asset is encumbered.

Most encumbrances run with the land. That is, they are tied to the land and will persist from owner to owner. Others exist at the pleasure of the owner. Encumbrances may have an effective date and expiration date. In the parcel data model, encumbrances are polygon features having their own legal descriptions. Encumbrances are characterized as:

- Overlapping—Encumbrances can overlap. For example, ingress and egress of an easement or a prescriptive right-of-way can overlap.

- Noncontinuous—There are many areas of land that are free from encumbrances.

The map above shows a parcel with a utility easement and a prescriptive road right-of-way. The encumbrances overlap and are noncontinuous, as described above.

The question of whether roads are an encumbrance or a fee simple interest varies from jurisdiction to jurisdiction. Brown (1995) defines a prescriptive easement as "the acquisition of an easement by adverse use under claim of right for a statutory period required by law."

In many states, prescriptive easements are a specified width such as 4 rods (66 feet). The description of an ownership parcel may extend to the center of the prescriptive right-of-way, but the public controls the use of land in the prescriptive easement. This is a case where one of the sticks in the bundle of rights for the parcel belongs to the public for a right-of-way. The owner may have future reversion rights if the right-of-way is vacated (abandoned).

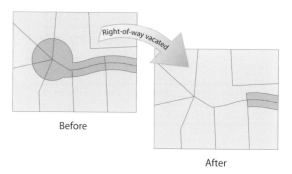

Before

After

The before and after maps above show one example from a parcel map where an encumbrance was vacated and adjoining parcels took reversion rights for their portions of the vacated right-of-way.

Should prescriptive areas be shown publicly held parcels in the ownership parcels or should the underlying owner be shown with the prescriptive right or reversion right shown as an easement? The parcel data model allows for either scenario, and it is up to you to decide how to map and manage prescriptive easements and reversion rights. If the prescriptive areas have separate ownership, then the ownership representation is continuous. If the underlying landowner is shown as holding the land with an easement on top, the ownership is represented as continuous polygon features with encumbrances to represent the full picture. The differences will be in the processes applied to determine the tax parcel and in how related tables and relationships are connected to the objects.

| Simple feature class **Encumbrance** | | Geometry | *Polygon* | | | |
|---|---|---|---|---|---|---|
| | | Contains M values | *No* | | | |
| | | Contains Z values | *No* | | | |
| Field name | Data type | Allow nulls | Prec-ision | Scale | Length | |
| OBJECTID | Object ID | | | | | |
| Shape | Geometry | Yes | | | | |
| EncumbranceID | String | Yes | | | 30 | The primary key |
| EncumbranceType | String | Yes | | | 30 | Types, such as easement, claim, lien, and right-of-way |
| EncumbranceOwner | String | Yes | | | 64 | Name of the owner |
| Area | Double | Yes | 0 | 0 | | The legal area of the parcel |
| AreaType | String | Yes | | | 20 | The units used for the legal area |
| Shape_Length | Double | Yes | 0 | 0 | | |
| Shape_Area | Double | Yes | 0 | 0 | | |

*Encumbrances are limitations on rights and uses of land.*

There are essential feature classes for parcel users that are slightly beyond the scope of a parcel data model. These are called Related Uses because they are closely related to parcels but are not likely to be managed by a parcel mapping group. Addresses are typically assigned by a city's legal addressing authority. Regulated uses and restrictions are outputs from the community planning process.

The feature classes in this section are examples to illustrate the connection between the parcel data model and related uses, such as addresses, regulations, and property restrictions. For general purposes of the parcel data model, these feature classes are grouped with other administrative feature classes in a feature class collection independent of parcel topology. Users may also wish to create more expansive data models for site addressing, regulated uses, and restrictions.

## SITE ADDRESSES

Maps and other representations of parcel information through an address point can serve many departments. Site addresses are points within a parcel that serve as a location for the site address information.

Site address points are a geolocation for a site address. Most site addresses are assigned to structures. For example, a building may have one site address that can span multiple parcels; a parcel may not have a site address, such as vacant land; or a parcel could have multiple site addresses, such as parcel with many buildings or businesses.

For some applications, there may also be important supplemental address points. For example, in rural environments there may be related points that identify the end of the driveway for emergency vehicles. In urban environments,

there may be points that identify entrances to and turns on major roads to gain access to the parcel. These related points are not included in this parcel data model design, but it is recognized that these can be important points.

This map illustrates structures on parcels with site address points. Parcel information can be linked to the site address point. The structures may have more than one address, as in condominiums. See Chapter 4, 'Addresses and locations', for more information.

| Simple feature class **SiteAddress** | | Geometry | Point |
| | | Contains M values | No |
| | | Contains Z values | No |

| Field name | Data type | Allow nulls | Length | |
|---|---|---|---|---|
| OBJECTID | OID | | | |
| Shape | Geometry | Yes | | |
| AddressText | String | Yes | 64 | The street number and all prefixes and suffixes, including the full street name |
| StreetNumber | String | Yes | 10 | Number assigned to building or land parcel along the street to identify location and ensure accurate mail delivery |
| StreetNumberSuffix | String | Yes | 10 | A subnumber to a street number |
| StreetPrefix | String | Yes | 10 | A predirectional field |
| StreetName | String | Yes | 64 | Official name of a street, assigned by a local governing authority |
| StreetType | String | Yes | 10 | Generally defined by the postal service; includes common street indications, such as street, avenue, and boulevard |
| StreetSuffix | String | Yes | 10 | The directional symbol representing the sector of a city where a street address is located |
| Municipality | String | Yes | 64 | A finer partitioning of geographic subdivisions of a county, usually associated with additional levels of government |

*Represents important addresses and their locations within a parcel. Can be used for simple parcel mapping or more sophisticated address management purposes.*

## REGULATED USES

Regulated uses represent limitations imposed on land by a public agency. These are independent of the chain of title. One common example is land use zoning.

The map on the right illustrates Euclidean zoning, which is based on district and use.

Information about restrictions on the nature, usage, and physical dimensions, including setbacks and density, for these districts would be described in a zoning ordinance.

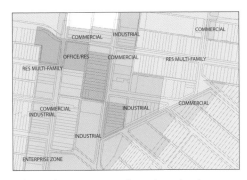

| Simple feature class **RegulatedUse** | | Geometry | *Polygon* | | |
|---|---|---|---|---|---|
| | | Contains M values | *No* | | |
| | | Contains Z values | *No* | | |

| Field name | Data type | Allow nulls | Prec-ision | Scale | Length |
|---|---|---|---|---|---|
| OBJECTID | OID | | | | |
| Shape | Geometry | Yes | | | |
| RegulatedID | String | Yes | | | 30 |
| RegulationType | String | Yes | | | 8 |
| RegulationClassification | String | Yes | | | 30 |
| RegulationDescription | String | Yes | | | 64 |
| RegulationAgency | String | Yes | | | 64 |
| Shape_Length | Double | Yes | 0 | 0 | |
| Shape_Area | Double | Yes | 0 | 0 | |

*Regulated use polygons capture information related to limitations or permissions for the use and enjoyment of land by a public agency or authority. Zoning is a common example of a regulated use.*

The primary key for the object class

Indicates the category, source, or location of the regulation, such as a zoning district

The district or classification of the regulation applied by the public agency

Describes the regulations applied to the polygon, such as setbacks

The public agency that enforces the regulated use

---

In the map on the right, the zoning district boundaries are contiguous with the parcel boundaries, but this may not always be the case.

## RESTRICTIONS

Restriction polygons capture information related to limitations or permissions for the use and enjoyment of land by the land right holder, such as a homeowners' association that prohibits members from parking recreational vehicles in the driveway or from having detached garages.

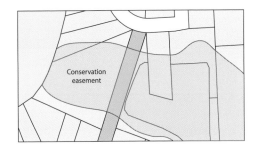

Conservation easement

| Simple feature class **Restriction** | | Geometry | *Polygon* | | | |
|---|---|---|---|---|---|---|
| | | Contains M values | *No* | | | |
| | | Contains Z values | *No* | | | |

| Field name | Data type | Allow nulls | Default value | Domain | Prec-ision | Scale | Length |
|---|---|---|---|---|---|---|---|
| OBJECTID | OID | | | | | | |
| Shape | Geometry | Yes | | | | | |
| RestrictionID | String | Yes | | | | | 30 |
| RestrictionType | String | Yes | Restrictive-Covenant | Restriction-Type | | | 20 |
| RestrictionDescription | String | Yes | | | | | 30 |
| RestrictionAgency | String | Yes | | | | | 64 |
| Shape_Length | Double | Yes | | | 0 | 0 | |
| Shape_Area | Double | Yes | | | 0 | 0 | |

*Restriction polygons capture information related to limitations or permissions for the use and enjoyment of land by the land right holder.*

The primary key for the object class

Indicates the category, source, or location of the restriction

Describes the restriction on the parcel

Person, individual, or organization to whom the restriction applies

"Administrative areas" is a generic term for many different kinds of overlays that may or may not coincide with parcel boundaries. Two kinds of boundaries are discussed here: map index and tax district. In practice, GIS users of this data model will create any number of additional administrative areas, depending on their application needs.

Administrative areas are any division of land for managing or governing programs or agencies. Very common examples include map indexes, school and tax districts, and service areas—water service, pumping stations, trash collection areas, and so on.

## MAP INDEX

A common type of administrative area is a map index, used in conjunction with a local government's series of map sheets of its jurisdiction. These are usually square areas defined at regular intervals, such as one-eighth, one-fourth, or one-half mile, or they may be based on a coordinate system, such as a state plane coordinate system, and defined by a constant east and north coordinate value. From the map index, a user can find where the hardcopy or online map for that area is stored.

| 1218 | 1219 | 1220 | 1221 |
| 1318 | 1219 | 1320 | 1321 |
| 1418 | 1419 | 1420 | 1421 |
| 1518 | 1519 | 1520 | 1521 |

| Simple feature class **MapIndex** | | Geometry | *Polygon* | | |
|---|---|---|---|---|---|
| | | Contains M values | *No* | | |
| | | Contains Z values | *No* | | |
| **Field name** | **Data type** | **Allow nulls** | **Prec- ision** | **Scale** | **Length** |
| OBJECTID | OID | | | | |
| Shape | Geometry | Yes | | | |
| MapSheetNumber | String | Yes | | | 60 |
| Shape_Length | Double | Yes | 0 | 0 | |
| Shape_Area | Double | Yes | 0 | 0 | |

*These are usually square areas defined at regular intervals, such as every mile, or based on a coordinate system, such as a state plane coordinate system, and defined by a constant east and north coordinate value.*

The label or other identifier of the cell within a map index system

## TAX DISTRICT

In the figure on the right, the boundaries define what schools children attend and which school taxes are levied on the property tax roll. Notice that the school district boundaries do not always follow the owner parcel boundaries but generally do follow tax parcel boundaries. The other administrative areas shown are neighborhoods, which generally follow owner parcel boundaries, although there are exceptions.

School districts are a kind of tax district. Counties, cities, villages, towns, and townships are other examples of administrative areas. These types of areas may benefit from parcel information as a reference, or they may be intended to follow parcel boundaries.

| Simple feature class **TaxDistrict** | | Geometry | *Polygon* | | | |
|---|---|---|---|---|---|---|
| | | Contains M values | *No* | | | |
| | | Contains Z values | *No* | | | |
| **Field name** | **Data type** | **Allow nulls** | **Precision** | **Scale** | **Length** | |
| OBJECTID | OID | | | | | |
| Shape | Geometry | Yes | | | | |
| AreaName | String | Yes | | | 60 | |
| ParentName | String | Yes | | | 60 | |
| DistrictName | String | Yes | | | 60 | |
| DistrictCode | String | Yes | | | 60 | |
| Shape_Length | Double | Yes | 0 | 0 | | |
| Shape_Area | Double | Yes | 0 | 0 | | |

*Tax districts are defined based on areas of similar value and characteristics for taxation purposes.*

The type of tax district
The name of a parent tax district
The name of the tax district
The common code used for the district

**5**

Three data layers are commonly used as a base reference for parcels: orthophotos, elevation, and a comprehensive representation of surveys for the study area. Orthophotos are useful for providing up-to-date, spatially referenced imagery to help locate structures in and around parcels, such as buildings and roads. Digital elevation datasets provide a relief map for a study area. Survey datasets provide a highly accurate control network to tie parcels to ground locations.

### RASTER DATASETS

For decades, many local governments have collected aerial imagery of their jurisdictions. Today, it is possible to obtain inexpensive satellite imagery with sufficient resolution to replace photogrammetry in many applications. In most areas, especially met-

ropolitan, the images are updated on a regular basis, such as every two years. Given enough time, the historical library of these records can be interesting for research and analysis.

In addition to aerial photographs and satellite imagery,

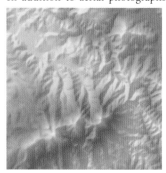

another form of raster data is a grid of elevation postings. Additional raster datasets can be derived from an elevation grid, such as hillshaded and watershed drainage grids. For example, the complete 30-meter hillshaded DEM for the United States is available online from the USGS through the Geography Network (www.geographynetwork.com) and can be freely added as a layer in a map document without downloading the data to a local server.

Whatever the application, a local government can acquire numerous raster datasets.

Chapter 7, 'Using raster data', provides examples and detailed design discussion.

*Detail of orthophoto base from Oakland County, Michigan*

## SURVEY DATASETS

Surveying is the discipline of collecting accurate measurements to determine the relative spatial locations of points on or near the surface of the earth. Named spatial locations are represented by one or more coordinate points.

To establish coordinates for points, surveyors use precise field instruments, procedures, and computations. They measure slope, horizontal, and vertical distances between points, and angles between lines of sight. Each subsequent survey updates point locations and adds to a computation network.

Measurements, computations, survey points, and coordinates, collectively called survey objects, can be managed in a comprehensive survey dataset. In addition to storing these objects, survey datasets can be used to update dependencies in a computation network as subsequent surveys are performed.

Survey datasets can be used to enhance feature classes with survey awareness, allowing stored features to be associated with survey coordinates. If the GIS supports the notion of survey-aware feature classes, then the survey-based data can be used to automatically correct the locations of dependent GIS features.

Today, a number of government agencies collect survey data as part of their routine work flow. This is expected to grow as the cost of global positioning satellite (GPS)-based surveys continues to drop and will improve the quality of parcel boundary information. The next step is to integrate these surveys with traditional GIS data using survey datasets. Several progressive government agencies will begin to incorporate survey data into their information holdings to gain higher-quality parcel representations.

Chapter 6, 'Surveying federal lands', provides more examples and discussion of survey datasets.

**Survey-aware feature classes**

| Feature class |
| --- |
| Corner |
| Boundary |
| TaxParcel |
| SimultaneousConveyance |
| SurveyFirstDivision |
| SurveySecondDivision |

*Survey-aware feature classes can participate in a topology. In these cases, all of the topologically integrated feature classes should be survey-aware.*

5

**GIS geodatabase**
## feature

*Vertices in survey-aware feature classes can be linked and, optionally, adjusted when im-proved survey point locations are*

**Measurement database**
## survey point

*Survey locations can be associated with feature geometry. When survey locations are adjusted, linked feature shapes are updated.*

**Measurement database**
## measurement

*A computation network stores dependencies among computations and refines positional accuracy with additional measurements.*

You may have noticed that certain terms, such as continuous, noncontinuous, overlapping, and nonoverlapping, appear numerous times in this chapter. These are important business rules and behaviors that can be enforced within the database using topology. Topology defines how features share geometry. Simply put, topology represents a set of spatial relationships that may exist between two or more features. These relationships include adjacency, intersection, overlap, and many others. Topology integrity rules are an important part of the geodatabase definition.

Modern GIS software allows users the flexibility and ease of defining their topology requirements in terms of data integrity rules. This section presents the key topological rules applied in the parcel data model.

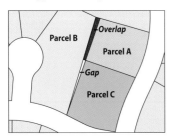

Tax and owner parcels are intended to be continuous and nonoverlapping. This does not mean they always are, but over the long term, errors tend to be corrected.

For example, the three parcels shown above have an overlap between Parcels A and B, and a gap between parcels B and C. The overlap and gap may be due to ambiguous legal descriptions or incorrect mapping representation. Either way, this situation results in five ownership parcel polygons in the GIS. The polygon between parcels B and C may be coded as a gap or unknown ownership and the polygon between parcels A and B may be coded as an overlap or conflict. Alternatively, the shaded areas may be assigned to one of the adjoining owners. These are decisions that each jurisdiction will need to make in its parcel mapping programs. The parcel data model accommodates a wide variety of solutions to this situation.

In a geodatabase topology, several feature classes can participate in a topology. One of the integrity rules that can be set is a coordinate rank that defines which features have the highest level of accuracy. When coordinates of features with a lower rank are within the cluster tolerance of the coordinates of more accurate features, they will be adjusted to the more accurate coordinates. Coordinate ranks for this parcel implementation indicate that boundary lines, having a rank of 1,

are the most accurate because they are entered using COGO. The coordinates of the other feature classes have a lower rank and will be adjusted to the boundary coordinates within the cluster tolerance.

Topology rules can be defined either within a single feature class or subtype or between two feature classes or subtypes, and each rule essentially reads like a complete sentence. In this list, there are two kinds of rules within a single class: Must not have dangles and Must not overlap. Another common rule is Must not have gaps; however, this rule is not used in this model because each of the feature classes is typically noncontinuous on a parcel map; that is, gaps often occur at common areas, such as roads. However, depending on your system and policies, you may find it useful to add this rule as well.

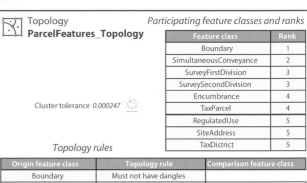

**Topology**
**ParcelFeatures_Topology**

*Participating feature classes and ranks*

| Feature class | Rank |
|---|---|
| Boundary | 1 |
| SimultaneousConveyance | 2 |
| SurveyFirstDivision | 3 |
| SurveySecondDivision | 3 |
| Encumbrance | 4 |
| TaxParcel | 4 |
| RegulatedUse | 5 |
| SiteAddress | 5 |
| TaxDistrict | 5 |

Cluster tolerance *0.000247*

*Topology rules*

| Origin feature class | Topology rule | Comparison feature class |
|---|---|---|
| Boundary | Must not have dangles | |
| TaxParcel | Boundary must be covered by | Boundary |
| SimultaneousConveyance | Boundary must be covered by | Boundary |
| SurveyFirstDivision | Boundary must be covered by | Boundary |
| TaxParcel | Must not overlap | |
| SimultaneousConveyance | Must not overlap | |
| SurveyFirstDivision | Must be covered by | SimultaneousConveyance |
| SurveyFirstDivision | Must not overlap | |
| SurveySecondDivision | Must be covered by | SurveyFirstDivision |
| SurveySecondDivision | Must not overlap | |

There are several types of rules between feature classes in this list. The rule SimultaneousConveyance boundary must be covered by Boundary means that all sides of the exterior of a simultaneous conveyance polygon feature must coincide with a Boundary line feature. Another rule, SurveyFirstDivision must be covered by SimultaneousConveyance, means that wherever a SurveyFirstDivision polygon appears, it must fit within a separate SimultaneousConveyance polygon.

Topology rules could also be applied to site addresses. For example, SiteAddress must be inside TaxParcel and TaxParcel contains point SiteAddress. These are symmetric rules, to make sure that every parcel has at least one address, and every address is located within a parcel.

**Survey-aware feature classes**

| Feature class |
| --- |
| Corner |
| Boundary |
| TaxParcel |
| SimultaneousConveyance |
| SurveyFirstDivision |
| SurveySecondDivision |

*Survey-aware feature classes can participate in a topology. In these cases, all of the topologically integrated feature classes should be survey-aware.*

**TaxParcel must not overlap**

**Boundary must not have dangles**

*Also SimultaneousConveyance, SurveyFirstDivision, and SurveySecondDivision*

## topology rules in the land parcel data model

**Corner** **must be covered by endpoint of** **Boundary**

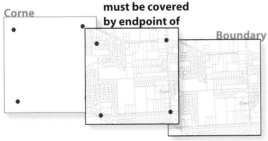

**TaxParcel** **boundary must be covered by** **Boundary**

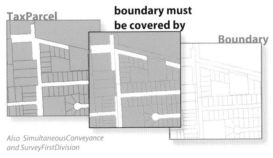

*Also SimultaneousConveyance and SurveyFirstDivision*

**Boundary** **endpoint must be covered by** **Corner**

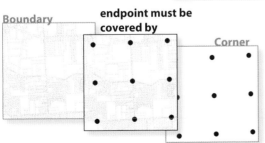

**SurveyFirstDivision** **must be covered by** **Simultaneous-Conveyance**

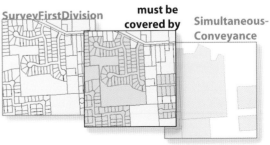

5

This parcel model decision tree contains a progression of questions and steps to help you decide which elements of the parcel data model your agency needs. The parcel data model is a rich set of feature classes that cover many contingencies for a variety of jurisdictions. However, your agency may only require a portion of the parcel data model. This decision tree gives you guidance on which of the feature classes you should select to include in your geodatabase. You can incrementally add feature classes as your project advances to meet your business requirements.

## Do you build on and manage a parcel framework?

The parcel framework is the primary division of parcels used for parcel mapping and reference. In the public domain states of the United States, the divisions of the PLSS—township, section, and section divisions—form the parcel framework for mapping and legal descriptions. In other areas of the United States, there may be municipal or town divisions with further divisions into map sheets or other regular divisions. Most mapping jurisdictions have some sort of parcel framework.

If you are outside the United States, you should modify the parcel framework of your data model for your local requirements.

## Do you manage survey information?

If you track and store distance, direction, source, and accuracy information about parcel lines from multiple surveys, then you are managing survey information.

You do not need to fully manage the measurements in a survey dataset to use parcel coordinate geometry and distance annotation on your parcel boundaries. In addition to managing the measurements between corners, you will probably manage information about the corners themselves, such as monument recovery notes.

## Do you manage tax parcels?

Tax parcels are most commonly managed by counties and local governments. These parcels have a related record in a tax or assessment roll and are used to support the tax assessment program.

## Do you manage ownership information?

Ownership parcels may be used as the foundation to build tax parcels. Ownership parcels will, by definition, provide a spatial representation of all deeds and surveys. All the land in the jurisdiction will be accounted for in an ownership mapping program, and it will be possible to generate chain of title information from the maps. In most U.S. counties, a typical land records system will begin with the tax parcels and could evolve to the ownership parcels.

## Do you manage rights and interests in land?

The rights and interests in land are the individual components of ownership. These components are sometimes thought of as a bundle of sticks that can be separated. For example, the mineral rights are often separated from the surface rights. Are grazing rights and hunting rights tracked and managed within your system? If they are, then you probably manage rights and interests.

## Do you manage data related to parcels at a local level?

Administrative areas are related to parcel information, such as school districts, tax districts, and municipal boundaries. These districts and administrative areas are often mapped based on parcel boundaries. For example, a school district might be defined by merging all of the parcels coded as being in that district; this is called a dissolve operation in GIS systems.

Sometimes these boundaries are captured independently of the parcel boundaries, such as with many school district boundaries. When these districts are combined with the parcels, they must be integrated to remove slivers and other inconsistencies.

# Parcel model decision tree

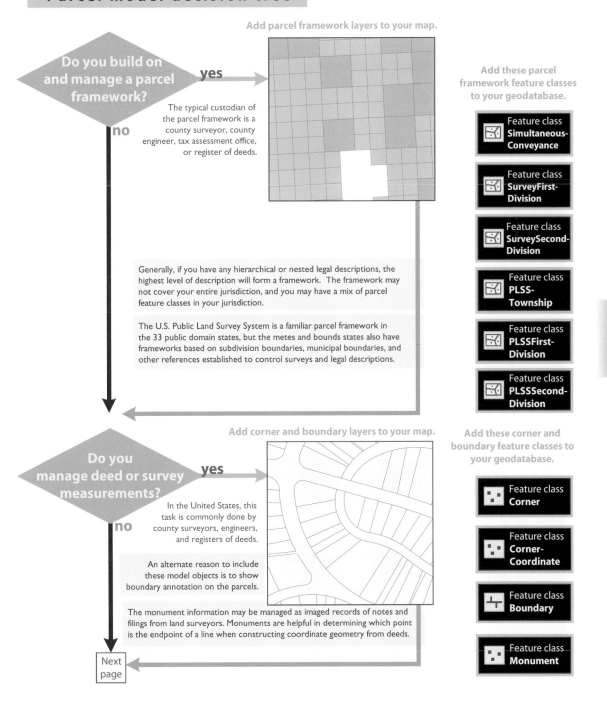

Add parcel framework layers to your map.

**Do you build on and manage a parcel framework?** — **yes**

The typical custodian of the parcel framework is a county surveyor, county engineer, tax assessment office, or register of deeds.

**no**

Add these parcel framework feature classes to your geodatabase.

Feature class **Simultaneous-Conveyance**

Feature class **SurveyFirst-Division**

Feature class **SurveySecond-Division**

Feature class **PLSS-Township**

Feature class **PLSSFirst-Division**

Feature class **PLSSSecond-Division**

Generally, if you have any hierarchical or nested legal descriptions, the highest level of description will form a framework. The framework may not cover your entire jurisdiction, and you may have a mix of parcel feature classes in your jurisdiction.

The U.S. Public Land Survey System is a familiar parcel framework in the 33 public domain states, but the metes and bounds states also have frameworks based on subdivision boundaries, municipal boundaries, and other references established to control surveys and legal descriptions.

Add corner and boundary layers to your map.

**Do you manage deed or survey measurements?** — **yes**

In the United States, this task is commonly done by county surveyors, engineers, and registers of deeds.

**no**

An alternate reason to include these model objects is to show boundary annotation on the parcels.

The monument information may be managed as imaged records of notes and filings from land surveyors. Monuments are helpful in determining which point is the endpoint of a line when constructing coordinate geometry from deeds.

Add these corner and boundary feature classes to your geodatabase.

Feature class **Corner**

Feature class **Corner-Coordinate**

Feature class **Boundary**

Feature class **Monument**

Next page

5

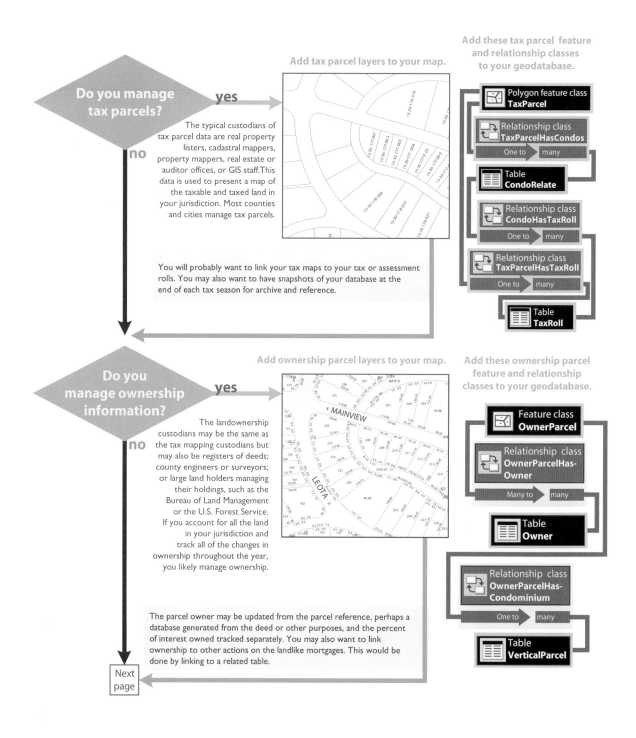

Add tax parcel layers to your map.

Add these tax parcel feature and relationship classes to your geodatabase.

**Do you manage tax parcels?**

**yes**

The typical custodians of tax parcel data are real property listers, cadastral mappers, property mappers, real estate or auditor offices, or GIS staff. This data is used to present a map of the taxable and taxed land in your jurisdiction. Most counties and cities manage tax parcels.

**no**

You will probably want to link your tax maps to your tax or assessment rolls. You may also want to have snapshots of your database at the end of each tax season for archive and reference.

Polygon feature class **TaxParcel**

Relationship class **TaxParcelHasCondos**
One to many

Table **CondoRelate**

Relationship class **CondoHasTaxRoll**
One to many

Relationship class **TaxParcelHasTaxRoll**
One to many

Table **TaxRoll**

Add ownership parcel layers to your map.

Add these ownership parcel feature and relationship classes to your geodatabase.

**Do you manage ownership information?**

**yes**

The landownership custodians may be the same as the tax mapping custodians but may also be registers of deeds; county engineers or surveyors; or large land holders managing their holdings, such as the Bureau of Land Management or the U.S. Forest Service. If you account for all the land in your jurisdiction and track all of the changes in ownership throughout the year, you likely manage ownership.

**no**

The parcel owner may be updated from the parcel reference, perhaps a database generated from the deed or other purposes, and the percent of interest owned tracked separately. You may also want to link ownership to other actions on the land like mortgages. This would be done by linking to a related table.

Feature class **OwnerParcel**

Relationship class **OwnerParcelHas-Owner**
Many to many

Table **Owner**

Relationship class **OwnerParcelHas-Condominium**
One to many

Table **VerticalParcel**

Next page

## Do you manage rights and interests in land?

**yes**

Typical custodians are large landholders and land management agencies, such as state landownership management agencies, the Bureau of Land Management, and the Forest Service in the United States. Some local governments may include encumbrances, such as utility easements, on their tax parcels, but most local governments do not map and manage mineral rights.

The domain of values for the mineral types will vary depending on what is commonly extracted or separated in your area. Likewise, the indication of the type of easement will depend on what most commonly occurs in your area, for example, utility, ingress and egress, and conservation are three commonly mapped easements.

**no**

Add rights and interests layers to your map.

Add these rights and interests feature and relationship classes to your geodatabase.

Feature class
**Separated-Right**

Relationship class
**RightsHave-References**

Many to   many

Table
**ParcelReference**

Feature class
**Encumbrance**

## Do you manage data related to parcels at a local level?

**yes**

These are the districts and administrative areas that may be derived from the parcel or map, form a defining limit for parcels, or define the authority or jurisdiction for parcel information. This category also includes map sheets, such as tax map system indices.

This information is usually managed by the same group that manages the parcel, either ownership or tax, and is often used by a wide variety of applications. For example, school districts might affect and be managed by the real property tax manager but may also be important for school bus routing and demographic information.

**no**

Add rights and interests layers to your map.

Add these tax parcel feature and relationship classes to your geodatabase.

Feature class
**SiteAddress**

Feature class
**RegulatedUse**

Feature class
**Restriction**

Feature class
**TaxDistrict**

Feature class
**MapIndex**

Finish

In the United States, local governments maintain a series of standardized parcel maps to cover a sizeable geographic area at large map scales. The map shown here illustrates many typical parts of a parcel map.

## CADASTRAL AND LAND RECORDS MAPPING

Government agencies need to create map sheets of all of the parcels in their jurisdiction at multiple scales. Every parcel must be shown whole on at least one sheet, if possible.

Some counties still maintain a map book and page hardcopy of their parcels. The boundaries for these areas are irregular and somewhat arbitrary. However, there is a need to be able to plot parcel maps based on the deed book and page boundaries. In many cases, the map pages often form the polygons of a map index layer, which is used in tax map production. This is the intent of the MapIndex feature class.

Some counties and cities provide tax assessor maps to the general public. These maps are included in some large-scale map series. You can come up with a number of different variations of the content, but the reason for the series remains the same: to regularly print maps of the extent of the municipality at a large scale. Some example data includes cadastral base maps; zoning maps; emergency fire hydrant maps; and water, sewer, and storm infrastructure maps.

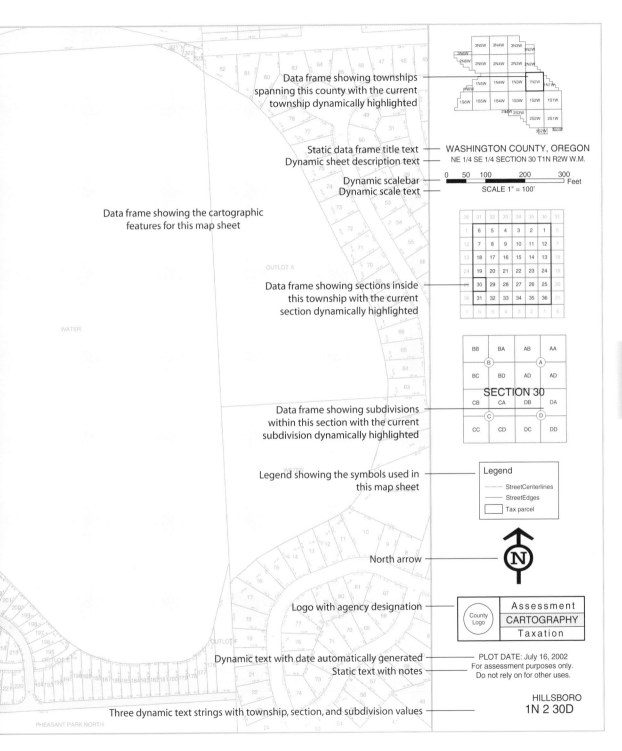

Data frame showing townships spanning this county with the current township dynamically highlighted

Static data frame title text — WASHINGTON COUNTY, OREGON
Dynamic sheet description text — NE 1/4 SE 1/4 SECTION 30 T1N R2W W.M.

Dynamic scalebar
Dynamic scale text — SCALE 1" = 100'

Data frame showing the cartographic features for this map sheet

OUTLOT A

WATER

Data frame showing sections inside this township with the current section dynamically highlighted

SECTION 30

Data frame showing subdivisions within this section with the current subdivision dynamically highlighted

WATER

Legend showing the symbols used in this map sheet

Legend
StreetCenterlines
StreetEdges
Tax parcel

North arrow

Logo with agency designation — County Logo | Assessment CARTOGRAPHY Taxation

Dynamic text with date automatically generated — PLOT DATE: July 16, 2002
Static text with notes — For assessment purposes only. Do not rely on for other uses.

HILLSBORO

Three dynamic text strings with township, section, and subdivision values — 1N 2 30D

PHEASANT PARK NORTH

5

Parcel maps and parcel information in databases are continuously updated over time. Real estate transactions, parcel splits, and new subdivisions occur almost continuously. This section describes a number of approaches for tracking historical parcel information in the database. When considering history tracking or data archiving, users generally want to know the state of the parcel fabric for a certain date, how a specific parcel has changed through time, and what the parent parcels in its lineage were.

## METHODS OF HISTORICAL TRACKING

The data archiving requirements of land records systems typically fall into two categories:

- How the database looks at the beginning of the tax year

- Tracking the complete transaction level history of parcels in addition to retrieving a view of the database at the beginning of the tax year

For the first group, the best solution might be to simply make a backup of the database at the beginning of each tax year and archive on backup media (such as CD or DVD.

Versioning also offers a convenient way to do snapshot history for users who want to keep historical data online. To use versioning for history tracking, you need only create a new version at whatever interval is required, such as yearly or monthly. These versions should be given a name that identifies them as historical versions so they are not inadvertently posted or deleted. To look at the state of the database on a particular date, the user would simply switch the display to the historical version with the closest date.

To accurately track the lineage or history of a parcel as it changes, it is necessary to archive parcel transactions. For land records management, a transaction can be based on a legal document resulting from an owner change, the subdividing of a piece of property, or the resurvey of boundary properties. Transactions can also be based on events such as the adjustment of property boundaries due to new or better control points. In any case, the transaction is not the individual edit of a line or polygon feature, but the culmination of all these edits in a single long transaction resulting in an updated parcel fabric. For instance, the steps involved in splitting a parcel would include adding new boundaries, updating the PIN, adding and adjusting annotation, and so on. Together, all of these steps are part of a single transaction and form the level of a database update some would like to track (see adjacent figure). It can also happen that multiple splits or merges with a given parcel take place in a single tax

year. Referring again to the adjacent figure, simply recording the database at the beginning of each tax year would not capture the existence of parcel 201.

In land records management, transactional history is maintained so that users may look back at the changes that were made to a parcel (or the area in which the current parcel now sits) through time. Title or deed searches require this level of detail so that, for example, historical records can be searched to assure there are no outstanding liens against a piece of property. Anyone who has been part of a land dispute would probably agree that the ability to track historical updates at this level of granularity can provide great benefit with the retrieval of accurate information on a single disputed piece of property.

## DATABASE DESIGN

The ability to track updates through time requires an archive of updated features in additional tables, as shown in the next figure. As changes are posted to the database, retired features are saved in the archive tables. The original state of the features is written to the archive feature classes and stamped

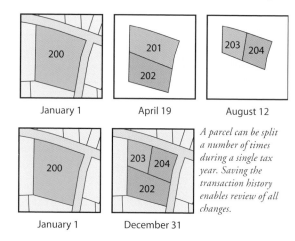

January 1      April 19      August 12

January 1      December 31

*A parcel can be split a number of times during a single tax year. Saving the transaction history enables review of all changes.*

with the current date and time in the OUT_DATE field. The updated state of the features is stamped with the current system date and time or the legal transaction date and time in the IN_DATE field. The IN_DATE and OUT_DATE fields can later be queried to determine the time frame in which a particular representation of the feature was active.

By using separate feature classes, the historical representations of the updated features can be archived independently of the active features. Using separate feature classes also allows the luxury of archiving only the features of interest. For parcel management, the parcel polygon and the boundary lines are generally the only feature classes of interest. The parcel polygons are maintained for area and PIN information, while the boundaries are maintained for bearing and distance of the historical lines. Labeling based on these attributes can be used to create a map that contains text as well as the features.

*Only minor changes need to be made to the database for data archiving. The fields added for archiving are highlighted in yellow.*

### Simple feature class — Boundaries
Geometry Polyline · Contains M values No · Contains Z values No

| Fieldname | Datatype | Allow nulls | Precision | Scale | Length |
|---|---|---|---|---|---|
| OBJECTID | Object ID | | | | |
| DIRECTION | String | Yes | | | 12 |
| DISTANCE | String | Yes | | | 10 |
| DELTA | String | Yes | | | 10 |
| RADIUS | String | Yes | | | 10 |
| TANGENT | String | Yes | | | 10 |
| ARCLENGTH | String | Yes | | | 10 |
| SIDE | String | Yes | | | 1 |
| IN_DATE | Date | Yes | 0 | 0 | 8 |
| SHAPE | Geometry | Yes | | | |
| SHAPE_Length | Double | Yes | 0 | 0 | |

### Simple feature class — Boundaries_History
Geometry Polyline · Contains M values No · Contains Z values No

| Fieldname | Datatype | Allow nulls | Precision | Scale | Length |
|---|---|---|---|---|---|
| OBJECTID | Object ID | | | | |
| DIRECTION | String | Yes | | | 12 |
| DISTANCE | String | Yes | | | 10 |
| DELTA | String | Yes | | | 10 |
| RADIUS | String | Yes | | | 10 |
| TANGENT | String | Yes | | | 10 |
| ARCLENGTH | String | Yes | | | 10 |
| SIDE | String | Yes | | | 1 |
| IN_DATE | Date | Yes | 0 | 0 | 8 |
| OUT_DATE | Date | Yes | 0 | 0 | 8 |
| SHAPE | Geometry | Yes | | | |
| SHAPE_Length | Double | Yes | 0 | 0 | |

### Simple feature class — TaxParcels
Geometry Polygon · Contains M values No · Contains Z values No

| Fieldname | Datatype | Allow nulls | Precision | Scale | Length |
|---|---|---|---|---|---|
| OBJECTID | Object ID | | | | |
| GPIN | String | Yes | | | 14 |
| LOT_NO | String | Yes | | | 7 |
| MAPID | Double | Yes | 0 | 0 | |
| LU_STNUM | Double | Yes | 0 | 0 | |
| LU_STDIR | String | Yes | | | 2 |
| LU_STNAME | String | Yes | | | 25 |
| LU_STTYPE | String | Yes | | | 4 |
| LU_ZIP1 | Double | Yes | 0 | 0 | |
| LU_ZIP_EXT | Double | Yes | 0 | 0 | |
| LU_DB | Double | Yes | 0 | 0 | |
| LU_DBPG | Double | Yes | 0 | 0 | |
| LU_MB | Double | Yes | 0 | 0 | |
| LU_MBPG | Double | Yes | 0 | 0 | |
| LU_SUB_DIV | String | Yes | | | 22 |
| L_APP_IMPR | Double | Yes | 0 | 0 | |
| L_APP_VALU | Double | Yes | 0 | 0 | |
| L_APP_MRKT | Double | Yes | 0 | 0 | |
| L_CRNT_OWN | String | Yes | | | 33 |
| L_MAIL_ADR | String | Yes | | | 25 |
| L_MAIL_CIT | String | Yes | | | 20 |
| L_MAIL_ZIP | String | Yes | | | 5 |
| BUILDING_TYPE | Long integer | Yes | 0 | | |
| TAX_DISTRICT | Long integer | Yes | 0 | | |
| LANDUSE | Long integer | Yes | 0 | | |
| IN_DATE | Date | Yes | 0 | 0 | 8 |
| SHAPE | Geometry | Yes | | | |
| SHAPE_Length | Double | Yes | 0 | 0 | |
| SHAPE_Area | Double | Yes | 0 | 0 | |

### Simple feature class — TaxParcels_History
Geometry Polygon · Contains M values No · Contains Z values No

| Fieldname | Datatype | Allow nulls | Precision | Scale | Length |
|---|---|---|---|---|---|
| OBJECTID | Object ID | | | | |
| GPIN | String | Yes | | | 14 |
| LOT_NO | String | Yes | | | 7 |
| MAPID | Double | Yes | 0 | 0 | |
| LU_STNUM | Double | Yes | 0 | 0 | |
| LU_STDIR | String | Yes | | | 2 |
| LU_STNAME | String | Yes | | | 25 |
| LU_STTYPE | String | Yes | | | 4 |
| LU_ZIP1 | Double | Yes | 0 | 0 | |
| LU_ZIP_EXT | Double | Yes | 0 | 0 | |
| LU_DB | Double | Yes | 0 | 0 | |
| LU_DBPG | Double | Yes | 0 | 0 | |
| LU_MB | Double | Yes | 0 | 0 | |
| LU_MBPG | Double | Yes | 0 | 0 | |
| LU_SUB_DIV | String | Yes | | | 22 |
| L_APP_IMPR | Double | Yes | 0 | 0 | |
| L_APP_VALU | Double | Yes | 0 | 0 | |
| L_APP_MRKT | Double | Yes | 0 | 0 | |
| L_CRNT_OWN | String | Yes | | | 33 |
| L_MAIL_ADR | String | Yes | | | 25 |
| L_MAIL_CIT | String | Yes | | | 20 |
| L_MAIL_ZIP | String | Yes | | | 5 |
| BUILDING_TYPE | Long integer | Yes | 0 | | |
| TAX_DISTRICT | Long integer | Yes | 0 | | |
| LANDUSE | Long integer | Yes | 0 | | |
| IN_DATE | Date | Yes | 0 | 0 | 8 |
| OUT_DATE | Date | Yes | 0 | 0 | 8 |
| SHAPE | Geometry | Yes | | | |
| SHAPE_Length | Double | Yes | 0 | 0 | |
| SHAPE_Area | Double | Yes | 0 | 0 | |

5

A common database design is to maintain only the PIN with the parcel feature class; all other attributes, such as owner and sales information, are placed in separate related tables. With this design, the sale of a property could result in no change to the parcel feature, since neither the shape nor PIN would change. Only the necessary fields of related owner tables and tax rolls would need to be updated.

If the related tables are maintained outside the GIS, then extra steps would be involved to ensure that parcels are accurately archived and available for query. For example, it might be necessary to create database views on the related tables (based on IN_DATE and OUT_DATE fields) before performing joins or relates to the parcel feature class for historical queries.

## HISTORICAL QUERIES

Once a versioned historical database has grown to include a significant number of versions, it opens up the potential for history-based queries, such as:

- Show me the database at "January 1, 2002".

- Show me how parcel feature "1234" has changed through time.

- Show me what is in the space of feature "5678" at "April 15, 2002".

In designing the database versioning to support queries like these, it is important to keep in mind who should have access to the historical data. For example, public access may be allowed to snapshot data but not to transaction data.

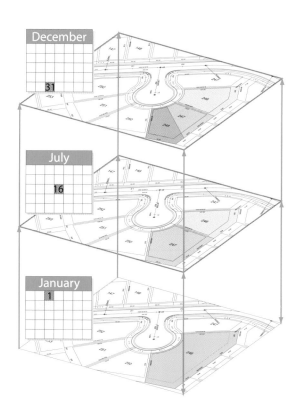

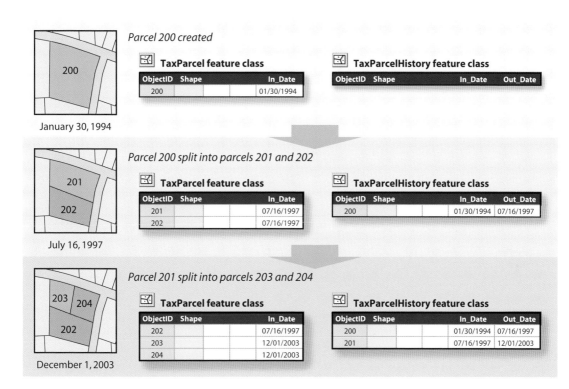

Parcel 200 created

TaxParcel feature class

| ObjectID | Shape | | | In_Date |
|----------|-------|--|--|---------|
| 200 | | | | 01/30/1994 |

TaxParcelHistory feature class

| ObjectID | Shape | | | In_Date | Out_Date |
|----------|-------|--|--|---------|----------|

January 30, 1994

Parcel 200 split into parcels 201 and 202

TaxParcel feature class

| ObjectID | Shape | | | In_Date |
|----------|-------|--|--|---------|
| 201 | | | | 07/16/1997 |
| 202 | | | | 07/16/1997 |

TaxParcelHistory feature class

| ObjectID | Shape | | | In_Date | Out_Date |
|----------|-------|--|--|---------|----------|
| 200 | | | | 01/30/1994 | 07/16/1997 |

July 16, 1997

Parcel 201 split into parcels 203 and 204

TaxParcel feature class

| ObjectID | Shape | | | In_Date |
|----------|-------|--|--|---------|
| 202 | | | | 07/16/1997 |
| 203 | | | | 12/01/2003 |
| 204 | | | | 12/01/2003 |

TaxParcelHistory feature class

| ObjectID | Shape | | | In_Date | Out_Date |
|----------|-------|--|--|---------|----------|
| 200 | | | | 01/30/1994 | 07/16/1997 |
| 201 | | | | 07/16/1997 | 12/01/2003 |

December 1, 2003

5

To store the transactional history of changes, the TaxParcel feature class is modified to include an In_Date field. The TaxParcelHistory class has the same structure as the TaxParcel feature class, with the addition of an Out_Date field.

When parcels are updated, the original parcels are written to the TaxParcelHistory feature class with Out_Date set to the current date. The In_Date field is changed to the current date in the Tax-Parcel feature class for each updated record.

The history of a particular location in the database is shown by performing an Identify against the archived feature class for Parcels. The In_Date field is being used as the primary display field.

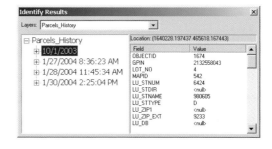

This chapter presented several general aspects and issues related to parcel data modeling, especially as applied in the United States using a specific example for Oakland County, Michigan. But this was essentially an introductory overview; a more comprehensive guide on land records data modeling is provided in *GIS and Land Records—The ArcGIS Parcel Data Model*, by Nancy von Meyer, available from ESRI Press.

The geodatabase implementation in Oakland County continues to evolve based on new requirements and capabilities. The current data model schema being used in Oakland County, Michigan, is referenced under the 'Further Resources' section on the next page.

## REFERENCES AND FURTHER READING

Black, Henry Campbell. 1991. *Black's Law Dictionary*. 6th ed. St. Paul, Minnesota: West Publishing.

Brown, Curtis M.; Wilson, Donald A.; and Robillard, Walter G. 1995. *Brown's Boundary Control and Legal Principles*. 4th ed. New York, New York: John Wiley and Sons.

Brown, Curtis M. 1969. *Boundary Control and Legal Principles*. 2nd ed. New York, New York: John Wiley and Sons.

Danielsen, Diann. 1993. The Cadastral Model in Parcel-Based Land Information Systems. Independent study report, Civil and Environmental Engineering Department, University of Wisconsin, Madison.

Epstein, Earl, and Brown, Patricia. 1990. Land Interests. In *Multipurpose Land Information Systems: The Guidebook*. Reston, Virginia: Subcommittee on Geodetic Control.

Federal Geographic Data Committee. 1999. Cadastral Data Content Standard for the National Spatial Data Infrastructure, Version 1.1. Reston, Virginia: Subcommittee on Cadastral Data.

*Modeling and Using History in ArcGIS: An ESRI Technical Paper*. 2002. Technical Paper, Redlands, California: ESRI.

Moyer, D. David, and Fisher, Kenneth Paul. 1973. *Land Parcel Identifiers for Information Systems*. Chicago, Illinois: American Bar Foundation.

Simpson, S.R. 1976. *Land Law and Registration*. Cambridge: Cambridge University Press.

Ting, L., and I. P. Williamson. 1999. The dynamic human-kind–land relationship and its impact on land administration systems. In *Proceedings of the Joint United Nations and FIG International Conference on Land Tenure and Cadastral Infrastructures for Sustainable Development*. Melbourne.

von Meyer, Nancy. 1989. A Conceptual Model for Spatial Cadastral Data in a Land Information System. Ph.D. diss., University of Wisconsin, Madison.

von Meyer, Nancy. 2002. Production, Analysis, and Publication: A Concept for Geographic Information Environments. White paper, Pendleton, South Carolina: Fairview Industries.

von Meyer, Nancy. 2004. *GIS and Land Records—The ArcGIS Parcel Data Model*. Redlands, California: ESRI Press.

Wattles, G.H. 1979. *Writing Legal Descriptions*. Orange, California: Gurdon H. Wattles Publications.

Williamson, I.P., and L. Ting. 1999. Land administration and cadastral trends—A framework for reengineering. In *Proceedings of the Joint United Nations and FIG International Conference on Land Tenure and Cadastral Infrastructures for Sustainable Development*. Melbourne.

## ACKNOWLEDGMENTS

Nancy von Meyer of Fairview Industries is the lead developer of this data model and provided much of the content in this chapter. Scott Oppmann, GIS Supervisor at Oakland County, Michigan, provided much of the map data in this chapter and shared his experience working with the parcel data model. Shawn Thornton from the GIS Division of Santa Fe County also provided data and feedback.

## CREDITS

Many of the graphics, photographs, and map data are courtesy of Santa Fe County, New Mexico; Fairview Industries; Oakland County, Michigan; Waukesha County, Wisconsin; and Cook County, Illinois. Wayne Hewitt of ESRI contributed content to this chapter.

## FURTHER RESOURCES

Follow the Land Parcels link on ESRI ArcOnline at http://support.esri.com/datamodels.

Visit the Oakland County, Michigan, GIS Web site for the most current version of the county's parcel data model at http://www.co.oakland.mi.us/maps/models.

5

*This chapter represents an alternate design goal for land parcels compared to that presented in Chapter 5, 'Parcels and the cadastre'. While that data model was directed toward applications in local government and tax assessment, this chapter is directed toward ownership and case management of public lands in the United States.*

**6**

From the late 1700s through the late 1800s, the newly formed United States government commissioned and implemented the survey of the vast territory west of the former British colonies to enable land sales to growing waves of settlers. Under the direction of the General Land Office, this became known as the Public Land Survey System. The PLSS established a reference grid for all subsequent land surveys in those areas.

In time, the General Land Office became the U.S. Bureau of Land Management (BLM), which is now responsible for systems to maintain and disseminate public land conveyance (patent) records, federal landownership status, and cadastral data. In support of these responsibilities, a team of U.S. federal agencies, including the BLM, the U.S. Forest Service (USFS), the Bureau of Indian Affairs, and the Minerals Management Service, have collaborated with states, counties, and private industry to develop the Land Records 2000 (LR2000) system and, more recently, the National Integrated Land System (NILS).

NILS is a system for the management of cadastral records and land parcel information in a GIS environment for purposes of land title research and land resource management. NILS is based on, and meets the requirements of, the Federal Geographic Data Committee's Cadastral Data Content Standard. The implementation of the NILS model includes conversion of the data from NAD27 to the NAD83 datum, as well as the development of a seamless national dataset. The survey and parcel data in NILS will serve as the foundation for a national multipurpose cadastre.

The data model described in this chapter is the transaction processing and maintenance data model for NILS. The data model and data designed for Web-based publication can be found at www.geocommunicator.gov.

# Surveying
# federal lands

When the United States was formed, a huge task lay ahead: the survey of the new lands to enable development and settlement. Settlement across the country was used to raise much-needed funds for the new United States government. The PLSS emerged as the primary survey framework for the new territories, while traditional surveys served as the cadastral framework for the eastern one-third of the United States.

In 1785, the United States legislature passed the Land Ordinance Act. This ordinance was the beginning of the rectangular survey system. Ohio was the first state to have all its land surveyed in this system, thus being the starting point for all subsequent surveys west of Ohio.

There have been several adjustments to the original Land Ordinance Act of 1785 to clarify and redefine certain points. In 1803, the United States acquired the Louisiana Territory. The land along the Mississippi River was surveyed in what were known as "French Tracts", metes and bounds with waterfront access to each tract. The rectangular system did not apply to French Tracts, or later in the acquisition of Texas.

The acquired lands west of Ohio had to be surveyed prior to disposal under various land disposal acts and laws (this excluded the French Tracts, Texas, and Spanish Land Grants). Before the 1876 Homestead Act, the land was surveyed in 40-acre plots so the homesteaders could make claim on the land prior to or upon their arrival (Oklahoma excluded). In addition, certain special surveys took place, such as mineral surveys defined by the 1872 Mining Act.

In short, all land in the eminent domain had to be surveyed so the government knew what land remained in the public domain and what land was given away, sold, or bargained to private ownership. The rectangular system that became known as the PLSS was the fastest, most logical system to dispose of the land with minimal landownership disputes.

As landownership has changed in the private sector, the shape of the physical survey also has changed due to subdivision for other owners. If the owner of one of the subdivisions wants to return the land to the government, the land is not always surveyed at the time of the reconveyance. In cases of vague or lost boundaries, the land is surveyed prior to acquisition so the limits of the land are clear. However, as land that has been in the public domain since the original survey (1800s) is conveyed out, the land must be surveyed prior to the passage of title so that the new landowner knows the limits to the title.

Surveys are triggered by land disputes, title conveyance, or adjustments made as a result of lost or poorly defined boundaries. Homesteads, mineral surveys, and other actions may be surveyed prior to any known title exchange with a specific use in mind but without necessarily having any interest from private ownership.

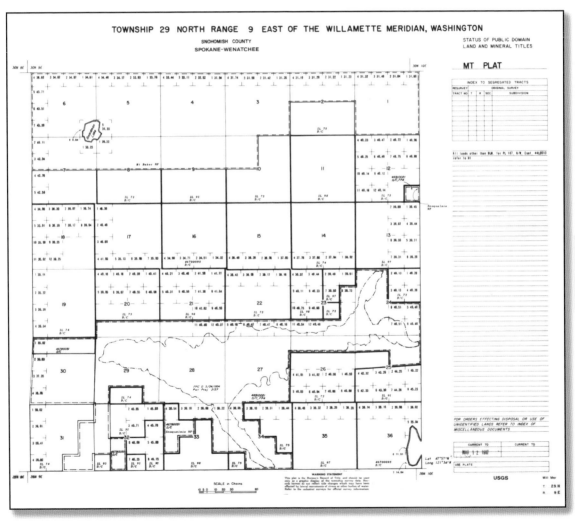

*Use plat showing oil and gas leases. Use plats present the information on a master title plat (MTP), which shows land title, rights, and segregations.*

The case study for this chapter is an enormous project: the management of PLSS reference data across most of the United States as well as the management of location and use of public lands throughout the entire United States. To place the data model design in context, it is important to understand the background and requirements of this project.

BLM is tasked with managing public land conveyance data, the ownership status of federal lands (both the real property and mineral property), and the cadastral framework of the PLSS. BLM is responsible for some 261 million acres of public land and 700 million acres of subsurface land. This includes responsibility for the official boundary surveys for all federal agencies in the United States and the PLSS.

## THE PUBLIC LAND SURVEY SYSTEM

The PLSS is a reference survey framework covering 32 states (shaded area in the U.S. map on the next page). PLSS establishes a set of baselines and principal meridians that define rectangular divisions of land. The PLSS created some 28,000 townships, and there are now about 130 million parcels in this land area. Each township requires approximately 5,000 geographic features made up of measurements, points, lines, and polygons.

To better perform its duties, the BLM engaged with the USFS and other agencies to develop the National Integrated Land System.

## THE NATIONAL INTEGRATED LAND SYSTEM

The goal of NILS is to provide a process to collect, maintain, and store parcel-based land and survey information that meets the common, shared business needs of land title and land resource management. Some 250 users manage surveys and measurements, and about 900 manage parcel information.

To accomplish its goal, the NILS project consists of four application modules: Survey Management (SM); Measurement Management (MM); Parcel Management legal description (PM); and GeoCommunicator (GC), a Web portal. At the time of this writing, these modules are not complete; NILS is an ongoing project with initial releases of each module but is still a work in progress.

### Survey and Measurement Management

The Survey Management module of NILS is a set of applications that provides surveyors with the ability to manage field-collected survey data to produce survey plats and field notes. It allows the exporting of data to an intermediate format for a variety of survey equipment and for importing field data back into the SM database. GIS, raster, and field data are all integrated within SM for data validation and decision making while in the field.

Measurement Management provides surveyors with tools to collect, analyze, and adjust record data from plats. MM enables combination and integration of data from a variety of sources to create a seamless measurement network from which legal descriptions are produced, also called the legal description fabric. The legal description fabric can then be used as the basis for the parcel fabric, which is used by land managers for decision making.

As part of the National Integrated Land System, the Land Survey Information System (LSIS) Web site at http://www.geocommunicator.gov/lsi provides a means for distributing land survey boundary information to the public.

### Parcel Management

Parcel Management is a desktop GIS application with tools for land managers to create and update parcel features and their legal descriptions. This includes a set of tools for managing work flows such as:

- Determining land status
- Verifying a parcel's legal description
- Eestablishing a case file for document control
- Creating legal descriptions
- Editing the legal description fabric, parcel fabric, and other components of the system
- Acquiring rights in title
- Handling applications for rights-of-way, temporary use permits (TUP), oil and gas leases, and others

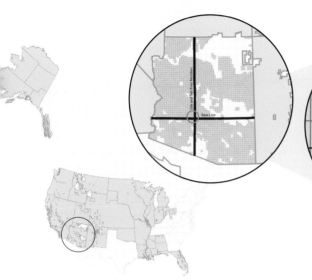

*PLSS townships are nominally 6 miles square, though some may be irregular, such as around large bodies of water or due to corrections for the earth's curvature.*

*Each township is divided into 36 sections, each 1 mile square.*

*PLSS defines a spatial hierarchy: These examples zoom into the state of Arizona (circle at lower left). A baseline and principal meridian are shown dividing Arizona (see inset above).*

*Standard sections contain 640 acres. Each section can be subdivided into halves and quarters, repeatedly, until each parcel of land is accurately described. Aliquot parts represent exact subdivisions of a section of land. Fractional sections, lots, and cadastral tracts may be used to describe uneven parcels of land.*

## The GeoCommunicator portal

GeoCommunicator is a comprehensive portal Web site that supports the cadastral, land record, and parcel communities by providing one-stop access to the Public Land Survey System and other survey-based data, land status information, case recordation parcel information, federal landownership, and other reference data. GeoCommunicator is part of the Geodata.gov network.

Geodata.gov is the Geospatial One-Stop portal and is one of 24 e-government initiatives sponsored by the Federal Office of Management and Budget to enhance government efficiency and improve citizen services.

*The PLSS point identifier, a concatenation of the legacy point identifier and the township ID, is a unique point identifier across the United States.*

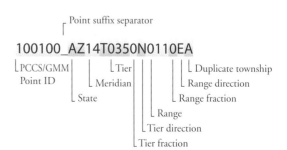

NILS and this data model are the result of the need for many agencies at the federal, state, and county level, as well as private industry involved in public land leases, to share accurate and timely information concerning public landownership, rights, and interests.

Only recently has GIS been capable of integrating with the much higher-resolution survey data. As the management of public land records has become increasingly complicated, this integration has become more urgent. Several agencies have responsibilities or strong interest in some part of the public land and have created multiple disconnected libraries of survey and parcel data. As the costs keep rising to maintain the accuracy and currency of this data, two of the agencies most concerned with management of public land records, BLM and USFS, began the project that became known as NILS.

## NILS

NILS provides the tools to manage land records and cadastral data from field to fabric. This means that users can compute lines and points from field survey measurement data and create legal land and parcel descriptions to be used in mapping and land record maintenance. The diagram on the next page illustrates the three-tiered approach for collecting and managing this data.

### Survey fabric

At the foundation is the survey fabric that contains survey points, coordinates, measurements, and computations. To construct this dataset, field survey measurement data is exported from the field measuring equipment to an intermediate interchange format, converted from angular measurements to points and directions, and imported into a survey dataset. Using ArcGIS Survey Analyst, this survey dataset can be linked to GIS features for the purpose of automatically updating the GIS features based on changes to the survey framework resulting from new field measurements.

The unit of work in survey management is a survey project (usually a single plat). In this data model, the survey fabric is used to construct and maintain the legal description fabric, for which the unit of work is a complete township.

### Legal description fabric

The legal description (LD) fabric consists of GIS features representing the surveyed features. These include polygon boundaries for the PLSS boundaries, such as townships, sections, and aliquot parts, as well as boundaries for non-PLSS features, such as metes and bound surveys and mineral surveys. These features in the LD fabric form the basic units for creating and maintaining the parcel fabric.

### Parcel fabric

The features in the parcel fabric are linked to the legal description fabric. In this manner, vertical integration is maintained across the three tiers. Topology rules add a means of validating this integration and will be defined between LD and parcel fabrics.

# Field to fabric

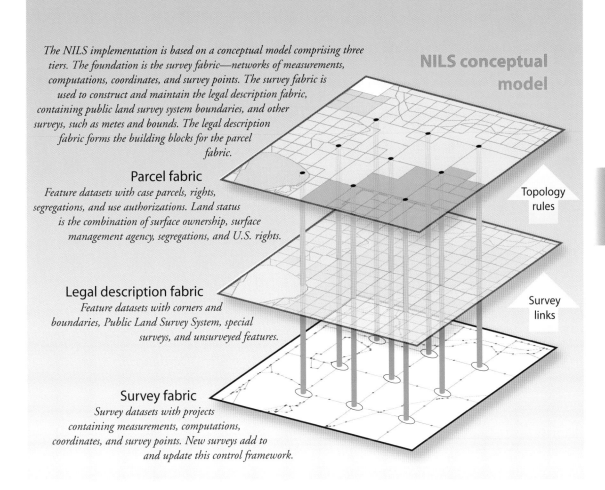

The NILS implementation is based on a conceptual model comprising three tiers. The foundation is the survey fabric—networks of measurements, computations, coordinates, and survey points. The survey fabric is used to construct and maintain the legal description fabric, containing public land survey system boundaries, and other surveys, such as metes and bounds. The legal description fabric forms the building blocks for the parcel fabric.

## NILS conceptual model

### Parcel fabric

*Feature datasets with case parcels, rights, segregations, and use authorizations. Land status is the combination of surface ownership, surface management agency, segregations, and U.S. rights.*

Topology rules

### Legal description fabric

*Feature datasets with corners and boundaries, Public Land Survey System, special surveys, and unsurveyed features.*

Survey links

### Survey fabric

*Survey datasets with projects containing measurements, computations, coordinates, and survey points. New surveys add to and update this control framework.*

6

Each of the four main components of NILS involves many functions, tasks, and work flows. The results of survey management feed into measurement management, which affects legal descriptions. Legal descriptions are then used in parcel management. Some of the tasks in each of the components can trigger a new request for survey, repeating the process flows again.

Each layer of the NILS conceptual model requires that numerous tasks be implemented. The diagram on the next page illustrates the key duties of each model component.

The survey fabric from the conceptual model involves two levels of information. The first level (Survey Management) comes directly from field survey equipment, and the second level (Measurement Management) is derived from SM for use in building the legal description.

## Survey Management

The purpose of the SM component of NILS is ultimately to generate survey plats of federally owned land. This means providing support for collecting and adjusting survey data and the creation of plats and field notes. One of the most common adjustments is the least squares adjustment (LSA), which merges new survey data with previous surveys. The SM component also ensures that data from different sources, such as theodolite and GPS, are integrated properly.

## Measurement Management

The MM component prepares the plat data for use in parcel management. Plat data from a field survey is in a particular form representing the individual field survey as absolute directions and distances referencing parallels and meridians. To be used for the generation of legal descriptions, the MM imports and combines plats into PLSS townships. Once a data entry has been verified through LSA, automated section subdivision is performed on standard sections in the PLSS township. Townships are further aggregated into regions, and regional least square adjustments are applied to align townships. These regions of townships generate the PLSS cadastral network with its associated computational network. Nominal locations are then generated for each subdivision, and legal descriptions are associated.

## Legal description

A parcel's legal description is the primary reference format for its location on earth. This could be expressed in terms of the PLSS or as metes and bounds from other survey control points in non-PLSS states. The LD component of NILS is responsible for creating and modifying a legal description from the survey (MM) component. This includes being able to update a legal description using COGO traverse data as well as to apply and validate the topology of the legal description fabric.

The LD fabric is maintained in a multiversioned dataset to support long transactions and multiple users. The reconcile and post tasks are part of the database administrator's role for resolving potential conflicts among the multiple users.

## Parcel Management

The main purpose of the PM component is the management of land status and cases. Land status is the cumulative state of ownership and rights to a parcel, which can become quite complicated. A case is like a file folder containing all the information pertaining to a given transfer of title. Data for both land status and cases are also multiversioned datasets to support long transactions and multiuser editing.

# Survey Management

**Work flow processes**
Request for survey
· *Search facilities.*
Field survey
· *Intervening corners*
· *Corner restoration*
· *Layout calculations*
· *Traverses*
Platting and field notes

**Task flow processes**
General field survey setup
Layout calculations
Corner restoration
Traverses
Field Survey LSA

**Functions**
Point alias.
Delta x and y.
Station and offset.
New deflection angle.
Direction distance intersection.
Distance distance intersection.
Double proportion.
Grant boundary adjustment.
Irregular boundary adjustment.
Broken boundaries.
1, 2, and 3 point control.
Import GPS.
Curve construction.
COGO fillet curve.
Curve fitting to 3 or more points.
Median curve.
Spiral curve.
TPS LSA
· *Manage observations.*
· *Statistical reports.*
· *Display LSA values.*
· *Traverse misclosure display.*
· *Robusting.*
· *Coordinate movement.*
· *Unadjusted coordinates.*

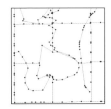

# Measurement Management

**Work flow processes**
SFF import
Computation translation
Maintenance
Survey point merge
Regional LSA
Section subdivision
· *Normal section subdivision*
· *Minor section subdivision*
· *Irregular section subdivision*
Protraction
· *Protraction*
· *Amended protraction*

**Task flow processes**
Review imports.
Review translations.
Maintain survey project.
Survey point merge.
Section subdivision.
Regional LSA.

**Functions**
Inverse
Direction and distance
Intersection
Single proportion
Geodetic calculator
COGO LSA
· *Manage observations.*
· *Statistical reports.*
· *Display LSA values.*
· *Traverse misclosure display.*
· *Robusting.*
· *Coordinate movement.*
· *Unadjusted coordinates.*
Import non-NILS data.
Point alias.
Automated section subdivision.
Statistical display.
Protraction.

# Legal Description

**Work flow processes**
LD import.
Create LD.
Review/Maintain LD.
LD delete.

**Task flow processes**
Verify attributes.
LD fabric management.
Reconcile/Post.
Validate topology.

**Functions**
Maintain/Review LD geometry.
Create LD from survey.
· *PLSS or metes and bounds*
Edit topology.
Verity attributes.
· *Attribute integrity*
· *Topology and attribute validation*
Link to survey fabric.
Update LD and parcel geometry based on survey linking and topology.
Subdivide sections with LD attributes.
Export LD.
LD point merge.
COGO traverse in a legal description.

# Parcel Management

**Work flow processes**
Case processing
Plat creation
· *Use authorizations, titles, and so on*
Land status
Case data export for publication
Case data creation and maintenance

**Task flow processes**
Case management
Case analysis
Case display
LD fabric management
Land status management
Land status analysis
Land status display
Document management

**Functions**
Browse maps.
Choose map themes.
Legal description tool.
Land status tools.
Case display tools.
Case management tools.
Case analysis tools.
Reporting.

LD—Legal description
LSA—Least squares adjustment
TPS—Theodolite-based field equipment
SFF—Standard file format

**6**

This diagram provides an overview of the thematic content for modeling NILS, including survey data, parcel and ownership feature classes, and cartographic and reference themes.

The vertical organization of the diagram reflects the concept of layering features as in the real world. Each theme is described below.

## Digital orthophotography

As with many other data models, digital orthophotography provides a useful backdrop to the other map layers. This can help in checking the accuracy of other GIS layers.

## Vector reference

Vector reference data is typically taken from other base map sources, such as topographic maps. Rivers, roadways, and other features commonly form borders of land parcels and can be helpful in constructing the parcel geometry.

## Survey fabric

The survey fabric consists of plat data generated from field survey measurements and represents the core of this data model. The survey fabric has high precision and accuracy in comparison with other GIS data. It cannot be directly edited as other GIS data, but only through controlled processes integrated with field survey data collection.

## Corners and record boundaries

These GIS features are built from the survey fabric. Corners and record boundaries are used as reference points and lines for constructing the polygon features in the legal description fabric.

## Legal description fabric

Legal descriptions are captured as polygon features and are used as the building blocks for defining the boundaries for ownership, rights, and interests.

## Cases

Case records are created or modified in the event of title transfer and subdivision. This data consists of polygon features derived from the legal description fabric and land status records. Cases may overlap.

## Rights and segregations

Many of the rights to a property are or can be separated from the ownership of the property, such as ditches and canals, rights-of-way, and mineral rights. Segregations are the removal of public lands from operation due to overriding factors. These are represented as polygon features that may overlap each other.

## Land status

Land status is the combination of surface ownership, surface management agency, segregations, and U.S. rights. This combination indicates allowed activities on the land with nonoverlapping polygons.

## Mining claims

Mining claims are represented as polygons for lodes or placer mines containing valuable mineral deposits.

## Use authorizations

Use authorizations represent mineral leases, such as for coal, oil, gas, and geothermal. Authorized leases of a given case group (type of lease) cannot overlap.

## Cartographic representation

For finished maps to be published, it is often necessary to displace or modify some of the geographic features for readability. Annotation may be added as well as legend and other map layout information.

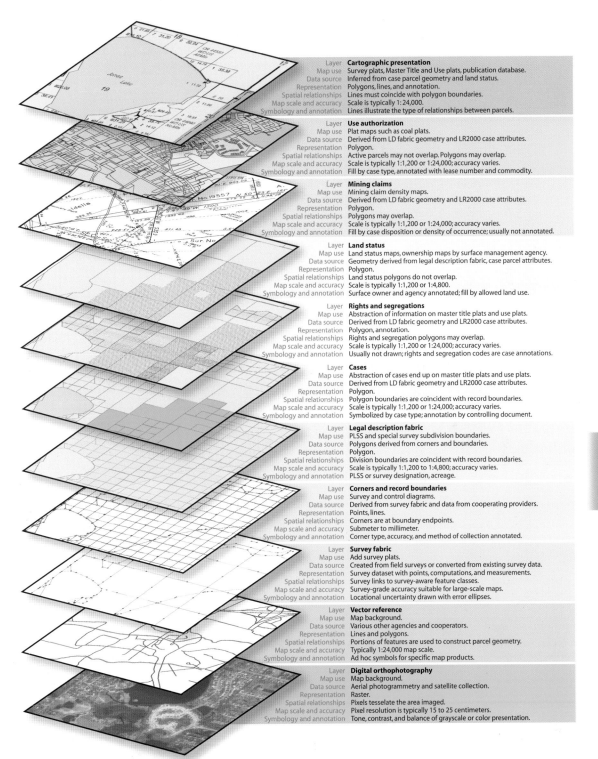

| Layer | **Cartographic presentation** |
|---|---|
| Map use | Survey plats, Master Title and Use plats, publication database. |
| Data source | Inferred from case parcel geometry and land status. |
| Representation | Polygons, lines, and annotation. |
| Spatial relationships | Lines must coincide with polygon boundaries. |
| Map scale and accuracy | Scale is typically 1:24,000. |
| Symbology and annotation | Lines illustrate the type of relationships between parcels. |

| Layer | **Use authorization** |
|---|---|
| Map use | Plat maps such as coal plats. |
| Data source | Derived from LD fabric geometry and LR2000 case attributes. |
| Representation | Polygon. |
| Spatial relationships | Active parcels may not overlap. Polygons may overlap. |
| Map scale and accuracy | Scale is typically 1:1,200 or 1:24,000; accuracy varies. |
| Symbology and annotation | Fill by case type, annotated with lease number and commodity. |

| Layer | **Mining claims** |
|---|---|
| Map use | Mining claim density maps. |
| Data source | Derived from LD fabric geometry and LR2000 case attributes. |
| Representation | Polygon. |
| Spatial relationships | Polygons may overlap. |
| Map scale and accuracy | Scale is typically 1:1,200 or 1:24,000; accuracy varies. |
| Symbology and annotation | Fill by case disposition or density of occurrence; usually not annotated. |

| Layer | **Land status** |
|---|---|
| Map use | Land status maps, ownership maps by surface management agency. |
| Data source | Geometry derived from legal description fabric, case parcel attributes. |
| Representation | Polygon. |
| Spatial relationships | Land status polygons do not overlap. |
| Map scale and accuracy | Scale is typically 1:1,200 or 1:4,800. |
| Symbology and annotation | Surface owner and agency annotated; fill by allowed land use. |

| Layer | **Rights and segregations** |
|---|---|
| Map use | Abstraction of information on master title plats and use plats. |
| Data source | Derived from LD fabric geometry and LR2000 case attributes. |
| Representation | Polygon, annotation. |
| Spatial relationships | Rights and segregation polygons may overlap. |
| Map scale and accuracy | Scale is typically 1:1,200 or 1:24,000; accuracy varies. |
| Symbology and annotation | Usually not drawn; rights and segregation codes are case annotations. |

| Layer | **Cases** |
|---|---|
| Map use | Abstraction of cases end up on master title plats and use plats. |
| Data source | Derived from LD fabric geometry and LR2000 case attributes. |
| Representation | Polygon. |
| Spatial relationships | Polygon boundaries are coincident with record boundaries. |
| Map scale and accuracy | Scale is typically 1:1,200 or 1:24,000; accuracy varies. |
| Symbology and annotation | Symbolized by case type; annotation by controlling document. |

| Layer | **Legal description fabric** |
|---|---|
| Map use | PLSS and special survey subdivision boundaries. |
| Data source | Polygons derived from corners and boundaries. |
| Representation | Polygon. |
| Spatial relationships | Division boundaries are coincident with record boundaries. |
| Map scale and accuracy | Scale is typically 1:1,200 to 1:4,800; accuracy varies. |
| Symbology and annotation | PLSS or survey designation, acreage. |

| Layer | **Corners and record boundaries** |
|---|---|
| Map use | Survey and control diagrams. |
| Data source | Derived from survey fabric and data from cooperating providers. |
| Representation | Points, lines. |
| Spatial relationships | Corners are at boundary endpoints. |
| Map scale and accuracy | Submeter to millimeter. |
| Symbology and annotation | Corner type, accuracy, and method of collection annotated. |

| Layer | **Survey fabric** |
|---|---|
| Map use | Add survey plats. |
| Data source | Created from field surveys or converted from existing survey data. |
| Representation | Survey dataset with points, computations, and measurements. |
| Spatial relationships | Survey links to survey-aware feature classes. |
| Map scale and accuracy | Survey-grade accuracy suitable for large-scale maps. |
| Symbology and annotation | Locational uncertainty drawn with error ellipses. |

| Layer | **Vector reference** |
|---|---|
| Map use | Map background. |
| Data source | Various other agencies and cooperators. |
| Representation | Lines and polygons. |
| Spatial relationships | Portions of features are used to construct parcel geometry. |
| Map scale and accuracy | Typically 1:24,000 map scale. |
| Symbology and annotation | Ad hoc symbols for specific map products. |

| Layer | **Digital orthophotography** |
|---|---|
| Map use | Map background. |
| Data source | Aerial photogrammetry and satellite collection. |
| Representation | Raster. |
| Spatial relationships | Pixels tesselate the area imaged. |
| Map scale and accuracy | Pixel resolution is typically 15 to 25 centimeters. |
| Symbology and annotation | Tone, contrast, and balance of grayscale or color presentation. |

6

An overview of the geodatabase structure to support the thematic content on the previous page is shown here. Details of the feature classes and topology rules are presented throughout the remainder of the chapter.

The database design for this case study consists of two principal datasets: one for the core NILS survey data and another for all feature classes related to legal descriptions and ownership. Related tables are shown outside the legal description feature dataset because they do not need a spatial reference.

Because of the geodetic scale of data encompassing the conterminous United States, the spatial reference chosen for the GIS feature dataset is simple geographic (longitude–latitude).

The survey dataset shown for the NILS survey core model depicts several custom tables created to support the NILS business requirements and work flow.

The feature dataset for legal description and ownership contains all other feature classes shown to participate in a single topology.

Four feature classes in this design are survey-aware: Corner, Monument, MeasuredCoordinate, and RecordBoundary. These features can be updated directly from the survey data as needed.

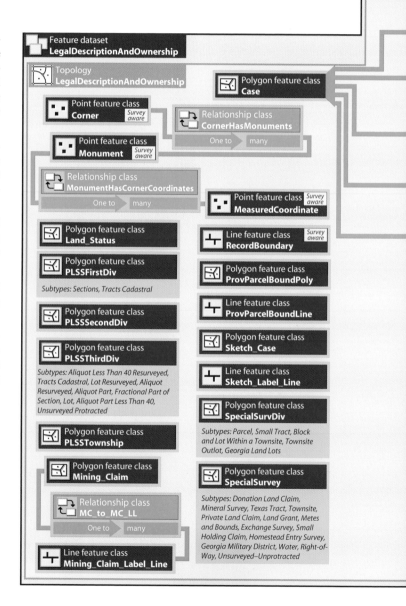

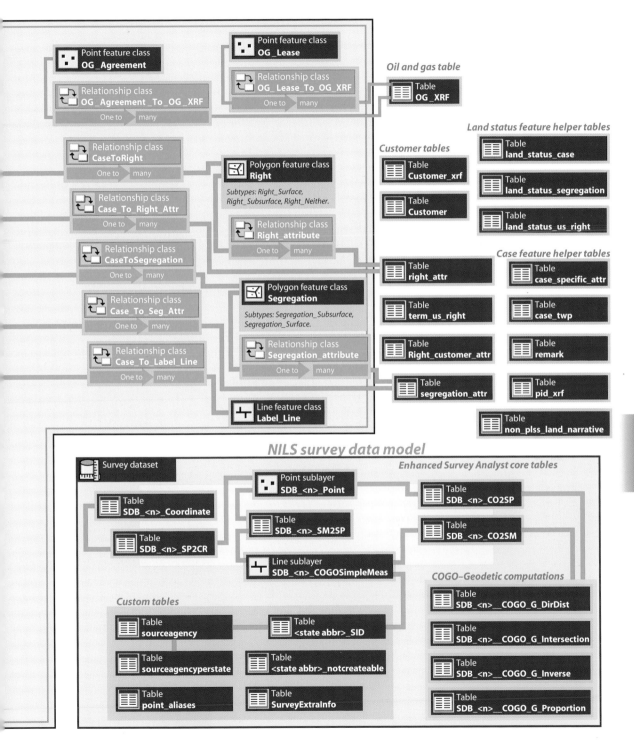

6

At the core of NILS is the field survey data, integrated with related GIS data. The locations of geographic features in the GIS can be updated from field surveys.

Survey data is fundamental to NILS, and the integration of this survey data with GIS data is essential. The figures at right show schematically how GIS data, such as parcel boundaries, can be linked and updated with survey data. The yellow survey and red survey in the figure on the lower right represent two survey projects conducted at different points in time that are part of the comprehensive survey database. The shaded polygon represents a land parcel that is linked to the survey data through survey-aware features. At the user's direction, an automated procedure snaps the land parcel boundaries to the coordinates from the yellow survey, as shown in the bottom right figure. With this capability, survey data can greatly improve the accuracy of GIS features' locations.

### Extensions to core ArcGIS survey dataset and tools

For the NILS project, the standard survey dataset was augmented with tables to store survey metainformation (data about the data), geodetic information, and additional information used in the NILS work flows. Survey points were augmented to hold:

- Multiple coordinates
- Provisional coordinates, such as for temporary boundaries
- Noncomputable points, which could be used for points you don't want to snap to when creating parcel features or COGO computations
- Control point metadata
- Substitution identifier

ArcGIS Survey Analyst includes a new geodetic engine, a new COGO package with geodetic COGO tools, least squares adjustment for COGO data, plat generation, and other features that support NILS.

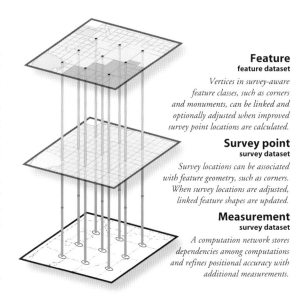

**Feature**
**feature dataset**

*Vertices in survey-aware feature classes, such as corners and monuments, can be linked and optionally adjusted when improved survey point locations are calculated.*

**Survey point**
**survey dataset**

*Survey locations can be associated with feature geometry, such as corners. When survey locations are adjusted, linked feature shapes are updated.*

**Measurement**
**survey dataset**

*A computation network stores dependencies among computations and refines positional accuracy with additional measurements.*

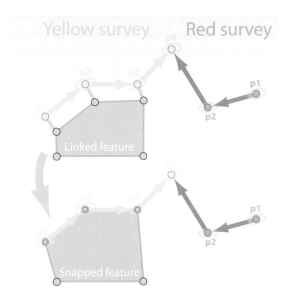

Yellow survey · Red survey

Linked feature

Snapped feature

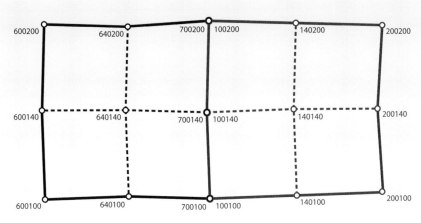

*A survey dataset is an integrated layer in the geodatabase and contains four data types—observed points, coordinates, measurements, and computations.*

*Survey points are named locations observed either through multiple surveys or derived through alternate sources.*

### Survey points

| Project ID | Point name | GIS coordinate |
|---|---|---|
| 1 | 600100 | (lat, lon, elev) |
| 1 | 640100 | (lat, lon, elev) |
| 1 | 700100 | (lat, lon, elev) |
| 1 | 600140 | (lat, lon, elev) |
| 1 | 640140 | (lat, lon, elev) |
| 1 | 700140 | (lat, lon, elev) |
| 1 | 600200 | (lat, lon, elev) |
| 1 | 640200 | (lat, lon, elev) |
| 1 | 700200 | (lat, lon, elev) |
| 2 | 100100 | (lat, lon, elev) |
| 2 | 140100 | (lat, lon, elev) |
| 2 | 200100 | (lat, lon, elev) |
| 2 | 100140 | (lat, lon, elev) |
| 2 | 140140 | (lat, lon, elev) |
| 2 | 200140 | (lat, lon, elev) |
| 2 | 100200 | (lat, lon, elev) |
| 2 | 140200 | (lat, lon, elev) |
| 2 | 200200 | (lat, lon, elev) |

*A PLSS survey project represents a unit of work as a township 6 by 6 miles with multiple surveys, each consisting of measurements, points, coordinates, and computations.*

### Survey projects

| Project ID | Name | Coordinate system |
|---|---|---|
| 1 | AZPM04T0340N0340E | NAD_1927_North_American... |
| 2 | AZPM04T0340N0350E | NAD_1927_North_American... |

*Point alias identifies identical setups to define the measurement network for PLSS township lineup.*

### Point alias

| Alias1 | Alias2 |
|---|---|
| 700100 | 100100 |
| 700200 | 100200 |

*Measurements in the PLSS are either observations from recorded plats or derived through the computational network. Directions are converted from azimuths to geodesic and distances from ground to ellipsoidal.*

### Measurements

| Project ID | From | To | Type | LineType |
|---|---|---|---|---|
| 1 | 600100 | 700100 | Observation | True mean |
| 1 | 700100 | 700200 | Observation | True mean |
| 1 | 700200 | 600200 | Observation | True mean |
| 1 | 600200 | 600100 | Observation | True mean |
| 1 | 640100 | 640140 | Computation | Geodesic |
| 1 | 600140 | 640140 | Computation | Geodesic |
| 1 | 700140 | 640140 | Computation | Geodesic |
| 1 | 640200 | 640140 | Computation | Geodesic |
| 2 | 100100 | 200100 | Observation | True mean |
| 2 | 200100 | 200200 | Observation | True mean |
| 2 | 200200 | 100200 | Observation | True mean |
| 2 | 100200 | 100100 | Observation | True mean |
| 2 | 140100 | 140140 | Computation | Geodesic |
| 2 | 100140 | 140140 | Computation | Geodesic |
| 2 | 200140 | 140140 | Computation | Geodesic |
| 2 | 140200 | 140140 | Computation | Geodesic |

*Computations in the PLSS define new points through relationships with other points. These points can then participate in other computations. In PLSS, a computed point can only be defined by one computation.*

### Computations

| Project ID | Name | New point | Type |
|---|---|---|---|
| 1 | 1 | 640100 | Single proportion |
| 1 | 2 | 600140 | Single proportion |
| 1 | 3 | 700140 | Single proportion |
| 1 | 4 | 640200 | Single proportion |
| 1 | 5 | 640140 | Intersection |
| 2 | 6 | 140100 | Single proportion |
| 2 | 7 | 100100 | Single proportion |
| 2 | 8 | 200140 | Single proportion |
| 2 | 9 | 140200 | Single proportion |
| 2 | 10 | 140140 | Intersection |

*Coordinates are either imported from an alternate source or generated through computations or adjustments of observations.*

### Coordinates

| Project ID | Point name | Type | GIS coordinate |
|---|---|---|---|
| 1 | 600100 | Imported | (lat, lon, elev) |
| 1 | 640100 | Computed | (lat, lon, elev) |
| 1 | 700100 | Imported | (lat, lon, elev) |
| 1 | 600140 | Computed | (lat, lon, elev) |
| 1 | 640140 | Computed | (lat, lon, elev) |
| 1 | 700140 | Computed | (lat, lon, elev) |
| 1 | 600200 | Imported | (lat, lon, elev) |
| 1 | 640200 | Computed | (lat, lon, elev) |
| 1 | 700200 | Imported | (lat, lon, elev) |
| 2 | 100100 | Imported | (lat, lon, elev) |
| 2 | 140100 | Computed | (lat, lon, elev) |
| 2 | 200100 | Imported | (lat, lon, elev) |
| 2 | 100140 | Imported | (lat, lon, elev) |
| 2 | 140140 | Computed | (lat, lon, elev) |
| 2 | 200140 | Computed | (lat, lon, elev) |
| 2 | 100200 | Imported | (lat, lon, elev) |
| 2 | 140200 | Computed | (lat, lon, elev) |
| 2 | 200200 | Imported | (lat, lon, elev) |

6

To meet the BLM requirements of keeping original values, NILS extended the Survey Analyst data model to include support for geodetic conversions; survey source information; and specific BLM business rules, such as section subdivision and minor subdivision.

## Measurements

A measurement is derived either through data import or the computational network. A measurement can be a direction, distance, or both. Directions are represented as azimuths with a reference to north.

With the PLSS being in geodetic representation, information about a measurement's native format, such as original direction type, distance type, coordinate system, and datum, is necessary to obtain correct geodesy parameters when applying geodetic computations. Each measurement is also attached to survey quality information through the survey source identifier (SID).

Some measurements represent tie lines to control stations and are not used to generate features, such as parcel boundaries.

## Measurements and survey source information

NILS measurements represent original measurements as presented on the survey plat. NILS stores these measurements in geographic coordinate system NAD83 based on the GRS 1980 ellipsoid. To reproduce original measurement values, NILS stores the necessary parameters to make this conversion. To constantly improve the PLSS network, NILS stores original survey source information, including error estimates used to update corner coordinates, in the PLSS cadastral network.

| Simple feature class **COGOSimpleMeas** | | | | | Geometry | Polyline | | |
|---|---|---|---|---|---|---|---|---|
| | | | | | Contains M values | No | | |
| | | | | | Contains Z values | No | | |
| **Field name** | **Data type** | **Allow nulls** | **Default value** | **Domain** | **Prec-ision** | **Scale** | **Length** | |
| SDB _OID | Object ID | | | | | | | |
| SDB _LatestMod | Long integer | Yes | | | 0 | | | |
| SDB _SurveyID | Long integer | No | | | 0 | | | Survey project identifier |
| SDB _SHAPE | Geometry | Yes | | | | | | Definition of feature geometry |
| MeasSubType | Short integer | No | | ArcSurvey _COGO _SMSubType | 0 | | | |
| Dir | Double | Yes | | | 0 | 0 | | Azimuth from data entry or computation |
| Length | Double | Yes | | | 0 | 0 | | Distance from data entry or computation |
| OrthoOffset | Double | Yes | | | 0 | 0 | | |
| VAngle | Double | Yes | | | 0 | 0 | | |
| VAngleOrthoOffset | Double | Yes | | | 0 | 0 | | |
| SDB _SHAPE _Length | Double | Yes | | | 0 | 0 | | |
| SID | String | Yes | | | | | 32 | Survey source identifier |
| TIE | Short integer | Yes | | | 0 | | | Survey tie line |
| OrigDirType | Short integer | Yes | | | 0 | | | Original type of direction |
| OrigDistType | Short integer | Yes | | | 0 | | | Original type of distance |
| Orig_Datum | Short integer | Yes | | | 0 | | | Original reference datum |
| Not_Meas | Short integer | Yes | | | 0 | | | Measurement not to be drawn |
| Org_Coordinate _System | String | Yes | | | | | 255 | Original coordinate system of measurement |

## Survey source information

Each survey performed on the PLSS has survey source information, which identifies the quality of the survey. This information is stored in the SID table.

The SID table holds error estimates on the measurements used in least squares adjustments. The sizes of the error estimates are based on the SID information estimates for a particular SID attached to each individual measurement.

The SID table also holds information about what type of survey was performed, when it was approved, and which agency or private contractor was responsible for it. Another important piece of information is whether a measurement was derived from a protraction or a field measurement.

**Table**
**SID**

| Field name | Data type | Allow nulls | Default value | Domain | Precision | Scale | Length | |
|---|---|---|---|---|---|---|---|---|
| State | String | Yes | | | | | 2 | The state of the survey |
| PM | Short integer | Yes | | | 0 | | | Principal meridian of the survey |
| SID | String | Yes | | | | | 32 | Survey source ID |
| SurveyorName | String | Yes | | | | | 64 | Name of the surveyor who made the survey |
| AAYear | Short integer | Yes | | | 0 | | | Survey acceptance year |
| AAMonth | Short integer | Yes | | | 0 | | | Survey acceptance month |
| AADay | Short integer | Yes | | | 0 | | | Survey acceptance day |
| ComYear | Short integer | Yes | | | 0 | | | Field survey completion year |
| ComMonth | Short integer | Yes | | | 0 | | | Field survey completion month |
| ComDay | Short integer | Yes | | | 0 | | | Field survey completion day |
| SSPCode | String | Yes | | | | | 2 | Survey source procedure code |
| SourceAgency | String | Yes | | | | | 32 | Survey source agency |
| Township | Double | Yes | | | | | 32 | Name of township for survey |
| Protraction | Short integer | Yes | | | 0 | | | Whether survey is a protraction |
| Curve | Short integer | Yes | | | 0 | | | Whether survey is a curve |
| Comment | String | Yes | | | | | 255 | Comment |
| OriginalSIDComments | String | Yes | | | | | 255 | Original SID comments |
| AngleErrorEstimate | String | Yes | | | | | 255 | Error estimate on angle measurement |
| LengthStdev | Double | Yes | | | 0 | 0 | | Error estimate on distance measurement |
| BearingStdev | Double | Yes | | | 0 | 0 | | Error estimate on azimuth measurement |
| LengthPPMStdev | Double | Yes | | | 0 | 0 | | Parts per million (PPM) error estimate on distance measurement |

6

Survey points represent locations for which you want to compute accurate locations by applying robust survey methods. Point locations are recorded as coordinates and error estimates based on the survey information used to compute the coordinates. Additional surveys enable you to recalculate the coordinate locations. Thus, each survey point can potentially have multiple coordinates.

A point can be located using one or more coordinates either imported or computed through the survey or computational network. Each survey-generated coordinate can have an error estimate and residual value attached. Further, a set of coordinates can become part of a mean coordinate computation.

The PLSS editor stores historical information about coordinates, such as whether they were the original coordinates, what coordinate system and datum were used, and whether

the information about error estimates and residuals was imported.

Depending on the data entry type, a coordinate can be tagged as provisional until a least squares adjustment of the survey network is performed. If more than one coordinate is present, a current coordinate is defined for use as the current survey point location. A selected set of coordinates is used to compute a mean coordinate location.

## Table
## Coordinate

| Field name | Data type | Allow nulls | Default value | Domain | Precision | Scale | Length | |
|---|---|---|---|---|---|---|---|---|
| SDB_OID | Object ID | | | | | | | |
| SDB_LatestMod | Long integer | Yes | | | 0 | | | |
| SDB_SurveyID | Long integer | No | | | 0 | | | |
| SDB_CompuOID | Long integer | No | | | 0 | | | |
| SDB_CompuCID | Long integer | No | | | 0 | | | |
| SDB_X | Double | Yes | | | 0 | 0 | | Latitudinal coordinate |
| SDB_Y | Double | Yes | | | 0 | 0 | | Longitudinal coordinate |
| SDB_Z | Double | Yes | | | 0 | 0 | | Elevation over chosen ellipsoid |
| M0 | Double | Yes | | | 0 | 0 | | Scale factor |
| Qxx | Double | Yes | | | 0 | 0 | | Square of estimated measurement error in easting |
| Qxy | Double | Yes | | | 0 | 0 | | Residual Qxy element in the covariance matrix |
| Qxz | Double | Yes | | | 0 | 0 | | Residual Qxz element in the covariance matrix |
| Qyy | Double | Yes | | | 0 | 0 | | Residual Qyy element in the covariance matrix |
| Qyz | Double | Yes | | | 0 | 0 | | Residual Qyz element in the covariance matrix |
| Qzz | Double | Yes | | | 0 | 0 | | Residual Qzz element in the covariance matrix |
| CreationRole | Long integer | No | | | 0 | | | |
| IncludeInMean | Short integer | Yes | | ArcSurvey_Point_YesNo | 0 | | | Whether a coordinate should be included in mean |
| Provider | Long integer | Yes | | | 0 | | | |
| ProvidingCoord | Long integer | Yes | | | 0 | | | |
| CreationDate | Date | Yes | | | 0 | 0 | 8 | Date point was created |
| Info | String | Yes | | | | | 128 | Information text field |
| Orig_Datum | Short integer | Yes | | | 0 | | | Identifies original datum of the point |
| Original_Coord | Short integer | Yes | | | 0 | | | If coordinate is an original control coordinate |
| Commented_Out | Short integer | Yes | | | 0 | | | If coordinate was used in least squares adjustment |
| Origin | Short integer | Yes | | | 0 | | | How coordinate was derived |
| Error_average | Double | Yes | | | 0 | 0 | | Average error from PCCS |
| Error_maximum | Double | Yes | | | 0 | 0 | | Maximum error from PCCS |
| ADJ | Short integer | Yes | | | 0 | | | If there is supporting information from adjustments |
| OrgStdev | Double | Yes | | | 0 | 0 | | Original standard deviation of adjustment data |
| Provisional | Short integer | Yes | | | 0 | | | If the coordinate is provisional |
| Org_Coordinate_System | String | Yes | | | | | 255 | Original coordinate system of the point |

Each point in the PLSS is identified by a unique point identifier, which consists of a six-digit PLSS point ID as the prefix and the suffix defined as meridian, tier, and range. The six-digit prefix for each point identifier was taken from one of two earlier coordinate frameworks used for NILS: the PLSS Coordinate Computation System (PCCS) or the Geographic Coordinate Data Base (GCDB) Measurement Management (GMM) system. A version of GMM called WinGMM was also used on the Microsoft Windows platform.

A point represents a control point, monument, or computed corner. Locations of control points are obtained from published coordinates of points.

The location of monument corners is obtained through least squares adjustments of plat measurements defining the survey network.

The computed corners are defined through the computational network, built from normal, irregular, and minor section subdivisions.

The point table further stores historical information about a point, such as from which coordinate system and datum it was derived, from which previous BLM system point data it was imported, and whether a point can be used in the computational network or for feature generation.

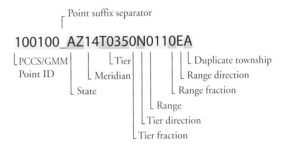

*PLSS point identifier—This is a concatenation of the legacy point identifier and the township ID to create a unique point identifier across the United States.*

| Simple feature class **Point** | | Geometry | Point | | |
|---|---|---|---|---|---|
| | | Contains M values | No | | |
| | | Contains Z values | No | | |

| Field name | Data type | Allow nulls | Prec-ision | Scale | Length | |
|---|---|---|---|---|---|---|
| SDB _OID | Object ID | | | | | |
| SDB _LatestMod | Long integer | Yes | 0 | | | |
| SDB _SurveyID | Long integer | No | 0 | | | |
| SDB _SHAPE | Geometry | Yes | | | | |
| SDB _UniqueID | Long integer | Yes | 0 | | | |
| Name | String | No | | | 32 | Point name with PLSS ID, meridian, tier, and range |
| X | Double | Yes | 0 | 0 | | Latitudinal coordinate |
| Y | Double | Yes | 0 | 0 | | Longitudinal coordinate |
| Z | Double | Yes | 0 | 0 | | Elevation over the chosen ellipsoid |
| M0 | Double | Yes | 0 | 0 | | Scale factor |
| Qxx | Double | Yes | 0 | 0 | | Square of the estimated measurement error in easting |
| Qxy | Double | Yes | 0 | 0 | | Residual Qxy element in the covariance matrix |
| Qxz | Double | Yes | 0 | 0 | | Residual Qxz element in the covariance matrix |
| Qyy | Double | Yes | 0 | 0 | | Square of the estimated measurement error in northing |
| Qyz | Double | Yes | 0 | 0 | | Residual Qyz element in the covariance matrix |
| Qzz | Double | Yes | 0 | 0 | | Residual Qzz element in the covariance matrix |
| CreationDate | Date | Yes | 0 | 0 | 8 | Date point was created |
| Control | Short integer | Yes | 0 | | | Defines if a point is a control point |
| Orig_Datum | Short integer | Yes | 0 | | | Identifies original datum of the point |
| Error _average | Double | Yes | 0 | 0 | | Average error from PCCS |
| Error _maximum | Double | Yes | 0 | 0 | | Maximum error from PCCS |
| System | Short integer | Yes | 0 | | | Whether data is from PCCS or WinGMM |
| Provisional | Short integer | Yes | 0 | | | Provisional coordinate |
| Controllable | Short integer | Yes | 0 | | | Points that may be used for computations |
| NotControllableReason | String | Yes | | | 255 | Reason a point cannot be used |
| AccessDeniedList | String | Yes | | | 255 | Points that cannot be used in any computations |
| Not_Point | Short integer | Yes | 0 | | | Points that cannot be used to generate features |
| Org_Coordinate _System | String | Yes | | | 255 | Original coordinate system of the point |

When a lease is initiated, a legal description is needed to identify the area within federal land. To generate the legal description, a survey may not be necessary in every case. Instead, a section or minor section subdivision can be performed using specified procedures. These procedures are a set of computations that subdivides sections into quarter or quarter-quarter sections stored in a computational network attached to the measured network. Every time the measurement network is adjusted, all computations are recomputed and all locations in the PLSS cadastral networks are updated.

To support the normal, irregular, and minor section subdivision in the PLSS, the PLSS editor supports a computational network, which is attached to the survey network. A new computed point is defined from a computation in the computational network. Four types of computations are currently supported.

- The direction–distance computation calculates a new point from a known location, direction, and distance. Specific to the PLSS, a new point can also be defined from the relationship between points instead of measurements only.

- For the intersection of two lines, each line can be defined from seven different constructions, the simplest being a line between two point IDs. This creates 49 possibilities for intersecting two lines.

- The inverse computation creates a measurement between two points from an inverse computation.

- The proportion computation distributes new points along a chosen geodetic line between two points from either variable or even distance, number of segments, or through a reference proportion located on a different line in the computational network.

When necessary, input parameter information about native measurement type, coordinate system, and datum are stored to obtain correct geodetic computations.

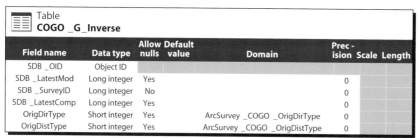

**Table**
**COGO _G_Inverse**

| Field name | Data type | Allow nulls | Default value | Domain | Prec-ision | Scale | Length | |
|---|---|---|---|---|---|---|---|---|
| SDB _OID | Object ID | | | | | | | |
| SDB _LatestMod | Long integer | Yes | | | 0 | | | |
| SDB _SurveyID | Long integer | No | | | 0 | | | |
| SDB _LatestComp | Long integer | Yes | | | 0 | | | |
| OrigDirType | Short integer | Yes | | ArcSurvey _COGO _OrigDirType | 0 | | | Original direction type |
| OrigDistType | Short integer | Yes | | ArcSurvey _COGO _OrigDistType | 0 | | | Original distance type |

**Table**
**COGO _G_DirDist**

| Field name | Data type | Allow nulls | Default value | Domain | Prec-ision | Scale | Length | |
|---|---|---|---|---|---|---|---|---|
| SDB _OID | Object ID | | | | | | | Reference to points and measurements |
| SDB _LatestMod | Long integer | Yes | | | 0 | | | |
| SDB _SurveyID | Long integer | No | | | 0 | | | |
| SDB _LatestComp | Long integer | Yes | | | 0 | | | |
| OrigDirType | Short integer | Yes | | ArcSurvey _COGO _OrigDirType | 0 | | | Original direction type |
| OrigDistType | Short integer | Yes | | ArcSurvey _COGO _OrigDistType | 0 | | | Original distance type |
| LineType | Short integer | Yes | | ArcSurvey _COGO _LineType | 0 | | | Line type |
| Datum | Short integer | Yes | | ArcSurvey _COGO _DatumType | 0 | | | Reference datum |
| Org _Coordinate _System | String | Yes | | | | | 255 | Original coordinate system of the point |

## Table
## COGO _G_Proportion

| Field name | Data type | Allow nulls | Default value | Domain | Precision | Scale | Length | |
|---|---|---|---|---|---|---|---|---|
| SDB _OID | Object ID | | | | | | | |
| SDB _LatestMod | Long integer | Yes | | | 0 | | | |
| SDB _SurveyID | Long integer | No | | | 0 | | | |
| SDB _LatestComp | Long integer | Yes | | | 0 | | | |
| ProportionCase | Short integer | Yes | | ArcSurvey _COGO _CaseType | 0 | | | Selected proportion type |
| OrigDirType | Short integer | Yes | | ArcSurvey _COGO _OrigDirType | 0 | | | Original direction type |
| CompDist | Double | Yes | | | 0 | 0 | | Computed distance |
| RecDist | Double | Yes | | | 0 | 0 | | Recorded distance |
| Datum | Short integer | Yes | | ArcSurvey _COGO _DatumType | 0 | | | Reference datum (NAD27 or NAD83) |
| NumberOfPoints | Double | Yes | | | 0 | 0 | | Number of result points |
| Numerator 1 | Double | Yes | | | 0 | 0 | | Distance of the first result point |
| Numerator 2 | Double | Yes | | | 0 | 0 | | Distance of the second result point |
| Numerator 3 | Double | Yes | | | 0 | 0 | | Distance of the third result point |
| Numerator 4 | Double | Yes | | | 0 | 0 | | Distance of the fourth result point |
| Numerator 5 | Double | Yes | | | 0 | 0 | | Distance of the fifth result point |
| Numerator 6 | Double | Yes | | | 0 | 0 | | Distance of the sixth result point |
| Numerator 7 | Double | Yes | | | 0 | 0 | | Distance of the seventh result point |
| Numerator 8 | Double | Yes | | | 0 | 0 | | Distance of the eighth result point |
| Increment | Double | Yes | | | 0 | 0 | | Incremental distance between points |
| Org_Coordinate _System | Double | Yes | | | | | 255 | Original coordinate system of the point |

## Table
## COGO _G_Intersection

| Field name | Data type | Allow nulls | Default value | Domain | Precision | Scale | Length | |
|---|---|---|---|---|---|---|---|---|
| SDB _OID | Object ID | | | | | | | |
| SDB _LatestMod | Long integer | Yes | | | 0 | | | |
| SDB _SurveyID | Long integer | No | | | 0 | | | |
| SDB _LatestComp | Long integer | Yes | | | 0 | | | |
| Line 1Type | Short integer | Yes | | ArcSurvey _COGO _LineType | 0 | | | Type of Line1 |
| Line 1Dir 1 | Double | Yes | | | 0 | 0 | | First direction for Line1 |
| Line 1Dir 2 | Double | Yes | | | 0 | 0 | | Second direction for Line1 |
| OrigLine 1DirType | Short integer | Yes | | ArcSurvey _COGO _OrigDirType | 0 | | | Original direction type for Line1 |
| Line 1Dist 1 | Double | Yes | | | 0 | 0 | | Distance measurement for Line1 |
| OrigLine 1DistType | Short integer | Yes | | ArcSurvey _COGO _OrigDistType | 0 | | | Original distance type for Line1 |
| Line 1Datum | Short integer | Yes | | ArcSurvey _COGO _DatumType | 0 | | | Reference datum for Line1 |
| Line 2Type | Short integer | Yes | | ArcSurvey _COGO _LineType | 0 | | | Type of Line2 |
| Line 2Dir 1 | Double | Yes | | | 0 | 0 | | First direction for Line2 |
| Line 2Dir 2 | Double | Yes | | | 0 | 0 | | Second direction for Line2 |
| OrigLine 2DirType | Short integer | Yes | | ArcSurvey _COGO _OrigDirType | 0 | | | Original direction type for Line2 |
| Line 2Dist 1 | Double | Yes | | | 0 | 0 | | Distance measurement for Line2 |
| OrigLine 2DistType | Short integer | Yes | | ArcSurvey _COGO _OrigDistType | 0 | | | Original distance type for Line2 |
| Line 2Datum | Short integer | Yes | | ArcSurvey _COGO _DatumType | 0 | | | Reference datum for Line2 |
| Computation 1 | Short integer | Yes | | ArcSurvey _COGO _IntersectionType | 0 | | | Line1 computation type |
| Computation 2 | Short integer | Yes | | ArcSurvey _COGO _IntersectionType | 0 | | | Line2 computation type |
| ResultPointCount | Long integer | Yes | | | 0 | | | Number of result points |
| ResultPointIndex | Long integer | Yes | | | 0 | | | Index of selected result point |
| Org_Coordinate _System | String | Yes | | | | | 255 | Original coordinate system of the point |

6

Corners and monuments are point feature classes used to represent the computed corners and control points referenced in surveys. Corners in the survey fabric are mirrored as point features in the legal description fabric for topology validation and data sharing.

A corner is a location in space, while a monument is a physical marker that identifies that location. Corners are determined from precise land surveys and may be updated as new surveys yield greater precision and accuracy to the location. Because of this, both corners and monuments are made survey aware in the data model for purposes of automated update using ArcGIS Survey Analyst software.

Monuments may be replaced over time due to weathering or damage or to establish a more precise location. Thus, multiple monuments may be associated with a single corner location in the GIS database. The Monument feature class represents a history of surveys and monument references over time.

A convention used in this data model is to put a state abbreviation prefix on certain feature classes. Because this data model is for use by a number of federal agencies, this is to distinguish multiple states' data in the database in support of work flow tasking and other data management functions.

| Simple feature class **<state abbr>_Corner** | | | | | | | | | Geometry *Point* / Contains M values *No* / Contains Z values *No* |
|---|---|---|---|---|---|---|---|---|---|

| Field name | Data type | Allow nulls | Default value | Domain | Precision | Scale | Length | Description |
|---|---|---|---|---|---|---|---|---|
| OBJECTID | Object ID | | | | | | | |
| Shape | Geometry | Yes | | | | | | |
| CreatedBy | String | Yes | | | | | 255 | Name of individual who created feature |
| DateCreated | Date | Yes | | | 0 | 0 | 8 | Date of feature creation |
| ModifiedBy | String | Yes | | | | | 255 | Name of individual who last modified feature |
| DateModified | Date | Yes | | | 0 | 0 | 8 | Date of last feature modification |
| DocumentHyperlink | String | Yes | | | | | 30 | Link to external document |
| PointIDUnique | String | Yes | | | | | 23 | Concatenated township and corner ID |
| CornerID | String | Yes | | | | | 6 | Primary key for the feature class polygon |
| Township | String | Yes | | | | | 16 | Concatenated tier and range name |
| CSourceAgent | String | Yes | BLM | ManagingAgency | | | 100 | Individual or organization that established the corner |
| ZCoordinate | Double | Yes | | | 0 | 0 | | Elevation in feet |
| Software | String | Yes | SA | Software | | | 10 | Collection software |
| YAccuracy | Long integer | Yes | | | 0 | | | Horizontal x accuracy from source survey data |
| XAccuracy | Long integer | Yes | | | 0 | | | Horizontal y accuracy from source survey data |
| ZAccuracy | Long integer | Yes | | | 0 | | | Elevation accuracy from source survey data |
| CornerType | String | Yes | U | Corner Type | | | 30 | A concatenation of corner classification and corner qualifier |
| CornerLabel | String | Yes | | | | | 100 | A name describing the legal location |
| CornerLocalLabel | String | Yes | | | | | 60 | Any number of alternative names or aliases for the corner |

*A corner is a legal location. It may mark the extremity of a parcel or a parcel framework polygon. A corner may have multiple monuments that serve as physical markers for the legal location of the corner.*

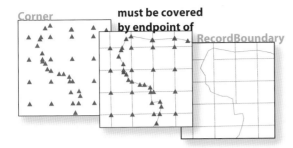

**Corner**     **must be covered**
**by endpoint of**
**RecordBoundary**

*This figure shows a topology rule governing the spatial relation-
ship between corners and record boundaries. Essentially, corners
must be located at the endpoints of record boundary features.*

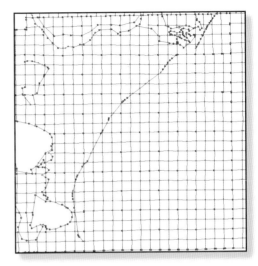

*Map of corners and record boundaries*

---

**Relationship class**
**<state abbr>_CornerHasMonuments**

| | |
|---|---|
| Type *Simple* | Forward label *Monument* |
| Cardinality *One to many* | Backward label *Corner* |
| Notification *None* | |

| **Origin feature class** | **Destination feature class** |
|---|---|
| Name *<state abbr>_Corner* | Name *<state abbr>_Monument* |
| Primary key *CornerID* | |
| Foreign key *CornerID* | |

**Coded value domain**
**Software**

| | |
|---|---|
| Field type *String* | |
| Split policy *Default value* | |
| Merge policy *Default value* | |

| Code | Description |
|---|---|
| CMM | Computation Measurement Management |
| GMM | Geographic Measurement Management |
| PCCS | PLSS Computational Coordinate System |
| SA | Survey Analyst |
| Other | Other |

**6**

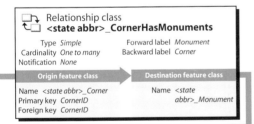

**Simple feature class**
**<state abbr>_Monument**

| | |
|---|---|
| Geometry | *Point* |
| Contains M values | *No* |
| Contains Z values | *No* |

| Field name | Data type | Allow nulls | Default value | Domain | Prec-ision | Scale | Length | |
|---|---|---|---|---|---|---|---|---|
| OBJECTID | Object ID | | | | | | | |
| Shape | Geometry | Yes | | | | | | |
| CreatedBy | String | Yes | | | | | 255 | Name of individual who created feature |
| DateCreated | Date | Yes | | | 0 | 0 | 8 | Date of feature creation |
| ModifiedBy | String | Yes | | | | | 255 | Name of individual who last modified feature |
| DateModified | Date | Yes | | | 0 | 0 | 8 | Date of last feature modification |
| DocumentHyperlink | String | Yes | | | | | 30 | Link to external document |
| CornerPointID | String | Yes | | | | | 30 | Pointer to identify which corner monument is attached to |
| CornerID | String | Yes | | | | | 6 | A primary key for the point feature |
| MonumentType | String | Yes | | | | | 30 | Material, composition, and characteristics of physical corner marker |
| MonumentDateSet | Date | Yes | | | 0 | 0 | 8 | The date the monument was set |
| CPSourceAgent | String | Yes | | | | | 100 | Control point source agent, such as register of deeds |
| CPSourceIndex | String | Yes | | | | | 100 | A value assigned to a monument record file |
| CPSourceType | String | Yes | | | | | 100 | Family of documents, files, images, or other sources |
| CPSourceDate | Date | Yes | | | 0 | 0 | 8 | Date of the monument record or file |
| CornerPointStatus | String | Yes | | | | | 100 | Monument's relationship to other monuments at same corner |

*Point feature that marks the ends of record
boundaries or the extremeties of a parcel or a
parcel framework polygon. A corner may or
may not be monumented, and there may be
one monument per corner.*

Measured coordinates are coordinate values that have been surveyed in the field and have known reliabilities and error estimates. The measured coordinates are often used as controls in the measurement management process.

Just as a corner can have multiple monuments, a single monument may also have multiple associated coordinates. The MeasuredCoordinate feature class has attributes for encoding metadata about each set of coordinates, such as the source, accuracy, reliability, vertical datum used, and other important context.

The MeasuredCoordinate feature class is survey aware, so updates to field survey data can directly update the associated coordinates in the GIS database.

*Historic township corner marker. Source: BLM*

Simple feature class
**\<state abbr>\_Monument**

| Field name | Data type | Length |
|---|---|---|
| OBJECTID | Object ID | |
| Shape | Geometry | |
| CreatedBy | String | 255 |
| DateCreated | Date | 8 |
| ModifiedBy | String | 255 |
| DateModified | Date | 8 |
| DocumentHyperlink | String | 30 |
| CornerPointID | String | 30 |
| CornerID | String | 6 |
| MonumentType | String | 30 |
| MonumentDateSet | Date | 8 |
| CPSourceAgent | String | 100 |
| CPSourceIndex | String | 100 |
| CPSourceType | String | 100 |
| CPSourceDate | Date | 8 |
| CornerPointStatus | String | 100 |

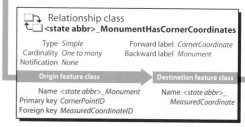

Relationship class
**\<state abbr>\_MonumentHasCornerCoordinates**

| | |
|---|---|
| Type *Simple* | Forward label *CornerCoordinate* |
| Cardinality *One to many* | Backward label *Monument* |
| Notification *None* | |

| Origin feature class | Destination feature class |
|---|---|
| Name *\<state abbr>\_Monument* | Name *\<state abbr>\_* |
| Primary key *CornerPointID* | *MeasuredCoordinate* |
| Foreign key *MeasuredCoordinateID* | |

*BLM cadastral survey marker. Source: BLM*

| | | | | | | | | | |
|---|---|---|---|---|---|---|---|---|---|

**Simple feature class**
**<state abbr>_MeasuredCoordinate**

Geometry *Point*
Contains M values *No*
Contains Z values *No*

*The corner point measured coordinate is an x,y; x,y,z; or z-value for a monument.*

| Field name | Data type | Allow nulls | Default value | Domain | Precision | Scale | Length | |
|---|---|---|---|---|---|---|---|---|
| OBJECTID | Object ID | | | | | | | |
| Shape | Geometry | Yes | | | | | | |
| CreatedBy | String | Yes | | | | | 255 | Name of individual who created feature |
| DateCreated | Date | Yes | | | 0 | 0 | 8 | Date of feature creation |
| ModifiedBy | String | Yes | | | | | 255 | Name of individual who last modified feature |
| DateModified | Date | Yes | | | 0 | 0 | 8 | Date of last feature modification |
| DocumentHyperlink | String | Yes | | | | | 30 | Link to external document |
| MeasuredCoordinateID | String | Yes | | | | | 30 | Primary key for the feature |
| PointIDUnique | String | Yes | | | | | 23 | Points to monument represented by coordinate |
| CSourceAgent | String | Yes | BLM | ManagingAgency | | | 100 | Corner source agent, such as register of deeds |
| ZCoordinate | Double | Yes | | | 0 | 0 | | The z coordinate value or elevation |
| YAccuracy | Long integer | Yes | | | 0 | | | |
| XAccuracy | Long integer | Yes | | | 0 | | | |
| ZAccuracy | Long integer | Yes | | | 0 | | | X accuracy, the x component of a 95% error ellipse |
| CoordinateValue | String | Yes | | | | | 30 | Y accuracy, the y component of a 95% error ellipse |
| CoordinateStatus | String | Yes | Active | | | | 30 | Z accuracy, the z component of a 95% error ellipse |
| CSourceIndex | String | Yes | | | | | 100 | Survey from which coordinate value originated |
| CSourceType | String | Yes | | | | | 100 | |
| CSourceDate | Date | Yes | | | 0 | 0 | 8 | Date of record, such as date of adjustment |
| CSourceComments | String | Yes | | | | | 100 | Additional notes about methods to obtain accuracy |
| Reliability | String | Yes | | | | | 30 | Measure of the total accuracy of coordinate value |
| AccuracyComments | String | Yes | | | | | 30 | Any statements about accuracy of coordinate value |
| CoordinateSystem | String | Yes | | | | | 30 | Reference frame for linear or angular quantities |
| VerticalDatum | String | Yes | North American Vertical Datum of 1988 | | | | 60 | Reference system for defining point elevations |
| CoordinateMethod | String | Yes | Total Station | | | | 30 | Technology used to establish coordinate value |
| CoordinateProcedure | String | Yes | Other | | | | 30 | Procedure using methods to measure coordinate value |
| VerticalUnits | String | Yes | International Feet | | | | 30 | Units of measure for elevation value |
| Software | String | Yes | | Software | | | 10 | |
| Township | String | Yes | | | | | 16 | |
| AvailFlag | String | Yes | | | | | 1 | |

6

Record boundary features represent the surveyed boundary from a survey dataset in the GIS. They also support COGO attributes so plat data can be quickly and easily added to the legal description fabric.

Record boundaries are mirrored with corresponding objects in the survey fabric for topology validation and to aid in sharing data with agencies that do not have Survey Analyst.

**RecordBoundary**

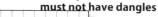
**must not have dangles**

The topology rule shown above means that RecordBoundary features must terminate at an intersection with another feature, which in this model must be a corner feature.

*Record boundaries are two-point line features that represent segments of the LD fabric features.*

## Coded value domain
### RecordBoundaryType

Field type *Long integer*
Split policy *Default value*
Merge policy *Default value*

| Code | Description |
|------|-------------|
| 0 | Township Line |
| 1 | Section Line |
| 2 | Subdivision Line |
| 3 | Special Line |
| 4 | Blank Line |

## Coded value domain
### RecordBoundaryStatus

Field type *String*
Split policy *Default value*
Merge policy *Default value*

| Code | Description |
|------|-------------|
| Ambulatory | Ambulatory |
| Tidal | Tidal |
| Disputed | Disputed |
| Adjudicated | Adjudicated |
| Connecting Line | Connecting Line |
| Computed | Computed |
| Constructed | Constructed |
| Duplicate | Duplicate |
| Archived | Archived |
| Unknown | Unknown |

## Coded value domain
### DirectionUnit

Field type *String*
Split policy *Default value*
Merge policy *Default value*

| Code | Description |
|------|-------------|
| Deg | Decimal Degrees |
| DMS | Degrees Minutes Seconds |
| Rad | Radians |
| Grad | Gradians |
| Gons | Gons |
| Other | Other |
| Unknown | Unknown |

## Coded value domain
### DistanceUnit

Field type *String*
Split policy *Default value*
Merge policy *Default value*

| Code and description |
|----------------------|
| Chains |
| US Survey Feet |
| International Feet |
| Meters |
| Pole |
| Arpent |
| Perch |
| Rod |
| Stick |
| Vara |
| Vara - California |
| Vara - Texas |
| Unknown |

## Coded value domain
### DistanceType

Field type *String*
Split policy *Default value*
Merge policy *Default value*

| Code and description |
|----------------------|
| Ground |
| Sea Level |
| Grid |
| Unknown |

## Coded value domain
### DirectionType

Field type *String*
Split policy *Default value*
Merge policy *Default value*

| Code and description |
|----------------------|
| Assumed |
| Astronomical North |
| Astronomical South |
| Geodetic North |
| Geodetic South |
| Magnetic North |
| Magnetic South |
| Unknown |

*A record boundary is the linear feature that represents the edge of a polygon feature, which may be a parcel or a parcel framework.*

## Simple feature class
### <state abbr>_RecordBoundary

Geometry *Polyline*
Contains M values *No*
Contains Z values *No*

| Field name | Data type | Allow nulls | Default value | Domain | Precision | Scale | Length | |
|------------|-----------|-------------|---------------|--------|-----------|-------|--------|---|
| OBJECTID | Object ID | | | | | | | |
| Shape | Geometry | Yes | | | | | | |
| CreatedBy | String | Yes | | | | | 255 | Name of individual who created feature. |
| DateCreated | Date | Yes | | | 0 | 0 | 8 | Date of feature creation. |
| ModifiedBy | String | Yes | | | | | 255 | Name of individual who last modified feature. |
| DateModified | Date | Yes | | | 0 | 0 | 8 | Date of last feature modification. |
| DocumentHyperlink | String | Yes | | | | | 30 | Link to external document. |
| RecordBoundaryID | String | Yes | | | | | 30 | The primary key for the line entity. |
| RecordBoundaryType | Long integer | Yes | 2 | RecordBoundaryType | 0 | | | Type of record boundary. |
| RecordBoundaryStatus | String | Yes | Constructed | RecordBoundaryStatus | | | 30 | Legal status of record boundary. |
| RecordBounds | String | Yes | | | | | 30 | Boundary location by call, document, or location. |
| OffsetLeft | Double | Yes | | | 0 | 0 | | Distance left of and perpendicular to boundary line. |
| OffsetRight | Double | Yes | | | 0 | 0 | | Distance right of and perpendicular to boundary line. |
| RecordBoundaryComment | String | Yes | | | | | 100 | Information about record boundary in public record. |
| Direction | String | Yes | | | | | 12 | The angle between a line and a reference line. |
| Distance | String | Yes | | | | | 10 | The quantity for linear measure distance of boundary. |
| DirectionType | String | Yes | Unknown | DirectionType | | | 30 | Basis of bearing (or azimuth) for direction. |
| DirectionUnit | String | Yes | DMS | DirectionUnit | | | 30 | Indicates the units for a direction. |
| DirectionQuadrant | String | Yes | | | | | 10 | Directions can be measured as a bearing or azimuth. |
| DistanceUnit | String | Yes | International Feet | DistanceUnit | | | 30 | Defines units of measure and distance reference plane. |
| DistanceType | String | Yes | Unknown | DistanceType | | | 30 | Describes the reference surface for the distance. |
| Radius | String | Yes | | | | | 10 | The distance from the center to any point on the curve. |
| Delta | String | Yes | | | | | 10 | The central angle of a circular curve. |
| Tangent | String | Yes | | | | | 10 | Distance between points of tangency and intersection. |
| ArcLength | String | Yes | | | | | 10 | The arc length is the long chord length. |
| Side | String | Yes | | | | | 1 | Side of curve where radius point is located. |
| RBSourceAgent | String | Yes | | | | | 30 | Person or agency determining record boundary values. |
| RBSourceIndex | String | Yes | | | | | 30 | Value assigned to document to identify source. |
| RBSourceType | String | Yes | | | | | 30 | Describes a family of documents, files, or images. |
| RBSourceDate | Date | Yes | | | 0 | 0 | 8 | Date of record boundary document or other record. |
| RBSourceReliability | Date | Yes | | | 0 | 0 | 8 | Date that record boundary reliability was established. |
| ProtractedFlag | String | Yes | N | YesNo | | | 255 | Perimeter of index area calculated from feature shape. |
| Township | String | Yes | | | | | 16 | Township containing this record boundary. |
| Shape_Length | Double | Yes | | | 0 | 0 | | |

Townships are the largest units of land area in the PLSS. Because of their size, the curvature of the earth, the presence of large water bodies, and the number of townships between principal meridians, all townships do not have the same dimensions.

The township is the fundamental unit of land area in the PLSS. Nominally six miles square in size, townships consist of 36 one-mile sections. Each township is named with its relative position from the state's PLSS baseline and meridian. The baseline runs east–west, while the meridian runs north–south.

Townships were typically surveyed starting in the southeastern corner. Adjustments were generally needed along the west and north boundaries to compensate for the curvature of the earth, with the effect that the western and northern (and especially the northwesternmost) sections were smaller than the southeastern sections.

*Method of numbering townships and sections from General Land Office, 1921*

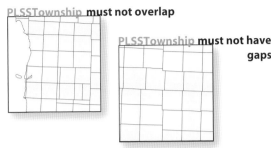

**PLSSTownship must not overlap**

**PLSSTownship must not have gaps**

*The topology rules in this figure indicate that townships must adjoin and fill the space without gaps or overlaps.*

---

Coded value domain
**Township Survey Status**

Field type *String*
Split policy *Default value*
Merge policy *Default value*

| Code | Description |
|---|---|
| Protracted | Protracted |
| Surveyed | Surveyed |
| Surveyed and Protracted | Surveyed and Protracted |

---

Coded value domain
**Principal Meridian**

Field type *String*
Split policy *Default value*
Merge policy *Default value*

| Code | Description | Code | Description | Code | Description |
|---|---|---|---|---|---|
| 00 | No Land Desc | 18 | Louisiana | 36 | Between Miamis |
| 01 | First Principal | 19 | Michigan | 37 | Muskingham River |
| 02 | Second Principal | 20 | Montana | 38 | Ohio River Base |
| 03 | Third Principal | 21 | Mount Diablo | 39 | Scioto River 1 |
| 04 | Fourth Principal | 22 | Navajo | 40 | Scioto River 2 |
| 05 | Fifth Principal | 23 | New Mexico | 41 | Scioto River 3 |
| 06 | Sixth Principal | 24 | St Helena | 43 | Twelve Miles |
| 07 | Black Hills | 25 | St Stevens | 44 | Kateel River |
| 08 | Boise | 26 | Salt Lake | 45 | Umiat |
| 09 | Chicksaw | 27 | San Bernardino | 46 | 4 th extended |
| 10 | Choctaw | 28 | Seward | 47 | West of Miamis |
| 11 | Cimmarron | 29 | Tallahassee | 48 | US Military Survey |
| 12 | Copper River | 30 | Uintah | 91 | Connecticut West Reserve in Ohio |
| 13 | Fairbanks | 31 | Ute | 92 | Ohio Company Purchase in Ohio |
| 14 | Gila-Salt River | 32 | Washington | 93 | Virginia Military Survey in Ohio |
| 15 | Humboldt | 33 | Willamette | 98 | Invalid Land Desc |
| 16 | Huntsville | 34 | Wind River | 99 | Undefined Land Desc |
| 17 | Indian | 35 | Ohio River Survey | | |

---

Coded value domain
**TownshipDuplicateCode**

Field type *String*
Split policy *Default value*
Merge policy *Default value*

| Code | Description |
|---|---|
| 0 | No Duplicate |
| A | First Duplicate |
| B | Second Duplicate |
| C | Third Duplicate |

---

Coded value domain
**TownshipRangeDirection**

Field type *String*
Split policy *Default value*
Merge policy *Default value*

| Code | Description |
|---|---|
| W | West |
| E | East |

---

Simple feature class
**<state abbr>_PLSSTownship**

Geometry *Polygon*
Contains M values *No*
Contains Z values *No*

| Field name | Data type | Allow nulls | Default value | Domain | Precision | Scale | Length | |
|---|---|---|---|---|---|---|---|---|
| OBJECTID | Object ID | | | | | | | |
| Shape | Geometry | Yes | | | | | | |
| CreatedBy | String | Yes | | | | | 255 | The name of the user or process that created the feature. |
| DateCreated | Date | Yes | | | 0 | 0 | 8 | The date on which the feature instance was created. |
| ModifiedBy | String | Yes | | | | | 255 | The name of the user who updated the feature. |
| DateModified | Date | Yes | | | 0 | 0 | 8 | Date feature was updated and posted to the enterprise database. |
| DocumentHyperlink | String | Yes | | | | | 30 | Used for ArcMap hyperlink capabilities |
| PLSSTownshipID | String | Yes | | | | | 30 | Primary key that identifies each township entity. |
| StateCode | String | Yes | | StateNameCodes | | | 2 | Code for state identifier. |
| PrincipalMeridian | String | Yes | | Principal Meridian | | | 2 | Named reference of beginning point for measuring east or west ranges. |
| TierDesignator | String | Yes | | | | | 3 | Number of rows of townships, north or south from a PLSS origin. |
| TierFraction | String | Yes | | | | | 1 | Fractions are created at gaps between surveyed township boundaries . |
| TierDirection | String | Yes | | | | | 1 | North or south designator. |
| RangeDesignator | String | Yes | | | | | 3 | Number of columns of townships, east or west from a PLSS origin. |
| RangeFraction | String | Yes | | | | | 1 | Fractions are created at gaps between surveyed township boundaries . |
| RangeDirection | String | Yes | | TownshipRangeDirection | | | 1 | East or west designator. |
| TownDupCode | String | Yes | | TownshipDuplicateCode | | | 1 | Optional flag for duplicate values. |
| Township | String | Yes | | | | | 16 | Concatenated tier and range name. |
| TownshipType | String | Yes | | Township Survey Status | | | 40 | Whether the township is surveyed, protracted, or unsurveyed. |
| Shape_Length | Double | Yes | | | 0 | 0 | | |
| Shape_Area | Double | Yes | | | 0 | 0 | | |

*A township is typically an area comprising 36 sections in a six-by-six array.*

6

PLSS townships are subdivided in a spatial hierarchy of first, second, and third divisions. These divisions are typically aliquot parts ranging in size from 640 acres to 160 to 40 acres, and subsequently all the way down to 2.5 acres.

To support land division tasks, PLSS townships may be divided into many levels. The first division is nominally a one-mile square unit of land called a "section." These nominally contain 640 acres.

The second division is also called a "quarter section." Each first division unit can have four, second divisions, which may vary in shape and size.

Two topology rules are shown at right. The first stipulates that each subdivision of a township must be bounded by features of the RecordBoundary class. This to ensure that PLSS subdivisions are coincident with the actual survey data, through the survey-aware RecordBoundary feature class.

The second topology rule stipulates that each PLSS subdivision feature is covered by a single PLSS township feature. This enforces that subdivisions nest in a proper spatial hierarchy.

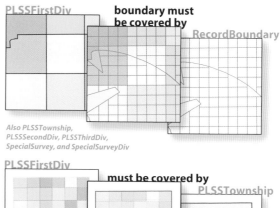

**PLSSFirstDiv** boundary must be covered by **RecordBoundary**

Also PLSSTownship, PLSSSecondDiv, PLSSThirdDiv, SpecialSurvey, and SpecialSurveyDiv

**PLSSFirstDiv** must be covered by **PLSSTownship**

Also PLSSSecondDiv and PLSSThirdDiv

PLSS first divisions are normally sections, square tracts of land nominally measuring one mile square and containing 640 acres.

| | | | | | | | | |
|---|---|---|---|---|---|---|---|---|
| **Simple feature class** <state abbr>_PLSSFirstDiv | | | | Geometry | Polygon | | | |
| | | | | Contains M values | No | | | |
| | | | | Contains Z values | No | | | |
| **Field name** | **Data type** | **Allow nulls** | **Default value** | **Domain** | **Prec- ision** | **Scale** | **Length** | |
| OBJECTID | Object ID | | | | | | | |
| Shape | Geometry | Yes | | | | | | |
| CreatedBy | String | Yes | | | | | 255 | The name of the user or process that created the feature |
| DateCreated | Date | Yes | | | 0 | 0 | 8 | The date on which the feature instance was created |
| ModifiedBy | String | Yes | | | | | 255 | The name of the user who updated the feature |
| DateModified | Date | Yes | | | 0 | 0 | 8 | Date feature was updated and posted to the enterprise database |
| DocumentHyperlink | String | Yes | | | | | 30 | Used for ArcMap hyperlink capabilities |
| PLSSFirstDivID | String | Yes | | | | | 30 | Primary key field |
| FirstDivisionDesignator | String | Yes | | | | | 3 | Letter, number, or combination that identifies first division |
| FirstDivisionFraction | String | Yes | | | | | 1 | Optional fraction designation code |
| FirstDivDupCode | String | Yes | | | | | 1 | Optional flag for duplicate values |
| Township | String | Yes | | | | | 16 | Concatenated tier and range name |
| FirstDivisionType | String | Yes | S | | | | 1 | Type of division |
| AreaSize | Double | Yes | | | 0 | 0 | | Area of the first division |
| AreaUnit | String | Yes | | AreaUnit | | | 255 | Units of the area measurement |
| AreaSource | String | Yes | | AreaSource | | | 1 | Source of the area |
| Shape_Length | Double | Yes | | | 0 | 0 | | |
| Shape_Area | Double | Yes | | | 0 | 0 | | |

Sections in first divisions drawn in ArcMap

The Legal Land Description (LLD) table in LR2000 is a source for acreage tracts in NILS. Since tracts may appear in more than one source, they sometimes need to be reconciled. The AreaSource field and coded value domain for first and second division features support identification of such cases.

The main purpose for the SecondDivision feature class is to help describe mining claims. Mining claims are nominally located within up to five quarter sections.

**Coded value domain**
**AreaUnit**

Field type *String*
Split policy *Default value*
Merge policy *Default value*

| Code | Description |
| --- | --- |
| Square Feet | Square Feet |
| Acres | Acres |
| Hectares | Hectares |
| Other | Other |

**Coded value domain**
**AreaSource**

Field type *String*
Split policy *Default value*
Merge policy *Default value*

| Code | Description |
| --- | --- |
| 0 | Acreage from LLD without adding the portions of the survey |
| A | Acreage calculated by query that added LLD acreages by special survey type |
| B | Acreage from official plat and agrees with LLD sum |
| C | Acreage from official plat and disagrees with LLD sum |
| D | Acreage from MTP or paper map |
| E | Acreage from GIS coverage or AutoCAD |
| F | Acreage computed by a subdivision program |

*PLSS second divisions are normally quarter sections. A quarter section is nominally a half mile square and contains 160 acres.*

**Simple feature class**
**<state abbr>_PLSSSecondDiv**

Geometry *Polygon*
Contains M values *No*
Contains Z values *No*

| Field name | Data type | Allow nulls | Default value | Domain | Precision | Scale | Length | |
| --- | --- | --- | --- | --- | --- | --- | --- | --- |
| OBJECTID | Object ID | | | | | | | |
| Shape | Geometry | Yes | | | | | | |
| CreatedBy | String | Yes | | | | | 255 | The name of the user or process that created the feature |
| DateCreated | Date | Yes | | | 0 | 0 | 8 | The date on which the feature instance was created |
| ModifiedBy | String | Yes | | | | | 255 | The name of the user who updated the feature |
| DateModified | Date | Yes | | | 0 | 0 | 8 | Date feature was updated and posted to the enterprise database |
| DocumentHyperlink | String | Yes | | | | | 30 | Used for ArcMap hyperlink capabilities |
| PLSSSecondDivID | String | Yes | | | | | 30 | The primary key field |
| SecondDivDesignator | String | Yes | | | | | 3 | Letter, number, or combination that identifies second division |
| SecondDivSuffix | String | Yes | | | | | 2 | Optional indicator for duplicate second divisions |
| SecondDivType | String | Yes | Quarter | | | | 30 | Type of division |
| SecondDivDupcode | String | Yes | | | | | 1 | Optional flag for duplicate values |
| FirstDivisionDesignator | String | Yes | | | | | 3 | Letter, number, or combination identifying first division |
| FirstDivisionFraction | String | Yes | | | | | 1 | Optional fraction designator code |
| FirstDivisionDupCode | String | Yes | | | | | 1 | Optional flag for duplicate values |
| Township | String | Yes | | | | | 16 | Concatenated tier and range name |
| AreaSize | Double | Yes | | | 0 | 0 | | Area of the second division |
| AreaUnit | String | Yes | | AreaUnit | | | 16 | Units of the area measurement |
| AreaSource | String | Yes | | AreaSource | | | 16 | Source of the area |
| Shape_Length | Double | Yes | | | 0 | 0 | | |
| Shape_Area | Double | Yes | | | 0 | 0 | | |

Some cases are referred to as "quarter-quarter sections" (for example, the northeast quarter of the southeast quarter). PLSS third divisions typically contain the 40-acre aliquot parts. Until NILS, this was the smallest subdivision of land held in a GIS. With new tools, the legal description fabric can now be subsequently divided into even smaller units—as well as irregular subdivisions, such as lots and fractional sections—and managed in the third division.

The smallest regular subdivisions of sections are created in the NILS geodatabase as PLSS third division polygon features. As the list of subtypes on the next page shows, this includes lots, aliquot parts 40 acres and smaller, fractional sections, and cadastral tracts.

In normal usage, aliquot parts (literally "equal parts") could refer to any regular subdivision of a section, including halves and quarters of a section. Halves of a section are represented as N, S, E, or W (such as "the north half of section 5).

Quarters of a section are represented as NW, SW, NE, and SE (such as "the northwest quarter of section 5). Sometimes, several aliquot parts are required to accurately describe a parcel of land. For example, ESW denotes the east half of the southwest quarter containing 80 acres, and SWNENE denotes the southwest quarter of the northeast quarter of the northeast quarter containing 10 acres. The aliquots shown in the database, such as SWNENE, usually translate into words found on the land document.

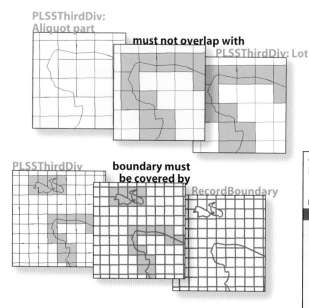

**PLSSThirdDiv: Aliquot part must not overlap with PLSSThirdDiv: Lot**

**PLSSThirdDiv: Aliquot part must not overlap**

**PLSSThirdDiv boundary must be covered by RecordBoundary**

Coded value domain
**PLSSAliquotDivisionType**

Field type *String*
Split policy *Default value*
Merge policy *Default value*

| Code | Description |
|------|-------------|
| L | L |
| A | A |
| B | B |
| U | U |
| O | O |
| LR | LR |
| AR | AR |
| BR | BR |
| TCI | TCI |

Coded value domain
**Nominal Locations**

Field type *String*
Split policy *Default value*
Merge policy *Default value*

| Code | Description | Code | Description |
|------|-------------|------|-------------|
| A | NENE | J | NWSW |
| B | NWNE | K | SWSW |
| C | SWNE | L | SESW |
| D | SENE | M | NESE |
| E | NENW | N | NWSE |
| F | NWNW | O | SWSE |
| G | SWNW | P | SESE |
| H | SENW | Q | ALL |
| I | NESW | Z | NOT RELEVANT |

## Simple feature class
### &lt;state abbr&gt;_PLSSThirdDiv

| | | Geometry | Polygon |
|---|---|---|---|
| | | Contains M values | No |
| | | Contains Z values | No |

*Contains all aliquot divisions of the PLSS below the second division calculated as equal divisions. Includes divisions 3–n (sixteenths and smaller).*

| Field name | Data type | Allow nulls | Default value | Domain | Prec-ision | Scale | Length | |
|---|---|---|---|---|---|---|---|---|
| OBJECTID | Object ID | | | | | | | |
| Shape | Geometry | Yes | | | | | | |
| CreatedBy | String | Yes | | | | | 255 | The name of the user or process that created the feature. |
| DateCreated | Date | Yes | | | 0 | 0 | 8 | The date on which the feature instance was created. |
| ModifiedBy | String | Yes | | | | | 255 | The name of the user who updated the feature. |
| DateModified | Date | Yes | | | 0 | 0 | 8 | The date feature was updated and posted to the enterprise database. |
| DocumentHyperlink | String | Yes | | | | | 30 | Used for ArcMap hyperlink capabilities. |
| PLSSAliquotID | String | Yes | | | | | 30 | Primary key identifier. |
| AliquotDesignator | String | Yes | | | | | 3 | Name of the aliquot division. |
| AliquotLevel | Long integer | Yes | 3 | | 0 | | | Level of subdivision; values greater than two are valid. |
| FirstDivisionDesignator | String | Yes | | | | | 3 | Letter, number, or combination identifying first division. |
| FirstDivisionFraction | String | Yes | | | | | 1 | Used for fractional and other optional suffixes. |
| FirstDivDupCode | String | Yes | | | | | 1 | Optional flag for duplicate values. |
| NominalLocation | String | Yes | | Nominal Locations | | | 1 | Nominal location code (A–P, Q, Z). |
| MinorSubdivision | String | Yes | | | | | 4 | Optional minor subdivision code (R–Y). |
| Quarter | String | Yes | | QuarterDomain | | | 2 | Second division designator. |
| SurveyType | String | Yes | A | | | | 3 | The type of survey marking the aliquot boundary. |
| SurveyNumber | String | Yes | | | | | 5 | Optional survey number. |
| SurveySuffix | String | Yes | | | | | 2 | Optional survey suffix. |
| SurveyNote | String | Yes | | | | | 3 | Optional survey note. |
| AreaSize | Double | Yes | | | 0 | 0 | | Area of the third division. |
| AreaUnit | String | Yes | | AreaUnit | | | 255 | Units of the area measurement. |
| AreaSource | String | Yes | | AreaSource | | | 1 | Source of the area. |
| LandDescriptionDupCode | String | Yes | | | | | 1 | Land description duplicate code |
| DiscrepencyCode | String | Yes | | | | | 1 | Used when GCDB and LLD locations differ. |
| SurveyRuleException | String | Yes | | | | | 3 | Exceptions to survey type rules; numbers reference specific rules. |
| Township | String | Yes | | | | | 16 | Concatenated tier and range name. |
| SubsurfaceOnly | String | Yes | | | | | 1 | Code indicating subsurface only survey. |
| ValidationCode | String | Yes | | | | | 1 | Code to report whether GCDB and LLD land descriptions match. |
| SubtypeCodeAliqDiv | Long integer | Yes | 2 | | 0 | | | Type field for distinguishing entities with different business rules. |
| Shape_Length | Double | Yes | | | 0 | 0 | | |
| Shape_Area | Double | Yes | | | 0 | 0 | | |

## Subtypes of &lt;state abbr&gt;_PLSSThirdDiv

Default subtype 2
Subtype field *SubtypeCodeAliqDiv*
List of defined default values and domains for subtypes in this class

| Subtype code | Subtype description | | Field name | Default value | Domain |
|---|---|---|---|---|---|
| 1 | Lot | ⇨ | AliquotLevel | 4 | AliquotPartLessThan40Level |
| | | | SurveyType | L | PLSSAliquotDivisionType |
| 2 | Aliquot Part | ⇨ | AliquotLevel | 2 | AliquotPartLevel |
| | | | SurveyType | A | PLSSAliquotDivisionType |
| 3 | Aliquot Part Less Than 40 | ⇨ | AliquotLevel | 4 | AliquotPartLessThan40Level |
| | | | SurveyType | B | PLSSAliquotDivisionType |
| 4 | Unsurveyed Protracted | ⇨ | AliquotLevel | 5 | |
| | | | SurveyType | U | PLSSAliquotDivisionType |
| 5 | Fractional Part of Section | ⇨ | AliquotLevel | 5 | |
| | | | SurveyType | O | PLSSAliquotDivisionType |
| 6 | Lot Resurveyed | ⇨ | AliquotLevel | 4 | AliquotPartLessThan40Level |
| | | | SurveyType | LR | PLSSAliquotDivisionType |
| 7 | Aliquot Resurveyed | ⇨ | AliquotLevel | 2 | AliquotPartLevel |
| | | | SurveyType | AR | PLSSAliquotDivisionType |
| 8 | Aliquot Less Than 40 Resurveyed | ⇨ | AliquotLevel | 4 | AliquotPartLessThan40Level |
| | | | SurveyType | BR | PLSSAliquotDivisionType |
| 9 | Tracts Cadastral | ⇨ | AliquotLevel | 2 | AliquotPartLevel |
| | | | SurveyType | TCI | PLSSAliquotDivisionType |

### Range domain
### AliquotPartLessThan40Level

| | |
|---|---|
| Field type | Long integer |
| Split policy | Default value |
| Merge policy | Default value |

| Minimum value | Maximum value |
|---|---|
| 4 | 16 |

### Range domain
### AliquotPartLevel

| | |
|---|---|
| Field type | Long integer |
| Split policy | Default value |
| Merge policy | Default value |

| Minimum value | Maximum value |
|---|---|
| 2 | 3 |

### Coded value domain
### QuarterDomain

| | |
|---|---|
| Field type | String |
| Split policy | Default value |
| Merge policy | Default value |

| Code | Description |
|---|---|
| NW | NorthWest |
| NE | NorthEast |
| SE | SouthEast |
| SW | SouthWest |

Each of the subtypes also share these default values and domains for the fields shown.

| Field name | Default value | Domain |
|---|---|---|
| NominalLocation | | Nominal Locations |
| Quarter | | QuarterDomain |
| AreaUnit | | AreaUnit |
| AreaSource | | AreaSource |

**6**

Special surveys are surveys based on rules outside the PLSS, such as metes and bounds surveys, homestead entry surveys, mineral surveys, and others. A special survey can be considered the first division of a survey and can contain subsequent divisions. These also do not follow PLSS rules and, hence, are special surveys.

Types of special surveys include:

- Metes and bounds surveys define boundaries of irregular areas of land.

- Homestead entry surveys were enacted under the Homestead Act of 1862. Persons who settled this land were given 160 acres, provided they lived upon and improved the land.

- Land grants were given by the U.S. Congress to each state in proportion to the number of representatives.

- An exchange survey is required whenever government lands are exchanged with nonpublic entities.

- Mineral surveys are required to patent a mining claim.

- Surveys are required for certain remote lands that are unsurveyed and in which protraction diagrams are used.

- Donation land claims applying to many federal land grants in Oregon by act of the U.S. Congress in 1850 require special surveys.

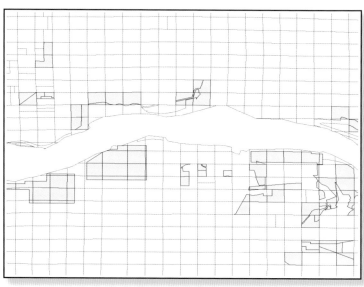

*The shaded areas in this map are special surveys. Special surveys fill holes in the legal description fabric, specifically the PLSS third division.*

| Field name | Data type | Allow nulls | Default value | Domain | Precision | Scale | Length | |
|---|---|---|---|---|---|---|---|---|

**Simple feature class**
**<state abbr>_SpecialSurvey**

Geometry *Polygon*
Contains M values *No*
Contains Z values *No*

*Boundaries not related to the PLSS. Facilitates representation of non-PLSS features and areas in locations not covered by PLSS. Features may or may not be in areas covered by PLSS.*

| Field name | Data type | Allow nulls | Default value | Domain | Precision | Scale | Length | Description |
|---|---|---|---|---|---|---|---|---|
| OBJECTID | Object ID | | | | | | | |
| Shape | Geometry | Yes | | | | | | |
| CreatedBy | String | Yes | | | | | 255 | Name of individual who created feature. |
| DateCreated | Date | Yes | | | 0 | 0 | 8 | Date of feature creation. |
| ModifiedBy | String | Yes | | | | | 255 | Name of individual who last modified feature. |
| DateModified | Date | Yes | | | 0 | 0 | 8 | Date of last feature modification. |
| DocumentHyperlink | String | Yes | | | | | 30 | Link to external document. |
| SpecialSurveyID | String | Yes | | | | | 30 | Primary key identifier. |
| SpecSurvDesignator | String | Yes | | | | | 3 | Designation for survey area, such as lot number. |
| FirstDivisionDesignator | String | Yes | | | | | 3 | Letter, number, or combination identifying the first division. |
| FirstDivisionFraction | String | Yes | | | | | 1 | Optional fraction designator code. |
| FirstDivDupCode | String | Yes | | | | | 1 | Optional flag for duplicate values. |
| NominalLocation | String | Yes | | Nominal Locations | | | 1 | Nominal location code (A–P, Q, Z). |
| MinorSubdivision | String | Yes | | | | | 4 | Optional minor subdivision code (R–Y). |
| SurveyType | String | Yes | E | | | | 3 | Type of survey marking the special survey boundary. |
| SurveyNumber | String | Yes | | | | | 5 | Optional survey number. |
| SurveySuffix | String | Yes | | | | | 2 | Optional survey suffix. |
| SurveyNote | String | Yes | | | | | 3 | Optional survey note. |
| AreaSize | Double | Yes | | | 0 | 0 | | Area of the special survey. |
| AreaUnit | String | Yes | | AreaUnit | | | 255 | Units of the area measurement. |
| AreaSource | String | Yes | | AreaSource | | | 1 | Source of the area. |
| LandDescriptionDupCode | String | Yes | | | | | 1 | Land description duplicate code. |
| DiscrepencyCode | String | Yes | | | | | 1 | Used when GCDB and LLD locations differ. |
| SurveyRuleException | String | Yes | | | | | 3 | Exceptions to survey type rules. Numbers reference specific rules. |
| Township | String | Yes | | | | | 16 | Concatenated tier and range name. |
| SubsurfaceOnly | String | Yes | | | | | 1 | Code indicating subsurface-only survey. |
| ValidationCode | String | Yes | | | | | 1 | Code to report whether GCDB and LLD land descriptions match. |
| SubtypeCodeSpecSurv | Long integer | Yes | 5 | | 0 | | | Subtype field to discriminate feature behaviors. |
| Shape_Length | Double | Yes | | | 0 | 0 | | |
| Shape_Area | Double | Yes | | | 0 | 0 | | |

**Subtypes of <state abbr>_SpecialSurvey**

Subtype field *SubtypeCodeSpecSurv*
Default subtype *5*

List of defined default values and domains for subtypes in this class

| Subtype code | Subtype description | Field name | Default value | Domain |
|---|---|---|---|---|
| 1 | Homestead Entry Survey | SurveyType | H | SpecialSurveyType |
| 2 | Land Grant | SurveyType | G | SpecialSurveyType |
| 3 | Exchange Survey | SurveyType | X | SpecialSurveyType |
| 5 | Metes and Bounds | SurveyType | E | SpecialSurveyType |
| 6 | Mineral Survey | SurveyType | M | SpecialSurveyType |
| 7 | Private Land Claim | SurveyType | R | SpecialSurveyType |
| 8 | Small Holding Claim | SurveyType | J | SpecialSurveyType |
| 9 | Texas Tract | SurveyType | TT | SpecialSurveyType |
| 10 | Townsite | SurveyType | N | SpecialSurveyType |
| 11 | Georgia Military District | SurveyType | GMD | SpecialSurveyType |
| 12 | Water | SurveyType | W | SpecialSurveyType |
| 13 | Right-of-Way | SurveyType | ROW | SpecialSurveyType |
| 14 | Unsurveyed–Unprotracted | SurveyType | Z | SpecialSurveyType |
| 15 | Donation Land Claim | SurveyType | Q | SpecialSurveyType |

**Coded value domain**
**SpecialSurveyType**

Field type *String*
Split policy *Default value*
Merge policy *Default value*

| Code | Description |
|---|---|
| FLL | French Long Lot |
| J | Small Holding Claim |
| N | Townsite |
| H | Homestead Entry Survey |
| G | Land Grant |
| X | Exchange Survey |
| E | Metes and Bounds |
| M | Mineral Survey |
| R | Private Land Claim |
| TT | Texas Tract |
| GMD | Georgia Military District |
| ROW | Right-of-Way |
| W | Water |
| Z | Unsurveyed–Unprotracted |
| Q | Donation Land Claim |

| Field name | Default value | Domain |
|---|---|---|
| NominalLocation | | Nominal Locations |
| AreaUnit | | AreaUnit |
| AreaSource | | AreaSource |

**6**

Provisional parcel boundaries are nonsurveyed boundaries often used as building blocks in legal descriptions. Examples include stream boundaries, ridge and fence lines, political boundaries, and others. These come from a variety of sources, such as USGS quad sheets, reference thematic layers, and heads-up digitizing from orthophotos.

Provisional parcel boundaries do not participate in topology. Over time, they may be surveyed and incorporated into the survey fabric, then removed from this feature class. NILS Parcel Management users most often create these when survey data is unavailable.

## Simple feature class
### <state abbr>_ProvParcelBoundLine

Geometry *Polyline*
Contains M values *No*
Contains Z values *No*

| Field name | Data type | Allow nulls | Default value | Domain | Prec-ision | Scale | Length | |
|---|---|---|---|---|---|---|---|---|
| OBJECTID | Object ID | | | | | | | |
| Shape | Geometry | Yes | | | | | | |
| CreatedBy | String | Yes | | | | | 255 | Name of individual who created feature |
| DateCreated | Date | Yes | | | 0 | 0 | 8 | Date of feature creation |
| ModifiedBy | String | Yes | | | | | 255 | Name of individual who last modified feature |
| DateModified | Date | Yes | | | 0 | 0 | 8 | Date of last feature modification |
| DocumentHyperlink | String | Yes | | | | | 30 | Link to external document |
| RecordBoundaryID | String | Yes | | | | | 30 | Identifier of source feature, if applicable |
| source | String | Yes | | ProvParcel-BoundarylineSource | | | 255 | Identifier of origin of source feature, if applicable |
| source_date | Date | Yes | | | 0 | 0 | 8 | Date source feature was created |
| survey_flag | String | Yes | | | | | 255 | Flag indicating if source feature was surveyed |
| direction | String | Yes | | | | | 12 | COGO field |
| distance | String | Yes | | | | | 10 | COGO field |
| delta | String | Yes | | | | | 10 | COGO field |
| radius | String | Yes | | | | | 10 | COGO field |
| tangent | String | Yes | | | | | 10 | COGO field |
| arclength | String | Yes | | | | | 10 | COGO field |
| side | String | Yes | | | | | 1 | COGO field |
| Shape_Length | Double | Yes | | | 0 | 0 | | |

*Provisional boundaries may be defined where surveys have not been completed but a geometry is required for mapping or parcel management purposes.*

### Coded value domain
**ProvParcelBoundarylineSource**

Field type *String*
Split policy *Default value*
Merge policy *Default value*

| Code | Description |
|---|---|
| CulturalFeature | CulturalFeature |
| Centerline | Centerline |
| Hydro | Hydro |
| Topo | Topo |
| Political | Political |

## Simple feature class
### <state abbr>_ProvParcelBoundPoly

Geometry *Polygon*
Contains M values *No*
Contains Z values *No*

| Field name | Data type | Allow nulls | Default value | Domain | Prec-ision | Scale | Length | |
|---|---|---|---|---|---|---|---|---|
| OBJECTID | Object ID | | | | | | | |
| Shape | Geometry | Yes | | | | | | |
| CreatedBy | String | Yes | | | | | 255 | Name of individual who created feature |
| DateCreated | Date | Yes | | | 0 | 0 | 8 | Date of feature creation |
| ModifiedBy | String | Yes | | | | | 255 | Name of individual who last modified feature |
| DateModified | Date | Yes | | | 0 | 0 | 8 | Date of last feature modification |
| DocumentHyperlink | String | Yes | | | | | 30 | Link to external document |
| RecordBoundaryID | String | Yes | | | | | 30 | Identifier of source feature, if applicable |
| source | String | Yes | | ProvParcelBoundary-PolySource | | | 255 | Identifier of origin of source feature, if applicable |
| source_date | Date | Yes | | | 0 | 0 | 8 | Date source feature was created |
| survey_flag | String | Yes | | | | | 255 | Flag indicating if source feature was surveyed |
| Shape_Length | Double | Yes | | | 0 | 0 | | |
| Shape_Area | Double | Yes | | | 0 | 0 | | |

*Polygons for provisional boundaries*

### Coded value domain
**ProvParcelBoundary-PolySource**

Field type *String*
Split policy *Default value*
Merge policy *Default value*

| Code and description |
|---|
| M&B |
| Traced |
| Bounded |
| Hydro |
| Topo |
| Political |

6

The Case feature class holds information that impacts land status. Cases can be for title transfer through land disposals (public to private) and acquisitions (private to public). Exchanges are the combination of disposals and acquisitions. Cases are also opened for land designations, such as withdrawals from public land for a National Park.

Whenever the title to a part of the public land is transferred, NILS will start a new case record. A Case feature represents the state of information available for the case record that was found in LR2000. Title transfers are primarily about surface ownership but may also include surface and subsurface rights. Land designations may restrict or allow surface and subsurface rights, and are usually determined by some goal such as cultural or natural preservation. Cases can and often do overlap spatially.

Cases are represented on the master title plat, which is a hardcopy product. During case processing, realty specialists at the BLM refer to MTPs for a given legal description to examine the cumulative effect of all pertinent cases to derive land status. Historical information is conveyed in the MTP by complex linework and annotation. NILS is not trying to replicate the complete hardcopy of MTP, but intends to provide the same case information for analysis. In any case, if the land status does not support a given case, that case cannot be authorized.

*Land conveyances (federal to private) are overlaid by land acquisitions, exchanges, and corrective documents. White areas are public domain. Cases are given light fill colors to distinguish types.*

**Subtypes of <state abbr>_Case**

Subtype field   *case_group*
Default subtype   *21*

List of defined default values and domains for subtypes in this class

| Subtype code | Subtype description | Field name | Default value | Domain |
|---|---|---|---|---|
| 21 | Acquisitions | case_type | 210099 | CaseType_21 |
| | | case_disp | 99 | CaseDisposition |
| | | admin_agency | BLM | ManagingAgency |
| 386 | Mineral Patents | case_type | 386200 | CaseType_386 |
| | | case_disp | 99 | CaseDisposition |
| | | admin_agency | BLM | ManagingAgency |
| 20 | Land Resource Management | case_type | 200099 | CaseType_20 |
| | | case_disp | 99 | CaseDisposition |
| | | admin_agency | BLM | ManagingAgency |
| 18 | Public Administration Procedures | case_type | 180099 | CaseType_18 |
| | | case_disp | 99 | CaseDisposition |
| | | admin_agency | BLM | ManagingAgency |
| 17 | Program Management | case_type | 179202 | CaseType_17 |
| | | case_disp | 99 | CaseDisposition |
| | | admin_agency | BLM | ManagingAgency |
| 16 | Planning, Programming, Budgeting | case_type | 160099 | CaseType_16 |
| | | case_disp | 99 | CaseDisposition |
| | | admin_agency | BLM | ManagingAgency |
| 25 | Disposition; Occupancy and Use | case_type | 256099 | CaseType_25 |
| | | case_disp | 99 | CaseDisposition |
| | | admin_agency | BLM | ManagingAgency |
| 0 | General Management | case_type | 009999 | CaseType_00 |
| | | case_disp | 99 | CaseDisposition |
| | | admin_agency | BLM | ManagingAgency |
| 37 | Multiple Use; Mining | case_type | 370099 | CaseType_37 |
| | | case_disp | 99 | CaseDisposition |
| | | admin_agency | BLM | ManagingAgency |
| 23 | Withdrawals | case_type | 230099 | CaseType_23 |
| | | case_disp | 99 | CaseDisposition |
| | | admin_agency | BLM | ManagingAgency |
| 24 | Land Classification | case_type | 240099 | CaseType_24 |
| | | case_disp | 99 | CaseDisposition |
| | | admin_agency | BLM | ManagingAgency |
| 26 | Disposition; Grants | case_type | 261099 | CaseType_26 |
| | | case_disp | 99 | CaseDisposition |
| | | admin_agency | BLM | ManagingAgency |
| 22 | Exchanges | case_type | 220099 | CaseType_22 |
| | | case_disp | 99 | CaseDisposition |
| | | admin_agency | BLM | ManagingAgency |
| 27 | Disposition; Sales | case_type | 270099 | CaseType_27 |
| | | case_disp | 99 | CaseDisposition |
| | | admin_agency | BLM | ManagingAgency |

The CaseID is an identifier provided by LR2000 that serves as NILS' link back to LR2000. It is important to keep NILS in sync with LR2000, and CaseID is the key.

CaseGroups are a useful way of categorizing the different types of cases along functional lines. For example, while many kinds of cases can overlap spatially, some cannot, such as withdrawals and land dispositions.

| Simple feature class <state abbr>_Case | | | | | | | | |
|---|---|---|---|---|---|---|---|---|
| | | | | Geometry | Polygon | | | |
| | | | | Contains M values | No | | | |
| | | | | Contains Z values | No | | | |
| Field name | Data type | Allow nulls | Default value | Domain | Prec-ision | Scale | Length | |
| OBJECTID | Object ID | | | | | | | |
| Shape | Geometry | Yes | | | | | | |
| CreatedBy | String | Yes | | | | | 255 | Name of person who created feature |
| DateCreated | Date | Yes | | | 0 | 0 | 8 | Date of feature creation |
| ModifiedBy | String | Yes | | | | | 255 | Person who last modified feature |
| DateModified | Date | Yes | | | 0 | 0 | 8 | Date of last feature verification |
| DocumentHyperlink | String | Yes | | | | | 30 | Link to external document |
| verified_by | String | Yes | | | | | 255 | Name of person who manually verified feature |
| verified_date | Date | Yes | | | 0 | 0 | 8 | Date of last feature verification |
| PID | String | Yes | | | | | 255 | ID created for each serial number |
| case_id | Long integer | Yes | | | 0 | | | Unique internal case identifier |
| serial_nr_full | String | Yes | | | | | 17 | Case serial number |
| case_group | Long integer | Yes | 21 | CaseGroup | 0 | | | Subtype field for case group |
| case_type | String | Yes | | | | | 6 | First six digits of case type |
| case_part | String | Yes | | | | | 2 | Last two digits of case serial number |
| case_disp | String | Yes | 99 | CaseDisposition | | | 30 | Current status of case |
| legal_description | Blob | Yes | | | 0 | 0 | 0 | Text legal description of case in XML format |
| admin_agency | String | Yes | BLM | ManagingAgency | | | 8 | Agency that has jurisdiction over case |
| stored_acreage | Double | Yes | | | 0 | 0 | | Acreage for case parcel |
| edit_geom_flag | Short integer | Yes | | | 0 | | | Flag for whether geometry has been manually edited |
| edit_attr_flag | Short integer | Yes | | | 0 | | | Flag for whether attribute has been manually edited |
| is_nominally_located | String | Yes | | | | | 1 | Boolean indicating if a case is nominally located |
| lr2000_system_id | String | Yes | | | | | 2 | Identifier for LR2000 system |
| Shape_Length | Double | Yes | | | 0 | 0 | | |
| Shape_Area | Double | Yes | | | 0 | 0 | | |

*Polygons that represent the geometry and attributes of case parcels*

| Coded value domain CaseDisposition | | |
|---|---|---|
| | Field type | String |
| | Split policy | Default value |
| | Merge policy | Default value |
| Code | Description | |
| 99 | Unknown | |
| 5 | Authorized | |
| 2 | Pending | |
| 9 | Closed | |
| 59 | Authorized and Completed | |
| 9C | Acquired Parcel | |

| Coded value domain CaseType_386 | | |
|---|---|---|
| | Field type | String |
| | Split policy | Default value |
| | Merge policy | Default value |
| Code | Description | |
| 386210 | LODE PAT - MINERALS ONLY | |
| 386403 | MILLSITE PATENT PLACER | |
| 386400 | MILLSITE PATENTS | |
| 386201 | MIN PAT APLN-LODE BLM | |
| 386202 | MIN PAT APLN-LODE FS | |
| 386401 | MIN PAT APLN-MILLSIT BLM | |
| 386402 | MIN PAT APLN-MILLSITE FS | |
| 386301 | MIN PAT APLN-PLACER BLM | |
| 386302 | MIN PAT APLN-PLACER FS | |
| 386501 | MIN PAT-POTASSIUM | |
| 386200 | MINERAL PATENT LODE | |
| 386300 | MINERAL PATENT PLACER | |
| 386100 | MINERAL SURVEY APLN | |
| 386310 | PLACER PAT - MIN ONLY | |

*CaseType_386 is just one of several domains for different case types. These are used to define subcategories for each case group.*

| Coded value domain ManagingAgency | | |
|---|---|---|
| | Field type | String |
| | Split policy | Default value |
| | Merge policy | Default value |
| Code | Description | |
| BLM | Bureau of Land Management | |
| BPA | Bonneville Power Administration | |
| BR | Bureau of Reclamation | |
| COE | Corps of Engineers | |
| USCG | U.S. Coast Guard | |
| USDA | U.S. Dept of Agriculture (except Forest Service) | |
| DOD | Dept of Defense (except Army Corp of Engineers) | |
| USDA FS | USDA Forest Service | |
| FWS | U.S. Fish and Wildlife Service | |
| BIA | Bureau of Indian Affairs | |
| NPS | National Park Service | |
| DOE | U.S. Dept of Energy (AEC and others) | |
| GSA | General Services Administration | |
| RES | Native Reservation | |
| Private | Private | |

6

The initial focus of NILS PM is to spatially enable the BLM's case processing for analysis. It is important to display cases in a way that is similar to master title and use plats. This data will eventually be used to display land status and for derivative map products. Label lines are an intermediate step to the eventual goal of creating high-quality cartographic output.

Case attributes are not readily used for labeling because information may be stored across multiple related object and feature classes, and labeling requirements vary for the different case groups. Therefore, the case information is processed to get the cartographically correct attributes for each case group. These label lines can be used for dynamic labeling or for annotation.

Label lines serve an additional purpose. Case information is driven by transactions from LR2000; therefore, the label lines provide a location for PM users to edit labeling and annotation for cartographic purposes without impacting the integrity of the case data.

On the MTP, case types are distinguished by line weight or pattern, history is conveyed by line offset, and case information is labeled at the bottommost line of a case. It was fairly easy to duplicate the bottommost line display for dynamic labels. Automatic labels were chosen over annotation features so any number of cases can be stacked and visible at any given time; these labels will need to adjust their position to be placed as low as possible within a case. The use of ordinary labels also allows noneditors to change an expression.

During the create process, after the case geometry is unioned, an algorithm is run to determine the cases. Metadata attributes, such as case_id and serial_nr_full, come directly from the case feature class. Attributes for the actual label (label_val_1, etc) may be obtained from the right_att object class, the seg_attr object class, and the case_remark object class. The field and object class with the appropriate values are specified in the pm_case_label_config table and are categorized by case group.

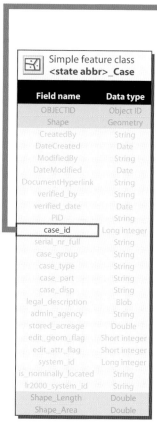

Simple feature class
**<state abbr>_Case**

| Field name | Data type |
|---|---|
| OBJECTID | Object ID |
| Shape | Geometry |
| CreatedBy | String |
| DateCreated | Date |
| ModifiedBy | String |
| DateModified | Date |
| DocumentHyperlink | String |
| verified_by | String |
| verified_date | Date |
| PID | String |
| case_id | Long integer |
| serial_nr_full | String |
| case_group | String |
| case_type | String |
| case_part | String |
| case_disp | String |
| legal_description | Blob |
| admin_agency | String |
| stored_acreage | Double |
| edit_geom_flag | Short integer |
| edit_attr_flag | Short integer |
| system_id | Long integer |
| is_nominally_located | String |
| lr2000_system_id | String |
| Shape_Length | Double |
| Shape_Area | Double |

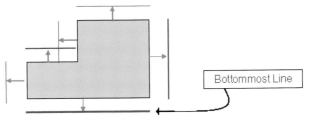

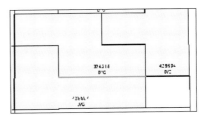

Plats are annotated along a polygon's bottom at center. By exploding a polygon into separated line segments as shown above, it becomes easier to determine the bottommost line. This way it is not confused with intersecting lines that it may meet at the bottom. Only the bottommost line is stored in the database.

*This figure shows an example of placing attributes from a Case feature along its label lines.*

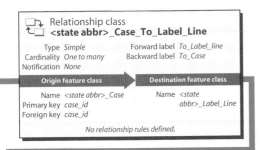

**Relationship class**
**<state abbr>_Case_To_Label_Line**

| | | | |
|---|---|---|---|
| Type | *Simple* | Forward label | *To_Label_line* |
| Cardinality | *One to many* | Backward label | *To_Case* |
| Notification | *None* | | |

| Origin feature class | Destination feature class |
|---|---|
| Name | *<state abbr>_Case* | Name | *<state abbr>_Label_Line* |
| Primary key | *case_id* | | |
| Foreign key | *case_id* | | |

*No relationship rules defined.*

**Simple feature class**
**<state abbr>_Label_Line**

Geometry *Polyline*
Contains M values *No*
Contains Z values *No*

*A label line's geometry is derived from case parcel feature geometry and is used for case parcel label placement.*

| Field name | Data type | Allow nulls | Default value | Domain | Prec-ision | Scale | Length | |
|---|---|---|---|---|---|---|---|---|
| OBJECTID | Object ID | | | | | | | |
| Shape | Geometry | Yes | | | | | | |
| CreatedBy | String | Yes | | | | | 255 | Name of individual who created feature |
| DateCreated | Date | Yes | | | 0 | 0 | 8 | Date of feature creation |
| ModifiedBy | String | Yes | | | | | 255 | Name of individual who last modified feature |
| DateModified | Date | Yes | | | 0 | 0 | 8 | Date of last feature modification |
| DocumentHyperlink | String | Yes | | | | | 30 | Link to external document |
| pid | String | Yes | | | | | 255 | Unique ID for each serial number |
| case_id | Long integer | Yes | | | 0 | | | Unique internal case identifier |
| case_group | String | Yes | | CaseGroup | | | 3 | First two characters of CaseType; coarse grouping of cases |
| case_type | String | Yes | | | | | 6 | Fill six digits of CaseType; more granular grouping |
| case_disp | String | Yes | 99 | CaseDisposition | | | 30 | Current status of use |
| label_val_1 | String | Yes | | | | | 30 | Value of first label to display |
| label_name_1 | String | Yes | | | | | 40 | Name of first label to display |
| label_val_2 | String | Yes | | | | | 30 | Value of second label to display |
| label_Name_2 | String | Yes | | | | | 40 | Name of second label to display |
| label_val_3 | String | Yes | | | | | 30 | Value of third label to display |
| label_name_3 | String | Yes | | | | | 40 | Name of third label to display |
| label_val_4 | String | Yes | | | | | 30 | Value of fourth label to display |
| label_name_4 | String | Yes | | | | | 40 | Name of fourth label to display |
| edit_geom_flag | Short integer | Yes | | | 0 | | | True if geometry has been manually edited |
| edit_attr_flag | Short integer | Yes | | | 0 | | | True if attributes have been manually edited |
| Shape_Length | Double | Yes | | | 0 | 0 | | |

Sometimes the information from LR2000 is augmented in NILS to support review and analysis during case processing. This additional information is not needed or available in LR2000 but can be preserved in the NILS database for later review.

Parcel management users require the ability to create ad hoc case features for analysis and review during application stages of a case. These cases have not and may not be entered into LR2000. The sketch feature class is the location for ad hoc case creation. It has the same attributes as the case and label line feature classes with the exception of case_id. If appropriate, the sketch and sketch label line can serve as the basis for the feature in the case feature class, once the case is serialized.

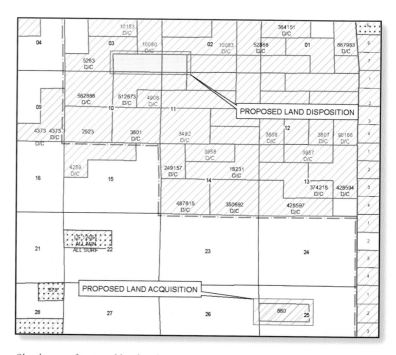

*Sketch cases of proposed land exchanges*

**Simple feature class**
**<state abbr>_Sketch_Case**

| Geometry | Polygon |
| Contains M values | No |
| Contains Z values | No |

*Polygons that represent the geometry and attributes of sketch cases*

| Field name | Data type | Allow nulls | Default value | Domain | Precision | Scale | Length | |
|---|---|---|---|---|---|---|---|---|
| OBJECTID | Object ID | | | | | | | |
| Shape | Geometry | Yes | | | | | | |
| CreatedBy | String | Yes | | | | | 255 | Name of individual who created feature |
| DateCreated | Date | Yes | | | 0 | 0 | 8 | Date of feature creation |
| ModifiedBy | String | Yes | | | | | 255 | Name of individual who last modified feature |
| DateModified | Date | Yes | | | 0 | 0 | 8 | Date of last feature modification |
| DocumentHyperlink | String | Yes | | | | | 30 | A link to external document |
| serial_nr_full | String | Yes | | | | | 17 | Case serial number |
| case_group | String | Yes | | CaseGroup | | | 3 | First two characters of CaseType |
| case_type | String | Yes | | | | | 6 | Full six digits of CaseType |
| case_part | String | Yes | | | | | 2 | Last two digits of case serial number |
| case_disp | String | Yes | 99 | CaseDisposition | | | 30 | Current status of case |
| legal_description | Blob | Yes | | | 0 | 0 | 0 | Text legal description of the case stored in XML format |
| admin_agency | String | Yes | BLM | ManagingAgency | | | 8 | Agency that has jurisdiction over the case |
| stored_acreage | Double | Yes | | | 0 | 0 | | Acreage for case parcel retrieved from LR2000 |
| edit_geom_flag | Short integer | Yes | | | 0 | | | True if geometry has been manually edited |
| edit_attr_flag | Short integer | Yes | | | 0 | | | True if attributes have been manually edited |
| system_id | Long integer | Yes | | | 0 | | | BLM system identifier from LR2000 |
| Shape_Length | Double | Yes | | | 0 | 0 | | |
| Shape_Area | Double | Yes | | | 0 | 0 | | |

**Simple feature class**
**<state abbr>_Sketch_Label_Line**

| Geometry | Polyline |
| Contains M values | No |
| Contains Z values | No |

*A label line's geometry is derived from case parcel feature geometry and is used for case parcel feature placement.*

| Field name | Data type | Allow nulls | Default value | Domain | Precision | Scale | Length | |
|---|---|---|---|---|---|---|---|---|
| OBJECTID | Object ID | | | | | | | |
| Shape | Geometry | Yes | | | | | | |
| CreatedBy | String | Yes | | | | | 255 | Name of individual who created feature |
| DateCreated | Date | Yes | | | 0 | 0 | 8 | Date of feature creation |
| ModifiedBy | String | Yes | | | | | 255 | Name of individual who last modified feature |
| DateModified | Date | Yes | | | 0 | 0 | 8 | Date of last feature modification |
| DocumentHyperlink | String | Yes | | | | | 30 | A link to external document |
| case_group | String | Yes | | CaseGroup | | | 3 | First two characters of CaseType |
| case_type | String | Yes | | | | | 6 | Full six digits of CaseType |
| label_val_1 | String | Yes | | | | | 30 | Value of first label to display |
| label_name_1 | String | Yes | | | | | 40 | Name of first label to display |
| label_val_2 | String | Yes | | | | | 30 | Value of second label to display |
| label_Name_2 | String | Yes | | | | | 40 | Name of second label to display |
| label_val_3 | String | Yes | | | | | 30 | Value of third label to display |
| label_name_3 | String | Yes | | | | | 40 | Name of third label to display |
| label_val_4 | String | Yes | | | | | 30 | Value of fourth label to display |
| label_name_4 | String | Yes | | | | | 40 | Name of fourth label to display |
| edit_geom_flag | Short integer | Yes | | | 0 | | | True if geometry has been manually edited |
| edit_attr_flag | Short integer | Yes | | | 0 | | | True if attributes have been manually edited |
| serial_nr_full | String | Yes | | | | | 17 | Case serial number |
| Shape_Length | Double | Yes | | | 0 | 0 | | |

*6*

The rights modeled in the Rights feature class and Rights_attribute object class are U.S. rights. The term_us_rights table is for third party rights. Rights are interests in the land that are reserved for the United States. There are many standard reservations, including ditches, canals, rights-of-way, and mineral rights.

Rights-of-way and easements are two different types of land use. A right-of-way gives temporary use (30 years or less) of the land for a specific use and is generally not surveyed by the government. Easements generally give title for any use across public or private land; the title states ". . . is given to the grantee and their assigned, to have and to hold with all rights, privileges, and improvements . . . for ever." In the case of an easement, the land is surveyed as the land leaves, returns, or is granted to the next owner, whether federal or private.

Rights in NILS do not exist independently of a case. A case geometry can have multiple rights. The related rights can have different geometries than the case. Each related right can have multiple right codes. The rights codes are stored in the rights_attr table.

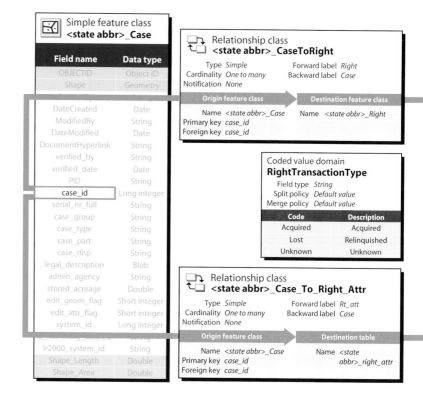

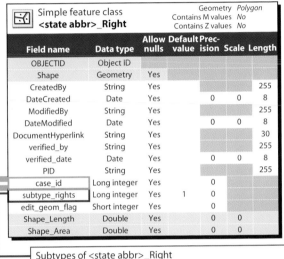

**Simple feature class**
**<state abbr>_Right**

| | |
|---|---|
| Geometry | Polygon |
| Contains M values | No |
| Contains Z values | No |

*Polygons that represent the geometry and attributes of use authorization cases*

| Field name | Data type | Allow nulls | Default value | Precision | Scale | Length | |
|---|---|---|---|---|---|---|---|
| OBJECTID | Object ID | | | | | | |
| Shape | Geometry | Yes | | | | | |
| CreatedBy | String | Yes | | | | 255 | Name of individual who created feature |
| DateCreated | Date | Yes | | 0 | 0 | 8 | Date of feature creation |
| ModifiedBy | String | Yes | | | | 255 | Name of individual who last modified feature |
| DateModified | Date | Yes | | 0 | 0 | 8 | Date of last feature modification |
| DocumentHyperlink | String | Yes | | | | 30 | Link to external document |
| verified_by | String | Yes | | | | 255 | Name of individual who manually verified feature |
| verified_date | Date | Yes | | 0 | 0 | 8 | Date of last feature verification |
| PID | String | Yes | | | | 255 | Unique ID created for each serial number |
| case_id | Long integer | Yes | | 0 | | | Unique internal case identifier |
| subtype_rights | Long integer | Yes | 1 | 0 | | | Estate type |
| edit_geom_flag | Short integer | Yes | | 0 | | | True if geometry has been manually edited |
| Shape_Length | Double | Yes | | 0 | 0 | | |
| Shape_Area | Double | Yes | | 0 | 0 | | |

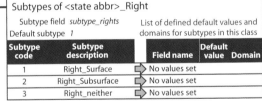

**Subtypes of <state abbr>_Right**

Subtype field *subtype_rights*
Default subtype *1*

List of defined default values and domains for subtypes in this class

| Subtype code | Subtype description | | Field name | Default value | Domain |
|---|---|---|---|---|---|
| 1 | Right_Surface | ⇨ | No values set | | |
| 2 | Right_Subsurface | ⇨ | No values set | | |
| 3 | Right_neither | ⇨ | No values set | | |

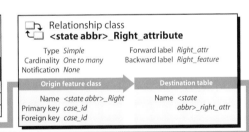

**Relationship class**
**<state abbr>_Right_attribute**

| | | | |
|---|---|---|---|
| Type | Simple | Forward label | Right_attr |
| Cardinality | One to many | Backward label | Right_feature |
| Notification | None | | |

| Origin feature class | Destination table |
|---|---|
| Name *<state abbr>_Right* | Name *<state abbr>_right_attr* |
| Primary key *case_id* | |
| Foreign key *case_id* | |

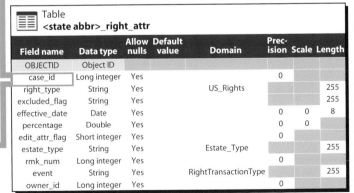

**Table**
**<state abbr>_right_attr**

*Separate rights table, since a case can have multiple rights.*

| Field name | Data type | Allow nulls | Default value | Domain | Precision | Scale | Length | |
|---|---|---|---|---|---|---|---|---|
| OBJECTID | Object ID | | | | | | | |
| case_id | Long integer | Yes | | | 0 | | | Unique internal case identifier. |
| right_type | String | Yes | | US_Rights | | | 255 | Type of interest. |
| excluded_flag | String | Yes | | | | | 255 | If true, this record is an exclusion of a right. |
| effective_date | Date | Yes | | | 0 | 0 | 8 | Date of action that affected the right. |
| percentage | Double | Yes | | | 0 | 0 | | Percent interest. |
| edit_attr_flag | Short integer | Yes | | | 0 | | | True if attributes have been manually edited. |
| estate_type | String | Yes | | Estate_Type | | | 255 | Valid values are surface, subsurface, or neither. |
| rmk_num | Long integer | Yes | | | 0 | | | ID for a specific remark, to distinguish among multiples. |
| event | String | Yes | | RightTransactionType | | | 255 | Type of transaction. |
| owner_id | Long integer | Yes | | | 0 | | | ID of right owner. |

Surveying federal lands · 265

A segregation is the removal, for a specified period, of public lands from the operation of one or more of the public land laws. Segregations are commonly associated with land withdrawals. For example, mining may technically be allowed in a given area, but could still be prohibited due to some other motivation, such as habitat restoration.

Segregations are modeled identically to rights; however, segregations are rights that are unavailable. Rather than saying what rights the U.S. has, segregations say what rights the U.S. is not allowing. Segregations can expire or be released.

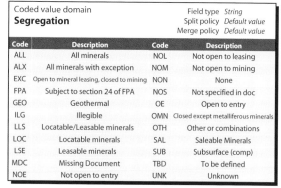

**Coded value domain**
**Segregation**

Field type  String
Split policy  Default value
Merge policy  Default value

| Code | Description | Code | Description |
|------|-------------|------|-------------|
| ALL | All minerals | NOL | Not open to leasing |
| ALX | All minerals with exception | NOM | Not open to mining |
| EXC | Open to mineral leasing, closed to mining | NON | None |
| FPA | Subject to section 24 of FPA | NOS | Not specified in doc |
| GEO | Geothermal | OE | Open to entry |
| ILG | Illegible | OMN | Closed except metalliferous minerals |
| LLS | Locatable/Leasable minerals | OTH | Other or combinations |
| LOC | Locatable minerals | SAL | Saleable Minerals |
| LSE | Leasable minerals | SUB | Subsurface (comp) |
| MDC | Missing Document | TBD | To be defined |
| NOE | Not open to entry | UNK | Unknown |

**Coded value domain**
**ReleaseSegregationExtent**

Field type  String
Split policy  Default value
Merge policy  Default value

| Code | Description |
|------|-------------|
| 08 | ALL MINERALS |
| 22 | ASPHALTIC MATERIAL |
| 21 | COAL LEASING |
| 06 | DESERT LAND ENTRY |
| 30 | EX LANDS OPENED |
| 39 | EXCHANGE |
| 40 | EXCHANGE  -FLPMA |
| 27 | EX -GENERAL EXCHANGE ACT |
| 24 | EX -TAYLOR GRAZING ACT |
| 15 | FPA -DISPOSAL  (NON -INPUT ) |
| 26 | FPA -RELEASE OF SEC   24 |
| 11 | FPA -ROW (NON -INPUT ) |
| 33 | GEOTHERMAL LEASING |
| 01 | HOMESTEAD |
| 09 | LEASING |
| 02 | LOCATION |
| 10 | NATIONAL FOREST LANDS |
| 25 | NATL WILD   & SCENIC RIV |
| 28 | NON -METALLIFEROUS MIN |
| 14 | OIL  & GAS LEASING |
| 34 | OIL SHALE LEASING |
| 19 | OPEN PUBLIC SALE LAWS |
| 16 | OPEN TO AGRI LAWS |
| 38 | OPEN TO MILLSITE LOC |
| 37 | OPEN TO PLACER LOCATION |
| 05 | PREFERENCE RIGHTS |
| 18 | PS -SUBJ FPA  (NON -INPUT ) |
| 32 | R &PP |
| 12 | SALEABLE MINERALS |
| 13 | SETTLEMENT |
| 04 | SETTLMNT   & LOCATION  -ALL |
| 03 | SMALL TRACT |
| 23 | SODIUM |
| 20 | STATE EXCHANGE |
| 31 | STATE SELECTION |
| 17 | SUBSURFACE   (COMP ) |
| 07 | SURFACE |
| 99 | TO BE DEFINED |
| 29 | TOWNSITE |

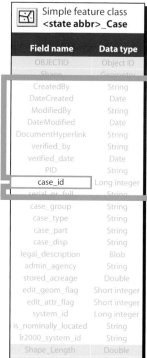

**Simple feature class**
**<state abbr>_Case**

| Field name | Data type |
|------------|-----------|
| OBJECTID | Object ID |
| Shape | Geometry |
| CreatedBy | String |
| DateCreated | Date |
| ModifiedBy | String |
| DateModified | Date |
| DocumentHyperlink | String |
| verified_by | String |
| verified_date | Date |
| PID | String |
| case_id | Long integer |
| serial_or_full | String |
| case_group | String |
| case_type | String |
| case_part | String |
| case_disp | String |
| legal_description | Blob |
| admin_agency | String |
| stored_acreage | Double |
| edit_geom_flag | Short integer |
| edit_attr_flag | Short integer |
| system_id | Long integer |
| is_nominally_located | String |
| lr2000_system_id | String |
| Shape_Length | Double |
| Shape_Area | Double |

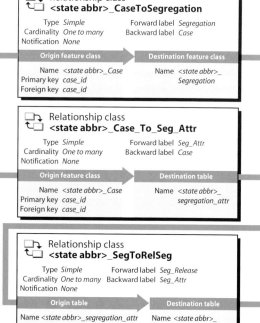

**Relationship class**
**<state abbr>_CaseToSegregation**

Type  Simple
Cardinality  One to many
Notification  None

Forward label  Segregation
Backward label  Case

**Origin feature class**
Name  <state abbr>_Case
Primary key  case_id
Foreign key  case_id

**Destination feature class**
Name  <state abbr>_Segregation

**Relationship class**
**<state abbr>_Case_To_Seg_Attr**

Type  Simple
Cardinality  One to many
Notification  None

Forward label  Seg_Attr
Backward label  Case

**Origin feature class**
Name  <state abbr>_Case
Primary key  case_id
Foreign key  case_id

**Destination table**
Name  <state abbr>_segregation_attr

**Relationship class**
**<state abbr>_SegToRelSeg**

Type  Simple
Cardinality  One to many
Notification  None

Forward label  Seg_Release
Backward label  Seg_Attr

**Origin table**
Name  <state abbr>_segregation_attr
Primary key  case_id
Foreign key  Case_ID

**Destination table**
Name  <state abbr>_segregation_release

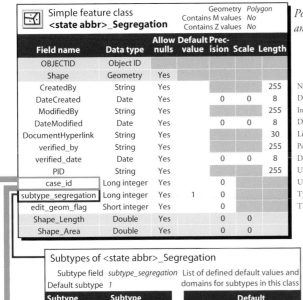

## Simple feature class
### <state abbr>_Segregation

Geometry: *Polygon*
Contains M values: *No*
Contains Z values: *No*

*Polygons that represent the geometry and attributes of segregations*

| Field name | Data type | Allow nulls | Default value | Precision | Scale | Length | |
|---|---|---|---|---|---|---|---|
| OBJECTID | Object ID | | | | | | |
| Shape | Geometry | Yes | | | | | |
| CreatedBy | String | Yes | | | | 255 | Name of person who created feature |
| DateCreated | Date | Yes | | 0 | 0 | 8 | Date of feature creation |
| ModifiedBy | String | Yes | | | | 255 | Individual who last modified feature |
| DateModified | Date | Yes | | 0 | 0 | 8 | Date of last feature modification |
| DocumentHyperlink | String | Yes | | | | 30 | Link to external document |
| verified_by | String | Yes | | | | 255 | Person who manually verified feature |
| verified_date | Date | Yes | | 0 | 0 | 8 | Date of last feature verification |
| PID | String | Yes | | | | 255 | Unique ID created for each serial number |
| case_id | Long integer | Yes | | 0 | | | Unique internal case identifier |
| subtype_segregation | Long integer | Yes | 1 | 0 | | | Types of segregations |
| edit_geom_flag | Short integer | Yes | | 0 | | | True if geometry was manually edited |
| Shape_Length | Double | Yes | | 0 | 0 | | |
| Shape_Area | Double | Yes | | 0 | 0 | | |

### Subtypes of <state abbr>_Segregation

Subtype field: *subtype_segregation*
Default subtype: *1*

List of defined default values and domains for subtypes in this class

| Subtype code | Subtype description | Field name | Default value | Domain |
|---|---|---|---|---|
| 1 | Segregation_Surface | ⇨ No values set | | |
| 2 | Segregation_Subsurface | ⇨ No values set | | |

## Relationship class
### <state abbr>_Segregation_attribute

Type: *Simple*
Cardinality: *One to many*
Notification: *None*
Forward label: *Segregation_attr*
Backward label: *Segregation_feature*

| Origin feature class | Destination table |
|---|---|
| Name <state abbr>_Segregation | Name <state abbr>_segregation_attr |
| Primary key case_id | |
| Foreign key case_id | |

*Separate segregations table, since a case can have multiple segregations*

## Table
### <state abbr>_segregation_attr

| Field name | Data type | Allow nulls | Default value | Domain | Precision | Scale | Length | |
|---|---|---|---|---|---|---|---|---|
| OBJECTID | Object ID | | | | | | | |
| case_id | Long integer | Yes | | | 0 | | | Unique internal case identifier |
| segregation | String | Yes | | Segregation | | | 16 | Rights that are excluded or unavailable |
| effective_date | Date | Yes | | | 0 | 0 | 8 | Date of action that affected the segregation |
| expiration_date | Date | Yes | | | 0 | 0 | 8 | Date of expiration for the segregation |
| managing_agency | String | Yes | BLM | ManagingAgency | | | 255 | Surface management agency |
| estate_type | String | Yes | Unknown | Estate_Type | | | 255 | Type of estate |
| edit_attr_flag | Short integer | Yes | | | 0 | | | True if attribute has been manually edited |
| seg_excluded_right | String | Yes | | | | | 50 | Rights excluded from the segregation |
| rmk_num | Long integer | Yes | | | 0 | | | ID for a specific remark, used for multiple remarks |

*Whenever a segregation is released, an entry is made in this table.*

## Table
### <state abbr>_segregation_release

| Field name | Data type | Allow nulls | Default value | Domain | Precision | Scale | Length | |
|---|---|---|---|---|---|---|---|---|
| OBJECTID | Object ID | | | | | | | |
| Case_ID | Long integer | Yes | | | 0 | | | Unique internal case identifier |
| Rel_Date | Date | Yes | | | 0 | 0 | 8 | Date the segregation was released |
| Rel_Segr_Code | String | Yes | | ReleaseSegregationExtent | | | 50 | Code representing the type of segregation released |

6

Land status is the combination of four types of information: surface ownership, surface management, segregations, and U.S. rights. Land status is the foundation of case processing. The attributes are derived through analysis of the parcel management cases, while the geometry is from the legal description fabric.

The federal government has maintained information on land since the inception of the United States. This information has been accumulated as a series of events on the land represented by Case features. Land status can be thought of in terms of four types of information: surface ownership, surface management (since the federal agency charged with management of a property may be different from the agency that owns it), segregations, and U.S. rights. Surface ownership is stored in terms of the type of agency rather than the specific name of the owner, as shown in the OwnershipClassification domain in the schema. The field admin_agency is for storing the name of the surface management agency.

Segregations and U.S. rights are held in separate tables for additional information. A single land status feature may be linked to any number of records of segregations and U.S. rights. The land status is derived by searching for all such events on the land that were conducted by various authorities, then determining the cumulative effect of all actions found.

Each Land_Status feature can be linked to Case features through the Land_Status_Case table. A Land_Status feature can have one or more Land_Status_Case records associated by Land_Status_ID. Each such Land_Status_Case is associated with one Case feature and has a process_order field to indicate the relative order of processing each case for the land status.

## Work in progress

Once all the case data has been populated in the Parcel Management module, NILS will support the derivation, storage, and mapping of land status. The geometry of a land status feature will be derived from the lowest level of legal description fabric building blocks.

NILS has a long-term strategy of deriving and managing land status, but in the interim, data in the Surface Management Agency (SMA) module in NILS is being displayed and managed by the BLM using varying methodologies among the state offices. This data is collected at 1:2,000,000, so it does not exactly align with legal description fabric and parcel management fabric data.

The BLM has the responsibility for federal ownership, although this is not the same as ownership; when overlaid with case data, it is an additional piece of information in determining land status.

SMA is not the same as "ownership" because it does not show all rights and interests.

*NILS map showing surface management agencies*

## Simple feature class
### <state abbr>_Land_Status

Geometry *Polygon*
Contains M values *No*
Contains Z values *No*

| Field name | Data type | Allow nulls | Default value | Domain | Precision | Scale | Length | |
|---|---|---|---|---|---|---|---|---|
| OBJECTID | Object ID | | | | | | | |
| Shape | Geometry | Yes | | | | | | |
| CreatedBy | String | Yes | | | | | 255 | Name of individual who created feature |
| DateCreated | Date | Yes | | | 0 | 0 | 8 | Date of feature creation |
| ModifiedBy | String | Yes | | | | | 255 | Name of individual who last modified feature |
| DateModified | Date | Yes | | | 0 | 0 | 8 | Date of last feature modification |
| DocumentHyperlink | String | Yes | | | | | 30 | Link to external document |
| derived_date | Date | Yes | | | 0 | 0 | 8 | Date that land status was derived |
| computed_date | Date | Yes | | | 0 | 0 | 8 | Date for which land status was derived |
| admin_agency | String | Yes | BLM | ManagingAgency | | | 255 | Agency that manages surface of parcel |
| owner_classification | String | Yes | Private | OwnershipClassification | | | 255 | Type of owner |
| edit_attr_flag | Short integer | Yes | | | 0 | | | True if attributes have been manually edited |
| Shape_Length | Double | Yes | | | 0 | 0 | | |
| Shape_Area | Double | Yes | | | 0 | 0 | | |
| LandStatus_ID | Long integer | Yes | | | 0 | | | |

*Land status represents a particular combination of key influences on a parcel. The geometry of a Land Status feature is from the LD fabric.*

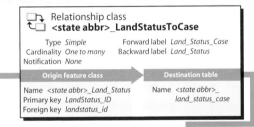

## Relationship class
### <state abbr>_LandStatusToCase

Type *Simple*  Forward label *Land_Status_Case*
Cardinality *One to many*  Backward label *Land_Status*
Notification *None*

**Origin feature class**
Name *<state abbr>_Land_Status*
Primary key *LandStatus_ID*
Foreign key *landstatus_id*

**Destination table**
Name *<state abbr>_land_status_case*

## Coded value domain
### OwnershipClassification

Field type *String*
Split policy *Default value*
Merge policy *Default value*

| Code | Description |
|---|---|
| CVT | City–Village–Town |
| County | County |
| Federal | Federal |
| Indian Tribe | Indian Tribe |
| International | International |
| Non-Profit | Nonprofit |
| Private | Private |
| State | State |
| Other | Other |
| PD | Public Domain |
| OC | Revested Oregon and California Railroad Lands |
| CB | Revested Coos Bay Wagon Road Lands |
| AQ | Land Acquired |
| LU | Land Utilization Projects |
| IND | Indian Trust and Fee Lands |
| HST | Historic State Lands |
| NF | Nonfederal |
| PE | Public Domain With Exception |
| AE | Acquired With Exception Right |

## Table
### <state abbr>_land_status_case

| Field name | Data type | Allow nulls | Precision | Scale | Length | |
|---|---|---|---|---|---|---|
| OBJECTID | Object ID | | | | | |
| case_id | Long integer | Yes | 0 | | | Unique internal case identifier |
| process_order | Long integer | Yes | 0 | | | Priority order for processing this case |

*Table identifying related cases and the priority order for each*

## Table
### <state abbr>_land_status_segregation

| Field name | Data type | Allow nulls | Precision | Scale | Length | |
|---|---|---|---|---|---|---|
| OBJECTID | Object ID | | | | | |
| initial_status | String | Yes | | | 255 | Starting segregation status |
| finish_status | String | Yes | | | 255 | Segregation status after status computation |
| estate_type | String | Yes | | | 255 | Either surface or subsurface |

*Table of additional information concerning segregations (removals from public land operation)*

## Table
### <state abbr>_land_status_us_right

| Field name | Data type | Allow nulls | Precision | Scale | Length | |
|---|---|---|---|---|---|---|
| OBJECTID | Object ID | | | | | |
| initial_status | String | Yes | | | 255 | Starting U.S. right status |
| initial_pct | Double | Yes | 0 | 0 | | Percentage owned by the United States |
| finish_status | String | Yes | | | 255 | U.S. rights after status has been computed |
| finish_pct | Double | Yes | 0 | 0 | | Percentage owned by the United States |
| estate_type | String | Yes | | | 255 | Either surface or subsurface |

*Table of additional information concerning U.S. rights reserved on a parcel*

6

Mining claims are just one of many types of land use, but they are significant enough to warrant a distinct feature class. Each mining claim may be located within up to five quarter sections, with a maximum area dependent on the mining claim commodity. While the mining claim has a precise location, BLM does not require that the location be a finer resolution than the quarter section.

A mining claim, which can be either lode or placer, may be located on federal land and must contain a valuable mineral deposit. Of most interest are mining claims having case dispositions either active or closed. If a claim becomes patented, it becomes closed, which triggers the creation of a Case feature. This, in turn, triggers a field survey that will refer to the new legal description rather than the PLSS or other survey framework.

Note that the fields case_id, case_group, and case_disp (case disposition) are identical in intent and business rules to those described for the Case feature class earlier in this chapter.

The Mining_Claim feature class also has a relationship to Customer_XRF table, shown later in this chapter, based on the case_id key field. Customer_XRF is, in turn, related to Customer through the customer_id key.

Relationship class
**<state abbr>_MC_to_MC_LL**

| | |
|---|---|
| Type *Simple* | Forward label *TO_MC_LL* |
| Cardinality *One to many* | Backward label *To_MC* |
| Notification *None* | |

| Origin feature class | Destination feature class |
|---|---|
| Name *<state abbr>_Mining_Claim* | Name *<state abbr>_* |
| Primary key *case_id* | *Mining_Claim_Label_Line* |
| Foreign key *case_id* | |

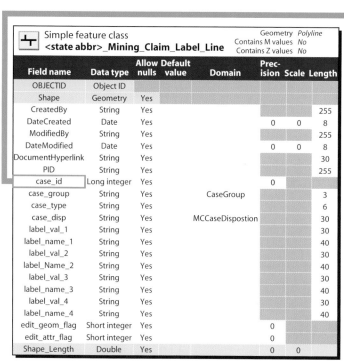

Simple feature class
**<state abbr>_Mining_Claim_Label_Line**

Geometry *Polyline*
Contains M values *No*
Contains Z values *No*

| Field name | Data type | Allow nulls | Default value | Domain | Precision | Scale | Length |
|---|---|---|---|---|---|---|---|
| OBJECTID | Object ID | | | | | | |
| Shape | Geometry | Yes | | | | | |
| CreatedBy | String | Yes | | | | | 255 |
| DateCreated | Date | Yes | | | 0 | 0 | 8 |
| ModifiedBy | String | Yes | | | | | 255 |
| DateModified | Date | Yes | | | 0 | 0 | 8 |
| DocumentHyperlink | String | Yes | | | | | 30 |
| PID | String | Yes | | | | | 255 |
| case_id | Long integer | Yes | | | 0 | | |
| case_group | String | Yes | | CaseGroup | | | 3 |
| case_type | String | Yes | | | | | 6 |
| case_disp | String | Yes | | MCCaseDispostion | | | 30 |
| label_val_1 | String | Yes | | | | | 30 |
| label_name_1 | String | Yes | | | | | 40 |
| label_val_2 | String | Yes | | | | | 30 |
| label_Name_2 | String | Yes | | | | | 40 |
| label_val_3 | String | Yes | | | | | 30 |
| label_name_3 | String | Yes | | | | | 40 |
| label_val_4 | String | Yes | | | | | 30 |
| label_name_4 | String | Yes | | | | | 40 |
| edit_geom_flag | Short integer | Yes | | | 0 | | |
| edit_attr_flag | Short integer | Yes | | | 0 | | |
| Shape_Length | Double | Yes | | | 0 | 0 | |

*Linear feature representing bottommost line of a mining claim polygon*

Name of individual who created feature
Date of feature creation
Name of individual who last modified feature
Date of last feature modification
Link to external document
Unique point identifier
Foreign key for case processing use
Case group to which this mining claim belongs
Case group subcategory
Case disposition code
Label value, first of up to four
Label name, first of up to four
Label value, second of up to four
Label name, second of up to four
Label value, third of up to four
Label name, third of up to four
Label value, fourth of up to four
Label name, fourth of up to four
Flag indicating geometry has been changed
Flag indicating other attribution has been changed

| Coded value domain **MCCaseDispostion** | |
|---|---|
| Field type | String |
| Split policy | Default value |
| Merge policy | Default value |

| Code | Description |
|---|---|
| P | Pending |
| A | Active |
| C | Closed |
| V | Voided |
| U | Unknown |

### Simple feature class
### <state abbr>_Mining_Claim

Geometry *Polygon*
Contains M values *No*
Contains Z values *No*

*Description of a mining claim that can be on up to five quarter sections*

| Field name | Data type | Allow nulls | Default value | Domain | Precision | Scale | Length | |
|---|---|---|---|---|---|---|---|---|
| OBJECTID | Object ID | | | | | | | |
| Shape | Geometry | Yes | | | | | | |
| CreatedBy | String | Yes | | | | | 255 | Name of individual who created feature |
| DateCreated | Date | Yes | | | 0 | 0 | 8 | Date of feature creation |
| ModifiedBy | String | Yes | | | | | 255 | Name of individual who last modified feature |
| DateModified | Date | Yes | | | 0 | 0 | 8 | Date of last feature modification |
| DocumentHyperlink | String | Yes | | | | | 30 | Link to external document |
| PID | String | Yes | | | | | 255 | Unique point identifier |
| case_id | Long integer | Yes | | | 0 | | | Foreign key for case processing |
| serial_nr_full | String | Yes | | | | | 17 | Mining claim serial number assigned |
| case_group | String | Yes | | CaseGroup | | | 3 | Applicable case group for this mining claim |
| case_type | String | Yes | | | | | 6 | Subcategory of the case group |
| case_disp | String | Yes | | MCCaseDisposition | | | 30 | Case disposition code |
| legal_description | Blob | Yes | | | 0 | 0 | 0 | Complete legal description of the mining claim |
| claim_name | String | Yes | | | | | 20 | Name assigned to the mining claim |
| commodity | String | Yes | | | | | 3 | Type of mineral for which the mining claim is created |
| date_of_recordation | Date | Yes | | | 0 | 0 | 8 | Date this record was entered |
| date_of_claim | Date | Yes | | | 0 | 0 | 8 | Date the mining claim took effect |
| edit_attr_flag | Short integer | Yes | | | 0 | | | Flag indicating one or more of the attributes have changed |
| edit_geom_flag | Short integer | Yes | | | 0 | | | Flag indicating the geometry has changed |
| lr2000_system_id | Long integer | Yes | | | 0 | | | Foreign key to related records in LR2000 |
| Shape_Length | Double | Yes | | | 0 | 0 | | |
| Shape_Area | Double | Yes | | | 0 | 0 | | |
| verified_by | String | Yes | | | | | 255 | Name of person verifying this record |
| verified_date | Date | Yes | | | 0 | 0 | 8 | Date this record was last verified |

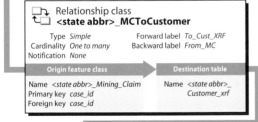

### Relationship class
### <state abbr>_MCToCustomer

| Type | *Simple* | Forward label | *To_Cust_XRF* |
|---|---|---|---|
| Cardinality | *One to many* | Backward label | *From_MC* |
| Notification | *None* | | |

| Origin feature class | Destination table |
|---|---|
| Name *<state abbr>_Mining_Claim* | Name *<state abbr>_Customer_xrf* |
| Primary key *case_id* | |
| Foreign key *case_id* | |

### Table
### MC_Customer_xrf

| Field name | Data type | Allow nulls | Precision | Scale | Length |
|---|---|---|---|---|---|
| OBJECTID | Object ID | | | | |
| case_id | Long integer | Yes | 0 | | |
| customer_id | Long integer | Yes | 0 | | |
| lr2000_system_id | String | Yes | | | 2 |

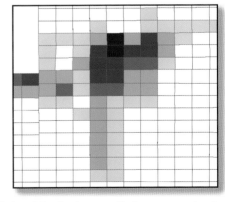

*Mining claim density map: Each quarter section is color coded according to the number of mining claims on record in that cell.*

6

Oil and gas leases and agreements represent authorizations for specific rights to control or possess public land. Other use authorization feature classes will be incorporated into NILS in the future, such as for coal, geothermal, and rights-of-way.

An authorized lease is of one commodity type only; thus, authorized multiple lessees within this case group cannot overlap. However, a given lease can have multiple lessees with varying fractional interests. Note that the case_id field is identical in intent and business rules to that described for the Case feature class described earlier.

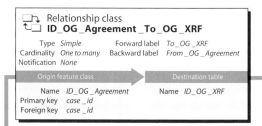

**Relationship class**
**ID_OG_Agreement_To_OG_XRF**

| | | | |
|---|---|---|---|
| Type | Simple | Forward label | To_OG_XRF |
| Cardinality | One to many | Backward label | From_OG_Agreement |
| Notification | None | | |

| Origin feature class | | Destination table | |
|---|---|---|---|
| Name | ID_OG_Agreement | Name | ID_OG_XRF |
| Primary key | case_id | | |
| Foreign key | case_id | | |

**Simple feature class**
**OG_Agreement**

Geometry: Point
Contains M values: No
Contains Z values: No

*Oil and gas agreement*

| Field name | Data type | Allow nulls | Default value | Domain | Prec- ision | Scale | Length | |
|---|---|---|---|---|---|---|---|---|
| OBJECTID | Object ID | | | | | | | |
| Shape | Geometry | Yes | | | | | | |
| CreatedBy | String | Yes | | | | | 255 | Name of individual who created feature |
| DateCreated | Date | Yes | | | 0 | 0 | 8 | Date of feature creation |
| ModifiedBy | String | Yes | | | | | 255 | Name of individual who modified feature |
| DateModified | Date | Yes | | | 0 | 0 | 8 | Date of last feature modification |
| DocumentHyperlink | String | Yes | | | | | 30 | Link to external document |
| verified_by | String | Yes | | | | | 255 | Name of person verifying this feature |
| verified_date | Date | Yes | | | 0 | 0 | 8 | Date feature was last verified |
| PID | String | Yes | | | | | 255 | Unique point identifier |
| case_id | Long integer | Yes | | | 0 | | | Foreign key for case processing |
| serial_nr_full | String | Yes | | | | | 17 | Case serial or lease number |
| legal_description | Blob | Yes | | | 0 | 0 | 0 | Complete legal description |
| unit_agreement_name | String | Yes | | | | | 20 | Name of the unit agreement |
| participating_area_name | String | Yes | | | | | 20 | Name of the participating area; might be null |
| commodity | String | Yes | | US_Rights | | | 3 | Leasable, locatable, or salable commodity of the lease |
| total_acreage | Double | Yes | | | 0 | 0 | | Total storage acreage of all leases in the agreements |
| case_group | String | Yes | 318 | CaseGroup_318 | | | 3 | Case group to which this feature belongs |
| case_type | String | Yes | | CaseType_318 | | | 6 | Case group subcategory |
| case_disposition | String | Yes | | UACaseDisposition | | | 3 | Case disposition code |
| effective_date | Date | Yes | | | 0 | 0 | 8 | Effective date of agreement |
| expiration_date | Date | Yes | | | 0 | 0 | 8 | Expiration data of agreement |
| termination_date | Date | Yes | | | 0 | 0 | 8 | Termination date of agreement |
| edit_geom_flag | Short integer | Yes | | | 0 | | | Flag indicating geometry has been changed |
| edit_attr_flag | Short integer | Yes | | | 0 | | | Flag indicating other attribution has been changed |
| lr200_system_id | String | Yes | | | | | 2 | Foreign key to related records in LR2000 |

## Simple feature class
**OG_Lease**

| | Geometry | Point |
|---|---|---|
| | Contains M values | No |
| | Contains Z values | No |

*Oil and gas lease*

| Field name | Data type | Allow nulls | Default value | Domain | Prec-ision | Scale | Length | |
|---|---|---|---|---|---|---|---|---|
| OBJECTID | Object ID | | | | | | | |
| Shape | Geometry | Yes | | | | | | |
| CreatedBy | String | Yes | | | | | 255 | Name of individual who created feature |
| DateCreated | Date | Yes | | | 0 | 0 | 8 | Date of feature creation |
| ModifiedBy | String | Yes | | | | | 255 | Name of individual who modified feature |
| DateModified | Date | Yes | | | 0 | 0 | 8 | Date of last feature modification |
| DocumentHyperlink | String | Yes | | | | | 30 | Link to external document |
| verified_by | String | Yes | | | | | 255 | Name of person verifying this feature |
| verified_date | Date | Yes | | | 0 | 0 | 8 | Date feature was last verified |
| PID | String | Yes | | | | | 255 | Unique point identifier |
| case_id | Long integer | Yes | | | 0 | | | Foreign key for case processing |
| serial_nr_full | String | Yes | | | | | 17 | Case serial or lease number |
| legal_description | Blob | Yes | | | 0 | 0 | 0 | Complete legal description |
| case_group | String | Yes | 31 | CaseGroup_31 | | | 3 | Case group to which this feature belongs |
| case_type | String | Yes | | CaseType_31 | | | 6 | Case group subcategory |
| case_disposition | String | Yes | | UACaseDisposition | | | 3 | Case disposition code |
| stored_acreage | Double | Yes | | | 0 | 0 | | Stored acreage of the lease |
| commodity | String | Yes | | US_Rights | | | 3 | Leasable, locatable, or salable commodity of the lease |
| lease_name | String | Yes | | | | | 20 | Name of the lease |
| royalty_rate | Double | Yes | | | 0 | 0 | | Money paid back to government for oil and gas not sold |
| rate_reduction | String | Yes | | YesNo | | | 1 | If royalty rate has been reduced |
| many_royalty_rates | String | Yes | | YesNo | | | 1 | If many royalty rates are applicable |
| held_by | String | Yes | | HeldBy | | | 3 | Production status on lease |
| effective_date | Date | Yes | | | 0 | 0 | 8 | Effective date of lease |
| expiration_date | Date | Yes | | | 0 | 0 | 8 | Expiration date of lease |
| termination_date | Date | Yes | | | 0 | 0 | 8 | Termination date of lease |
| edit_geom_flag | Short integer | Yes | | | 0 | | | Flag indicating geometry has been changed |
| edit_attr_flag | Short integer | Yes | | | 0 | | | Flag indicating other attribution has been changed |
| lr2000_system_id | String | Yes | | | | | 2 | Foreign key to related records in LR2000 |

*6*

## Relationship class
**ID_OG_Lease_To_ID_OG_XRF**

| | |
|---|---|
| Type | *Simple* |
| Cardinality | *One to many* |
| Notification | *None* |

| | |
|---|---|
| Forward label | *To_OG_XRF* |
| Backward label | *From_OG_Lease* |

| Origin feature class | Destination table |
|---|---|
| Name | *ID_OG_Lease* |
| Primary key | *case_id* |
| Foreign key | *case_id* |

| |
|---|
| Name | *ID_OG_XRF* |

## Coded value domain
**HeldBy**

| | |
|---|---|
| Field type | *String* |
| Split policy | *Default value* |
| Merge policy | *Default value* |

| Code | Description |
|---|---|
| 653 | Held by Loc In Prod Unit |
| 650 | Held by Production - Actual |
| 651 | Held by Production - Allocated |

## Table
**ID_OG_XRF**

| Field name | Data type | Allow nulls | Default value | Domain | Prec-ision | Scale | Length | |
|---|---|---|---|---|---|---|---|---|
| OBJECTID | Object ID | | | | | | | |
| case_id | Long integer | Yes | | | 0 | | | |
| agreement_snf | String | Yes | | | | | 17 | Serial_nr_full of agreement, primary key |
| agreement_type | String | Yes | | | | | 6 | |
| og_snf | String | Yes | | | | | 17 | Serial_nr_full of agreement or lease, foreign key |
| og_type | String | Yes | | | | | 6 | |

Numerous additional tables are maintained in the NILS geodatabase to support various parcel management tasks and functions. In some cases, these tables are used to store data received from the LR2000 system. With the exception of pid.xrf, these exist to support the end user.

The LR2000 is an external, opaque system to the NILS PM module. Some data from LR2000 is stored in the NILS geodatabase to support parcel management tasks and functions. For example, some of the tables exist to hold information that varies in quantity and is essential for understanding a case, such as case_specific_attr (specifically document numbers) and term_us_right. Additional information useful for understanding a case is held in case_twp, remark, and non_plss_land_narrative.

Other tables, such as Customer_xrf and Right_customer_attr, hold cross-references for many-to-many relationships. The Customer table holds enterprisewide data.

The pid_xref table is used to store links between systems; this is for system support rather than user support.

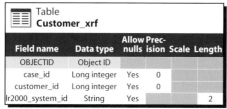

*Table used to cross-reference mining claim customers between LR2000 and PM*

| Table Customer_xrf | | | | | |
|---|---|---|---|---|---|
| **Field name** | **Data type** | **Allow nulls** | **Prec- ision** | **Scale** | **Length** |
| OBJECTID | Object ID | | | | |
| case_id | Long integer | Yes | 0 | | |
| customer_id | Long integer | Yes | 0 | | |
| lr2000_system_id | String | Yes | | | 2 |

Foreign key to related case feature
Unique identifier for each customer
Unique identifier for customer in LR2000

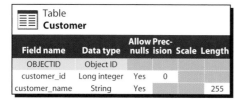

*Table used to hold copy of selected data from LR2000 for use within the GIS*

| Table Customer | | | | | |
|---|---|---|---|---|---|
| **Field name** | **Data type** | **Allow nulls** | **Prec- ision** | **Scale** | **Length** |
| OBJECTID | Object ID | | | | |
| customer_id | Long integer | Yes | 0 | | |
| customer_name | String | Yes | | | 255 |

Unique identifier for each customer
Name of customer

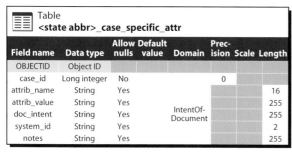

*Stores miscellaneous case information*

| Table <state abbr>_case_specific_attr | | | | | | | |
|---|---|---|---|---|---|---|---|
| **Field name** | **Data type** | **Allow nulls** | **Default value** | **Domain** | **Prec- ision** | **Scale** | **Length** |
| OBJECTID | Object ID | | | | | | |
| case_id | Long integer | No | | | 0 | | |
| attrib_name | String | Yes | | | | | 16 |
| attrib_value | String | Yes | | | | | 255 |
| doc_intent | String | Yes | | IntentOf- Document | | | 255 |
| system_id | String | Yes | | | | | 2 |
| notes | String | Yes | | | | | 255 |

Unique internal case identifier
Type of attribute in attrib_value
Value of the attribute attrib_name
Code representing document's intent
BLM system identifier from LR2000
Additional text

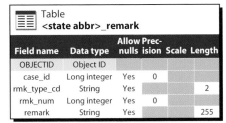

Table
**<state abbr>_remark**

| Field name | Data type | Allow nulls | Precision | Scale | Length | |
|---|---|---|---|---|---|---|
| OBJECTID | Object ID | | | | | |
| case_id | Long integer | Yes | 0 | | | Unique internal case identifier |
| rmk_type_cd | String | Yes | | | 2 | Source; segregation, right, or use authorization |
| rmk_num | Long integer | Yes | 0 | | | Remark ID to distinguish among multiple remarks |
| remark | String | Yes | | | 255 | Remark text |

*Contains original content of action codes. Remarks that cannot be parsed are written to this table.*

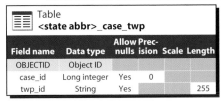

Table
**<state abbr>_case_twp**

| Field name | Data type | Allow nulls | Precision | Scale | Length | |
|---|---|---|---|---|---|---|
| OBJECTID | Object ID | | | | | |
| case_id | Long integer | Yes | 0 | | | Unique internal case identifier |
| twp_id | String | Yes | | | 255 | Township identifier |

*Table used in conjunction with the case feature classes to support multiple townships within a case*

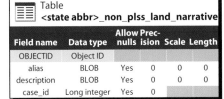

Table
**pid_xrf**

| Field name | Data type | Allow nulls | Precision | Scale | Length | |
|---|---|---|---|---|---|---|
| OBJECTID | Object ID | | | | | |
| pid | String | Yes | | | 255 | Unique point identifier |
| sys_val | String | Yes | | | 255 | System dependent value, Case ID, or other identifier |
| sys_val_name | String | Yes | | | 255 | Name of system to which value belongs, such as LR2000 |

*Cross-reference table for parcels (used by system, not by users)*

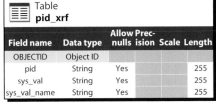

Table
**<state abbr>_non_plss_land_narrative**

| Field name | Data type | Allow nulls | Precision | Scale | Length | |
|---|---|---|---|---|---|---|
| OBJECTID | Object ID | | | | | |
| alias | BLOB | Yes | 0 | 0 | 0 | Other description |
| description | BLOB | Yes | 0 | 0 | 0 | Legal description |
| case_id | Long integer | Yes | 0 | | | Unique internal case identifier |

*Supports other nonstandard text descriptions of land, such as metes and bounds*

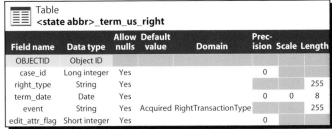

Table
**<state abbr>_term_us_right**

| Field name | Data type | Allow nulls | Default value | Domain | Precision | Scale | Length | |
|---|---|---|---|---|---|---|---|---|
| OBJECTID | Object ID | | | | | | | |
| case_id | Long integer | Yes | | | 0 | | | Unique internal case identifier |
| right_type | String | Yes | | | | | 255 | |
| term_date | Date | Yes | | | 0 | 0 | 8 | Date the new right will take effect |
| event | String | Yes | | Acquired RightTransactionType | | | 255 | |
| edit_attr_flag | Short integer | Yes | | | 0 | | | True if attribute has been manually edited |

*Additional information on rights held by the United States in a case*

Table
**Right_customer_attr**

| Field name | Data type | Allow nulls | Default value | Domain | Precision | Scale | Length | |
|---|---|---|---|---|---|---|---|---|
| OBJECTID | Object ID | | | | | | | |
| case_id | Long integer | Yes | | | 0 | | | Unique internal case identifier |
| customer_id | String | Yes | | | | | 255 | Foreign key to Customer table |
| right_code | String | Yes | | | | | 2 | Code identifying the type of right |
| admin_agency | String | Yes | BLM | ManagingAgency | | | 255 | Agency responsible for surface management |
| percentage | Double | Yes | | | 0 | 0 | | Percentage of the land for which the right belongs to the customer |

*Additional information on rights held by a customer in a case*

Essentially all the feature classes in the NILS data model participate in a single topology. This is for data validation and geometry sharing with the focus on creating a seamless land grid for data integrity and data sharing.

The legal description topology rules shown here ensure the data integrity of the survey framework classes. While many feature classes participate in this topology, the basic rules are simple:

- PLSS townships must not overlap or have gaps.

- PLSS subdivisions must not overlap or have gaps.

- PLSS subdivisions must be covered by PLSS townships.

- RecordBoundary features must outline all PLSS subdivisions and cases.

- Corner features must be at the ends of record boundaries.

Other rules are designed to handle cases of SpecialSurvey features within the PLSS framework. These rules are presented in context throughout the remainder of the chapter.

**Survey-aware feature classes**

| Feature class |
|---|
| Corner |
| Monument |
| MeasuredCoordinate |
| RecordBoundary |

*Survey-aware feature classes can participate in a topology. In these cases, all of the topologically integrated feature classes should be survey aware.*

## Topology
**LegalDescription_Topology**

Cluster tolerance  *0.000005 degrees*
~ *0.5 meter*

### Participating feature classes and ranks

| Feature class | Rank | Feature class | Rank | Feature class | Rank |
|---|---|---|---|---|---|
| MeasuredCoordinate | 1 | PLSSSecondDiv | 5 | Right | 8 |
| Monument | 1 | PLSSThirdDiv | 6 | Segregation | 8 |
| RecordBoundary | 2 | SpecialSurvey | 6 | Use_Authorization | 8 |
| Corner | 2 | SpecialSurvDiv | 7 | Land_Status | 9 |
| PLSSTownship | 3 | Case | 8 | | |
| PLSSFirstDiv | 4 | Mining_Claim | 8 | | |

### Topology rules

| Origin feature class | Topology rule | Comparision feature class |
|---|---|---|
| PLSSThirdDiv : Aliquot Part | Must not overlap | |
| PLSSTownship | Must not overlap | |
| SpecialSurvey : Land Grant | Must not overlap | |
| Land_Status | Must not overlap | |
| PLSSThirdDiv : Aliquot Part | Must not overlap with | PLSSThirdDiv : Aliquot Part Less Than 40 |
| PLSSThirdDiv : Aliquot Part | Must not overlap with | PLSSThirdDiv : Lot |
| PLSSThirdDiv : Aliquot Part | Must not overlap with | PLSSThirdDiv : Tracts Cadastral |
| PLSSThirdDiv : Lot | Must not overlap with | PLSSThirdDiv : Aliquot Part Less Than 40 |
| PLSSThirdDiv : Aliquot Resurveyed | Must not overlap with | PLSSThirdDiv : Fractional Part of Section |
| PLSSThirdDiv : Aliquot Resurveyed | Must not overlap with | PLSSThirdDiv : Unsurveyed Protracted |
| PLSSThirdDiv : Aliquot Resurveyed | Must not overlap with | SpecialSurvey : Texas Tract |
| PLSSThirdDiv : Aliquot Resurveyed | Must not overlap with | SpecialSurvey : Townsite |
| PLSSThirdDiv : Aliquot Resurveyed | Must not overlap with | SpecialSurvey : Private Land Claim |
| PLSSThirdDiv : Aliquot Resurveyed | Must not overlap with | SpecialSurvey : Metes and Bounds |
| PLSSThirdDiv : Aliquot Resurveyed | Must not overlap with | SpecialSurvey : Exchange Survey |
| PLSSThirdDiv : Aliquot Resurveyed | Must not overlap with | SpecialSurvey : Small Holding Claim |
| PLSSThirdDiv : Aliquot Resurveyed | Must not overlap with | Special Survey : Homestead Entry Survey |
| PLSSThirdDiv : Aliquot Resurveyed | Must not overlap with | SpecialSurvey : Georgia Military District |
| PLSSThirdDiv : Aliquot Resurveyed | Must not overlap with | SpecialSurvDiv |
| PLSSThirdDiv : Unsurveyed Protracted | Must not overlap with | PLSSThirdDiv : Aliquot Less Than 40 Resurveyed |
| PLSSThirdDiv : Unsurveyed Protracted | Must not overlap with | PLSSThirdDiv : Fractional Part of Section |
| PLSSThirdDiv : Unsurveyed Protracted | Must not overlap with | PLSSThirdDiv : Lot |
| PLSSThirdDiv : Unsurveyed Protracted | Must not overlap with | PLSSThirdDiv : Aliquot Part Less Than 40 |
| PLSSThirdDiv : Unsurveyed Protracted | Must not overlap with | PLSSThirdDiv : Lot Resurveyed |
| PLSSThirdDiv : Unsurveyed Protracted | Must not overlap with | SpecialSurvDiv |
| PLSSTownship | Must not have gaps | |
| PLSSTownship | Boundary must be covered by | RecordBoundary |
| PLSSFirstDiv | Boundary must be covered by | RecordBoundary |
| PLSSSecondDiv | Boundary must be covered by | RecordBoundary |
| PLSSThirdDiv | Boundary must be covered by | RecordBoundary |
| SpecialSurvey | Boundary must be covered by | RecordBoundary |
| Case | Boundary must be covered by | RecordBoundary |
| Segregation | Boundary must be covered by | RecordBoundary |
| Use_Authorization | Boundary must be covered by | RecordBoundary |
| Right | Boundary must be covered by | RecordBoundary |
| Land_Status | Boundary must be covered by | RecordBoundary |
| RecordBoundary | Must not have dangles | |
| Corner | Must be covered by endpoint of | RecordBoundary |
| PLSSThirdDiv | Must be covered by | PLSSTownship |
| PLSSFirstDiv | Must be covered by | PLSSTownship |
| PLSSSecondDiv | Must be covered by | PLSSTownship |
| MiningClaim | Must be covered by | RecordBoundary |

6

## REFERENCES

Brown, Curtis M.; Wilson, Donald A.; and Robillard, Walter G. 1995. *Brown's Boundary Control and Legal Principles*. 4th ed. New York, New York: John Wiley and Sons.

Brown, Curtis M. 1969. *Boundary Control and Legal Principles*. 2nd ed. New York: New York: John Wiley and Sons.

Epstein, Earl, and Brown, Patricia. 1990. Land Interests. In *Multipurpose Land Information Systems: The Guidebook*. Reston, Virginia: Subcommittee on Geodetic Control.

Federal Geographic Data Committee. 1999. Cadastral Data Content Standard for the National Spatial Data Infrastructure, Version 1.1. Reston, Virginia: Subcommittee on Cadastral Data.

General Land Office. 1921. *Primer of Instructive Information Relative to Legal Subdivisions and Plats of Public Land Surveys*. Washington, D.C.: U.S. Department of the Interior, Bureau of Land Management, Eastern States.

Linklater, Andro. 2002. *Measuring America: How an Untamed Wilderness Shaped the United States and Fulfilled the Promise of Democracy*. New York: Walker Publishing Company.

Moyer, D. David, and Fisher, Kenneth Paul. 1973. *Land Parcel Identifiers for Information Systems*. Chicago, Illinois: American Bar Foundation.

National Integrated Land System (NILS) Home Page. Last modified June 30, 2003. URL: http://www.blm.gov/nils/.

NILS Parcel Management Use Cases (Preliminary Draft). 2002. Washington, D.C.: Bureau of Land Management. URL: http://www.blm.gov/nils/parcel/PMUseCases-PreliminaryDraft.pdf.

Simpson, S.R. 1976. *Land Law and Registration*. Cambridge: Cambridge University Press.

Ting, L., and I. P. Williamson. 1999. The dynamic human-kind–land relationship and its impact on land administration systems. In *Proceedings of the Joint United Nations and FIG International Conference on Land Tenure and Cadastral Infrastructures for Sustainable Development*. Melbourne.

von Meyer, Nancy. 1989. A Conceptual Model for Spatial Cadastral Data in a Land Information System. Ph.D. diss., University of Wisconsin, Madison.

von Meyer, Nancy. 2002. Production, Analysis, and Publication: A Concept for Geographic Information Environments. White paper, Pendleton, South Carolina: Fairview Industries.

Wattles, G.H. 1979. *Writing Legal Descriptions*. Orange, California: Gurdon H. Wattles Publications.

Williamson, I.P., and L. Ting. 1999. Land administration and cadastral trends—A framework for reengineering. In *Proceedings of the Joint United Nations and FIG International Conference on Land Tenure and Cadastral Infrastructures for Sustainable Development*. Melbourne.

## CREDITS

Thanks to Ron Taylor of the Colorado BLM for background on public lands and surveys, rights-of-way, and easements. Ron also provided many of the graphics and map data used in this chapter. Jennifer Cadkin, Mark Williams, and Carsten Bjornsson of ESRI provided significant content for this chapter.

## FURTHER RESOURCES

Follow the Land Parcels link from ESRI ArcOnline at http://support.esri.com/datamodels for more information on data models.

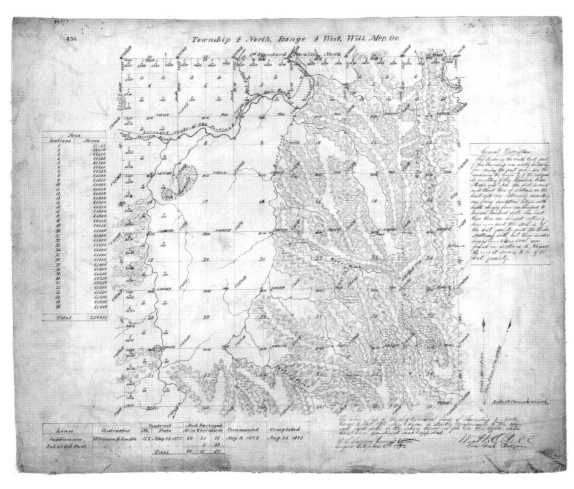

*Raster data has a simple structure that can be readily applied for many different purposes. This chapter presents four types of applications that illustrate common ways raster data is currently used in GIS: scanned maps, orthophotos, elevation models, and time series analysis.*

**7**

Raster data is used for visualization and geoprocessing in many different applications. Hardcopy maps are often scanned into digital form for backdrops to other geographic data or as sources for extracting vector features through a data conversion process. One of the quickest ways to compile a GIS database is through conversion of scanned hardcopy maps. The case study for scanned maps in this chapter comes from the National Geographic Society (NGS).

Orthophotos are also used for map backdrops, as well as for updating vector geographic data. With modern high-resolution satellite imagery and ever more abundant aerial photography, the quality and quantity of orthophotos has improved dramatically in recent years, while costs have dropped. The case study for orthophotos comes from the Texas Natural Resources Information System (TNRIS), which publishes 1-meter aerial photography of the entire state for public access on the Web.

One of the oldest uses of raster data is for elevation mapping. The data source for this application consists of elevation postings at regular intervals over large areas. Each raster cell can then be colored according to the elevation range in which it falls. Digital elevation models, as these are called, can be used to derive shaded-relief maps, determine the paths of water through a landscape, derive contours, study line-of-sight viewsheds, and perform many other applications related to terrain and hydrologic analysis. This case study is from the U.S. Geological Survey's National Elevation Dataset (NED), freely available on the Web.

Much like the weather maps on television, a sequence of raster dataset observations of an area at set time intervals can be used to animate a map. This is useful for studying the expansion patterns of urban areas, the paths and effects of hurricanes, storm precipitation across a watershed, and many other events recorded as time series. This case study is based on a time series of raster images of Hurricane Mitch as it moved across the Atlantic Ocean to the United States in 1998, captured in satellite imagery by the U.S. National Oceanic and Atmospheric Administration (NOAA) .

# Using raster data

Raster datasets represent important information assets for GIS application and use. Raster data is collected with increasing frequency and data volume. Many users have managed raster datasets as a collection of compressed raster files but are recognizing the need to apply relational database technology for integrating the management of raster data with their other critical GIS data assets. Therefore, raster database design and management as integrated GIS management tasks are growing in significance.

Images and other raster datasets are important GIS data resources that can be expensive to build and maintain. The tactic of using relational databases to manage image data is becoming increasingly widespread. In recent years, DBMS and GIS have evolved to support massive data collections that can be simultaneously accessed by many users.

## WHY PUT IMAGES IN A DATABASE?

There are several good reasons for taking advantage of the functionality and strengths of standard relational DBMS coupled with GIS technology. These are some of the most important benefits:

- Huge datasets requiring multiuser access—When many users are accessing the same raster files simultaneously, better performance is possible from a properly tuned, centralized database than from a file-based system. This is especially important with massive raster datasets. For example, EarthSat has loaded a database with 15-meter satellite imagery over the entire earth, 6.5 terabytes in database size (see figures on the next page), for high-performance Web access.

- Data management—A database allows common data management and retrieval for all GIS data, including raster, vector, metadata, and tabular data. A database also provides access to large images (many gigabytes to many terabytes) of continuous spatial data, such as the 30-meter resolution DEM composite of North America.

- Data security—A DBMS permits multiple security levels to be established and enforced. Users can be given access to the imagery relevant to the job on which they are working.

- Data query—A DBMS enables a common query environment. Queries can help locate all data related to an area during a particular time period or for a particular subject matter, depending on the metadata provided with the datasets. With raster catalogs, additional attribution can

be associated with each dataset to support more extensive queries as well.

- Incremental updates—With ArcSDE, it is possible to update just a portion of a raster dataset without having to rebuild it entirely. Only the affected portions of a continuous image need to be rebuilt. (Pyramids are discussed in more detail later in the chapter.)

Here are three example use cases.

### Base maps for enterprise GIS

A water supply company had considerable legacy engineering data stored on paper and Mylar maps. It needed to be able to supply these to its users as background images to be combined with vector data into a seamless hybrid map. Eventually, these images would be replaced by vector data. The images were scanned as 1-bit TIFF images. The company manages approximately 3,000 images (40 gigabytes) centrally using ArcSDE and supplies them as background images to users running ArcMap. Users continually add new layers and update existing vector data with new information derived from the imagery.

### Data management and distribution

An association of governments needed a central repository of imagery that could be easily accessed by its members as well as by the public on the Web. It provides the images in downloadable formats, as well as through an interactive mapping Web site that allows interested parties to view the images online. The data is in 8-bit, 3-band, 1-meter digital orthophoto quarter quadrangles (DOQQ). So far, it has stored one terabyte of imagery in SQL Server using ArcSDE, with more images to be added as the areas are rephotographed by satellites and aircraft.

## Additional feature attribution

An organization may have pictures of locations it needs to attach to vector features in the GIS. This could be pictures of a house linked to a land parcel, a pump or valve linked to a hydraulic network, or property damage linked to the location of a flood or other natural catastrophe.

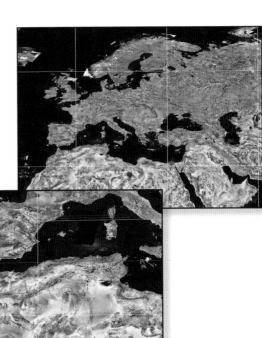

*Views of Europe and the coast of Spain from EarthSat 15-meter imagery. These images were generated from a database of the entire earth that is 6.5 terabytes in size.*

**7**

Raster datasets represent geographic features by dividing the world into discrete square or rectangular cells laid out in a grid. Each cell has a location relative to an origin and a value describing some entity being observed. For example, the cell values in an aerial photograph represent the amount of light reflected from the earth's surface. Cell values can also be any measured or calculated value, such as elevation, slope, rainfall, vegetative type, and temperature.

Raster datasets are two-dimensional arrays of cells (or pixels). Each cell's height and width are the same throughout the raster dataset, and cells may be square or rectangular. A raster dataset spans a rectangular area.

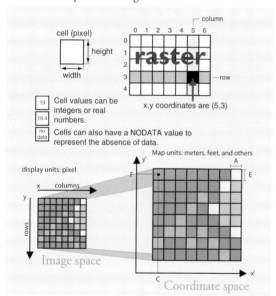

Each cell has a single numeric value. This value can represent any of several qualities of a location, such as reflectance, color, precipitation, or elevation.

Raster data is organized in rows and columns and is spatially referenced. You can determine the coordinate of a cell by counting columns from the left and rows from the top.

Raster data is stored as arrays of cells (pixels) and can be displayed on the map's coordinate system. Raster datasets of geographic areas are automatically processed by the GIS with a display transformation that converts cell units to map coordinates.

## TYPES OF RASTER DATA

The data stored in a raster dataset can be categorized as one of the four types shown below.

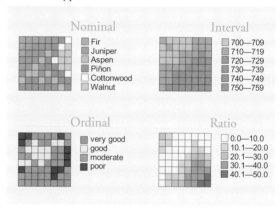

Nominal data values are categorized and have names. The data value is an arbitrary type code. Examples are soil types and land use.

Ordinal data values are categorized, have names, and are ranked numerically. Examples are land suitability classifications and soil drainage rankings.

Interval data values are numerically ordered, and the interval difference is meaningful. Examples are voltage potential and difference in concentration.

Ratio data values measure a continuous phenomenon with a natural zero point. Examples are rainfall and population.

Nominal and ordinal data represent discrete categories. They are best represented with integer cell values.

Interval and ratio data present continuous phenomena and are usually measured with real number cell values.

| 21 | 17 | 17 | 18 | 22 | 18 |
|---|---|---|---|---|---|
| 18 | 16 | 17 | 19 | 24 | 19 |
| 21 | 19 | 19 | 19 | 22 | 22 |
| 26 | 23 | 21 | 20 | 18 | 21 |
| 24 | 23 | 18 | 16 | 20 | 19 |
| 18 | 14 | 16 | 17 | 19 | 20 |

Discrete cell values

| 21.1 | 17.3 | 17.2 | 18.1 |
|---|---|---|---|
| 18.5 | 16.2 | 17.3 | 19.1 |
| 21.0 | 19.1 | 19.4 | 19.2 |
| 26.3 | 23.1 | 21.6 | 20.5 |

Real cell values

## RASTER BANDS

Some raster datasets have a single band (a measure of a single characteristic) of data, while others have multiple bands. When you create a map layer from a raster image, you can choose to display a single band of data or form a color composite from multiple bands. Three types of single-band data are shown here.

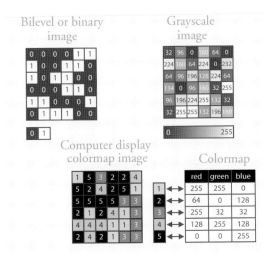

Bilevel or binary image

Grayscale image

Computer display colormap image

Colormap

In a binary image, each cell has a value of 0 or 1. This type of data is often used for scanning maps with simple linework, such as parcel maps.

In a grayscale image, each cell has a value from 0 to another number, such as 255 or 2047. These are often used for black-and-white aerial photographs.

One way to represent colors on an image is with a colormap. A set of values is arbitrarily coded to match a defined set of red–green–blue (RGB) values.

With multiple bands, each band usually represents a segment of the electromagnetic spectrum collected by a sensor. Bands can represent any portion of the electromagnetic spectrum,

including ranges not visible to the eye—the infrared or ultraviolet sections of the spectrum.

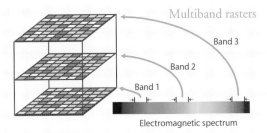

Multiband rasters

Band 3

Band 2

Band 1

Electromagnetic spectrum

Any three of the available bands can be chosen to create RGB composites, so more information can be presented on computer displays that employ a red–green–blue color rendition model.

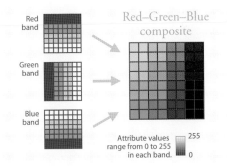

Red band

Green band

Blue band

Red–Green–Blue composite

Attribute values range from 0 to 255 in each band.

## OPTIMIZING DISPLAY WITH PYRAMIDS

You have the option to create pyramids for raster datasets. These comprise a set of raster datasets downsampled by progressive factors of two. The downsampled datasets are intended to shorten the display time for larger areas requiring lower display resolution. The term "pyramid" is a conceptual naming convention; the overall raster data extent remains the same, but the cells change in size.

7

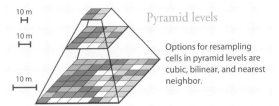

Pyramid levels

Options for resampling cells in pyramid levels are cubic, bilinear, and nearest neighbor.

ArcMap selects the appropriate pyramid level for the current display scale, thereby improving display speed.

One of the major design decisions in managing raster data is whether to keep all the data in a single dataset or in a catalog of, potentially, many datasets. In some cases, the application requirements will dictate which approach to use, while in other cases, the choice may not be as obvious.

A raster dataset is any valid raster format organized into one or more bands. Each band consists of an array of pixels, and each pixel has a value. A raster dataset has at least one band. More than one raster dataset can be mosaicked together into a larger, single, continuous raster dataset. Note that when partially overlapping raster datasets are mosaicked, the overlapping area contains only one set of cell values.

A raster catalog is a collection of raster datasets defined in a table format in which each record defines an individual raster dataset in the catalog. A raster catalog can be large and contain thousands of images. A raster catalog is typically used to display adjacent, fully overlapping, or partially overlapping raster datasets without having to mosaic them into one large raster dataset.

When working with multiple raster datasets, there are three possible storage methods: Store each raster dataset individually, mosaic them all into one large raster dataset, or store them as members of a raster catalog.

Storing the raster datasets individually is often the best method when the datasets are not adjacent to each other or are rarely used on the same project. Mosaicking your inputs together to form one large, single extent of raster data is appropriate for many applications, but a raster catalog may be desired for any of these reasons:

- The extents of the raster datasets partially or fully overlap, and you want the common areas to be preserved.

- The raster datasets represent a collection of observations of the same area at different times in a time series.

- You do not need to see the entire area at one time (raster catalogs display a wire frame at smaller scales).

- You want to manage a collection of images as an integrated set.

- You are constantly adding new images to your geodatabase.

- You want to record and manage additional attribute columns that describe each image.

Rasters can also be an attribute of a feature. This means that a field of type raster can exist as one of the columns within a feature class. This is similar to having a hyperlink of a file-based image in a field, except the raster image is stored and managed within the geodatabase.

When working with large raster datasets, it may be best to divide the overall extent into segments that can be loaded in parallel. For example, the EarthSat digital globe database was divided into six mosaics within a raster catalog. This allowed the data to be loaded in six parallel tasks, greatly reducing the time needed to perform the loading. TNRIS also includes a raster catalog of orthophoto mosaics gathered over the entire state at 1-meter resolution.

For managing and accessing raster data, there are notable differences in functionality and performance between personal geodatabases (PGDB) and multiuser DBMS. This will be discussed further, following the next page.

# Raster datasets and catalogs

You have two main options for organizing your raster datasets: either as single seamless images (datasets) or collections (catalogs) of datasets.

*A geodatabase can contain distinct raster datasets and raster catalogs of such datasets.*

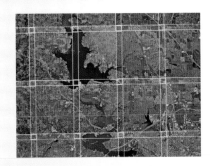

| | Raster dataset | Raster catalog |
|---|---|---|
| *Description* | A single picture of an object or a seamless image covering a spatially continuous area. This may be a single original image or the result of many images appended together. | A collection of raster datasets displayed as a single layer. These must all be in the same coordinate system and should have the same data type. |
| *Geodatabase* | Display and analysis time can be much faster with raster datasets stored in a database. Databases support better query, multiuser access, security, and data management. | Display and analysis time can be much faster with a raster catalog table containing all its datasets rather than just references to external files or separate dataset tables. Databases support better query, multiuser access, security, and data management. |
| *Map layers* | One map layer. | One map layer. |
| *Homogeneous or heterogeneous data* | Homogeneous data: a single format, data type, and file. | Heterogeneous data: multiple formats, data types, and file sizes. |
| *Metadata* | Stored once and applies to complete dataset. | Stored as attribute columns for each raster dataset in the raster catalog. |
| *Pyramiding* | Only build a single pyramid on one large raster. | Build a pyramid for each raster dataset member. |
| *Pros* | Fast to display at any scale. Mosaic saves space, since there is no overlapping data. Displays with better blending at mosaicked image seams. | Can manage multirow raster tables for many purposes. Can specify one layer for display. Easy to update. Easy to add new rasters. |
| *Cons* | File-based and PGDB raster datasets are slower to update because the entire file has to be rewritten. | File-based raster catalogs with different data types may not render well. |
| *Recommendations* | Use raster datasets when overlaps between mosaicked images do not need to be retained and for fast display of raster files. | Use raster catalog for massive image repositories, retaining overlaps between datasets, managing time series data, and when differences among adjoining images prevent mosaicking. |

7

Whether using raster datasets or raster catalogs, you have a choice of storage facilities for your data, basically, whether to use files, a personal geodatabase, or an ArcSDE geodatabase. The default option is to use raster format files independently of any database, but there are many good reasons for managing your raster data in a geodatabase.

Raster data managed in an ArcSDE geodatabase offers an enterprise level of functionality, such as security, multiuser access, and data sharing.

In the past, you would physically import the raster data into your DBMS using ArcSDE and build it to enable the most efficient queries and updates. However, with its new storage structure, the raster data is said to be managed (fully controlled) by the geodatabase.

When using the personal geodatabase, the raster data is always stored as referenced raster dataset files on disk. The raster data accessed from a personal geodatabase is said to be managed when it has been converted from its original location and format into an ERDAS IMAGINE® (.img) file inside a special folder located next to the personal geodatabase. Deleting managed raster data deletes the associated ERDAS IMAGINE files stored in the special raster geodatabase folder.

The personal geodatabase can also reference raster dataset files of any supported format from their existing locations without having to completely manage the individual image files. This type of reference does not require the raster data to be imported, which can significantly reduce data preparation time, but results in slower performance for many operations. Deleting a row (raster dataset) of a nonmanaged geodatabase will not delete the referenced raster files. The nonmanaged approach serves well for prototyping, but carries potential security and other risks that may not be prudent in a multiuser application.

A personal geodatabase is good in the following situations:

- For quick raster catalog prototyping (managed or nonmanaged).

- When only a moderate number of users will access and use the data. Only one user at a time can edit the data.

- When the application does not require an enterprise RDBMS. This greatly lowers costs for software purchase, maintenance, and administration.

- When the application does not already require an ArcSDE geodatabase or does not need its higher performance.

An ArcSDE geodatabase can be the best choice for these reasons:

- ArcSDE geodatabases have the best display performance on large raster datasets (can be multiple terabytes of data).

- It is the preferred option for raster dataset mosaics or any other datasets larger than two gigabytes.

- Multiuser access is allowed for both updating and reading.

- Incremental updates are allowed. PGDB updates to raster datasets require replacement of the entire dataset, as with updates to external raster files.

- Both lossy and lossless compression are allowed. PGDB uses only ERDAS IMAGINE compression.

- Massive storage is allowed, in terms of size and number of users.

- ArcSDE provides the best centralized data storage technology for sharing raster data across an organization or with the public.

For many users, a personal geodatabase will be sufficient and will be simpler and less expensive to administer. But the ability of ArcSDE to support large numbers of users, as well as to incrementally update and rebuild pyramids, may provide a significant enough advantage to drive your choice.

# ArcSDE and personal geodatabases

You have two main geodatabase options for storing your raster data: in personal geodatabases or in ArcSDE.

*In the personal geodatabase, the raster data is always stored as referenced raster dataset files on disk, not within the Access database. Alternatively, you can use ArcSDE to manage huge raster data collections as an integrated data source in a DBMS that supports multiuser access, security, and high performance.*

|  | ArcSDE geodatabase | PGDB |
|---|---|---|
| *Description* | ArcSDE integrated with Oracle, IBM DB2, Informix, or Microsoft SQL Server DBMS. | ArcGIS Desktop software integrated with Microsoft Access (run time) database software. |
| *Application* | Sophisticated applications accessing small to large data volumes with any number of simultaneous users. | Efficient for small to medium raster data sizes, small numbers of users, and for prototyping ArcSDE applications. |
| *Data volume* | No size limits. The storage requirements depend on the file format. | Depending on file format used for external files, size limit may be 2 or more gigabytes. Datasets held inside the database are compressed. |
| *Multiuser access* | Any number of users and editors. Limits depend on network server configuration and administration. | Realistically supports a few simultaneous users. |
| *Updates* | Allows for incremental updates. | Updates require rewriting affected raster datasets; similar to updating external raster files. |
| *Management* | Raster data is always compressed and stored within the geodatabase, yielding the greatest performance. | External raster datasets can be converted for use inside PGDB in a compressed format. Data left in its native file format is slowest to process. |
| *Pros* | Supports huge data volumes, fast display, better multiuser performance, common data management and retrieval for all spatial data, tools for establishing security levels, and a common query environment. | With PGDB, you can take advantage of raster datasets and catalogs for capabilities such as image selection with attribute and spatial queries, time series datasets, pyramids, and more. |
| *Cons* | Price and DBMS administration overhead. Initial data loading is easy but time-consuming. | Can be slow and hard to update, lacks real DBMS backbone. More than a few simultaneous users impairs performance. |
| *Recommendations* | Use ArcSDE for faster performance, no size limits, and for more than a few simultaneous users reading the database. | Personal geodatabases are simpler to use. Use personal geodatabases for small and moderately sized raster datasets. They are recommended for prototyping. |

**7**

In an enterprise geodatabase, two factors in your control greatly affect raster data performance: the use of pyramids and compression. You have a range of choices with regard to each of these capabilities, and you may need to consider several factors and the application requirements to make the best use of these choices.

Tiling, indexing, and pyramiding all work together to improve raster data performance. Each time a raster dataset is queried, the spatial index returns only the minimum set of tiles in the most appropriate pyramid level necessary to satisfy the extent and resolution of the query. Compression, which is highly recommended, reduces the amount of data transferred between the client and the server, making it possible to store large (on the order of several terabytes), seamless raster datasets and raster catalogs and serve them quickly to a client for display.

Of the database tasks just mentioned, tiling and indexing are often best left to the default settings. However, pyramids and compression involve factors in your control that should be discussed in more detail.

## Pyramids

Pyramids are reduced resolution representations of your dataset used to improve performance. Pyramids speed up the display of raster data by varying the level of detail in accordance with the extent of data to be viewed. For example, when viewing an entire dataset covering a large area, the level of detail need not be very great. In contrast, the detail must be as finely resolved as possible when zoomed in close to a small area. The database server chooses the most appropriate pyramid level automatically, based on the user's display scale.

Pyramids are created by resampling the original data into a set of lower-resolution representations. When you enable pyramiding for a raster dataset, the main parameter you need to consider is the resampling method to be used. Nearest neighbor should be used for nominal data or raster datasets with colormaps, such as land use or pseudocolor images. Bilinear interpolation or cubic convolution should be used for continuous data, such as satellite imagery or aerial photography.

It is important to prototype to determine the most appropriate resampling technique for your data. Remember that pyramid resampling only affects the display, not the original data.

## Data compression

The primary benefit of compressing your data is to reduce storage space. An added benefit is greatly improved performance because you are transferring fewer packets of data from the server to the client application.

Data compression affects the tiles of raster data before storing them in the geodatabase. The compression can be lossy (JPEG and JPEG 2000), or lossless (LZ77). Lossless compression means that the values of cells in the raster dataset are not changed or lost. The amount of reduction in data size will depend on the type of pixel data; the more homogeneous the image, the higher the compression ratio.

Lossy compression is well suited for background images not intended for analysis. It results in faster data loading and retrieval. Less storage space is needed, since the compression ratios can be 5:1 or 10:1 with JPEG and up to 20:1 with JPEG 2000.

Lossless compression should be chosen for the following reasons:

- The raster datasets are to be used for deriving new data or for visual analysis.

- The required compression is no more than 3:1.

- You want to preserve the information content of the original data.

- Your inputs have already been lossy compressed.

Although enterprise geodatabase storage can accommodate raster data without compression, it is generally recommended. If you are unsure of which to use, at least choose the default of LZ77 (lossless).

# JPEG compression by map scale

*Percentages reflect the target amount of original data preserved by the algorithm.*
*Higher percentages are needed at larger map scales (smaller denominators).*

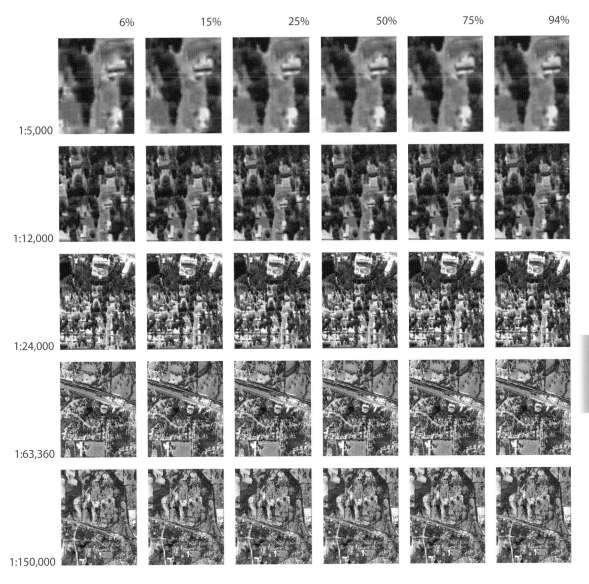

The work flow steps for designing and building a geodatabase of raster data are straight-forward. These seven steps outline a general methodology that can be adapted to a wide variety of projects.

Designing and implementing a GIS using raster data is no different than it would be for any other GIS. The only difference is now you will be using raster data instead of, or in addition to, vector feature data.

## BASIC DESIGN METHODOLOGY

When working with raster data, your work flow could be the following:

### 1. Identify purpose or objective.

Why do you need raster data? How do you wish to use raster data in the GIS? Uses generally fall in either or both of two categories: data for analysis and data for display. For example, raster data for analysis may involve a watershed analysis or terrain analysis, updating some topographic features in other datasets, or updating land cover classes to assess the new location of a housing development. An example of data for display is the common use of orthophotos as a background for a map.

### 2. Identify the data.

If you're looking to extract information from imagery, consider the resolution you require and whether you need one or more spectral bands. You may consider whether the data can come from an aircraft or satellite. If you're going to work with elevation data, you may consider the most appropriate methods for collection, such as LIDAR, contour lines, or radar interferometry. If you intend to create a collection of scanned maps, you need to identify what those maps are, such as scanned documents, CAD drawings, or topographic maps.

### 3. Refine the requirements.

Determine more detailed requirements based on:

- Cost—What are your budget limits? Can you afford the data you want? Is there an alternative within your budget?

- Availability—Does the data already exist? How often is the data updated? Will you receive updates as individual tiles or a single update with complete coverage? Can you receive this data in a timely manner?

- Licenses—Can you share or distribute this data? Can you use this data in multiple projects? What can you do with the information or data derived from the original data? Can you serve this to the public using the Internet?

- Resolution—Will the available level of detail provide the required information?

- Storage—What database or file formats will be used? How large is each file? Will you use pyramids? How much total disk space is needed?

- Extent—Can you cover the area of interest with one raster image, or will you need multiple raster datasets?

- Accuracy—Will the available data resolution provide you with the required spatial accuracy? What is the level of accuracy promoted by the data vendor? How will the data be verified and validated?

- Accessibility and pricing—Is or will the data be accessible on a network? Will you charge fees for usage or downloads? Who will have access to the data? How will you control access and sales?

### 4. Acquire and review data.

This can involve placing orders for the data with a company capable of providing it, scanning the maps you need, or acquiring the source data and building the corresponding raster datasets. It is important that you have a system for checking the quality of the data, whether created in-house or acquired from outside sources. You may have to check for missing data (such as dropped lines or pixels), poorly represented data, or if the data is georeferenced for your area of interest.

## 5. Prepare the data.

Building the database could require the prior extraction or conversion from one data format to another, such as from LIDAR elevation points to a DEM. It could also involve some preprocessing, such as georeferencing or rubbersheeting.

## 6. Design and build the database.

This could involve one of four main choices:

- Building a large, seamless raster dataset (mosaic) from multiple images

- Building a separate, distinct raster dataset from each source image (essentially, each dataset would be accessed independently of the others)

- Building a raster catalog containing all the imagery as multiple rows in one or more tables

- Retaining the data in separate image files

Additional considerations include which compression method to use and whether to use a personal geodatabase or a multiuser geodatabase management system.

You will need to create some level of metadata, depending on your intended distribution and access to the data. For example, what kinds of queries should users expect to use to find your raster data over the Web? If using raster catalogs, you may consider additional catalog fields to allow more extensive querying capabilities.

## 7. Deploy and maintain the geodatabase.

One of the main reasons for going through this entire loading process is to enable many people to use the data for many purposes and projects. This requires administration and management.

In most situations, you will plan on reusing your dataset or database. You will have to plan for updates, modifications, and the ability to build on your initial implementation.

**7**

# CASE STUDIES

Of the many possible applications of raster data, this chapter explores four: orthophotos, digital elevation models, scanned maps, and time series. These are among the most common applications of raster data and are broadly representative of many other cases. A raster database was built for each scenario to illustrate key design alternatives.

## Orthophotos

The TNRIS orthophotos of 1-meter imagery are an enormous asset to the public because they have free Web-based access. Collected since 2000, this orthoimagery is periodically updated, making it an excellent complement to the USGS topographic map series.

## Digital elevation models

The NED is also an excellent complement to the USGS topographic map series. The imagery you will see later in this chapter is derived from the elevation data to show terrain by darkening one side of hills and valleys (called hillshaded relief).

## Scanned maps

The National Geographic Society has been producing beautiful maps of countries and regions across the globe for decades. It has taken on the task of scanning all the USGS topographic maps across the United States.

## Time series

In 1998, Hurricane Mitch hit the mid-Atlantic coast of the United States. Satellites managed by NOAA gathered numerous photos of the hurricane's progress over the Atlantic Ocean and after it hit land. Each image was put into a raster catalog, enabling time series display and analysis from ArcMap.

## CASE STUDY COMPARISONS

The figure below summarizes the parameters by which these case studies are compared and the choices made.

## Compression

Lossy compression was chosen for the Texas orthophotos and the National Geographic scanned maps because these datasets were not intended for detailed visualization and analysis. NED employs lossless compression because it is used by a large user community extensively for terrain analysis. The

| | Raster catalog or dataset? | Mosaic? | Compression | Pyramids | Layer display |
|---|---|---|---|---|---|
| **Orthophotos**<br>**TNRIS** | Catalog | Yes | Lossy (JPEG25) | Cubic | RGB |
| **Elevation model**<br>**USGS NED** | Dataset | Yes | Lossless (LZ77) | Cubic or Bilinear | Hillshaded relief |
| **Scanned maps**<br>**NG TOPO!** | Catalog | Yes | Lossy (JPEG50) | Bilinear | Colormaps |
| **Time series**<br>**NOAA—Hurricane Mitch** | Catalog | No | Lossless (LZ77) | Nearest neighbor | Movie, wire frame off |

Hurricane Mitch data is lossless to improve the visual effect and analytical capabilities.

## Pyramids

The choice of pyramid sampling algorithm for each case study depends mainly on the net effect. Either bilinear interpolation or cubic convolution could be chosen for any of these. But nearest neighbor was chosen for Hurricane Mitch for fastest performance of the timed sequence display.

## Layer display

For orthophotos, each of the RGB values is taken from a particular imagery band, essentially showing three bands at a time.

For elevation data, a stretch renderer or color ramp is commonly used to portray hypsometric colors for different elevation ranges. With geoprocessing, a hillshade dataset can also be generated from the elevation data for displaying shaded relief. This will be discussed in more detail in the NED case study later in the chapter.

Scanned maps are generally rendered in color to look like the hardcopy source from which they are scanned; the Hurricane Mitch movie is achieved through GIS map viewer settings for time sequencing.

The state of Texas manages a strategic GIS database with comprehensive coverage for key topographic map layers. One of the primary layers is a digital color orthophoto base for the entire state at 1-meter resolution. Two primary requirements are to support base mapping for natural resource management and provide public access and download for portions of the database, including the orthophoto layers.

The Texas Natural Resource Information System is a state government division of the Texas Water Development Board. It acts as a clearinghouse for the state's maps, aerial photography, and digital natural resources data. TNRIS has a significant database of raster data, including both digital elevation and color orthophotography. TNRIS needs a way to manage and view these datasets.

The orthophoto dataset contains approximately 17,000 color infrared orthophotos at 1-meter resolution. The original size of this imagery is roughly 2.7 terabytes. TNRIS chose to build a raster catalog of one-quarter degree mosaics (four mosaics per 1-degree cell) for two main reasons: irregular update cycles and the need to preserve the original extent of the USGS 1:24,000 topographic map series.

Orthophoto updates are received by TNRIS at irregular intervals from many organizations, including a number of local governments, counties, and collaborative partnerships. A major partnership was established between TNRIS and USGS for data collection to support *The National Map*. Each organization provides updates according to its own internal data collection timelines. There is no regular, statewide update schedule but, rather, a continuous series of updates for various extents.

Given the variable data update cycles, building a single, large mosaic would require significant update time and management. Also, the base map requirements are based on the existing 1:24,000-scale USGS map sheets. TNRIS specifically chose to receive raster updates in one-quarter degree mosaics (four mosaics per 1-degree cell) that align with the USGS 1:24,000-scale maps.

The TNRIS orthophoto design met the following requirements:

- Frequent updates occur for portions of the state coverage.

- Raster catalog tile extents preserve the desired base map extents.

- Complete images with any overlap areas are preserved.

- All the mosaics can be contained in a central multiuser geodatabase (in SQL Server managed using ArcSDE).

- Each image can be exported separately or as part of a larger area of interest.

- The raster catalog enables query by attribute or location.

Raster
**[Raster catalog in ArcSDE for TNRIS]**

| Field name | Data type | Allow nulls | Default value | Domain | Length | Desc-ription | Spatial reference | Geometry type | Avg Num Pts | Grid 1 | Grid 2 | Grid 3 | Contains z values | Contains m values | Default shape field | Prec-ision | Scale |
|---|---|---|---|---|---|---|---|---|---|---|---|---|---|---|---|---|---|
| NAME | Text | Yes | | | | | | | | | | | | | | | |
| RASTER | Raster | | | | | | NAD 1927 UTM Zone 14N | | | | | | | | | | |
| FOOTPRINT | Geometry | Yes | | | | | NAD 1927 UTM Zone 14N | Polygon | 0 | 536870911.25 | | | No | No | Yes | | |
| OID | Object ID | | | | | | | | | | | | | | | | |
| METADATA | Blob | Yes | | | | | | | | | | | | | | | |
| FOOTPRINT.AREA | Double | No | | | | | | | | | | | | | | 0 | 0 |
| FOOTPRINT.LEN | Double | No | | | | | | | | | | | | | | 0 | 0 |

A prototype geodatabase was developed for testing that contained 3,052 images and totaled 440 GB in a raster catalog. A number of file formats and compressions were tested. Lossy compression was chosen to increase performance and lower the storage requirements. To determine the best level of compression, the prototype raster dataset was compressed at various levels and viewed at different mapping scales. The prototype results were used to create the chart shown earlier in this chapter in the 'Pyramids and data compression' topic.

The target compression level was determined based on the 1-meter data resolution and the intended map scales. Generally, the expected map scales for presentation would not exceed 1:10,000. By viewing the image resolution in the previous chart, it was determined that the JPEG 25 compression was acceptable.

For image pyramid generation, the bilinear interpolation or cubic convolution are the recommended resampling algorithms for continuous data, such as satellite imagery and aerial photography. Although bilinear interpolation is performed more quickly, the results are not as sharp looking as those from cubic convolution. TNRIS chose the cubic convolution resampling method for building its pyramids.

In ArcMap, the rasters can be viewed using a single map layer specification. Because of the large number of raster datasets in the catalog, image viewing is set to display the catalog as a wire frame when more than 10 images appear in the view extent.

*Sample of TNRIS orthophoto imagery*

7

Raster elevation data may be stored and managed within a geodatabase. This type of data can be used for surface elevation display, but it is generally maintained for analysis. Watershed modeling, defining the direction of water flows, determining the grade in a construction project, analyzing a surface for slope and aspect, creating hillshade views, and generating three-dimensional surface views are a few common examples of elevation data use.

An example of an enterprise design to manage elevation in a raster dataset is the National Elevation Dataset produced by the United States Geological Survey.

The NED provides elevation data covering the continental United States, Alaska, Hawaii, and the island territories in a seamless format with a consistent projection, resolution, elevation units, and horizontal and vertical datums. This dataset was mainly built from digital elevation models at a scale of 1:24,000 over the conterminous United States and islands, and 1:63,360 for Alaska. A series of quadrangle-based DEMs were mosaicked into a single, continuous national raster dataset.

The original final resolution of the NED was one arc-second (approximately 30-meter pixels) for the conterminous United States and two arc-seconds (approximately 60-meter pixels) for Alaska. In addition to the standard 30-meter data, the NED is continuously updated with 10-meter and 3-meter sources, gradually migrating the nationwide DEM to these finer resolutions.

As of December 2003, approximately 43 percent of the conterminous United States was available in 10-meter resolution, and a coverage over Puget Sound, Washington, was at 3-meter resolution. See the NED Release Notes for more details (ftp://edcftp.cr.usgs.gov/pub/data/ned/).

Managing the NED as a single raster dataset is a key requirement. The issues that had to be addressed included overlap, compression, and resampling.

## Overlap

DEM data does not overlap. Assembling a continuous raster dataset is much easier.

## Compression

A lossless compression, such as LZ77, is required. A lossless compression technique means that the data size is larger. However, the raster values are better preserved for analysis.

## Resampling type for building pyramids

DEM data is continuous; therefore, cubic convolution should be chosen to build the pyramids because it displays with a smooth, crisp appearance. In certain cases, bilinear interpolation may reveal a smoother appearance, which may be regarded as favorable. However, keep in mind that the primary purpose of DEM data is analysis.

## Further details

Additional details of the NED dataset include:

- The 54,000 quadrangles of DEMs for the United States, including Alaska and Hawaii, are mosaicked into a single raster dataset 60 GB in size, forming one GIS layer.

- An automated system for updating NED is employed to make data corrections that minimize artifacts, perform edgematching, and fill sliver areas with missing data. These are incremental updates to the raster dataset, including pyramids.

- Data is stored in Oracle and accessed using ArcSDE. The NED is served over the Web using ArcIMS®.

- From October 2002 to September 2003, nearly seven terabytes of NED data copies were downloaded over the Web, while a significant fraction of this amount was distributed on physical media.

Another project of a similar nature under way at USGS is the compilation and hosting of the National Land Cover Dataset (NLCD), which distinguishes among vegetation types, built areas, and water areas (http://seamless.usgs.gov).

*NED shaded relief maps available online from the Geography Network*
*for the state of Washington and the central Washington mountains*

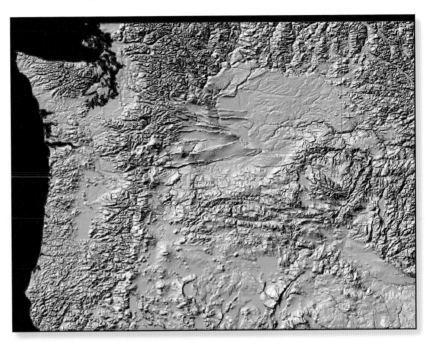

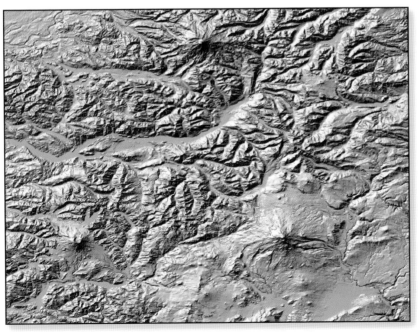

Scanned maps may be stored and managed within ArcGIS as raster data. You may want to scan maps to provide information to create or edit vector data, to add as attribute information for a feature, or to add value to your map as background information. In this chapter, the storage of scanned topographic maps for use as base maps is discussed.

The National Geographic Society scanned all of the 1:24,000 scale USGS topographic maps for the entire United States. This resulted in an enormous number of data files and is distributed as the National Geographic TOPO! series.

The project goal for this case study was to mosaic these maps together for each state and deliver them as a raster catalog of mosaicked images to be used as background for mapping. Because of the size of the mosaics, a raster catalog of mosaicked maps for each state was used to organize all the individual states into a single countrywide database using ArcSDE.

Scanned maps are best used at the scale range for which they were originally created. For example, viewing a 1:24,000 map at a scale of 1:100,000 will not allow you to see clearly all the details on the map or read all of its labels. Also, if viewing this same map at a scale of 1:5,000, it will appear blocky, because zooming in to a larger scale does not allow you to see more detail on the map.

Maps should be scanned at an appropriate resolution. Scanning a map at too high a resolution (for example, 1,000 dpi) may not introduce any more information or resolution, but will result in a much larger dataset. On the other hand, if you scan the map at too low a resolution (such as 72 dpi), then you may not capture all of the information contained on the map clearly and text may not be legible at the target scale.

The original scanned map raster datasets were in a TPS format, and each raster dataset had its own colormap. Not every state and map sheet used the same colormap. Because each mosaicked raster dataset can only have one colormap associated with it, any one chosen colormap would not be appropriate for the complete raster dataset. To solve this dilemma, the raster datasets were converted into 3-band TIFF files using an RGB color scheme. Because of the change in the color scheme, the file sizes increased. For example, after conversion into RGB raster format, a prototype built using 1,000 scanned maps with an original size of approximately 60 GB increased to 100 GB.

The National Geographic TOPO! datasets were also reprojected to a geographic coordinate system (latitude–longitude). Because the original USGS topographic maps were projected to Universal Transverse Mercator (UTM), text symbology did not appear straight, and a seamless image could not be built to cross UTM zones. Using a geographic coordinate system overcomes these two problems. Subsequently, they were converted to geographic latitude–longitude coordinates using the NAD83 datum.

JPEG compression was used to store the raster datasets with a quality setting of 50. It was determined through prototyping that this still provided an adequate level of detail at the intended map scale while reducing the overall raster dataset file size.

Pyramids were chosen to speed up the raster display. Normally, for continuous data, such as this RGB representation, cubic convolution would be the best option. However, in this case, the bilinear interpolation displayed with the highest quality. This is one example of why you should prototype a small portion of your raster dataset before making any permanent decisions.

Details of the raster data in the geodatabase:

- Scanned raster datasets were mosaicked into a single raster dataset for each state. A raster catalog of the entire United States contains all raster datasets, accessed as a single GIS layer.

- JPEG 50 compression was used with bilinear interpolation pyramid resampling.

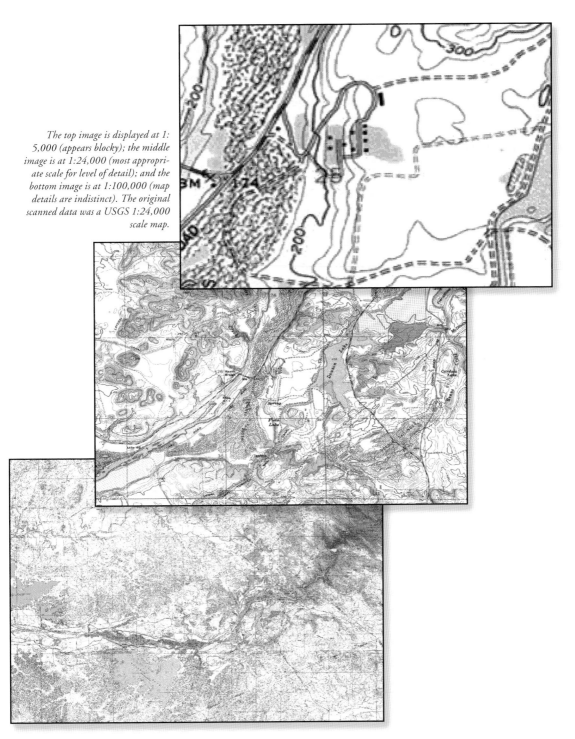

The top image is displayed at 1:5,000 (appears blocky); the middle image is at 1:24,000 (most appropriate scale for level of detail); and the bottom image is at 1:100,000 (map details are indistinct). The original scanned data was a USGS 1:24,000 scale map.

Using a geodatabase raster catalog, you can show a time series of images that can be viewed in sequence as an animation. When creating a time series raster catalog, first be sure that all the images you will place in the raster catalog cover the same spatial area. Second, make sure that the raster datasets are sorted in the raster catalog in the order you want them to be displayed.

A raster catalog can be used to manage a time series of raster datasets. This generally refers to raster data collected as observations at different times at a single location. Examples include collecting satellite imagery over a short period of time to monitor natural disasters, such as flooding or fires, or over longer periods of time to show the patterns of urban sprawl or the changes in a forested area due to cutting and regrowth.

This case study is based on a dataset of satellite imagery captured using a Geostationary Operational Environmental Satellite (GOES), collected over 17 days to capture the movements of Hurricane Mitch in 1998.

NOAA of the U.S. Department of Commerce develops and manages the GOES satellites. GOES was originally designed to monitor the earth's atmosphere and surface over a large region. The first GOES satellite was launched in 1975, and every few years additional GOES satellites have been launched to replace ageing GOES satellites and to provide additional information and coverage. Because GOES satellites are geostationary, each continually collects data over the same area of the earth. This has provided the opportunity to gather continually changing information such as weather system information. GOES can be used to monitor potential severe weather conditions, such as hurricanes and thunder-

storms; estimate rainfall or snowfall; map the movement of sea ice; detect forest fires; and monitor volcano plumes.

This dataset was downloaded from NOAA's National Climatic Data Center (http://cdo.ncdc.noaa.gov/ GOESBrowser/goesbrowser). It includes 33 images, collected at 12:00 AM and PM universal coordinated time (UTC), from October 14, 1998, until October 31, 1998.

Loading this data into a raster catalog to use in ArcGIS was straightforward. By loading each dataset into a raster catalog, the data could be managed together. New datasets can be appended at any time, and the dataset can be viewed as an animation to show the movement of the hurricane over time. A raster catalog can contain data with various extents, spatial resolutions, and data types; therefore, different raster datasets can be added to enhance the present raster dataset.

The LZ77 compression was used to store the raster datasets in the raster catalog because it is a lossless compression. Although this data is not intended for statistical analysis, storage size was not a primary issue, and high image quality was important for display. Nearest neighbor was chosen for pyramid resampling because it makes the best display.

---

**Raster**
**[Raster catalog in ArcSDE for Hurricane Mitch]**

| Field name | Data type | Allow nulls | Default value | Domain | Length | Description | Spatial reference | Geometry type | Avg Num Pts | Grid 1 | Grid 2 | Grid 3 | Contains z values | Contains m values | Default shape field | Precision | Scale |
|---|---|---|---|---|---|---|---|---|---|---|---|---|---|---|---|---|---|
| OBJECTID | Object ID | | | | | | | | | | | | | | | | |
| NAME | Text | Yes | | | 255 | | | | | | | | | | | | |
| METADATA | Blob | Yes | | | 0 | | | | | | | | | | | | |
| DATA_TIME | Date | Yes | | | | | | | | | | | | | | | |
| SHAPE | Geometry | Yes | | | | | GCS WGS 1984 | Polygon | 0 | 2147 | | | No | No | Yes | | |
| RASTER | Raster | | | | | Raster Column | Unknown | | | | | | | | | 0 | 0 |
| SHAPE.AREA | Double | No | | | | | | | | | | | | | | 0 | 0 |
| SHAPE.LEN | Double | No | | | | | | | | | | | | | | 0 | 0 |

Because of the raster dataset sizes (under 2 GB combined), they could have been loaded into a personal geodatabase. Loading data into an ArcSDE geodatabase can take longer than loading data into a personal geodatabase but results in much faster display time.

Displaying the raster catalog as a movie is a simple process. There is a setting in ArcMap on the raster catalog's layer properties dialog box you can specify to automatically display each raster dataset in the raster catalog in a time sequence.

Four case studies highlighted some of the key parameters and decisions to consider for storing and managing small and large amounts of raster data in the geodatabase. The main decisions involve the use of raster catalogs, level of compression, and pyramid methods. There is no single approach that works best in all cases. Prototyping is effective at determining the best approach to use in each case.

## SUMMARY

Raster data is being collected with increasing frequency at greater levels of resolution. Full function geodatabases will be required to manage and use this data. Corresponding improvements in relational database technology support multiuser access to huge datasets over the Internet.

Innovations such as the Geography Network complement desktop GIS tools by allowing GIS users to access and link to data sources from within a map editor without downloading. The example that highlighted this capability was the USGS NED, which allows users to link to a 60 GB nationwide hillshaded relief dataset in Sioux Falls, South Dakota, from within ArcMap.

The National Geographic Society (and a number of other Web-based map generators) have scanned all the topographic quadsheets into a seamless map of the United States.

A timed sequence (movie) of hurricane data showed the capability for GIS to handle raster time series. While this example involved continuous data, it was stored with lossless compression and nearest neighbor pyramid resampling—an approach normally used with discrete data. This approach worked well in this case, providing high-quality visualization with the fastest possible refresh rate for screen display.

One of the key decisions in raster data management involves the use of raster catalogs, essentially a table in which each raster dataset is a record either containing or linking to the actual raster content.

The NED and National Geographic TOPO! both consisted of large mosaics covering the entire extent of their data. However, TNRIS made a raster catalog of mosaics across the entire state of Texas to improve data management. EarthSat, mentioned in the chapter's introduction, even used a raster catalog to speed up the loading time of its 6.5 terabyte global database, which took just 2.5 weeks for the initial database loading. This was done by dividing the complete dataset into

six raster datasets within a single raster catalog and loading the six raster datasets in parallel.

## REFERENCES AND FURTHER READING

Estimating the Size of Your Tables and Indexes: The Raster Data Tables. In *ArcSDE Configuration and Tuning Guide for Oracle*. 2004. Redlands, California: ESRI Press.

Migrating Existing Data to Geodatabase. In *Building a Geodatabase*. 2004. Redlands, California: ESRI Press.

*Raster Data in ArcSDE 9.0*. 2004. White paper, Redlands, California: ESRI Press.

Storing Raster Data. In *ArcSDE Configuration and Tuning Guide for Oracle*. 2004. Redlands, California: ESRI Press.

*Understanding ArcSDE*. 2004. Redlands, California: ESRI Press.

Zeiler, Michael. 1999. Cell-Based Modeling With Rasters. In *Modeling Our World*. Redlands, California: ESRI Press.

## ACKNOWLEDGMENTS

Thanks to all the case study data providers. The TNRIS team included Drew Decker; Marcy Berbrick; Erika Boghici; David Pimentel; Brent Porter; Felicia Retiz; Chris Williams; Ron Pigott of the Texas Water Development Board; Dawn Ortiz of the University of Texas Center for Space Research; and Michael Ouimet of the Texas Department of Information Resources in Austin, Texas. Support from the National Geographic Society included R.J. Kern and Matthew Heller. Thanks to Axel Graumann of the NOAA National Climatic Data Center for the Hurricane Mitch data and to Sara Jean Paulson, Susan Greenlee, Dean Gesch, and David Greenlee of the USGS Earth Resources Observation Systems (EROS) Data Center for helping with the National Elevation Dataset. Jason Willison and Melanie Harlow of ESRI contributed content to this chapter.

## FURTHER RESOURCES

The USGS maintains a seamless server for distribution of *The National Map* data at http://seamless.usgs.gov/. This provides access to NED, NLCD, SRTM data, and high-resolution urban area orthoimagery.

Visit http://www.tnris.state.tx.us for more information about TNRIS and http://maps.nationalgeographic.com/topo/ for access to the National Geographic TOPO! Web site. NOAA's main Web site is http://www.noaa.gov/.

7

*Base maps require a data model that supports the generation of high-quality digital cartographic products with varying levels of detail for a desired range of map scales. Base maps provide a framework for GIS data use and analysis, and commonly used GIS data from many domains may be combined with cartographic attributes to build the base map. This chapter presents a case study for a topographic base map at 1:24,000 scale, building on work in progress at TNRIS, based in Austin, Texas.*

8

In 1884, John Wesley Powell, director of the USGS, envisioned the first National Map of the United States. It was to cover densely populated areas at a scale of 1:62,500 (15-minute quad), important mining districts at 1:125,000, and other terrain at 1:250,000. It was to include several types of information that are still today considered base map layers: transportation, hydrography, place names, boundaries, and elevation. Expected to take 24 years, the map wasn't completed until 1990.

Certainly, you would expect that cartographic methods and standards have evolved considerably since 1884. With the growth and use of GIS in the past decade, cartographic technology and methods have changed even more. GIS-based cartography is now an important GIS application, and it is increasingly possible and appropriate for GIS professionals to adapt cartographic compilation methods for use in their GIS data automation tasks. Most GIS users want to provide high-quality interactive maps in their GIS.

This chapter has several objectives. The first objective is to describe the essential content of a base map within the context of a GIS and in support of the USGS National Map vision. Although there are many kinds of base maps, this chapter focuses on a topographic map because this is possibly the most complex and inclusive type of base map, the superset of most others that might be constructed.

The second objective is to demonstrate how high-quality cartographic capabilities can be added to any existing GIS data model. GIS techniques that support high-quality cartography are presented throughout the chapter.

The third objective is to present a design for managing a complex feature classification and descriptive system, a key issue for national mapping agencies. Project and feature-level metadata for source tracking will also be discussed.

At the end of this chapter, you can read about the application of this cartographic data model at TNRIS. This case study presents several interesting design choices that simplify some map layers to streamline the data compilation work for cartographic needs.

# Cartography
# and the base map

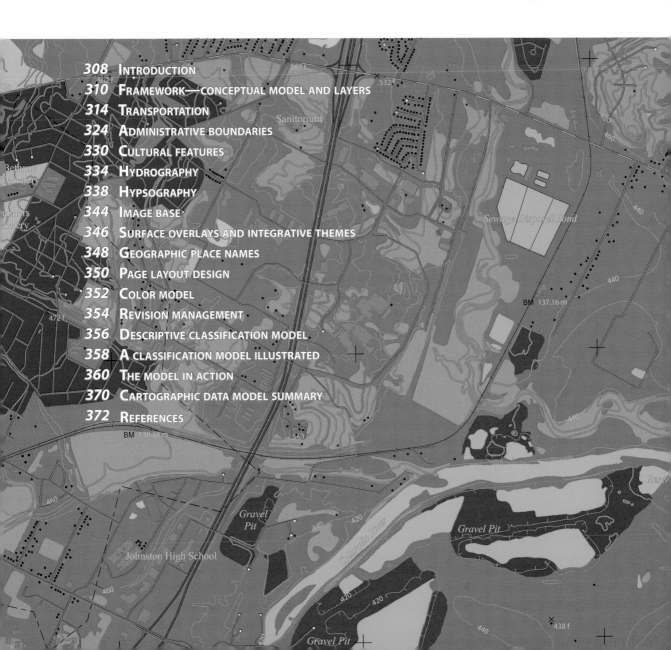

Base maps serve multiple purposes. As a purely cartographic product, such as reference maps, they provide a spatial reference framework for the reader to locate and identify objects in the surrounding terrain. Within a GIS, the base map layers provide a reference framework for a number of critical feature and raster layers used in GIS applications and support advanced cartographic symbols and label text.

Base maps are used for a wide range of activities, including infrastructure planning and management, demographic analysis, and outdoor recreation. The cartographic representations contained in base maps can be derived from the same multipurpose thematic layer designs used for traditional GIS as described throughout this book.

One way to think about base maps is that they are a potential application you can add to your GIS by extending your data model in specific ways to support advanced cartographic representations.

### Extending base maps with GIS

Traditionally, base maps have been purely cartographic products. The earliest base maps portrayed roads, railways, canals, structures, other landmarks, and boundaries against a backdrop of vegetation, rivers, lakes, elevation points, and contour lines. GIS first emerged as a tool for thematic geographic analysis, but often fell short in meeting the demanding specifications for creating finished cartographic products. However, GIS has changed.

Using current GIS technology, common spatial representations can be used for both advanced cartographic display and GIS analysis. For example, local roads are represented as lines at 1:24,000; lakes as polygons; and so on. Traditional GIS data models for these layers can be extended with symbol and label attributes to become a cartographic data model as well.

Extending any traditional GIS data model enables the data to be used effectively for thematic and other GIS analysis, as well as high-quality cartographic map products. The GIS provides numerous useful tools for editing and managing the integrity of multipurpose data used in topographic mapping.

The methods described in this chapter are meant to build on many of the data models presented in this book by adding specifications for map layers, symbols, and layer properties, as well as properties for map elements and the page layout

for a topographic map series. Each section focuses on the cartographic extensions that could be reasonably applied to any geodatabase schema that contains the proper geographic representations for features, such as streams, lakes, contours, and roads. You'll find more discussion on map layers and cartographic symbols than on features and table structures.

### Common themes

Some of the commonly used layers in topographic base maps include:

- Geographic names
- Transportation (roads, railroads, airports)
- Boundaries (state, county)
- Hydrography (rivers, streams, lakes)
- Land cover (vegetation)
- Cultural features (regional centers, urban areas)
- Elevation (contours, spot elevations, DEMs)
- Orthoimagery
- Landsat 7 satellite imagery

This list may vary from state to state and across nations. For example, TNRIS does not include land cover and groups geographic names with cultural points in its base map in a different manner from the USGS National Map specification. In any case, these are the themes to be discussed throughout this chapter.

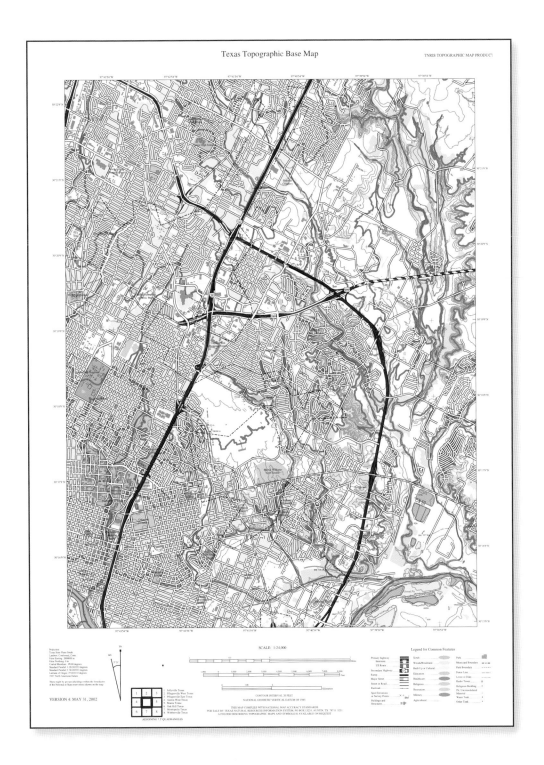

Texas Topographic Base Map

TNRIS TOPOGRAPHIC MAP PRODUCT

SCALE: 1:24,000

CONTOUR INTERVAL 20 FEET
NATIONAL GEODETIC VERTICAL DATUM OF 1983

Legend for Common Features

VERSION 4: MAY 31, 2002

THIS MAP COMPLIES WITH NATIONAL MAP ACCURACY STANDARDS
FOR SALE BY TEXAS NATURAL RESOURCES INFORMATION SYSTEM, PO BOX 13231, AUSTIN, TX 78711-3231
A FOLDER DESCRIBING TOPOGRAPHIC MAPS AND SYMBOLS IS AVAILABLE ON REQUEST

ADJOINING 7.5' QUADRANGLES

8

For governments trying to improve the quality and currency of their maps while reducing duplication of effort across departments and agencies, base maps are strategic products in their own right. Bringing together all the layers shown here requires an integrative approach within each state. This is intended as a representative model that is expected to vary somewhat across local and state agencies.

The conceptual model is organized around the base map thematic layers described here. Many of these themes appear in other chapters of this book, which contain more detailed models. Content from this data model may be integrated with these other models, and vice versa.

## Transportation

This includes roads, railroads, transportation infrastructure, and cartographic features. A sophisticated theme may include transportation networks for route finding; however, this data model is focused on identification of transportation features for cartographic purposes. TNRIS obtained most of this data from the Texas Department of Transportation (TxDOT) and from the USGS geographic names information system (GNIS).

## Boundaries

Boundaries include administrative areas, such as municipal and other legal jurisdictions. This could include census boundaries, if the data is available (see Chapter 3, 'Census units and boundaries').

## Cultural

This theme includes any cultural features not already in other themes, such as hospitals, schools, museums, and other significant buildings or landmarks.

## Hydrography

Hydrography includes surface water and features for managing water, such as rivers, lakes, canals, wells, and water treatment plants (see Chapter 2, 'Streams and river networks').

## Hypsography

Hypsography includes elevation points, contour lines, TINs, DEMs, and shaded relief based on the DEMs.

## Surface overlays

This theme could have any number of different features, depending on the purposes for the map. Examples include land cover (vegetation), soil type, and surface geology. These could come from many sources, including advanced very high resolution radiometer (AVHHR) used by NOAA. The Natural Resources Conservation Service (NRCS) provides county-level soil surveys over most or all the United States.

## Image base

Useful for either the map background or ground reference, this might include satellite and orthophotos; scanned maps, such as USGS digital raster graphs (DRG); and other thematic images (see Chapter 7, 'Using raster data').

## Reference

Primarily intended for cartographic support for location finding, this data includes map grids or graticules and other labeled tics at the map's edge.

## Page layout design

The elements of a cartographic product might include a North arrow, a legend, source attribution, inset or locator maps, and so on.

## CROSS-CUTTING THEMES

Labels and other annotation are part of almost all the above themes. Since annotation of, for example, river names might be handled differently for cartographic purposes than annotation of administrative areas, it is expected that each feature class may have corresponding annotation classes.

Place names are also important across many themes. This chapter presents a simple approach for a comprehensive names table. A more elaborate approach is discussed in Chapter 4, 'Addresses and locations'.

Similarly, revision information is often desired for features in various themes. This can be designed to keep track of when, why, and by whom various data was modified. One design for revision tracking is provided in this chapter.

**Reference**

| | |
|---|---|
| Layer | **Reference** |
| Map use | Location finding |
| Data source | USGS, ArcMap graticules, and PLSS |
| Representation | Map grids, labeled tics at map edge |
| Spatial relationships | Continuous data for the United States where it applies |
| Map scale and accuracy | Acceptable for 1:10,000 through 1:2,000,000-scale products |
| Symbology and annotation | Organizational standard for text sizes, tics, and lines |

| | |
|---|---|
| Layer | **Transportation** |
| Map use | Represents how goods and people move between destinations. |
| Data source | TxDOT, USGS, GNIS. |
| Representation | Routes, infrastructure, cartographic representations, and annotation. |
| Spatial relationships | At least one node of road segments must connect to another road. |
| Map scale and accuracy | Acceptable for 1:10,000 through 1:30,000-scale products. |
| Symbology and annotation | Organizational standard based on USGS 1:24,000-scale products. |

| | |
|---|---|
| Layer | **Cultural** |
| Map use | Represents cultural features and landmarks |
| Data source | USGS, GNIS |
| Representation | Points, lines, areas, and annotation |
| Spatial relationships | None |
| Map scale and accuracy | Acceptable for 1:10,000 through 1:30,000-scale products |
| Symbology and annotation | Organizational standard based on USGS 1:24,000-scale products |

| | |
|---|---|
| Layer | **Boundaries** |
| Map use | Administrative and legal boundaries: parks, military reservations |
| Data source | USGS, Census TIGER files, councils of governments |
| Representation | Lines with areas to support annotation |
| Spatial relationships | None for TNRIS |
| Map scale and accuracy | Acceptable for 1:10,000 through 1:30,000-scale products |
| Symbology and annotation | Organizational standard based on USGS 1:24,000-scale products |

| | |
|---|---|
| Layer | **Hydrography** |
| Map use | Surface water and features for moving, storing, and managing water |
| Data source | USGS, GNIS |
| Representation | Points, lines, and areas |
| Spatial relationships | None for TNRIS |
| Map scale and accuracy | Acceptable for 1:10,000 through 1:50,000-scale products |
| Symbology and annotation | Organizational standard based on USGS 1:24,000-scale products |

| | |
|---|---|
| Layer | **Hypsography** |
| Map use | Represents terrain |
| Data source | USGS |
| Representation | Elevation points, contour lines, TINs, DEMs, and hillshades |
| Spatial relationships | Contour lines are only connected to other lines of the same elevation |
| Map scale and accuracy | Acceptable for 1:10,000 through 1:50,000-scale products |
| Symbology and annotation | Organizational standard based on USGS 1:24,000-scale product |

| | |
|---|---|
| Layer | **Surface overlays** |
| Map use | Other useful themes, such as land cover, land use, and soils. |
| Data source | Potentially many, including USGS, NRCS, AVHHR, and local sources. |
| Representation | Areas and rasters. |
| Spatial relationships | Different types do not overlap. |
| Map scale and accuracy | Acceptable for 1:10,000 through 1:50,000-scale products. |
| Symbology and annotation | Organizational standard based on USGS 1:24,000-scale products. |

| | |
|---|---|
| Layer | **Image base** |
| Map use | Map background and reference. |
| Data source | Aerial photos, satellite imagery, USGS DRGs, other historical images. |
| Representation | Raster. |
| Spatial relationships | Pixels cover the image area. |
| Map scale and accuracy | Pixel size is 1 to 2.5 meters; useful for products of 1:4,000 to 1:65,000. |
| Symbology and annotation | Color or grayscale. |

| | |
|---|---|
| Layer | **Page layout design** |
| Map use | Map collar, data use, and color specification |
| Data source | ArcMap template and style maintained at organizational level |
| Representation | Map template and style for every product variation |
| Spatial relationships | None |
| Map scale and accuracy | 1:24,000 |
| Symbology and annotation | Organizational standard based on USGS 1:24,000-scale map products |

8

The major data elements for creating and maintaining the topographic base map are shown in this diagram. A key aspect of this data model is organizing the data for cartography. Multiple map layers can use data from a single feature class, and a given map layer can use data from more than one feature class or table. While the details of these feature classes, tables, and map layers may vary among data providers, the broad groupings are likely to be consistent.

These diagrams summarize the most important feature classes and tables used to implement the conceptual model shown previously. An important element of the cartographic data model is captured in the layer definitions (yellow boxes) shown here. In the rest of the case studies, there was no attempt to capture specifications for cartographic representations as part of each data model. However, the map layers play an important role in most GIS applications.

## Boundaries

This dataset contains administrative boundaries for government, military, and legal jurisdictions, together with their cartographic place names as annotation. A topology is created for the boundary feature classes to ensure coincidence and tessellation as appropriate.

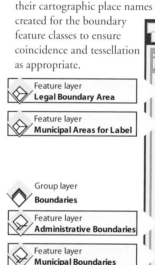

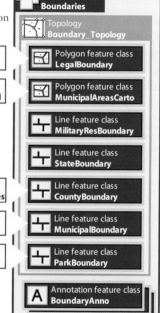

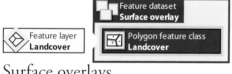

## Surface overlays

This dataset typically contains vegetation or land cover layers if vector features are used. A topology created with this feature class can be used to help construct a clean dataset without overlapping polygons. If raster data is used, colors can be used to symbolize the pixels.

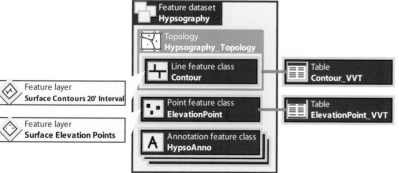

## Hypsography

The hypsography dataset contains spot elevation points, contour lines, and their annotation (elevation values). A topology is created for contours to ensure nonintersection. When contours are derived from a DEM, such a topology is not necessary.

## Transportation

The transportation dataset contains the road and railway classes appropriate to 1:24,000 scale. Infrastructure contains airports, depots, customs facilities, and other related features. A topology is shown for road, ramp, and highway classes only but may be extended to include railroads.

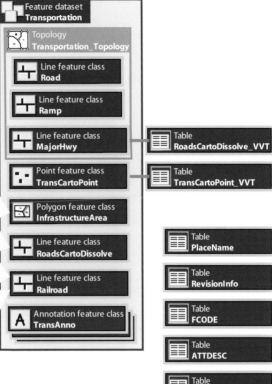

## Reference

This reference dataset contains an index to the USGS 1:24,000-scale topographic map quad sheets. Other grids may be included according to users' needs.

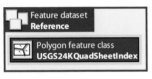

## Hydrography

Hydrography points model springs and wells; lines model streams and shorelines; and areas model lakes and other water bodies.

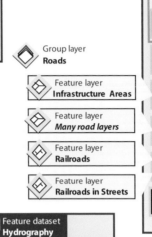

## Tables

The nonspatial tables shown here are used to hold place names, revision tracking information, and to support construction of valid feature descriptions. VVTs are described later in this chapter.

## Cultural

Cultural points model landmarks, lines model specific boundaries, and areas model land use zones. A topology is used to ensure coincidence of adjacent feature boundaries. Annotation features are used to display the place names for each type of feature.

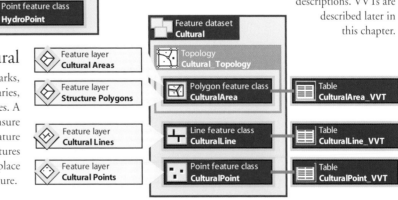

8

The road network is one of the most important feature layers on a base map. In this data model, transportation consists mainly of road centerline data and cartographic cues. At a scale of 1:24,000, essentially every road and significant trail are included. Capturing the type and vertical level of each road segment permits sophisticated and accurate cartographic rendering of complex interchanges. Labeling can be simple and effective. Topology can be used to help manage the integrity of the road network.

Transportation data is important for urban and regional planning, disaster preparedness, service delivery, emergency 911 (E-911) response planning, zoning, and general map reference.

A topographic base map typically shows the complete road and rail network based on centerline data. The type of each road or rail feature determines its symbology. This data model serves not only to distinguish the symbology of different road types but also to support a set of topological rules for ensuring the spatial integrity of the road network.

Because this chapter deals extensively with cartography, both feature classes and map layers are shown in relation to each other. It is the layers that determine the cartographic appearance of a map.

The logical data model for the transportation portion of the topographic base map data model includes:

- Schema definitions

- Classification of road and railroad types

- Map layers used to represent different elevation levels, such as for complex overpasses

- Symbology and labeling of roads and railroads for high-quality cartographic rendering

- Use of topology to ensure data quality

In addition, you will find a number of practical tips for improving the cartographic quality of transportation features on a base map.

## SCHEMA OF ROAD FEATURE CLASSES

The three feature classes on the next page are used to hold dozens of road types. The main distinction between MajorHwys and Roads is that MajorHwys are for restricted access roads, which connect to other MajorHwys and Roads via Ramps.

Notice the Type and OverpassLevel fields in each of these classes; they will be used to support multiple map layers for cartographic rendering.

The fourth feature class, TransJunctions, may be created as an artifact of the topological network for roads and railroads. These point features are useful for locating breaks in road features during routine editing and ensuring proper connectivity between MajorHwys, Ramps, and Roads.

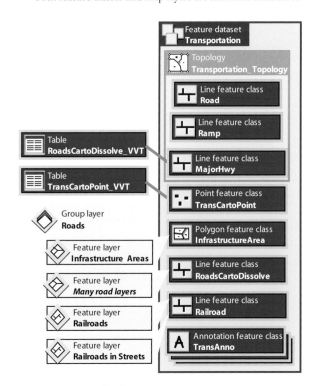

*Restricted access highways*

## Simple feature class
### MajorHwy

| | Geometry | | Polyline |
|---|---|---|---|
| | Contains M values | | No |
| | Contains Z values | | No |

| Field name | Data type | Allow nulls | Default value | Domain | Prec-ision | Scale | Length |
|---|---|---|---|---|---|---|---|
| OBJECTID | Object ID | | | | | | |
| Shape | Geometry | Yes | | | | | |
| TYPE | Long integer | Yes | | | 0 | | |
| TRANSID | Long integer | Yes | | | 0 | 0 | |
| SOURCE | Long integer | Yes | | | 0 | 0 | |
| OverpassLevel | Long integer | Yes | 0 | | 0 | | |
| Enabled | Short integer | Yes | 1 | EnabledDomain | 0 | | |
| Shape_Length | Double | Yes | | | 0 | 0 | |

Type of highway
Permanent unique identifier
Basis for a join to the RevisionInfo table
Road level for drawing order

*Ramps*

## Simple feature class
### Ramp

| | Geometry | | Polyline |
|---|---|---|---|
| | Contains M values | | No |
| | Contains Z values | | No |

| Field name | Data type | Allow nulls | Default value | Domain | Prec-ision | Scale | Length |
|---|---|---|---|---|---|---|---|
| OBJECTID | Object ID | | | | | | |
| Shape | Geometry | Yes | | | | | |
| TYPE | Long integer | Yes | 900 | | 0 | | |
| TRANSID | Long integer | Yes | | | 0 | 0 | |
| SOURCE | Long integer | Yes | | | 0 | 0 | |
| OverpassLevel | Long integer | Yes | 0 | | 0 | | |
| Enabled | Short integer | Yes | 1 | EnabledDomain | 0 | | |
| Shape_Length | Double | Yes | | | 0 | 0 | |

Type of ramp
Permanent unique identifier
Basis for a join to the RevisionInfo table
Road level for drawing order

*Road and street features*

## Simple feature class
### Road

| | Geometry | | Polyline |
|---|---|---|---|
| | Contains M values | | No |
| | Contains Z values | | No |

| Field name | Data type | Allow nulls | Default value | Domain | Prec-ision | Scale | Length |
|---|---|---|---|---|---|---|---|
| OBJECTID | Object ID | | | | | | |
| Shape | Geometry | Yes | | | | | |
| TYPE | Long integer | Yes | 904 | | 0 | | |
| CLASS | Long integer | Yes | | | 0 | | |
| TRANSID | Long integer | Yes | | | 0 | 0 | |
| SOURCE | Long integer | Yes | | | 0 | 0 | |
| OverpassLevel | Long integer | Yes | 0 | | 0 | | |
| Enabled | Short integer | Yes | 1 | EnabledDomain | 0 | | |
| Shape_Length | Double | Yes | | | 0 | 0 | |

Type of road or street (for symbology)
Class of road feature (for labeling)
Permanent unique identifier
Basis for a join to the RevisionInfo table
Road level for drawing order

*Produced by the geometric network*
*and used to ensure only ramp features*
*connect to restricted access highways*

## Simple feature class
### TransJunction

| | Geometry | | Point |
|---|---|---|---|
| | Contains M values | | No |
| | Contains Z values | | No |

| Field name | Data type | Allow nulls | Default value | Domain | Prec-ision | Scale | Length |
|---|---|---|---|---|---|---|---|
| OBJECTID_1 | Object ID | | | | | | |
| Shape | Geometry | Yes | | | | | |
| OBJECTID | Long integer | Yes | | | 0 | | |
| Enabled | Short integer | Yes | | | 0 | | |

**8**

The schema and layer definitions to support cartographic rendering of roads are presented here. This involves the creation of several additional feature classes whose data is derived from the other transportation feature classes. Although these additional feature classes may seem like overhead, this approach helps support high-quality road symbols and enforce independence of road data from its cartographic representation, which leads to more robust and adaptive databases and applications.

Roads can take on many classifications. This data model uses a domain table that identifies 74 types of U.S. roads, spread across five major categories. These categories have different names in most countries, but generally follow a similar pattern.

At the scale of 1:24,000 for which this data model is intended, cul-de-sacs (usually a rounded termination on a local street) are represented by a point feature class, Trans-CartoPoints, with a corresponding layer called Cul De Sacs having the symbol shown below.

All other street classifications are organized for cartographic purposes in a line feature class called RoadsCartoDissolve. This class contains all the features merged from the Roads, MajorHwys, and Ramps feature classes. While the separate feature classes are important for data maintenance, such as to take advantage of topology tools, the RoadsCartoDissolve feature class is most useful and efficient for rendering and labeling the road network for a cartographic product.

The field VVT_ID is the attribute identifier that holds the classification for each of the 74 types of roads in the RoadsCartoDissolve feature class. This is the primary key of a related table, RoadsCartoDissolve_VVT, which holds a detailed definition of each road type. A more detailed description of the VVT approach is discussed near the end of this chapter.

In addition to road classification, the vertical level of each road segment helps determine its symbology. In this data model, the attribute OverpassLevel is placed on each transportation class. Each road segment then takes on a positive or negative integer value corresponding to its relative drawing order above or below other road levels. In this way, any number of overpass roads and underpass tunnels can be accurately rendered. When copying the data to the Roads-CartoDissolve class, the OverpassLevel values are placed in the Level_ field.

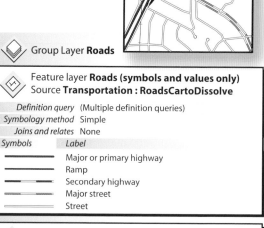

Group Layer **Roads**

Feature layer **Roads (symbols and values only)**
Source **Transportation : RoadsCartoDissolve**

| | |
|---|---|
| *Definition query* | (Multiple definition queries) |
| *Symbology method* | Simple |
| *Joins and relates* | None |
| *Symbols* | *Label* |

| | |
|---|---|
| ――――― | Major or primary highway |
| ――――― | Ramp |
| ――――― | Secondary highway |
| ――――― | Major street |
| ――――― | Street |

Feature layer **Cul De Sacs (symbols and values only)**
Source **Transportation : TransCartoPoint**

| | |
|---|---|
| *Definition query* | None |
| *Symbology method* | Simple |
| *Joins and relates* | None |
| *Symbol* | ○ |

## Coded value domain
## Roads

| | |
|---|---|
| Field type | Double |
| Split policy | Default value |
| Merge policy | Default value |

| Code | Description | Code | Description | Code | Description |
|---|---|---|---|---|---|
| 0 | Restricted Access Highway, Interstate | 23 | Street, Ranch to Market Spur | 49 | Secondary Highway, State Route |
| 1 | Restricted Access Highway, US Route | 24 | Street, Ranch Road Spur | 50 | Secondary Highway, State Route Alternate |
| 2 | Restricted Access Highway, Off State Business Route | 25 | Street, US Route Alternate | 51 | Secondary Highway, State Route Loop |
| 3 | Restricted Access Highway, US Route Alternate | 26 | Street, Recreational Road Spur | 52 | Secondary Highway, State Route Spur |
| 4 | Restricted Access Highway, US Route Spur | 27 | Street, Principal Arterial | 53 | Secondary Highway, Off Interstate Business Route |
| 5 | Restricted Access Highway, State Route | 28 | Street, County Road (CR Networks) | 54 | Secondary Highway, Off US Business Route |
| 6 | Restricted Access Highway, State Route Alternate | 29 | Street, City Street (City Networks) | 55 | Major Street, US Route |
| 7 | Restricted Access Highway, State Route Loop | 30 | Street, Frontage | 56 | Major Street, Off State Business Route |
| 8 | Restricted Access Highway, State Route Spur | 31 | Street, Service | 57 | Major Street, Off Farm or Ranch Business Route |
| 9 | Restricted Access Highway, Off Interstate Business Route | 32 | Street, Access | 58 | Major Street, Farm to Market |
| 10 | Restricted Access Highway, Off US Business Route | 33 | Street, US Route Spur | 59 | Major Street, Ranch to Market |
| 11 | Ramp | 34 | Street, State Route | 60 | Major Street, Ranch Road |
| 12 | Ramp, Collector | 35 | Street, State Route Alternate | 61 | Major Street, Farm to Market Spur |
| 13 | Ramp, Turnaround | 36 | Street, State Route Loop | 62 | Major Street, Ranch to Market Spur |
| 14 | Street, US Route | 37 | Street, State Route Spur | 63 | Major Street, Ranch Road Spur |
| 15 | Street, Off State Business Route | 38 | Street, Off Interstate Business Route | 64 | Major Street, US Route Alternate |
| 16 | Street, Off Farm or Ranch Business Route | 39 | Street, Off Interstate Business Route | 65 | Major Street, Principal Arterial |
| 17 | Street, Farm to Market | 40 | Trail, Jeep | 66 | Major Street, County Road (CR Networks) |
| 18 | Street, Ranch to Market | 41 | Trail, Motocross | 67 | Major Street, City Street (City Networks) |
| 19 | Street, Ranch Road | 42 | Trail, Bicycle | 68 | Major Street, US Route Spur |
| 20 | Street, Park Road | 43 | Trail, Hiking | 69 | Major Street, State Route |
| 21 | Street, Recreational Road | 44 | Trail, Footpath | 70 | Major Street, State Route Alternate |
| 22 | Street, Farm to Market Spur | 45 | Secondary Highway, US Route | 71 | Major Street, State Route Loop |
| | | 46 | Secondary Highway, Off State Business Route | 72 | Major Street, State Route Spur |
| | | 47 | Secondary Highway, US Route Alternate | 73 | Major Street, Off Interstate Business Route |
| | | 48 | Secondary Highway, US Route Spur | 74 | Major Street, Off US Business Route |

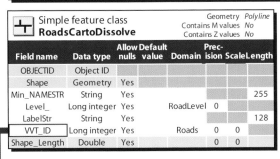

## Simple feature class
## RoadsCartoDissolve

| | |
|---|---|
| Geometry | Polyline |
| Contains M values | No |
| Contains Z values | No |

| Field name | Data type | Allow nulls | Default value | Domain | Precision | Scale | Length |
|---|---|---|---|---|---|---|---|
| OBJECTID | Object ID | | | | | | |
| Shape | Geometry | Yes | | | | | |
| Min_NAMESTR | String | Yes | | | | | 255 |
| Level_ | Long integer | Yes | | RoadLevel | 0 | | |
| LabelStr | String | Yes | | | | | 128 |
| VVT_ID | Long integer | Yes | | Roads | 0 | 0 | |
| Shape_Length | Double | Yes | | | 0 | 0 | |

*Lines that are dissolved from the roads, ramps, and major highways based on VVT_ID and Name attributes to support rapid map rendering and labeling*

Name of point feature
Drawing level of point feature
Label string
Feature type key

## Table
## RoadsCartoDissolve_VVT

| Field name | Data type | Allow nulls | Precision | Scale | Length |
|---|---|---|---|---|---|
| OBJECTID | Object ID | | | | |
| VVTID | Long integer | Yes | 0 | | |
| FCODE | Long integer | Yes | 0 | | |
| ACODES | String | Yes | | | 254 |
| DESCRIPTIO | String | Yes | | | 254 |

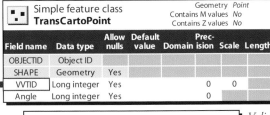

## Simple feature class
## TransCartoPoint

| | |
|---|---|
| Geometry | Point |
| Contains M values | No |
| Contains Z values | No |

| Field name | Data type | Allow nulls | Default value | Domain | Precision | Scale | Length |
|---|---|---|---|---|---|---|---|
| OBJECTID | Object ID | | | | | | |
| SHAPE | Geometry | Yes | | | | | |
| VVTID | Long integer | Yes | | | 0 | 0 | |
| Angle | Long integer | Yes | | | 0 | | |

*Point features that support high-quality cartography, such as cul-de-sacs*

Type of feature, defined in a valid value table
Display angle

## Table
## TransCartoPoint_VVT

| Field name | Data type | Allow nulls | Precision | Scale | Length |
|---|---|---|---|---|---|
| OBJECTID | Object ID | | | | |
| VVTID | Long integer | Yes | 0 | 0 | |
| FCODE | Long integer | Yes | 0 | | |
| ACODES | String | Yes | | | 254 |
| DESCRIPTIO | String | Yes | | | 254 |

*Valid values for the TransCartoPoints feature class*

Unique ID within valid value domain
Feature type name
List of attribute names and associated values valid for this feature type
Description for this kind of feature

## Coded value domain
## RoadLevel

| | |
|---|---|
| Description | Overpass level |
| Field type | Long integer |
| Split policy | Default value |
| Merge policy | Default value |

| Code | Description |
|---|---|
| 0 | Ground Level |
| -2 | Tunnel 2 Levels Down |
| -1 | Tunnel 1 Level Down |
| 1 | Overpass 1 Level Up |
| 2 | Overpass 2 Levels Up |
| 3 | Overpass 3 Levels Up |
| 4 | Overpass 4 Levels Up |
| 5 | Overpass 5 Levels Up |
| 6 | Overpass 6 Levels Up |

**8**

It is possible to accurately represent highway overpasses, interchanges, bridges, and so forth, using a combination of road types and levels. These, in turn, are used to control the drawing order of all road segments from bottom (typically ground-level roads) to top (overpasses). This is an example of a complex layer definition used to model and represent road network connectivity.

Two primary design methods are used in transportation layers: drawing cased roads based on linear geometry and representing road structures, such as overpasses, complex highway interchanges, and bridges.

In the map on the right, you'll notice that highways are drawn in red with a thin black road casing around them, and city streets are white with a thin black road casing. This effect is achieved by drawing each road twice—initially with a black road casing that is slightly thicker than the red or white interior line used to "fill" the interior space.

You'll also notice that this map accurately depicts how roads are stacked on one another at their crossings. Roads that pass over others are drawn on top. The strategy is to add attributes that describe the road level, which can be used to specify the drawing order that represents the road structures. This can be useful for urban mapping applications.

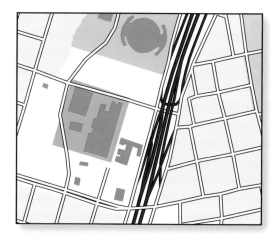

*Road casings and levels can be rendered using linear road features with simple linework and special cartographic attributes.*

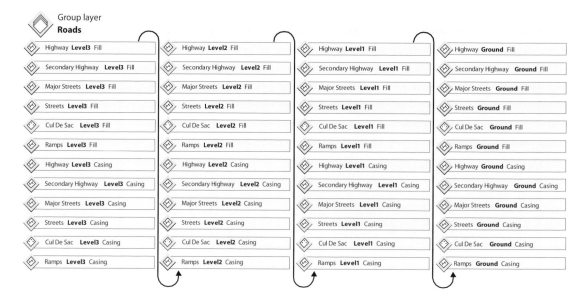

Group layer
**Roads**

| | | | |
|---|---|---|---|
| Highway **Level3** Fill | Highway **Level2** Fill | Highway **Level1** Fill | Highway **Ground** Fill |
| Secondary Highway **Level3** Fill | Secondary Highway **Level2** Fill | Secondary Highway **Level1** Fill | Secondary Highway **Ground** Fill |
| Major Streets **Level3** Fill | Major Streets **Level2** Fill | Major Streets **Level1** Fill | Major Streets **Ground** Fill |
| Streets **Level3** Fill | Streets **Level2** Fill | Streets **Level1** Fill | Streets **Ground** Fill |
| Cul De Sac **Level3** Fill | Cul De Sac **Level2** Fill | Cul De Sac **Level1** Fill | Cul De Sac **Ground** Fill |
| Ramps **Level3** Fill | Ramps **Level2** Fill | Ramps **Level1** Fill | Ramps **Ground** Fill |
| Highway **Level3** Casing | Highway **Level2** Casing | Highway **Level1** Casing | Highway **Ground** Casing |
| Secondary Highway **Level3** Casing | Secondary Highway **Level2** Casing | Secondary Highway **Level1** Casing | Secondary Highway **Ground** Casing |
| Major Streets **Level3** Casing | Major Streets **Level2** Casing | Major Streets **Level1** Casing | Major Streets **Ground** Casing |
| Streets **Level3** Casing | Streets **Level2** Casing | Streets **Level1** Casing | Streets **Ground** Casing |
| Cul De Sac **Level3** Casing | Cul De Sac **Level2** Casing | Cul De Sac **Level1** Casing | Cul De Sac **Ground** Casing |
| Ramps **Level3** Casing | Ramps **Level2** Casing | Ramps **Level1** Casing | Ramps **Ground** Casing |

The order in which these layers are rendered on the map is essential to achieve the proper cartographic result. To draw an overpass correctly, the uppermost road features should be rendered after the lower road features. This requires classification of the initial centerline data, delineating and coding each road element to have the correct OverpassLevel field value. This should also be ground-truthed or photo-verified by knowledgeable local experts.

Once the data has been correctly delineated and coded for overpass levels and copied into the RoadsCartoDissolve class, simple queries can be used to select the appropriate subsets of casing and fill elements in the desired order. For example, the query for a highway overpass is simply "road type 0 to 10 and level = 1," where a road type of 0 to 10 refers to restricted access highways, and a level equal to 1 refers to the first level above ground level.

Finally, there is a priority ranking among the road types at each vertical level. Where a major road crosses a minor road, the symbol for the major road takes precedence. For this reason, all the casing and fill layers are ordered as shown below. Within each column and across the columns from left to right, the layers are shown in stack order. Thus ground fill layers are rendered on top of ground casing layers, level 1 layers are rendered after ground layers, and so on. Still, you may prefer to make some slight variation in this ordering to improve the appearance at a particular type of intersection with your own data.

Notice this approach requires no special programming to achieve the proper cartographic effect. The main effort involved is to edit the highway intersections in sufficient detail that standard queries can distinguish ramps, local streets, and highways at multiple levels. Once all the layers have been defined for your specific types of roadways, the map can be reused as a template simply by pointing the layers to a different database.

Note that a 1:24,000-scale map should have its reference scale set to 1:24,000 (reference scale is a property of the data frame in ArcMap). Since the reference scale affects the size of map elements as you zoom in or out of the map, this is essential to set correctly, particularly if you are editing road levels or annotation.

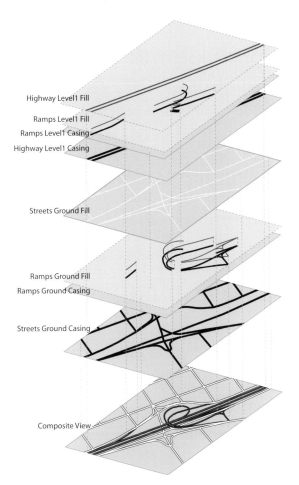

Highway Level1 Fill

Ramps Level1 Fill

Ramps Level1 Casing

Highway Level1 Casing

Streets Ground Fill

Ramps Ground Fill

Ramps Ground Casing

Streets Ground Casing

Composite View

*8*

Different types of highways are distinguished by their iconic shields displaying the highway number, while city streets are labeled with their names. These labels are either centered on or parallel to the road feature. GIS software supports several approaches, such as automatic labeling and the use of annotation feature classes.

## Dynamic labeling

In this example, autolabeling with ArcGIS was used to define and render the correct highway shields or street names on corresponding road features. The figure at right shows the highway symbols, placement, and other parameters defining the "label classes" created for this purpose. For each major category of road used in the data, a representative symbol is chosen to complement the choice of line color and weight used for the line feature. In the case of local streets, the placement option is slightly different from that of highways, since street names are normally offset slightly above the roads they name.

**TIP** The default labeling approach typically places one label (such as a U.S. highway shield) on the map for each highway feature, but often just one such label is not enough. To fix this, users may turn on labeling for both fill and casement layers, then move the second instance of the name down in layer priority so it draws after other important information is placed. More often than not, this results in the second label using white space well away from the first label placement. This can be made to work independently of scale and interactively without external labeling engines such as Maplex.

## Annotation

Some users may wish to go beyond autolabeling to create annotation feature classes for greater flexibility in label placement. The one class shown in the schema overview, TransAnno, is a placeholder for potentially many annotation classes.

Because of the need to handle multiple vertical levels of tunnels and overpasses, the actual set of annotation classes for this case study includes:

- RailroadOwnerAnno
- GroundInterstateAnno
- Overpass1InterstateAnno
- Overpass2InterstateAnno
- GroundUSRouteAnno
- Overpass1USRouteAnno
- Overpass2USRouteAnno
- GroundStateRouteAnno
- Overpass1StateRouteAnno
- Overpass2StateRouteAnno
- GroundCountyRoadAnno
- Overpass1CountyRoadAnno
- Overpass2CountyRoadAnno
- GroundStreetAnno
- Overpass1StreetAnno
- Overpass2StreetAnno

Other annotation classes may also be created, such as for Farm-to-Market (FM) routes, Ranch-to-Market (RM) routes, and Ranch Roads (RR), all common in Texas.

While annotation potentially requires more preparation time than dynamic labeling, it leads to much faster display. This is because the annotation is simply retrieved from the database and placed where intended, while labeling involves dynamic placement calculations every time the map is redrawn. The more text required in your map, the better annotation is likely to perform.

**TIP** There are two ways of making these classes in ArcGIS. The simpler is to build up the label classes, then convert them to annotation classes. The other way is to create each annotation feature class independently and set its parameters directly.

Note that ArcGIS 9 allows the user to create subtypes of annotation classes. Therefore, all of these annotations can be handled with a single annotation class. With this capability, it would make the most sense to have a single annotation class for each feature dataset.

## Annotation feature class

| | |
|---|---|
| **A** | Annotation feature class **TransAnno** |

**Geometry**
Contains M values  *No*
Contains Z values  *No*

| Field name | Data type | Allow nulls | Prec-ision | Scale | Length |
|---|---|---|---|---|---|
| OBJECTID | Object ID | | | | |
| SHAPE | Geometry | Yes | | | |
| FeatureID | Long integer | Yes | 0 | | |
| ZOrder | Long integer | Yes | 0 | | |
| AnnotationClassID | Long integer | Yes | 0 | | |
| Element | Blob | Yes | 0 | 0 | 0 |
| SHAPE_Length | Double | Yes | 0 | 0 | |
| SHAPE_Area | Double | Yes | 0 | 0 | |

---

Text for Layer **Roads (apply to sublayers as needed)**

*Method*  Define classes of labels, each with different properties

*Label Class Name* **Interstate**
Arial, Bold, 8.0 Pts

*SQL Query*  VVT_ID = 0
*Expression*  [PlaceName.LABELSTR]
*Placement*  On the line
 Best placement along the line
 Labels follow the curve of the line = False
 Orientation: Orient to the page
 Angle: Horizontal

*Weights and Rank*  Remove duplicate labels   Label Weight:  High
 Return overlapping labels: True   Feature Weight: None
 Buffer: 0   Rank: 18 of 22

*Label Class Name* **USRoute**
Arial, Bold, 8.0 Pts

*SQL Query*  VVT_ID = 1 OR VVT_ID = 3 OR VVT_ID = 14 OR
 VVT_ID = 45 OR VVT_ID = 55
*Expression*  [PlaceName.LABELSTR]
*Placement*  On the line
 Best placement along the line
 Labels follow the curve of the line = False
 Orientation: Orient to the page
 Angle: Horizontal

*Weights and Rank*  Remove duplicate labels   Label Weight:  High
 Return overlapping labels: True   Feature Weight: None
 Buffer: 0   Rank: 14 of 22

*Label Class Name* **StateRoute**
Arial, Bold, 8.0 Pts

*SQL Query*  VVT_ID=5 OR VVT_ID=34 OR VVT_ID=49 OR VVT_ID=69
*Expression*  [PlaceName.LABELSTR]
*Placement*  On the line
 Best placement along the line
 Labels follow the curve of the line = False
 Orientation: Orient to the page
 Angle: Horizontal

*Weights and Rank*  Remove duplicate labels   Label Weight:  High
 Return overlapping labels: True   Feature Weight: None
 Buffer: 0   Rank: 15 of 22

Street Name
*Label Class Name* **Street**
Times New Roman, Normal, 6.0 Pts

*SQL Query*  (VVT_ID >13 AND VVT_ID < 34) OR
 (VVT_ID > 34 AND VVT_ID < 45) OR
 (VVT_ID > 64 AND VVT_ID < 67)
*Expression*  [PlaceName.LABELSTR]
*Placement*  Above the line
 Best placement along the line
 Labels follow the curve of the line = False
 Orientation: Orient to the page
 Angle: Along the line

*Weights and Rank*  Remove duplicate labels   Label Weight:  High
 Return overlapping labels: True   Feature Weight: None
 Buffer: 0   Rank: 16 of 22

**8**

Railroads are modeled with one feature class and two feature layers. This gives you the flexibility to model a railroad network as well as meet cartographic requirements, such as when railroads follow along streets. Topology rules are defined controlling the overlap of roads and railroads. Infrastructure areas model large facilities, such as airports, at a small scale.

## Railroads

In this data model, there are three types of railroad features: railroads, sidings, and railroads in streets. These are divided into two layer groups so that railroad-in-road features can be rendered after (on top of) street layers, while the regular railroad and siding features are typically rendered before (beneath) street layers.

The most appropriate labeling for railroads in the United States is to place the owner name along each feature, similar in style and placement to street names.

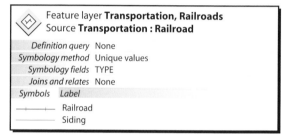

Feature layer **Transportation, Railroads**
Source **Transportation : Railroad**

| | |
|---|---|
| Definition query | None |
| Symbology method | Unique values |
| Symbology fields | TYPE |
| Joins and relates | None |
| Symbols | Label |
| ⊢——⊢ | Railroad |
| ———— | Siding |

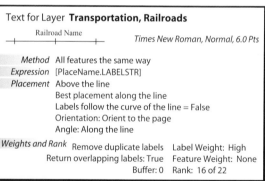

Text for Layer **Transportation, Railroads**

Railroad Name    *Times New Roman, Normal, 6.0 Pts*

| | |
|---|---|
| Method | All features the same way |
| Expression | [PlaceName.LABELSTR] |
| Placement | Above the line |
| | Best placement along the line |
| | Labels follow the curve of the line = False |
| | Orientation: Orient to the page |
| | Angle: Along the line |
| Weights and Rank | Remove duplicate labels    Label Weight: High |
| | Return overlapping labels: True    Feature Weight: None |
| | Buffer: 0    Rank: 16 of 22 |

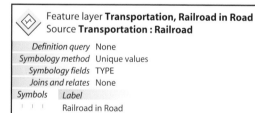

Feature layer **Transportation, Railroad in Road**
Source **Transportation : Railroad**

| | |
|---|---|
| Definition query | None |
| Symbology method | Unique values |
| Symbology fields | TYPE |
| Joins and relates | None |
| Symbols | Label |
| ı  ı  ı | Railroad in Road |

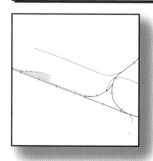

Simple feature class **Railroad**

| | | Geometry | Polyline |
|---|---|---|---|
| | | Contains M values | No |
| | | Contains Z values | No |

| Field name | Data type | Allow nulls | Default value | Domain | Prec-ision | Scale | Length | |
|---|---|---|---|---|---|---|---|---|
| OBJECTID | Object ID | | | | | | | |
| Shape | Geometry | Yes | | | | | | |
| TYPE | Long integer | Yes | 1601 | | 0 | | | Type of railroad line |
| SOURCE | Double | Yes | | | 0 | 0 | | Basis of a join to the RevisionInfo table |
| TransID | Long integer | Yes | | | 0 | | | Permanent unique identifier |
| OwnerName | String | Yes | | | | | 32 | Name of railroad company |
| Shape_Length | Double | Yes | | | 0 | 0 | | |

*Railroad lines*

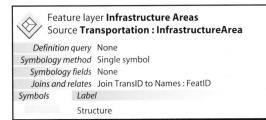

Feature layer **Infrastructure Areas**
Source **Transportation : InfrastructureArea**

| | |
|---|---|
| *Definition query* | None |
| *Symbology method* | Single symbol |
| *Symbology fields* | None |
| *Joins and relates* | Join TransID to Names : FeatID |
| Symbols | *Label* |
| | Structure |

Text for Layer **Infrastructure Areas**

| Area Name | *Times New Roman, Normal, 8.0 Pts* |
|---|---|

| | |
|---|---|
| *Method* | All features the same way |
| *Expression* | [PlaceName.LABELSTR] |
| *Placement* | Remove duplicate labels |
| Weights and Rank | |

| | |
|---|---|
| Return overlapping labels: True | Label Weight: High |
| Buffer: 0 | Feature Weight: None |
| | Rank: 9 of 22 |

Simple feature class
**InfrastructureArea**

Geometry *Polygon*
Contains M values *No*
Contains Z values *No*

| Field name | Data type | Allow nulls | Default value | Domain | Prec- ision | Scale | Length |
|---|---|---|---|---|---|---|---|
| OBJECTID | Object ID | | | | | | |
| Shape | Geometry | Yes | | | | | |
| TYPE | Long integer | Yes | | | 0 | | |
| CLASS | Long integer | Yes | 8500 | | 0 | | |
| SOURCE | Double | Yes | | | 0 | 0 | |
| JURIS | Long integer | Yes | 8012 | | 0 | | |
| TransID | Long integer | Yes | | | 0 | 0 | |
| Shape_Length | Double | Yes | | | 0 | 0 | |
| Shape_Area | Double | Yes | | | 0 | 0 | |

*Large area features that represent transportation infrastructure, such as airports or shipyards.*

Type of feature
Class of feature
Basis of a join to the RevisionInfo table
Agency responsible for a feature
Permanent unique identifier

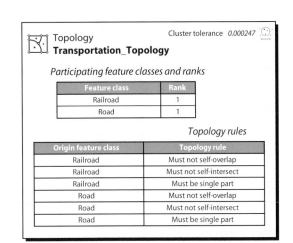

Robert Mueller
Municipal Airport

## Infrastructure

Infrastructure areas are generally large transportation features such as airports or shipyards. Notice these are not outlined; this is to reduce clutter and confusion in the map.

**TIP** As a general rule to reduce clutter, none of the area features in this data model are outlined. The only time outlines are used for area features is when the outlines are linear features themselves, such as city boundaries (more on this in the Administrative Boundaries theme).

## Defining Topology

The goal of topology creation with these three feature classes is to ensure proper connectivity of the road network. The RoadsCartoDissolve feature class in this data model was created to hold all streets, ramps, and highways in a single class, thus simplifying the processes of rendering and labeling for cartographic purposes. However, for data maintenance these three classes are kept distinct from each other to facilitate topological analysis.

The rules shown here are to enforce that any single road feature does not loop back on itself and that there are no internal junctions within a single feature (must be single part). Besides reducing errors in the data, these rules enable more effective generalization of transportation networks (editing the data to produce smaller-scale products).

One of the artifacts of the geometric network creation tools in ArcGIS is the generation of junction features at the intersection of linear features in the topology.

**TIP** The junction features created by the topology are useful in the editing stages of delineating and coding highway ramps and overpasses. You can select these points and specific features by road type and location to help find classification errors (for example, to get only ramps).

Topology
**Transportation_Topology**

Cluster tolerance *0.000247*

*Participating feature classes and ranks*

| Feature class | Rank |
|---|---|
| Railroad | 1 |
| Road | 1 |

*Topology rules*

| Origin feature class | Topology rule |
|---|---|
| Railroad | Must not self-overlap |
| Railroad | Must not self-intersect |
| Railroad | Must be single part |
| Road | Must not self-overlap |
| Road | Must not self-intersect |
| Road | Must be single part |

**8**

Boundaries are used on base maps to distinguish between different kinds of zones, such as cities, counties, state and local parks, and military and tribal reservations. This theme corresponds to Political Boundaries in the Texas base map. This theme could also tie in with census data, for example, to link administrative units with the extensive demographic tables collected by the census.

Administrative jurisdiction boundaries are important in the support of road construction and maintenance, E-911 response planning, services distribution, urban planning, taxation, water and wastewater utilities, and general map production.

Administrative boundaries can represent a broad set of classes. Texas separates administrative areas into two distinct themes: district boundaries (school districts, voting precincts, legislative districts) and political boundaries (municipalities, counties, federal lands, and state and local parks). This base map data model illustrates the political boundaries theme but could easily be extended to include district boundaries as well.

This theme has some overlap with census data, since that theme includes many of the same kinds of boundary classes. Census data is normally considered a separate, distinct theme, partly because it is collected and distributed as a complete package by the U.S. Census Bureau and partly because the locational accuracy of the census data does not always match the accuracy requirements for state and local data sources. However, the ability to link local and regional administrative units with their associated demographic statistics may justify the effort to integrate the data. More discussion of the census data model is found in Chapter 3, 'Census units and boundaries'.

As with some other base map themes, some administrative boundaries tend to change frequently, requiring continual updates from many state and local agencies. This leads to the need for greater integration among these agencies. Each state would benefit from propagating a common model for boundary feature classes to its county and municipal governments.

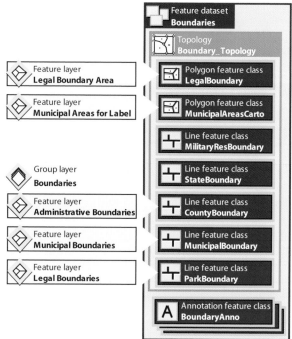

## Defining topology

Some administrative areas can be mosaicked to form a tessellated area covered completely by administrative areas, while others cannot. For areas that tessellate like this, topology can be used to improve map quality.

Notice that most of the administrative feature classes participate in the same topology. These topology rules ensure that counties do not overlap other counties, states do not overlap other states, and linear features on boundaries are coincident with the boundaries of their respective area features.

The Must not have gaps rule can, optionally, be used in cases where you are not sure if you have complete coverage of administrative features.

Topology
**Boundary_Topology**

Cluster tolerance  *0.000247*

*Participating feature classes and ranks*

| Feature class | Rank | Feature class | Rank |
|---|---|---|---|
| CountyBoundary | 1 | MunicipalBoundary | 1 |
| MilitaryResBoundary | 1 | LegalBoundary | 1 |
| ParkBoundary | 1 | MunicipalAreasCarto | 1 |
| StateBoundary | 1 | | |

*Topology rules*

| Origin feature class | Topology rule | Comparison feature class |
|---|---|---|
| CountyBoundary | Must not self-overlap | |
| ParkBoundary | Must be covered by boundary of | LegalBoundary |
| MilitaryResBoundary | Must be covered by boundary of | LegalBoundary |
| StateBoundary | Must not self-overlap | |
| MunicipalBoundary | Must be covered by boundary of | MunicipalAreasCarto |

Boundaries may be captured as both line and polygon features. The linear boundary feature classes are used primarily for cartographic purposes. Boundary lines are symbolized based on their boundary type as presented in the administrative domains, such as AdminBoundaries. Administrative polygons are used for both data maintenance and cartography.

The coded value domains below are used by some or all of the administrative feature classes. AdminBoundaries and AdminJurisdiction provide a range of political boundary types, while AdminLegalBoundaries provides a list of park and military reservation functions.

The field CULTID in these feature classes is the permanent unique key used for relating each feature to records in the Names table.

**Simple feature class**
**StateBoundary**

| | | Geometry | Polyline |
| --- | --- | --- | --- |
| | | Contains M values | No |
| | | Contains Z values | No |

| Field name | Data type | Allow nulls | Default value | Domain | Precision | Scale | Length |
| --- | --- | --- | --- | --- | --- | --- | --- |
| OBJECTID_1 | Object ID | | | | | | |
| Shape | Geometry | Yes | | | | | |
| ID | Long integer | Yes | | | 0 | 0 | |
| TYPE | Long integer | Yes | | AdminBoundaries | 0 | | |
| SOURCE | Long integer | Yes | | | 0 | 0 | |
| CULTID | Long integer | Yes | | | 0 | 0 | |
| JURISD | Long integer | Yes | | AdminJurisdiction | 0 | | |
| DISPUTED | Long integer | Yes | | TrueFalse | 0 | | |
| Shape_Length | Double | Yes | | | 0 | 0 | |

*State boundary line*

**Coded value domain**
**AdminLegalBoundaries**

Description *Types of Legal Boundaries*
Field type *Long integer*
Split policy *Default value*
Merge policy *Default value*

| Code | Description |
| --- | --- |
| 8040 | National Park |
| 8041 | National Forest |
| 8042 | National Wildlife Area |
| 8043 | National Wilderness Area |
| 8044 | Indian Reservation |
| 8045 | Military Reservation |
| 8046 | Federal Prison |
| 8047 | Misc. Federal Reservation |
| 8048 | Non-National Forest System Lands |
| 8049 | Forest Administration Area |
| 8050 | Forest Service Ranger District |
| 8051 | Land owned by Forest Service but outside of proclamation boundary |
| 8052 | Misc. State Reservation |
| 8053 | State Park |
| 8054 | State Wildlife Area |
| 8055 | State Forest |
| 8056 | State Prison |
| 8057 | Misc. County Reservation |
| 8060 | Large Park, City, County, or Private |
| 8061 | Small Park, City, County, or Private |
| 8058 | Ahupuaa (Hawaii) |
| 8059 | Hawaiian Homestead |

**Coded value domain**
**AdminBoundaries**

Description *Types of Admin Boundaries*
Field type *Long integer*
Split policy *Default value*
Merge policy *Default value*

| Code | Description |
| --- | --- |
| 8020 | State |
| 8021 | County |
| 8022 | Local or Regional |
| 8023 | National |
| 8024 | International Waters |

**Coded value domain**
**AdminJurisdiction**

Description *Types of Jurisdictions*
Field type *Long integer*
Split policy *Default value*
Merge policy *Default value*

| Code | Description |
| --- | --- |
| 8012 | Unknown |
| 8013 | County |
| 8014 | Local |
| 8015 | Private |
| 8010 | Federal |
| 8011 | State |

## Simple feature class: CountyBoundary

Geometry: Polyline
Contains M values: No
Contains Z values: No

County boundary lines

| Field name | Data type | Allow nulls | Default value | Domain | Precision | Scale | Length | Description |
|---|---|---|---|---|---|---|---|---|
| OBJECTID_1 | Object ID | | | | | | | Object ID |
| Shape | Geometry | Yes | | | | | | |
| ID | Long integer | Yes | | | 0 | 0 | | ID—Relic from shapefile <not needed> |
| TYPE | Long integer | Yes | | AdminBoundaries | 0 | | | Type of boundary |
| SOURCE | Long integer | Yes | | | 0 | 0 | | Basis for join to RevisionInfo table |
| CULTID | Long integer | Yes | | | 0 | 0 | | Permanent unique ID |
| JURISD | Long integer | Yes | | AdminJurisdiction | 0 | | | Agency responsible for a feature |
| SHAPE_LENG | Double | Yes | | | 0 | 0 | | Length in common map units |
| DISPUTED | Long integer | Yes | | TrueFalse | 0 | | | Indicates whether the boundary is disputed |
| NAME | String | Yes | | | | | 64 | Name of county |
| Shape_Length | Double | Yes | | | 0 | 0 | | |

## Simple feature class: MunicipalBoundary

Geometry: Polyline
Contains M values: No
Contains Z values: No

Municipal boundary lines

| Field name | Data type | Allow nulls | Default value | Domain | Precision | Scale | Length | Description |
|---|---|---|---|---|---|---|---|---|
| OBJECTID_1 | Object ID | | | | | | | Object ID |
| Shape | Geometry | Yes | | | | | | |
| ID | Long integer | Yes | | | 0 | 0 | | ID—Relic from shapefile <not needed> |
| SOURCE | Long integer | Yes | | | 0 | 0 | | Basis for a join to the RevisionInfo table |
| CULTID | Long integer | Yes | | | 0 | 0 | | Permanent unique ID |
| JURISD | Long integer | Yes | | AdminJurisdiction | 0 | | | Agency responsible for a feature |
| DISPUTED | Long integer | Yes | | TrueFalse | 0 | | | Indicates whether the boundary is disputed |
| Shape_Length | Double | Yes | | | 0 | 0 | | |

## Simple feature class: ParkBoundary

Geometry: Polyline
Contains M values: No
Contains Z values: No

Park boundary lines

| Field name | Data type | Allow nulls | Default value | Domain | Precision | Scale | Length | Description |
|---|---|---|---|---|---|---|---|---|
| OBJECTID_1 | Object ID | | | | | | | Object ID |
| Shape | Geometry | Yes | | | | | | |
| TYPE | Long integer | Yes | | AdminLegalBoundaries | 0 | | | Type of park |
| SOURCE | Long integer | Yes | | | 0 | 0 | | Basis for a join to the RevisionInfo table |
| CULTID | Long integer | Yes | | | 0 | 0 | | Permanent unique ID |
| JURISD | Long integer | Yes | | AdminJurisdiction | 0 | | | Agency responsible for boundary |
| DISPUTED | Long integer | Yes | | TrueFalse | 0 | | | Indicates whether the boundary is disputed |
| Shape_Length | Double | Yes | | | 0 | 0 | | |

## Simple feature class: MilitaryResBoundary

Geometry: Polyline
Contains M values: No
Contains Z values: No

Boundaries for military reservations

| Field name | Data type | Allow nulls | Default value | Domain | Precision | Scale | Length | Description |
|---|---|---|---|---|---|---|---|---|
| OBJECTID_1 | Object ID | | | | | | | Object ID |
| Shape | Geometry | Yes | | | | | | |
| ID | Long integer | Yes | | | 0 | 0 | | ID—Relic from shapefile <not needed> |
| TYPE | Long integer | Yes | | AdminLegalBoundaries | 0 | | | Type of boundary |
| SOURCE | Long integer | Yes | | | 0 | 0 | | Basis for a join to the RevisionInfo table |
| CULTID | Long integer | Yes | | | 0 | 0 | | Permanent unique ID |
| JURISD | Long integer | Yes | | AdminJurisdiction | 0 | | | Agency responsible for a feature |
| Shape_Length | Double | Yes | | | 0 | 0 | | |

8

The polygon feature classes for boundaries are used in the map for cartographic labeling and to complement the linear boundary feature classes. Census data is a possible source for cultural area features. While not intended for cartographic output, a link with census data will enable you to include extensive summary demographic statistics with your administrative area units.

Boundary polygons are used for interior labeling, possibly with leader lines for small polygons. By judiciously using linear feature labels along boundaries and area feature labels in municipal area interiors, all map views can be well labeled.

The LegalBoundaries feature class serves much the same purpose as the MunicipalAreasCarto feature class but is intended for land use features other than municipalities. The LegalBoundaries feature class is designed for dynamic boundaries, for which revision tracking and dispute status may be important (this is less likely for municipal boundaries). These areas also tend to be less prominent than municipal areas and, thus, use a smaller text label font size.

**TIP** Boundary polygons can be generated from linear feature classes in ArcMap using the Construct Feature tool. Linear features can be made from polygon features using the Planarize tool.

**TIP** When the map includes boundaries between neighboring districts, such as counties or states, place linear boundary feature labels for the neighboring regions directly across the boundary from each other.

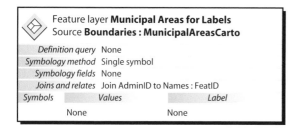

Feature layer **Municipal Areas for Labels**
Source **Boundaries : MunicipalAreasCarto**

| | |
|---|---|
| Definition query | None |
| Symbology method | Single symbol |
| Symbology fields | None |
| Joins and relates | Join AdminID to Names : FeatID |

| Symbols | Values | Label |
|---|---|---|
| None | None | |

Text for Layer **Municipal Areas**

City Name     *Times New Roman, Normal, 11.0 Pts*

| | |
|---|---|
| Method | All features the same way |
| Expression | [PlaceName.LABELSTR] |
| Placement | One label per feature |

Weights and Rank

| | |
|---|---|
| Return overlapping labels: True | Label Weight: High |
| | Feature Weight: None |
| Buffer: 0 | Rank: 6 of 22 |

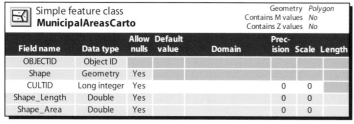

Simple feature class
**MunicipalAreasCarto**

Geometry *Polygon*
Contains M values *No*
Contains Z values *No*

| Field name | Data type | Allow nulls | Default value | Domain | Prec-ision | Scale | Length |
|---|---|---|---|---|---|---|---|
| OBJECTID | Object ID | | | | | | |
| Shape | Geometry | Yes | | | | | |
| CULTID | Long integer | Yes | | | 0 | 0 | |
| Shape_Length | Double | Yes | | | 0 | 0 | |
| Shape_Area | Double | Yes | | | 0 | 0 | |

*Municipal area features to support placing labels within the areas*

Permanent unique ID

Austin

## Feature layer **Legal Boundaries**
### Source **Boundaries : LegalBoundary**

| | |
|---|---|
| *Definition query* | None |
| *Symbology method* | Single symbol |
| *Symbology fields* | None |
| *Joins and relates* | Join AdminID to Names : FeatID |

| Symbols | Values | Label |
|---|---|---|
| | 8040-43, 47-55, 57-58, 61 | Park, Forest, or Preserve |
| | 8056, 8046 | Prison |
| | 8044 | Indian Reservation |
| | 8045 | Military |

## Text for Layer **Legal Boundary Areas**

Area Name    *Times New Roman, Normal, 8.0 Pts*

| | |
|---|---|
| *Method* | All features the same way |
| *Expression* | [PlaceName.LABELSTR] |
| *Placement* | Remove duplicate labels. |

*Weights and Rank*

Return overlapping labels: True  
Buffer: 0

Label Weight: High  
Feature Weight: None  
Rank: 8 of 22

## Simple feature class
### **LegalBoundary**

Geometry *Polygon*  
Contains M values *No*  
Contains Z values *No*

*Polygons for regions that need to be labeled with an interior label*

| Field name | Data type | Allow nulls | Default value | Domain | Precision | Scale | Length |
|---|---|---|---|---|---|---|---|
| OBJECTID | Object ID | | | | | | |
| Shape | Geometry | Yes | | | | | |
| TYPE | Long integer | Yes | 8040 | AdminLegalBoundaries | 0 | | |
| SOURCE | Double | Yes | | | 0 | 0 | |
| CULTID | Long integer | Yes | | | 0 | 0 | |
| JURISD | Long integer | Yes | 8012 | AdminJurisdiction | 0 | | |
| Disputed | Long integer | Yes | 0 | TrueFalse | 0 | | |
| Shape_Length | Double | Yes | | | 0 | 0 | |
| Shape_Area | Double | Yes | | | 0 | 0 | |

Type of feature  
Basis of a join to the RevisionInfo table  
Permanent unique ID  
Agency responsible for a feature  
Indicates whether the boundary is disputed

**TIP** Make sure boundary tints are distinct and do not conflict with thematic tints of other map layers, such as cultural line tints.

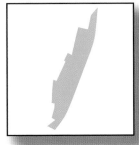

## Annotation feature class
### **BoundaryAnno**

Geometry  
Contains M values *No*  
Contains Z values *No*

| Field name | Data type | Allow nulls | Precision | Scale | Length |
|---|---|---|---|---|---|
| OBJECTID | Object ID | | | | |
| SHAPE | Geometry | Yes | | | |
| FeatureID | Long integer | Yes | 0 | | |
| ZOrder | Long integer | Yes | 0 | | |
| AnnotationClassID | Long integer | Yes | 0 | | |
| Element | BLOB | Yes | 0 | 0 | 0 |
| SHAPE_Length | Double | Yes | 0 | 0 | |
| SHAPE_Area | Double | Yes | 0 | 0 | |

*The BoundaryAnno feature class is a placeholder for potentially many annotation feature classes. It is shown here as a reminder that you can convert any administrative class labels into annotation features for more flexible formatting and placement.*

8

The cultural theme captures important landmarks, building footprints, communications and power lines, and other significant cultural features not already in another theme.

The cultural theme in this base map data model is intended to capture significant features used in topographic mapping products not already accounted for in other themes. Point features include schools, churches, towers, and landmarks. Linear features include significant walls, fences, and communications and power lines. Area features include building footprints and built-up (urban) areas, with different colors used to distinguish educational, religious, health care, agricultural, and recreational land uses.

Cultural features are shown as part of a dataset containing both cultural and surface water (hydrographic) feature classes. This is to take advantage of topology to prevent cultural areas, such as landmarks, from overlapping water bodies.

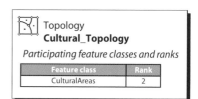

Topology
**Cultural_Topology**

*Participating feature classes and ranks*

| Feature class | Rank |
| --- | --- |
| CulturalAreas | 2 |

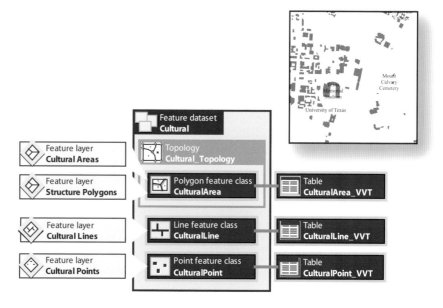

As with the transportation theme, cultural feature classes use valid value tables to define the set of detailed classifications of feature types. In this data model, two key feature layers are based on the CulturalAreas feature class, one for structure polygons, such as buildings, and the second layer for all other types of cultural areas. These are handled by separate layers because building structure labels might be drawn on top of another nearby cultural feature.

You may have noticed the Rank field in the lower right corner of Text for Layer definitions on these pages. This rank refers to the priority for the labeling only, not for feature rendering.

**TIP** Notice that Structure Polygons are dark gray but not black; it is important to make sure labels are always readable on top of their associated features. Make sure all of your labels can float over the map and still be readable.

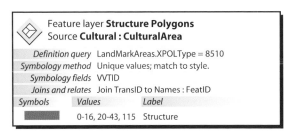

Feature layer **Structure Polygons**
Source **Cultural : CulturalArea**

| | |
|---|---|
| *Definition query* | LandMarkAreas.XPOLType = 8510 |
| *Symbology method* | Unique values; match to style. |
| *Symbology fields* | VVTID |
| *Joins and relates* | Join TransID to Names : FeatID |

| Symbols | Values | Label |
|---|---|---|
| | 0-16, 20-43, 115 | Structure |

Text for Layer **Structure Polygons**

Structure Name     *Times New Roman, Normal, 8.0 Pts*

| | |
|---|---|
| *Method* | All features the same way |
| *Expression* | [PlaceName.LABELSTR] |
| *Placement* | One label per feature |

Weights and Rank

Return overlapping labels: True

Label Weight: High
Feature Weight: None
Buffer: 0     Rank: 10 of 22

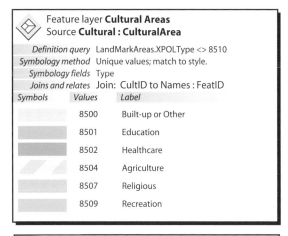

Feature layer **Cultural Areas**
Source **Cultural : CulturalArea**

| | |
|---|---|
| *Definition query* | LandMarkAreas.XPOLType <> 8510 |
| *Symbology method* | Unique values; match to style. |
| *Symbology fields* | Type |
| *Joins and relates* | Join: CultID to Names : FeatID |

| Symbols | Values | Label |
|---|---|---|
| | 8500 | Built-up or Other |
| | 8501 | Education |
| | 8502 | Healthcare |
| | 8504 | Agriculture |
| | 8507 | Religious |
| | 8509 | Recreation |

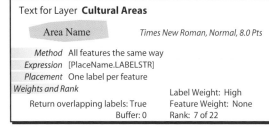

Text for Layer **Cultural Areas**

Area Name     *Times New Roman, Normal, 8.0 Pts*

| | |
|---|---|
| *Method* | All features the same way |
| *Expression* | [PlaceName.LABELSTR] |
| *Placement* | One label per feature |

Weights and Rank

Return overlapping labels: True

Label Weight: High
Feature Weight: None
Buffer: 0     Rank: 7 of 22

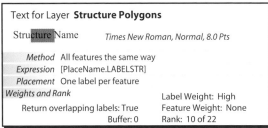

Simple feature class
**CulturalArea**

Geometry     Polygon
Contains M values     No
Contains Z values     No

| Field name | Data type | Allow nulls | Prec-ision | Scale | Length |
|---|---|---|---|---|---|
| OBJECTID | Long integer | Yes | 0 | | |
| Shape | Geometry | Yes | | | |
| SOURCE | Double | Yes | 0 | 0 | |
| CultID | Double | Yes | 0 | 0 | |
| VVTID | Long integer | Yes | 0 | 0 | |
| XPOLType | Long integer | Yes | 0 | | |
| Shape_Length | Double | Yes | 0 | 0 | |
| Shape_Area | Double | Yes | 0 | 0 | |

Basis for a join to the RevisionInfo table
Permanent unique ID
Type of landmark area
Superclass for landmark areas

*Valid values for CulturalArea feature class*

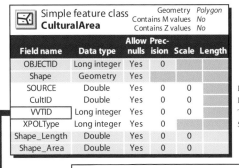

Table
**CulturalArea_VVT**

| Field name | Data type | Allow nulls | Prec-ision | Scale | Length |
|---|---|---|---|---|---|
| OBJECTID | Object ID | | | | |
| VVTID | Long integer | Yes | 0 | 0 | |
| FCODE | Long integer | Yes | 0 | | |
| ACODES | String | Yes | | | 254 |
| DESCRIPTIO | String | Yes | | | 254 |

Unique ID within valid value domain
Feature type name
List of attribute names and associated values valid for this feature type
Description for this kind of feature

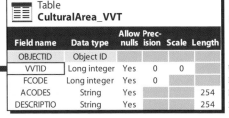

8

Cultural points and lines are generally prominent structures, as shown in these layer definitions.

Cultural point features are generally rendered in black, while line features may have other colors. It is important, when choosing colors for these features, to ensure there is sufficient contrast and lack of color conflict between these features and other layers they may overlay.

**TIP** Points are rotated to match real-life orientation. In ArcGIS, use the Advanced Rotation symbology method.

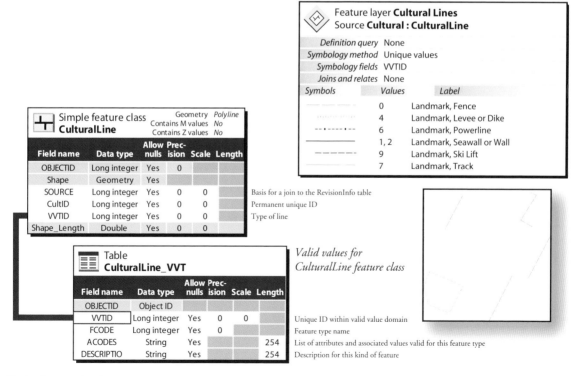

Feature layer **Cultural Lines**
Source **Cultural : CulturalLine**

| | |
|---|---|
| Definition query | None |
| Symbology method | Unique values |
| Symbology fields | VVTID |
| Joins and relates | None |

| Symbols | Values | Label |
|---|---|---|
| ———— | 0 | Landmark, Fence |
| ·············· | 4 | Landmark, Levee or Dike |
| — · — · · — | 6 | Landmark, Powerline |
| ———— | 1, 2 | Landmark, Seawall or Wall |
| — — — — | 9 | Landmark, Ski Lift |
| | 7 | Landmark, Track |

Simple feature class
**CulturalLine**

| | | |
|---|---|---|
| Geometry | Polyline |
| Contains M values | No |
| Contains Z values | No |

| Field name | Data type | Allow nulls | Precision | Scale | Length |
|---|---|---|---|---|---|
| OBJECTID | Long integer | Yes | 0 | | |
| Shape | Geometry | Yes | | | |
| SOURCE | Long integer | Yes | 0 | 0 | |
| CultID | Long integer | Yes | 0 | 0 | |
| VVTID | Long integer | Yes | 0 | 0 | |
| Shape_Length | Double | Yes | 0 | 0 | |

Basis for a join to the RevisionInfo table
Permanent unique ID
Type of line

Table
**CulturalLine_VVT**

| Field name | Data type | Allow nulls | Precision | Scale | Length |
|---|---|---|---|---|---|
| OBJECTID | Object ID | | | | |
| VVTID | Long integer | Yes | 0 | 0 | |
| FCODE | Long integer | Yes | 0 | | |
| ACODES | String | Yes | | | 254 |
| DESCRIPTIO | String | Yes | | | 254 |

*Valid values for CulturalLine feature class*

Unique ID within valid value domain
Feature type name
List of attributes and associated values valid for this feature type
Description for this kind of feature

## Feature layer **Cultural Points**
## Source **Cultural : CulturalPoint**

| | |
|---|---|
| *Definition query* | None |
| *Symbology method* | Unique values; match to style. |
| *Symbology fields* | VVTID |
| *Joins and relates* | None |

| Symbols | Values | Label |
|---|---|---|
| | 25 | Tower, TV |
| | 29 | Tower, Communications |
| | 27 | Tower, Microwave |
| | 26 | Tower, Antenna |
| | 24 | Tower, Radio |
| | 23 | Tower |
| | 22 | Building, School |
| | 21 | Building, Religious |
| | 20 | Building, General Case |
| | 19 | Satellite Dish, Large |
| | 16 | Pit, Unconsolidated Material |
| | 14 | Cliff Dwelling |
| | 13 | Historical Marker |
| | 12 | Drill Hole |
| | 6 | Tank |
| | 1,5 | Mine or Mine Shaft |
| | 4 | Quarry |
| | 3 | Prospect |
| | 0 | Mine Entrance or Adit |

## Text for Layer **Cultural Points**

*Method* Define classes of features and label each class differently.

| Place Name | *Class Name* **Label by Name** |
|---|---|
| | *Times New Roman, Normal, 7.0 Pts* |

*SQL Query* [None]
*Expression* [PlaceName.LABELSTR
*Placement* Anywhere, above and right preferred
*Weights and Rank*  One label per feature  Label Weight: High
Return overlapping labels: True  Feature Weight: High
Buffer: 0  Rank: 11 of 22

| Place Type | *Class Name* **Label by Type** |
|---|---|
| | *Times New Roman, Normal, 7.0 Pts* |

*SQL Query* [VVT_ID] = 6 OR [VVT_ID] = 23 OR [VVT_ID] = 24
*Expression* [VVT_ID]
*Placement* Anywhere, above and right preferred
*Weights and Rank*  One label per feature  Label Weight: High
Return overlapping labels: True  Feature Weight: High
Buffer: 0  Rank: 12 of 22

## Simple feature class
## **CulturalPoint**

| | |
|---|---|
| Geometry | *Point* |
| Contains M values | *No* |
| Contains Z values | *No* |

*Point landmarks*

| Field name | Data type | Allow nulls | Prec-ision | Scale | Length | |
|---|---|---|---|---|---|---|
| OBJECTID | Long integer | Yes | 0 | | | |
| Shape | Geometry | Yes | | | | |
| ROTATION_A | Short integer | Yes | 0 | | | Rotation angle for symbol display |
| SOURCE | Long integer | Yes | 0 | 0 | | Basis for a join to the RevisionInfo table |
| CultID | Long integer | Yes | 0 | 0 | | Permanent unique ID |
| VVT_ID | Long integer | Yes | 0 | 0 | | Type of landmark |

## Table
## **CulturalPoint_VVT**

*Valid values for CulturalPoint feature class*

| Field name | Data type | Allow nulls | Prec-ision | Scale | Length | |
|---|---|---|---|---|---|---|
| OBJECTID | Object ID | | | | | |
| VVTID | Long integer | Yes | 0 | 0 | | Unique ID within valid value domain |
| FCODE | Long integer | Yes | 0 | | | Feature type name |
| ACODES | String | Yes | | | 254 | List of attributes and associated values valid for this feature type |
| DESCRIPTIO | String | Yes | | | 254 | Description for this kind of feature |

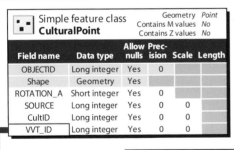

8

Water features are important in topographic base maps. They can identify sources of drinking water for hikers and resources for planning purposes as well as important facilities, such as water treatment plants and sewage ponds. You can also incorporate relevant portions of the Arc Hydro data model described in Chapter 2, 'Streams and river networks', that is useful for a base map.

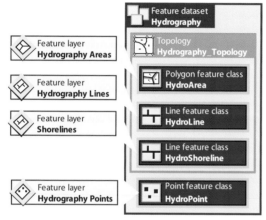

Accurate, complete maps of surface water features are important for water resources, land use, and urban planning; flood control; and agriculture. In some ways, this is one of the simpler themes in the base map: There are just a few feature classes, and each map layer corresponds to a separate feature class.

Hydrographic features include point sources, such as wells, springs, tanks, and windmills; linear objects, such as streams, canals, aqueducts, and dams; and areal objects, such as lakes, reservoirs, ponds, and marshes. Each of these may have a number of characteristics. This data model provides two descriptors for classification and cartographic purposes: the TYPE and CLASS fields. The TYPE field is for the principle function of the point, linear, or areal feature, while the CLASS field takes on values related to the type of water or its flow.

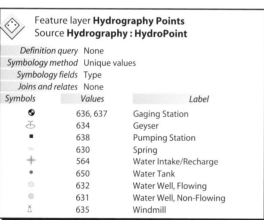

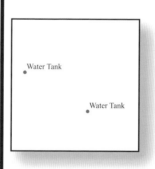

Coded value domain
**HydroPoints**

Description *Types of hydro points*
Field type *Long integer*
Split policy *Default value*
Merge policy *Default value*

| Code | Description |
|---|---|
| 564 | Water Intake |
| 565 | Dam or Weir |
| 630 | Rock |
| 631 | Well, non-flowing |
| 632 | Well, Flowing |
| 635 | Well, Windmill |
| 636 | Gaging Station |
| 637 | Gaging Station, Tidal |
| 638 | Pumping Station |
| 650 | Water Tank |
| 651 | Cistern |
| 652 | Filtration Pond |
| 653 | Tailings Pond |
| 654 | Sewage Disposal Area |
| 655 | Aquaculture Pond |
| 656 | Duck Pond |

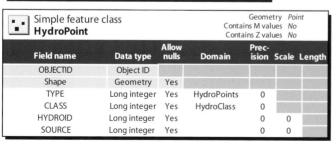

*Point hydrography features, such as wells, discharge, recharge, or monitoring stations.*

Type of hydro point
Class of water flow
Permanent unique ID
Basis for a join to the RevisionInfo table

Hydrography point features are given symbols representing their primary function and class. The list shown for the Hydrography Points map layer on the previous page is sufficient for this case study; however, you may wish to shorten or extend this list to better suit your own environmental context.

Streams and rivers can be depicted both as linear and areal features. This is due to scale, such as to distinguish either the stream centerline or its channel. Streams, rivers, and lakes are either perennial, intermittent, or dry.

Notice in the Text for Layer Hydrography Lines figure on the right that two methods of displaying the label are shown. The first method is to show the actual name of the feature for the label; this approach is only used for streams and rivers (Type = 571). The other approach is to display the feature type as its label; this is standard practice for aqueducts, dams, and other nonstream features.

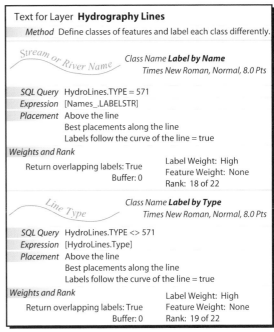

Text for Layer **Hydrography Lines**

*Method* Define classes of features and label each class differently.

*Stream or River Name*

Class Name **Label by Name**
Times New Roman, Normal, 8.0 Pts

*SQL Query* HydroLines.TYPE = 571
*Expression* [Names_.LABELSTR]
*Placement* Above the line
Best placements along the line
Labels follow the curve of the line = true

*Weights and Rank*

Return overlapping labels: True
Buffer: 0

Label Weight: High
Feature Weight: None
Rank: 18 of 22

*Line Type*

Class Name **Label by Type**
Times New Roman, Normal, 8.0 Pts

*SQL Query* HydroLines.TYPE <> 571
*Expression* [HydroLines.Type]
*Placement* Above the line
Best placements along the line
Labels follow the curve of the line = true

*Weights and Rank*

Return overlapping labels: True
Buffer: 0

Label Weight: High
Feature Weight: None
Rank: 19 of 22

Feature layer **Hydrography Lines**
Source **Hydrography : HydroLine**

| | |
|---|---|
| *Definition query* | None |
| *Symbology method* | Unique values, Many fields |
| *Symbology fields* | Type, Class |
| *Joins and relates* | HydroID joined to Names : FeatID |

| Symbols | Values | Label |
|---|---|---|
| | 500, 0 | Closure Line |
| | [550,552,571], 610 | Stream or Channel, Perennial |
| | [550,552,571], 611 | Stream or Channel, Intermittent |
| | [574,576], 610 | Aqueduct |
| > < | [574,576], 611 | Aqueduct, Elevated |
| | [574,576], 612 | Aqueduct, Tunnel |
| | 575, 0 | Flume |
| | 577, 0 | Siphon |
| | 580, 0 | Dam or Wier |

Coded value domain
**HydroClass**

| | |
|---|---|
| Description | *Types of flow* |
| Field type | *Long integer* |
| Split policy | *Default value* |
| Merge policy | *Default value* |

| Code | Description |
|---|---|
| 615 | Mineral or Hot |
| 616 | Salt |
| 617 | Fresh |
| 618 | Artesian |
| 610 | Perennial |
| 611 | Intermittent |
| 612 | Dry |

Coded value domain
**HydroLines**

| | |
|---|---|
| Description | *Lines water flows in* |
| Field type | *Long integer* |
| Split policy | *Default value* |
| Merge policy | *Default value* |

| Code | Description |
|---|---|
| 550 | Channel, Undredged |
| 551 | Processing or Closure Line |
| 552 | Canal or Ditch |
| 571 | River or Stream |
| 572 | Braided Stream |
| 574 | Aqueduct or Pipeline |
| 575 | Flume |
| 576 | Penstock |
| 577 | Siphon |
| 578 | Channel, Dredged |
| 580 | Dam or Weir |

Simple feature class
**HydroLine**

Geometry *Polyline*
Contains M values *No*
Contains Z values *No*

*Lines along which water is conveyed*

| Field name | Data type | Allow nulls | Domain | Precision | Scale | Length | |
|---|---|---|---|---|---|---|---|
| OBJECTID | Object ID | | | | | | |
| Shape | Geometry | Yes | | | | | |
| TYPE | Long integer | Yes | HydroLines | 0 | | | Type of hydro line |
| CLASS | Long integer | Yes | HydroClass | 0 | | | Class of water flow |
| HYDROID | Long integer | Yes | | 0 | 0 | | Permanent unique ID |
| SOURCE | Long integer | Yes | | 0 | 0 | | Basis for join to RevisionInfo |
| Shape_Leng | Double | Yes | | 0 | 0 | | User-defined length of feature |
| Shape_Length | Double | Yes | | 0 | 0 | | |

**8**

Shorelines complete the discussion of hydrography lines. This section also covers hydrography areas, which have a rich classification and symbology scheme. As with the other hydrography features, hydrography areas are classified in terms of major and minor codes (TYPE and CLASS fields), which allow many kinds of hydrography areas to be represented in a simple, extensible way in the GIS database.

Shorelines are another type of hydrography line. These are managed as a separate feature class because it is often important to know their material composition for boat navigation, recreation, or other purposes. Shoreline features are also used to model coastlines of water bodies that border a map's area of interest.

Hydrography areas have the widest variability among the hydro features in this data model, as evident in the legend of symbols for HydroAreas on the next page. Among these symbols, you will see some that represent a combination of HydroAreas TYPE and CLASS, such as the entry about halfway down, "511,612 Marsh, Wetland, or Swamp, Submerged". The 511 refers to the marsh or wetland, while 612 is from the HydroClasses list on the previous page, meaning

"dry." Farther down the list are several entries for Lake or Pond, each with a different HydroClass value.

As with HydroLines, the text labels for HydroAreas may be either the name of the feature (for rivers, lakes, or large seas) or the feature type name.

**TIP** When choosing colors for hydrography features and text, be sure that area fills are lighter in color tint than boundary features, and that text is darker than either the fill or the boundary.

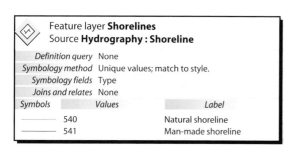

Feature layer **Shorelines**
Source **Hydrography : Shoreline**

| | |
|---|---|
| *Definition query* | None |
| *Symbology method* | Unique values; match to style. |
| *Symbology fields* | Type |
| *Joins and relates* | None |

| Symbols | Values | Label |
|---|---|---|
| ——— | 540 | Natural shoreline |
| ——— | 541 | Man-made shoreline |

Coded value domain
**HydroShore**

Description  *Types of shorelines*
Field type  *Long integer*
Split policy  *Default value*
Merge policy  *Default value*

| Code | Description |
|---|---|
| 540 | Natural |
| 541 | Man-made |
| 543 | Indefinite |
| 546 | Apparent |
| 542 | Closure Line |

Coded value domain
**HydroShoreClass**

Description  *Types of shore materials*
Field type  *Long integer*
Split policy  *Default value*
Merge policy  *Default value*

| Code | Description |
|---|---|
| 621 | Boulders |
| 622 | Sand |
| 623 | Gravel |
| 624 | Mud |
| 625 | Shell |
| 626 | Coral |
| 627 | Rock |
| 628 | Concrete |
| 629 | Cliff |

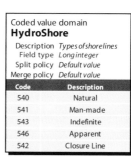

Simple feature class
**HydroShoreline**

Geometry  *Polyline*
Contains M values  *No*
Contains Z values  *No*

| Field name | Data type | Allow nulls | Domain | Precision | Scale | Length |
|---|---|---|---|---|---|---|
| OBJECTID | Object ID | | | | | |
| Shape | Geometry | Yes | | | | |
| TYPE | Long integer | Yes | HydroShore | 0 | | |
| CLASS | Long integer | Yes | HydroShoreClass | 0 | | |
| HYDROID | Long integer | Yes | | 0 | 0 | |
| SHOREMAT | Long integer | Yes | | 0 | | |
| SOURCE | Long integer | Yes | | 0 | 0 | |
| Shape_Leng | Double | Yes | | 0 | 0 | |
| Shape_Length | Double | Yes | | 0 | 0 | |

*Shorelines*

Type of shoreline
Class of shoreline
Permanent unique ID
Shore material
Basis for a join to the RevisionInfo table
User-defined length of feature

## Feature layer **Hydrography Areas**
## Source **Hydrography : HydroArea**

| | |
|---|---|
| *Definition query* | None |
| *Symbology method* | Unique values, Many fields |
| *Symbology fields* | Type, Class |
| *Joins and relates* | HydroID joined to Names : FeatID |

| Symbols | Values | Label |
|---|---|---|
| | 500, 0 | Alkali Flat |
| | 501, 0 | Reservoir |
| | 502, 0 | Reservoir, Covered |
| | 503, 0 | Glacier or Permanent Snowfield |
| | 504, 0 | Salt Flat |
| | 505, 0 | Inundation Area |
| | 506, 0 | Aquaculture Pond |
| | 507, 0 | Industrial Water Impoundment |
| | 508, 0 | Area to be Submerged |
| | 509, 0 | Sewage Disposal Plant |
| | 510, 0 | Tailings Pond |
| | 511, 612 | Marsh, Wetland, or Swamp, Submerged |
| | 511, 0 | Marsh, Wetland, or Swamp |
| | 511, 611 | Marsh, Wetland, or Swamp, Wooded |
| | 512, 0 | Mangrove |
| | 513, 0 | Cranberry Bog |
| | 514, 0 | Tidal Flat |
| | 515, 0 | Bay, Estuary, Gulf, or Ocean |
| | 516, 0 | Shoal |
| | 517, 0 | Soda Evaporator |
| | 518, 0 | Duck Pond |
| | 526, 0 | Filtration Pond |
| | 527, 0 | Foul Area |
| | 571, 610 | River or Stream |
| | 580, 610 | Lake or Pond, Perennial |
| | 580, 611 | Lake or Pond, Intermittent |
| | 580, 612 | Lake or Pond, Dry |
| | 580, 616 | Lake or Pond, Salt |
| | 583, 0 | Spoil, Dredged, or Dump Area |

## Text for Layer **Hydrography Areas**

*Method* Define classes of features and label each class differently.

*Water Body Name* — Class Name **Label by Name**
Times New Roman, Normal, 8.0 Pts

| | |
|---|---|
| *SQL Query* | HydroAreas.TYPE = 571 OR HydroAreas.TYPE = 580 OR HydroAreas.TYPE = 515 |
| *Expression* | [PlaceName.LABELSTR] |
| *Placement* | One label per features |

*Weights and Rank*

| | |
|---|---|
| Return overlapping labels: True | Label Weight: High |
| Buffer: 0 | Feature Weight: None |
| | Rank: 17 of 22 |

*Water Body Type* — Class Name **Label by Type**
Times New Roman, Normal, 8.0 Pts

| | |
|---|---|
| *SQL Query* | HydroAreas.TYPE <> 571 OR HydroAreas.TYPE <> 580 OR HydroAreas.TYPE <> 515 |
| *Expression* | [HydroAreas.Type] |
| *Placement* | One label per feature |

*Weights and Rank*

| | |
|---|---|
| Return overlapping labels: True | Label Weight: High |
| Buffer: 0 | Feature Weight: None |
| | Rank: 19 of 22 |

### Coded value domain **HydroAreas**

| | |
|---|---|
| Field type | *Long integer* |
| Split policy | *Default value* |
| Merge policy | *Default value* |

| Code | Description |
|---|---|
| 500 | Alkali Flat |
| 501 | Reservoir |
| 502 | Reservoir, Covered |
| 503 | Glacier or Permanent Snowfield |
| 504 | Salt Evaporator |
| 505 | Inundation Area |
| 506 | Aquaculture Pond |
| 507 | Industrial Water Impoundment |
| 508 | Area to be Submerged |
| 509 | Sewage Disposal Pond |
| 510 | Tailings Pond |
| 511 | Marsh, Wetland, Swamp, or Bog |
| 512 | Mangrove Area |
| 513 | Cranberry Bog |
| 514 | Tidal Flat |
| 515 | Bay, Estuary, Gulf, Sea, or Ocean |
| 516 | Shoal |
| 517 | Soda Evaporator |
| 518 | Duck Pond |
| 520 | Cable Area |
| 521 | Pipeline Area |
| 522 | Cable and Pipeline Area |
| 523 | Pipeline Obstruction Area |
| 524 | Gut |
| 525 | Dry Dock Area |
| 526 | Filtration Pond |
| 527 | Foul Area |
| 528 | Mine Danger Area |
| 571 | Stream or River |
| 580 | Lake or Pond |
| 581 | Reef |
| 582 | Sand in Open Water |
| 583 | Spoil, Dredged, or Dump Area |

### Simple feature class **HydroArea**

| | |
|---|---|
| Geometry | *Polygon* |
| Contains M values | *No* |
| Contains Z values | *No* |

| Field name | Data type | Allow nulls | Domain | Precision | Scale | Length | |
|---|---|---|---|---|---|---|---|
| OBJECTID | Object ID | | | | | | |
| Shape | Geometry | Yes | | | | | |
| TYPE | Long integer | Yes | HydroAreas | 0 | | | Type of feature |
| CLASS | Long integer | Yes | HydroClass | 0 | | | Class of flow |
| HYDROID | Long integer | Yes | | 0 | 0 | | Permanent unique ID |
| SOURCE | Long integer | Yes | | 0 | 0 | | Basis for join to RevisionInfo |
| Shape_Leng | Double | Yes | | 0 | 0 | | User-defined length of feature |
| Shape_Length | Double | Yes | | 0 | 0 | | |
| Shape_Area | Double | Yes | | 0 | 0 | | |

*Area water features*

**8**

Cartography and the base map · 337

Vector topographic data includes elevation points and contour lines, which have many applications, including hydrographic modeling, flood hazard mapping, slope analysis, transportation planning, and recreation.

Elevation points are usually benchmarks for ground control reference or elevations of significant features. What constitutes a significant feature can vary with the surrounding terrain. For example, a hill that rises 200 feet above a valley may be significant in a relatively flat region but completely unnoticeable in a mountainous region.

Contours are lines of constant elevation. These may be derived from DEMs or from stereophotogrammetry. Topology is used to verify that contour lines do not self-intersect or cross other contours.

## Elevation points

Elevation point features can be based on numerous types of data, as shown in the feature layer definition diagram and the domain table on the next page. The symbols can have three textual elements: the term "BM" for benchmarks, the elevation numeric value, and the units of measurement. In ArcGIS, these elements can be combined to form a character marker symbol that allows flexible construction and font size of the numeric value, units, and benchmark code. The text content of a character marker symbol scales as you zoom in or out of the map.

**TIP** Always include units of measurement in elevation point symbols; while it may be obvious to the cartographer that the elevations are in feet or meters, it is almost certain that the values will be less obvious to some readers.

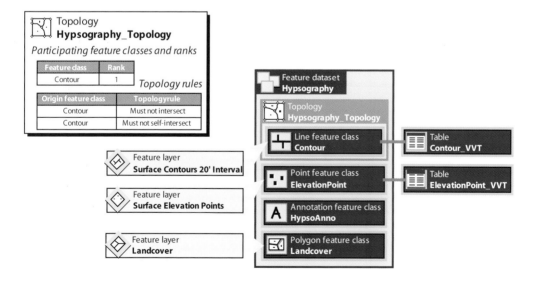

## Feature layer **Surface Elevation Points**
## Source **Hypsography : ElevationPoint**

| Definition query | None |
| --- | --- |
| Symbology method | Unique values; match to style. |
| Symbology fields | VVTID |
| Joins and relates | None |

| Symbols | Values | Label |
| --- | --- | --- |
| `·` | 12 | Boundary Monument, No Tablet |
| BM `·` | 13 | Boundary Monument, Tablet |
| × | 4 | Horizontal Control Station, Better than 3rd Order, Checked Spot Elevation |
| BM △ | 5 | Horizontal Control Station, Better than 3rd Order, Vertical Angle Benchmark |
| △ | 2,3 | Horizontal Control Station, Less than 3rd Order |
| BM ⊙ | 11 | Horizontal and Vertical Control Station, Better then 3rd Order |
| ⊙ | 10 | Horizontal and Vertical Control Station, Less than 3rd Order |
| × | 0,1 | Spot Elevation, Less than 3rd Order |
| × | 6,7 | Vertical Control Station, No Tablet |
| BM × | 8,9 | Vertical Control Station, Tablet |

---

## Text for Layer **Surface Elevation Points**

× ELEV units          *Arial, Normal, 6.0 Pts*

| Method | All features the same way |
| --- | --- |
| Expression | [ELEVATION] & " " & [UNITS] |
| Placement | Anywhere; above and right preferred |
| Weights and Rank | One label per feature          Label Weight: High |
| | Return overlapping labels: True          Feature Weight: High |
| | Buffer: 0          Rank: 21 of 22 |

---

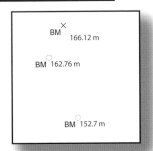

BM × 166.12 m

BM ○ 162.76 m

BM ○ 152.7 m

---

## Coded value domain
## **ElevationPoints**

| Description | *Types of Elevation Points (VVT)* |
| --- | --- |
| Field type | *Double* |
| Split policy | *Default value* |
| Merge policy | *Default value* |

| Code | Description |
| --- | --- |
| 0 | Spot Elevation, Ground Level, Less than 3rd Order |
| 1 | Spot Elevation, On Bridge, Less than 3rd Order |
| 2 | Horizontal Control Station, Less than 3rd Order, Checked Spot Elevation |
| 3 | Horizontal Control Station, Less than 3rd Order, Vertical Angle Benchmark |
| 4 | Horizontal Control Station, Better than 3rd Order, Checked Spot Elevation |
| 5 | Horizontal Control Station, Better than 3rd Order, Vertical Angle Benchmark |
| 6 | Vertical Control Station, No Tablet, Recoverable |
| 7 | Vertical Control Station, No Tablet, Permanent |
| 8 | Vertical Control Station, Tablet, Recoverable |
| 9 | Vertical Control Station, Tablet, Permanent |
| 10 | Horizontal and Vertical Control Station, Less than 3rd Order |
| 11 | Horizontal and Vertical Control Station, Better than 3rd Order |
| 12 | Boundary Monument, No Tablet |
| 13 | Boundary Monument, Tablet |

---

## Simple feature class
## **ElevationPoint**

Geometry **Point**
Contains M values **No**
Contains Z values **No**

| Field name | Data type | Allow nulls | Default value | Domain | Precision | Scale | Length | |
| --- | --- | --- | --- | --- | --- | --- | --- | --- |
| OBJECTID | Object ID | | | | | | | |
| Shape | Geometry | Yes | | | | | | |
| ELEVATION | Double | Yes | | | 0 | 0 | | Elevation of point |
| UNITS | String | Yes | | | | | 4 | Units of measurement |
| SOURCE | Long integer | Yes | | | 0 | 0 | | Basis for a join to the RevisionInfo table |
| SURFID | Long integer | Yes | | | 0 | | | Permanent unique ID |
| VVTID | Long integer | Yes | 0 | ElevationPoints | 0 | 0 | | Type of elevation point |

*Valid values for*
*ElevationPoint feature class*

---

## Table
## **ElevationPoint_VVT**

| Field name | Data type | Allow nulls | Precision | Scale | Length | |
| --- | --- | --- | --- | --- | --- | --- |
| OBJECTID | Object ID | | | | | |
| VVTID | Long integer | Yes | 0 | | | Unique ID within valid value domain |
| FCODE | Long integer | Yes | 0 | | | Feature type name |
| ACODES | String | Yes | | | 254 | List of attributes and associated values valid for this feature type |
| DESCRIPTIO | String | Yes | | | 254 | Description for this kind of feature |

**8**

For cartographic purposes, contour lines are divided into several groups, as shown in the feature layer definition below. The choice of index elevations depends on the contour interval, which, in turn, depends on both the map scale and the relative relief of the terrain.

Contour labeling seems straightforward until you try to do it. Due to the wide variability in density and curvature of contour lines for a given terrain, it is difficult to write a general purpose algorithm for placing all contour labels in "good places."

Since contour lines should be rendered beneath most other map layers, you may need to make some layers partially transparent to allow the contours to show through. In this example, contours were rendered after (on top of) surface overlays and administrative areas, and before (beneath) hydrography, transportation, and administrative line features. Elevation points are rendered last, to be on top of all other layers.

**TIP** For the best labeling results, annotation should be placed manually to manage proper orientation (parallel and centered on contour line) and to distribute labels for best readability (avoid labeling in areas of dense contours, and stagger labels when close together).

**TIP** Here is an approach that works well for labeling a specific set of contours, although it involves a couple of intermediate geoprocessing tasks:

1. Create some graphic lines perpendicular to the contour lines, intersecting them where they would ideally be labeled.
2. Buffer those graphic lines, creating a new feature class. Experiment to get the best buffer distance that allows the complete elevation value to display without a lot of excess space.
3. Create another polygon feature class that has only one polygon surrounding the desired contour features.
4. Union the feature class created in step 3 with the buffers from step 2 as a geoprocessing operation.
5. Start editing the result of step 4:
   a. Select the big polygon with all the holes.
   b. Switch the selection.
   c. Delete the holes that are now selected.
   d. Stop editing and save your edits.

6. Intersect the contours with the buffers (in ArcGIS, this is done using the Geoprocessing wizard). This produces lines that will be the segments to be labeled.
7. Intersect the contours with the polygon feature from step 5 to produce a line feature class that has the segments that should be labeled.
8. In each of the feature classes resulting from steps 6 and 7, add a new field called LabelYN (short integer). Set the values in the feature class from step 6 to be 0 (zero), and from step 7 to be 1 (one).
9. Finally, merge the feature classes resulting from steps 6 and 7 to create the final output.
10. By setting a label query to display the labels only for contour features with LabelYN=1, the desired contours will be labeled.

---

Feature layer **Surface Contours 20' Interval**
Source **Hypsography : Contours**

| | |
|---|---|
| *Definition query* | [Index20] = 1 |
| *Symbology method* | Unique values; many fields |
| *Symbology fields* | VVTID, LabelYN |
| *Joins and relates* | None |

| Symbols | Values | Label |
|---|---|---|
| | 0, 0 | Intermediate |
| | 1, 0 | Intermediate, Depression, Carrying |
| | 2, 0 | Intermediate, Depression |
| | 3, 0 | Intermediate, Carrying |
| | 4, 0 | Index |
| | 5, 0 | Index, Depression, Carrying |
| | 6, 0 | Index, Depression |
| | 7, 0 | Index, Carrying |
| | 8, 0 | Supplemental |
| | 9, 0 | Supplemental, Depression, Carrying |
| | 10, 0 | Supplemental, Depression |
| | 11, 0 | Supplemental, Carrying |
| | 12, 0 | Submerged |
| | 13, 0 | Submerged, Depression, Carrying |
| | 14, 0 | Submerged, Depression |
| | 15, 0 | Submerged, Carrying |
| | 16, 0 | Ice Surface |
| | 17, 0 | Ice Surface, Depression, Carrying |
| | 18, 0 | Ice Surface, Depression |
| | 19, 0 | Ice Surface, Carrying |

## Simple feature class
### Contours

| | | | | | Geometry | Polyline |
| | | | | | Contains M values | No |
| | | | | | Contains Z values | No |

| Field name | Data type | Allow nulls | Default value | Domain | Prec-ision | Scale | Length | |
|---|---|---|---|---|---|---|---|---|
| OBJECTID | Object ID | | | | | | | |
| Shape | Geometry | Yes | | | | | | |
| ELEVATION | Double | Yes | | | 0 | 0 | | Elevation of contour line |
| SOURCE | Double | Yes | | | 0 | 0 | | Basis for a join to the RevisionInfo table |
| UNITS | String | Yes | f | Units | | | 4 | Units of measurement |
| SurfID | Long integer | Yes | | | 0 | | | Permanent unique ID |
| LabelYN | Short integer | Yes | 0 | EnabledDomain | 0 | | | Whether a segment should be labeled |
| Index20 | Short integer | Yes | | | 0 | | | Whether a segment is a 20-foot interval |
| VVTID | Double | Yes | 0 | Contours | 0 | 0 | | Type of contour line |
| Shape_Length | Double | Yes | | | 0 | 0 | | |

## Table
### Contours_VVT

*Valid values for Contours feature class*

| Field name | Data type | Allow nulls | Prec-ision | Scale | Length | |
|---|---|---|---|---|---|---|
| OBJECTID | Object ID | | | | | |
| VVTID | Double | Yes | 0 | | | Unique ID within domain |
| FCODE | Long integer | Yes | 0 | | | Feature type name |
| ACODES | String | Yes | | | 254 | List of valid attributes and values |
| DESCRIPTIO | String | Yes | | | 254 | Description for this kind of feature |

## Text for Layer **Contour Lines 20' Interval**

*Method* Define classes of features and label each class differently.

~~~~~~ ELEV ~~~~~~   *Class Name* **Default**
                     Arial, Normal, 6.0 Pts

*SQL Query* [LabelYN] = 1
*Expression* [Elevation]
*Placement* Centered on line
            Best location along line
            Follow along the line = No

*Weights and Rank*  One label per feature    Label Weight: High
            Return overlapping labels: True  Feature Weight: None
                        Buffer: 0    Rank: 22 of 22

## Coded value domain
### Contours

| | | Field type | Double |
| | | Split policy | Default value |
| | | Merge policy | Default value |

| Code | Description |
|---|---|
| 0 | Contour, Intermediate |
| 1 | Contour, Intermediate, Depression, Carrying |
| 2 | Contour, Intermediate, Depression |
| 3 | Contour, Intermediate, Carrying |
| 4 | Contour, Index |
| 5 | Contour, Index, Depression, Carrying |
| 6 | Contour, Index, Depression |
| 7 | Contour, Index, Carrying |
| 8 | Contour, Supplemental |
| 9 | Contour, Supplemental, Depression, Carrying |
| 10 | Contour, Supplemental, Depression |
| 11 | Contour, Supplemental, Carrying |
| 12 | Contour, Underwater |
| 13 | Contour, Underwater, Depression, Carrying |
| 14 | Contour, Underwater, Depression |
| 15 | Contour, Underwater, Carrying |
| 16 | Contour, Ice Surface |
| 17 | Contour, Ice Surface, Depression, Carrying |
| 18 | Contour, Ice Surface, Depression |
| 19 | Contour, Ice Surface, Carrying |

*HypsoAnno is a placeholder for potentially numerous annotation classes, each one corresponding to a contour label type. With ArcGIS, these are most conveniently generated from the label class definitions themselves.*

## A Annotation feature class
### HypsoAnno

| | | | | | Geometry | |
| | | | | | Contains M values | No |
| | | | | | Contains Z values | No |

| Field name | Data type | Allow nulls | Default value | Domain | Prec-ision | Scale | Length |
|---|---|---|---|---|---|---|---|
| OBJECTID | Object ID | | | | | | |
| SHAPE | Geometry | Yes | | | | | |
| FeatureID | Long integer | Yes | | | 0 | | |
| ZOrder | Long integer | Yes | | | 0 | | |
| AnnotationClassID | Long integer | Yes | | | 0 | | |
| Element | Blob | Yes | | | 0 | 0 | 0 |
| SHAPE_Length | Double | Yes | | | 0 | 0 | |
| SHAPE_Area | Double | Yes | | | 0 | 0 | |

**8**

Hypsography, or topographic relief, can be expressed as raster data, such as DEMs, or as vector data, such as elevation points and contour lines. DEMs are used as source data for numerous derived products, such as hillshaded relief, watershed delineation, and contour lines.

Topographic relief can be one of the most distinctive aspects of a base map. This theme adds elevation detail to a map in both raster and vector forms.

The most essential form of topographic data is the digital elevation model. This consists of a grid of elevation points with uniform spacing. A wealth of analytical tools has evolved to take advantage of this form of data, such as for delineating watersheds, flood modeling, slope determination and hillshading, communication tower placement, viewshed analysis, and utilities planning. Many base maps use a DEM with 30-meter spacing between elevation points, based on data collected by the U.S. Geological Survey and other data providers. Plans include enhancing this data to 10-meter spacing interval.

There are three main methods of terrain depiction in maps. The first is just to show that local relief exists. This can be achieved using a hillshaded DEM overlay with a transparency between 60 and 75 percent. The symbology of the hillshade should use a subtle color ramp, such as from yucca yellow to 40 percent gray, from the esri.style color palette.

The second method is to show relief and elevation with hypsometric coloring using two grids, a DEM and a hillshade. One way to make this work is to render the DEM with a gradation of color well suited for your elevation ranges, then overlay with any polygon layers that are important with a transparency between 30–45 percent. Finally, overlay the hillshade with a transparency of 35–55 percent.

The third method to show terrain is a naturalistic depiction of relief and elevation. This is like the second way just mentioned but with the addition of a vegetation or land cover grid that is classified by vegetation or land cover type, with each type rendered in the most natural color according to its nature. This layer can be overlaid on the DEM with a transparency of 40–75 percent—you'll need to experiment for best results.

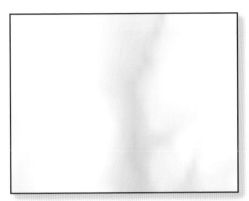

*Digital elevation model of central Austin; yellows represent higher elevations, and greens represent lower.*

*The same DEM with the addition of hillshade and cultural layers; the hillshade adds a sense of depth to the map.*

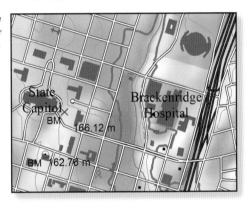

|  Raster Dataset | Geometry *Raster* | *Digital elevation model used for hypsometric tinting* |
|---|---|---|
| **DEM** | Resolution *30 meter* | |

8

| Raster Dataset | Geometry *Raster* | *Hillshade derived from DEM* |
|---|---|---|
| **Hillshade** | Resolution *30 meter* | |

Aerial photography and satellite imagery are widely used as backdrops for overlaid features. They have also become a cost-effective means of collecting and updating vast amounts of information on a regular basis. To georeference this data, including all the other data sources present in a GIS, a network of ground survey control points is also needed. Two main approaches to building this control network are to use ground-based data collection and remotely sensed data collection.

Image base refers to three types of remotely sensed data: aerial photography from which orthoimagery is derived; satellite imagery; and scanned maps.

## ORTHOIMAGERY

Aerial photography provides a wealth of data that would be prohibitively expensive to collect from ground level. This information is used as a general map background as well as for land cover change detection, property appraisals, environmental analysis, feature extraction to create other geographic themes, and many other purposes.

To be useful in a GIS, this image data is orthorectified. This involves first correcting distortions introduced by the photographic equipment and the airplane's flight path, then imposing an earth-based coordinate system.

## SATELLITE IMAGERY

Digital imagery from earth-observing satellites can be collected on a constant, ongoing basis and is useful in creating irrigated farmland maps, assessing urban growth patterns, and planning park management programs. For emergency response, postdisaster imagery may be useful in documenting losses and future planning of mitigation efforts.

## SCANNED MAPS

The earliest forms of digital maps were scanned from paper or Mylar maps. These are often useful for historical comparison. Scanned maps may be found in various formats; for example, the USGS DRG format was used for scanned topographic quad sheets.

**TIP** To improve readability of vectors and text over imagery, try toning down raster layers by reducing contrast (-22) and increasing brightness (+26). This shows vector and text overlays better, and the image prints with less ink.

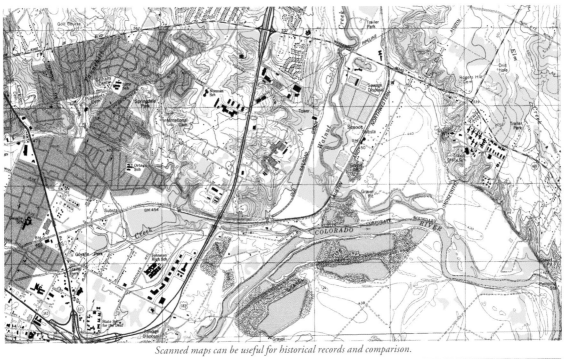

*Scanned maps can be useful for historical records and comparison.*

*DOQQ imagery is useful for proofing and updating the base map.*

Many other themes can be imagined and created in addition to those described so far. The surface overlays theme provides a placeholder for any number of additional themes, such as land cover, soils, and flood hazard zones. Other, more complicated themes are good candidates for cross agency coordination, such as critical infrastructure, wetlands delineation, census data, parcel index, place names, and addressing.

## Land cover

This theme is used for distinguishing broad categories of vegetation and surface material. The exact content of this theme may vary widely across regions, states, and countries. Such an overlay can be useful for wildlife management, flood control, drought management, nutrient and pesticide runoff modeling, city and county planning, and fire protection.

The schema structure for Land Cover is shown on the following page. The Type field holds a value corresponding to the type of land cover.

In this data model, land cover polygons are not expected to overlap, so a topology is created to enforce this condition. However, it is conceivable that land cover areas could overlap, depending on the land cover types created and the nature of the land. In this case, a topology would not be needed.

## ADDITIONAL OVERLAYS

In addition to land cover, several other overlays are considered useful enough to mention here, although they were not included in the example schema.

### Soil survey

The U.S. Department of Agriculture's Natural Resources Conservation Service has compiled county-level Digital Soil Survey Geographic (SSURGO) datasets updated from older 1:24,000 paper surveys. These are useful in land appraisal, site selection, agriculture, construction, transportation planning, and estimation of groundwater contamination susceptibility.

### Flood hazard

Flood hazard information is used in repetitive flood claims. TNRIS plans to compile a dataset of 100-year and 500-year floodplain boundaries. This would be used to support activities related to construction and financing, transportation risk planning, disaster preparedness, and floodplain insurance.

| | Feature layer **Surface Cover** | |
|---|---|---|
| | Source **LandCover : LandCover** | |
| *Definition query* | None | |
| *Symbology method* | Unique values; match to style. | |
| *Symbology fields* | Type | |
| *Joins and relates* | None | |
| Symbols | Values | Label |
| | 251 | Scrub |
| | 250 | Woods/Brushland |
| | 255 | Sand |
| | 254 | Scattered Trees |
| | 257 | Lava |
| | 258 | Gravel |

## INTEGRATIVE THEMES

Certain other themes that are useful overlays are more complicated than those mentioned above, requiring multiagency coordination and integration. These include critical infrastructure, addressing, parcel index, and census data.

### Critical infrastructure

In the United States and many other nations, it is increasingly important to distinguish "critical infrastructure" for purposes of emergency preparedness and management, including mitigation, planning, monitoring, response, and recovery.

This could include a wide range of facilities in the transportation, energy, agriculture, telecommunications, chemical, defense, public health, and other sectors. Such a resource requires considerable integration of available data among multiple agencies. For security purposes, public access to portions of this data may be restricted.

### Census boundaries and demographics

The U.S. Census Bureau publishes extensive locational and demographic data on a regular basis. The locational data consists of built and natural features that form boundaries for census blocks, block groups, tracts, and jurisdictional boundaries. The demographic data is tabular in nature, but each record can be linked to a given census block, block group, tract, or jurisdictional area. Census maps and associated demographics are used by all levels of government, as well as private businesses, to plan and provide services.

Since this data is collected and published at the national level, it would be useful and cost-effective for each state and local government to create a single resource that can be shared among the agencies at that level. This data could then be overlaid on other base map themes according to the user's immediate requirements.

| Simple feature class **Landcover** | | | | | Geometry *Polygon*<br>Contains M values *No*<br>Contains Z values *No* | | | |
|---|---|---|---|---|---|---|---|---|
| **Field name** | **Data type** | **Allow nulls** | **Default value** | **Domain** | **Prec-ision** | **Scale** | **Length** | |
| OBJECTID | Object ID | | | | | | | |
| Shape | Geometry | Yes | | | | | | |
| TYPE | Long integer | Yes | 250 | Landcover | 0 | | | |
| SOURCE | Long integer | Yes | | | 0 | 0 | | |
| SURFID | Long integer | Yes | | | 0 | 0 | | |
| Shape_Length | Double | Yes | | | 0 | 0 | | |
| Shape_Area | Double | Yes | | | 0 | 0 | | |

*Vegetative and nonvegetative natural land cover*

Type of land cover
Defines an M:1 relationship class to add source information from RevisionInfo table
Unique identifier

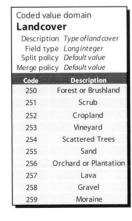

Coded value domain
**Landcover**

| Description | *Type of land cover* |
|---|---|
| Field type | *Long integer* |
| Split policy | *Default value* |
| Merge policy | *Default value* |

| Code | Description |
|---|---|
| 250 | Forest or Brushland |
| 251 | Scrub |
| 252 | Cropland |
| 253 | Vineyard |
| 254 | Scattered Trees |
| 255 | Sand |
| 256 | Orchard or Plantation |
| 257 | Lava |
| 258 | Gravel |
| 259 | Moraine |

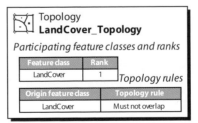

Topology
**LandCover_Topology**

*Participating feature classes and ranks*

| Feature class | Rank |
|---|---|
| LandCover | 1 |

Topology rules

| Origin feature class | Topology rule |
|---|---|
| LandCover | Must not overlap |

**8**

A key design question you'll encounter is how sophisticated your place names data model needs to be. Geographic features have names, often several, that are used for map labeling and other applications, such as maintaining a place name gazetteer. In addition, many cartographic agencies have the responsibility of maintaining the official place names registry for a jurisdiction. With increasing frequency, many place names databases need to hold geographic locations for place names—either a geographic feature or something as simple as a latitude–longitude coordinate.

Each base map will have some strategy for text and label placement on the map. Two key design tasks are to define the text label properties for each map layer and collate all the text for all map layers into an integrated labeling specification for the map. This includes setting text symbol properties (colors, fonts, point sizes, and so on), as well as specifications for how features are labeled (for example, whether names are splined along roads or whether administrative areas are labeled within the area, along adjacent boundaries, or both), and how to deal with labeling priorities and conflicts.

Labeling can be as simple as adding a name field to a feature or defining label properties for each map layer. Many data models manage place names as annotation feature classes. This often has difficult data maintenance issues for extents where names undergo considerable change. More sophisticated designs can be implemented where the place names database (built to hold official names, alternate names, and proposed names) is integrated with the GIS.

The more sophisticated design was not used in this data model. However, if you have an interest in such a design, you can investigate some useful methods presented in the address data model in Chapter 4, 'Addresses and locations'. This comprehensive address data model has design concepts similar to geographic place names. For example, the address

data model includes a comprehensive names table and illustrates how names can be associated with multiple feature classes in the geodatabase. It also demonstrates how each feature could be associated with many possible addresses (including its name) and how a name could potentially belong to many features.

More work in this area is needed, but early results look promising. Here is a design for a names database that is independent of the GIS.

## National GNIS

The larger the organization, the greater the need for a consistent, up-to-date, shared resource of place names. In response to this need, and to consolidate the numerous place names databases currently in use, the USGS and the U.S. Board on Geographic Names have embarked on a long-term program called the Geographic Names Information System, a national database of geographic place names.

GNIS Phase 1, a compilation of names appearing on USGS 1:24,000 topographic maps, has been completed for all 50 states. Phase 2, now in progress, consists of virtually all other known place names, particularly names from other federal maps, names that are historical but no longer used, and those with variant spellings. GNIS now contains infor-

| Table **PlaceName** | | | | | | | |
|---|---|---|---|---|---|---|---|
| Field name | Data type | Allow nulls | Default value | Precision | Scale | Length | |
| OBJECTID | Object ID | | | | | | |
| FEAT_ID | Long integer | Yes | | 0 | 0 | | Foreign key to ObjectID of associated feature |
| NAMESTR | String | Yes | | | | 254 | Place name in all uppercase for use in searching |
| LABELSTR | String | Yes | | | | 254 | Place name in upper/lowercase for map display |
| GNISSTATUS | Long integer | Yes | 0 | 0 | | | Status of place name in GNIS |
| VERIMETHOD | Long integer | Yes | 902 | 0 | | | Foreign key to list of revision verification methods |
| VERIDATE | Date | Yes | 0 | 0 | 8 | | Date revision was verified |

*Geographic place names*

mation on approximately 2 million physical and cultural geographic features in the United States.

The information for any geographic name in the GNIS Web site includes:

- Federally recognized feature name

- Feature type

- Elevation (where available)

- Estimated 1994 population of incorporated cities and towns

- States and counties in which the feature is located

- Latitude and longitude of the feature location

- List of USGS 7.5-minute x 7.5-minute topographic maps on which the feature is shown and names other than the federally recognized name by which the feature may be or have been known

- Links to sites offering map viewers for graphical display of the feature

- Links to sites offering information about the watershed area in which the feature is located

The Web site also allows users to download a set of additional gazetteer data to further extend the usefulness of the GNIS data.

This is a promising step, but more work is needed. Many public federal spatial data sources do not contain names or links to names. The sample data in this model has names from state and local sources, as well as manual data entry for hydrographic areas.

**PlaceName table**

The NAMESTR field values are in all uppercase letters, making it easier to match names in queries. The LABELSTR field values are in mixed, upper- and lowercase letters, to be used to produce labels or annotation. VERIMETHOD and VERIDATE are fields used in verifying the correctness of the names data. The GNISSTATUS field refers to the inclusion of each record in the national GNIS.

Chapter 4, 'Addresses and locations', contains another example of a names table, in this case, to support names for addressing of streets, parcels, buildings, and other points of interest. Users are encouraged to anticipate as many uses for the names data as possible when deciding on the most appropriate schema for their own organizations. Also, keep in mind that managing names in a normalized names table

allows for testing consistency between GIS layers that may be integrated from multiple agencies.

8

The design of a map and its surrounding map elements helps determine the effectiveness and elegance of a cartographic product. Most of the elements in the map specification used for this case study are easily assembled using out-of-the-box ArcMap capabilities, while three of the elements are manually constructed. Templates created to implement a map specification further simplify the task of generating the final output.

Page layout for maps is not yet captured as part of the geodatabase. This section provides tips for cartographic elements and their placement on the map page. It is time to summarize the choices made and steps taken to create the topographic map discussed early in this chapter.

## Elements of a map specification

The specification for the finished map in this case study contains several elements:

- Title, logo, contact information, and version date

- Map window, latitude–longitude reference graticule with tic marks and labels

- Geodetic datum and projection parameter descriptions

- North arrow, magnetic declination, and quadrangle locator

- Scale text and bars, contour interval, and legend

Of these, the magnetic declination indicator, quadrangle locator, and legend were assembled manually, and they can also be automated with programming. The rest were created using the ArcMap default style and property sheets (refer to Basemap.style, included with the case study database).

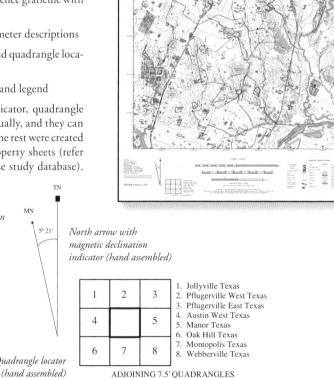

Projection:
Texas State Plane South
Lambert_Conformal_Conic   *Projection information*
False Easting: 2000000 m   *(stock component)*
False Northing: 0 m
Central Meridian:  99.00 degrees
Standard Parallel 1: 28.383333 degrees
Standard Parallel 2: 30.283333 degrees
Latitude of Origin: 27.833333 degrees
1927 North American Datum

There might be private inholdings within the boundaries
of the national or state reservations shown on the map.

**VERSION 4: MAY 31, 2002**

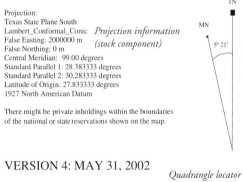

TN

MN

5° 21'

*North arrow with
magnetic declination
indicator (hand assembled)*

*Quadrangle locator
(hand assembled)*

| 1 | 2 | 3 |
| 4 |   | 5 |
| 6 | 7 | 8 |

1. Jollyville Texas
2. Pflugerville West Texas
3. Pflugerville East Texas
4. Austin West Texas
5. Manor Texas
6. Oak Hill Texas
7. Montopolis Texas
8. Webberville Texas

ADJOINING 7.5' QUADRANGLES

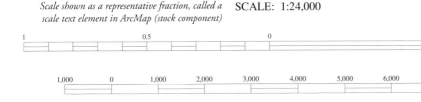

Scale shown as a representative fraction, called a
scale text element in ArcMap (stock component)

SCALE: 1:24,000

Graphical scalebars
(stock components)

CONTOUR INTERVAL 20 FEET

*Contour interval text (stock)*

NATIONAL GEODETIC VERTICAL DATUM OF 1983

*Datum text (stock)*

THIS MAP COMPLIES WITH NATIONAL MAP ACCURACY STANDARDS
FOR SALE BY TEXAS NATURAL RESOURCES INFORMATION SYSTEM, PO BOX 13231, AUSTIN, TX 78711-3231
A FOLDER DESCRIBING TOPOGRAPHIC MAPS AND SYMBOLS IS AVAILABLE ON REQUEST.

The legend and other manually created components can be reused on any number of maps. Thus, the investment in making the first finished map can be leveraged with other map sheets in the series (more than 4,000 in Texas).

A GPS-ready latitude–longitude graticule was chosen for the reference grid, since this is the most widely used and understood by the general public. A grid of tics was used instead of a mesh of lines because this leaves the map much less cluttered and easier to read. The tics are distinctive enough from the other symbology to find easily but discreet enough that they do not distract the map reader.

## Create a template

With the ability to automate much, if not all, of the map specification elements, a GIS-based map document can be made into a template for a given map product. This template can be used with any number of GIS datasets, as long as each dataset schema supports the layer definitions in the map template. In addition, multiple templates could be designed for the same datasets. For example, one template could be used for topographic base maps, and a different template might be used for thematic maps using much of the same data layered on the digital orthophoto reference layer.

Legend for Common Features

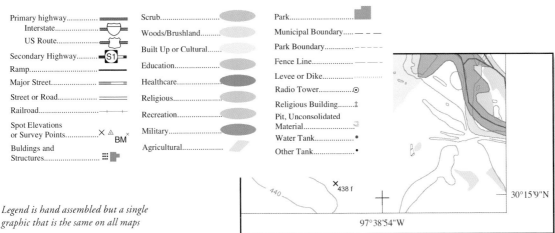

*Legend is hand assembled but a single
graphic that is the same on all maps*

The colors on a topographic map are designed to visually discriminate thematic layers; identify objects through natural colors; and emphasize important features, such as major roads and rivers. Here are some of the colors used in the TNRIS prototype with their RGB values.

The colors selected for this map represent a conscious intent to think differently about a topographic map.

## Contemporary topographic map colors

The design of this map with respect to colors attempts to address the evolution of how topographic maps are used. Colors are selected to balance the natural with the built environment. Highways, roads, and place names are prominent, but elements, such as graticules, are less prominent because they are not how most people find locations. This evolution will continue with the widespread adoption of GPS technology.

The colors were chosen to be pleasant yet still convey cultural expectations. Areas such as parks and open space should be green. Urban areas are a stucco color (versus gray pavement or a boysenberry stain as on traditional topographic maps). Certain kinds of cultural features now in the USGS data, such as educational, religious, and recreation areas, are given different colors that are easier to locate on maps.

In general, this set of distinct colors was chosen to be small enough to learn easily, particularly if users already knew something about topographic maps. They were chosen to be unambiguous so major kinds of geographic features could be easily distinguished from their neighbors if a strong difference existed; and if two kinds of activity were similar, the difference for their colors would be less distinct. Buildings were specifically treated with gray instead of black so black text labels for those buildings could overstrike the buildings, if necessary, and not lose their legibility.

While this discussion has emphasized the use of colors in filling polygons, these colors are also used in point, line, and other symbols.

# Topographic base map color model
## Colors defined with RGB values

R: 189
G: 247
B: 135

Scattered trees background

R: 204
G: 246
B: 255

Surface water

R: 245
G: 202
B: 122

Native American reservations

R: 215
G: 194
B: 158

Lava background

R: 10
G: 147
B: 252

Natural shorelines and hydro text

R: 255
G: 235
B: 190

Built up and infrastructure areas

R: 78
G: 78
B: 78

Lava foreground

R: 211
G: 255
B: 190

Background for some hydro areas

R: 232
G: 190
B: 255

Education area

R: 225
G: 225
B: 225

Gravel background

R: 137
G: 112
B: 68

Foreground for some hydro areas

R: 122
G: 182
B: 245

Health care area

R: 164
G: 121
B: 22

Contour lines

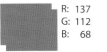
R: 109
G: 187
B: 67

Foreground for some hydro areas

R: 230
G: 230
B: 0

Religious area

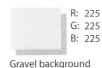
R: 255
G: 0
B: 0

Fences and road fills

R: 0
G: 0
B: 0

Black, used for many symbols

R: 182
G: 252
B: 179

Recreation area

R: 156
G: 156
B: 156

Major street fills

R: 153
G: 204
B: 153

Park areas

R: 211
G: 255
B: 190

Agriculture area, green strip, or woods

Structure polygons
R: 104
G: 104
B: 104

R: 225
G: 190
B: 153

Prison areas

R: 255
G: 255
B: 190

Agriculture area, yellow stripe

R: 102
G: 205
B: 171

Submerged contour lines

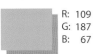
R: 222
G: 140
B: 140

Military areas

R: 215
G: 215
B: 158

Scrub

R: 170
G: 170
B: 170

Boundary line, wide backgrounds

8

It is important to not only manage current data, but it is also becoming increasingly important to enable the review and comparison of historical data with current data. Now that GIS databases can store the evolution of data over time, organizations should consider the most appropriate methods for managing historical updates to the database.

It has been difficult in the past to keep complete and current documentation for GIS projects describing such details as:

- Which features were edited for a given purpose

- The source of the updates

- The collection method used

- The accuracy of the new data (and the method it was based on)

- Possibly feature-level metadata, such as a voice clip, scanned fax, XML data, or other documents providing context for the change to a particular feature

It can be tedious, if not difficult, to collect and maintain this kind of information, but this documentation can provide crucial information for later audits of a geographic dataset. It may become important to identify and revise a particular set of edits later because of a change in policies, procedures, or business requirements. It may also become important to substantiate past decisions, for example, to help resolve conflicts between the maintenance authority and its customers.

An important step toward this goal is the ability to manage versioned data in the geodatabase to maintain an archive of all previous states of each dataset. The initial driver for this capability has been to support the editing of a single GIS database by multiple users at the same time.

## Revision information

This base map data model implements the basic concept of storing revision information. To accomplish this, many of the feature classes have an attribute called Source (long integer). This is a foreign key to the RevisionInfo table (see schema below). The ObjectID serves as a revision ID and primary key field for joins with other tables having a Source foreign key.

This table can be used across local, state, and federal levels of government. However, the level of government can affect the frequency of database updates. For example, for 1:24,000 topographic map data at the local level, the number of updates on any given day might be high. For 1:24,000 map data at the state and regional levels, however, updates might be aggregated and summarized monthly or even less frequently.

### Table
### RevisionInfo

| Field name | Data type | Allow nulls | Precision | Scale | Length | |
|---|---|---|---|---|---|---|
| OBJECTID | Object ID | | | | | |
| CollMeth | Long integer | Yes | 0 | | | Collection method (key to lookup table) |
| AccMeas | Long integer | Yes | 0 | | | Accuracy measurement |
| PosAcc | Long integer | Yes | 0 | | | Positional accuracy value |
| Source | Long integer | Yes | 0 | | | Foreign key to associated revision information sources |
| EntryDate | Date | Yes | 0 | 0 | 8 | Date revision was begun |
| IDDate | Date | Yes | 0 | 0 | 8 | Date feature name verified |
| PosAccDate | Date | Yes | 0 | 0 | 8 | Date positional accuracy verified |
| LastVerDate | Date | Yes | 0 | 0 | 8 | Date of last verification |
| EndDate | Date | Yes | 0 | 0 | 8 | Retirement date |
| MinScale | Long integer | Yes | 0 | | | Minimum applicable map scale |
| MaxScale | Long integer | Yes | 0 | | | Maximum applicable map scale |
| Authority | Long integer | Yes | 0 | | | Maintenance authority (key to lookup table) |
| FMID | Long integer | Yes | 0 | 0 | | Feature metadata ID, foreign key to metadata table |

*Revision tracking metadata*

The RevisionInfo table is intended to support GIS data as it moves between local, state, and federal agencies. The Source field in this table, as well as the Authority field, are expected to vary in usage across different states; the Source field could be a link to additional reference information, and the Authority field could indicate the responsible agency associated with each revision record.

Other fields, such as those having to do with collection method, accuracy, and appropriate scales of use, are most likely to be known and maintained at the local level.

The feature-level metadata identification (FMID) field is a foreign key to additional tables not shown here. This needs to be managed consistently throughout all levels of government for uniform access to the metadata.

8

In a data model with a relatively flat hierarchy of feature types, database designers can use domains (lookup tables) to help distinguish and describe features. The use of subtypes can add another level of hierarchy to the classification scheme. Many agencies have developed more complex taxonomies of feature types with rich descriptions. Prudent database design, however, leans in the direction of reducing the number of feature classes for several reasons. This section presents an approach for managing a rich set of feature types within a limited number of feature classes.

It can be challenging for a cartographer to model hundreds or possibly thousands of different types of geographic features in a GIS, as many cartographic products require. Supporting a rich classification scheme in a database runs counter to conventional wisdom for database design, which is to reduce the number of tables for performance reasons.

One of the most complex classifications is contained in the Digital Geographic Information Exchange Standard (DIGEST), an international standard primarily used among North Atlantic Treaty Organization (NATO) national mapping agencies. One component of DIGEST is the Feature and Attribute Coding Catalog (FACC) data dictionary, which defines a system for associating meaning with geographic features.

This standard is based on a set of feature codes, which can then be further modified by other parameters. For example, an intermittent stream would be described as "River/Stream, hydrological category = intermittent" (BH140, hyc=6). A church would be described as "Building, function = house of worship, house of worship type = church" (AL015, bfc=7, hwt=4). In FACC, the primary feature code, such as BH140 and AL015, is called the FCODE, while additional parameters, such as hyc, bfc, and hwt, are called ACODEs. This system provides a standard, general, and extensible mechanism for describing features. The use of ACODEs to parameterize the feature codes overcomes the limitations of a single linear or hierarchical coding system.

The FACC designation for a feature can be considered as an attribute of the feature. It is a complex attribute, because it consists of an FCODE and one or more ACODEs, but it is logically a single property. A set of line features, with their FACC code, could be modeled like this:

| ID | Shape | FACC |
|----|-------|------|
| 101 | xy...xy | BH140, hyc=6 |
| 102 | xy...xy | BH140, hyc=8 |
| 103 | xy...xy | BH140, hyc=8, exs=32 |

In this case, the feature class represents a drainage network of rivers, streams, and canals. Each drainage network element is coded with the appropriate FACC feature code.

As this example illustrates, FACC defines a standard for assigning meaning to features, but it does not dictate any particular organization of features into classes or the actual structure of a GIS data model. In particular, it is not necessary that the logical or physical schema of a GIS database design reflect the logical structure of the coding standard. FCODEs do not define feature classes, and ACODEs do not define feature class fields. The only requirement is that a standard code or description (such as in FACC) can be associated with any feature represented in the database.

It is not appropriate to use the descriptive logic of FACC or another coding standard to control the structure of the GIS data model. Other aspects, such as the geographic representation of features (lines organized in a network, areas which share topology, and so on); the need to model real-world

| OBJECTID* | VVTID | FCODE | ACODES | DESCRIPTIO |
|-----------|-------|-------|--------|------------|
| 1 | 0 | 2 | DEP 0\|CAR 0 | Contour, Intermediate |
| 2 | 1 | 2 | DEP 1\|CAR 1 | Contour, Intermediate, Depression, Carrying |
| 3 | 2 | 2 | DEP 1\|CAR 0 | Contour, Intermediate, Depression |
| 4 | 3 | 2 | DEP 0\|CAR 1 | Contour, Intermediate, Carrying |
| 5 | 4 | 3 | DEP 0\|CAR 0 | Contour, Index |
| 6 | 5 | 3 | DEP 1\|CAR 1 | Contour, Index, Depression, Carrying |
| 7 | 6 | 3 | DEP 1\|CAR 0 | Contour, Index, Depression |
| 8 | 7 | 3 | DEP 0\|CAR 1 | Contour, Index, Carrying |
| 9 | 8 | 4 | DEP 0\|CAR 0 | Contour, Supplemental |
| 10 | 9 | 4 | DEP 1\|CAR 1 | Contour, Supplemental, Depression, Carrying |
| 11 | 10 | 4 | DEP 1\|CAR 0 | Contour, Supplemental, Depression |
| 12 | 11 | 4 | DEP 0\|CAR 1 | Contour, Supplemental, Carrying |
| 13 | 12 | 5 | DEP 0\|CAR 0 | Contour, Underwater |
| 14 | 13 | 5 | DEP 1\|CAR 1 | Contour, Underwater, Depression, Carrying |
| 15 | 14 | 5 | DEP 1\|CAR 0 | Contour, Underwater, Depression |
| 16 | 15 | 5 | DEP 0\|CAR 1 | Contour, Underwater, Carrying |
| 17 | 16 | 6 | DEP 0\|CAR 0 | Contour, Ice Surface |
| 18 | 17 | 6 | DEP 1\|CAR 1 | Contour, Ice Surface, Depression, Carrying |
| 19 | 18 | 6 | DEP 1\|CAR 0 | Contour, Ice Surface, Depression |
| 20 | 19 | 6 | DEP 0\|CAR 1 | Contour, Ice Surface, Carrying |

*Contours_VVT is a lookup table that can be used for data validation and symbology definition. For example, FCODE=2 refers to intermediate contours. Two ACODE values, DEP and CAR, further qualify the feature classification.*

objects; or the feature extraction specifications are usually more important factors to consider in defining feature classes in a database design. A better method is to use associated tables that contain the feature and attribute codes.

## VALID VALUE TABLE APPROACH

The solution to this issue is called the valid value table approach. In this design, an auxiliary lookup table (the VVT) is associated with each feature class. Examples in this chapter include RoadsCartoDissolve_VVT, TransCartoPoints_VVT, CulturalLines_VVT, CulturalPoints_VVT, CulturalAreas_VVT, Contours_VVT, and ElevationPoints_VVT.

A portion of Contours_VVT data is shown on the previous page. The VVTID is the key field used for joins with the Contours table. Each record has a single value for FCODE and one or more values separated by a vertical bar "|" symbol for ACODEs. In this table, there are two ACODEs, DEP and CAR, for each FCODE value.

This table was used to construct and enumerate a taxonomy of contour types. Once the types are enumerated, the VVTID and Description values are plugged into the geodatabase properties as a domain value lookup table.

This approach requires no additional programming and uses the most efficient method for managing the description lookup.

However, this simple use of the VVT table is for assigning feature symbols and drawing rules, not for rich feature descriptions. Some VVT tables have as many as 20 ACODEs qualifying a single FCODE, and it becomes increasingly important to support queries against individual ACODE values. In this latter case, some additional user programming is required to extend and enable the editor and query tools to have visibility into the VVT table and its ACODES column directly. An ArcGIS feature coding extension has been written for this purpose and is available online (see the technical paper, Feature Coding Standards and Geodatabase Design, ESRI 2002, and the 'Further resources' section at the end of this chapter).

Taking the VVT concept one step further, it is possible to use a small set of auxiliary tables to define a complete feature classification system for the entire GIS database. Such a foundation could be used to validate individual VVT tables, such as the one just described. The schema for these tables is shown below, with examples on the next page.

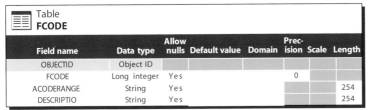

Table
**FCODE**

| Field name | Data type | Allow nulls | Default value | Domain | Precision | Scale | Length |
|---|---|---|---|---|---|---|---|
| OBJECTID | Object ID | | | | | | |
| FCODE | Long integer | Yes | | | 0 | | |
| ACODERANGE | String | Yes | | | | | 254 |
| DESCRIPTIO | String | Yes | | | | | 254 |

*VVT reference table of all valid ACODE values for each FCODE*

Unique feature classification code
Set of all valid ACODEs and values for one FCODE
Feature classification description

Table
**ATTDESC**

| Field name | Data type | Allow nulls | Default value | Domain | Precision | Scale | Length |
|---|---|---|---|---|---|---|---|
| OBJECTID | Object ID | | | | | | |
| ACODE | String | Yes | | | | | 8 |
| DESCRIPTIO | String | Yes | | | | | 254 |

*VVT reference table of unique ACODEs and their descriptions*

ACODE name
Description of this ACODE name

Table
**ATTVAL**

| Field name | Data type | Allow nulls | Default value | Domain | Precision | Scale | Length |
|---|---|---|---|---|---|---|---|
| OBJECTID | Object ID | | | | | | |
| ACODE | String | Yes | | | | | 8 |
| VALUE_ | Long integer | Yes | | | 0 | | |
| DESCRIPTIO | String | Yes | | | | | 254 |
| NOTES | String | Yes | | | | | 254 |

*VVT reference table of valid ACODE values, independent of the feature type*

ACODE name
One valid value of this ACODE
Description of this ACODE value
Alternate or supplemental description of this ACODE

**8**

The tables on these pages effectively define a complete feature classification foundation. One set of these tables could be used to support any number of cartographic products on multiple GIS databases. The beauty of this design is the flexibility with which features can be classified. Few database tables are needed to manage a rich classification system that allows a variable number of parameters to define any given feature type. This leads to simpler data models that would not need structural modifications just to accommodate an evolving classification scheme.

Three tables define any given feature classification system, FCODE, ATTDESC, and ATTVAL. These tables are to be populated by the user/database administrator for use by the ArcGIS feature coding extension mentioned previously.

To populate these tables, first start with the ATTDESC and ATTVAL tables, creating them as simple tables in a spreadsheet or personal database document. Next, create an intermediate table listing the ACODEs used by each FCODE, with one FCODE–ACODE pair per record. It is then relatively straightforward to write a program that walks through this intermediate table and the ATTVAL table to generate the ACODERANGE column of the FCODE table. Some FCODEs may require manual editing, such as those for Buildings in the table shown here (see last four records in the diagram).

Each of these FCODEs has the same ACODE but with a different range of values. However, these descriptions can also be added programmatically, as long as the FCODE and each ACODE have descriptions.

The FCODE table would be manually edited further to add the FCODE descriptions and remove invalid ACODE values. It is generally a good idea to have the fewest number of ACODE fields necessary for each FCODE. The more ACODEs there may be for a single FCODE, the more difficult becomes the task of validating all the values and combinations of values across all the ACODEs for a given FCODE record.

## IMPLICATIONS OF A VVT APPROACH

If your database requires the use of an extensive classification system, such as with DIGEST FACC or USGS Digital Line Graph (DLG), then you should consider using VVTs. The approach described here can accommodate both the FACC and DLG classification schemes and helps ensure semantic integrity in the database design. It also offers advantages for enhanced database use and for multiscale and multipurpose database specifications.

| OBJECTID* | FCODE | ACODERANGE | DESCRIPTIO |
|---|---|---|---|
| 1 | 0 | CUL [0,1] | Road, End Point |
| 2 | 1 | JUN [0,1] | Road, Junction |
| 3 | 2 | DEP [0,1]|CAR [0,1] | Contour, Intermediate |
| 4 | 3 | DEP [0,1]|CAR [0,1] | Contour, Index |
| 5 | 4 | DEP [0,1]|CAR [0,1] | Contour, Supplemental |
| 6 | 5 | DEP [0,1]|CAR [0,1] | Contour, Underwater |
| 7 | 6 | DEP [0,1]|CAR [0,1] | Contour, Ice Surface |
| 8 | 7 | GRD [0,1] | Spot Elevation |
| 9 | 8 | TRD [0,1]|PRM [0,1]|HTP [0,1] | Horizontal Control Station |
| 10 | 9 | TAB [0,1]|PRM [0,1] | Vertical Control Station |
| 11 | 10 | TRD [0,1] | Horizontal and Vertical Control Station |
| 12 | 11 | TAB [0,1] | Boundary Marker, Better than 3rd Orde |
| 26 | 12 | BLD [0,4,7,10,11,22,23,24,25,26,30,31,32,33,34,35] | Building, General |
| 27 | 13 | BLD [16,17,18] | Building, Religious |
| 28 | 14 | BLD [19,20,21,43] | Building, Healthcare |
| 29 | 15 | BLD [8,14,28,29] | Building, Sports or Entertainment |

*The FCODE table defines the complete set of ACODEs and ACODE values that are valid for each FCODE (partial table content shown).*

*The ATTDESC table lists and describes each ACODE (partial table content shown).*

| OBJECTID* | ACODE | DESCRIPTIO |
|---|---|---|
| 1 | CUL | Cul De Sac or Dead End |
| 2 | JUN | Junction Type |
| 3 | DEP | Depression Status for Contours |
| 4 | CAR | Carrying Status for Contours |
| 5 | GRD | Spot Elevation Ground Relationship |
| 6 | TAB | Survey Point Tablet Status |
| 7 | TRD | Elevation point 3rd Order or better Status |
| 8 | PRM | Survey Point Permanent Status |
| 9 | HTP | Spot Elevation Horizontal Type |
| 10 | MIN | Mines |
| 11 | BDG | Building Point Types |
| 12 | LMP | Landmark points |
| 13 | TOW | Tower Points |
| 14 | LLM | Landmark Lines |
| 15 | RCL | Recreational Landmark Lines |

## Enhanced database use

Having a more sophisticated classification system embodied in the GIS can lead to more expressive queries, feature symbology, and quality assurance during data entry and update. By incorporating FCODEs and ACODEs (or major and minor codes, as with USGS DLG) into the schema, you can take advantage of these codes when selecting features for export. These tables essentially form a coded value domain for enforcing data integrity across combinations of multiple attributes on features and other objects. Thus, a user can assign major and minor code values to the data yet be prevented from assigning invalid combinations. For example, a user should be able to create "a new road that is paved and has a median" but not to create "a new road that is dirt and has a median."

*The ATTVAL table lists and describes every value of each ACODE (partial table content shown).*

## Multiscale use

Using major and minor codes are usually independent of feature geometry type (point, line, polygon). This is especially useful for multiscale databases in which features may change in geometry type as the display scale changes. For example, a building could be represented as a polygon at a large scale, as a point at a smaller scale, and be aggregated with other nearby buildings into a built-up area polygon at a still smaller scale. With the VVT approach, the feature–attribute combinations are not representation dependent and can be applied regardless of the geometry type needed at any given moment.

## Multipurpose use

VVTs could be used for multiple data and cartographic products as well. For example, a VVT could be used to define how features are shown on different types of maps and to help define different symbology for each of these products. This can be achieved by adding columns to the VVT table itself, such as a column for the product type or other context. With appropriate queries, the map's appearance could then reflect the user's current purpose with the least effort to change data layers.

| OBJECTID* | ACODE | VALUE_ | DESCRIPTIO | NOTES |
|---|---|---|---|---|
| 1 | CUL | 0 | Dead End | |
| 2 | CUL | 1 | Cul De Sac | |
| 3 | JUN | 0 | On/Off Ramp | |
| 4 | JUN | 1 | | Other |
| 5 | DEP | 0 | | Not Depression Contour |
| 6 | DEP | 1 | Depression | |
| 7 | CAR | 0 | | Not Carrying Contour |
| 8 | CAR | 1 | Carrying | |
| 9 | GRD | 0 | | Ground Level |
| 10 | GRD | 1 | On Bridge | |
| 11 | TAB | 0 | No Tablet | |
| 12 | TAB | 1 | Tablet | |
| 13 | TRD | 0 | Less than 3rd Order | |
| 14 | TRD | 1 | Better than 3rd Order | |
| 15 | PRM | 0 | Recoverable | |
| 16 | PRM | 1 | Permanent | |
| 17 | HTP | 0 | Checked Spot Elevation | |
| 18 | HTP | 1 | Vertical Angle Benchmark | |
| 19 | LLM | 0 | Fence | |
| 20 | LLM | 1 | Wall | |
| 21 | LLM | 2 | Sea Wall | |
| 22 | LLM | 3 | Conveyor | |
| 23 | LLM | 4 | Levee or Dike | |
| 24 | LLM | 5 | Corrall | |
| 25 | LLM | 6 | Power Line | |
| 26 | REC | 0 | Track | |
| 27 | REC | 1 | Slide | Bobsled or Luge |
| 28 | REC | 2 | Ski Lift | |
| 29 | LLM | 7 | Historical Line | |
| 30 | MIN | 0 | Entrance | |
| 31 | MIN | 1 | Shaft | |
| 32 | LMP | 0 | Coke Oven | |
| 33 | LMP | 1 | Prospect | |
| 34 | LMP | 2 | Drill Hole | |
| 35 | LMP | 3 | Historical Marker | |

TNRIS collects data for its statewide mapping program through collaboration with many state agencies, federal agencies, and local governments. To make the most use of its limited budget and staff resources, TNRIS sought to fully automate its strategic base map database, called StratMap, by streamlining several of the design concepts presented in this chapter.

Much of the base map cartographic product described so far in this chapter has been based on the organization and symbology of data for the standard USGS topographic map series. While the TNRIS project team favored these design concepts, all of which were implemented in a working prototype, its firm goal was to fully automate the map production process, which necessitated a simpler design. Another guiding principle for TNRIS was to make updates to the source database to update associated map products, both at the state level and for the USGS National Map.

## A TALE OF TWO SERIES

In thinking about the most maintainable organization of data for its map products, the TNRIS team took into account both the intended use of the maps, as well as the availability of high-resolution (1 meter) aerial photography. Instead of producing a single map series, TNRIS settled on two: one based on a simplification of the USGS topographic map series and another series having a detailed DOQQ backdrop. The simplified topographic map presents an easy-to-read view of many types of physical features, while the DOQQ-based series supports fine resolution and dynamic data, such as urban detail.

This approach has led to several simplifications in the base map design that may be of as much interest to readers as the concepts presented earlier. These simplifications can be summarized as:

- Refinement and update of the USGS GNIS data to support map layers for landmarks and other cultural point features

- Elimination of data collection and rendering for footprints of buildings in favor of the DOQQ backdrop with GNIS names overlaid

- Use of database views to distinguish the various categories of streets and highways for display in the map editor

- Elimination of topology creation or maintenance

- Elimination (for now) of the VVT approach in favor of simple feature classifications and symbology

- Use of standard feature labeling instead of feature-linked annotation

- Licensing of Geographic Data Technology (GDT) data for labeling of city streets

### GNIS and the Texas Names Gazetteer

Fundamental to both map series, TNRIS augments GNIS (a tabular dataset) by making the names into geographic features to support labeling of key buildings and other landmarks in orthophotos. These place name features are called the Texas Names Gazetteer. With this gazetteer, errors are more easily found, and updates to the names dataset directly affect related map products.

GNIS data collection in Texas continues in a multiyear, multiphase project with the USGS. TNRIS staff have compiled well over one hundred reference sources for the names and, as a result, have found it necessary to prioritize the types of features included in the names database. The most important are schools, hospitals and clinics, parks, malls, courthouses and other key government buildings, and populated places (PPLs), which include metropolitan utility districts and colonias (small, primarily Hispanic villages). The emphasis is on widely recognized structures and other important landmarks that can serve as aids to navigation. Hydrographic features, such as rivers, springs, and dams, are also included. Over time, other interesting and useful landmarks, such as museums, libraries, and golf courses, may be added.

### DOQQ backdrop

In addition to its use in proofing vector data, the use of high-resolution aerial photography addresses an important need—offering more current and correct data for the highly dynamic urban landscape. It is easier to simply update the photo than to redraw and proof building footprints.

## Database views

The practice of using multiple layers for transportation features, as described earlier, can be carried out in a number of ways. In the early prototype, on-the-fly relationships were used for each of the many transportation layers. Each relate resulted in a query of the roads feature class to select a particular subset of road features. With a large database of detailed road features, however, on-the-fly relationships did not provide adequate performance. Instead, the database administrator created database views for subgroups of road features. Corresponding map layers for these views were created, one map layer per database view. This provided the performance needed in the production database.

## Topology

TNRIS chose not to create any topologies. This was largely because TNRIS does not have authority to alter the data for many of the feature classes but is simply publishing the data compiled from its many sources.

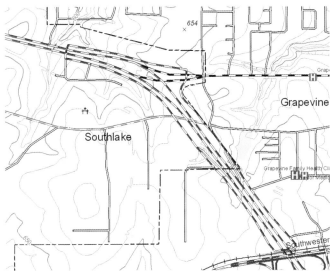

*Detail of Southlake and Grapevine, Texas, showing organization and symbology for 1:24,000 scale topographic base map*

## Valid Value Tables

The TNRIS team chose to use a simple classification scheme for their features, precluding the need for the VVT approach described earlier in this chapter. This allows them to keep the database structure similar to the map structure, which their customers are using when they place orders. It also reduces the potential for classification errors when entering data into the database.

## Feature labeling versus annotation

The TNRIS team chose to use automatic labeling based on feature attributes, rather than using annotation features. For area features such as city, county, and state boundaries, they created both polygon and line feature classes, the polygon for shading and for a centered label, and the line features for labeling along the boundary.

## Licensing GDT data

For a fee, TNRIS licensed the use of Geographic Data Technology city street data for the state of Texas. This was not for the actual street lines, which come from TxDOT, but for the local street names, which are not included in the TxDOT data. TNRIS makes the GDT line features transparent but turns on labels, thus annotating the TxDOT street data.

*Detail of Southlake–Grapevine DOQQ and vector features for map series that can be used effectively at larger scales than 1:24,000. Note the different colors used for easier identification of major roads, rail, and landmark points against the DOQQ backdrop.*

The same thematic layers and broad categories of feature classes presented at the beginning of this chapter still hold, but the specific feature classes and map layers have changed for the current TNRIS work in progress, primarily for simpler organization.

TNRIS and StratMap require a simple data model that can support integration of multiple data sources because the source content comes from several state, regional, and local agencies. The Texas Department of Transportation provides the greatest share of data, but TNRIS has literally hundreds of sources for all the feature classes shown here.

## Landmarks and Boundaries

These feature classes capture the principal cultural layers. The Texas Names Gazetteer is integrated with landmark points, allowing easier proofing and updating. Multiple layers are created for most of these classes, one for use over DOQQ and a second for use without DOQQ.

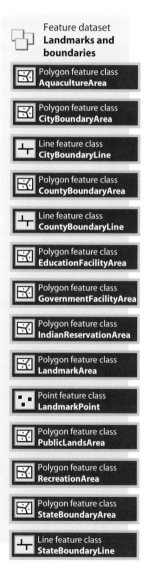

Feature dataset
**Landmarks and boundaries**

Polygon feature class
**AquacultureArea**

Polygon feature class
**CityBoundaryArea**

Line feature class
**CityBoundaryLine**

Polygon feature class
**CountyBoundaryArea**

Line feature class
**CountyBoundaryLine**

Polygon feature class
**EducationFacilityArea**

Polygon feature class
**GovernmentFacilityArea**

Polygon feature class
**IndianReservationArea**

Polygon feature class
**LandmarkArea**

Point feature class
**LandmarkPoint**

Polygon feature class
**PublicLandsArea**

Polygon feature class
**RecreationArea**

Polygon feature class
**StateBoundaryArea**

Line feature class
**StateBoundaryLine**

## Hydrography and Hypsography

Rivers, streams, and water bodies are collected at 1:100,000 from NHD, and at 1:24,000 from enhanced NHD. An extensive springs dataset is incorporated into the Texas Names Gazetteer, as well as surface water names. Contour intervals vary from 5 to 40 feet.

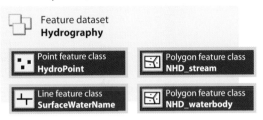

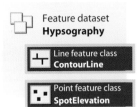

## Infrastructure

Infrastructure features are for important land uses not normally considered cultural.

## Transportation

Highways, streets, and railroads are provided by TxDOT. These are accurate enough to overlay on 1-meter orthophotos. Multiple layers are created for major highways and railroads, one for use over DOQQ and a second for use without DOQQ.

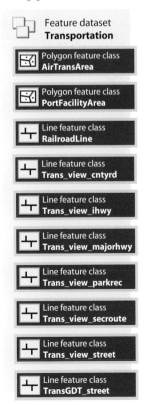

## Reference

Reference datasets include an index to the USGS 1:24,000 topographic map quad sheets, a DOQQ index, and a 1-degree latitude–longitude grid, which is an index to the DOQQ image catalog.

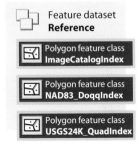

8

TNRIS transportation data is based on TxDOT, GDT, and other sources. The TxDOT data is detailed and is updated on a regular basis. This is well suited for overlaying on 1–meter resolution orthophotos.

The transportation feature dataset has certain distinctions worth mentioning, including the use of database views, a single elevation for all roads, the use of multiple fill layers to achieve dashed-line road symbols, simplification of symbology for use over orthophotos, and the use of GDT street data for labeling.

## Database views

TNRIS uses six categories of roads: interstate highways; U.S. and state highways; secondary routes, such as FMs and RRs, county roads; park and recreation roads; and local streets. These categories are revealed to the GIS as database views. A database view is a named selection of records from a relational database such as Oracle, IBM DB2, or Microsoft SQL Server. These views appear as separate tables to ArcSDE and are much faster in operation than using on-the-fly selection queries from ArcMap.

## Single elevation for all roads

Notice the close-up view of a highway interchange in the figure on the next page. TNRIS creates multiple layers for drawing the different classes of roads but has fewer such layers for transportation than was discussed earlier in this chapter. This is to simplify and streamline data updates and map generation. For example, all road and ramp segments in the interchange shown appear to be at the same elevation in this figure. At a scale of 1:24,000, the detail of representing all overpasses and underpasses correctly was considered unnecessary, and at larger scales (zoomed into the map), the orthophoto can provide this level of detail.

## Creating dashed-line road symbols

The red–white dash pattern used for major highways is accomplished by assigning two fill layers, the first having the red dash and the second having the white dash, as can be seen in the figure's layer list.

## Orthophoto symbolization

The TxDOT transportation data is sufficiently detailed for 1:24,000-scale topographic maps and as overlays on 1-meter orthophotos at much larger scales (up to 1:10,000 scale). A different representation is used for some transportation features when the roads are displayed over an orthophoto backdrop. Given the red tint in many aerial photographs, the dashed red symbol used for major highways is difficult to read over DOQQs, so these roads are changed to a solid white fill.

## Local street labels

Notice the local street names in this figure. These are the labels from GDT street data, for which the GDT street lines themselves have been made transparent, so the TxDOT road lines are the principal data source.

## Transportation areas

TNRIS includes air and water facilities, such as airports and seaports, to be part of the transportation feature dataset as separate feature classes. The layers made visible are shown at the bottom of the layer list in the figure.

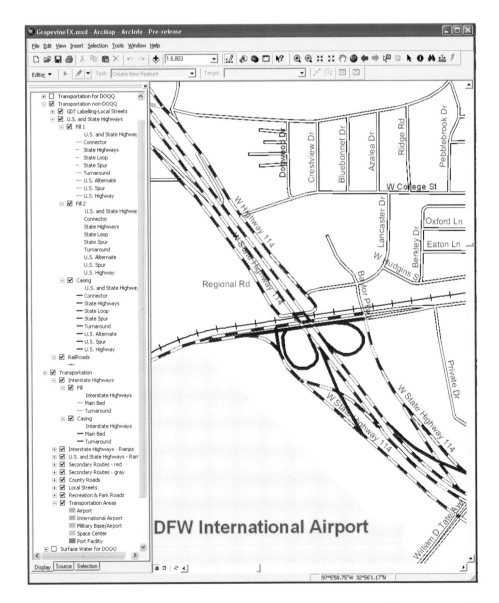

Landmarks and boundaries in the TNRIS database are grouped together in the same feature dataset. Integrated with the landmark data is the Texas Names Gazetteer, which is a geographic extension and refinement of GNIS.

The TNRIS landmarks and boundaries dataset has its own set of issues: how to label the edges as well as the centroid of administrative areas, how to symbolize over an orthophoto, and how to deal with multiple noncoincident boundary features along the same path. Again, keep in mind this organization is still a work in progress and is subject to change. In particular, the boundary types are in flux at the time of this writing.

### Administrative area boundaries

TNRIS uses both polygon and line features and layers to represent administrative areas, such as city, county, regional council of governments, and state jurisdictions. The polygon feature provides an anchor for interior labeling of the area, while the line feature provides an anchor for labeling parallel to, and on both sides of, a county or state line. City polygon features only are shown in the figure on the next page; the line features are added as needed for cartographic finishing.

### Orthophoto symbolization

The orthophoto shown earlier illustrates the symbolization used for landmark features when viewed over DOQQ. Most of the point symbols in the layer list for the map at right are colored yellow for viewing over DOQQ.

### Dealing with multiple, almost coincident features

Many jurisdictions throughout the state have overlapping interests in certain boundaries. A common case of this is where TxDOT maintains a county boundary database in support of its road maintenance and other contracts. The pertinent city and county governments will also have their version of the county boundaries. Since these are collected and maintained independently of each other, these boundaries often do not coincide. Since TNRIS does not have authority to change these boundaries, it finesses this issue by using lines for the boundaries that are thick enough to mask most discrepancies.

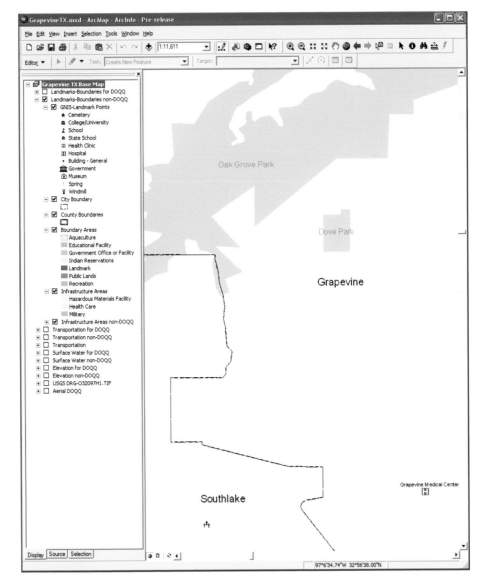

Hydrography for TNRIS comes primarily from the U.S. National Hydro Dataset. This has, until recently, been collected at a scale of 1:100,000 but is now being enhanced and updated with 1:24,000 data. Hypsography for contour lines and spot elevations is based on USGS data at a scale of 1:24,000.

## NHD hydrography

For layer display, TNRIS simplifies the hydrographic features from Arc Hydro into a small number of classes based on the NHD data from the USGS. This includes stream flow lines, pipelines, connections, and water bodies. Several types of water bodies are shown in the figure on the next page's layer list.

## Springs database

An extensive database of springs is also maintained by the Texas Water Development Board in conjunction with the USGS. Since these point features are also included in the Texas Names Gazetteer, they are displayed as part of the landmarks layer described earlier.

## Hypsography

Contour data is taken and refined from USGS DLG sources, with contour intervals varying from 5 to 40 feet. A simple set of contour line types is used for these layers.

A single class of elevation point features is used, based on spot elevation data from USGS DLGs.

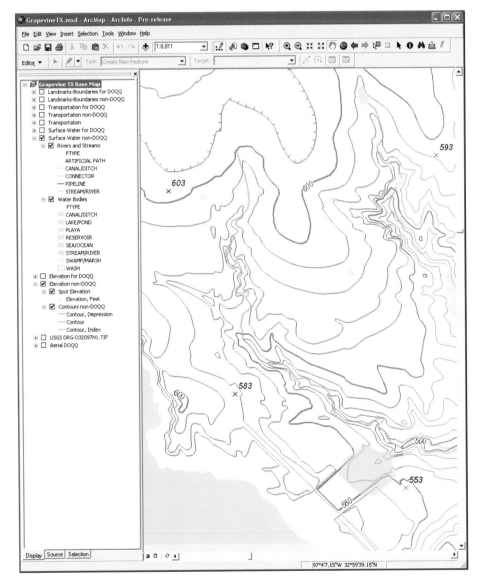

To meet the cartographic requirements that might be imposed on a GIS, a complete cartographic data model should be considered. This data model potentially consists of several kinds of extensions to the landscape data model.

*It tells the truth by lying, like a poem*
*With bold hyperbole of shape and line —*
*A masterpiece of false simplicity.*
*Its secret meanings must be mulled upon,*
*Yet all the world is open to a glance.*
*With colors to fire the mind, a song of names,*
*A painting that is not at home on the walls*
*But crumpled on a station wagon floor,*
*Worn through at folds, tape patched*
*and chocolate smudged*
*(What other work of art can lead you home?)*
*— A map was made to use.*

*Juliana O. Muehrcke*

Cartographic products are inevitably representations of reality chosen carefully by the cartographer to make the map as readable as possible. For example, a road next to a river might be displaced on the map from its actual physical location to distinguish it from the river it follows and to accurately place these objects relative to one another ("the road runs along the west side of the river"). For millennia, cartographic maps have been the product of human manual skill and labor. But in recent decades, it has become possible to automate more and more aspects of cartography.

In the context of a topographic base map data model, you have now seen numerous elements of a cartographic data model. This is an additive data model in the sense that it can be added to essentially any kind of landscape data model, where the term landscape refers to a locationally accurate representation of some area of interest. A cartographic data model can include any number of the following elements: additions to the schema and content of geographic feature classes, a descriptive classification scheme, a cartographic data collection specification, a map layout specification, and any number of map layers. These are discussed further below.

## Additions to schema

Several of the feature classes in this base map data model have additional attributes used just for cartographic purposes. The OverpassLevel attribute on transportation classes is intended to support accurate depiction of street and highway overpasses and underpasses. The VVTID attribute of numerous feature classes is a foreign key to a classification record used to control symbology. The VVT tables are necessary to support this use. The RoadsCartoDissolve feature class is an entire feature class made to support accurate representation of streets and highways. These are just a few of the ways that the base map schema has been extended.

## Additional features

In many cases, new features must be added to the database to reflect cartographic adjustments to locationally accurate features without losing the accurate source data. For example, new features may be created from geoprocessing original source features, such as to generalize selected features for use at a different scale.

## Descriptive classification system

A detailed, hierarchical feature classification scheme is an important part of many cartographic data models, particularly for national mapping agencies (NMAs), which generally require the use of established standard coding schemes for feature types and attribute values, as discussed earlier in the chapter.

## Cartographic specification

At a scale of 1:24,000, lakes of at least 1 square kilometer in area can be drawn as polygons; if they have less area, then they may be drawn as point locations or omitted entirely. A cartographer applies data collection rules such as this to virtually every type of feature in the database.

## Map layout specification

As demonstrated previously, there are many elements in a hardcopy map layout, such as the grids and graticules, magnetic North arrow direction, map legend, and so on. These could be based on a national standard, such as the USGS 1:24,000 topographic map series, or you could design your own. Implementing such a map layout specification may involve still more additions to the geodatabase schema, but the more that can be integrated within the database, the easier it will be to share it with other data providers and users.

## Map layers

Finally, the map layers themselves in the GIS can form an important part of a cartographic data model. In the transportation feature dataset of this base map data model, there were numerous map layers used to represent road casing and fill for each overpass or underpass level in the dataset. Each of these layers invoked a query to the database and imposed a particular symbology on the query result. Map layer properties also determine the valid scale range and transparency for displaying a given feature class. The layers essentially implement the cartographic specification rules.

All of these elements together complete the cartographic data model. You are free to use any combination of these that suit your application requirements, keeping in mind standard practices and guidelines for achieving high-quality cartographic results.

8

## REFERENCES AND FURTHER READING

Data Users Guide 1: Digital Line Graphs From 1:24,000-Scale Maps. 1990. Reston, Virginia: U.S. Department of the Interior, U.S. Geological Survey.

Dent, Borden D. 1998. *Cartography: Thematic Map Design*. McGraw-Hill.

Digital Geographic Information Exchange Standard, Part 4, Annex C, Alphabetized Content Listing of All Features and Attributes, edition 2.1. 2000. Washington, D.C.: Digital Geographic Information Working Group. URL: http://www.digest.org/html/DIGEST_2-1_Part4_AnnexC.pdf.

*Digital Texas: 2002 Biennial Report on GIS Technology*. 2002. Austin: Texas Geographic Information Council.

*Feature Coding Standards and Geodatabase Design*. 2002. ESRI Technical Paper, URL: http://arconline.esri.com/arconline/whitepapers/ao_/Feature_Coding_Standards_and_Geodatabase_Design.pdf.

Imhoff, Euard. 1982. *Cartographic Relief Presentation*. De Gruyter, New York.

National Mapping Program Technical Instructions, Part 2 Attribute Coding, Standards for Revised Primary Series Quadrangle Maps. 2001. Reston, Virginia: U.S. Department of the Interior, U.S. Geological Survey, National Mapping Division.

National Mapping Program Technical Instructions, Part 3 Attribute Coding, Standards for Digital Line Graphs. 1998. Reston, Virginia: U.S. Department of the Interior, U.S. Geological Survey, National Mapping Division.

National Mapping Program Technical Instructions, Part 5 Publication Symbols, Standards for 1:24,000- and 1:25,000-Scale Quadrangle Maps. 2002. Reston, Virginia: U.S. Department of the Interior, U.S. Geological Survey, National Mapping Division.

National Mapping Program Technical Instructions, Part 6 Publication Symbols, Standards for 1:24,000- and 1:25,000-Scale Quadrangle Maps. 2001. Reston, Virginia: U.S. Department of the Interior, U.S. Geological Survey, National Mapping Division.

National Mapping Program Technical Instructions, Standards for 1:24,000-Scale Digital Line Graphs and Quadrangle Maps. 2001. Reston, Virginia: U.S. Department of the Interior, U.S. Geological Survey, National Mapping Division.

StratMap Texas, Digitally Remastered: Draft Transportation Data Description, Version 4. 2000. Austin, Texas: GIS/Trans, Ltd.

## ACKNOWLEDGMENTS

Deep thanks to the TNRIS staff: Drew Decker, Marcy Berbrick, Erika Boghici, David Pimentel, Brent Porter, Felicia Retiz, and Chris Williams; to Ron Pigott of the Texas Water Development Board, to Dawn Ortiz of the University of Texas Center for Space Research, and to Michael Ouimet of the Texas Department of Information Resources in Austin, Texas, for sharing data, time, and experience working with the TNRIS data models. Charlie Frye and Aileen Buckley of ESRI provided content for this chapter.

## FURTHER RESOURCES

Follow the Basemap link from ESRI ArcOnline at http://support.esri.com/datamodels for further information on this data model.

The Feature Coding Extension for ArcGIS version 8.3 and higher is available at http://arcobjectsonline.esri.com. Click on Samples in the Topics list (left column), then on Geodatabase, then on ArcGIS Extension for feature coding standards. Links to download the Visual Basic and C++ versions will then appear.

The U.S. EPA is collecting and updating nationwide land cover data and other themes as part of its Multi-Resolution Land Characteristics Consortium. See http://www.epa.gov/mrlc/data.html for more information.

Many geographic name inventories have been compiled at the national level; one of these is the USGS Geographic Names Information System. See http://geonames.usgs.gov/ for more information.

8

*The physical data model is the implementation of your logical model in an actual geodatabase. Creating the physical data model is an iterative process in which the logical design is applied to a prototype geodatabase, data is loaded, and the system is tested. Lessons learned from this cycle are applied in one or more subsequent pilot geodatabases. When the system performs to your expectations, it is ready to implement as a production geodatabase.*

**9**

**A**fter you have finished the conceptual and logical data models, the next stage of the process is creating the physical data model or implementing the geodatabase schema. While the conceptual and logical models are independent of a specific GIS technology, creating a physical data model requires an implementation platform. This chapter deals with the process of implementing a physical data model using ESRI ArcGIS software.

There are several starting points in the process. The one you choose will depend in part on how closely your logical data model matches an existing geodatabase data model, the degree to which your data model matches your existing GIS data, the simplicity or complexity of your model, and whether you choose to use a visual Computer-Aided Software Engineering (CASE) tool to represent the geodatabase schema.

You should plan to prototype your schema in a personal geodatabase for initial testing, then refine your schema and create a pilot geodatabase for further testing. The design of the final, or production, geodatabase will be informed by the lessons learned during the prototype and pilot phases.

# Building geodatabases

The process of implementing a physical data model unfolds in six stages, each of which is repeated to create a prototype, pilot, and, finally, a production geodatabase. First you start with a logical geodatabase design and apply it to a geodatabase. Second, you modify the newly created schema. Third, you load data into the schema. Fourth, you build topological relationships. Fifth, you test the geodatabase. Sixth, you revise the schema and repeat the cycle again until the production geodatabase is done.

When you create a geodatabase from a logical model, you should plan to implement the geodatabase in a three-phase project. The first phase is a prototype, in which you first put your logical model into practice. The next is a more complete pilot geodatabase that builds on the lessons learned from creating the prototype. Testing in each of these phases will help you refine your model, which can finally be implemented as a production geodatabase. It is important to invest time in testing and revising the prototype and pilot geodatabases.

### 1. Obtain or develop a design

As you have seen earlier in this book, a number of geodatabase schemas have been developed by groups of designers from different disciplines. It may be that one of the existing schemas matches your needs closely enough that you can copy and modify it. If so, you would start at the first option on the geodatabase implementation work flow overview diagram, option A, and use a template to begin implementing your geodatabase.

Because physical data model implementation is an iterative process, once you have implemented and tested a geodatabase, you may revisit its design, regardless of how you began the physical data model design process. If there is not already a schema that fits your logical design, you might decide that existing GIS data contains most of the schema elements that you have planned to implement. In this case, you might choose option B as a starting point.

If you have a simple logical data model design, and you are not interested in using a CASE tool to design the data model, you can begin implementing the physical data model from scratch in ArcCatalog and choose option C as your starting point. If you are proficient with a CASE tool, you may choose to start at option D. This approach has the disadvantage that some of the spatial geodatabase properties, such as topologies, network connectivity rules, and raster catalogs, cannot

be expressed with the Unified Modeling Language (UML) used by the CASE tool.

### 2. Modify the design

After the initial schema is generated, the next stage is to modify the schema in ArcCatalog. Depending on your starting point, you may make many or few modifications to the schema at this point. The amount of work at this stage is proportional to the difference between the template or the geodatabase you have created and the logical model you designed. If you started using a CASE tool, it is best to make your schema design changes using the tool before you create the database schema or in the next iteration. The exceptions to this rule are the schema elements that cannot be created using CASE tools, notably topology.

### 3. Load data

The next stage of the process, in most cases, is to load data into the geodatabase. You might skip this stage if you created the basic schema by importing existing data into a new geodatabase. In the data loading phase, you may use tools in ArcCatalog and ArcMap to load data, depending on whether you are loading simple features or features with advanced geodatabase behavior (such as validation rules, relationship classes, and custom object behavior). You may also create new features to fill an empty feature class (particularly for dimension features; annotation features, in some cases; or features that are derived from existing features). For example, you might create polygons from points and lines, using topology, or you might generalize a feature class or merge many features together with no attributes to create quick-drawing layers for large map extents. You might also, at this stage, create new standard or feature-linked annotation feature classes by designing labels in ArcMap and converting them to annotation.

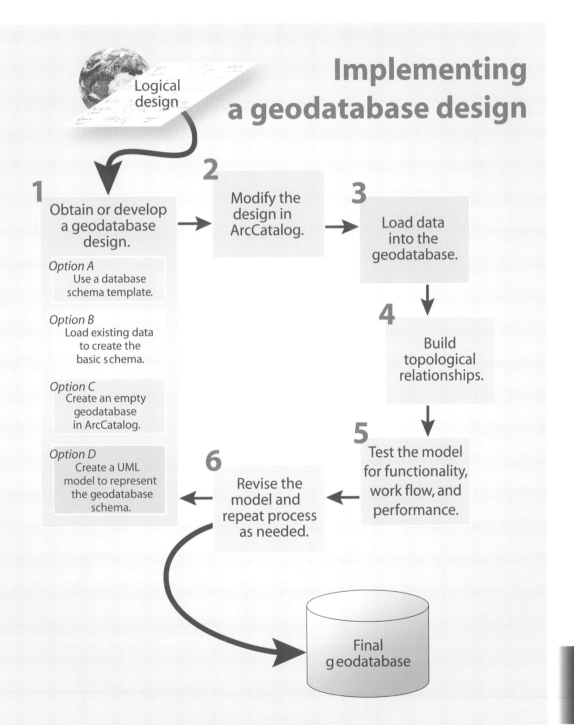

**Implementing a geodatabase design**

Logical design

**1** Obtain or develop a geodatabase design.

*Option A*
Use a database schema template.

*Option B*
Load existing data to create the basic schema.

*Option C*
Create an empty geodatabase in ArcCatalog.

*Option D*
Create a UML model to represent the geodatabase schema.

**2** Modify the design in ArcCatalog.

**3** Load data into the geodatabase.

**4** Build topological relationships.

**5** Test the model for functionality, work flow, and performance.

**6** Revise the model and repeat process as needed.

Final geodatabase

*9*

### 4. Build topological relationships

Once your initial data has been loaded, the next stage is to implement topological relationships. These could be geodatabase topologies or geometric networks (although a given feature class cannot participate in more than one topology or geometric network). You should use the minimum number of topology rules necessary to enforce the topological relationships you need. Remember that topology rules may be applied to subtypes, as well as to feature classes. Topologies may be validated in their entirety or a section at a time, depending on the size of your database and your work flow.

### 5. Test the model

The next stage is to test your geodatabase. Test work flows, create sample data products (layers, maps, reports, charts, 3D visualizations), perform analyses, trace networks, edit features, check for topological errors, and fix topology errors by editing features. If you are implementing a multiuser geodatabase, make sure that all of the feature classes and subtypes are loaded (although it may be reasonable to load a clipped subset of your data for testing purposes, at least for the first iteration of the process), create versions, edit and reconcile versions, and load the system with a realistic number of editors and data viewers.

### 6. Revise the model

This process should be repeated at least once, probably two or more times, especially for enterprise geodatabases implemented with ArcSDE in a commercial multiuser RDBMS. Prototyping in a personal geodatabase is quicker and simpler than prototyping on an RDBMS, but once your schema has been tested and is proved conceptually solid, you should still plan to test a multiuser pilot geodatabase. This will help you ensure that versioning work flows, multiuser editing, and performance are satisfactory.

In the following pages, each stage in the geodatabase implementation process will be broken down into smaller parts and discussed in detail.

### SHARING A GEODATABASE SCHEMA

Once you have gone through the process of designing and creating a geodatabase, you may want to share your design with colleagues. You can extract the schema of a finished database into a personal geodatabase or export a schema-only XML workspace document. Either can be shared and used by others to create schemas for new geodatabases. The Geodatabase Designer and Geodatabase Diagrammer tools allow you to export reports and diagrams of your geodatabase schema.

### A GEODATABASE IS PART OF A GIS

A production geodatabase is part of a larger system, the GIS. While it is important to invest in the design and refinement of the geodatabase, it is equally important to remember that the geodatabase will not operate in a vacuum. People will use client applications to connect to the geodatabase to view, edit, analyze, and present data. Such connections will typically occur over a network and may involve many round-trip requests to the database. Planning for realistic levels of use and designing the hardware, DBMS, network and the parts of the client systems to work together efficiently will greatly improve the performance of the system.

Allhough planning your computer and network infrastructure and tuning your DBMS are beyond the scope of this book, there are some geodatabase design choices and a number of additional things that you can do on the client-side to help your system use network and geodatabase resources efficiently.

## Designing for performance

Geodatabase designs that tend to perform well:

- Use subtypes, rather than additional feature classes, to differentiate types of objects.

- Keep feature classes that are not topologically related out of feature datasets.

- Use relationship classes sparingly, especially composite relationship classes.

- Use event messaging sparingly.

For more information on planning your computer and network infrastructure and tuning your DBMS, see *Inside a Geodatabase* and the ESRI white papers, *Multiuser Geographic Information Systems With ArcInfo 8* and *System Design Strategies*.

## Maintenance for performance

Good database maintenance is essential for good system performance.

- Keep indexes up-to-date on primary and foreign keys.

- Compress (compact) the database on a regular schedule.

- Perform typical RDBMS maintenance regularly.

## GIS client tips for performance

On the client-side in your GIS, there are a number of strategies that can effectively improve performance. Most of these help by using network and geodatabase resources efficiently.

- Create thumbnail images of data to preview in ArcCatalog.

- Use the Map Cache in ArcMap.

- Add all related feature classes and tables to the map when editing.

- Avoid large numbers of layers with definition queries.

- Use annotation rather than labeling.

- Set scale-dependent rendering for labels, annotation, and large feature classes.

- Use simpler symbology and avoid large-patterned area fills.

- Create maps with layers, default extents, and symbology tailored to specific tasks.

The starting point for the geodatabase implementation process is a good logical database design that specifies how geographic features are spatially and logically related to one another and to tables, annotation, and dimensions.

How you implement a geodatabase from a logical design will depend on your available resources. You may or may not have a data model template, existing data, or UML modeling tools. Regardless of which path you take, the key things to have at this stage are a solid logical model and some information about the projection and extent of the data to be stored in the geodatabase.

## Option A: Use a template

The preferred method for implementing a geodatabase design is to extract the schema of an existing geodatabase and customize it for your own instance. Any geodatabase schema can be easily copied. Use the Extract Data wizard on the Disconnected Editing toolbar in ArcMap to extract the schema from the desired geodatabase. For details, see the *Extract Data Wizard* document on the ESRI data model download Web site at http://support.esri.com/datamodels and the ArcGIS Desktop Help.

If you use a UML or XML metadata interchange (XMI) template, you will start in ArcCatalog. Create a new personal geodatabase, add the CASE Schema Creation Tool to ArcCatalog, select the geodatabase, and click the tool to import the schema. You can specify which parts of the schema to implement in the new geodatabase. The result will be an empty geodatabase with a schema that matches or is a subset of the XMI or UML template. However, this method cannot be used to transfer topologies and other spatial properties. For details, see the *Repository to the Geodatabase* document on the ESRI data model download Web site.

You can also use an XML Workspace Document to create the schema for a dataset or feature class with the Import XML Workspace Document tool in ArcCatalog.

## Option B: Load existing data

If your logical model closely matches your existing GIS data, you can create the database schema by importing existing feature classes into a geodatabase. You will need to know the spatial reference for your data, especially for new feature datasets. The spatial reference of standalone feature classes can be derived from the feature classes that you import but the extent of a dataset must be made large enough to include the extent of all feature classes that will be in it. Use the tools in ArcCatalog or the ArcSDE command line to import data.

## Option C: Create an empty geodatabase

If you have a simple logical model that differs substantially from your existing GIS data, you can create a new geodatabase in ArcCatalog and manually create the feature datasets, feature classes, tables, and so on, that make up the schema. You do not need a template, existing data, or a UML modeling tool to start. When you create the schema from scratch, there will be less work in the next stage. Once you have created a schema, you can use it as a template for future versions.

## Option D: Create a UML model

Several of the template geodatabases are represented in UML diagrams. With a CASE tool, such as Visio or Rational Rose, you can adapt these models and create your geodatabase schema. UML models represent portions of a geodatabase schema in a diagram that makes it easy to see the relationships between the objects. This method requires proficiency with a UML modeling tool.

## SETTING THE SPATIAL REFERENCE

Regardless of how you start, you must set the spatial reference of datasets and feature classes. The spatial reference information includes the coordinate system, datum, extent, and storage precision of the data. This information is shared by all feature classes within a dataset and makes topological relationships possible. The spatial reference cannot be changed later, so take the time to calculate an adequate extent and precision for your data. The extent of the spatial reference must contain the x,y domains of all feature classes that you add to the dataset.

If you extract a schema from a template, you will set the spatial reference in the process of extracting the schema. If you create the schema by loading your existing data, you will set the spatial reference in the process of loading the data. If you create new, empty schema elements in ArcCatalog, you will set the spatial reference for feature datasets and standalone feature classes when you create them. If you create a new geodatabase using a CASE tool, you will be prompted to set the spatial reference by the Schema wizard.

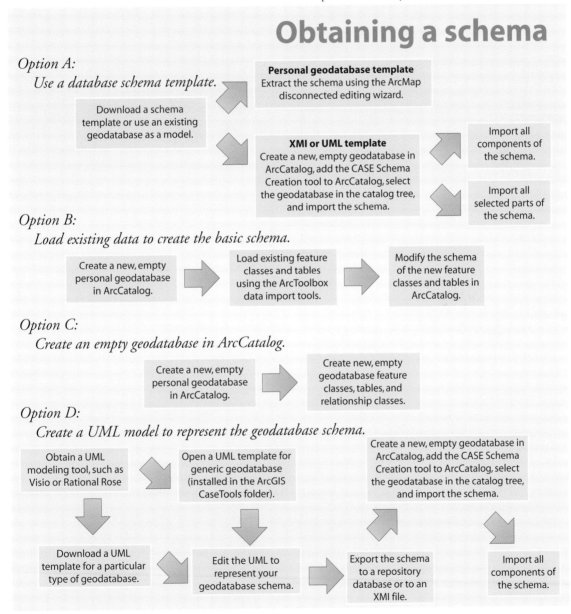

# Obtaining a schema

**Option A:**
*Use a database schema template.*

Download a schema template or use an existing geodatabase as a model.

**Personal geodatabase template**
Extract the schema using the ArcMap disconnected editing wizard.

**XMI or UML template**
Create a new, empty geodatabase in ArcCatalog, add the CASE Schema Creation tool to ArcCatalog, select the geodatabase in the catalog tree, and import the schema.

Import all components of the schema.

Import all selected parts of the schema.

**Option B:**
*Load existing data to create the basic schema.*

Create a new, empty personal geodatabase in ArcCatalog.

Load existing feature classes and tables using the ArcToolbox data import tools.

Modify the schema of the new feature classes and tables in ArcCatalog.

**Option C:**
*Create an empty geodatabase in ArcCatalog.*

Create a new, empty personal geodatabase in ArcCatalog.

Create new, empty geodatabase feature classes, tables, and relationship classes.

**Option D:**
*Create a UML model to represent the geodatabase schema.*

Obtain a UML modeling tool, such as Visio or Rational Rose

Open a UML template for generic geodatabase (installed in the ArcGIS CaseTools folder).

Create a new, empty geodatabase in ArcCatalog, add the CASE Schema Creation tool to ArcCatalog, select the geodatabase in the catalog tree, and import the schema.

Download a UML template for a particular type of geodatabase.

Edit the UML to represent your geodatabase schema.

Export the schema to a repository database or to an XMI file.

Import all components of the schema.

**9**

Modifying the schema is an extension of the process of creating it. Depending on how you created the schema, you may have relatively few or many modifications to make in this phase.

The extent to which you need to modify the database schema will depend on how you began the process of creating the geodatabase and the difference between the database you created and your logical model. You will probably need to make more changes if you started with a template geodatabase and fewer if you designed the database schema in a CASE tool or built it from scratch with ArcCatalog. Different templates were constructed with different assumptions and may be more or less detailed than your logical model.

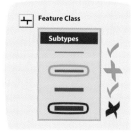

### Adding or removing feature classes

If you started from a template or loaded existing data to create the schema, you may need to create some additional feature classes. A template may also have contained feature classes or tables that do not correspond to your logical model. You can use ArcCatalog to create or delete feature classes in the geodatabase to match your logical model. If you delete a feature class that participates in a relationship, the relationship class will also be deleted. You can also define new subtypes of features or remove subtypes that do not match your model.

### Modifying feature classes

You may need to change the name of an existing feature class or add or remove attribute fields to make a feature class match your logical model. You can use ArcCatalog to rename feature classes, add new fields, or delete unnecessary fields. You may need to move existing data into new fields by calculating new field values, which can be done using the field calculator in ArcMap, or by SQL in your RDBMS. Once they've been created, field names and data types cannot be changed. You can change some properties

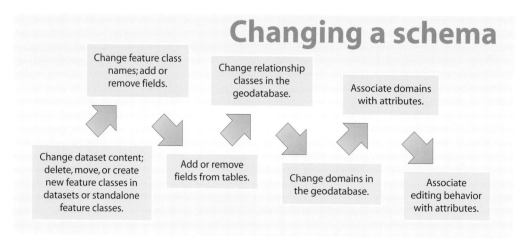

# Changing a schema

Change feature class names; add or remove fields.

Change relationship classes in the geodatabase.

Associate domains with attributes.

Change dataset content; delete, move, or create new feature classes in datasets or standalone feature classes.

Add or remove fields from tables.

Change domains in the geodatabase.

Associate editing behavior with attributes.

of existing fields, such as the alias, which is the name the field will be shown with in ArcMap, and the default value, domain, and subtype field.

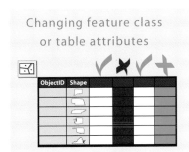

### Adding or removing fields from tables

Tables, like feature classes, may also need to be renamed, created to fill gaps from a template schema, or deleted where they are not part of your logical model. Similarly, existing tables may need to have fields added or deleted. Use ArcCatalog to make these schema changes. If you are using a CASE tool, make such schema changes in your geodatabase UML diagram.

### Changing relationship classes

A template geodatabase may contain relationship classes that you do not need. You can delete these in ArcCatalog. Conversely, you may need to create a new relationship class between two classes of objects in your geodatabase.

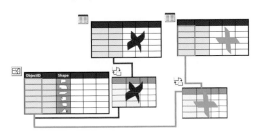

### Changing domains

You may find that the domains included with a template geodatabase do not match those defined in your logical model. You can add or remove values from coded value domains or change the ranges of range domains in ArcCatalog. If necessary, you can add new domains to your geodatabase or delete existing domains that are not applicable.

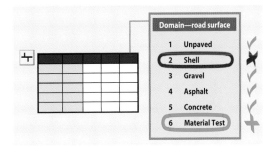

### Associating domains with attributes

You can associate domains with an attribute of a table, feature class, or subtype in ArcCatalog. If new attributes are added, or new feature classes or subtypes are added, you may need to associate one or more domains with their attributes. Likewise, if you add new domains to the schema, you will need to associate them with an attribute of a feature class or subtype before they will be useful.

### Associating editing behavior with attributes

You can associate behavior, such as default values and merge or split policies with an attribute of a table, feature class, or subtype. These types of editing behavior can speed editing by setting appropriate values in the fields of new features. Merge policies control what values are assigned to an attribute of the resulting feature when two features are merged. Split policies control what values are assigned to an attribute of the resulting features when a given feature is split.

9

The next step is to load data into the geodatabase. There are several ways to get data into a geodatabase. If the data already exists in a digital form outside the geodatabase, then you can import or load it. If the data is not already in digital form, it can be digitized, scanned, or derived from other data.

The methods you choose to get data into your geodatabase will depend on the type of data, the amount of data, and whether the data contains simple features or features with validation behavior, such as network features.

The two quickest ways of getting data into a geodatabase are importing and loading. Importing a feature class or table creates a duplicate of the imported feature class in the target geodatabase. Loading data copies features from one feature class to an existing feature class schema in the geodatabase. The existing schema may be empty or may already contain features. In most cases, if you have created an empty geodatabase schema, you will be using data loading tools to put data into existing feature classes. There are desktop tools for loading data in ArcMap and ArcCatalog and tools for loading data with ArcSDE.

There are some other ways to get data into a geodatabase. Deriving the contents of a feature class from one or more other feature classes is one. There are a few different ways to create such derived data. A generalization tool could be used to create a generalized river feature class from more detailed data for cartographic purposes, or many features could be merged to provide a faster drawing overview layer. Annotation can be derived from attributes of features, using annotation editing tools in ArcMap or by converting feature labels into annotation. Features can be digitized into a feature class during an edit session. Polygons can be created from existing features using topology.

## Loading features

You can load features from a variety of types of vector data using the ArcGIS Desktop user interface tools.

The data loading tool in ArcCatalog is meant to load simple feature data outside an edit session. This loader allows you to use a SQL query to specify which features to load and allows you to load into a subtype or a feature class. It cannot be used to load data into feature classes that participate in a geometric network, although you can load data with

the tool and create the network afterward. You can also export feature classes from existing geodatabases as XML recordset or workspace documents and import these into a new geodatabase.

The object loader is a tool that you can add to ArcMap using the Customize dialog box. It allows you to load data into a target feature class during an edit session. It applies any object-specific behavior and validation rules during the process, and it supports loading data into geometric networks. Because it works in an edit session and employs validation checks, this data loader can be significantly slower than the ArcCatalog data loader. If you extract the schema from a template geodatabase with a geometric network, it may be preferable to keep the geometric network and use the Object Loader in ArcMap to load the data. If you delete the network to load data faster, you will need to rebuild it from scratch in ArcCatalog.

For large volumes of data that need to be loaded into ArcSDE geodatabases, the SDE data loaders are very efficient, although they require you to be more familiar with your data and with the tools themselves than the desktop tools.

## Loading annotation

You can use tools in ArcMap to import annotation from existing coverages or CAD drawings or from SDE3, Vector Product Format (VPF), or PC ARC/INFO® annotation. You can create annotation by converting labels in ArcMap into annotation, either in a new annotation feature class or an existing one. Annotation features may be created one at a time using the edit tools, or they may be created for many features at once using the Annotate Selected Features tool in ArcMap.

## Loading dimension features

Dimension features, like annotation, may be created one at a time using the edit tools, or for many features at once using the Dimension Selected Features tool in ArcMap.

Dimension features can also be copied from an existing geodatabase.

**Loading rasters**

Rasters can be loaded into the geodatabase as raster catalogs or mosaics. There are tools in ArcToolbox™ and ArcSDE for loading rasters into a geodatabase, although they require that you be more familiar with your data and with the tools themselves than the ArcGIS Desktop tools.

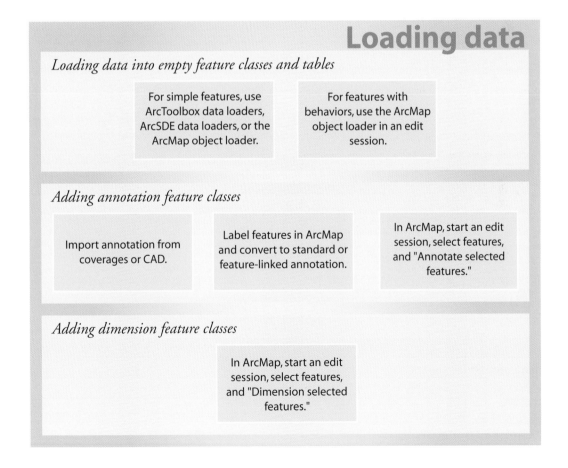

## Loading data

*Loading data into empty feature classes and tables*

For simple features, use ArcToolbox data loaders, ArcSDE data loaders, or the ArcMap object loader.

For features with behaviors, use the ArcMap object loader in an edit session.

*Adding annotation feature classes*

Import annotation from coverages or CAD.

Label features in ArcMap and convert to standard or feature-linked annotation.

In ArcMap, start an edit session, select features, and "Annotate selected features."

*Adding dimension feature classes*

In ArcMap, start an edit session, select features, and "Dimension selected features."

9

It is useful to create topological relationships after features have been loaded into the geodatabase. This is partly a matter of necessity, since UML modeling tools do not yet support geodatabase topology, and partly a matter of convenience. While UML modeling tools support creating geodatabase schemas with geometric networks, the data loading process is faster without one.

Geodatabase datasets may contain two types of topological relationships among features and feature classes: geometric networks and topologies. Although both sorts of topological relationships may be considered elements of the geodatabase schema, it is better to defer creating this part of the schema until after the data loading stage. Geometric networks can be created using the CASE schema creation tools, but they generally should be dropped before loading large amounts of data, as the connectivity and feature validation process for geometric networks substantially increases data loading time. It is best to load data into feature classes with the simple data loaders and create the geometric network after the data has been loaded. Topologies cannot be created using the CASE tools. It is usually best to create topologies after all of the feature classes that participate in the topology have been loaded because a topology must be revalidated after a new feature class is added. However, sometimes it is worth the extra steps to create a topology before some of the feature classes that will participate in it exist, if the topology is going to be used to create the features in that feature class.

In versioned geodatabases, changing the feature classes that participate in a topology or geometric network is a major schema change that requires all versions to be reconciled with the default version, then deleted. This cannot happen while people are using the geodatabase and can disrupt work flows that rely on versioning, so this change should be done before versions are created. The behavior and utility of the topology or network for editing and analysis purposes should be thoroughly tested before the production geodatabase is built.

## Creating a geometric network

You create a geometric network in ArcCatalog using the Build Geometric Network wizard or by using the CASE tools to reapply the schema to the geodatabase after the data has been loaded. When you build a geometric network, you first specify the feature classes that will participate in the network. Feature classes that are already part of another network or topology cannot be added to a new geometric network. If the Build Geometric Network wizard detects a field named "enabled", it will ask whether to preserve existing enabled values. The "enabled" field is used by the geometric network tools to manage network tracing. If you choose to enable all features, then the value of this field for each feature will be set to 1, which means "true." You might choose to preserve existing enabled values because the features have already been part of a geometric network and you want to retain the information about whether they are enabled. If you do so, all valid values (1 or 0) will be retained in this field, and invalid values will be set to 1.

Next you name the network, then identify which line feature classes, if any, will be complex edge features in the network. Complex edge features are not split where other features connect to them. Simple edge features always connect to exactly two junctions, and they are split by intersections with other features. In a water network, you might represent a long section of water main as a single complex edge feature, with a number of simple edge features representing water laterals connected at junctions along its length.

The next step is to enable snapping and set a snapping tolerance. If features do not connect exactly, they can be moved to within a snapping tolerance that you specify to connect to a nearby feature. You can specify which feature classes can be moved in the snapping process.

Next you will identify sources and sinks, for purposes of tracing flow in the network. You might identify certain junction features in a network as sources, such as pump stations, or sinks, such as the mouth of a river or a household water meter. You can add weights to the network to take advantage of the trace analysis tools in ArcMap. If you choose to add weights, you can associate each weight with an attribute field for each feature class.

After the network is created, you can open the Geometric Network Properties dialog box in ArcCatalog to set up connectivity rules for the edge and junction feature classes or subtypes in the network. You can define connectivity rules between edges and between edges and junctions. For the edge–junction rules, you can define the number of edges to which a given junction can connect, and the number of junctions to which an edge can connect. This is called the cardinality of the rule. For edge–edge rules, you can define the types of junctions that can connect to each pair of types of edges and select a default type of junction that will automatically be created when edges are connected together.

## Creating a topology

You can create a topology in ArcCatalog using the New Topology wizard. The first step is to name the topology and specify a cluster tolerance. The cluster tolerance is a distance within which vertices and endpoints of features will be snapped together. The cluster tolerance is applied when the topology is first validated to ensure that parts of features that fall within a small distance of parts of other features are made coincident.

The next step is to select the feature classes that will participate in the topology. Only feature classes that do not already participate in a topology or geometric network can be added to a new topology.

Then you would define the number of ranks for the topology and assign each feature class a rank in the topology. Topology ranks give you finer control over which features will be moved in the process of snapping vertices within the cluster tolerance. The highest rank is 1, and you can have up to 50 ranks. Parts of lower ranking features will be snapped to higher ranking features in the validation process. If your feature classes have z-values in their geometry, you can also specify z ranks.

The next step is to choose the topology rules to be applied to your feature dataset. If you are working from a template, you can save the topology rules out into a rule (.rul) file and load them into your new topology. You can also manually specify each topology rule. After the rules are specified, the topology is complete. You can validate the whole topology upon completing it, or you can validate parts of it while editing in ArcMap. For large datasets, validating the entire topology can take some time.

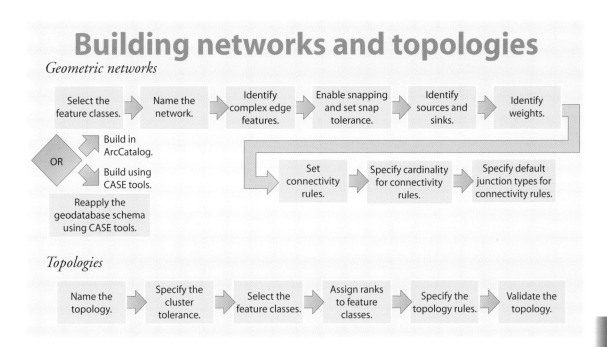

# Building networks and topologies

*Geometric networks*

Select the feature classes. → Name the network. → Identify complex edge features. → Enable snapping and set snap tolerance. → Identify sources and sinks. → Identify weights.

OR → Build in ArcCatalog.
OR → Build using CASE tools.

Reapply the geodatabase schema using CASE tools.

Set connectivity rules. → Specify cardinality for connectivity rules. → Specify default junction types for connectivity rules.

*Topologies*

Name the topology. → Specify the cluster tolerance. → Select the feature classes. → Assign ranks to feature classes. → Specify the topology rules. → Validate the topology.

**9**

While you may detect flaws in the implementation of your logical model in the data loading or topology creation stages, it is essential that you spend time thoroughly testing the geodatabase in prototype and pilot phases. Testing the geodatabase involves creating representative data products, testing editing and analysis operations, and testing work flows and multiple user access and response. Thumbnails in ArcCatalog and maps with scale-dependent rendering can improve performance.

A geodatabase is part of a GIS system. When you test your geodatabase design, you should do so with an eye to the range of uses that will be expected of the whole system. You should create data products, such as maps, charts, and reports, that are representative of your organization's everyday needs. Test any custom features and applications that will be part of the system. Test standard work flows and versioned data editing. Test with multiple users making typical and large requests of the geodatabase.

In the course of testing, you may encounter performance issues. Some of these may be remedied by adapting your geodatabase design. Others may be addressed by modifying other parts of the GIS to reduce the demand on the geodatabase. Such changes include creating maps that include only those layers necessary for a particular job, setting scale-dependent rendering for large layers and annotation feature classes in ArcMap, and using thumbnails to preview data in ArcCatalog.

## TEST DIFFERENT TYPES OF MAPS

A map is a key information product of a GIS database, and your organization will probably need to create several different types of maps. It is essential to test that the schema you create enables the efficient creation and use of the various maps your organization relies upon.

### Reporting

Some maps are produced as parts of a reporting work flow. Create a range of typical maps to test that the necessary feature classes, tables, and attributes are available in your geodatabase. Test that reports, charts, and derived data tables can be produced, and that address tables can be geocoded against the database.

### Geometric networks

Geometric networks are typically used to analyze connectivity and measure such things as flow, pressure, or cost between points. Create maps using your geometric network data and perform traces, connect and disconnect, and enable and disable network elements. Test connectivity rules to ensure that they are correctly applied and look for legitimate types of connections that may have been overlooked in the modeling phase. Check that the correct domains are applied to different subtypes.

### Editing

Maps designed for editing data should include all the feature classes and related tables that will be edited but should not contain more feature classes than necessary. Create, delete, and modify the geometry and attributes of features and related rows in tables. Edit topologies to ensure that the rules support the relationships you need to maintain the spatial integrity of your data. Fix topology errors using editing and error repair tools. Simple symbology, scale-dependent rendering, and consistent use of the Map Cache usually improves editing performance.

### Publication

Large, richly detailed and heavily annotated maps may be an occasional or everyday product for your organization. Test that the necessary feature classes and the attributes needed to symbolize them are available. Check that typical label expressions can be created or that the necessary annotation or dimension feature classes exist. Cartographic requirements often lead to additional feature classes (such as for annotation and symbolized boundary lines).

Some databases are periodically published in whole or in part to the Web or on removable media with ArcReader™. Make sure that the feature classes needed for publication are available and that unnecessary or confidential feature classes or attributes are removed for such data products. Simplified versions of some data may be maintained as part of your schema for such purposes.

## TEST CUSTOM APPLICATIONS

In addition to testing whether custom applications function, you should test whether they will scale effectively to a multiuser environment. One common bottleneck in a multiuser geodatabase occurs when custom applications make needless or excessive requests of the geodatabase. These applications may function on a development machine with a local database, but in a multiuser production environment, they may rapidly overtax the system. Queries or connection requests embedded in loops and editing applications that attempt to save after every edit create extra network traffic and database requests.

## TESTING VERSIONED WORK FLOWS

Multiuser geodatabases use versions to manage simultaneous editing of the same feature classes by multiple users.

Versions may also be used to manage work flows or history. Test your versioning scheme to ensure that different versions can be edited, that child versions can be reconciled and posted back to their parent versions, and that conflicts are correctly identified and resolved. Test any editing scenarios that involve topologies and versions to find feature classes that frequently produce conflicts. Test disconnected or distributed editing scenarios.

## TEST WITH MULTIPLE USERS

A geodatabase may have many users. Be sure to test the system with a representative number of users making typical and unusually large requests of the database. Be sure to apply all of the tests mentioned above with multiple users. Performance issues that are not apparent with a single user can be detected and resolved through appropriate stress testing in the prototype and pilot phases.

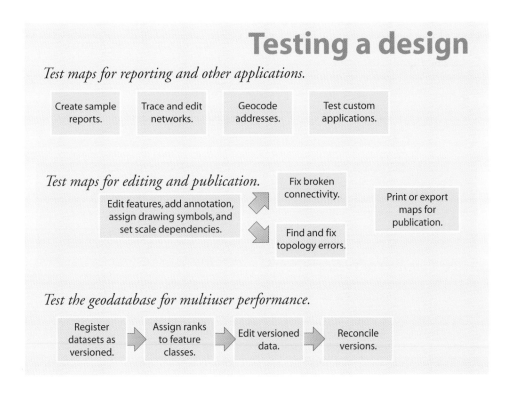

# Testing a design

*Test maps for reporting and other applications.*

- Create sample reports.
- Trace and edit networks.
- Geocode addresses.
- Test custom applications.

*Test maps for editing and publication.*

- Edit features, add annotation, assign drawing symbols, and set scale dependencies.
- Fix broken connectivity.
- Find and fix topology errors.
- Print or export maps for publication.

*Test the geodatabase for multiuser performance.*

- Register datasets as versioned.
- Assign ranks to feature classes.
- Edit versioned data.
- Reconcile versions.

**9**

Record problems you discover during the testing phase and revise the database schema so it meets all of your design requirements. Regardless of where you started the process, after the prototype phase, you will have a geodatabase template to work from. This will speed up the process of creating the next geodatabase schema because you can extract and modify the prototype geodatabase schema. If you are working with a CASE tool, you should implement your changes in the UML model and re-create the schema.

During the testing phase, you are likely to find a variety of problems. Some may be due to incorrect mapping of logical design onto physical design, while others may be due to errors or oversights in the logical design. A third class of problem occurs where the physical design is correct, but the work flow to complete a task is needlessly cumbersome. Performance issues are a fourth class of problem that you may encounter. Regardless of the type, it is important to record and address problems during the prototype and pilot phases.

Errors in the physical design can usually be addressed by making changes to the physical model. Such problems, when found in the prototype phase, should be fixed in the design and retested in the pilot phase. Depending on the magnitude of the problem, you may be able to make the needed schema changes to your test geodatabase, or you may need to re-create the geodatabase and reload data. If you are using a CASE tool, you should make your schema modifications using the tool so your geodatabase diagram does not become out of sync with the actual design.

Work flow and performance problems can sometimes be addressed through changes to the geodatabase schema, but they may also be resolved by changing other parts of the GIS. A feature class that is needed for cartographic representations at a small scale may be created by merging and generalizing features of a more detailed feature class. The generalized data with few attributes will be displayed more quickly with fewer round trips to the geodatabase. Map documents, editing practices, and even feature geometry can be tailored to specific tasks to improve performance.

## EXAMPLE: CONDOMINIUM DATA MODEL

Examples of some of the problems just mentioned can be drawn from the schema diagram shown on the next page. This part of the schema from Chapter 5, 'Parcels and the cadastre', illustrates two relationships that OwnerParcel features may have with other tables. In this model, an OwnerParcel feature for a condominium subdivision can be associated with VerticalParcel records that correspond to the condominium units. This schema is intended for and used by a county tax jurisdiction that isn't concerned with the building or floor plan outlines of each unit, or the VerticalParcel table would have been made a polygon feature class. But suppose that you do need to represent individual condominium units as features because, in your case, condominium values are assessed based on their surface area and location within a building (the better the view out the window, the higher the market value of the condominium unit). Still another reason for making condominium units into features is to accurately represent the outlines of buildings and land within condominiums that are collections of detached homes or office buildings. To address either of these cases, you would have to replace the VerticalParcel table with a polygon feature class, perhaps called simply CondominiumUnit. Each condominium unit feature might have additional attribution helping to justify the value associated with the parcel.

Conversely, you might not need the VerticalParcel table or relationship at all. In this case, you should remove this table and relationship.

## EXAMPLE: MAINTENANCE VERSUS PUBLISHING

Another reason for revising or augmenting your data model can arise from the need to support Web-based public access to your database. Suppose you prototyped a set of feature classes and tables for handling street and building addresses. The data model described in Chapter 4, 'Addresses and location', has a normalized structure to support data maintenance. Suppose you built this model, and during the prototyping, another department in your organization realized your data could be used for geocoding property records they had in simple tables. Chapter 4 anticipates just this kind of situation, and points out that it is a maintenance data model not designed or efficient for geocoding.

By this time, you might be thinking you should change your data model to make it more efficient for geocoding (assuming you were in a position to be able to help out the other department), but then you would lose the functionality for data entry and update validation that is important in address databases (and many others).

A better approach would be to design a separate geodatabase to use for geocoding that reduces the schema to the minimum number of tables and attributes that are absolutely necessary. Then, on a periodic basis, you could transfer the data from your maintenance database to the geocoding database.

This practice would be the "best practice" when it comes to serving data to the public over the Web. Any such publishing database should be designed for best performance of queries rather than updates, and be organized in a system that can support high-volume network traffic, which is usually not necessary for a maintenance database.

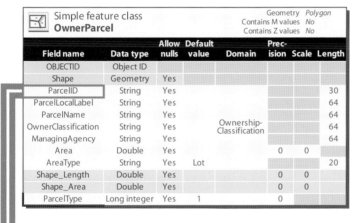

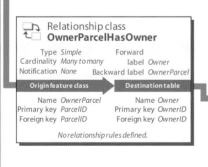

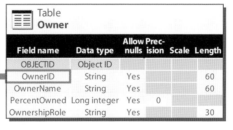

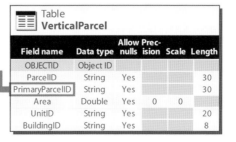

*Sample feature classes from Chapter 5, 'Parcels and the cadastre'.*

Depending on your application, you may wish to change the number and types of relationships, either for performance or functionality. An alternative design might need to be tested. You may want to model condominium units (VerticalParcel table) as polygon features rather than records in a table if, for example, your organization already records the outlines of vertical parcels.

9

Creating a geodatabase from a logical model is an iterative process. Once you have a design, it is important to create and test prototype and pilot versions before creating the final production geodatabase.

## SUMMARY

The process of creating a geodatabase from a logical data model has several entry points, depending on how you want to approach the process and what resources are available. Typically, regardless of the entry point, there are six major steps in the process. These include applying the logical design to a new geodatabase, modifying the schema, loading data into the schema, building topological relationships, testing, and revising the geodatabase. The revision step marks the point where the process begins again. The whole set of steps should be repeated at least twice so you have the opportunity to test, learn from, and revise a prototype and pilot version before you create a production geodatabase.

## REFERENCES

There are a number of resources that contain more detailed information on how to create and maintain a geodatabase. Much of this information can be found in the ArcGIS documentation set or the online Help. Focused help with parts of the process is available in Tips and Tricks documents on the Data Models page of the ESRI Web site. Detailed information about ArcSDE, data loading, versioning, topology, and system design is available in white papers on the White Papers page of the ESRI Web site.

### ESRI documentation

Two books with useful information on the process of designing and building geodatabases are *Building a Geodatabase,* and the *Geodatabase Workbook*, parts of the standard ESRI printed and PDF documentation sets.

### Data model tips and tricks

Several brief documents with step-by-step instructions for parts of the geodatabase creation process are available on the ESRI Web site in the Data Models section. These include:

- *How to Create a Geodatabase From a Microsoft Repository Database or XMI File.* 2004. URL: http://downloads.esri.com/support/documentation/ao_/RepositoryToGeodatabase.pdf.

- *How to Create a New Geodatabase Using the Extract Data Wizard.* 2004. URL: http://downloads.esri.com/support/documentation/ao_/ExtractDataWizard.pdf.

- *How to Load Data Into the Geodatabase.* 2004. URL: http://downloads.esri.com/support/documentation/ao_/LoadDataGeodatabase.pdf.

- *How to Set the Spatial Reference for a Feature Dataset or Standalone Feature Class in a Geodatabase.* 2004. URL: http://downloads.esri.com/support/documentation/ao_/SpatialReferenceGeodatabase.pdf.

### ESRI white papers

The White Papers page of the Knowledge Base section of the ESRI Web site contains many technical papers on a variety of subjects. Specific white papers that are relevant for creating a geodatabase include:

- *ArcGIS: Working With Geodatabase Topology.* 2003. URL: http://downloads.esri.com/support/whitepapers/ao_/geodatabase-topology.pdf.

- Hoel, Erik; Menon, Sudhakar; and Morehouse, Scott. 2003. *Building a Robust Relational Implementation of Topology.* URL: http://downloads.esri.com/support/whitepapers/ao_/BuildingRobustTopologies.pdf.

- *Multiuser Geographic Information Systems With ArcInfo 8*. 2000. URL: http://downloads.esri.com/support/whitepapers/ao_/Multiuser_GIS_with_AI8.pdf.

- Peters, Dave. *System Design Strategies*. 2004. URL: http://downloads.esri.com/support/whitepapers/sde_/SystemDesignStrategiesMarch2004.pdf.

- *Raster Data in ArcSDE 8.3*. 2003. URL: http://downloads.esri.com/support/whitepapers/sde_/arcsde83_raster.pdf.

- *Versioning*. 2004. URL: http://downloads.esri.com/support/whitepapers/ao_/Versioning_2.pdf.

- *Versioning Workflows*. 2004. URL: http://downloads.esri.com/support/whitepapers/ao_/Versioning_Workflows_2.pdf.

- *Working With the Geodatabase Using SQL*. 2004. URL: http://downloads.esri.com/support/whitepapers/ao_/GeodatabaseUsingSQL_2.pdf.

- *XML Schema of the Geodatabase*. 2004. URL: http://downloads.esri.com/support/whitepapers/ao_/XML_Schema.pdf.

## FURTHER RESOURCES

Many of the resources listed above can be downloaded from one of the following Web pages:

http://support.esri.com

The Knowledge Base section contains links to white papers and product documentation. The Data Models section contains links to the data model case studies and the Tips and Tricks documents.

The ESRI developer Web site:

http://arcgisdeveloperonline.esri.com

and ArcScripts Web site:

http://arcscripts.esri.com

contain numerous tools, utilities, and samples that are useful in designing a geodatabase, loading data, and documenting the database.

## ACKNOWLEDGMENTS

Bob Booth of ESRI wrote this chapter and Scott Crosier of ESRI made many of the graphics.

**9**

# Books from ESRI Press

*Continued on next page*

When ordering, please mention book title and ISBN (number that follows each title)